The Great Ideas of
Clinical Science

The Great Ideas of Clinical Science

17 Principles That Every Mental Health
Professional Should Understand

Edited by
Scott O. Lilienfeld and William T. O'Donohue

Routledge
Taylor & Francis Group
New York   London

Routledge is an imprint of the
Taylor & Francis Group, an informa business

Routledge
Taylor & Francis Group
270 Madison Avenue
New York, NY 10016

Routledge
Taylor & Francis Group
2 Park Square
Milton Park, Abingdon
Oxon OX14 4RN

© 2007 by Taylor & Francis Group, LLC
Routledge is an imprint of Taylor & Francis Group, an Informa business

Printed in the United States of America on acid-free paper
10 9 8 7 6 5 4 3 2 1

International Standard Book Number-10: 0-415-95038-4 (Hardcover)
International Standard Book Number-13: 978-0-415-95038-1 (Hardcover)

Library of Congress Cataloging-in-Publication Data

The great ideas of clinical science : 17 principles that every mental health professional should understand / Scott O. Lilienfeld, William T. O'Donohue, editors.
    p. ; cm.
    Includes bibliographical references.
    ISBN 0-415-95038-4 (hb : alk. paper)
    1. Clinical psychology.   I. Lilienfeld, Scott O., 1960- . II. O'Donohue, William T.
    [DNLM: 1. Psychology, Clinical. 2. Research.   WM 105 G786 2007]

RC467.G74 2007
616.8--dc22

                                            2006012727

Visit the Taylor & Francis Web site at
http://www.taylorandfrancis.com

and the Routledge Web site at
http://www.routledgementalhealth.com

Contents

Foreword

In the fullness of time, our progress in understanding the natural order advances through the process of science, and psychology is no exception. To gain perspectives on this progress, one needs to take the long view of a historian. In so doing, one will come to appreciate the role of great ideas and creative individuals, while at the same time realizing that our cumulative progress is greater than any one idea or individual. In this era of substantive and sometimes emotional disagreements among some segments of clinical psychology over the role of science, it is easy to lose sight of that view, but it should not be lost. In fact, we have made enormous progress since the proclamation of the Boulder model of clinical psychology over 50 years ago.

The scientist practitioner model of clinical psychology was clearly a "great idea" that undergirds most of the chapters in this outstanding compendium. But it is often forgotten that in the 20-year period following the publication of the Boulder model (Raimy, 1950; Shakow et al., 1947), most psychologists did not have the foggiest notion of how this model could be implemented. Thus, I remember a day in the late 1960s when a distinguished visitor came to present a lecture billing himself as a "scientist practitioner," and proceeded to recount how he spent his mornings in the animal laboratory studying licking behavior in rats, and his afternoons in the clinic administering projective tests. It seemed to this (young) psychologist at that point that something was missing! This incident occurred in an era when applied work of any kind was largely disparaged and ridiculed by psychological scientists in positions of power in psychology departments. As a result, clinical psychologists in academia were second-class citizens (and those in practice worse), and programs of clinical training were afforded few resources, and even less flexibility in training scientist practitioners. For example, course credit was not awarded for clinical supervisory experiences. The consequences of this early clinical–experimental split, as it was called then, were several and included the early creation of professional schools of psychology, first in universities, and then free standing. This was followed by a shift toward a more professional focus in the American Psychological Association (APA) and, in the late 1980s, the formation of a new society now called the Association for Psychological Science (APS), in which scientists could once again run their own affairs and set their own agenda.

These consequences were ironic in a sense because the "great idea" of the Boulder model began to really take hold in the 1970s as a result of a succession of creative and remarkable advances in our methods and our knowledge, most of which are detailed in this book. For example, we learned how to expand the scientific method to the clinic and to apply the great logic of science to clinical practice in a variety of different ways, including the use of single-case experimental case designs (Barlow & Hersen, 1973; Hersen & Barlow, 1976). Indeed, Lazarus and Davison (1971) detailed the manner in which case studies could contribute to our knowledge, and they recapitulate that creative thinking with a chapter in this book (see Chapter 7). Through the pioneering work of Gordon Paul and others, we learned how to evaluate psychological therapies and began to prove that some therapies were better than others (see Chapter 6). We discovered that judgmental biases are a part of being human, a basic finding for which a psychologist, Daniel Kahneman, won the Nobel Prize (Kahneman, Slovic, & Tversky, 1982) and that clinicians are subject to these biases just like everyone else (see Chapter 2). Psychologists also played a major role in the creation of our current system of classifying mental disorders that allowed us to identify and assess various manifestations of psychopathology with a precision that had not been approached previously (American Psychiatric Association, 2000; see Chapter 5). All of these ideas and more are detailed in the first section of this book.

At the same time, psychological science was flourishing in a manner such that its application to clinical problems became all the more apparent. Thus, advances in learning theory have provided one of the more satisfactory accounts of the development of at least some forms of psychopathology (Bouton, Mineka, & Barlow, 2001) as further detailed in this volume (see Chapter 9). Similarly, advances in the study of personality traits (see Chapter 12), and in cognitive neuroscience (see Chapter 13), allowed for a deeper and broader understanding of psychopathology and its treatment and added more substance to the scientific base for psychological practice. For example, to better understand emotional disorders we are now turning to emotion science, which details the evolutionary pressures responsible for an adaptive emotional life that can sometimes go horribly awry (e.g., Campbell-Sills & Barlow, in press). In this era we have all but solved the great nature–nurture debate by detailing the intricate dance of genes and the environment in any causal models of behavior (see Chapter 10). In the context of our development, we understand more fully that mind/body dualism is a fiction because biochemical interventions influence thought, feelings, and behaviors in the same way that psychological interventions change brain function and, it seems, brain structure. Most of these ideas are detailed in this book in a manner that is inspiring when one thinks of the state of our science and profession as little as 40 years ago.

The future will probably witness equally stunning achievements. What seems apparent in the near future is that we are arriving at a new understanding of the relationship of personality and psychopathology that will influence our conceptions of psychopathology and systems of classification. Thus, discrete, thin slices of psychopathology that comprise our current nosology will give way to more broadly conceived dimensions or spectrums of psychopathology based on cognitive and affective neuroscience as well as our deepening knowledge of the influences of culture (see Chapters 16 and 17). And, scientists and practitioners will come together, overcoming current disagreements to produce important data on translating advances in psychological science directly to the clinic. In this way will practitioners be full partners in what will become a truly evidence-based practice of psychology, fulfilling the vision of participants in the Boulder conference over 50 years ago.

This creative and unique book details many of these great ideas of the past 50 years, incorporating some chapters by individuals who originally helped to advance the ideas. In so doing, it becomes easier to take the long view and to glimpse the future, a time when our understandings of the mysteries of human nature will accelerate and deepen, much to our benefit.

David H. Barlow, Ph.D.
Center for Anxiety and Related Disorders
Boston University

REFERENCES

American Psychiatric Association. (2000). *Diagnostic and statistical manual of mental disorders* (4th ed.) (Text Revision). Washington, D.C.: Author.

Barlow, D. H., & Hersen, M. (1973). Single case experimental designs: Uses in applied clinical research. *Archives of General Psychiatry, 29*, 319–325.

Bouton, M. E., Mineka, S., & Barlow, D. H. (2001). A modern learning-theory perspective on the etiology of panic disorder. *Psychological Review, 108*, 4–32.

Campbell-Sills, L., & Barlow, D. H. (in press). Incorporating emotion regulation into conceptualizations and treatments of anxiety and mood disorders. In J.J. Gross (Ed.), *Handbook of emotion regulation.* New York: Guilford Press.

Hersen, M., & Barlow, D. H. (1976). *Single case experimental designs: Strategies for studying behavior change.* New York: Pergamon Press.

Kahneman, D., Slovic, P., & Tversky, A. (1982). *Judgment under uncertainty: Heuristics and biases.* Cambridge, UK: Cambridge University Press.

Lazarus, A. A., & Davison, G. C. (1971). Clinical innovation in research and practice. In A. E. Bergin & S. L. Garfield (Eds.), *Handbook of psychotherapy and behavior change: An empirical analysis* (pp. 196–213). New York: Wiley.

Raimy, V. C. (Ed.). (1950). *Training in clinical psychology.* Englewood Cliffs, NJ: Prentice Hall.

Shakow, D., Hilgard, E. R., Kelly, E. L., Luckey, B., Sanford, R. N., & Shaffer, L. F. (1947). Recommended graduate training program in clinical psychology. *American Psychologist, 2*, 539–558.

About the Editors

Scott O. Lilienfeld, Ph.D., is associate professor of psychology at Emory University in Atlanta. Dr. Lilienfeld is founder and editor of the new journal, *Scientific Review of Mental Health Practice* and is past (2001–2002) president of the Society for a Science of Clinical Psychology, which is Section III within Division 12 (Society of Clinical Psychology) of the American Psychological Association (APA). He also served as the Division 12 program chair for the 2001 APA Convention. He is a member of eight journal editorial boards, including the *Journal of Abnormal Psychology, Psychological Assessment,* and *Clinical Psychology Review,* and he has served as an external reviewer for over 50 journals and several grant proposals. Dr. Lilienfeld has published approximately 150 articles, book chapters, and books in the areas of personality disorders (especially psychopathic and antisocial personality disorders), personality assessment, anxiety disorders, psychiatric classification and diagnosis, and the scientific foundations of clinical psychology. His work on psychological pseudoscience has been featured in the *New York Times, Los Angeles Times, Boston Globe, Washington Post,* the *New Yorker,* and *Scientific American.* In addition, he has appeared on ABC's *20/20,* CNN, National Public Radio, Canadian Public Radio, and numerous other radio stations. In 1998, Dr. Lilienfeld received the David Shakow Award for outstanding early career contributions to clinical psychology from APA Division 12.

William T. O'Donohue, Ph.D., is a licensed clinical psychologist who is widely recognized for his proposed innovations in mental health service delivery, in treatment design and evaluation, and in knowledge of empirically supported cognitive behavioral therapies. He is a member of the Association for the Behavioral and Cognitive Therapies and served on the board of directors of this organization. Dr. O'Donohue has an exemplary history of successful grant funding and government contracts. Since 1996, he has received over $1.5 million in federal grant monies from sources including the National Institute of Mental Health and the National Institute of Justice. In addition, Dr. O'Donohue has published his work prolifically. He has edited over 20 books, written 35 book chapters on various topics, and published reviews for 7 books. Furthermore, he has published more than 75 articles in scholarly journals. Dr. O'Donohue is currently directing a major grant-funded project involving integrated care. This project is a treatment development/ outcome evaluation project. Specially trained psychologists are placed into primary care and five sets of variables are examined: (1) patient satisfaction; (2) provider satisfaction; (3) clinical change; (4) functional change; and (5) medical utilization change. Dr. O'Donohue is a national expert in training clinicians in integrated care and developing quality improvement projects in integrated care.

Contributors

Roger K. Blashfield, Ph.D., is a professor in the Department of Psychology at Auburn University. He earned his B.S. at Ohio State and his Ph.D. at Indiana University. Before going to Auburn, he was on the faculty of the Pennsylvania State University and the University of Florida (psychiatry). His area of research interest is the classification of psychopathology.

Danny R. Burgess is an advanced doctoral student in the Department of Psychology at Auburn University. He earned his B.S. at the University of Southern Mississippi. His doctoral dissertation focuses on the clinical utility of the Five Factor Model versus the Axis II of DSM-IV-TR versus Axis V of the DSM-IV-TR when characterizing personality disorders.

Yulia E. Chentsova-Dutton, Ph.D., is an assistant professor of psychology at Colby College. Her research interests include cultural shaping of emotions, the effect of contextual cues on emotional responding, and cultural influences on emotion responding in different types of psychopathology.

Nicholas A. Cummings, Ph.D., Sc.D., is a former president of the American Psychological Association who has been predicting and influencing the future of mental health practice for 50 years. He wrote and implemented the nation's first prepaid psychotherapy insurance benefit in 1959, establishing it as the prototype of benefits to follow. In response to his prescience, he has founded over two dozen organizations, including American Biodyne (1980–1992), the nation's first and only psychologically driven managed behavioral healthcare organization (MBHO). He is the recipient of five honorary doctorates and numerous awards, including psychology's highest, the Gold Medal for a Lifetime of Contributions to Practice. He is the author or editor of 44 books and over 450 book chapters and refereed journal articles. He is currently Distinguished Professor, University of Nevada, Reno; president, Cummings Foundation for Behavioral Health; board chair, The Nicholas & Dorothy Cummings Foundation; and founding board chair, CareIntegra.

Gerald C. Davison is professor and chair of the University of Southern California's Department of Psychology. In 2006 he served as president of the Society of Clinical Psychology (Division 12 of APA) and as chair of the Council of Graduate Departments of Psychology. His textbook, *Abnormal Psychology*, co-authored with Kring, Neale, and Johnson, recently appeared in its 10th edition and has been used at hundreds of universities here and abroad. In 1993 he won the USC Associates Award for Excellence in Teaching, a university-wide prize, and in 2003 was the recipient of the Lifetime Achievement Award of the Association of Behavioral and Cognitive Therapies. His research focuses on experimental and philosophical analyses of psychopathology, assessment, and therapeutic change.

David Faust, Ph.D., is a professor in the Department of Psychology, University of Rhode Island, and holds an affiliate appointment in the Department of Psychiatry and Human Behavior, Brown University Program in Medicine. Dr. Faust is the former director of psychology at the Rhode Island Hospital. His areas of interest include clinical decision making, neuropsychology, philosophy of science and epistemology, and psychology and law, and he is the senior editor of the upcoming revision of Ziskin's classic treatise on psychology and law.

Katherine A. Fowler, M.A., received her B.S. in psychology from Florida State University in 1999, and is currently an advanced graduate student in clinical psychology at Emory University in Atlanta, GA. Her current research interests include the interface of personality and psychopathology, and personality disorders, with a particular focus on psychopathic personality. She plans to graduate with her doctorate in spring 2007.

Howard N. Garb, Ph.D., directs the largest psychological screening program for the U.S. Air Force. Screening is conducted during basic training, and the purpose is to identify trainees with severe psychopathology. Dr. Garb received a double-major Ph.D. in clinical psychology and research methodology and psychological measurement from the University of Illinois at Chicago. He completed an NIMH postdoctoral fellowship in clinical psychology and research methodology and program evaluation at Northwestern University. He has published extensively in the areas of psychological assessment and clinical judgment.

Sherryl H. Goodman, Ph.D., received her Ph.D. in clinical psychology in 1978 from the University of Waterloo under the mentorship of Dr. Donald Meichenbaum. She then joined the faculty at Emory University where she is currently a professor in the Department of Psychology with a joint appointment in the Department of Psychiatry and Behavioral Sciences. She served as director of clinical training from 1996 to 2003. Her research interests, grounded in the field of developmental psychopathology, concern the mechanisms by which mothers with depression may transmit psychopathology to their children. Dr. Goodman is also interested in the epidemiology of child and adolescent psychopathology, with a particular focus on risk and protective factors. She is currently directing research on: (a) maternal depression as an early life stress for infants; (b) vulnerabilities to depression in preschool-aged children of depressed mothers; (c) the development of a measure of children's perceptions of parental sadness; (d) children's understanding of sadness in others; and (e) women's narratives on their experiences of parenting and depression. She is the coeditor with Ian Gotlib of the 2002 book, *Children of depressed parents: Alternative pathways to risk for psychopathology* (American Psychological Association Press) and with Corey Keyes of the in-press book, *Handbook of women and depression* (Cambridge University Press). Dr. Goodman is a fellow of the American Psychological Association and of Div. 12, is a former associate editor of the *Journal of Family Psychology* and is an associate editor of the *Journal of Abnormal Psychology*. She is dedicated to the integration of science and practice in the field of clinical psychology through training and advocacy.

Michael N. Hallquist, M.A., is a doctoral student in clinical psychology at the State University of New York at Binghamton. His interests are in the areas of pain and behavioral medicine, hypnosis, body dysmorphic disorder, and personality disorders. He has published numerous scholarly works and presented papers on these topics.

Allan R. Harkness, Ph.D., is an associate professor in the Psychology Department at The University of Tulsa in Tulsa, OK. He served as Director of Clinical Training at Tulsa from 1996 to 2001, and chair of the department from 2001 to 2004. He received his Ph.D. after completing the clinical psychology program at the University of Minnesota in 1989. Dr. Harkness specializes in the application of personality individual differences science in clinical psychology. He has published in the *Journal of Personality and Social Psychology, Psychological Assessment, Journal of Abnormal Psychology*, and the *Journal of Personality Assessment*, amongst others. He has authored numerous book chapters on personality assessment.

Stephen S. Ilardi, Ph.D., received his Ph.D. in clinical psychology from Duke University in 1995, and now serves on the faculty of the doctoral training program at the University of Kansas. His major research focus has been the understanding of maladaptive cognitive processes in depression, with an emphasis on integrating theory and methods of cognitive neuroscience, while his most recent work has looked to extend this perspective through the development of a novel integrative intervention for depression. Dr. Ilardi was the recipient of the Society of Clinical Psychology's Blau Award for Early Career Contributions to Clinical Psychology.

Leslie Karwoski, M.A., is completing her Ph.D. in clinical psychology at the University of Kansas. Her main areas of research interest are affective disorders and clinical treatment outcomes. Her research presentation at the 2005 meetings of the Society for a Science of Clinical Psychology (SSCP: APA Division 12, Section III) was awarded "Best Poster" honors.

Arnold A. Lazarus, Ph.D., ABPP, is a distinguished professor emeritus of psychology at Rutgers University and is the executive director of The Lazarus Institute in Skillman, New Jersey. Previously, he was on the faculties of Stanford, Yale, and Temple University Medical School, and is the recipient of many honors and awards for the multimodal approach to therapy that he developed. He has authored 17 books and over 350 professional articles and chapters, and has served as president of several professional societies and associations.

Steven Jay Lynn, Ph.D., is a professor of psychology at the State University of New York at Binghamton, and a diplomate in clinical and forensic psychology (ABPP). A former president of the American Psychological Association (APA) Hypnosis Division, Dr. Lynn is the author or editor of 16 books and more than 230 articles on hypnosis, abnormal psychology, memory, psychotherapy, dissociation, anomalous experiences, and science and pseudoscience. He is a recent recipient of the Chancellor's Award, State University of New York, for Excellence in Scholarship, Creativity, and Professional Activities. Dr. Lynn serves on eleven editorial boards, including the *Journal of Abnormal Psychology*.

Abigail Matthews, M.A., is a doctoral candidate in clinical psychology at the State University of New York at Binghamton. Her interests are in the areas of eating disorders and depression, and she has published and presented papers on these topics.

M. Teresa Nezworski, Ph.D., is an associate professor in the School of Brain and Behavioral Sciences at the University of Texas at Dallas and director of psychological services at the Callier Center. She has a joint appointment as clinical professor in the Graduate School of Biomedical Sciences at UT Southwestern Medical Center. Dr. Nezworski completed the doctoral training programs in both experimental child psychology and clinical psychology at the University of Minnesota in 1983. She teaches courses in assessment and psychopathology, and provides supervision to doctoral interns and clinical staff working with patients with communication disorders and comorbid mental health conditions including autism spectrum disorders, posttraumatic head injury, hearing impairment, tinnitus/hyperacusis, selective mutism, and so on. She is particularly interested in factors contributing to diagnostic error and the misinterpretation of psychological test results.

Gordon L. Paul, Ph.D., is the Hugh Roy and Lillie Cranz Cullen Distinguished Professor of Psychology and director of the Clinical Research Unit at the University of Houston, where he also teaches in the graduate clinical program. He has served on the boards of 7 major clinical journals and is a frequent consulting editor for 19. A practicing licensed psychologist and certified health-services provider with both inpatient and outpatient supervisory experience, he has consulted to more than 200 organizations and served as a member of or advisor to numerous taskforces, study sections, and review groups at regional, state, and national levels. He continues as an advisor to several policymaking groups and to advocacy organizations on behalf of people suffering from severe emotional and behavioral problems. An advocate of the scientist-professional model for clinical psychology, Dr. Paul's research and teaching have been at the forefront of those demonstrating the utility of psychosocial principles for the assessment and nonpharmacological treatment of problems ranging from anxiety to schizophrenia. Awards for excellence in graduate training have recognized these accomplishments, as have election to fellow status in numerous professional organizations and selection for more than 35 honorary biographical publications and expert listings, including *Good Housekeeping's* Best Mental Health Experts (among 37 experts in schizophrenia). Early publications on research methodology and on anxiety-related problems became citation classics and his more recent work on inpatient assessment and treatment has been the basis for numerous awards, among them, the Society for a Science of Clinical Psychology's Distinguished Scientist Award and the American Psychological Association, Division 12's Distinguished Scientific Contributions to Clinical Psychology Award.

Kevin Rand currently is pursuing an internship at Duke University Medical Center and did his graduate work at the University of Kansas. His research interests include the influences of hope on performance and well-being, treatments for depression and anxiety, and perfectionism. He also is interested in the theoretical linkage of psychology with other domains of scientific inquiry.

John Ruscio, Ph.D., is associate professor of psychology at The College of New Jersey. Among the nearly three dozen peer-reviewed journal articles, books, and book chapters that he has authored or co-authored, many involve his interest in clinical judgment. Theory and research on decision making suffuse the critical-thinking text that he published with Wadsworth, now in its second edition and titled *Critical thinking in psychology: Separating sense from nonsense.* Several of Dr. Ruscio's articles about clinical judgment have appeared in the *Scientific Review of Mental Health Practice,* where he currently serves as an associate editor. Dr. Ruscio is also on the editorial board at the *Journal of Abnormal Psychology.*

Neil Schneiderman, Ph.D., is the James L. Knight Professor of Psychology, Medicine, Psychiatry and Behavioral Sciences, and Biomedical Engineering; Director, Division of Health Psychology in the Department of Psychology; and Director of the University of Miami Behavioral Medicine Research Center. He has been a long-term director of the National Institutes of Health (NIH) program projects in Psychoneuroimmunology and HIV/AIDS, as well as in Biobehavioral Bases of Coronary Heart Disease Risk and Management. These program projects have been associated with NIH pre- and post-doctoral training grants under his direction. Dr. Schneiderman has served as editor-in-chief of *Health Psychology* and of the *International Journal of Behavioral Medicine*. He has also served as president of the Division of Health Psychology of the American Psychological Association, Academy of Behavioral Medicine Research, and the International Society of Behavioral Medicine. He is recipient of the Distinguished Scientist Award from the American Psychological Association and from the Society of Behavioral Medicine. Dr. Schneiderman has published more than 300 articles in the areas of stress, endocrine and immune responses in cardiovascular disease, diabetes, HIV/AIDS, and prostate cancer.

Scott D. Siegel is completing his Ph.D. in clinical health psychology at the University of Miami and is currently on psychology internship at the Puget Sound VA Medical Center. He has published in the areas of cancer, cardiovascular disease, fatigue, stress, health, and immunity.

Richard J. Siegert, Ph.D., is a clinical psychologist and neuropsychologist who has research interests in psychometrics, cognition in neuro- logical and psychiatric disorders, and rehabilitation for such disorders. Since 2000, he has worked with Tony Ward on the theoretical implica- tions of evolutionary approaches to human behavior for understanding psychopathology. They have published together on this topic in the journals *Aggression and Violent Behavior, Australian Psychologist*, and *Review of General Psychology*, as well as several book chapters. Richard is an associate professor with the University of Otago at the Wellington School of Medicine and Health Sciences, where he is the head of the Rehabilitation Teaching and Research Unit.

William Timberlake, Ph.D., is professor of psychological and brain sciences at Indiana University, a core member of the Programs in Cognitive Science, Neuroscience, and Animal Behavior, and an adjunct professor of biology. He is a fellow of the American Association for the Advancement of Science, the American Psychological Society, and the American Psychological Association. He served on the Psychobiology and Graduate Research Traineeship Panels at the National Science Foundation, on the editorial boards of eight journals, and was three times an associate editor of *Animal Learning & Behavior*. For a decade he was codirector of the Center for the Integrative Study of Animal Behavior and the Program in

Animal Behavior at Indiana, and served on the board of fellows of the Poynter Center for the Study of Ethics & American Institutions. He held visiting appointments at Harvard, University of California at San Diego, Reed College, Cambridge University, and Oregon Health Sciences University. His research is concerned with the integration of learning and evolution.

Jeanne L. Tsai, Ph.D., is an assistant professor of psychology at Stanford University. She is director of the Stanford Culture and Emotion Lab (http://www-psych.stanford.edu/-tsailab/). Her research examines how cultural ideas and practices shape the emotions that people actually feel, emotions that people want to feel, and the implications these processes have for mental health and well-being across the life span. Her work is funded by the National Institute of Mental Health and the National Institute on Aging.

Erin C. Tully, M.A., received her B.S. from the University of Pittsburgh (psychology major) in 2000 and her M.A. in psychology (clinical) from Emory University in 2002. She is completing her graduate training at Emory University under the mentorship of Dr. Sherryl Goodman and, at the time of this writing, anticipated being awarded her doctoral degree in the summer of 2006. As a research fellow with the National Institute of Mental Health's (NIMH) undergraduate research program, she began a program of research studying mechanisms of risk and vulnerability for internalizing disorders, particularly in offspring of women with depression. She has continued this line of research throughout her graduate training and in 2005 was awarded a National Research Service Award by the NIMH to study vulnerabilities for psychopathology in young children of depressed mothers. She is embarking on a program of research on the developmental psychopathology of internalizing disorders and developing a conceptual model for studying vulnerabilities for depression that incorporates affect regulation abilities, psychophysiological functioning, and information processing along with exposure to risk factors.

Irwin D. Waldman, Ph.D., is a professor in the Department of Psychology, Emory University. Dr. Waldman is a clinical psychologist with developmental interests, who examines the genetic and environmental etiology of disruptive behavior disorders (e.g., ADHD, conduct disorder) in childhood and adolescence. His current research explores the role of candidate genes in the development of externalizing behavior problems, as well as genetic and environmental influences on comorbidity and on the links between normal variation in symptoms and in personality in the general population and extreme variants in clinical samples.

Tony Ward, Ph.D., MA (Hons), DipClinPsyc, is a clinical psychologist by training and has been working in the clinical and forensic field since

1987. He was formerly Director of the Kia Marama Sexual Offenders' Unit at Rolleston Prison in New Zealand, and has taught both clinical and forensic psychology at Victoria, Canterbury, and Melbourne Universities. He is currently the Director of Clinical Training at Victoria University of Wellington. Professor Ward's research interests fall into five main areas: rehabilitation models and issues; cognition and sex offenders; the problem behavior process in offenders; the implications of naturalism for theory construction and clinical practice; assessment and case formulation in clinical psychology. He has published over 180 journal articles, books, and book chapters. His most recent book (co-authored with Devon Polaschek and Tony Beech) is *Theories of sexual offending*, John Wiley & Sons Ltd. (2006).

John C. Williams, M.A., is a doctoral student in clinical psychology at the State University of New York at Binghamton. His interests are in the areas of mindfulness, hypnosis, and the assessment of acceptance. He has published and presented papers on these topics.

James M. Wood, Ph.D., is a professor of psychology at the University of Texas at El Paso. He received his Ph.D. in clinical psychology in 1990 from the University of Arizona. He has taught graduate courses in psychometrics, multivariate statistics, personality assessment, and psychopathology. He has published numerous articles in the area of psychological assessment as well as on interrogative suggestibility and child forensic interviewing. He is particularly interested in issues in applied professional decision making.

Introduction

What Are the Great Ideas of Clinical Science and Why Do We Need Them?

SCOTT O. LILIENFELD AND WILLIAM T. O'DONOHUE

As the eminent psychology historian Ludy Benjamin (2001) observed, "A common lament among psychologists today, particularly among those with gray hair, is that the field of psychology is far along a path of fragmentation or disintegration" (p. 735). Indeed, the two editors of this book, although still managing to stave off the inevitable progression toward heads of completely gray hair, have heard much the same plaint on myriad occasions.

THE RESISTANCE TO A COMMON CORE OF PSYCHOLOGICAL KNOWLEDGE

The field of psychology, so the story goes, possesses little or no intellectual coherence. From this perspective, psychology might meet Kuhn's (1962) definition of a preparadigmatic field, in which there is considerable debate about such fundamentals as the domain of inquiry, legitimate research methods, and standards of evidence. We should therefore focus, the narrative continues, on training specialists rather than generalists, because there is no general body of psychological knowledge from which to draw. Indeed, many contemporary psychologists doubt that a core body of psychological knowledge exists (Griggs,

Proctor, & Bujak-Johnson, 2002; see Henriques, 2004, for an interesting discussion). A problem with this view is that it raises a troubling and embarrassing question: In what way, then, are we psychologists experts? How do we justify all the benefits and honorifics associated with our professional status if indeed we do not possess unique knowledge and skills (O'Donohue & Henderson, 1999)?

Still others suspect that such a core body of psychological knowledge exists but are reluctant to specify it, perhaps out of fear that by doing so they would hold graduate programs accountable to unduly stringent curricular standards. We can find no better illustration of this point than the conclusions drawn from the 1958 Miami Beach Conference on Graduate Education in Psychology (Roe, Gustad, Moore, Ross, & Skodak, 1959; see also Benjamin, 2001). Eight days of prolonged discussion yielded the following unintentionally humorous consensus: "First, there is a common core [of psychological knowledge]. Second, we should not specify what this is lest we in any way discourage imaginative innovation in graduate training" (p. 44).

Regrettably, precious little appears to have changed in the intervening 38 years. Indeed, the accreditation standards of professional graduate psychology programs have shifted increasingly toward abandoning the effort to develop a core curriculum (Benjamin, 2001). For example, in the recent accreditation standards of the American Psychological Association, clinical psychology graduate programs are evaluated not by how well they fulfill consensually adopted educational and training criteria, but by how well they adhere to their own individually constructed criteria (American Psychological Association, Committee on Accreditation, 2002). Nevertheless, this renunciation of core content may have baleful consequences for the profession. As one of us (along with several colleagues) argued,

> Although we welcome creativity and innovation in how clinical psychology programs elect to meet fundamental educational goals, this does not mean that the nature of these goals should be left largely to programs themselves. We believe that psychology has advanced to the point where at least the rudiments of a core "critical thinking curriculum in clinical science" can be identified for all clinical programs. By permitting clinical programs to select their own training models and evaluating how well they hew to these models, accreditation bodies are abdicating their responsibility to ensure that future generations of clinical psychologists become thoughtful and informed consumers of the scientific literature. (Lilienfeld, Fowler, Lohr, & Lynn, 2005, p. 207)

Nevertheless, this is not to say that psychologists should just become adept at critical thinking—that psychologists are in some sense philosophers skilled at uncovering assumptions, analyzing weaknesses in definitions, detecting contradictions, evaluating claims, and analyzing the soundness of arguments. These skills are indeed extremely important. Still, the question remains, given all proferred candidates for belief, which ideas still stand after such winnowing criticism has been applied? In this book, we have attempted to identify the survivors.

FRAGMENTATION BETWEEN SCIENCE AND PRACTICE

Although intellectual fragmentation poses a threat to virtually all domains of psychology, this threat appears to be especially acute in clinical psychology and allied disciplines, including counseling psychology, school psychology, and social work. Indeed, if there is one thing on which clinical psychologists can agree, it is that there is little on which clinical psychologists can agree. The past few decades have witnessed an increasing schism between researchers and practitioners marked by mutual mistrust. Much of this "scientist-practitioner gap" (Fox, 1996; Tavris, 2003), as it has come to be known, reflects a deep-seated disagreement concerning the nature of knowledge claims.

Whereas scientists agree that controlled research should be the final arbiter of truth claims in clinical psychology, many practitioners believe that their subjective clinical experience should be accorded such privileged status. Moreover, some practitioners dismiss the relevance of research findings on psychotherapy and assessment to their everyday practice, maintaining that these findings should be disregarded when they conflict with clinical intuition, clinical anecdotes, subjective experience, or some combination thereof. The partisan divide has probably been exacerbated by the tendency of some scientists to express a condescending attitude toward clinicians, and the tendency of some clinicians to express an unwillingness to examine scientific evidence that could constrain their favored practices. To many outside observers, the "war" between researchers and practitioners, as psychologist and science writer Carol Tavris (2003) termed it, appears about as amenable to common ground as a political debate between Michael Moore and Rush Limbaugh.

The problems do not end there. Even within competing camps of researchers and practitioners, sharp and often acrimonious debates rage over a plethora of fundamental questions. When making clinical decisions, should we place greater trust in data from actuarial formulas or from intuitions derived from personal experience? Are single case reports worthless as evidence, or can they offer valuable insights in some cases? Does the current system of classifying mental disorders do more good than harm? Are different schools of psychotherapy associated with important differences in efficacy? Are genetic influences critical in the causes of mental disorders, or has their importance been overestimated? Are evolutionary explanations of psychopathology useful, or are they merely fanciful "just so stories" cooked up to account for behavior that we can't otherwise explain? Do mental disorders remain essentially fixed across generations, or do they morph over time in accord with prevailing social and cultural expectations? The list, although not endless, is certainly formidable.

Understandably, graduate students in clinical psychology and cognate disciplines sometimes leave their courses profoundly confused about the status of their discipline. With so much disagreement concerning so many foundational issues, many of them conclude that there is no core body of knowledge in clinical science with which to turn. Others go even further, taking the present state of intellectual chaos as an implicit license to "do almost anything" as clinicians. After all, with so little consensual knowledge regarding psychotherapy, assessment, and diagnosis, why be constrained by the injunctions of a relative handful of researchers in the Ivory Tower?

YES, THERE IS A CORE BODY OF CLINICAL SCIENCE KNOWLEDGE

This perplexing and troubling state of affairs suggests a pressing need for common ground between researchers and practitioners, as well as within these two groups. The recent passing of the most influential clinical scientist of the second half of the 20th century, Paul E. Meehl of the University of Minnesota (see Waller & Lilienfeld, 2005), affords an auspicious occasion for reminding researchers, practitioners, and students that the field of clinical science *does* possess a number of basic unifying principles. As Meehl (1973) noted wryly in the preface to his book, *Psychodiagnosis:*

> If one really believes that there is no appreciable validity in the existing corpus of psychological knowledge that bears upon mental health problems, as to either substance or method, then the obvious conclusion is that we should liquidate our training programs and turn to making an honest living selling shoes. I record my prediction that this "thin beer" phase of clinical psychology is a passing fad. . . . (p. xxi)

We concur wholeheartedly with Meehl that such a body of dependable knowledge in clinical science exists. The significant ongoing debates regarding specific questions in psychotherapy, assessment, and diagnosis should not overshadow the fundamental domains of agreement among established scholars of clinical science. There is, we contend, substantially more consensus than meets the eye. But what comprises this core body of clinical science knowledge?

In a classic article in the *Journal of Consulting and Clinical Psychology,* Meehl (1978) delineated five "noble traditions" of clinical psychology: descriptive psychopathology, behaviorism and learning theory, psychodynamics, psychometrics, and behavior genetics. Although not hewing rigidly to Meehl's list (for example, readers of this book will find no explicit mention of psychodynamics as a core concept, although they will find residues of it in several chapters), we have been inspired by it to generate a more fine-grained list of what we, and what we suspect most clinical scientists, would regard as the 17 "Great Ideas" of clinical science. These ideas comprise the framework for this volume.

WHAT MAKES AN IDEA GREAT?

Although we will not attempt to offer a definitive answer to the question of what makes an idea "great," we'll outline the admittedly rough criteria we've adopted for the purposes of this volume. Fortunately, Fathali Moghaddam (2005) has recently provided helpful guidance in this regard. According to Moghaddam, great ideas in psychology possess four key features: they (1) influence our perceptions of human nature, (2) exert an applied impact, (3) stimulate research, and (4) stand the test of time. We concur with his criteria, although we would offer a friendly amendment to his fourth criterion by noting that great psychological ideas have survived repeated scientific tests over long spans of time. We (and Moghaddam, we suspect) would not, of course, wish to commit the logician's *ad antiquitem fallacy* of concluding that an idea must be meritorious merely because it has endured for numerous generations. Astrology, for example, has survived largely intact for five millennia despite the wholesale absence of any scientific support for its claims (Hines, 2003).

To Moghaddam's four useful criteria, we would add a fifth: the capacity of an idea to generate *consilience* (Wilson, 1998) across diverse domains of knowledge, especially those at different levels of scientific explanation (e.g., physiological, psychological, social). Most or all of the great ideas in this volume, we maintain, have fostered connections among disparate intellectual approaches.

We regard these 17 Great Ideas as the fundamental concepts—philosophical, conceptual, and methodological—that every mental health researcher and practitioner should know. The eminent analytic philosopher Wilfred Van Orman Quine (see Quine & Ullian, 1978) suggested that our belief systems can be thought of as consisting of a core belief, with some beliefs highly connected to others, many strands flowing to and from them. Core beliefs, according to Quine, are of particular importance because they prop up so many other peripheral beliefs. We believe that the 17 Great Ideas we present here are central to the clinical scientist's web of belief. They are key to how the clinical scientist sees the world; they animate research programs; they help define what are taken as legitimate research questions; they serve as sources of theories; they help define what is and is not legitimate evidence; they assist in devising new therapies or evaluating proffered ones; and they play a key role in case formulation. In short, we regard them as forming the bedrock foundation for the education and training of all aspiring clinical scientists.

We believe that the knowledge imparted by these Great Ideas is directly relevant to the ethical aspiration of "First do no harm," often taken to be a succinct distillation of the physician's Hippocratic Oath. Such knowledge allows the clinician to appreciate the complexity and substantive matters that need to be considered when rendering important clinical decisions. We have argued elsewhere (O'Donohue & Henderson, 1999; see also Chapter 1, this volume) that professionals possess *epistemic duties*—obligations to acquire and apply specialized knowledge. These 17 Great Ideas comprise the backbone of this knowledge set for the clinical scientist.

Almost certainly, many thoughtful readers will quarrel with our selection of precisely 17 Great Ideas, not to mention these specific 17 ideas. Such debate is healthy, and we eagerly await recommendations from readers concerning candidates for other Great Ideas of clinical science.

Nevertheless, we humbly believe that most readers will agree that these 17 concepts embody most, if not virtually all, of the core body of dependable knowledge that the field of clinical psychology has accumulated. Moreover, we believe that these 17 Great Ideas offer the promise of bridging the ever-widening gulf between researchers and practitioners by offering a *lingua franca* for enhancing dialogue between these two increasingly isolated groups. We hope that we are not expecting too much by suggesting that this volume may provide one modest step toward narrowing the scientist–practitioner gap from a Grand Canyon to a flowing ravine.

REFERENCES

American Psychological Association. (2002). *Report of the Committee on Accreditation*. Washington, DC: Author.

Benjamin, L.T. (2001). American psychology's struggles with its curriculum: Should a thousand flowers bloom? *American Psychologist, 56,* 735–742.

Fox, R. E. (1996). Charlatanism, scientism, and psychology's social contract. *American Psychologist, 51,* 777–784.

Griggs, R. A., Proctor, D. L., & Bujak-Johnson, A. (2002). The nonexistent common core. *American Psychologist, 57,* 452–453.

Henriques, G. (2004). Psychology defined. *Journal of Clinical Psychology, 60,* 1207–1221.

Hines, T. (2003). *Pseudoscience and the paranormal*. Amherst, NY: Prometheus Books.

Kuhn, T. (1962). *The structure of scientific revolutions*. Chicago: University of Chicago Press.

Lilienfeld, S. O., Fowler, K. A., Lohr, J. M., & Lynn, S. J. (2005). Pseudoscience, nonscience, and nonsense in clinical psychology: Dangers and remedies. In R. H. Wright & N. A. Cummings (Eds.), *Destructive trends in mental health: The well-intentioned path to harm* (pp. 187–218). New York: Routledge.

Meehl, P. E. (1973). Preface. In P. E. Meehl (Ed.), *Psychodiagnosis: Selected papers* (vii–xxii). Minneapolis: University of Minnesota Press.

Meehl, P. E. (1978). Theoretical risks and tabular asterisks: Sir Karl, Sir Ronald, and the slow progress of soft psychology. *Journal of Consulting and Clinical Psychology, 46,* 806–834.

Moghaddam, F. M. (2005). *Great ideas in psychology.* Oxford, England: Oneworld Publications.

O'Donohue, W., & Henderson, D. (1999). Epistemic and ethical duties in clinical decision-making. *Behavior Change, 16,* 10–19.

Quine, W. V., & Ullian, J. S. (1978). *The web of belief.* New York: Random House.

Roe, A., Gustad, J. W., Moore, B. V., Ross, S., & Skodak, M. (1959). *Graduate education in psychology.* Washington, D.C.: American Psychological Association.

Tavris, C. (2003). Mind games: Psychological warfare between therapists and scientists. *The Chronicle of Higher Education (Review), February 28,* B7–9.

Waller, N. G., & Lilienfeld, S. O. (2005). Paul Everett Meehl: The cumulative record. *Journal of Clinical Psychology, 61,*1209–1229.

Wilson, E. O. (1998). *Consilience: The body of knowledge.* New York: Knopf.

PART

I

How to Think Clearly
About Clinical Science

1

Science Is an Essential Safeguard Against Human Error

WILLIAM T. O'DONOHUE, SCOTT O. LILIENFELD, AND KATHERINE A. FOWLER

As behavioral health professionals, we justify our professional titles—that of clinical psychologist or any of its cognates (e.g., counseling psychologist, psychiatrist, social worker, psychiatric nurse, marriage and family counselor, psychotherapist) by our specialized knowledge. Simply put, we ought not merely believe something to be true but should actually know it to be true on the basis of good evidence. Our clients hire us largely out of their beliefs that we possess specialized knowledge and skills. Our knowledge of the evidence relating to human behavior and its problems, including our knowledge of the limitations of this evidence, is the warrant that justifies all the benefits that we acquire in our professional role: pay, honorific titles, and special abilities to perform certain acts (such as admitting patients to hospitals). If we do not in fact possess such special knowledge and abilities, then we are in effect engaged in a deceptive sham in which we are illegitimately acquiring our special role and treatment (Dawes, 1994; O'Donohue & Lilienfeld, in press). In such cases, clients are placing their trust, futures, and interests in the hands of individuals who may not have earned it.

In this chapter, we discuss the advantages and the necessity of adopting a scientific perspective concerning psychopathology and its treatment. We argue that there is persuasive scientific evidence that we as human

3

cognitive agents can come all too easily to plausible, but erroneous, beliefs. For example, we can believe that x is associated (e.g., correlated) with y when it is not or that x causes y even when it does not (e.g., that a certain treatment reliably produces certain outcomes). Furthermore, we contend that specialists and experts, such as behavioral health professionals, possess a special duty to remain vigilant against erroneous ways of thinking and to hold beliefs that are justified by the best scientific evidence available.

Most centrally, we maintain that science—an applied epistemology (approach to knowledge) that features specialized ways of forming beliefs—is the best way to minimize error in our web of beliefs. Science, we propose, is the best safeguard we have at our disposal against commonplace biases and lapses in reasoning to which we are all prone. As Carl Sagan (1995) observed, the protections afforded by science are especially crucial when testing our most cherished beliefs, such as those derived from our own preferred theoretical orientations. We also argue that science provides the most trustworthy basis for solving the myriad problems we confront in behavioral health—problems related to what causes disorders and how to measure and treat them.

Thus, clinical science entails that behavioral health professionals possess what we call an *epistemic duty*—a duty to know. Moreover, this epistemic duty is best enacted through a critical knowledge of the scientific method in psychology and the relevant scientific literature (see also McFall, 1991). We agree with McFall (1991) that many popular competing views of an appropriate epistemology for behavioral health are mistaken. Finally, we contend that science offers the best way to meet our epistemic duties and to solve the growing problems that face us as a profession.

KNOWLEDGE

To be effective clinical scientists, we must base our actions and decisions on knowledge. We should not simply guess or believe, but instead *know* how nature, in this case human nature, actually operates to influence behavior. Epistemology is the branch of philosophy that addresses such questions as "What is knowledge?" and "What are the best ways to acquire knowledge?" One of its main tasks in the former case is to distinguish knowledge from other forms of belief, such as mere opinion, armchair speculation, false belief, and unwarranted belief.

Although epistemology can be dated back as far as Plato in the fourth century B.C., there have been dramatic changes in the study of knowledge in the 20th and now 21st centuries. Because something called "science" has produced an unprecedented accumulation of accurate knowledge, epistemologists have turned to the question of "What is special about science that has made it so fertile in producing such knowledge?" This is one of the central questions of a specialty area known as the philosophy of science.

We live in an era in which scientific triumphs are taken increasingly as commonplace. Therefore, it may be worthwhile to reflect briefly on the fundamental shifts in knowledge and daily life that have accrued from the "scientific revolution."

Before the scientific revolution, we did not know whether the sun revolved around the earth or vice versa. We did not understand gravity or other laws of motion. Electricity was unknown. So were the causes and cures of most diseases. Without an understanding of microscopic organisms, such as bacteria and viruses, and their interactions with parts of the human body, little could be done to understand—let alone treat or prevent—much sickness and causes of death. The number and nature of chemical elements were poorly understood. As a consequence, what is now known as material science was also unknown. Thus, the technology that flows from material science to produce everything from Post-it® notes, to enduring and safe toys, to car bodies that are lightweight (for gas mileage), rust-resistant, and strong (for safety), could not be developed. Advances in botany facilitated the agricultural revolution, so that many people were freed from farming and left to pursue activities that satisfied other human needs, such as acquiring knowledge. Advances in engineering have allowed computer hardware to become inexpensive and amazingly efficient. It is fair to say that our everyday Western society—especially much of its comforts, relative safety, and efficacy—is so imbued with science and technology that they have become part of the background that we take for granted. Moreover, we have so counted on science as a problem-solving mechanism that when we experience such problems as oil shortages, impending flu pandemics, and potential terrorist attacks, we look to scientists to help us solve them.

It is also easy to take for granted many of the previous scientific achievements in behavioral health. In the first world, few if any mental health hospitals can today be called "snake pits." However, before the rise of effective antipsychotic medications in the 1950s, the situation was far different. The delusions and hallucinations of individuals with schizophrenia were so unmanageable that patients were put in cells, chained to chairs, or, if not controlled, yelling and spreading their feces on the walls. As most readers of abnormal psychology textbooks know, the word "bedlam" derived from a cockney pronunciation of Bethelem—a mental hospital in England in which chaos reigned supreme. In addition, effective technologies based on learning principles have been developed to help mentally retarded and autistic children learn a wide range of functional skills, including language. Even bedwetting can be successfully treated with bell and pad technologies (see Chambless et al., 2006; O'Donohue & Fisher, in press).

Thus, we have come a long way with the diagnosis and treatment of many behavioral health problems. Other such problems have been refractory, either because they have received scant scientific attention (for example, many of the paraphilias or personality disorders) or because the efforts to resolve these problems have yet to yield positive results (Laws & O'Donohue; 2001; O'Donohue, Fowler, & Lilienfeld, 2005).

Why Is Science Necessary?

One of the major reasons why science is necessary is that humans often form firmly held beliefs that are mistaken. This tendency is hardly limited to practicing clinicians, as academic researchers are probably just as prone to such errors as everyone else (Meehl, 1993). Compounding the problem of firmly held but erroneous beliefs is the fact that most people are blissfully unaware of their own cognitive biases. For example, Pronin, Gilovich, and Ross (2004) found evidence for what they termed "bias blind spot," whereby most people are adept at pointing out cognitive biases in others but incapable of recognizing the same biases in their own reasoning. Nevertheless, good scientists, including good clinical scientists, are aware of their propensities toward bias and rely on scientific methods to compensate for them. As noted earlier, it is especially crucial to avail ourselves of these scientific methods when our favored theoretical beliefs are at stake.

There are numerous examples of erroneous beliefs in history, from earth-centered views of the universe, to misestimating the size of the earth, to believing that human physiology was a function of the moon and four basic humors, to believing that there were only four kinds of elements—earth, water, fire, and air. Psychologists and philosophers have studied and begun to categorize the myriad ways in which human cognition is subject to error. We will discuss three of the most important errors here (see also Chapter 2).

Confirmation Bias

"The mother of all biases," *confirmation bias,* is probably the central bias that the scientific method was developed to circumvent. We can define this bias as the tendency to selectively seek out and recall information consistent with one's hypotheses and to neglect or reinterpret information inconsistent with them.

Several investigators have found that clinicians fall prey to confirmation bias when asked to recall information regarding clients. For example, Strohmer, Shivy, and Chiodo (1990) asked counselors to read three versions of a case history of a client, one containing an equal number of descriptors indicating good self-control and poor self-control, one containing more descriptors indicating good than poor self-control, and one containing more descriptors indicating poor than good self-control. One week after reading this case history, psychotherapists were asked to offer as many factors they could remember that "would be helpful in determining whether or not [the client] lacked self-control" (p. 467).

Therapists offered more information that would be helpful for confirming than disconfirming the hypothesis that the client lacked self-control, even in the condition in which the client was characterized mostly by good self-control descriptors.

Researchers, too, are prone to confirmation bias. For example, Mahoney (1977) asked 75 journal reviewers with strong behavioral orientations to evaluate hypothetical manuscripts that contained identical research designs but strikingly different results. In some cases, these results were consistent with traditional behavioral views (reinforcement strengthens motivation), whereas in other cases they contradicted these views (reinforcement undermines motivation). Reviewers were far more likely to evaluate the paper positively if it confirmed their preexisting views (e.g., "A very fine study," "An excellent paper . . .") than if it disconfirmed them (e.g., "There are so many problems with this paper, it is difficult to decide where to begin," "a serious, mistaken conclusion").

Similarly, there is evidence that clinicians are prone to the related phenomenon of *premature closure* in diagnostic decision making: they frequently reach conclusions on the basis of too little information (Garb, 1989). For example, Gauron and Dickinson (1969) reported that psychiatrists who observed a videotaped interview frequently formed diagnostic impressions within 30 to 60 seconds. Premature closure may be both a cause and a consequence of confirmation bias. It may produce confirmation bias by effectively halting the search for data that could refute the clinicians' preexisting hypotheses. It may result from confirmation bias because clinicians may reach rapid conclusions by searching selectively for data that confirm these hypotheses.

Illusory Correlation

Clinicians, like all individuals, are prone to *illusory correlation*, which we can define as the perception of (a) a statistical association that does not exist or (b) a stronger statistical association than is present. Illusory correlations are especially likely to arise when individuals hold powerful a priori expectations regarding the covariation between certain events or stimuli. Such correlations are almost certainly in part a product of our propensity to detect meaningful patterns in random data (Gilovich, 1991). Although this tendency is often adaptive in that it can help us to make sense of our confusing external worlds, it can lead us astray in certain situations (see also Chapter 2).

For example, many individuals are convinced that a strong correlation exists between the full moon and psychiatric hospital admissions, even though research has demonstrated convincingly that this association is a mental mirage (Rotton & Kelly, 1985). Moreover, many parents of autistic children are certain that the onset of their children's disorder coincides with the administration of mercury-bearing vaccines, although large and carefully conducted epidemiological investigations disconfirm this association (Herbert, Gaudiano, & Sharp, 2002).

In a classic study of illusory correlation, Chapman and Chapman (1967) examined why psychologists perceive clinically meaningful associations between signs (e.g., large eyes) on the Draw-A-Person (DAP) test (a commonly used human figure drawing task) and psychiatric symptoms (e.g., suspiciousness), even though research has demonstrated that these associations do not exist (Kahill, 1984). They presented undergraduates with DAP protocols that were purportedly produced by psychiatric patients with certain psychiatric symptoms (e.g., suspiciousness). Each drawing was paired randomly with two of these symptoms, which were listed on the bottom of each drawing. Undergraduates were asked to inspect these drawings and estimate the extent to which certain DAP signs co-occurred with these symptoms.

Chapman and Chapman found that participants "discovered" that certain DAP signs tended to co-occur consistently with certain psychiatric symptoms, even though the pairing between DAP signs and symptoms in the original stimulus materials was entirely random. For example, participants perceived large eyes in drawings as co-occurring with suspiciousness, and broad shoulders in drawings as co-occurring with doubts about manliness. Interestingly, these are the same associations that tend to be perceived by clinicians who use the DAP (Chapman & Chapman, 1967). Illusory correlation has been demonstrated with other projective techniques, including the Rorschach (Chapman & Chapman, 1969) and sentence completion tests (Starr & Katkin, 1969). Illusory correlation may be most likely when, as in the case of the DAP, individuals hold strong a priori expectations regarding the associations between stimuli.

Hindsight Bias

Individuals tend to overestimate the likelihood that they would have predicted an outcome once they have become aware of it, a phenomenon known as *hindsight bias* (Fischhoff, 1975) or the "I knew it all along effect." Arkes et al. (1981) examined the effects of hindsight bias on medical decision making. Physicians were assigned randomly to one of five groups, each of which was given the same case history. The foresight group was asked to assign a probability estimate to each of four potential medical diagnoses. Each of the four hindsight groups was told that one of the four diagnoses was correct, and was then asked to predict the likelihood that they would have selected that diagnosis. The hindsight groups assigned the least likely diagnoses indicated a much greater likelihood that they would have chosen those ostensibly "correct" diagnoses in question compared with the foresight group. Hindsight bias bears implications for practitioners' diagnostic judgments. Instead of analyzing present data independently, professionals may inadvertently corroborate past diagnoses. In other words, access to a previous diagnosis may corrupt the independence of a "second opinion." There is no prescribed way to avoid hindsight bias in clinical situations, although Ruscio (2006) suggested testing predictions of future events and attending to their outcomes as a general remedy for minimizing such bias.

Hindsight bias is closely related to the phenomenon of *deterministic reasoning* in diagnostic decision making. Case formulations typically include the construction of causal hypotheses to account for a patient's pathology. For example, early in psychotherapy, many clinicians assess the patient's life history dating to childhood. The practitioner may view the patient's history through the lens of current psychopathology, leading to erroneous causal conclusions. The connections between past events and current functioning may seem so self-evident that the therapist makes little effort to consider other potential causal factors.

Hindsight bias and deterministic reasoning can result in overconfidence in clinical judgment. When asked to estimate the probability that they have produced correct judgments, undergraduate participants and clinicians are often overconfident (Garb, 1998; Smith & Dumont, 1997). This effect is most marked with complex or difficult tasks. Overconfidence bears many clinical implications, including risks to patients or others if suicide risk or dangerousness are incorrectly ruled out.

We can view science as an essential, although not perfect, corrective to these and other forms of erroneous belief formation. Through its methods, it helps us to avoid falling prey to these widespread, but understandable, human fallibilities and instead form beliefs that possess a higher probability of verisimilitude (that is, truth-likeness).

For example, randomized double-blind controlled trials are a partial control against confirmation bias, because such trials minimize the probability that investigators will inadvertently influence participants to produce the results for which they fervently hope. Systematic correlational designs help to minimize illusory correlation because such designs ensure the accurate computation of the covariation among variables. Carefully controlled longitudinal designs mitigate against hindsight bias because they collect data at multiple time points, thereby preventing researchers from reconstructing the past in accord with their hypotheses. The bottom line: Science is an essential safeguard against error, albeit not a foolproof one.

What Is Science?

Surprisingly, there has not been a clear, consistent answer to this question. Scholars who have attempted to address this question have emerged with divergent images (conceptions) of science. In this section, we will briefly review five major images of science:

1. Science as Error Correction (Sir Karl Popper)
2. Science as Exemplars of Effective Puzzle Solving (Thomas Kuhn)

3. Science as Persuasion
4. Science as Anarchy (Paul Feyerabend)
5. Indigenous Images of science by influential psychologists or psychotherapists (Freud, Rogers, Skinner)

We review these multiple and at times competing images for two major
reasons. First, we hope to debunk oversimplified characterizations of
science that are often proffered by psychological researchers. Arguments
in our field often rise to the meta-level and, in so doing, questions such
as "What is science?" and "Is this good science?" frequently arise. In these
contexts, the debate often becomes rather simplistic. For example, some
researchers assert dogmatically that science is defined exclusively by x,
where x is some property such as collecting quantitative information,
performing statistical tests, finding confirmatory data, attempting falsifi-
cations, and so on. However, a more thoroughgoing understanding of
science studies reveals that the matter is far more nuanced and complex.
Second, a review of these divergent images of science illustrates some
of the excitement of the science enterprise. As we will soon discover,
science is not a boring, sterile, or mechanistic endeavor. Instead, it is open,
dynamic, and inescapably human.

Two other issues deserve mention before we discuss the various images
of science in more detail:

1. To what extent are these images *descriptive* (capturing how actual
   science has worked in the past) or *prescriptive* (capturing what good
   scientists ought to do)? Practicing scientists are usually more interested
   in the latter. They often ask themselves, "How can I do science better?"
   They want prescriptions rather than historical descriptions. Regrettably,
   in contrast to most "hard" sciences (e.g., physics, chemistry) there has
   been little descriptive analysis of past episodes of psychological science
   (Smith, 1983, is a notable exception). As a consequence, most mainstream philosophers of science have ignored psychology.
2. What is the scope of these claims about science? Philosophers of science
   have mainly been interested in physics, biology, and chemistry and have
   accorded psychology, including clinical psychology, scant attention.
   Generalizations that are apt for certain sciences, such as physics, may
   therefore not be as apt for psychology.

Image 1: Science Works to Find and Correct Error

According to the prominent philosopher of science Sir Karl Popper
(1959), science begins with problems. Indeed, one reason we value
science is that it often deals with practical problems to which it can
provide at least some tentative solutions. For example, we want our
children to live healthy lives. Science, both basic and applied, offers us
information about germs, technologies to create clean drinking water

and treat sewage properly, inoculations to decrease the probability of childhood illnesses, exercise and nutrition to create health, and so on. Many critiques of science (Hess, 2004) neglect the crucial point that science has allowed us to advance nearly universal human values, such as the well-being of children.

Popper also saw problem solving as a key evolutionary activity (see also Chapter 11 in this volume). To him, problem solving and knowledge were key biological phenomena. Survival and reproduction are problems that give rise to a wide variety of often interrelated subproblems. Survival leads to concerns about acquiring food, which can lead to problems about raising crops, which gives rise to further questions about plant diseases, and so on. Popper thought that one of the major ways that humans differ from other animals is that we can form conjectures or hypotheses about solutions to our problems and then test them so that, if false, they "die in our stead." For Popper, science progresses by falsifying claims.

According to Popper (1999, p. 4), problems also arise when an organism's "expectations" about its environment (either innate or acquired experientially) turn out to be wrong. We can form these erroneous expectations because of some of the cognitive errors we discussed previously. The iterative process of formulating and testing expectancies is the method of trial-and-error or error elimination (see also Campbell, 1974). Nature eliminates errors by extinguishing unsuccessful problem solutions by means of natural selection. Since the origin of the earth, approximately 98% of species have become extinct (Ehrlich & Ehrlich, 1981). Even when species survive, they do so not because of perfect solutions to problems, but because their tentative solutions are "good enough." Eiseley (1958) put this point nicely:

> . . . [the] evolutionary past of every species of organism—the ghostly world of time in which animals are forever slipping from one environment to another and changing their forms and features as they go. . . . But the marks for the passage linger, and so we come down to the present bearing the traces of all the curious tables at which our forerunners have sat and played the game of life. Our world, in short, is a marred world, an imperfect world, a never totally adjusted world, for the simple reason that it is not static. The games are still in progress and all of us, in the words of Sir Arthur Keith, bear the wounds of evolution. Our backs hurt, we have muscles which no longer move, we have hair that is not functional. All of this bespeaks another world, another game played far behind us in the past. We are indeed products of "descent with modification." (p. 197)

Error elimination. At its most fundamental level, Popper's evolutionary epistemology is represented by the following problem-solving schema:

$$P1 \rightarrow TT \rightarrow EE \rightarrow P2.$$

. . . we start from some problem P1, proceed to a tentative solution or tentative theory TT, which may be (partly or wholly) mistaken; in any case it will be subject to error-elimination, EE, which may consist of critical discussion or experimental tests; at any rate, new problems are not in general intentionally created by us, they emerge autonomously from the field of new relationships which we cannot help bringing into existence with every action, however little we intend to do so. (Popper, 1972, p. 119)

Popper asserted that many people mistakenly view science as "the craving to be right." Scientific knowledge differs only from other knowledge in the methods by which errors are systematically identified and rectified (Popper, 1962, p. 216). Accordingly, the "difference between the amoeba and Einstein" is that "the amoeba dislikes to err while [Einstein] consciously searches for his errors in the hope of learning by their discovery and elimination" (Popper, 1972, p. 70).

The growth of scientific knowledge is thus characterized by "the repeated overthrow of scientific theories and their replacements by better and more satisfactory ones" (Popper, 1962, p. 215). The function of science is "not to save the lives of untenable systems but, on the contrary, to select the one which is by comparison the fittest, by exposing them all to the fiercest struggle for survival" (p. 42). The "fittest" theories—the ones with less error, the ones that Popper argued have highest truth-likeness—help the human species to adapt best to its environment. Accordingly, science is constantly in a state of flux in light of the fact that nature is "highly irregular, disorderly, and more or less unpredictable." Final truth is never attained because all tests that could potentially falsify a given account of reality can never be conducted. At best, a conjecture can have high truth-likeness—that is, behave like the truth, but still contain some error.

Munz (1985), a student of Popper's, provided an interesting conjecture regarding the noncognitive, affiliative function of dogmatically held—even false—beliefs:

With the emergence of consciousness, we get a further change in the nature of change. Conscious organisms can create falsehoods; they can lie and delude and deceive both themselves and others. . . . In this way, cultures are created. The most elementary strategy used in the development of cultures is the artificial protection of knowledge from criticism. Certain pieces of knowledge, though obviously not all knowledge, are set aside and protected from critical appraisal. The thunder is identified with a god, the shadow of a man with his soul, and twins with cucumbers. Rational doubts are nipped in the bud by the mere absence of competing alternative proposals. Such protected knowledge can be used as a social bond. People who subscribe to it are members of a society; people who don't are outside that society. In this way, a lot of knowledge is siphoned off and used for non-cognitive purposes—that is, as catechism. But such siphoning-off though initially obviously counter-adaptive, is an oblique advantage. A society so constituted is larger than a group of people bonded by nothing but the web of kinship and is therefore capable of effective division of labour and cooperation. (p. 282)

This is an interesting point about which clinical scientists need to be mindful. Individuals can hold beliefs for emotional and other "psychological" reasons rather than "rational" reasons. This conjecture may also explain some of the causes of "psychoreligions"—such as therapeutic fads and crazes—that pervade the behavioral health field (see Lilienfeld, Lynn, & Lohr, 2003; Singer & Lalich, 1996).

Let us take an example from Popper's (1999) writings to illustrate how a conjecture or a theory can be falsified. According to Popper, the best hypotheses are those that are "risky," meaning that they are posed in such a way that they are most susceptible to falsification. The riskier the prediction, the greater the number of observations that could falsify it. Taking "all ravens are black" as our theoretical statement, "all ravens are black" not only rules out the possibility of a white raven, but also of a red, green, or blue one. In fact, it rules out every color other than black. According to Popper, the statement "all ravens are black" contains greater empirical content than, say, the statement "no raven is white" or "no raven is blue or green." According to the calculus of probability, the statement "all ravens are black" is more improbable (risky) than any of the others. It is much more prone to falsification because of the greater number of potential falsifiers, and hence rationally superior, holding the greatest promise of yielding profitable returns. In principle, finding a raven of any color other than black is a potential falsifier of the theory "all ravens are black." However, should a nonblack (e.g., purple) raven turn up in our search to find a nonblack raven, then the theory "all ravens are black" would be falsified (Popper, 1999, p. 20).

Of course, many extant theories in most realms of science have yet to be falsified. How then do scientists decide which theories are superior? Using the theories of Newton's and Einstein's theory of gravitation as a case in point, Popper (1999) offered the following guidance:

> The interesting thing is that the theory says all the more, the greater number of its potential falsifiers. It says more, and can clear up more problems. Its *explanatory potential* or its *potential explanatory power* is greater. . . . From this standpoint, we may once again compare Newton's and Einstein's theories of gravitation. What we find is that the empirical content and the potential explanatory power of Einstein's theory are much greater than those of Newton's. . . . Einstein's theory is thus more risky. It may be in principle falsified by observations that do not touch Newton's theory. The empirical content of Einstein's theory, its quantity of potential falsifiers, is thus considerably greater than the empirical content of Newton's theory. . . . But even if the relevant observations have not yet been made, we can say that Einstein's theory is *potentially* superior to Newton's. It has the greater empirical content and the greater explanatory potential. (p. 20, italics in original)

What kinds of potentially erroneous beliefs should most concern clinical scientists? When conducting clinical practice, including assessment, diagnosis, and psychotherapy, we can make the following kinds of errors:

1. *False descriptive beliefs.* We can claim, for example, that our client never thought of suicide in the preceding week, when she thought of it five times.
2. *False causal beliefs.* We can believe that our client's erectile dysfunction is caused by performance anxiety, when it is caused by a neurological problem.
3. *False ontic beliefs.* We can believe that things exist when in fact they do not. We may believe that there is something such as an "inner child," when there is not ("ontic" refers to the nature of the real world).
4. *False relational claims.* We can believe that therapy x produces more change in certain types of clients than therapy y, when this is not the case.
5. *False predictions.* We can believe that therapy x in certain situations will result in the greatest change for this client, when it will not.
6. *False ethical beliefs.* We can believe that it is ethically permissible to engage in a certain kind of extratherapeutic relationship with a client, when it is not.

The good Popperian clinical scientist is concerned about all of these types of errors and attempts to maximize constructive criticism/feedback to identify and correct them. The best clinical scientists are concerned with errors in their belief systems—especially their most cherished beliefs—and thoroughly and honestly search for critical feedback to identify and minimize these errors. In the words of the Nobel Prize–winning physicist Richard Feynman (1985), science is "bending over backwards to prove ourselves wrong."

Image 2: Science as Solving Puzzles by Following Successful Exemplars

In his classic book, *The Structure of Scientific Revolutions*, the influential meta-scientist Thomas Kuhn (1970) advanced a view of scientific change in which science cycles through a series of stages. One of his core insights is that most scientists adopt a paradigm—a problem-solving exemplar, and attempt to apply lessons learned from this success to new unsolved problems.

Stage 1: Immature or Preparadigmatic Science. The first stage in Kuhn's model is immature science. According to Kuhn (1970), immature science is characterized by "frequent and deep debates over legitimate methods, problems, and standards of solution, though these serve rather to define schools than to produce agreement" (pp. 47–48). During this stage there is no consensus, and no agreed-upon facts or method.

Moreover, there may not be agreement on what subject matter is worthy of research (e.g., ontology), and there is a proliferation of competing schools of thought (Bird, 2000).

Stage 2: Normal or Paradigmatic Science. The second stage in the cyclical process of scientific change is normal science. During normal science, the field demonstrates cumulative progress (O'Donohue, 1993). What is more, normal science denotes a consensus in the scientific community: there are agreed-upon facts and methods, there is agreement on what subject matter is worthy of research, and what were once competing schools of thought usually settle into a single "paradigm."

Even though there are at least 21 different meanings of the term "paradigm" (see Masterman, 1970), it is generally used in one of two ways:

> On the one hand, it stands for the entire constellation of beliefs, values, techniques, and so on shared by the members of a given community. On the other, it denotes one sort of element in that constellation, the concrete puzzle-solutions which, employed as models or examples, can replace explicit rules as a basis for the solution of the remaining puzzles of normal science. (Kuhn, 1996, p. 175)

This "settling into a single paradigm" usually occurs in the wake of "some notable scientific achievement" (Kuhn, 1974, p. 460). For example, Kuhn stated that Newton's *Optiks*, which postulated that light consists of material corpuscles, "was the notable scientific achievement" that marked the first paradigm in optical science (Kuhn, 1996). Newton's *Optiks* was generally regarded as being "better than its competitors in solving . . . problems that . . . practitioners (had) come to recognize as acute" (Kuhn, 1996, pp. 23). Of course, this doesn't mean that the paradigm has to "explain all of the facts [which could confront it]"; a paradigm is only required to explain those deemed most important by a given community (Kuhn, 1996, pp. 17–18).

Paradigmatic science is largely a conservative endeavor, consisting of "mopping-up operations" and "puzzle-solving" (Kuhn, 1962, p. 24, pp. 35–42). Both of these procedures operate to "broaden and deepen the explanatory scope" of a paradigm (Gholson & Barker, 1985). Specifically, "mopping-up" and "puzzle-solving" involve: (1) striving to bring a paradigm "into closer agreement with nature" (Kuhn, 1963, p. 360); (2) attempts at increasing the accuracy and scope of the paradigm so as to include new phenomena (Kuhn, 1996, p. 25; Losee, 1980); and (3) better articulating the "paradigm theory . . . resolving some of its residual ambiguities" (Kuhn, 1996, p. 27).

Stage 3: Anomalies and Crisis. Normal science proceeds unabated just as long as the paradigm satisfactorily explains the phenomena to which it is applied (Losee, 1980). However, "new" and "unsuspected phenomena" are often uncovered by scientific research (Kuhn, 1996, p. 52).

At some point, normal science is almost always forced to confront "anomalous" data (Hoyningen-Huene, 1993). In contrast to Popper,

Kuhn argued that these anomalies don't necessarily provide falsifying counterexamples of the prevailing paradigm. Anomalies may arise because of instrumental or "human" error. In fact, when such anomalies arise it initially is the scientist, not the paradigm, who is to blame, (Bird, 2000). Kuhn (1962) stated:

> Normal science . . . often suppresses fundamental novelties because they are necessarily subversive of its basic commitments . . . [however], when the profession can no longer evade anomalies that subvert the existing tradition of scientific practice [the paradigm is in crisis]. (pp. 5–6)

Crisis. When enough anomalies accumulate, scientists begin questioning whether the dominant paradigm is appropriate. The prevailing paradigm is now said to be in a state of crisis. In other words, during a crisis blame is shifted from scientists to the paradigm, and a "sense of professional insecurity is generated" (Bird, 2000, p. 43). At times of crisis, there is a "blurring of a paradigm and the consequent loosening of the rules for normal research" (Kuhn, 1970, p. 84). When a crisis occurs, it becomes patent that normal science cannot continue as before. The paradigm is said to have "drowned in a sea of anomalies," and a point is reached when the old paradigm has to be discarded, giving way to a new paradigm (Kuhn, 1996). Contrary to the steady progress of normal science, this replacement of one paradigm for another is a cataclysmic (revolutionary) event (Gholson & Barker, 1985).

Stage 4: Revolutionary or Extraordinary Science. Kuhn (1962) defined what he meant by "scientific revolutions":

> Scientific revolutions are here taken to be those non-cumulative developmental episodes in which an older paradigm is replaced in whole or in part by an incompatible new one. (p. 91)

By "incompatible" Kuhn (1962) suggested that "after a revolution scientists are responding to a different world" (p. 111), making competing paradigms largely "incommensurable" (p. 102). Kuhn called this psychological phenomenon a "Gestalt switch" (Kuhn, 1996). For Kuhn, proponents of paradigms often hold such radically different presuppositions about the world that they perceive it in qualitatively distinct ways. For example, if Kepler (who embraced the Copernican, heliocentric theory of the solar system) and Tycho Brahe (who embraced the Aristotelian-Ptolemaic, geocentric theory of the solar system) were standing on a hill at dawn, "Tycho sees the rising sun but Kepler sees the rotation of the Earth" (Bird, 2000, p. 99).

Where Is Behavioral Science in Kuhn's Model?

Many authors have argued that psychology is in an immature or pre-paradigmatic stage of development given its absence of intellectual coherence. Nevertheless, the frequently posed question of whether psychology has a paradigm is wrongly put because it is too broad. Kuhn (personal communication, April, 1989) stated that:

> . . . [P]sychology is probably too much of a catchall field to generalise about. I've no reason to suppose that the same answers would be forthcoming if the same questions were addressed, say, to learning theory, clinical psychology, perceptual psychology, and intelligence testing. What the answers would be if the field were appropriately subdivided, I'm not the one to say. You have to know the field(s) from the inside to do that.

How did Kuhn account for the developmental delay of psychology and the other social sciences? Kuhn argued that because of the large relevance of these disciplines for urgent practical problems, they lack isolation from the demands of everyday concerns. According to him,

> . . . [T]he insulation of the scientific community from society permits the individual scientist to concentrate his attention upon problems that he has good reason to believe he will be able to solve. Unlike the engineer, and many doctors, and most theologians, the scientist need not choose problems because they urgently need solution and without regard for the tools available to solve them. In this respect, also, the contrast between natural scientists and many social scientists proves instructive. The latter often tend, as the former almost never do, to defend their choice of a research problem—e.g., the effects of racial discrimination or the causes of the business cycle—chiefly in terms of the social importance of achieving a solution. Which group would one then expect to solve problems at a more rapid rate? (Kuhn, 1970a, p. 164)

Thus, for Kuhn, scientists are usually engaged in puzzle solving, which uses successful exemplars as hints for solving new problems. This is the core of what Kuhn meant by paradigmatic or normal science. "Paradigm" is a word that has had wide currency in psychology and the other behavioral disciplines, but is often misused. To use this word properly according to Kuhn, one would need to be able to articulate: (1) an actual puzzle solution and (2) other scientists who used this puzzle solution as an exemplar for further puzzle solutions.

A good case can be made that this occurred in the rise of behavior therapy (see O'Donohue et al., 1999). B. F. Skinner, in his single-subject work with cumulative recorders, showed that the three-term contingency (the discriminative stimulus, the behavioral response, and the contingent consequence—i.e., the operant paradigm) resulted in regular relations (reinforcement, punishment, shaping, differential extinctions with various schedules of reinforcement). Early behavior therapists used this puzzle-solving exemplar and applied it to other problems (e.g., the treatment of an electively mute schizophrenic), using single-subject methodologies with considerable initial success (Lindsey & Skinner, 1959; Ullmann & Krasner, 1965). Thus, the image of science Kuhn proposed is that good scientists understand successful problem solving and creatively apply these solutions to novel problems.

Image 3: Science as Methodological Anarchy

Paul Feyerabend, a student of Karl Popper's, offered an interesting, controversial, and unconventional image of science. He argued that science possesses no single method: If one looks at any rule that scientists or philosophers of science have constructed (such as to develop conjectures and attempt to falsify them), one can find clear episodes in the history of science that violated this rule yet were successful at solving problems. Thus, Feyerabend argued paradoxically that to maximize the likelihood of problem solving, one should have no rules. Here are some of his key claims:

- Science is an essentially anarchistic enterprise: theoretical anarchism is more humanitarian and more likely to encourage progress than its law-and-order alternatives.
- The only principle that does not inhibit progress is: *anything goes.*
- The consistency condition that demands that new hypotheses agree with accepted *theories* is unreasonable because it preserves the older theory, and not the better theory. Hypotheses contradicting well-confirmed theories offer us evidence that cannot be obtained in any other way. Proliferation of theories is beneficial for science, whereas uniformity impairs its critical power.
- There is no idea, however ancient and absurd, that is not capable of improving our knowledge.
- No theory ever agrees with all the *facts* in its domain, yet it is not always the theory that is to blame. Facts are constituted by older ideologies, and a clash between facts and theories may be proof of progress.
- Science is much closer to myth than a scientific philosophy is prepared to admit. (Feyerabend, 1975).

For Feyerabend, science is anarchistic and should have no rules. Moreover, it should respect, understand, and learn from other discourses (e.g., ethics, history, art). In this image of science, clinical scientists should function as more than scientists, because there are other domains worthy of interest and applicable to clinical pursuits. In addition, this image of science sees science as a radically creative enterprise, attempting always to see limits in any rule or prescribed method. To solve problems, good scientists are opportunistic and borrow or invent new methods.

Again, one can see how Skinner was Feyerabendian in important respects. He did not use puzzle boxes, the dominant instrumentation of his day. Rather, he invented the operant chamber ("Skinner box") and the cumulative recorder. He did not use the same dependent variable but again innovated and used the rate of responding. He did not use group designs but, rather, invented single-subject experimental designs. In so doing—perhaps because of his lack of rule following—he discovered important regularities in behavior.

The key lesson here is that clinical scientists should always question their accepted methods, consider innovations in rules and methods, and judge these by problem solving effectiveness, not by whether they conform to the current standard.

Image 4: Science as Argument and Persuasion

In this fourth image, the function of science is to persuade others that one's findings and arguments are compelling. Indeed, one of the central purposes of language is persuasion (Quine & Ullian, 1970). For over two millennia, originating with the Sophists (lawyers by modern standards) in ancient Greece and Rome, "the art of persuasion" has been studied formally under the philosophical tradition known as "rhetoric" (Luks, 1999). In science and in other activities that rely heavily on rhetoric (e.g., law, education, philosophy, politics, literature), the central goal of the scientist is, implicitly or explicitly, to persuade one's audience—and first oneself. "Rhetorically, the creation of knowledge is a task beginning with self-persuasion and ending with the persuasion of others" (Gross, 1990, p. 3).

Many philosophers of science have argued for key "underdetermination theses" (e.g., Kuhn, 1962; Popper, 1972; Quine, 1961). An underdetermination thesis means that the move from some point to another is not a matter of logic, and therefore not necessarily truth preserving. Let us examine a few of these theses.

Quine (1961) and Popper (1972) argued for semantic underdetermination. That is, the move from some raw perception to some words that are used to refer or describe the raw perception (e.g., "The cat is on the mat") is underdetermined. Another way of saying this is that the perception does not logically entail the semantic "reference." Instead, there is always "a jump" from a purely logical point of view. As another example, all laws and theories are underdetermined by empirical evidence. Because not every piece of copper in the world has been tested to determine whether it conducts electricity, the claim that "all copper conducts electricity" is not entailed by actual empirical evidence. Again, this is another logical jump, whose legitimacy is a matter of persuasion.

These underdetermination theses imply that these moves are not matters of logical necessity, but matters of persuasion. The scientist must first "persuade" herself that what she sees is a correctly functioning thermometer that is actually displaying the value of 98.6°F. Furthermore, the scientist must persuade herself and others that given the alternatives the evidence best supports the statement that "all copper conducts electricity." These are matters of judgment, not logical necessity.

Rhetoric is also used in key "external" matters. For example, through rhetoric, scientists prescribe what empirical and conceptual problems are worthy of study, funding, and publication. The view that some methods or procedures are legitimate ways to discover knowledge is key to science. This issue, too, is not a deductive affair but a matter of rhetoric and persuasion. In psychology, debates about hypothetico-deductive, single-subject designs, as well as the use of inferential statistics, regularly occur, and listeners are variously persuaded about which are legitimate methodologies to best produce knowledge. Important consensuses emerge that allow the field to move beyond certain debates to other more circumscribed issues (note the similarity with the move Kuhn describes in a discipline moving from preparadigmatic status to paradigmatic status).

Moreover, according to this image of science, the psychological experiment is an attempt at persuasion. Take, for example, the issue of whether Therapy X is effective. The investigator needs to be mindful of reasons why he or others might be unconvinced that this therapy works. Good experimental design allows these concerns to be handled in a convincing fashion. Random sampling is a move designed to persuade those concerned by the claim that "The sample was biased and so therefore the results are unpersuasive due to their unrepresentativeness." Random assignment is a move designed to persuade those concerned by the claim "The groups might have been different from the start." The no-treatment control condition is a move designed to persuade those concerned by the claim "The problem would have spontaneously remitted." (Note that all control conditions are designed to rule out plausible rival hypotheses. But again "plausibility" is not a matter of logic, but a matter of judgment and persuasion.) The "importance" of the results is also a matter of persuasion. For example, is the magnitude of the effect clinically significant? Was the procedure "cost-effective"? Were possible iatrogenic effects (complications caused by diagnosis, treatment, or both) measured and found to be insignificant? Did patients find the treatment to be acceptable? These are all matters of persuasion. Finally, if the author *persuades* peer reviewers and the editor that these and other matters have been handled adequately, the paper is published.

In these examples, each of these methodological moves is fallible. For example, despite random sampling, the sample might still be biased. Random assignment still sometimes produces groups that differ initially in key ways. Thus, one is not logically compelled to accept that these problems have been definitively handled by these methodological moves. Rather, the scientists designing the experiments hope that these are persuasive, although they cannot logically compel assent.

The word "rhetoric" often carries a negative connotation; it is often taken to mean attempting to persuade through trickery or other invalid means. Gross (1990) clearly did not use this phrase in this way. Clearly, the use of what are seen as "valid" and "rational" methods are warranted as these in the usual case are highly persuasive, For example, the randomized controlled trial is usually fairly persuasive regarding questions about therapy outcome (but see Antonuccio for an interesting critique). However, that is not to say that style and other presentation aspects are irrelevant. Feyerabend's (1975) analysis of Galileo's arguments for the Copernican system revealed that Galileo used "propaganda, emotion, ad hoc hypotheses and appeal to prejudices of all kinds" (p. 153). Feyerabend argued that early in a theory's development, at a time when the theory is drastically underdetermined by evidence, matters of "style, elegance of expression, simplicity of presentation, tension of plot and narrative, and seductiveness of content become important features of our knowledge" (1975, p. 157).

Each of these persuasive tasks is neither isolated nor independent. Scientists work in a community, and consensus emerges from argument. This is the scientist's aim. Gross (1990) stated that:

> To rhetoricians, science is a coherent network of utterances that has also achieved consensus among practitioners. . . . But to say that scientific knowledge represents a consensus concerning the coherence and empirical adequacy of scientific utterances, that the various methods of science are essentially consensus-producing, is not to denigrate science; it is rather to pay tribute to the supreme human achievement that consensus on complex issues represents. . . . The truths of science, then, are achievements of argument. (p. 203)

In this image of science, good scientists understand what persuasive burdens they have. What is in doubt, and what sort of moves would clear up this doubt? Good scientists ask these questions about themselves and others.

According to this image of science, science is first and foremost an exercise in self-persuasion. The better this goal is accomplished, the better the next step of persuading others can be accomplished. Good scientists realize that they are prone to the cognitive biases discussed previously and attempt to persuade themselves that their beliefs are not due to these biases. Furthermore, they realize what the barriers to persuading others can be and strategize to overcome them. There are many competing belief systems and there is, in some important sense, a marketplace of ideas. Good scientists must compete in this marketplace and be effective salespersons. Part of the aptness of the sales metaphor is that individuals "buy" ideas not only on rational but on emotional considerations. An understanding of the psychology of belief formation and acceptance is key. This does not make science a glib, superficial, or cheap enterprise, but grounds science in the art of argument, counterargument, and persuasion.

O'Donohue and Lloyd (2005) suggested that psychotherapy itself is a persuasive activity. Therapists must first persuade themselves and then their clients of the correctness of the case formulation of the diagnoses, of the treatment, of the appropriateness of termination, and so on.

Image 5: Psychologists Have Constructed Their Own Images of Science

O'Donohue and Halsey (1997) tried to capture the differing views of science of Skinner, Rogers, and Ellis, all of whom obviously have exerted a significant influence on clinical psychology. For example, Freud claimed that his method was scientific. This assertion may surprise some who believe that psychoanalysis can be easily dismissed as unscientific or even pseudoscientific (Cioffi, 1998). Freud characterized his scientific method as deducing useful constructs from careful clinical observations and verifying them as useful, accurate constructs because they are utilized in therapeutic successes. Freud (1925) stated that:

> The view is often defended that sciences should be built up on clear and sharply defined basal concepts. In actual fact no science, not even the most exact, begins with such definitions. The true beginning of scientific activity consists rather in describing phenomena and in proceeding to group, classify, and correlate them. Even at the stage of description, it is not possible to avoid applying certain abstract ideas to the material in hand, ideas derived from various sources and certainly not the fruit of the new experience only. (p. 60)

Carl Rogers (1968), the founder of client-centered therapy and a leader of the humanistic movement in psychology, although attempting to synthesize empathic understanding to fully explore the private world of meanings with more conventional accounts of science, stated that:

> Unless I am willing to define these terms operationally, to design a research which will put them to the test, or to encourage others to design such researches; and unless the various extraneous variables are controlled, and the findings support the hypotheses, then we are only in the realm of pattern perception and not of confirmation. (Rogers, 1968, p. 67)

Skinner, having influenced behavioral analysis and behavior therapy, has been criticized by some as being *scientistic* (that is, as adhering "fetishistically" to a scientific methodology even when it is not appropriate) rather than scientific. But his initial claims for scientific status were greeted by some with skepticism because of his single-subject methodology. Skinner's recommendations for successful scientific practice include a focus on the individual organism, the use of rate of responding as the dependent variable, and an eschewal of statistics, all of which were and still are fairly unconventional.

We wish to draw four conclusions from this cursory review of the claims for scientific status of these three scholars, who have had substantial influence on clinical psychology:

1. They do not appear to be influenced directly by any of the classic philosophers of science, instead developing indigenous accounts of the scientific status of their psychologies (Albert Ellis, who cited explicitly the influence of Popper and the neo-Popperian, W. W. Bartley, was an exception);
2. These accounts of what constitutes science differ widely from one another and widely from the philosophers of science discussed earlier. Feyerabend (and Chairman Mao) would be happy, as a thousand methodological flowers are blooming;
3. These accounts give their psychotherapist adherents some warrant for claiming scientific status for their endeavors. The demarcation line cannot be easily drawn by stating, for example, that x performs psychoanalysis; therefore, x is not scientific;
4. More work needs to be conducted on the metascience (scientific study of science itself) of clinical psychology to sort out such questions as: (a) What are legitimate metascientific criteria for clinical science? (b) What are the problems with any of the metascientific claims of a school of psychotherapy (see Faust, 2005, for a discussion)?

SOME PRELIMINARY CONCLUSIONS ABOUT SCIENCE

Because we did not evaluate all of the major images of science, the conclusions that we can offer are preliminary. Nevertheless, we propose that each image of science captures a valid aspect of the sprawling enterprise of science. It is clear from our view that science is a multifaceted, complex problem-solving activity. It can involve maximizing criticism to identify and minimize error. It often uses exemplars of past similar successful solutions, which at times break existing rules, especially methodological rules. It also understands and respect discourses that lie outside the boundaries of traditional science. Fundamentally, the "science game" relies on persuasion, especially artful argumentation. Science is neither mechanistic nor simple. However, it is unprecedented in its problem-solving effectiveness.

CONCLUSION

Science provides the basis for our specialized knowledge and skills. Clinical science is dedicated to effectively solving the problems associated with behavioral health such as "What causes this disorder?" and "How can it be effectively treated?" We have epistemic duties to our clients to know this key information and to deliver the most effective and scientifically informed clinical services. Science is a complex and multifaceted activity, which attempts to solve problems by efficiently eliminating errors in our web of beliefs and compensating for cognitive biases to which we are all prone. Both clinical researchers and therapists are vulnerable to these biases, but good clinical scientists—whether they operate in the laboratory or consulting room—are keenly aware of this vulnerability. Moreover, good clinical scientists avail themselves of the tools of science, such as randomized double-blind designs, systematic correlational designs, and carefully controlled longitudinal studies, to minimize these biases. Science advances by creatively applying past successes, by creating new methods and rules, and by persuading through argumentation. Most of all, it advances by constructive criticism of our most cherished assumptions.

KEY TERMS

Epistemology: The study of knowledge. A specialty area in philosophy that attempts to answer questions such as: What is knowledge? How is knowledge gained? and more recently: What is special about science that accounts for its unprecedented ability to produce knowledge?

Epistemic duties: The responsibility to possess knowledge, particularly the special knowledge associated with expert or professional status.

Philosophy of science: The subdivision of philosophy that investigates special questions associated with science, such as, what distinguishes science from nonscience? What is good science? What accounts for changes in science (e.g., revolutions)? What is scientific explanation?

Science: A human activity associated with unprecedented growth of knowledge. Nevertheless, its precise definition remains controversial.

SUGGESTED READINGS

Carey, S. (1997). *A beginner's guide to scientific method.* New York: Wadsworth.

Curd, M., & Cover, J. A. (1998). *Philosophy of science: The central issues.* New York: W.W. Norton and Company.

Hempel, C. G. (1966). A case: Semelweiss, puerperal fever. In C. G. Hempel, *Philosophy of natural science.* New York: Prentice Hall (pp. 3–5).

McFall, R. M. (1991). Manifesto for a science of clinical psychology. *The Clinical Psychologist, 44 (6):* 75–88.

O'Donohue, W. T., & Lilienfeld, S. O. (in press). The epistemological and ethical dimension of clinical science. In T. Treat (Ed.), *A festschrift for Richard McFall.*

Pfohl, R. F. (Ed.). (2004). *Cognitive illusions: A handbook on fallacies and biases in thinking, judgment, and memory.* New York: Taylor and Francis.

REFERENCES

Bird, A. (2000). Thomas Kuhn. Princeton University Press: Princeton, New Jersey.

Bird, A. (2000). Thomas Kuhn. Chesham: Acumen, Princeton: Princeton University Press.

Campbell, B. (1974). Emotion and survival: An evolutionary perspective. *Journal of Primary Therapy*, Vol 1(3), Win. pp. 236–248.

Chambless, D. L., Baker, M. J., Baucom, D. H., Beutler, L., Calhoun, K. S., Crits-Christoph, P., Daiuto, A., DeRubeis, R., Detweiler, J., Haaga, D. A. F., Bennett Johnson, S., McCurry, S., Mueser, K. T., Pope, K. S., Sanderson, W. C., Shoham, V., Stickle, T., Williams, D. A., & Woody, S. A. (1998). Update on empirically validated therapies, II. *The Clinical Psychologist*, 51, 3–16.

Cioffi, F. (1998). Freud and the Question of Pseudo-Science. Chicago: Open Court.

Dawes, R. M. (1994). Psychological Measurement, Psychological Review. Vol. 101(2), 278–281.

Ehrlich, P. R. & Ehrlich, A. (1981). Extinction: The Causes and Consequences of the Disappearance of Species. New York: Random House.

Eiseley, L. (1958). Darwin's Century. Anchor Books: New York.

Feyerabend, P. (1975). Against Method: An Outline of an Anarchistic Theory of Knowledge. New York. New Left Books.

Feyerabend, P. (1993). Against Method. London: Verso; 3rd edition.

Feynman, R. (1985). QED: The strange theory of light and matter.

Fischhoff, B. (1975). Hindsight is not equal to foresight: The effect of outcome knowledge on judgment under uncertainty. *Journal of Experimental Psychology: Human Perception and Performance*, Vol 1(3), 288–299.

Garb, H. N. (1989). Clinical Judgment, Clinical Training, and Professional Experience. Psychological Bulletin, Vol. 105(3), 387–396.

Garb, H. N. (1998). *Studying the clinician: Judgment research and psychological assessment*. Washington, DC: American Psychological Association, 173–206.

Gauron, E. F., & Dickinson, J. K. (1969). The influence of seeing the patient first on diagnostic decision-making in psychiatry. *American Journal of Psychiatry*, 126, 199–205.

Gholson, B., & Barker, P. (1985). Kuhn, Lakatos, and Laudan: applications in the history of physics and psychology, *American Psychologist*, 40, pp. 755–769.

Gross, A. G., (1990). Reinventing Certainty: The Significance of Ian Hacking's Realism, *Proceedings of the Biennial Meeting of the Philosophy of Science Association* Vol. 1990, Volume One: Contributed Papers (1990), pp. 421–431.

Herbert, J. D., Sharp, I. R., & Gaudiano, B. A. (2002). Separating fact from fiction in the etiology and treatment of autism: A scientific review of the evidence. *Scientific Review of Mental Health Practice*, 1, 23–43.

Hess, D. J. (2004). Medical modernisation, scientific research field and the epistemic politics of health social movements. *Sociology of Health & Illness*, Vol 26(6), 695–709.

Hoyningen-House, P. (1993). *Reconstructing Scientific Revolutions: Thomas S. Kuhn's Philosophy of Science*. Chicago: University of Chicago Press.

Kuhn, T. S. (1962). The Structure of Scientific Revolutions (Chicago, University of Chicago Press).

Kuhn, T. S. (1963). "The Function of Dogma in Scientific Research," in *Scientific Change*, edited by A. Crombie (London: Heinemann: 347–69).

Kuhn, T. S. (1970). The Structure of Scientific Revolutions. University of Chicago Press: Chicago.

Kuhn, T. S. (1970). Notes of Lakatos PSA: Proceedings of the Biennial Meeting of the Philosophy of Science Association. 1970, pp. 137–146.

Kuhn, T. S. (1970a). The Structure of Scientific Revolutions, 2nd ed. (Chicago, University of Chicago Press).

Kuhn, T. S. (1974). Second thoughts on paradigms, in: F. Suppe (Ed.) The Structure of Scientific Theories, pp. 459–482 (Urbana, Illinois: University of Illinois Press).

Kuhn, T. S. (1996). The Structure of Scientific Revolutions University of Chicago Press, 3rd ed.

Luks, F. (1999). Post-Normal Science and the Rhetoric of Inquiry: Deconstruction normal science? Futures 31(7): 705–719.

Masterman, M., (1970). "The Nature of a Paradigm," pp. 59–89 in Lakatos and Musgrave, eds. Criticism and the Growth of Knowledge. Cambridge University Press: Cambridge.

McFall, R. M. (1991). Manifesto for a science of clinical psychology. *The Clinical Psychologist*, 44(6), 75–88.

Meehl, P. E. (1993). Philosophy of Science: Help or Hindrance? Psychological Reports, Vol 72(3), 707–733.

Munz, P. (1985). Our knowledge of the growth of knowledge: Popper or Wittgenstein. London: Routledge.

O'Donohue, W. T. (1993). The spell of Kuhn on psychology: An exegetical elixir, Philosophical Psychology, 6(3), 267–287.

O'Donohue, W., & Halsey, L. (1997). The substance of the scientist-practitioner relation: Freud, Rogers, Skinner & Ellis. *New Ideas in Psychology*, 15(1), 35–53.

O'Donohue, W., & Henderson, D. (1999). Epistemic and ethical duties in clinical decision-making. *Behavioral Change*, 16(1), 10–19.

O'Donohue, F., & Lilienfeld, 2005.

O'Donohue, W., & Lloyd, A. (2005). Ethos of contemporary clinical psychology. In R. H. Wright & N. A. Cummings (Eds.). *Destructive trends in psychology: The well intentioned road to harm.* New York: Brunner-Routledge (Taylor and Francis Group).

O'Donohue, W., Lilienfeld, S., & Fowler, K. (Eds.). (in press). *Sage handbook of personality disorders.* Thousand Oaks, CA: Sage Publications, Inc.

O'Donohue, W., Laws, R. D., Hollin, C. R., (Eds.). Handbook of Forensic Psychology, New York: Basic Books.

O'Donohue, W., Fisher, J., (in press). Clinician's Handbook of Evidence Based Practice Guidelines: The Role of Practice Guidelines in Systematic Quality Improvement. New York: Kluwer Academic Publishing.

Popper, K. R. (1959). The Logic of Scientific Discovery. Oxford, England: Basic Books, 1959, pp. 480.

Popper, K. (1962). The Logic of Scientific Discovery. Hutchinson: London.

Popper, K. (1972). Objective Knowledge: An Evolutionary Approach Clarendon Press: Oxford.

Popper, K. (1999). Falsificationism, Scientific Inquiry, pp. 65–71. Edited by Robert Klee. Oxford University Press: New York, Oxford. Princeton, NJ: Princeton University Press.

Pronin, E., Gilovich, T., Ross, L. (2004). Objectivity in the Eye of the Beholder: Divergent Perceptions of Bias in Self Versus Others. Psychological Review, Vol 111(3), 781–799.

Quine, W. V. (1961). From a Logical Point of View, Cambridge Massachusetts, London, Harvard University Press, second edition, revised.

Quine, W. V. O., and Ullian, J. S. (1970). The Web of Belief, New York: Random House.

Rogers, C. R., Coulson, W. R. (1968). Man and the science of man. Columbus, Ohio: Charles E. Merrill.

Sagan, C. (1995). The Demon-Haunted World: Science as a Candle in the Dark, Random House, 115–24.

Smith, L. D. (1983). Behaviorism and logical positivism: A revised account of the alliance (Volumes I and II) Dissertation Abstracts International, Vol 44(6-A), pp. 1900.

Starr, B. J., Katkin, E. S. (1969). The clinician as an aberrant actuary: Illusory correlation and the incomplete sentences blank. Journal of Abnormal Psychology, 74(6), 670–675.

Ullman & Krasner. (1965). Case studies in behavior modification. New York: Holt, Rinehart, & Winston.

2

The Clinician as Subject

Practitioners Are Prone to the Same Judgment Errors as Everyone Else

JOHN RUSCIO

In the *New York Times* best-selling book *Word Freak*, Stefan Fatsis (2001) chronicled his journey into the world of competitive Scrabble players. The tale he tells about the development of expert judgment holds lessons that extend well beyond the realm of Scrabble. Players must memorize a tremendous amount of information, beginning with game rules and the frequencies and point values of the letters in a set of Scrabble tiles. This much is fairly simple, but studying the lists of acceptable words presents a more daunting task: There are about 120,000 words allowed in U.S. tournaments, and the addition of about 40,000 British words yields a total of 160,000 words allowed in international tournaments. It takes many years of devoted study to approach complete word knowledge, and even the leading experts engage in a continual struggle to retain this information and create multiple, complex interconnections so that as many words as possible can be retrieved quickly in different game scenarios.

As impressive as these feats of memory may seem, successful expert-level play also demands sophisticated information processing. Increasingly thorny judgments and decisions must be made as one learns to master such strategic issues as rack and board management and the handling of the end game. Experts do much more than scan their memory stores for possible word plays. For example, many of the words played by experts are unrecognizable to laypersons, and even competitive players can be uncertain whether a particular play is an allowable word. This raises the question of whether to gamble a challenge of an opponent's play: If the word is invalid, it is removed and the opponent forfeits that turn. If the word is valid, one loses his or her own turn. If one opts not to challenge, another decision is whether to play a word or exchange one or more tiles. Particularly if no high-scoring or defensively important plays can be identified, it can be wise to forfeit a turn to exchange some unwanted letters for new ones. If one opts to make a play, this forces the decision of when to terminate the search for the best available play. These decisions, along with many others, must be made using limited information. One's retrievable word knowledge is incomplete, and information regarding an opponent's tiles and those that remain in the bag is bounded by probabilistic constraints. Likewise, decisions must be made rapidly, as there is a penalty for running over the 25-minute limit each player is allotted per game. With massive amounts of study and practice, some Scrabble players achieve a state in which their command of strategic decisions and generation of optimal or near-optimal plays appears effortless. Through a rigorous course of training and experience, the deliberative, short-sighted, and relatively foolhardy style of play exhibited by novices is replaced by the wisdom and automaticity characteristic of experts.

The process by which Scrabble players hone their judgment provides many useful clues about how to improve clinical judgment. Clinical practitioners must acquire and retain a wealth of factual knowledge as well as decision-making strategies for applying this knowledge effectively. Learning and using the full breadth and depth of theory and research related to the assessment, classification, and treatment of mental disorder within the constraints of applicable ethical and legal codes certainly does not constitute a game, yet many of the challenges of clinical work are analogous to those of an intricate game. A broad array of potentially relevant client characteristics, alternative interventions, and therapeutic goals constitutes the panoply of variables to consider. Relations among variables, especially causal relations, are seldom established unequivocally by previous research or experience. In light of available assessment tools and techniques, it can be difficult to obtain pertinent information in a reliable and valid manner. For a number of reasons, one will often have to make probabilistic inferences regarding gaps or apparent inconsistencies in the data. The nature of the judgments and decisions to be made, and the available options, is often open-ended. Ethical and legal codes proscribe some courses of action, but the breadth of tolerable practices remains vast. Tough choices must be made, and they can have significant consequences.

The complexity of the situation faced by clinical practitioners often demands the use of shortcuts to make critical judgments and decisions. Otherwise, the cognitive limits of human information processing could easily be exceeded. Likewise, inattention to potential cognitive biases can lead to judgment errors that might otherwise have been prevented. Although people vary in their aptitude for memorization and strategic thinking, the formidable knowledge base and skill set involved in competitive Scrabble or clinical practice must be built through training and experience. In what follows, suggestions for the development of expert clinical judgment will be drawn from an examination of cognitive limitations and biases, the disproportionate influence of personal experience, and the requirements for successful experiential learning.

Before proceeding, it is worth underscoring the approach and emphases of this chapter. Rather than attempting to catalogue exhaustively the types of errors that have been identified in the judgment literature, I have selected a handful of exemplars based on their applicability to clinical practice. Likewise, I have presented illustrative instances of judgment errors instead of descriptions of relevant research studies. I have provided citations for readers interested in pursuing additional reading, but the emphasis here is on the detection and prevention of judgment errors in clinical practice. Finally, and perhaps most important, this chapter's focus on judgment errors is not intended in a pejorative sense. Human fallibility stems from universal cognitive limitations and biases, not from foibles unique to practitioners. As the chapter subtitle states, clinicians are prone to the *same* judgment errors as everyone else. In everyday life, individuals are relatively free to use flawed reasoning. In the role of an expert, however, one assumes an added responsibility to "get it right." Training and experience are expected to correct errors in experts' intuitive understanding of their disciplines, including both the factual knowledge base and the implementation of appropriate techniques through sound reasoning. The examination of error in this chapter is intended to introduce students in the mental health professions to the sources, types, and prevention of common judgment errors to which everyone is susceptible and that can adversely impact clinical work.

COGNITIVE LIMITATIONS AND BIASES

One of the most fundamental principles guiding research on judgment and decision making is that human information processing is constrained by certain cognitive limitations. For example, there are limits to the amount of information that can be retrieved into and held in working memory (e.g., Miller, 1956), the complexity of the operations that can be performed on this information (e.g., Halford, Baker, McCredden, & Bain, 2005; Ruscio & Stern, in press), and the speed with which information can be processed (e.g., Sternberg, 1969). Whereas a computer will be unable to solve a problem when its memory capacity is exhausted or will spend as long as necessary to work out a solution when its memory is sufficient and its processing speed is the limiting factor, clinicians seldom have the option of either reaching no judgment or taking longer to make a decision. When working with a client, many provisional judgments must be made rapidly, on the basis of a wealth of information of mixed or ambiguous validity, to proceed with an assessment or treatment during an ongoing session.

When a judgment must be reached, cognitive limitations often necessitate the use of mental shortcuts, or *heuristics* (Turk & Salovey, 1988; Tversky & Kahneman, 1974). By simplifying the task, these strategies afford a judgment—even if a normatively suboptimal one. Usually, there is an inherent trade-off between accuracy and efficiency (but see Gigerenzer, Todd, & the ABC Research Group, 1999, for exceptions in which both accuracy and efficiency can be improved). Of particular interest is that the errors resulting from the use of heuristics are not always random. Predictable types of mistakes are sometimes observed, in which case the use of a mental shortcut can be understood as causing a cognitive bias.

Representativeness and Availability Heuristics

Two heuristics have received the lion's share of attention in the literature, as they manifest themselves in myriad judgment errors. The *representativeness heuristic* produces similarity-based judgments made on the superficial basis of "like goes with like" (Kahneman & Tversky, 1972). For instance, effects are presumed to resemble their causes. Such relationships often, but do not always, hold. Consider the popular notion that mental disorders with a "biological basis" are more appropriately treated with medication than with psychotherapy, whereas psychotherapy should be reserved for disorders with no biological basis. Setting aside the often vague meaning of "biological basis"—here it will be used to signify that biological factors play a role in the etiology of a disorder—the underlying assumption appears to be that a biological problem suggests the need for a biological solution (and vice versa). This clear case of representative thinking gives rise to a number of logical problems and conceptual puzzles.

Pitting interventions against one another in this way creates a false dichotomy between different levels of analysis (biological and psychological) at which one can conceptualize and test theories of psychopathology. There is no logical inconsistency between the existence of biological bases for a disorder and an understanding of that disorder in terms of psychological mechanisms. Unless one is a mind-body dualist, it should be easy to see that all mental functioning, normal or abnormal, must have a basis in the brain (see also Chapters 13 and 15). However, even though all mental disorders are biologically *mediated* (i.e., situated somewhere in neural tissue), this does not guarantee that either the original cause(s) or the successful treatment of a disorder is biological in nature. Thus, the notion that some disorders have a biological basis whereas others do not is logically flawed. Instead, it is more appropriate to ask about the nature of the biological basis for each disorder and to pursue possible treatments based on promising knowledge at any level of analysis.

In addition, the apparent correlation between the existence of biological bases for disorders and the availability of biological treatments may be spurious. Whereas the discovery of biochemical anomalies among individuals suffering from a particular mental disorder often prompts the development and testing of new medications, the absence of known biological anomalies prohibits such focused research on biological interventions. Thus, present *knowledge* of biological bases may be associated with the availability of biological treatment options, with no causal connection between the nature or extent of biological bases and the utility of biological interventions. In the end, of course, efficacy and effectiveness research are required to evaluate the appropriateness of any treatment. The naïve, "like goes with like" belief that disorders with known biological bases are most appropriately treated using medications may hinder the search for fruitful treatments.

Whereas representative thinking uses similarity as a cue, the *availability heuristic* produces judgments of frequency or probability on the basis of the ease with which instances can be retrieved from memory (Tversky & Kahneman, 1973). Whereas the ease of recall generally provides a useful clue to how common or rare a class of events is, this heuristic can sometimes lead to biased or erroneous judgments. Unusual occurrences often attract greater attention than more mundane happenings, with the result that one might be able to retrieve instances of these relatively rare events more easily than objectively more frequent events. This can be especially true of vivid, emotionally compelling events that seem noteworthy in large part because of their rarity (Nisbett & Ross, 1980). For example, when Schreiber (1973) published *Sybil*, few (if any) individuals diagnosed with multiple personality disorder (MPD, now listed in *DSM-IV* as dissociative identity disorder) had reported childhood abuse or as many as 16 alternate personalities. Highly unusual features such as these not only helped to captivate a large audience but also served as models for future reports because many people—including professionals and laypersons—formed an MPD schema on the basis of this exceptional case. Many (if not most) subsequent MPD reports included childhood abuse and increasing numbers of alters (Spanos, 1996). Despite the absence of compelling evidence that childhood abuse is correlated with diagnoses of MPD (Lilienfeld et al., 1999; Spanos, 1996)—let alone etiologically relevant—when clinicians rely on the availability heuristic in evaluating this putative association, they can retrieve many instances consistent with an abuse-MPD link.

Even if there is no statistical association between abuse and MPD, such an *illusory correlation* (Chapman & Chapman, 1967; see also Chapter 1) may persist due to the operation of the availability heuristic. A clinician who specializes in the diagnosis and treatment of MPD can expect to encounter a number of patients who report incidents of childhood abuse during a life history interview. After all, childhood abuse is not uncommon among clinical patients (or, for that matter, among mentally healthy individuals; Renaud & Estess, 1961). The availability of these instances in memory may be mistaken as evidence to support the abuse-MPD link. What is *not* available in memory are the frequencies with which individuals not diagnosed with MPD do and do not report abuse. Potentially available, but not especially salient, in memory is the frequency with which individuals diagnosed with MPD do not report abuse. Without comparing the relative frequencies of abuse histories among individuals diagnosed with MPD to individuals not diagnosed with MPD, one cannot determine whether these variables covary (see also Chapter 16).

The operation of the availability heuristic explains how illusory correlations can be formed from equivocal observations, and additional research suggests that such illusions can persist in the face of contradictory evidence. Chapman and Chapman (1967) demonstrated that laypersons and clinical psychologists share many false beliefs about relations between characteristics of human figure drawings and the personality traits of the individuals who drew them. For example, the empirically unfounded belief that people who draw large or exaggerated eyes tend to be suspicious or paranoid is one illusory correlation used in the Chapmans' work. When provided with evidence of a *negative* relationship (e.g., a series of drawings and personality traits paired such that paranoid individuals tend to be less likely to draw large or exaggerated eyes), individuals still reported that they "learned" from these data that a *positive* relationship holds. The fact that laypersons and clinicians share many illusory correlations regarding projective tests, coupled with the fact that these illusions can persist despite experience with contradictory evidence, may help to explain the popularity of projective test indices of limited validity (Chapman & Chapman, 1969; Wood, Nezworski, Lilienfeld, & Garb, 2003; see also Chapter 4).

Bad Habits: Confirmation and Hindsight Biases

The representativeness and availability heuristics are mental shortcuts that sacrifice accuracy for efficiency, yet they only result in biased judgment under certain circumstances. Other aspects of the normal cognitive repertoire, however, include more intrinsically biased ways of thinking, which Faust (1986) labeled "bad habits" (see also Chapter 3). One such bad habit, known as *confirmation bias*, involves selectively seeking, attending to, and attaching greater weight to information that supports rather than refutes one's own beliefs (Nickerson, 1998; see also Chapter 1). For example, some clinicians who work with victims of trauma use techniques to recover allegedly repressed memories (Poole, Lindsay, Memon, & Bull, 1995), and Sagan (1995) suggests that the nature of the material obtained using these techniques often bears an uncanny resemblance to the expectations of the practitioner. There are at least three specializations within this niche, each of which involves belief in the high frequency and pathogenicity of a particular type of trauma: child sexual abuse, satanic ritual abuse, and alien abduction. Patients whose therapists emphasize alien abduction tend to recover memories of being abducted by aliens, seldom of being sexually abused as a child or of being abused by satanic cults. To the extent that a similar correspondence holds for clinicians in each of these specializations, this would place considerable strain on coincidence as an explanation, even after one acknowledges the potential influence of referral biases (i.e., patients may seek out or be referred to practitioners who share their core beliefs). The most parsimonious explanation may be that confirmation bias guides the memory recovery process, which proceeds in the service of strongly held preconceptions rather than in a more objective search for veridical information (Lynn, Lock, Loftus, Krackow, & Lilienfeld, 2003).

When confirmation bias goes unchecked, open-minded consideration of multiple perspectives can become the exception rather than the rule: Support for a single working hypothesis is sought and incoming information passes through filters that operate to distort or remove potentially troublesome data. Whether intentionally or not, we expose ourselves to situations and environments that favor our prior beliefs. For example, we tend to associate with people who think as we do, read books and articles that support our views, and join professional organizations and attend conferences to interact with others who share our beliefs. Information is often packaged in ways that will most appeal to people who hold certain beliefs—and that will not challenge those beliefs. Different chapters in the same edited book, like different presenters within a symposium at a conference, seldom take opposing positions. By choosing which book to read or which session to attend, one can avoid dissonance-provoking confrontations with alternative viewpoints. More generally, consumers of information are increasingly able to select information sources that share their preconceptions. Although it can be comforting to experience agreement on positions regarding important issues, there are serious drawbacks to consider.

First, one might mistake a carefully selected survey of opinion—a highly biased sample—for genuine, generalizable agreement. It is easy to overestimate the extent of support for a position, or the expertise of fellow supporters, when one only consults articulate, like-minded individuals. For example, in the fall of 2004, National Public Radio aired a story on the skyrocketing sales of political books during the U.S. presidential campaign. A number of book publishers observed that sales were brisk, yet none believed that these books were influencing readers' political views. Instead, they suspected that people were buying and reading books by authors that shared their views to gain ammunition—in the form of the authors' credentials as well as the readers' favorite anecdotes or factoids—for political discussions and debates.

Second, to avoid discrepant views is to squander valuable opportunities to learn, especially when one holds mistaken beliefs that are correctable.

Often, one stands to benefit far more from engaging rather than evading the expertise of those with whom one disagrees. If the best arguments and evidence, presented in the most compelling fashion, fail to adequately support an opposing position, one can place greater confidence in one's own. In contrast, the case for an alternative stance may warrant changing one's position. Without giving a fair hearing to those who hold different views, one might foolishly cling to misguided beliefs.

The bad habit of confirmation bias manifests itself in many judgments and decisions that clinicians are called on to make routinely. For instance, when gathering information to reach a diagnosis, a preliminary hypothesis is often formed remarkably quickly (Garb, 1998). This working hypothesis can steer one toward a search for supportive information rather than the more normatively appropriate testing of competing hypotheses (Faust, 1986). Assessment performed in a confirmatory mode is likely to yield information that is consistent with an initial hunch, but this consistency is interpretationally ambiguous because the same information may be equally consistent with other, unconsidered hypotheses. The failure to adequately consider alternative hypotheses is known as *premature closure*. A clinician aware of this danger could pose multiple hypotheses and determine how to tease them apart most effectively. Performing assessment in a more explicitly hypothesis-testing mode is more likely to yield evidence that genuinely supports correct ideas and contradictory evidence that serves to rule out false ones.

Another bad habit of human judgment, *hindsight bias*, involves mistaking a perceived understanding of the past for an ability to predict or control future events (Hawkins & Hastie, 1990). Once knowledge of an event's outcome becomes available, one has a feeling of having "known it all along" (Fischhoff, 1975). This phenomenon has also been described as "creeping determinism" (Fischhoff, 1980), as a chain of events can appear to have unfolded in an inevitable sequence. Because it is easy to construct plausible explanations for events after they have occurred, it is unwise to place much confidence in such accounts, much less to deem an outcome inevitable. The remarkable ability to recognize patterns, which enables us to craft a good story by imposing order on chaos, is a perceptual skill of inestimable adaptive value. However, an apparatus adept at organizing information into coherent patterns carries with it the liability of occasional mistakes, patterns that are only apparent and not real. Given the survival imperative of successfully learning environmental contingencies, one might expect human beings to be imbued with a positive bias toward the recognition of potential patterns even when this entails frequent false positive identifications. The frequency with which people commit the *post hoc ergo propter hoc* fallacy (B follows A, therefore B was caused by A) attests to such a hypersensitivity of our pattern recognition faculties. For example, reasoning that "I tried this treatment and felt better, therefore the treatment works" is to commit this fallacy. Beyerstein (1997) described many alternative explanations that cannot be ruled out when attempting to draw conclusions on the basis of personal experience, testimonials, or other anecdotal evidence.

Similarly, Meehl (1973) described as a common fallacy observed in clinical case conferences the "assumption that content and dynamics explain why this person is abnormal" (p. 244). Engaging the services of a clinical practitioner establishes that the client is currently experiencing problems that, even if not diagnosable as mental disorder, involve at least some of the symptoms. The individual's present mental state constitutes an outcome in need of an explanation, and one's therapeutic orientation often guides the conceptualization of the case. For example, clinicians who believe that traumatic exposure is the root cause of most mental anguish tend to search for trauma in a life history interview. Because even most mentally healthy individuals have experienced events that can be described—whether by client or therapist—as traumatic, a sufficiently effortful search will nearly always yield information that is consistent with the clinician's etiological theory. Confirmation bias can be influential in guiding the selective search for this information, but hindsight bias is the culprit when one concludes that the uncovered trauma explains the client's current mental problems. This outcome only seems inevitable in hindsight, and there may be either no causal connection between the trauma and present mental state or a connection that is more subtle or complicated than presumed. Either way, the premature acceptance of the first plausible narrative may preclude a more thorough assessment of other factors necessary for the most accurate case formulation or the best treatment plan. The true test of understanding is not the construction of a plausible explanation for past events, but the successful prediction of future events (Dawes, 1993).

THE DISPROPORTIONATE INFLUENCE OF PERSONAL EXPERIENCE

Mental health disciplines such as psychology, psychiatry, and social work grant professional degrees that certify expertise in clinical practice. In an article aptly titled "Credentialed Persons, Credentialed Knowledge," Meehl (1997) considered the evidential support required to substantiate such claims to expertise. Any field of study necessarily begins with the anecdotal evidence of its practitioners' personal experiences. In clinical work, experience can include training exercises as well as supervised and independent practice; the term "personal experience" does not mean "single case" (see Chapter 7 for a discussion of the inferential value of single cases). Of course, anecdotes all too readily suggest faulty conclusions and unwarranted generalizations, especially when parsed impressionistically (Faust, 1984; Meehl, 1992). To overcome the short-comings of human judgment, pioneers of a new discipline must promote a balance between open-minded speculation and skeptical inquiry within an atmosphere of dispassionate investigation. Recognizing that scientific methodology—including research design and data analysis—has been crafted to counter cognitive limitations and biases in teasing apart fact and fiction, Meehl (1997) emphasized the importance of collecting data systematically and testing relationships between variables using appropriate statistical analyses.

For a variety of reasons, clinicians' personal experience often exerts a strong influence on their judgments even when more reliable and valid information is available. Because it is acquired firsthand, knowledge gained through personal experience in clinical practice is often more emotionally resonant than the comparatively pallid reporting of research results that one encounters in the literature. Because more vivid information is more easily retrieved from memory, the application of the availability heuristic provides one avenue by which personal experience can be assigned substantial weight in reaching clinical judgments and decisions.

To grant center stage to one's personal experience, however, can be to devalue the more informative collective experience of many other clinicians who have worked with a much larger and broader sample of clients. Acknowledging the informational value of clinical experience does not give privileged status to *personal* experience relative to the experience of everyone else. Systematic research, for example, constitutes the synthesis of many people's experiences, often a much larger and more representative sampling of pertinent experiences than one has encountered firsthand. In addition, knowledge obtained through personal experience is seldom subjected to adequate statistical testing. As a result, illusory correlations may take root and actual relationships that are in any way subtle or counterintuitive may escape notice. Although theory and research on mental health are far from satisfactory—much less complete—in many important respects, the extant literature can often provide sounder guidelines for practice than a comparatively narrow consideration of one's personal experiences. An exercise such as the following might reveal a double standard of evidence skewed toward the acceptance of one's own experience and the rejection of others' experience:

> Suppose that rather than having had certain experiences and reached a certain judgment myself, someone else presented me with the same conclusion on the basis of the same evidence. That is, the haphazard nature of the sampling, the unavailability of an unknown portion of the original data due to memory limitations and biases, the nonrandom assignment of clients to conditions that vary nonsystematically, the reliability and validity of objective and subjective outcome data (as it is recalled, not as it was initially assessed), and the steps in the reasoning process would be identical to what is going through my mind right now. The only difference would be that I did not personally experience any of this. Rather, I would be learning about the fully equivalent experiences of someone else, stated in unambiguous detail. Would I accept the judgment on these terms?

Through an exercise of this sort, one might remove the *personal* aspect of the relevant experiences and more objectively accord them the weight they merit in the judgment process.

In addition to the potential roles that availability bias and evidential double standards may play, a widespread misunderstanding within the mental health community can serve—intentionally or otherwise—to dismiss the knowledge available from research literature. When the collective experience of clinical investigators is discredited in this way, practitioners are forced to rely more heavily on the anecdotal evidence of their personal experience.

The misunderstanding at issue is captured in the maxim that "probability is irrelevant to the unique individual." Variants of this claim involve the substitution of "statistics" or "research" for "probability." Regardless of its precise phrasing, the idea is that knowledge of the long-run frequency of occurrence for many similar people, under similar circumstances, is of no bearing in a specific situation that is not to be repeated. For example, statistics reported in the research literature suggest that the probability of successfully alleviating an individual's specific phobia is maximized through exposure-based treatment (Barlow, 2002). It is not unusual, however, for a mental health expert to disregard this finding, administering some other treatment (e.g., long-term psychoanalysis) on the grounds that a particular client's case is special—that the probability/statistics/research do not apply to this unique individual. There are two ways of understanding such a claim.

First, one might interpret this as a claim that, despite the clinician's awareness that exposure therapy best addresses specific phobias, he or she perceives something sufficiently probative *in this instance* to countervail the prescribed treatment. Following Meehl's (1954) classic treatise on prediction, this is referred to as a "broken leg" case: An otherwise sound statistical prediction that a certain professor is likely to attend a movie one evening *should* be modified in light of the fact that the professor had just broken a leg and is in a cast that cannot fit in a movie seat. Despite the existence of such cases, research has revealed that practitioners overidentify "broken leg" counterexamples, departing too frequently from the predictions of a statistical formula derived from real-world outcome data and making more errors in the process (Grove, Zald, Lebow, Snitz, & Nelson, 2000). Meehl (1998) noted that this fact is predictable from the more general finding that, when given the same pool of valid information and evaluated against the same criteria, statistical predictions derived from outcome data are as or more accurate than clinical predictions *even when the clinicians are provided with the statistical predictions and are allowed to copy them.* If clinicians adopted the statistical predictions except in those instances where they could correctly identify exceptions, then their accuracy would be higher than that of the formula. Because this does not happen, the clinicians must be identifying too many exceptions. It is important to recognize what this means: Appeals to the uniqueness of the individual as grounds for countervailing the dictates of probability will, on balance, *increase* judgment errors (see Chapter 3 for more on statistical prediction).

Second, one might interpret this as a claim that, *in general*, probability is irrelevant to understanding or predicting the behavior of an individual. A simple thought experiment, originally presented by Meehl (1973), exposes the speciousness of this interpretation. Suppose that you are to play Russian roulette once, meaning that you will put a revolver to your head and pull the trigger. Would you prefer that there be one bullet and five empty chambers in the revolver, or five bullets and one empty chamber? You are, after all, a unique person who will either live or die, and this event will not be repeated. The only basis for preferring that there be just one bullet is that the *probability* of death is one in six rather than five in six. Clearly, probability is extremely relevant despite any unique aspects of this event.

The same reasoning applies when making clinical judgments—present knowledge (based on personal experience or more systematic research) can only establish the conditional probabilities of various outcomes given a certain decision. The rational way to reach important judgments is to choose the option with the best probability of success. Granted, actual clinical work complicates the subjective assessment of probabilities, as it is extremely challenging to identify, gather, and integrate the wealth of information pertinent to making many of the important decisions that arise, and knowledge of the relations between predictors and outcomes is usually quite modest. Nonetheless, the obstacles faced by practitioners do not negate the basic principle—carefully considering probability is *essential* for minimizing the chance of making a judgment error in each unique case.

THE CHALLENGE OF EXPERIENTIAL LEARNING

Expertise in any endeavor requires, among other things, a considerable amount of dedicated practice. Some skills, such as the motor coordination involved in playing a musical instrument, can be improved through repetitive practice exercises. Over time, the automaticity of performance increases and less effort is required to avoid making amateurish mistakes. Other types of skills, such as the creativity involved in composing new works of music, would not benefit from the same sort of repetitive practice. Instead, useful exercises might incorporate trial-and-error explorations of potential melodies, harmonizing, instrumentation, tempo, and so forth. With tasks as multifaceted and open-ended as this, there is no guarantee that experiential learning will occur. Certain requirements must be met, and there may be ways to structure practice sessions to maximize the rewards reaped for a fixed commitment of effort.

Some aspects of the earliest stages of clinical practice, when a large volume of information must be memorized, may bear greater similarity to the development of motor coordination than the development of musical creativity. An aspiring practitioner must learn about the signs and symptoms of a large number of mental disorders, an ever-expanding collection of assessment tools and treatment techniques (and, ideally, the empirical support for each), and the ethical and legal codes that apply to practitioners in a given locale, for example. Whereas the working vocabulary of mental health practice is acquired through rote learning, many interpersonal skills are honed through experiential learning in supervised training with actual clients and (later) through independent practice. With respect to the development of expert clinical judgment, how effective is experiential learning?

Reducing judgment errors by learning through experience requires attention to concrete, immediate, and unambiguous feedback on the accuracy (or inaccuracy) of prior judgments. Much of the feedback typically available to practitioners, however, is intrinsically ambiguous and temporally distal. For example, if a client does not arrive at several scheduled appointments and remains unreachable thereafter, one could interpret this outcome as a personal failure to form a strong therapeutic alliance. Or, one could assume that the client moved away on short notice and either lost his or her therapist's contact information or forgot to contact the therapist's office. Or, perhaps the client was cured. In either case, the feedback accumulates long after the sessions with this client have ended, and it becomes increasingly difficult to draw firm conclusions about what specific actions may have led to the early termination of therapy.

Practitioners also are exposed to and attend to more positive than negative feedback. Because it can be considerably more interpersonally awkward and difficult, displeased clients can be less likely to communicate blame to their therapists than pleased clients are to express gratitude. At least as important, even when feedback is available, the normal self-serving biases of human judgment can mount a variety of defenses against ego-threatening information while allowing more flattering information to arrive unfettered (Faust, 1986). Moreover, hindsight bias can make poor outcomes seem inevitable rather than the result of judgment errors. Even if a case is handled badly and therapeutic change is either nil or negative, there are many ways that a clinician can deflect this otherwise negative feedback. For instance, one might console oneself with the fact that the prognosis is poor for individuals suffering from chronic posttraumatic stress disorder, and especially poor for those with a comorbid substance abuse disorder. Even the most honestly self-critical therapist may not be able to distinguish the effects of some subtle errors in judgment from the effects of prior difficulties that ordinarily are not amenable to treatment. The net result of ambiguous feedback, time delay in the receipt of feedback, the scarcity of negative feedback, and hindsight bias is that there may be precious few opportunities to learn through experience.

Given these factors, it should not be terribly surprising that the accuracy of clinical judgment tends not to improve with clinical experience (Garb,

1989; see also Chapter 3 for a discussion of clinical judgment). This is consistent with what Dawes (1994) refers to as the *myth of expanding expertise.* Many people—clinicians included—simply assume that skills improve with experience and fail to consider the requirements for such learning to occur. Whereas skills acquired through rote memorization can be assessed relatively directly and easily, those built through experiential learning are considerably more difficult to assess. In place of reliable and valid measures of genuine improvement in clinical judgment, the myth of expanding expertise may fill the void with the presumption of gains attributable to experiential learning.

PROMOTING EXPERIENTIAL LEARNING

A return to the world of competitive Scrabble suggests some strategies that might be adapted to promote more effective experiential learning in clinical practice. As in chess, Scrabble players are provided with numerical ratings of their skill level. These ratings, updated with each game played, are calculated based on such factors as the outcome of the game and the skill level of the opposing player. Given the psychometric proficiency of psychologists and others in related disciplines, it is not inconceivable that a rating system could similarly be devised to quantify therapists' track records. Although clients are not directly analogous to opposing players, a good rating system could account for clients' current mental health, history, and complicating factors so that therapists who succeed with more difficult cases earn higher ratings. It is easy to imagine abuses of a rating scheme, but it also is possible to imagine beneficial uses of a well-constructed system, especially if access to ratings is appropriately restricted to those with educational, training, research, or other approved purposes. Clinical trainees and less effective therapists could seek opportunities to learn from expert mentors, and researchers could study expert therapists for clues about how they achieve their success. Particularly if such a system were developed and maintained by mental health professionals themselves, much might be learned about therapeutic success and truly expert clinical judgment. At the same time, the increasing demand for health care accountability suggests that the imposition of a rating system on therapists by insurers or government agencies is not out of the question. This possibility may provide some incentive for clinicians to devise a satisfactory system of their own before being forced into one that they find less palatable.

Perhaps more striking than the quantification of Scrabble players' expertise are some of the behavioral differences between Scrabble novices and experts observed by Fatsis (2001). Whereas beginners tend to clear a board and begin a new game quickly after one has ended, presumably believing that the best way to improve their play is through practice, experts study each game for opportunities to prevent the repetition of suboptimal plays in the future. In addition to studying the board itself at the end of the game, an expert takes meticulous notes on each play so that it can be evaluated in the context of the game at that moment. As Meehl (1997) and others argued, clinicians might learn more effectively if they tabulated and quantified their experiences. This practice could be useful for the generation and testing of hypotheses in real-world contexts. Even if not done formally as a research project, more informal tallies of the frequencies with which certain types of hunches or approaches do and do not bear fruit, or with which certain variables do and do not co-occur, could be highly informative for oneself or others.

Another tool that is increasingly used by current and aspiring Scrabble experts is to compare actual or hypothetical plays with the "optimal" plays generated by an expert system. These plays are optimal in the sense that a computer program—provided with complete Scrabble word knowledge and algorithms to score plays—can determine, probabilistically, what play is likely to yield the best final game score margin across a large number of games that all begin with precisely the same specifications (e.g., layout of tiles on the board, each player's current score, one or both players' racks of tiles). One can use such a program to ask whether a certain play is optimal or whether the computer can devise a better play, or one can compare two or more alternative plays (e.g., playing a word, playing a different word, exchanging certain tiles) to learn which would have been best. The ability to simulate follow-up data to evaluate every judgment is a powerful tool for Scrabble players to exploit. Clinicians do not have the same opportunity, but just as they could tally observations for subsequent analysis, they could take better advantage of opportunities to gather systematic data on various criterion measures with which to evaluate critical judgments retrospectively. Such criterion data could be collected on an ongoing basis, at termination, or subsequent to termination.

A final recommendation for improving judgment is not only consistent with observations of expert Scrabble players but also strongly supported by the literature on correcting judgment errors and overconfidence (e.g., Arkes, 1991). Scrabble experts are continually searching for weaknesses in their own play, striving to grow as players through ruthless self-appraisal. A key component of their success in learning through experience is the use of hypothetical counterfactuals such as "What mistakes have I made?" and "How might I prevent similar errors in the future?" In clinical work, one could examine cases with especially poor outcomes (e.g., the death of Candace Newmaker during rebirthing therapy; Mercer, 2002) to formulate hypotheses about how to prevent harmful judgment errors. Janis (1972) used this approach to identify the groupthink phenomenon as a culprit in many disastrous foreign policy decisions and recommended the institutionalization of a "devil's advocate." Of course, one can adopt that role with regard to one's own judgment. Like everyone else, clinicians are in a position to learn more about their trade by habitually asking themselves "Why might I be wrong?" (see also Chapter 1 for a discussion of science as a process of error-elimination).

CONCLUSION: TIPS FOR REDUCING JUDGMENT ERRORS

An understanding of the cognitive biases and logical fallacies discussed in this chapter suggests a number of concrete steps that can be taken to minimize judgment errors in clinical practice.

1. *Scrutinize similarity-based arguments.* Because the representativeness heuristic can make claims taking the form "like goes with like" appear quite reasonable, one must be especially careful to evaluate the logic and evidence bearing on such assertions.
2. *Conceptualize problems in multiple ways.* The availability heuristic can lead one astray when the instances most easily retrieved from memory provide a biased sample of data. Reconceptualizing an issue may provide new memory cues that elicit complementary information that reduces the initial bias and provides a firmer basis for reaching a judgment.
3. *Formulate and test multiple working hypotheses.* To prevent the premature closure that can result from the operation of confirmation and hindsight biases, it is important to generate multiple hypotheses and to tease them apart rigorously. Deliberately constructing and evaluating plausible alternative explanations can prevent many of the judgment errors resulting from a search for information to support an impression that was formed quickly.
4. *Recognize that personal experience is anecdotal evidence.* It is all too easy to allow personal experience to disproportionately influence clinical judgments. Whereas research systematically aggregates the experience of many practitioners with many clients, one's personal experience may involve a smaller, more haphazard, and less rigorously evaluated knowledge base. Considering whether one's own conclusions would be acceptable if presented by someone else may help to identify instances in which personal experience is being given undue weight (see also Chapter 7 for a discussion of anecdotal evidence in clinical science).
5. *Learn and apply basic principles of probability.* Because clinical work involves probabilistic relationships between variables, practitioners need to recognize that probability, statistics, and research evidence do apply to unique individuals. At least as important is learning the basic rules of probability and knowing when and how to apply them (e.g., using Bayes' Theorem to combine base rates with individuating information).
6. *Identify exceptions to statistical trends with caution.* A statistical trend represents a "signal" that can be detected despite the "noise" of individual differences and contextual variables. Although judgments informed by such trends will not be accurate in all cases, the literature strongly suggests that practitioners identify too many exceptions. Judgment errors can result from attaching too much significance to a client's uniqueness, which is often of little predictive value precisely because it is impossible to establish statistical associations involving truly unique characteristics. Discovering meaningful ways in which a client's

case shares features with others enables a savvy practitioner to more successfully play the odds by taking advantage of statistical trends.
7. *Play "devil's advocate" to one's own judgments.* Finally, asking why one might be wrong can suggest the need for additional information, help to differentiate between relevant and irrelevant information, or lead to a more appropriate way to integrate the available information when reaching a judgment. The more one learns about the limitations and biases of human reasoning, the more opportunities are afforded to prevent judgment errors by actively checking for mistaken premises or faulty logic in one's own thinking.

KEY TERMS

Availability heuristic: A mental shortcut for judging the probability or frequency of an event by using the ease with which instances can be retrieved from memory as a guide.

Confirmation bias: The tendency to selectively seek, attend to, or attach greater weight to information that supports rather than refutes one's beliefs.

Experiential learning: The development of expert knowledge or judgment through a process that requires concrete, immediate, and unambiguous feedback.

Hindsight bias: The presumption that the ability to construct a plausible explanation of past events implies a causal understanding that can be used to successfully predict future events.

Representativeness heuristic: A mental shortcut for reaching judgments based on perceived similarity or "goodness of fit" rather than actual probabilistic or causal relationships.

RECOMMENDED READINGS

Faust, D. (1986). Research on human judgment and its application to clinical practice. *Professional Psychology: Research and Practice, 17,* 420–430.

Garb, H. N. (1998). *Studying the clinician: Judgment research and psychological assessment.* Washington, DC: American Psychological Association.

Meehl, P. E. (1973). Why I do not attend case conferences. In P. E. Meehl (Ed.), *Psychodiagnosis: Selected papers* (pp. 225–302). Minneapolis: University of Minnesota Press.

Meehl, P. E. (1997). Credentialed persons, credentialed knowledge. *Clinical Psychology: Science and Practice, 4,* 91–98.

Turk, D. C., & Salovey, P. (1988). *Reasoning, inference, and judgment in clinical psychology.* New York: Free Press.

REFERENCES

Arkes, H. R. (1991). Costs and benefits of judgment errors: Implications for debiasing. *Psychological Bulletin, 110,* 486–498.

Beyerstein, B. L. (1997). Why bogus therapies seem to work. *Skeptical Inquirer, 21,* 29–34.

46

The Great Ideas of Clinical Science

Barlow, D. H. (2002). *Anxiety and its disorders: The nature and treatment of anxiety and panic* (2nd ed.). New York: Guilford.

Chapman, L. J., & Chapman, J. P. (1967). Genesis of popular but erroneous diagnostic observations. *Journal of Abnormal Psychology, 72*, 193–204.

Chapman, L. J., & Chapman, J. P. (1969). Illusory correlation as an obstacle to the use of valid psychodiagnostic observations. *Journal of Abnormal Psychology, 74*, 271–280.

Dawes, R. M. (1993). Prediction of the future versus an understanding of the past: A basic asymmetry. *American Journal of Psychology, 106*, 1–24.

Dawes, R. M. (1994). *House of cards: Psychology and psychotherapy built on myth.* New York: Free Press.

Fatsis, S. (2001). *Word freak: Heartbreak, triumph, genius, and obsession in the world of competitive Scrabble players.* Boston: Houghton Mifflin.

Faust, D. (1984). *The limits of scientific reasoning.* Minneapolis: University of Minnesota Press.

Faust, D. (1986). Research on human judgment and its application to clinical practice. *Professional Psychology: Research and Practice, 17*, 420–430.

Fischhoff, B. (1975). Hindsight ≠ foresight: The effect of outcome knowledge on judgment under uncertainty. *Journal of Experimental Psychology: Human Perception and Performance, 1*, 288–299.

Fischhoff, B. (1980). For those condemned to study the past: Reflections on historical judgment. In R. A. Shueder & D. W. Fiske (Eds.), *New directions for methodology of behavioral science: Fallible judgment in behavioral research* (pp. 79–93). San Francisco: Jossey-Bass.

Garb, H. N. (1989). Clinical judgment, clinical training, and professional experience. *Psychological Bulletin, 105*, 387–396.

Garb, H. N. (1998). *Studying the clinician: Judgment research and psychological assessment.* Washington, DC: American Psychological Association.

Gigerenzer, G., Todd, P. M., & the ABC Research Group (1999). *Simple heuristics that make us smart.* New York: Oxford University Press.

Grove, W. M., Zald, D. H., Lebow, B. S., Snitz, B. E., & Nelson, C. (2000). Clinical versus mechanical prediction: A meta-analysis. *Psychological Assessment, 12*, 19–30.

Halford, G. S., Baker, R., McCredden, J. E., & Bain, J. D. (2005). How many variables can humans process? *Psychological Science, 16*, 70–76.

Hawkins, S. A., & Hastie, R. (1990). Hindsight: Biased judgments of past events after the outcomes are known. *Psychological Bulletin, 107*, 311–327.

Janis, I. L. (1972). *Victims of groupthink: A psychological study of foreign-policy decisions and fiascos.* Oxford, England: Houghton Mifflin.

Kahneman, D., & Tversky, A. (1972). Subjective probability: A judgment of representativeness. *Cognitive Psychology, 3*, 430–454.

Lilienfeld, S. O., Lynn, S. J., Kirsch, I., Chaves, J. F., Sarbin, T. R., Ganaway, G. K., et al. (1999). Dissociative identity disorder and the sociocognitive model: Recalling the lessons of the past. *Psychological Bulletin, 125*, 507–523.

Lynn, S. J., Lock, T., Loftus, E. F., Krackow, E., & Lilienfeld, S. O. (2003). The remembrance of things past: Problematic memory recovery techniques in psychotherapy. In S. O. Lilienfeld, S. J. Lynn, & J. M. Lohr (Eds.), *Science and pseudoscience in clinical psychology* (pp. 205–239). New York: Guilford.

Meehl, P. E. (1954). *Clinical versus statistical prediction: A theoretical analysis and a review of the evidence.* Minneapolis: University of Minnesota Press.

Meehl, P. E. (1973). Why I do not attend case conferences. In P. E. Meehl (Ed.), *Psychodiagnosis: Selected papers* (pp. 225–302). Minneapolis: University of Minnesota Press.

Meehl, P. E. (1992). Cliometric metatheory: The actual approach to empirical, history-based philosophy of science. *Psychological Reports, 71*, 339–467.

Meehl, P. E. (1997). Credentialed persons, credentialed knowledge. *Clinical Psychology: Science and Practice, 4*, 91–98.

Meehl, P. E. (1998, May). *The power of quantitative thinking.* Invited address as recipient of the James McKeen Cattell Award at the annual meeting of the American Psychological Society, Washington, DC.

Mercer, J. (2002). Attachment therapy: A treatment without empirical support. *Scientific Review of Mental Health Practice, 1*, 105–112.

Miller, G. A. (1956). The magical number seven, plus or minus two: Some limits on our capacity for processing information. *Psychological Review, 63*, 81–97.

Nickerson, R. S. (1998). Confirmation bias: A ubiquitous phenomenon in many guises. *Review of General Psychology, 2*, 175–220.

Nisbett, R. E., & Ross, L. 1980. *Human inference: Strategies and shortcomings of social judgment.* Englewood Cliffs, NJ: Prentice-Hall.

Poole, D. A., Lindsay, D., Memon, A., & Bull, R. (1995). Psychotherapy and the recovery of memories of childhood sexual abuse: U.S. and British practitioners' opinions, practices, and experiences. *Journal of Consulting and Clinical Psychology, 63*, 426–437.

Renaud, H., & Estess, F. (1961). Life history interviews with one hundred normal American males: "Pathogenicity" of childhood. *American Journal of Orthopsychiatry, 31*, 786–802.

Ruscio, J., & Stern, A. R. (in press). The consistency and accuracy of holistic judgment: Clinical decision making with a minimally complex task. *Scientific Review of Mental Health Practice.*

Sagan, C. (1995). *The demon-haunted world: Science as a candle in the dark.* New York: Random House.

Schreiber, F. R. (1973). *Sybil.* Chicago: Henry Regnery.

Spanos, N. P. (1996). *Multiple identities and false memories: A sociocognitive perspective.* Washington, DC: American Psychological Association.

Sternberg, S. (1969). The discovery of processing stages: Extensions of Donders' method. In W. G. Koster (Ed.), *Attention and performance II* (pp. 276–315). Amsterdam: Elsevier-North Holland.

Turk, D. C., & Salovey, P. (1988). *Reasoning, inference, and judgment in clinical psychology.* New York: Free Press.

Tversky, A., & Kahneman, D. (1973). Availability: A heuristic for judging frequency and probability. *Cognitive Psychology, 5*, 207–232.

Tversky, A., & Kahneman, D. (1974). Judgment under uncertainty: Heuristics and biases. *Science, 185*, 1124–1131.

Wood, J. M., Nezworski, M. T., Lilienfeld, S. O., & Garb, H. N. (2003). *What's wrong with the Rorschach? Science confronts the controversial inkblot test.* San Francisco: Jossey-Bass.

3

Decision Research Can Increase the Accuracy of Clinical Judgment and Thereby Improve Patient Care

DAVID FAUST

AN ALLEGORY

A Friend's Dilemma

Suppose that you are sitting at home one day when you receive a call from your best friend, who informs you that she is faced with a frightful decision that must be made tomorrow, Saturday, at 9:00 am sharp. She must select one of two doors: Behind one is a hungry tiger that will devour her and behind the other is safety and perhaps even some bounty. Your friend wants your help in deciding which door to pick, a decision task that obviously involves prediction and for which accuracy is paramount. (The answer to the dilemma appears at the end of this chapter.)

This is not a time to worry about the aesthetics of the methodology you use to assist your friend. Within the bounds of ethics, you wish to maximize the likelihood of a correct decision, and you do not really care about the means used to achieve this result. If standing on your head (perhaps in order to peer under the doors) works, you are prepared to do so. Thus, the selection of methodology comes down to what is feasible or accessible and what works best, and not, for example, what fits with one's personal style or offers your friend temporary reassurance because it *seems* most fitting or humane.

Suppose we also know that the state of the universe (at least in this corner of the world) is not solely a product of randomness or chance but rather has some orderliness to it. More particularly in this case, the evildoer who has put your friend in this terrible dilemma has not tossed a coin to position the tiger but has made a decision or choice. As such, if you had a perfect understanding of the human mind, or this human mind, you might well be able to predict which choice had been made with nearly perfect accuracy. However, despite your extensive training and experience in psychology and your high level of competence, you lack such well-formulated knowledge, although you do know a good deal about the human psyche.

You have just enough time to perform a little background research: This sadist has put quite a few other individuals through the same trials, and the results are on record. Your research produces a few findings. You know, of course, that random selection would yield a 50% accuracy rate, which is a yardstick against which to evaluate the success of predictive methods. You discover that expert psychological consultants who have tried to predict doors through their knowledge of the human mind, or the human mind in question, have achieved a 65% accuracy rate, a considerable improvement over chance. You also find, however, that in 70% of the cases overall, the tiger is behind the left door and, further, on weekends, this figure increases to 80%. Thus, if selections are made by chance, the likelihood of a (fatal) mistake is 50%. If expert judgment based on theory or conceptualization of the mind is used, the rate is reduced substantially, falling to 35%, but if mere frequency data are used and it is the weekend, the error rate is reduced a good deal further, dropping to 20%. The relative merits of the different methods are thereby clear: In comparison to the use of frequency data, almost twice as many errors will be made using expert judgment, despite its validity, and two to three times more errors using random selection. Certainly one would not argue that this information should be withheld from one's friend because it is a little bruising to a psychologist's self-identity to find that frequency data has outperformed expert judgment. Rather, we would probably be thrilled that we had uncovered information that might save our friend's life and that, if applied across cases (and assuming no change in pattern of door selection), would save many lives.

DECISION TASKS FACING THE CLINICIAN AND APPLICATION OF THE ALLEGORY

I do not mean to sound flippant about human welfare by using this allegory; it is because the stakes can be so high in clinical decision making that the allegory is suitable. Among the range of important tasks facing the clinician, various undertakings, including some of the most critical ones, involve explicit or implicit prediction. Explicit prediction might involve testifying in court that a person will be able to achieve gainful employment, or deciding in the office setting whether a client will make a suicide attempt. Implicit prediction involves tasks that, on the surface, might not seem to be predictive in nature but for which, ultimately, decision making rests on forecasts. For example, selecting one mode of intervention over another surely involves considering the outcomes the alternatives might achieve. Deciding to proceed slowly with a client to gradually build up trust before raising more anxiety-provoking topics is probably done with the anticipation that such an approach carries less risk and a greater likelihood of an eventual positive outcome than an alternative approach. Likewise, in large part, diagnosis has clinical utility to the extent it helps us predict something (e.g., what is likely to happen or not happen and thus how to plan more effectively; which intervention is most likely to be successful). Even an interpretive statement in a therapy session generally is offered with the expectation/prediction that it is more likely to achieve a positive than a negative result. My use of the term "implicit prediction" is intended to capture the notion that many judgment tasks that we do not necessarily think of or frame as predictive nevertheless contain an important predictive element. Arguably, the majority of clinical tasks and activities involve explicit or implicit prediction, much like the selection of Door A or Door B. It is not overblown to state that the accuracy of prediction can have major, if not life-and-death, consequences, as might be the case with mistaken release of a patient who falsely denies homicidal intent.

Given the frequency and potential importance of prediction in clinical work, it seems sensible to argue, likewise, that within the bounds of feasibility and ethics, we should implement the best methods. Again, the aim is not personal ego gratification or style points but getting it right as often as possible.

The Conditions Under Which Theories Increase Predictive Accuracy

If the aim is predictive accuracy, it is critical to ask how this goal could be accomplished. A question that naturally arises is the extent to which, or the conditions under which, theories assist in achieving predictive power. Unquestionably, *at times*, scientific theories help us realize remarkable predictive accuracy, but note this qualification. In some circumstances, theories benefit prediction minimally, if at all, and may even *decrease* accuracy if they lead us away from more fruitful approaches. In the previous allegory, theory did enhance predictive accuracy beyond chance levels, but another approach proved to be better. Hence, someone depending on theory might well achieve results inferior to those accomplished with other methods.

I do not wish to enter into debates here about whether all thinking is "theory laden." Thinking presumes conceptualization of some type and, of course, does not occur in a vacuum. However, it does not follow that distinctions between the level of inference and theorizing involved in judgment cannot be made or are meaningless. It is meaningful to distinguish between prediction that proceeds in some manner through the lens (or structure) of a psychological theory about mind or behavior and prediction that bypasses such theories and rests on other foundations, such as fundamental principles of probability. For example, when attempting to predict the likelihood of violent behavior, the effort may rest at least partly on a theoretical framework about the human psyche and the manner in which individuals with a certain makeup respond to particular stressors and situations. Alternatively, one may rely on mere frequency data that links standing on a few specified variables to the occurrence of violent acts. Although it is understood that the original *identification* of possible predictor variables may depend on theory, this does not mean that such theory (versus a formal analysis) determines which variables are ultimately used or combined or how one goes from standing on those variables to an estimate of likelihood. It is a mistake to argue that, as both are theory laden, there is no meaningful distinction between an approach to prediction or formulation that depends substantially on theory and one that basically ignores theory and rests on such foundations as mere frequency data. One predictive formulation is heavily theory laden, in this case permeated by a theory that probably involves some conceptualization of the human mind and behavior, and the other disregards, perhaps entirely, ideas about how the mind works and rests on a very different strategy.

The conditions under which theory-based predictions achieve high levels of accuracy are fairly well understood. Three basic requirements need to be met, and falling short on any one of them will usually preclude a high degree of accuracy and may enfeeble predictive utility almost completely. The major parameters that influence outcome must be known, there must be a way to measure those parameters accurately, and the theory needs to be well corroborated or, as contemporary philosophers generally put it, should have a high degree of verisimilitude (i.e., truth-likeness) (Popper, 1983). The third requirement might sound vague, and I will sidestep it because it would require fairly detailed explication and because it should be apparent that in clinical psychology, we rarely meet either of the first two conditions, anyway. For example, the measurement of density in physics is a good deal more precise than that of repressive tendencies or avoidance in psychology. This is not a negative commentary about the rate of progress in psychology: Areas of science that have realized these accomplishments in even select domains have usually required many years; the subject matter of psychology contains distinctive features that make it especially challenging; and, fortunately, our field has developed alternative methods that do enhance accuracy and are readily available.

Questionable Assumptions About Ontological-Epistemological Isomorphism and Related Beliefs

In contemplating predictive tasks, many leading spokespersons in psychology and many practitioners tend to conflate ontological and epistemological issues and, therefore, seem to reach questionable conclusions about preferred predictive methods. *Ontological* refers to questions or assumptions about the nature of the world or what is out there, whereas *epistemological* refers to methods of knowing or for acquiring knowledge about the nature of the world. For example, the assertion that the moon is composed mainly of rock is an ontological claim, whereas the assertion that certain geologic methods can help to determine the composition of the moon is an epistemological claim.

Whether, or the extent to which, ontological and epistemological claims should maintain isomorphism or parallel elements in an idealized system is not a simple issue. However, in the real or practical world the two can diverge markedly without necessarily causing problems, despite what common belief or intuition might suggest. Intuitive assumptions about the need to align ontological and epistemological thought are potentially mistaken and seem to foster what are perhaps some of the most problematic and entrenched beliefs about preferred predictive strategies in clinical psychology.[1] For example, suppose one's ontological belief is that the human mind is complex (and who would argue otherwise?). It might seem to follow that, to be successful, assessment methods should attempt to capture that complexity, or that the clinician should attempt to integrate a complex data set or all of the data. However, this seeming night does not necessarily follow this preceding day.

At one time, astronomers found that treating planetary motion as an ellipse provided a sufficiently close approximation to facilitate impressive predictive accuracy. Before certain advancements were made, more complex models, although recognized by some as necessary to capture the true state of nature with greater fidelity, performed worse than this erroneous but close oversimplification. Likewise, when predicting human behavior, it is entirely possible that complex formulations will

---

[1] I am not suggesting that psychologists necessarily gather together to have drawn-out debates about whether ontological and epistemological assumptions need to maintain strict parallelism with one another, but whether one has such discussions or not or directly raises the latest thoughts of philosophers of science, we surely have positions, and often sophisticated ones, on methods of knowing. One can hold a position on the relation between methods of knowing and the nature of the world without speaking in the formal language of the philosopher or directly adopting certain formal philosophical concepts or distinctions.

ultimately maximize accuracy and do a better job of capturing the true state of nature than more simplified approaches. However, this does not mean that, *at present*, attempts to construct such complex formulations necessarily produce more accurate predictions than simpler approaches. Given the current state of knowledge, certain basic assumptions about the operation of the human psyche (e.g., that it is complex and involves multidimensional interfaces), even if fundamentally correct, do not necessarily dictate which methods are most effective at present for appraising and predicting human behavior, and they may even misdirect us toward inferior approaches.

I will argue that: (a) We do know a good deal about how to increase predictive accuracy in psychology (under the current state of knowledge or conditions of practice), and (b) most of the available help can be reasonably conceptualized as a decision technology that is negligibly based on theoretical conceptualizations about the human mind and behavior. Our tendency to reject or ignore this decision technology is somewhat puzzling because the evidence in favor of its usefulness is overwhelming (e.g., see Dawes, Faust, & Meehl, 1989). Furthermore, in many walks of life, we readily embrace technologies, even when their theoretical underpinnings are limited or minimally address the state of nature, or when our grasp of their underlying mechanisms or theoretical bases is limited. For example, the scientific community often has a minimal understanding of the mechanisms by which many helpful medicines achieve their benefits, especially when they are first discovered. Likewise, we readily use such devices as cars, cell phones, and computers, even if we know nearly nothing about the internal combustion engine or the difference between a transistor and more advanced circuitry.

Furthermore, at times there seems to be a potentially destructive blurring between helping people and the methods used to help people when the latter activate certain stereotypes. There is probably no disagreement that the manner in which one tries to help can sometimes be more important than the help provided. Thus, for example, if a doctor attending to a patient with a myocardial infarction drives that person's anxiety up so high that death results, trying to get the patient to take an aspirin might have been the right move but not the major determinant of outcome.

However, the emphasis on form over function, so to speak, can be taken too far, or such concerns can be misplaced. For example, it has been repeatedly argued that if one is personally responsible for an important decision involving someone else, then personalized methods for deciding should be used rather than depending on some general body of knowledge. Consequently, it may be asserted that even if we know one intervention works better than another in 85% of cases with closely related features, we should look more closely at idiosyncrasies or personal aspects of the situation in deciding a course of action (even when there is almost no evidence that attempting to do so improves decision making and considerable evidence that such an approach, if anything, is far more likely to increase the frequency of error). Or it might be argued that using a number to reach a decision is treating a person like a number, which is inhumane. In certain situations, individuals do use some mechanism to distance themselves from others in order to rationalize unfair treatment and, conceivably, a number could be used that way. However, equating the use of numbers with inhumane treatment per se is patently absurd. Only a mad person would argue that an ophthalmologist preparing to perform delicate laser surgery on the cornea to preserve someone's sight is engaging in cruel and inhuman treatment because she used the computer to calculate the exact size and contour of the eye and the intensity of exposure needed. Returning to the initial allegory, if mere frequency data decrease the chances of death by two- or threefold, is it more humane to throw out the numbers and use a "warmer" method? There is no question that numbers and technologies can be misused, but it is a serious breech of ethics to disregard information that can help clients merely because it is quantitative. Surely our friend would rather be "reduced to a number" if that greatly increases the chances of survival over being eaten alive.

EXAMPLES OF HELPFUL DECISION PROCEDURES

Use of Base Rates

We tend to think that predictive variables should hold some causal or intrinsic relation to the condition of interest. For example, when identifying depression, we tend to rely on such things as symptoms associated with the disorder, modes of thinking related to negative mood, or certain biological states that are conceptually or empirically linked with the condition. Our focus, often with good reason, is on characteristics that are either viewed as a manifestation of the disorder or as existing somewhere on a causal chain linked to the disorder. When attempting to predict outcomes of various sorts, we also tend to focus on similar classes of variables.

Given these mental predilections, we tend to ignore or underweight what is often an exceptionally useful, if not the most useful, predictive variable: simple frequency data. Research suggests that individuals, clinicians included, tend to weight frequency data properly only when it appears in isolation (Kahneman & Tversky, 1973; Kennedy, Willis, & Faust, 1997). For example, if we are told that 10% of students in School District X have attention-deficit/hyperactivity disorder (ADHD) and are asked to generate the probability that a randomly selected student has ADHD, the 10% frequency or base rate will dictate the assigned probability. However, there is a decided inclination to underweight or completely disregard frequency data to the extent that individuating information is also provided, even if that information has little or no relation to the outcome of interest. For example, merely being told that someone is a certain height or gender, regardless of whether such characteristics bear any relation to the relevant outcome, tends to draw attention away from frequency data, even when the latter are highly probative.

Much of the following material on base rates can be traced to the seminal article of Meehl and Rosen (1955; reprinted in Waller, Yonce, Grove, Faust, & Lenzenweger, 2006). Base rates are commonly the single most useful diagnostic indictor or predictive variable. A base rate refers to the frequency of a condition or event, whether it involves human affairs (e.g., how often individuals drink lemonade, argue with their neighbors, or develop serious mental disorders) or other types of occurrences (e.g., how often tires go flat between 10,000 and 20,000 miles of use, volcanoes erupt in the northwestern United States, or lobsters have blue shells). When one refers to "playing the base rate," this means one guesses that the most frequent outcome will occur. For example, if 70% of children like apples, one playing the base rate will guess that a randomly selected child will prefer apples. If 5% of children like lima beans, one guesses that a randomly selected child will not favor this food. Sometimes what is most frequent is nonoccurrence. For example, one playing the base rates would guess that it will not rain in Death Valley during the coming day.

Use of Base Rates with Dichotomous Decisions

In addressing and illustrating the use of base rates, for purposes of clarity I will start with a basic circumstance and proceed to more complex situations. Suppose we are presented with a dichotomous choice, such as whether Mental Disorder X is present or absent, Mental Disorder X versus Y is present, or whether Intervention A or B should be implemented. Many clinical situations involve dichotomous choices, such as deciding whether a criminal defendant is faking serious mental disorder or is actively schizophrenic, whether we should take an individual as a therapy patient, or whether we should move for involuntary hospitalization. Further suppose, for the moment, that the benefits of different types of correct decisions and the costs of different forms of error are about equal. For example, the costs associated with a false-positive error (e.g., diagnosing a condition as present when it is not present) about equals the costs of a false-negative error (e.g., missing a condition that is present). In most such circumstances, our primary aim is to maximize overall judgmental accuracy. (In contrast, if costs are unevenly distributed, we might be more interested in avoiding one or the other type of error, even if it impacted somewhat negatively on overall accuracy rate.)

With dichotomous decisions, random selection results in an overall accuracy rate of 50%. A 50% accuracy rate also happens to be the worst result that one can achieve playing the base rates, and occurs when the frequency of the two alternatives are equal. As the frequency of one or the other possibility deviates from 50%, the accuracy achieved playing the base rates increases accordingly. For example, if Condition A occurs 75% of the time and Condition B 25% of the time, guessing Condition A every time results in a 75% accuracy rate. Alternatively, if an adolescent who is going to be home late calls to inform his worried parents only 25% of the time, guessing that no call will be made results in an overall accuracy rate of 75%. Here, nonoccurrence is the more frequent "outcome," and thus one who is primarily interested in overall accuracy and who is playing the base rates guesses that the event will not take place.

Frequencies are sometimes very high or very low, in which case playing the base rates results in very high accuracy rates. If, for example, 99% of individuals who score below 75 on an IQ test will not graduate from a 4-year college, then guessing that someone with such a score will not do so should produce a 99% accuracy rate. As will be discussed, even when base rates achieve high accuracy rates, a policy of blind and unbending adherence to them in clinical practice can be very dangerous and is rarely advisable. Keeping this caution in mind, it is the case that numerous things in psychology occur often or very often, or rarely or very rarely, and thus one can often achieve impressive accuracy rates by merely playing the base rates. In many instances, the base rates are, far and away, the single most useful diagnostic or predictive indicator.

Suppose now that a clinician has access to both base rate information, such as the frequency with which a certain group of individuals succeed in some occupation, and to one or another diagnostic sign or indicator, such as a score on a measure of mental ability that this occupation tends to emphasize. The base rate and the test score may point in the same direction. For example, the base rate for success may be 75% and the individual may obtain a test result that surpasses some cut-off for predicting success. When both base rate and indicator agree, there is no need to select one over the other. Suppose, however, that the two disagree, as would be the case when someone's test score falls below the cut-off. In such circumstances, the two indicators point in opposing directions and the decision maker must select or elevate one over the other; the indicators conflict and, given the decision task at hand, they cannot be "integrated" or "synthesized."

It is striking how often those who write about psychological assessment advocate strategies or positions that, in effect, preclude, disregard, or even reject the possibility that direct conflict or contradiction will occur among the collected data, when it really is an extraordinarily common occurrence. When one advocates synthesis or integration of *all of the data*, such a position generally presumes, at some level, that all of the data can be aligned or are consistent, if only one is sage enough to detect the underlying pattern. With rare exceptions, however, if one gathers even a modicum of information, some of the data will be *contradictory*.

For example, in a neuropsychological battery, if one administers 20 tests (which is not unusual) and the tests average, say, a 75% accuracy rate (which is not an overly pessimistic figure), one in four of the tests, or about five in total, will produce erroneous results. If 15 of the tests produce the correct result and 5 a false result that flatly contradicts the other 15 tests, how can one possibly integrate all of the data into a fully aligned and synthesized array? Rather, some of the results are correct and some are incorrect—there are direct contradictions among the data—and the incorrect ones should be discarded and not combined or synthesized with the other results. My point is that obtaining inconsistent or flatly contradictory data is very common and, to the extent possible, should be managed by exercising properly directed selectivity, or by trying to identify what to keep and what to reject. It is not best handled by adopting the appealing but ultimately unjustified belief that there is no ultimate or intrinsic inconsistency among the data and that everything can be synthesized or integrated. As will be seen, the difference between a position that acknowledges the need for selectivity versus one that calls for integration of all of the data is hardly academic, as it may well lead to markedly contrasting and differentially effective judgment strategies.

If a test score and the base rate point in opposing directions, and the primary aim is to maximize overall accuracy, logic dictates reliance on whichever method or indicator is more accurate. For example, if the test is correct 60% of the time and playing the base rate achieves 80% accuracy, one should use the base rate over the test. It also follows that for a sign or test to outperform the base rate, it must achieve a level of accuracy that exceeds the frequency of the more common occurrence (or non-occurrence). For example, assume a test is 70% accurate in identifying posttraumatic stress disorder (PTSD), and that the base rate for PTSD in the setting of application is 60%. All else being equal, when a conflict arises between the conclusion that results from playing the base rates versus using the test, it should be resolved in favor of the test. However, if the frequency of PTSD is greater than 70% or lower than 30%, and consequently playing the base rates (in the first instance by guessing "yes" and in the second instance by guessing "no") achieves greater than 70% accuracy, inconsistencies should be resolved in favor of the base rates.

As these examples illustrate, the operating characteristics of tests (and other types of diagnostic and predictive indicators) vary depending on the base rate in the setting of application, and hence their utility cannot be properly appraised without taking the base rate into account. For example, a test that achieves a 75% accuracy rate may be very helpful in a setting in which a condition occurs 50% of the time, but of no help and even a hindrance in a setting in which the base rate is 95%. Determining whether one should or should not use a test often requires one to compare the success it achieves with that attained using the base rate. For this reason, the utility of a test is not a constant but varies in relation to the base rate. (As will be discussed, the same applies to a test's accuracy rate, that is, accuracy rates vary as base rates vary.) Furthermore, at times, such as when dichotomous choices are called for and use of the base rates leads to the highest accuracy rate, it may well be better to *not* administer a test. If the test aligns with the base rate it will not change the decision, and if it contradicts the base rate it should be disregarded.

There is no purpose served, and time and expense wasted, by administering a test that ought not be allowed to change anything. Even if the test is valid, if one administers and uses it for purposes of decision making, it is only likely to *decrease* judgmental accuracy. Here, rather than trying to collect more information and "integrate all of the data," less is more.

The same principles apply if more than two distinctions are relevant. For example, if there are three possibilities and one must identify the most likely one, then playing the base rates dictates selection of the most frequent outcome. As the number of choices multiply, extremely high base rates are less common, although alternative diagnostic methods, such as tests, are also likely to decrease in accuracy as they are equally required to distinguish among a greater number of competing possibilities.

The Use of Base Rates to Sharpen Judgments About the Likelihood of Outcomes

In many clinical situations, we are not primarily interested in making dichotomous choices but in determining the likelihood of possible or alternative outcomes. Suppose we need to appraise a psychiatric inpatient's potential for violent behavior over the next 72 hours. We are not only or particularly interested in whether violence or nonviolence is the more probable outcome. Even if nonviolence is more likely, simply knowing this fact does not provide a sufficient safeguard because the range of probability under which it is more probable extends so broadly, from anywhere above 50% to 100%. Stating matters in the inverse, this leaves a range of probability for violent behavior that extends from a low of 0% to a high of 49.999 . . . %; and much of this range likely represents unacceptable risk (especially if effective preventative actions are possible and are not particularly dangerous). In such circumstances we are usually much more concerned with achieving as accurate a determination of likelihood as possible to guide decision making. For example, we may decide that anything that exceeds, say, a 2% risk of violent behavior justifies preventative actions.

Here, rather than using base rates to identify the more likely outcome, one uses them to estimate the likelihood of an outcome, usually by combining the base rates with other valid predictors (to the extent such predictors are available). Incorporation and proper utilization of base rates in this context may greatly sharpen estimates of likelihood and sometimes will reduce error multifold. Of course, if base rates are unavailable they cannot be used in combination with other indicators (and vice versa).

To illustrate the potential impact of base rates on estimates of likelihood when combined with other indicators, suppose we are interested in determining the chances that a certain intervention, which carries moderate risks and is expensive, will produce a positive response for patients with a very troubling disorder. Alternative interventions are available that are less risky and less expensive but that have much lower success rates. A test has been developed that helps to identify those likely to benefit from treatment. Assume that a positive result on the test is associated with a 70% likelihood of a good treatment response, and a negative test result with a 30% likelihood of a good response. A patient obtains a positive result and is informed that this places her odds of a good response at 70%. Considering the risks and downside of the treatment, even these 7-in-10 odds do not convince the patient to proceed, a perfectly understandable and justifiable decision given the available information.

Further assume, however, that base rate information is available about response to treatment. Different sets of base rates have been gathered for different groups of patients as positive response rates vary among them. Our particular patient matches a group that falls within a certain age range, has shown good prior adaptive functioning, has experienced no prior episodes of the disorder in question, and that responds remarkably well to the treatment, demonstrating a success rate of 90%. Presume in addition that the base rate and the test result are not merely redundant; rather, each makes an independent contribution to decision accuracy. (Certain tests do not provide independent information but mainly capitalize on base rates, and thus may not add to the predictive accuracy achieved through the use of base rates alone.) The base rate for success is much higher then the rate found among those with a positive test result, and when the two are combined one obtains a probability of success that easily exceeds 90%. Looking at the other side of the coin, the chances of an unsuccessful treatment response fall well below 10%, or more than three times below the level associated with the positive test result. The patient finds her excellent chances of a good response very reassuring, goes ahead with the treatment, and is quite likely to achieve a much better outcome then she would have if she had pursued alternative treatment or no treatment.

As shown by this example, when the base rate and another valid indicator, such as a test score, point in the same direction or toward the same outcome (and are not merely redundant with each other), the likelihood of that outcome exceeds the probability indicated by the stronger predictor alone. For example, if the base rate is 90% (and thus allows one to predict with 90% accuracy) and a test is 70% accurate, and if both point in the same direction, the likelihood of the outcome exceeds 90%. The converse also holds; if both point toward nonoccurrence, the odds of nonoccurrence are greater than the odds indicated by the more accurate of the two methods. When the accuracy achieved with the base rates far exceeds that achieved by a test score or sign, an occurrence that is not unusual, the probability indicated by the test score should be adjusted considerably. For example, a 65% likelihood may need to be changed to 95%, or a 35% likelihood of some adverse event may need to be adjusted downward to 5%, or reduced sevenfold. In one circumstance in which I was involved, a test result suggesting a

10% likelihood of a suicide attempt needed to be adjusted downward by nearly one thousand–fold [!] given the 1 per 10,000 base rate among the population of interest; and the correction in the likelihood allowed for a much more rational and beneficial distribution of services. The magnitude of adjustment that is indicated may not be intuitively obvious and, as will be argued, is ultimately best determined by using formal procedures that are readily available and relatively simple.

When a base rate and a test point in *opposing* directions, the resultant joint likelihood is lower than that indicated by the more powerful predictor. Going back to our example of testing and treatment response, if the base rate for a positive treatment response is 90% and the test result is negative, that 90% likelihood must by adjusted downward (assuming, as before, that the test's predictive capacity is not merely a product of redundancy with the base rate). Once again, when there are large discrepancies in predictive accuracy achieved by the base rate compared with other signs or indicators, changes in probabilities may be considerable but difficult to judge intuitively, and are best arrived at formally. For example, although an unfavorable test result might indicate only a 35% likelihood of a positive outcome, a high base rate can still produce a figure that is much greater than 35% and that may well exceed 50% or even 75%.

One who is not inclined toward formal calculation of probabilities should still be able to apply these basic principles. For example, one should shift the probability indicated by the most powerful predictor upward when another nonredundant predictor points in the same direction, and downward when the other predictor points in the opposing direction. Furthermore, the magnitude of the upward or downward shift depends on how much better one predictor is than the other; that is, the more superior one predictor is to the other, all else being equal, the less the level of adjustment in the superior predictor that needs to be made. For example, if one predictor is 95% accurate and the other 65% accurate and the two are in opposition, the first will need to be adjusted minimally in the direction of the second, considerably weaker indicator.

As noted, fairly simple mathematical procedures are available to determine the exact level of adjustment necessary (see Meehl & Rosen, 1955; and Chapter 9 of Waller, Yonce, Grove, Faust, & Lenzenweger, 2006 [in which the same 1955 Meehl & Rosen article is also reproduced]). More generally, base rates and other diagnostic signs and indicators are not necessarily competitors and can be combined to reach more accurate judgments about the likelihood of outcomes, which in turn can provide very helpful guides to decision makers. For example, a 1% versus a 20% likelihood of violent behavior, or a 65% versus 85% likelihood of a positive response to a particular treatment, may change decisions entirely. In the latter case, we may be comparing different treatment options, and shifts in probabilities may completely change the relative standing or ranking of the alternatives under consideration.

Use of Base Rates in Differential Diagnosis

Base rates also can assist greatly with differential diagnosis. Again, starting with a basic situation and then proceeding to greater complexity, assume we have narrowed the possibilities to two conditions and that diagnostic signs and indicators point to both with equal strength. For example, suppose we are trying to distinguish between a mild traumatic brain injury (MTBI) and depression (a differential diagnosis that often arises in neuropsychology), and that the symptoms that are present, such as slowed mental processes and sleep disruption, have an equal strength of association with both conditions. Using these symptoms alone, one has a 50–50 chance of making the correct identification. However, assume that in the setting of interest, such as a clinic that specializes in certain patient groups, the frequency of depression is about 10 times higher than MTBI. In such circumstances, if one assumes that the patient has depression and not MTBI, one will be right in 10 of 11 cases, achieving an impressive hit rate of about 91%, as follows if the ratio between depressive disorder and MTBI is about 10 to 1, or 91% to 9%.

All else being equal, to the extent that base rates for conditions diverge, betting on the more frequent condition will achieve increasing levels of accuracy. For example, assume again that diagnostic indicators point equally toward two conditions, A and B. If Condition A occurs twice as often as Condition B, playing the base rates will result in about a 67% accuracy rate; whereas, if Condition A occurs 100 times more often than Condition B, playing the base rates will result in about a 99% accuracy rate.

When one must select from among two possible conditions and the base rates and diagnostic indicators conflict, then all else being equal, one looks toward the stronger of these two informational sources. (If the base rates and diagnostic indicators point in the same direction, then of course there is no need to select one over the other.) For example, if Condition A is four times more frequent than Condition B, reflecting a ratio of 4:1, then opposing signs must achieve a greater rate of differentiation before we would defer to them over the base rates. If a test favors Condition B over A at a ratio of 3:1, the test is a weaker indicator than the base rate and Condition A remains a better bet—a situation that is reversed if the test favors Condition B over A at a ratio of greater than 4:1. Such a decision policy is just another instantiation of the principle that, all else being equal, one resolves conflict between indicators by going with the stronger one.

Questions about cost or practicality aside, when deciding among conflicting indicators, level of predictive strength should be the deciding factor, not their appearance, their fit with our cognitive aesthetics, or the implicit belief that they must mesh with some theory, theoretical causal mechanism, or representative aspect of the disorder to be identified. For example, whether a variable is bland frequency data, an objective or projective test score, or some type of interview finding, should not, in and of itself, enter into decisions about their use. It is counterproductive to prejudge indicators because one prefers certain forms or classes (e.g., personality inventories, projective instruments, or statistical frequencies). Rather, equal standards of evidence should be applied across the board. After all, it would be irrational to argue, for example, that "I know the base rates are 10% more accurate than Test A, but I do not like base rates and so unless they beat tests by at least 20% I will not use them." Unfortunately, it seems that the type or class of indicator often enters into these decisions or even overwhelms more careful appraisal of demonstrated value.

The same principles used to select among two disorders apply when there are more diagnostic possibilities. For example, Condition A may occur 2 times more often than Condition B and 10 times more often than Condition C, or at a ratio of 10:5:1. Thus, guessing Condition A each time will result in 10 correct identifications for every 16 cases, or about a 63% accuracy rate. To bet against Condition A and instead select Condition B, the signs must show at least twice the strength of association with B in comparison to A; to bet on Condition C over Condition A, the strength of association must be at least 10 times greater, and so on.

In most instances, we are not limited to a single alternative indicator or test score, rather, multiple valid indicators are potentially available. This situation calls for no change in basic approach. When combining one indicator with others produces a composite of greater accuracy than the strongest variable in isolation, one compares the accuracy of the composite to the accuracy achieved using the base rates. When the two are in conflict, one goes with the superior predictor.

When combining indicators, one should be extremely cautious about assuming that their predictive power is strictly additive, as this is almost never the case. Rather, as a result of such factors as redundancy, their combined effectiveness may be considerably less than their sum total. For example, three variables that achieve respective accuracy rates of 50%, 60%, and 70%, when used in isolation, may achieve only a 75% accuracy rate when combined. Furthermore, it is not uncommon for the accuracy achieved by combining multiple variables to fall *below* that of the single strongest variable within the group; and for related reasons the optimal number of variables that should be used in forming composites is often much smaller than assumed (both of these points are addressed in greater detail below). Finally, it is often difficult to determine the strength of composites intuitively, there being a decided tendency to think that their predictive power is greater than is actually the case. Therefore, formal mathematical procedures are preferred for determining strength of association, as it is unfair to expect the unaided human mind to match the exactitude of such powerful methods.

When considering alternative diagnoses, one again may be most interested in determining relative likelihoods as accurately as possible rather than selecting one over the other(s). Obtaining these likelihoods can provide helpful guides to action. For example, certain diagnostic alternatives may turn out to be so improbable that they are not worth pursuing. In some cases, the probabilities may be low but not remote, the risks of missing the condition serious, and relatively inexpensive, effective, and low risk interventions may be available, in which case the course of action is usually clear. In other instances, two or three alternatives may not be exclusive of one another and may be sufficiently probable to justify further workup of each.

Here, as before, rather than placing base rates and other indicators in a contest of strength (when they conflict with each other), one combines them to obtain more exact estimates of likelihood. Again, when the base rates and other valid, nonredundant indicators point in the same direction, the joint likelihood exceeds that of the strongest indicator, and when the two are in opposition the reverse holds. As before, the level of adjustment necessitated by base rates can be considerable and counterintuitive, especially when the difference in predictive strength across the base rates and other indicators is substantial. Even when the magnitude of change is not that great, the relative likelihood and rank ordering of different possibilities may shift, thereby redirecting important decisions. The reader is again referred to Meehl and Rosen (1955) and to Chapter 9 of Waller et al. (2006) for formal procedures that can be used to combine base rates and other diagnostic indicators.

Which Base Rate?

Base rates for the same condition or event can vary considerably across groups or subgroups. For example, the frequency of presenile dementias obviously differs for 10–30- and 60-year-olds. Consequently, in many cases, base rates for the general population are not nearly as helpful as base rates for subgroups within that population. If one is trying to determine the likelihood that a violent criminal with a long history of antisocial behavior and arrest is likely to reoffend, the frequency of criminal activity among the U.S. population as a whole or, even more so, pacifist monks in U.S. monasteries, is not likely to be helpful or representative of the current individual with whom we are dealing.

One seeks the base rates for the narrowest applicable group, with narrowness in this case defined by features that: (a) impact the base rates and (b) are pertinent to the individual under consideration. For example, in the case of our criminal, the broadest group might be defined as the general population. Within that population, those with a history of prior criminal behavior commit subsequent crimes with a much higher frequency than those without such a history; hence, this is a dimension that alters the base rate. This dimension or characteristic is also pertinent to the individual because he can be rated on it. Other dimensions, such as a history of not just one but multiple crimes, and of hard drug use, may also alter the base rate and be pertinent as well. Some variables may alter the base rate but may not be pertinent to the individual under consideration. For example, the base rate may differ across persons with college versus graduate school education, but the individual we are considering may have dropped out in the 10th grade, and, consequently, the distinction is not relevant to him. Other variables may not be associated with a change in the base rate and do not help to narrow the group. For example, obsequious behavior before the parole board may have no association with subsequent criminal behavior.

It might seem as if a long list of variables would or should be used to narrow down groups. However, for practical and psychometric reasons, extending the list very far is usually not done or is not particularly helpful, especially if one can identify the variables that show the strongest association with changes in the base rates (i.e., are maximally valid for the purpose to which they are being applied) and are as independent from one another as possible. Proceeding in this fashion, a restricted set of variables, often five or fewer, will approach or achieve maximal benefit, at which point adding further variables will be of little or no help. Additional variables often yield little or no gain because they are too redundant with other variables. For example, a history of multiple violent crimes and of certain antisocial characteristics may each be associated with a change in the base rates, but they may co-occur so often that only one of the two needs to be used, the second adding almost nothing new. Adding variables to the data base can also be very costly and, especially when limited gains are achieved, may not be worth the effort. Suppose that one is already using three variables that each have four levels, resulting in 64 cells. Would one add a fourth variable with four levels that preliminary research suggests would create a statistically significant but only trivial change in the base rates (because one has already approached maximal benefit) and yet would create 192 additional cells and consequently require a massive normative study?

In many instances, the available data base for narrowing groups is not as complete as we would like. For example, important variables may not be accounted for or incorporated into the analysis. Nevertheless, narrowing the group by just one or two dimensions can still improve the applicability and utility of the base rates considerably. For example, suppose that 50% of individuals within the general population succeed in a certain occupation, but that a subgroup with superior intelligence achieves an 85% success rate. If our client demonstrates this exceptional capacity, the 50% overall likelihood of failure should be adjusted more than threefold, to 15%.

Sources of Information on Base Rates

Base rate information is available in many sources, although this may not be recognized if the conceptualization of base rates is too narrow. In addition to such obvious sources as epidemiological research on the frequency of various disorders or conditions (e.g., Kessler & Merikangas,

2004), many studies, although not necessarily using the term *base rates*, provide such data. As noted, base rates are not restricted to the frequency of disorders but refer more broadly to the frequency of events, conditions, or outcomes. Thus, for example, studies examining the rate of positive response to particular psychotherapeutic or pharmacologic interventions; the percentage of individuals who, having experienced two major depressive episodes, will experience a future episode; and the frequency with which individuals pleading insanity produce indications of malingering on a personality test all provide base rate data pertinent to clinicians' everyday activities and decision making.

Although high quality or precise base rate information is obviously preferable, various factors may degrade the data, such as limitations in sampling procedures or uncertainty about methods for identifying the outcome or event in question. For example, studies reporting rates of recidivism or of sexual abuse may be questionable due to limitations in detection methods or varying willingness to disclose events. Alternatively, the defining features of disorders adopted in diagnostic manuals may change over time, schizophrenia and PTSD serving as examples. As a result, the obtained base rates may differ considerably depending on the procedures and criteria used. In some cases, methods of identification, level of knowledge (or lack thereof), or vagaries in the things counted may render obtained base rate information of questionable or minimal use. In other cases, base rate information is unambiguous, dependable, and consistent across studies.

These problems with the potential quality of information notwithstanding, there are *many* instances in which helpful information is available on base rates, and imperfections in the quality of information do not alter the basic principles underlying the use of base rates. Furthermore, even knowing the range within which the base rates may fall can sometimes be helpful or sufficient, as when decisions would not change anywhere within the range. For example, although the estimates of permanent effects from very mild head injuries vary, the upper end of the obtained range across well-conducted research falls well below 25% (e.g., see Dikmen, Machamer, Winn, & Temkin, 1995). Thus, one can tell a patient a few days out from such an event that he is likely to have a good outcome. Furthermore, in this circumstance, soft predictors of a negative outcome are unlikely to override the base rate.

COMBINING INFORMATION

Combining All of the Information Versus All of the Useful Information: A Key Distinction

I have come to believe, having sampled various leading textbooks in assessment, asked many psychologists and students what they were taught, and read the courtroom transcripts of hundreds of psychologists, that there is widespread endorsement of the belief that one should "integrate all of the data" or perform some such synthetic exercise. Such advice almost surely has a subtle *erroneous* component, but it is a subtle error with teeth, one that can have surprisingly powerful adverse consequences. I believe that the erroneous component would be eliminated by merely changing this near-mantra a little to: Use *all* of the data *that enhance accuracy* and *none* that do *not*. This difference between integrating all of the data and restricting ourselves to all of the data that are helpful has major potential implications for decision making.

Ironically, almost every psychologist knows that not all of the data are necessarily helpful, and thus the broad acceptance of this dictate to integrate *all* (or nearly all) of the data is puzzling. I served in a legal case in which a boy's family had driven a few hundred miles on the morning he was to be tested, starting out well before sunrise to get there for the 8:30 am appointment. This boy performed well on an initial series of memory tests. However, later that morning, when asked to memorize an orally presented story, the child literally fell asleep as the passage was read to him. Amazingly, the technician finished the oral presentation, woke the boy up, and asked him for his recollection. The resultant raw score of zero and scaled score of one was then combined with a few other subtest scores to calculate a cumulative index that, as one might anticipate, fell within the deficient range. Would we say that this procedure was laudable because we should integrate all of the data and the raw score of zero was among that data?

We should not integrate all of the data because some data do not contribute to greater accuracy and may even move us further from it. As already noted, across a psychological assessment (whether based on formal testing, interview, or both), it is exceptional to obtain results that do not contain inconsistencies or flat-out contradictions. Thus, if 9 tests correctly indicate that a child has brain damage and the 10th indicates she does not, at some level the results are contradictory and the last test should be discarded. The possible objection that we are often involved in identifying hypothetical constructs and, therefore, definitive contradiction does not occur, will not advance matters very far or sidestep the issue. We are not solely involved with hypothetical constructs and commonly direct our attention to identifying or predicting *events* (e.g., whether someone will kill themselves or someone else, be able to keep a job, obtain passing grades in graduate school, or crash a school bus). The difference between an A average and an F average is not hypothetical, and the same holds even with matters for which there may be some conceptual fuzziness around the boundaries (e.g., what is and is not violent behavior).[2]

---

[2] Even if we are dealing with hypothetical constructs, if our construct will allow a direct contradiction on a core matter, it is not reassuring because it probably signals some form of serious trouble in the formulation.

I am not questioning whether developing an idiographic and in-depth understanding of a person may be a useful goal. But for now I wish to focus on specific diagnostic or predictive tasks, such as judging whether someone is being physically abused, should be hospitalized, may benefit from psychotherapy, or would be likely to respond better to an antidepressant or neuroleptic agent. With such predictive tasks, a ceiling in predictive accuracy is commonly approached or reached once one identifies a limited set of the most valid and least redundant predictors, often no more than three to five variables. There may be additional or even numerous other valid variables, but incorporating them into the formulation will probably yield little or no benefit (making their use inefficient) and may well *decrease* accuracy. Additional variables tend to be redundant (and therefore do not add unique predictive variance). Furthermore, when weaker predictors are combined with stronger predictors, especially using clinical judgment or subjective methods, the influence of the better predictors may be lessened or overridden. Hence, accuracy can suffer.

An idealized example illustrates how reduction in accuracy can occur, even when one is adding valid (but weaker) variables to stronger variables. Imagine Variable A predicts with 100% accuracy and Variable B with 95% accuracy. Thus, Variable B obviously will not improve accuracy. Furthermore, every time one defers to Variable B over A, error will result, because conflict between the two variables can only occur when they point in different directions, and every time B points in a different direction than A, it is wrong. (And if the decision maker never defers to Variable B, then Variable B is not being used.) Although the example is idealized, the same basic phenomenon can occur when one starts adding weaker variables into a mix of stronger variables. When these weaker variables conflict with the stronger variables, the weaker ones are usually wrong, and to the extent that they influence decision making, they tend to drive accuracy downward.

Clinicians often proceed as if validity were cumulative, which it often is not, especially if one has started with the best combination of predictors and then added more and more variables. The result of such thinking is insufficient selection or selectivity, which commonly diminishes the quality of judgment. If validity were strictly cumulative, then 101 variables that each accounted for 1% of the variance would together account for 101% of the variance. It could be argued that the almost venerated advice to "integrate all of the data" is one of the single most malignant norms within our profession and, ironically, is nearly a sure-fire way to hinder or reduce judgmental accuracy.

Incremental Validity as a Primary Determinant for Including or Excluding Variables

Although things may well change in the future as theories in psychology become much more advanced, at present incremental validity (Sechrest,

1963) should usually be the leading guide for deciding whether to include or exclude information for decision making. Incremental validity refers to the potential positive impact of adding new information to other information. If a new variable, when added, increases accuracy, it is said to have incremental validity (see also Chapter 4).

To maximize incremental validity, one attempts to identify the variables that are most valid and least redundant. For example, even if Variable A and variable B are the most valid available predictors, the two may overlap to such an extent that one adds minimally to the other. To use an extreme example, suppose one is making some overall determination about health status, and that weight is a relevant variable. If one assesses weight with two accurate scales, one that uses pounds and the other kilograms, the second measure adds nothing to the first measure or to the overall appraisal of health status. In such circumstances, the combination of A and B may prove inferior to the combination of either A or B with a third variable that, although not as strong as A or B, shows considerably less overlap with these two variables. Such psychometric realities may clash with the seemingly self-evident belief that adding as many valid variables as possible is the best approach.

Knowing What to Count Is Often More Important Than Weighting Variables and Analyzing Patterns

Once the most valid and least redundant variables are identified, one might ask whether they should be weighted differentially or how important it is to consider patterns within the data. The short answer is that at present, given the state of the science, knowing what to count (i.e., identifying which variables to include) is often more important than trying to assign differential weights or discern patterns, even if one merely adds variables or assigns them equal weights. The reasons for this paradox are complex. First, linear composites of variables, or even equal unit weights, often produce the same outcomes or conclusions as optimally weighted variables (Dawes, 1979; Dawes & Corrigan, 1974). Furthermore, the potential advantages gained by optimal weighting are frequently attenuated or negated as one moves from the sample of derivation and validation to new settings, as such weights tend to be sensitive to perturbations in sample characteristics.

Conclusions based on linear composites or simply summing variables also often produce the same conclusions as judgments that rest on (or attempt to take into account) patterns or configurations within the data. For example, according to various studies, decisions that psychologists report depend heavily on the analysis of configurations or complex patterns within the data can be reproduced in the great majority of instances with mathematical decision models or procedures that merely add up variables (see Faust, 1984). These models reproduce the outcome of decisions and are not intended to capture decision processes. However, if decisions based on the configural analyses that clinicians perform can often be reproduced through additive procedures, one must question the extent to which such analyses contribute to judgmental accuracy. Also, the types of pattern or configural analyses that are actually accomplished often turn out to be far less complex, or properly integrate far less data, than decision makers assume.

There is a tendency to underestimate the difficulties involved in pattern analysis or complex data integration. Studies show that the human mind has difficulties properly integrating or deciphering interrelations among only three or four variables, much less the many variables or results that a psychological assessment might generate (Faust, 1984). Furthermore, measurement error and related factors often produce arrays of data and contrasts in test scores that are substantially a product of artifact rather than true variation. It can be a supremely difficult task to differentiate one from the other and, therefore, to discern true patterns with satisfactory accuracy. Given both these innate limits in human cognitive capacities and the tremendous challenges that may present themselves when one attempts to decipher patterns among multiple variables, the potential advantages of complex pattern analysis are commonly neutralized or reversed in comparison with alternative strategies (e.g., identifying a relatively small set of the most valid and least redundant variables and summing them).

In many instances, when reaching decisions or predictions, errors of exclusion are less serious than errors of inclusion. If one fails to include a valid variable, there are often multiple other valid (and at least partially redundant) variables that can be used instead. For example, there are a number of relatively effective (and largely overlapping) questionnaires that can be used to evaluate depression. Thus, mistakenly selecting a variable that is a little less valid over a slightly stronger variable will often affect judgmental accuracy only minimally. In contrast, incorporating a weaker or invalid variable, an error of inclusion, can have a robust negative impact, especially when information is integrated by means of clinical judgment. If an invalid variable contradicts a valid variable in a sizeable percentage of cases, then to the extent this problematic variable influences judgment the consequences will generally be adverse. A composite that excludes this weaker or invalid variable might correctly indicate an 85% likelihood of positive outcome with a certain intervention, but the probability may be distorted downward to, say, 60% if the faulty variable is not excluded. Another intervention with a likely positive outcome of 70% might be implemented instead, doubling the chances (from 15% to 30%) that the patient will not benefit from the treatment.

Hence, trying to do too much, such as incorporating too many variables or attempting complex pattern analysis, may decrease judgmental accuracy in comparison to doing less. Doing less might involve focusing on the proper inclusion and exclusion of a limited set of variables and, once having identified what to use, essentially just adding the variables together. In acting this way we are in a position somewhat akin to past astronomers who knew that planetary motion was not strictly elliptical. Assuming or acting as if it were so, however, generated more accurate results than approaches that attempted to integrate what were surely the greater complexities of nature's true state. Similarly, there is little question that the human mind and behavior contain complex elements, and that knowing and predicting in psychology may well ultimately be best performed by taking patterns and configurations into account that almost surely exist in nature. But to go from a recognition of ultimate complexity to present-day assumptions about the best way to predict mixes up ontology and epistemology; it could be described as conflating the epistemological situation of today with that which may well be true tomorrow. For the present, given the current status of our theories and methods of knowing, simplifying approaches often work as well or better than more complex approaches.

The commonly advocated strategy of integrating all of the data and focusing on patterns and configurations, which sounds so appealing, can easily lead us astray. Einhorn (1986) expressed this painful compromise beautifully in an article entitled "Accepting Error to Make Less Error." Einhorn was not suggesting that we should happily accept errors in clinical decision making or cease efforts to improve predictive capacities through research. Rather, he meant that given current realities, the best methods do not eliminate error, and thus we know that a commitment to use them will produce errors. However, by not accepting error, we abandon the best available methods for alternatives that almost inevitably produce no better, and often inferior, overall results. If accepting error results in less error, we must discipline ourselves to act accordingly.

Some Strategies for Situations in Which Research on Incremental Validity Is Lacking

Data sets on incremental validity are often unavailable or limited to only some of the relevant variables. Lacking such information (a state of affairs that is nearly scandalous), a few guides can still prove helpful. First, we should be mindful that a relatively small set of predictors is usually all that is needed to approach or reach a ceiling in predictive accuracy. Second, there are often multiple valid predictors available, and if we try to identify strong predictors, minor errors (e.g., picking the second most valid predictor rather than the most valid one) will usually have little impact. It is more important to avoid including weak or, even worse, invalid predictors. For example, if there is a solid body of evidence on a number of valid predictors and, in contrast, limited or questionable research that suggests that some other variable *might* be a strong predictor, we should be conservative and avoid the temptation to include the questionable variable. (If further research confirms the utility of this other variable, then of course one's procedure can be modified.) Third, even simple correlation matrices may provide useful information about redundancy. For example, if Variables A and B are highly correlated and Variable C is similarly valid but has lower correlations with A and B, there is a strong argument for elevating the composite of Variables A and C or B and C over A and B (For a helpful discussion of considerations that apply to selecting or combining variables, see Goldberg, 1991.)

TAKE FULLER ADVANTAGE OF
HELPFUL DECISION METHODS

It is asking a lot of even the most capable mind, without formal help, to combine base rates with the diagnosticity of signs to determine the exact likelihoods that result. It is asking even more when one needs to determine the precise validity of signs, the relative level of redundancy among signs, and, based on this analysis, the optimal combination of variables for particular decision tasks. These are the very types of determinations that well-developed decision procedures rest on and thus that are, in effect, performed for the decision maker (Goldberg, 1991).

Take, for example, actuarial procedures. Meehl (1996), who was the first to bring the relative merits of actuarial (statistical) methods to a wide audience of psychologists, described their two basic defining features. Specifically, actuarial decisions: (a) rest on empirically established relations, and (b) are prespecified or based on routinized, objective methods, meaning that the same data always lead to the same conclusion. In a properly developed actuarial procedure, the validity of the various predictors is analyzed, as is redundancy among the variables and the combination of variables that achieves the greatest success. Variables are included in relation to their level of validity and their independent contribution to predictive accuracy. Base rates are often among the variables considered in developing such actuarial procedures, and thus are taken into account as well. Given the predictive utility of base rates, they often produce incremental validity and hence are incorporated into actuarial methods. Actuarial formulae and other such decision rules (e.g., optimal cut-scores for tests) perform the very types of analyses the clinician needs to maximize accuracy, and do so precisely, something that should not be expected of subjective judgment. Such decision rules, when developed and applied appropriately and judiciously, are almost sure to increase predictive accuracy and thereby improve patient care. They are welcome aids to practice and not threats.

Decision aids, procedures, and principles need not, and should not, be viewed as controlling. They certainly are not a substitute for values or ethics but, rather, provide one means by which we can increase the chances of actualizing what we value. These methods produce results that can help to inform judgment but that should not be applied blindly and regardless of circumstance. Although evidence suggests strongly (Dawes,

Faust, & Meehl, 1989) that individuals countervail actuarial decision aids too often and consequently reduce overall judgment accuracy, even strong supporters of such procedures do not argue for blind, uniform adherence to them (see also Chapter 2). Rather, proponents caution against an overly liberal approach to disregarding the results of decision aids and for a carefully formulated policy for deciding when to bet against them (such as when, for example, the cost of one type of error is far greater than that of another type).

Consistent with Einhorn's (1986) thesis, the application of base rates, the incorporation of incremental validity into decision policies, and the use of actuarial and related decision aids will all lead to errors. But their disregard, and dependence instead on unaided clinical judgment, will lead to more errors. The practice of accepting decision aids and procedures when they agree with our judgment and rejecting them when they do not is the same as not using them at all and fails to take advantage of their benefits.

The development and testing of decision rules provide explicit information about how well they do and do not work, and the results (say, a 75% accuracy rate) may strike us as inferior to the success we believe we can achieve using clinical judgment. Such beliefs are almost surely illusory, as hundreds of studies show the overall advantages of such procedures over clinical judgment (Dawes et al., 1989; Grove & Meehl, 1996; Grove, Zald, Lebow, Snitz, & Nelson, 2000) and, further, that subjective impressions about judgmental accuracy are usually inflated (see also Chapter 2). Many factors (e.g., skewed feedback and the tendency to recall our initial judgments as more consistent with outcome than is actually the case) all conspire to make it seem as if our accuracy is greater than is actually the case. Hence, if an actuarial procedure achieves 75% accuracy and we are fooled into thinking that we are 85% accurate (when our true rate is, say, 70%), we will reject the actuarial method for our own less successful approach. Perhaps the most fundamental lesson of science is that appearances can deceive, and I believe that almost anyone who looks at the direct evidence on such matters as clinical judgment, confidence, and accuracy, and the efficacy of properly developed decision procedures, would come away with the belief that these methods have much to offer even the best of us.

Rather than thinking of all of the reasons that a judgment founded on the base rates or an actuarial decision rule might be wrong, a preferred mental habit might be to generate legitimate reasons why our judgments might be wrong and the decision procedure correct. Focusing on why we might be right and the decision aid wrong tends to maintain or further inflate our demonstrated tendencies to be more confident than is warranted. Alternatively, bringing to mind reasons we might be wrong and the decision procedure right makes this contrary evidence more salient and can bring our confidence into better alignment with our accuracy. Finally, rather than considering all the reasons decision rules could be seen as a form of negative commentary on our field and capabilities, we might consider these accomplishments, which rest mainly on the efforts of psychologists, as a source of pride and as a major contribution of our field to the betterment of human welfare.

Clients entrust us to act in their best interests, which requires more than goodwill. It requires properly informed, disciplined, and directed goodwill (see also Chapter 1). For acts of clinical decision making and prediction, properly informed goodwill incorporates the science of clinical decision making. The answer to the originally posed allegory and choice is therefore clear: The individual's well-being is in our hands.

KEY TERMS

Clinical judgment: A method for combining or interpreting information that rests on subjective judgment or data integration in the "head."

Actuarial judgment: A method for combining or interpreting information in which clinical judgment is eliminated in reaching conclusions. Rather, actuarial decision making is defined by two necessary characteristics: (a) Data combination is routinized or automatic (i.e., the same data always lead to the same conclusion), and (b) conclusions rest exclusively on empirically established relations. An example of actuarial judgment is when statistically identified cut-off scores are strictly followed in determining whether an individual has a certain condition, and the conclusion is not modified by clinical judgment.

Statistical judgment: (See the definition of actuarial judgment)

Base rate: The frequency with which something occurs. For example, if 10% of a certain group is depressed, the base rate is 10%.

Incremental validity: Whether, or the extent to which, new sources of information or additional variables produce an increase in accuracy in comparison to the level of accuracy achieved without this additional information.

SUGGESTED READINGS

Arkes, H. R. (1981). Impediments to accurate clinical judgment and possible ways to minimize their impact. *Journal of Consulting and Clinical Psychology, 49,* 323–330.

Dawes, R. M., Faust, D., & Meehl, P. E. (1989). Clinical versus actuarial judgment. *Science, 243,* 1668–1674.

Faust, D., & Nurcombe, B. (1989). Improving the accuracy of clinical judgment. *Psychiatry, 52,* 197–208.

Meehl, P. E. (1996). *Clinical versus statistical prediction: A theoretical analysis and a review of the evidence* (New Preface). Lanham, MD: Rowan & Littlefield/ Jason Aronson. (Original work published 1954).

Meehl, P. E., & Rosen, A. (2006). Antecedent probability and the efficiency of psychometric signs, patterns, or cutting scores. In N. G. Waller, L. J. Yonce, W. M. Grove, D. Faust, & M. F. Lenzenweger (Eds.), *A Paul Meehl reader: Essays on the practice of scientific psychology* (pp. 213–236). Mahwah, NJ: Lawrence Erlbaum Associates. (Reprinted from *Psychological Bulletin,* 1955, *52,* 194–216)

Waller, N. G., Yonce, L. J., Grove, W. M., Faust, D., & Lenzenweger, M. F. (2006). Problem sets and solutions for Bayes Theorem, base rates and prediction. In N. G. Waller, L. J. Yonce, W. M. Grove, D. Faust, & M. F. Lenzenweger (Eds.), *A Paul Meehl reader: Essays on the practice of scientific psychology* (pp. 237–247). Mahwah, NJ: Lawrence Erlbaum Associates.

AUTHOR NOTES

I wish to express my sincere thanks to Dr. Leslie Yonce for her skillful and generous help in the preparation of this manuscript.

Many of the ideas in this chapter originate from Paul Meehl's work and thinking, in particular the sections on base rates and the advantages of statistical decision methods. Although I credit Meehl in various sections of the chapter, I must confess to having read so much of his work and conversed with him on so many occasions that it is sometimes difficult to recognize or recall when "my" ideas originated from him in whole or part. Suffice it to say that to the extent that this chapter contains worthwhile ideas, Meehl deserves the bulk of the credit.

REFERENCES

Dawes, R. M. (1979). The robust beauty of improper linear models in decision making. *American Psychologist, 34,* 571–582.

Dawes, R.M., & Corrigan, B. (1974). Linear models in decision making. *Psychological Bulletin, 81,* 95–106.

Dawes, R. M., Faust, D., & Meehl, P. E. (1989). Clinical versus actuarial judgment. *Science, 243,* 1668–1674.

Dikmen, S. S., Machamer, J. E., Winn, H. R., & Temkin, N. R. (1995). Neuropsychological outcome at 1-year post head injury. *Neuropsychology, 9,* 80–90.

Einhorn, H. J. (1986). Accepting error to make less error. *Journal of Personality Assessment, 50,* 387–395.

Faust, D. (1984). *The limits of scientific reasoning.* Minneapolis: University of Minnesota Press.

Goldberg, L. R. (1991). Human mind versus regression equation: Five contrasts. In W. M. Grove & D. Cicchetti (Eds.), *Thinking clearly about psychology. Essays in honor of Paul E. Meehl: Vol. 1. Matters of public interest* (pp. 173–184). Minneapolis: University of Minnesota Press.

Grove, W. M., & Meehl, P. E. (1996). Comparative efficiency of informal (subjective, impressionistic) and formal (mechanical, algorithmic) prediction procedures: The clinical-statistical controversy. *Psychology, Public Policy, and Law, 2,* 292–323.

Grove, W. M., Zald, D. H., Lebow, B. S., Snitz, B. E., & Nelson, C. (2000). Clinical vs. mechanical prediction: A meta-analysis. *Psychological Assessment, 12,* 19–30.

Kahneman, D., & Tversky, A. (1973). On the psychology of prediction. *Psychological Review, 80,* 237–251.

Kennedy, M. L., Willis, W. G., & Faust, D. (1997). The base-rate fallacy in school psychology. *Journal of Psychoeducational Assessment, 15,* 292–307.

Kessler, R. C., & Merikangas, K. R. (2004). The National Comorbidity Survey Replication (NCS-R): Background and aims. *International Journal of Methods in Psychiatric Research, 13,* 60–68.

Meehl, P. E. (1996). *Clinical versus statistical prediction: A theoretical analysis and a review of the evidence* (New Preface). Lanham, MD: Rowan & Littlefield/ Jason Aronson. (Original work published 1954).

Meehl, P. E., & Rosen, A. (2006). Antecedent probability and the efficiency of psychometric signs, patterns, or cutting scores. In N. G. Waller, L. J. Yonce, W. M. Grove, D. Faust, & M. F. Lenzenweger (Eds.), *A Paul Meehl reader: Essays on the practice of scientific psychology* (pp. 213–236). Mahwah, NJ: Lawrence Erlbaum Associates. (Reprinted from *Psychological Bulletin*, 1955, *52,* 194–216).

Popper, K. R. (1983). *Postscript: Vol. I. Realism and the aim of science.* Totowa, NJ: Rowman & Littlefield.

Sechrest, L. (1963). Incremental validity: A recommendation. *Educational and Psychological Measurement, 23,* 153–158.

Waller, N. G., Yonce, L. J., Grove, W. M., Faust, D., & Lenzenweger, M. F. (2006). Problem sets and solutions for Bayes Theorem, base rates and prediction. In N. G. Waller, L. J. Yonce, W. M. Grove, D. Faust, & M. F. Lenzenweger (Eds.), *A Paul Meehl reader: Essays on the practice of scientific psychology* (pp. 237–247). Mahwah, NJ: Lawrence Erlbaum Associates.

Psychometrics

Better Measurement
Makes Better Clinicians

JAMES M. WOOD, HOWARD N. GARB, AND
M. TERESA NEZWORSKI

Psychological testing is one of the brightest jewels in the crown of clinical psychology. In the early 1900s, when clinical psychologists were struggling to find their identity, the introduction of intelligence testing earned them prestige that they had never before enjoyed. In the 1950s, when large numbers of clinical psychologists first began to work in psychiatric settings, personality testing helped to establish their legitimacy.

Today, the number and variety of psychological measures are enormously greater than in the past. Traditional tests remain popular, such as the Wechsler intelligence tests and the MMPI/ MMPI-2, but important new measures have risen to prominence. Clinicians today use the Beck Depression Inventory-II (BDI-II; Beck, Steer, & Brown, 1996) to screen clients for depression and the Outcome Questionnaire-45 (OQ-45; Lambert & Finch, 1999) to monitor patients' week-to-week progress in therapy, and forensic evaluators use the Violence Risk Assessment Guide (VRAG; Quinsey, Harris, Rice, & Cormier, 1998) to predict criminals' propensity to future violence.

Using these three relatively new measures as exemplars, we will focus on a fundamental question: With all the options available, how can clinicians be intelligent consumers, selecting the tests and measures that will be most helpful to them and their clients? All tests are not equally useful and scientifically sound. Some, such as these three tests, have proven their worth and have an established scientific grounding. Others, such as the Rorschach Inkblot Test, are substantially less helpful and have a dismal scientific track record.

Over the past century, psychologists have developed a sophisticated set of principles and methods known as *psychometrics* that can be used to construct tests and evaluate their quality. Scientifically rigorous and clinically useful, psychometrics has aptly been called one of the "noble traditions" of clinical psychology (Meehl, 1997; see also Introduction). Six concepts form its core: validity, norms, standardized administration, base rates, reliability, and utility. In this chapter we discuss each of these concepts in turn. Psychologists who understand the central ideas of psychometrics will have taken an important step toward becoming well-informed consumers of tests and measures.

VALIDITY: DOES THE TEST MEASURE WHAT IT IS SUPPOSED TO?

The concept of *validity* is summed up by the question "How strong is the evidence that this test measures what it is supposed to?" For example, numerous studies have shown that depressed patients receive high scores on the BDI-II (the depression questionnaire mentioned previously). Furthermore, patients' scores return to normal levels as their symptoms improve. Such evidence supports the validity of the BDI-II as a measure of depression.

Psychometricians emphasize that the validity of a test score is not a static characteristic and can change depending on the specific purpose for which it is used (Messick, 1995). For example, the BDI-II may be highly valid when used to screen for depression, but less valid if used by itself to make specific diagnoses.

Types of Validity

The psychometric tradition firmly rejects *testimonials* as a basis for evaluating test validity. Even if 100 experienced psychologists were to vouch that in their clinical experience the BDI-II is a wonderful test, these testimonials would not be considered strong evidence of validity because, as a century of experience has shown, such *informal validations* can be highly misleading (Garb, Wood, Lilienfeld, & Nezworski, 2005; see also Chapter 7 for a discussion of the hazards of relying on testimonial evidence). A recent example illustrates the problem. During the 1980s and 1990s, the Depression Index of the widely used Comprehensive System for the Rorschach Inkblot Test (known colloquially as the "Rorschach") became widely used as a measure of depression. However, although the Depression Index achieved broad acceptance among psychologists who worked in clinical and forensic settings, systematic studies eventually demonstrated that it bears little or no relationship to depression (Jorgensen, Andersen, & Dam, 2000).

Because informal validation is undependable, the psychometric approach emphasizes the necessity of rigorous, systematic studies to determine whether a test is valid. Five types of validity are of central importance. The first is *content validity*, which corresponds to the question: "Is the *content* of the test appropriate for what is being measured?" For example, the questions on the BDI-II inquire about a wide range of depressive symptoms, such as sadness, feelings of worthlessness, and thoughts of suicide. Because the content of these questions is clearly relevant to depression and broad enough to cover most features of the disorder, the BDI-II is said to possess content validity as a measure of depression.

The second type is *convergent validity*, which corresponds to the question: "Does the test correlate with *other tests that measure the same attribute or diagnosis?*" For example, research shows that the BDI-II typically exhibits moderate-to-high correlations with other tests that measure depression, a finding that supports its convergent validity (Dozois & Dobson, 2002).

Third is *discriminant validity*, which corresponds to the question: "Does the test show *low* correlations with *tests that measure other attributes or diagnoses?*" For example, research shows that the BDI-II typically exhibits moderate correlations with tests that measure *anxiety* (Dozois & Dobson, 2002). These findings indicate that the BDI-II, like most measures of depression, has poor discriminant validity in respect to anxiety and cannot discriminate between patients with depression and patients with anxiety disorders.

Fourth is *concurrent validity*, which corresponds to the question: "Does the test correlate with current *nontest behaviors or symptoms?*" For example, as already noted, scores on the BDI-II are related to clinical diagnoses of depression, a finding that supports its concurrent validity.

Fifth are *predictive and postdictive validity*, which respectively correspond to the questions "Does the test *predict* relevant behaviors or symptoms in the *future?*" and "Does the test *postdict* relevant behaviors or symptoms in the *past?*" Predictive validity is not pertinent for some tests. For example, the BDI-II is not typically used to predict future depression, so its predictive validity is of minimal interest. However, if a study were to report that BDI-II scores correlate with later recurrence of depression, this would be an example of predictive validity. Some instruments such as the VRAG (the measure of violence potential mentioned earlier) are specifically designed to predict future behavior. Several follow-up studies have shown that the VRAG can identify criminals who are likely to commit violent crimes in the future (Quinsey et al., 1998), a finding that supports the predictive validity of the VRAG.

All of the forms of validity discussed here can be summarized under the overarching concept of *construct validity*. A *construct* is the *hypothesized attribute* that a test is intended to measure. For example, the BDI-II is intended to measure the construct of depression. Taken together, research findings regarding content, convergent, concurrent, and postdictive validity indicate that the BDI-II does in fact measure depression and therefore possesses construct validity, but only so long as clinicians using the test recognize its limited discriminant validity.

Standards for validity have evolved over time. In the first decades of the 20th century, psychological tests were often assumed to be valid if they possessed content validity. However, some popular tests of that era were found to perform poorly, even though their content seemed adequate. Thus, psychometricians today recognize that content validity by itself does not guarantee that a test is of good quality. Instead, tests are expected to prove themselves *empirically*, by demonstrating convergent, discriminant, concurrent, postdictive, and (when applicable) predictive validity in groups of real patients. Furthermore, experience has shown that it is often unwise to rely on merely one or two studies to establish the validity of a test, particularly if the test is likely to be used for important clinical or forensic decisions. Instead, multiple studies by independent researchers are usually necessary before a test can be considered well validated for a particular purpose.

Statistical Measures of Validity

Validity coefficient. Several statistics can be used to assess a test's validity. The most frequently used is the correlation coefficient (Pearson's r). A test's *validity coefficient* (that is, its correlation with the phenomenon it's intended to measure) can range, at least in theory, from 1.00 (indicating that the test measures the phenomenon with perfect accuracy) through 0.00 (indicating that the test and the phenomenon are unrelated) to −1.00 (indicating perfect disagreement). However, in practice, validity coefficients typically range between 0.00 and 1.00.

A test is commonly said to have "acceptable" validity if its validity coefficient is .30 or higher. However, this threshold is actually quite low: A test with a validity coefficient of .30 bears only a weak relationship to the phenomenon it is supposed to measure. For this reason, a threshold of .40 or .50 for validity coefficients is probably more suitable for most tests. For example, the correlation of IQ scores with school grades is about .50, a level of validity high enough to justify the use of intelligence tests in school settings.

Sensitivity, specificity, positive predictive power, and negative predictive power. Although the correlation coefficient is widely used as a validity statistic, four other statistics are generally more relevant when measuring a dichotomous or dichotomized outcome, such as presence or absence of a disorder. These are: sensitivity, specificity, positive predictive power, and negative predictive power. Other statistics are also important (e.g., statistics associated with signal detection theory), but they are used less frequently and will not be described here.

For purposes of discussion, we will assume that the dichotomous outcome of interest is presence or absence of a disorder. Each of the four statistics addresses a different clinically relevant question. *Sensitivity* addresses the question: "If an individual has a particular disorder, what is the probability that the test will correctly identify that disorder?" For example, the BDI-II correctly identifies approximately 95% of depressed patients as depressed, so its sensitivity is .95 (Arnau, Meagher, Norris, & Bramson, 2001).

Specificity addresses the question: "If an individual does *not* have a particular disorder, what is the probability that the test will correctly identify the individual as *not* disordered?" For example, the BDI-II correctly identifies approximately 90% of nondepressed individuals as *not* depressed, so its specificity is .90 (Arnau et al., 2001).

Positive predictive power addresses the question: "If the test identifies an individual as having a disorder, what is the probability that the individual *really has* the disorder?" For example, approximately 50% of individuals identified as depressed by the BDI-II really are depressed, so its positive predictive power is .50 (Arnau et al., 2001).

Negative predictive power addresses the question: "If the test identifies an individual as *not* having a disorder, what is the probability that the individual *really does not* have the disorder?" For example, approximately 99% of individuals identified as nondepressed by the BDI-II really are nondepressed, so its negative predictive power is .99 (Arnau et al., 2001).

The helpfulness of these statistics can be illustrated by two examples. First, suppose a patient has completed the BDI-II and been identified by the test as depressed. What is the probability that the test is correct? The answer is provided by the positive predictive power: Even though the test indicates depression, the probability is only about .50 that the patient really is depressed. Thus, the clinician should realize that he or she cannot uncritically accept the BDI-II score as equivalent to a diagnosis of depression.

As a second example, suppose a patient has taken the BDI-II and been identified as nondepressed. What is the probability that this test result is correct? In this case, the negative predictive power supplies the answer: The probability that the patient is *not* depressed is about .99—close to certainty. Notice that the negative predictive power of the BDI is much more substantial than its positive predictive power, an issue to which we will return later in this chapter.

Validity and Error

For a test to be error-free, its validity would have to be perfect, with validity coefficient, sensitivity, and specificity all equal to 1.00. In fact, the large majority of tests used in clinical practice possess only modest validity (validity = .30 to .50) and have substantial margins of error. The error in most psychological test scores is much greater than the margin of error—plus or minus 3%—in a typical election-year poll of voters' presidential preferences.

To correctly interpret scores and avoid misdiagnoses, clinical psychologists must be mindful of the validity of every test they use. For example, as already mentioned, if a patient's score on the BDI-II indicates depression, there is only about a 50% probability that the patient is actually clinically depressed. The score is informative but imperfect, and a clinician who unquestioningly accepted it would be wrong half the time.

There is reason to believe that psychologists are not always mindful of validity. For example, the interpretation of one score on a patient's Rorschach may sometimes seem to contradict the interpretation of another score. In such cases, devotees of the test may expend considerable ingenuity, energy, and imagination to explain the paradox and show how *both* interpretations are in fact correct. However, in such displays of interpretive inventiveness, one never hears the obvious remark: "Well, it may be that one or even both of these interpretations is simply wrong. After all, the Rorschach scores we are discussing have an average validity of .30 at best, so there are bound to be many errors" (see also Chapter 3). Such frank admissions would be refreshing, because psychometrics tells us that error plays a large role in Rorschach interpretation, so that inaccuracies and contradictions are inevitable.

Incremental Validity

Even a test that is valid may be of little clinical use in certain circumstances. For example, a clinician who has conducted a thorough interview and diagnosed a patient as seriously depressed usually has little need to administer the BDI-II, because the test is unlikely to add any new information that will change the diagnosis. In the case of this client, we would say that the BDI-II lacks *incremental validity* for detecting depression, above and beyond what can be learned from a diagnostic interview (Sechrest, 1963; see also Chapter 3 for a discussion of incremental validity).

As another example, research has shown that the OQ-45, the measure of therapy outcome previously mentioned, often uncovers new and important information about clients that their therapists have failed to detect during their weekly sessions (Hannan et al., 2005). In other words, the OQ-45 has demonstrated *incremental validity* above and beyond the information typically gathered from therapy sessions.

Unfortunately, there is little systematic research on the incremental validity of most tests used in psychological practice. However, several studies have examined the incremental validity of the Minnesota Multiphasic Personality Inventory (MMPI) and the Rorschach Inkblot Test. This research indicates that if a clinician already has access to interview data and biographical information, the addition of MMPI scores can produce a small but significant improvement in the clinician's judgments concerning a patient (Garb, 2003). However, if the clinician already has access to interview data and biographical information, the addition of the Rorschach does not improve clinical judgments. Thus, the MMPI, but not the Rorschach, has incremental validity when added to interviews and biographical information.

NORMS: STANDARDS OF COMPARISON

For a psychological test to be useful in clinical work, validity is absolutely necessary—but not sufficient. For example, suppose you are told that a particular patient scored 24 on the BDI-II. Although the BDI-II possesses excellent validity, you cannot interpret this score without appropriate standards of comparison, known as *norms*. For instance, if you are told that depressed patients typically score above 15 on the BDI-II, and that most nondepressed individuals score below 21 (Arnau et al., 2001), then these *norms* allow you to conclude that the patient with the score of 24 is probably depressed. Validity and norms stand together like two pillars, providing the underlying support for meaningful interpretation of clinical tests.

Normative Statistics

Although the norms for a test may include a wide variety of statistics, we will focus on a subset that is particularly important in clinical work. First are the mean and standard deviation for a group of nonpatients who have taken the test, known as the *normative sample*. For example, the mean of the BDI-II among normal nondepressed adults is about 7, with a standard deviation of 7 (Arnau et al., 2001). Thus, if a patient receives a score of 12 on the BDI-II, comparison with the norms indicates that he or she has scored well within the normal range and is probably not depressed.

Another set of useful normative statistics are the means and standard deviations of *relevant patient groups*. For example, the mean of the BDI-II among depressed patients has been reported as about 28 with a standard deviation of 10 (Arnau et al., 2001). Thus, if a patient receives a score of 24 on the BDI-II, comparison with the norms indicates that he or she has scored similarly to depressed patients and is also likely to be depressed.

Another important statistic is the *cutoff* between normal and disordered individuals. As already mentioned, most depressed individuals score above 15 on the BDI-II and most normal individuals score below 21. Thus, it is clear that patients who score 21 or higher are probably depressed, and patients who score 15 or lower are probably *not* depressed. But what about the "fuzzy" group of patients who score somewhere from 16 to 20? Research suggests that among primary medical patients, the highest diagnostic accuracy is achieved if 17/18 is selected as a cutoff, so that patients who score 18 or higher are classified as depressed, and patients who score 17 or lower are classified as nondepressed (Arnau et al., 2001).

The identification of a test cutoff can be a complicated procedure because the best cutoff may differ from one population to another. In general, the less common a disorder is in a particular group, the higher one will want to set the cutoff. For example, although the best cutoff (i.e., the one yielding the highest rate of correct classifications) appears to be 17/18 among primary medical patients, a cutoff of 19/20 appears to work better among college students (Dozois, Dobson, & Ahnberg, 1998) because depression is somewhat less common among college students than among primary medical patients.

Group-Specific Norms

As already noted, the norms for most tests include the mean and standard deviation for a normative sample composed of nonpatients sampled from the community. However, means and standard deviations may be substantially different in different groups of normal individuals. For example, normal 20-year-olds give substantially more correct answers on intelligence tests than normal 60-year-olds do. Thus, if the intelligence test scores for a 60-year-old patient are compared with norms based on 20-year-olds, the patient is likely to appear to be of relatively low intelligence, even though in fact he or she may be average or above-average compared with other individuals of the same age.

To avoid such problems, many tests provide *group-specific norms*, that is, separate means and standard deviations for different normal groups. For instance, because of the age-related differences we have just described, intelligence tests typically provide group-specific norms for different age groups. As another example, because normal males and normal females score differently on the Minnesota Multiphasic Personality Inventory-2 (MMPI-2), group-specific norms for each gender have been developed.

Group-specific norms are also often necessary for individuals who differ with respect to language, culture, ethnic group, or education. For example, in the United States, children who speak only English tend to score higher on tests of verbal intelligence than do children who speak both English and Spanish (Figueroa, 1989; Sattler & Altes, 1984). It would be a serious mistake to conclude that a bilingual child is of low intelligence simply because his or her test score is low compared with norms based on monolingual English-speaking children. Instead, group-specific norms may be necessary to allow comparison of the bilingual child's test scores with other bilingual children.

Norms and Error

As the discussion of group-specific norms illustrates, use of inappropriate or inaccurate norms can lead to serious test error. Major problems with norms have afflicted some of clinical psychology's most prominent intelligence and personality tests over the past century. For example, the norms of the first modern intelligence test were seriously flawed, so that many normal adults appeared mentally impaired when compared with them. The problem attracted national attention when the mayor of Chicago was administered the test and identified as supposedly "feeble-minded" (Zenderland, 1998, p. 246).

A second, more recent example involved the norms of the original MMPI, which were in use for approximately 40 years, from the early 1950s until about 1990. The norms for several MMPI scales were apparently in error, so that some individuals in the normal or near-normal range were mistakenly identified as disturbed (Greene, 2000). Fortunately, the MMPI-2 (the current version of the test) seems to have eliminated this problem.

A third example, even more recent, involves the norms of the Comprehensive System for the Rorschach that have been in use from the 1980s to the present. There is substantial evidence that these norms are seriously flawed, so that clinicians who rely on them will tend to overdiagnose patients with depression, thought disorder, and narcissism (Wood, Nezworski, Garb, & Lilienfeld, 2001).

In all of these historical examples, flawed norms have tended to "overpathologize," that is, to make relatively normal people appear psychologically disturbed. In fact, incorrect norms can be, and often are, more harmful than low validity. For example, a test of depression with absolutely no validity (validity coefficient = 0.00) but accurate norms will misclassify only about 2.5% of patients as depressed (assuming that the diagnostic cutoff is set two standard deviations above the mean of normal individuals). In contrast, a test of depression with perfect validity (validity coefficient = 1.00) but flawed norms may misclassify 25% or even 50% of patients as depressed, depending on where the diagnostic cutoff is erroneously set. For example, the flawed norms of the Comprehensive System for the Rorschach, already described, appear to lead to enormous misclassification rates, in some cases identifying about one-sixth of nonpatient adults as depressed, one-third as narcissistic, and one-half as thought disordered. Similar misclassification rates appear to occur when the Comprehensive System for the Rorschach is used with children (Wood et al., 2001).

STANDARDIZED ADMINISTRATION AND SCORING

From the earliest days of psychological research in the 1800s, psychologists have known that small variations in the way an experiment or test is administered can powerfully affect its results. Accordingly, well-designed tests are *standardized*, that is, they include detailed administration procedures that must be followed every time the test is given. Deviations from standardized procedures can introduce serious error into test results.

Standardization of test *scoring* is also an important consideration. Questionnaires with a structured response format (for example, requiring a True or False response) have the advantage that they can be scored in a relatively straightforward manner, thus reducing opportunities for scorer error. In contrast, intelligence tests are more complicated to score, and projective tests such as the Rorschach are more complicated yet. The more complicated a scoring system, the more vulnerable it is to scorer error.

BASE RATES AND ERROR

All the sources of test error discussed thus far can be controlled, or at least reduced, by conscientious effort. For instance, variations in test administration can be largely eliminated by following standardized testing procedures. However, there remains an important source of error that lies outside the control of psychologists, no matter how conscientious they may be. If a disorder is even moderately uncommon—that is, if its *base rate* is low or somewhat low—then a test designed to screen for the disorder is likely to have only mediocre positive predictive power. Thus, when the test identifies individuals as disordered, it will often be wrong. Known as the *base rate problem*, this source of error is particularly important to clinical psychologists because most of the disorders that they assess are abnormal, and so by definition uncommon (see also Chapter 3 for a discussion of base rates).

To understand the base rate problem, we can imagine the hypothetical situation shown in Figure 4.1. Let us assume that 100 medical patients in a primary care clinic are administered the BDI-II, and that 10 of these patients are clinically depressed. The base rate of depression among these patients is 10% (10/100)—about what would be expected in a

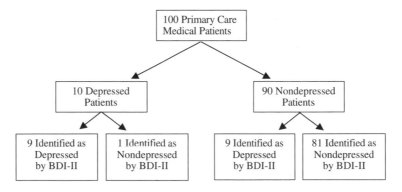

Figure 4.1. Diagnoses of Depression and BDI-II Classification for 100 Hypothetical Primary Care Medical Patients

primary care medical setting (Arnau et al., 2001). Because the sensitivity of the BDI-II is .95, it will correctly identify approximately 9 of the 10 depressed patients as depressed (see Figure 4.1). In addition, because the specificity of the BDI-II is .90, it will correctly identify approximately 81 of the 90 nondepressed patients (90%) as nondepressed *but misidentify the remaining 9 nondepressed patients as depressed.* These 9 misclassified patients are called *false positives.*

In total, the BDI-II will identify approximately 18 patients as depressed. Of these, 9 will truly be depressed and 9 will be false positives. To calculate the positive predictive power of the BDI-II in this group of patients, we can ask "If the test identifies a patient as depressed, what is the probability that the patient really is depressed?" The answer is .50 (9/18), which is not very impressive. Thus, when the BDI-II identifies a patient as depressed, it is wrong about half the time, as already mentioned in our earlier discussions.

The crucial point here is not that the BDI-II is a poor test. In fact, it is an exceptionally good test. However, even a test of high quality is likely to have poor positive predictive power when the base rate of a disorder is 10% or lower. The situation is even worse when the base rate is 1% or lower. For example, in a classic article published more than 50 years ago, Meehl and Rosen (1955) pointed out that because suicide is a rare event, even an excellent test designed to identify suicide attempters is bound to have very poor positive predictive power: An overwhelming number of the individuals identified as attempters will *not* attempt suicide.

Although the base rate problem is sobering, we should not conclude that psychological testing is a hopeless enterprise. A clinician who assesses the primary care medical patients in our example would be wise to continue using the BDI-II as a *screening instrument,* that is, as a tool to help identify patients *likely* to have problems. In the example, the BDI-II is nearly always correct when it identifies patients as *nondepressed* (negative predictive power = .99). Thus, the clinician can safely rely on the BDI-II when it identifies patients as not depressed. Furthermore, in the relatively few cases when the test indicates that depression is present, the clinician can follow up with a detailed interview. In half the cases (9 out of 18), depression will turn out to be the correct diagnosis. Even in the false positive cases, some other disorder besides depression is likely to be found. In particular, many patients who score as false positives on the BDI have a diagnosable anxiety disorder (Dozois & Dobson, 2002). Thus, despite its limited positive predictive power, the BDI-II can be a highly useful tool in clinical settings, alerting the clinician to cases that require detailed diagnostic workups.

RELIABILITY: CONSISTENCY OF SCORES

Many psychometric textbooks devote their opening chapters to reliability. We have delayed introducing this fundamental topic only because, in our view, its importance cannot be fully appreciated without a prior understanding of validity.

The concept of *reliability* can be summed up by the question: "How *consistent* are the results of this test?" There are two reasons that reliability is important. First, reliability is absolutely essential to validity. For instance, if a depression test is administered to a patient twice in one day and classifies the patient as depressed one time and nondepressed the next, the results would raise questions not only about the test's consistency but also about its validity, as one of the results must be wrong. An unreliable test cannot be valid.

Second, reliability is important because it can help to identify specific sources of error in a test. For example, if two psychologists administer an intelligence test to the same child but assign wildly discrepant scores, the inconsistency suggests that there may be problems with the test's scoring rules, or that one of the psychologists deviated from standardized scoring procedures.

Types of Reliability

Three types of reliability are commonly reported for psychological tests. Contrary to what one might assume, these three types sometimes yield markedly different estimates. First is *test-retest reliability*, which corresponds to the question: "Does the test yield consistent results *over time?*" For example, researchers in one study administered the BDI-II to the same group of patients on two different occasions a week apart (Beck et al., 1996). The patients' scores at the first testing correlated .93 with their scores at the second testing, indicating that the one-week test-retest reliability of the BDI-II was excellent.

Second is *interrater reliability*, which corresponds to the question: "Does the test yield consistent results among *different raters?*" For example, in a study of a well-known intelligence test, the responses of 60 children were scored by three different raters (Wechsler, 2003). The scores assigned by the different raters correlated .91 with one another, indicating that the interrater reliability of the test was excellent. Interrater reliability is highly relevant to intelligence tests, projective tests such as the Rorschach, and behavioral ratings, but less relevant to questionnaires such as the BDI-II, which do not require the use of raters.

Third is *internal reliability*, which corresponds to the question: "Are the items that make up the test *consistent with one another?*" For instance, because the 21 items of the BDI-II are all intended to measure depression, we would expect them to be correlated with one another. There are three alternative strategies for evaluating whether the items of a test are *internally consistent* (that is, whether they correlate with one another). One strategy is to divide the test into two distinct parts, one part consisting of even-numbered items and the other of odd-numbered items, and then calculate the correlation of one part with the other, known as *odd-even reliability.* The second strategy is to calculate the correlation of the first half of the test with the second half, known as *split-half reliability.* The third and most common strategy involves calculating the correlations among all items simultaneously and adjusting this number to arrive at *coefficient alpha,* also known as *Cronbach's alpha.* For instance, several studies have found that the internal reliability (internal consistency) of the BDI-II as measured by coefficient alpha is about .92 (Dozois & Dobson, 2002), which is considered to be excellent.

In general, the test-retest reliability, interrater reliability, and internal reliability of a test used in clinical practice should be .80 or higher. However, under some circumstances, high consistency is neither expected nor desirable. For example, the test-retest reliability of the BDI-II is considerably lower than .80 when the two administrations of the test occur a year apart. Because depression is often a cyclical disorder, patients depressed at the first testing are not expected to be depressed a year later, and therefore the one-year test-retest reliability *should* be low. As another example, extremely high internal reliability can sometimes indicate that test items are too narrowly similar (Loevinger, 1954). For instance, a depression questionnaire that consists entirely of questions about low self-esteem will probably have high internal consistency because its items all correlate highly with one another. However, its validity will be poor because it fails to inquire about other important symptoms of depression, such as sadness and hopelessness.

Utility: How Useful Is the Test?

Finally we come to *utility,* which might be considered the "bottom line" for any procedure used in clinical practice. The concept of utility can be summed up by the question: "Does use of this test result in better patient outcomes or more efficient delivery of services?" For example, we would say that the BDI-II has utility in primary care medical settings if its use leads to better identification and treatment of depressed patients, or to more efficient use of clinicians' time.

Unfortunately, we cannot say with *certainty* that the BDI produces these benefits, because its utility, and indeed the utility of most psychological tests, has never been systematically examined by researchers. For example, research has never demonstrated that the two personality tests most commonly used in clinical practice, the MMPI-2 and the Rorschach, actually improve patient outcomes or increase psychologists' efficiency. It is sobering to consider that the Rorschach—which lacks incremental validity, has flawed norms, and takes 2.5 hours to administer, score, and interpret—may actually reduce psychologists' efficiency and worsen patient outcomes.

Utility is the neglected child of the psychometric family (Hunsley & Bailey, 1999). However, an important exception is the OQ-45, the questionnaire previously mentioned that monitors therapy patients' mental health status.

During the past decade, several studies have evaluated whether use of this questionnaire improves patient outcomes. In a summary of this research, Lambert and his colleagues (2003) concluded that when therapists are provided with weekly feedback from the OQ-45, deterioration rates for patients identified as being at risk are cut nearly in half.

CONCLUSION

Psychometrics is one of the most successful and scientifically impressive accomplishments of psychology. Guided by its principles, psychologists have created an impressive array of tests for a substantial number of clinical and research purposes. Furthermore, the psychometric approach has proven highly exportable and been widely adopted by other disciplines. For instance, medical tests are now routinely evaluated using the same ideas—validity, norms, reliability, utility—that are described in this chapter.

In this chapter, we have outlined the fundamental concepts of psychometrics. We strongly encourage readers to develop deeper understanding of these ideas through additional reading and study. A clinician familiar with the psychometric framework will be well prepared to evaluate tests and select those most likely to prove helpful for clients. Few topics in clinical psychology are at once as intellectually stimulating and as clinically practical as the noble tradition of psychometrics.

Note: The views expressed in this chapter are those of the authors and are not the official policy of the Department of Defense or the United States Air Force.

KEY TERMS

Psychometrics: The science of constructing and evaluating tests.
Validity: Formally defined as the strength of evidence supporting an inference based on a test score. Less formally, validity addresses the question: "Does this score measure what it is suppposed to?"
Norms: Numbers that allow comparison of an individual's test score with the scores of a relevant group. For example, norms for the BDI-2 include means and standard deviations of BDI-2 scores for both nonpatient and depressed groups.
Standardization: Establishment of detailed and explicit rules for administration and scoring of a test.
Reliability: The degree to which a test yields consistent results. The term can apply to consistency between judges or raters (interrater reliability), consistency over time (test-retest reliability), or consistency among test items (internal reliability).
Base rate: The percentage of individuals in a population who have a particular condition, such as depression.

Utility: Formally defined as the degree to which use of a test or treatment improves patient outcomes or efficiency. Informally defined as the *usefulness* of the test or treatment.

RECOMMENDED READINGS

American Psychological Association (1999). *Standards for psychological and educational testing.* Washington, DC: Author.

Anastasi, A., & Urbina, S. (1997). *Psychological testing* (7th ed.). Upper Saddle River, N. J.: Prentice Hall.

Nunnally, J. C., & Bernstein, I. H. (1994). *Psychometric theory* (3rd ed.). New York: McGraw-Hill.

Streiner, D. L., & Norman, G. R. (2003). *Health measurement scales: A practical guide to their development and use* (3rd ed.). Oxford: Oxford University Press.

Wiggins, J. S. (1973). *Personality and prediction: Principles of personality assessment.* Reading, MA: Addison-Wesley.

REFERENCES

American Psychological Association (1999). *Standards for psychological and educational testing.* Washington DC: Author.

Arnau, R. C., Meagher, M. W., Norris, M. P., & Bramson, R. (2001). Psychometric evaluation of the Beck Depression Inventory-II with primary care medical patients. *Health Psychology, 20,* 112–119.

Beck, A. T., Steer, R. A., & Brown, G. K. (1996). *Manual for the Beck Depression Inventory-II.* San Antonio, TX: The Psychological Corporation.

Dozois, D. J. A., & Dobson, K. S. (2002). Depression. In M. M. Antony & D. H. Barlow (Eds.), *Handbook of assessment and treatment planning for psychological disorders* (pp. 259–299). New York: Guilford.

Dozois, D. J. A., Dobson, K. S., & Ahnberg, J. L. (1998). A psychometric evaluation of the Beck Depression Inventory-II. *Psychological Assessment, 10,* 83–89.

Figueroa, R. A. (1989). Psychological testing of linguistic-minority students: Knowledge gaps and regulations. *Exceptional Children, 56,* 145–152.

Garb, H. N. (2003). Incremental validity and the assessment of psychopathology in adults. *Psychological Assessment, 15,* 508–520.

Garb, H. N., Wood, J. M., Lilienfeld, S. O., & Nezworski, M. T. (2005). Roots of the Rorschach controversy. *Clinical Psychology Review, 25,* 97–118.

Greene, R. L. (2000). *The MMPI-2: An interpretive manual* (2nd ed.). Needham Heights, MA: Allyn & Bacon.

Hannan, C., Lambert, M. J., Harmon, C., Nielsen, S. L., Smart, D. W., Shimokawa, K., et al. (2005). A lab test and algorithms for identifying clients at risk for treatment failure. *Journal of Clinical Psychology/In Session, 61,* 155–163.

Hunsley, J., & Bailey, J. M. (1999). The clinical utility of the Rorschach: Unfulfilled promises and an uncertain future. *Psychological Assessment, 11,* 266–277.

Jorgensen, K., Andersen, T. J., & Dam, H. (2000). The diagnostic efficiency of the Rorschach depression index and the schizophrenia index: A review. *Assessment, 7,* 259–280.

Lambert, M. J., & Finch, A. E. (1999). The Outcome Questionnaire. In M. E. Maruish (Ed.), *The use of psychological testing for treatment planning and outcomes assessment* (2nd ed., pp. 831–869). Mahwah, NJ: Lawrence Erlbaum Associates.

Lambert, M. J., Whipple, J. L., Hawkins, E. J., Vermeersch, D. A., Nielsen, S. L., & Smart, D. W. (2003) Is it time for clinicians to routinely track patient outcome? A meta-analysis. *Clinical Psychology: Science and Practice, 10,* 288–301.

Loevinger, J. (1954). The attenuation paradox in test theory. *Psychological Bulletin, 51,* 493–504.

Meehl, P. E. (1997). Credentialed persons, credentialed knowledge. *Clinical Psychology: Science and Practice, 4,* 91–98.

Meehl P. E., & Rosen A. (1955). Antecedent probability and the efficiency of psychometric signs, patterns, or cutting scores. *Psychological Bulletin, 52,* 195–216.

Messick, S. (1995). Validity of psychological assessment. *American Psychologist, 50,* 741–749.

Quinsey, V. L., Harris, G. T., Rice, M. E., & Cormier, C. A. (1998). *Violent offenders: Appraising and managing risk.* Washington, DC: American Psychological Association.

Sattler, J. M., & Altes, L. M. (1984). Performance of bilingual and monolingual Hispanic children on the Peabody Picture Vocabulary Test-Revised and the McCarthy Perceptual Performance Scale. *Psychology in the Schools, 21,* 313–316.

Sechrest, L. (1963). Incremental validity: A recommendation. *Educational and Psychological Measurement, 23,* 153–158.

Wechsler, D. (2003). *WISC-IV technical and interpretive manual.* San Antonio, TX: The Psychological Corporation.

Wood, J. M., Nezworski, M. T., Garb, H. N., & Lilienfeld, S. O. (2001). The misperception of psychopathology: Problems with the norms of the Comprehensive System for the Rorschach. *Clinical Psychology: Science and Practice, 8,* 350–373.

Zenderland, L. (1998). *Measuring minds: Henry Herbert Goddard and the origins of American intelligence testing.* Cambridge, UK: Cambridge University Press.

5

Classification Provides an Essential Basis for Organizing Mental Disorders

ROGER K. BLASHFIELD AND DANNY R. BURGESS

All areas of science start with a classification system to organize the central concepts in these disciplines. In biology, for instance, the classification of plants and animals, as well as three other "kingdoms" of living things, serves as the organizational basis for knowledge in the related fields of zoology, botany, microbiology, bacteriology, virology, and so on. When students take chemistry in high school, they are asked to memorize at least part of the classification of elements as shown in a "periodic table" to organize our knowledge about the basic building blocks of physical chemistry. In mathematics, glossaries list the symbols, often designated by Greek letters, representing the standard mathematical functions, such as summation, finding a derivative, and the determinant of a matrix.

The field of psychopathology is no different. The classification of mental disorders is *the* basis for organizing scientific knowledge in the field. Undergraduate courses in abnormal psychology, for instance, virtually always follow the outline of a classification of mental disorders. Offices of practicing mental health professionals have copies of the official classification system for both professionals and their staff to use. Clients/patients who receive any type of treatment for depression, anxiety disorders, alcohol abuse, and so on, are assigned diagnoses contained in this official classification system. Newspapers, magazines, and the Internet contain a number of articles about different mental disorders that laypeople can use to help understand the psychological difficulties that affect their lives. In all of these venues, the idea of "classification" is the underlying authority for understanding mental disorders by students, professionals, patients, and laypeople.

Yet the classification of mental disorders is controversial. The cover of a 1999 issue of *The New Republic* was titled "Selling Shyness: How Doctors and the Drug Companies Created the 'Social Phobia' Epidemic." The article inside the magazine by Cottle (1999) was critical of the classification enterprise and the means by which drug companies manipulated the definition of disorders to increase sales (see also Talbot, 2001). When Peter Kramer's (1993) best-selling book, *Listening to Prozac*, was published, critics worried about the tendency of the American public to overpathologize normal behaviors and to search for "cosmetic psycho-pharmacology" (Rothman, 1994). More recently, Carey (2005) published a piece in the *New York Times* titled "Who's Mentally Ill? Deciding Is All in the Mind." The title implies that the classification of mental disorders is subjective, lacks a scientific basis, and involves value judgments about the deviant elements of a society.

To give the reader an appreciation of the classification of mental disorders, this chapter is organized into six segments: (1) a brief overview of a few individuals who are well recognized in the mental health fields for their excellence in studies of classification; (2) an overview of four important books about the classification of mental disorders as well as four books about classification as a general topic; (3) a historical overview of the evolution of official classification systems in the United States and in the world; (4) a discussion of the purposes of classification systems; (5) an analysis of how well the most recent official classifications of mental disorders meet these purposes; and (6) a brief set of comments about the impact of recent changes in the classification of mental disorders.

IMPORTANT AUTHORS

In histories of psychiatry, the individual most closely associated with the development of modern approaches to psychiatric classification was Emil Kraepelin. Kraepelin was born in Germany during the middle of the 19th century. After attending medical school, Kraepelin became the head of an insane asylum in Estonia. He had studied with the famous 19th-century psychologist Wilhelm Wundt while he was in medical school. Wundt had emphasized careful, strictly enforced experimental methods for observing and recording human behavior. Kraepelin applied Wundt's experimental methods to studying patients with mental disorders. He was an innovative writer, and he organized the chapters of his textbooks around forms of mental disorders that appeared to have the same longitudinal course. What we now think of as Kraepelin's classifications of psychopathology are literally nothing more than the table of contents for his textbooks of psychiatry (Menninger, 1963).

The second major writer on classification during the 20th century was Robert Kendell (Cooper, 2003). Kendell was a British psychiatrist who initially worked at the Institute of Psychiatry in London and later moved to Scotland. His most famous book, *The Role of Diagnosis in Psychiatry* (Kendell, 1975; see list of recommended readings), is still one of the best discussions of classification written in the 20th century. Kendell's initial writing about classification was stimulated by a debate in Great Britain between a group of psychiatrists who favored a dimensional view of depression versus another group who advocated a categorical approach (Kendell, 1968). A dimensional view assumes that the psychopathology can be described in quantitative terms by continua. Patients are not assigned diagnoses on an all-or-none basis but, rather, are described in terms of degree of severity (e.g., a patient is not considered depressed or not depressed, but rather as more depressed than others). With a dimensional approach, the psychopathology of patients differs not in kind but in degree, thus providing a descriptive, quantitative view of the patient's level of functioning. In contrast, the categorical view assigns patients to discrete, mutually exclusive categories that are defined by homogeneous characteristics. A patient is either depressed or not depressed, phobic or not phobic. The psychopathology is described in qualitative terms, such that patients with similar symptom patterns become members of a certain set or category. This debate between categorical versus dimensional models remains an active issue concerning the classification of personality disorders (Trull & Durrett, 2005; see also "A Dimensional Alternative to the Classification of Mental Disorders" later).

The third individual who has had a substantial impact on modern classification was Robert Spitzer, a psychiatrist at the New York State Psychiatric Institute. Spitzer became the head of the task force that generated the most substantial and innovative changes in psychiatric classification since the work of Kraepelin. Spitzer served as the head of the committees that created both the *Diagnostic and Statistical Manual of Mental Disorders (third edition)* (DSM-III, American Psychiatric Association [APA], 1980) and the DSM-III-Revised Version (DSM-III-R, APA, 1987). Spitzer's goal with the creation of the DSM-III and DSM-III-R was to increase the reliability of the classification system, such that there would be an increase in diagnostic agreement among users. Spitzer and Fleiss (1974) reviewed the reliability literature associated with the DSM-I (APA, 1952) and DSM-II (APA, 1968) and found poor reliability, mainly because of the use of vaguely worded prose to define mental disorders in earlier DSMs. Therefore, Spitzer proposed to use more precise descriptors to define mental disorder categories in hopes that clinicians and researchers would find the classification system more useful and specific. Recently, Spitzer's contributions to the classification of mental disorders were chronicled in an article for the lay public published in January 2005 issue of *The New Yorker* (Spiegel, 2005).

A number of other important individuals are currently focusing their careers on issues associated with psychiatric classification. In our opinion, the three most innovative and thoughtful of these contemporary writers are W. John Livesley, who is a Canadian psychiatrist best known for his writings on the personality disorders (e.g., Livesley, et al., 1992); John Sadler, who is an American psychiatrist with an extensive background in philosophy who writes about the relationship of values and classification systems (Sadler, 2005; see list of recommended readings); and Thomas Widiger, who is an American psychologist and strong advocate for a dimensional approach to classification (Costa & Widiger, 2002). Any of the substantial corpuses of writings by these three individuals can be immensely informative to readers wishing to learn more about psychiatric classification.

IMPORTANT BOOKS ABOUT CLASSIFICATION

The beginning of the reference section lists eight important books about classification. The first four of these focus on psychiatric classification. The short monograph by Kendell (1975) is the central book in this collection of four. Kendell's analysis of the issues associated with classification and diagnosis is simple, easy to read, and, like many simple things, quite complicated when fully thought through. The flip side to Kendell's approach is Kutchins and Kirk's (1997) book, which is an attack on the DSMs and on the enterprise of classification. Their criticisms force the reader to examine aspects of psychiatric classification that are often taken for granted. Two more advanced level books about classification are the Millon and Klerman (1986) edited volume, which contains a number of thoughtful and highly innovative views of the issues surrounding classification and the more recent book by Sadler (2005), which discusses the role of values in decisions about how the DSMs were created and organized.

For readings about classification as a general topic, we suggest four books, two of which concern biological classification. The book by Mayr and Ashlock (1991) is a readable and well-organized presentation of the complex issues associated with forming classifications of living organisms. The book by Hull (1988) is somewhat similar to the Sadler (2005) in that it is written by a philosopher of science who provides a critical, historical analysis of the debates concerning three quite different theories of biological classification. The remaining two books by Gelman (2003) and Murphy (2002) are graduate-level textbooks written for cognitive psychologists about the issues of concept formation and how children learn to use concepts to organize their understanding of the world.

EVOLUTION OF 20TH-CENTURY
CLASSIFICATION SYSTEMS

In 1891 in Vienna, Austria, the International Statistical Institute determined that an international classification of causes of death was needed, mainly because of the inconsistencies in disease terminology. The first classification was adopted in 1893 and was used to distinguish between general and localized diseases. In 1900, a second edition of the classification was implemented and officially named the International List of Causes of Death. Further editions were implemented about every 10 years, and by the sixth edition the World Health Organization (WHO) assumed the responsibility for the newly titled International Classification of Diseases, Injuries, and Causes of Death. By the seventh edition, the classification was referred to as the International Classification of Diseases (ICD).

The first official classification system of mental disorders adopted in the United States was published in 1917 when the American Psychiatric Association was founded. The structure of that classification system was modeled after the sixth edition of Kraepelin's textbook. The next major change in psychiatric classification occurred after World War II. Psychiatrists who had been drafted during World War II learned that the Army was using one classification, the Navy had another, the Veterans Administration system used a third, and none of these three was identical to the system officially recognized by the American Psychiatric Association. As a result, American psychiatrists, under the leadership of William Menninger, created a consensual system that all psychiatrists in the United States agreed to use. This system was called the *Diagnostic and Statistical Manual of Mental Disorders*, or DSM (APA, 1952). During the 1950s, international psychiatry decided to follow the American lead, and an international consensus was reached on how to classify mental disorders. This system was published as part of the World Health Organization's (WHO's) official classification of all medical diseases in the ICD. The eighth edition of the ICD (WHO, 1967) and the second edition of the DSM (APA, 1968) were virtually identical classifications of mental disorders. The changes occurring across ICD editions have not been as substantial as those of the DSM editions. The ICD-9 was published in 1977 and was quite similar to the DSM-II/ICD-8.

Despite the international consensus about the ICD-8/DSM-II, a large and vocal group of critics attacked these classifications. These critics focused on the belief that all mental disorders are considered diseases, ensuring the dominance of psychiatry among the mental health professions. The classification and diagnosis of mental disorders were assumed to be fundamental components of the medical model made apparent through the use of medical terms within the mental health arena: patient, diagnosis, treatment, and prognosis, to name a few. The medical approach was seen by these critics as inappropriate and demeaning toward those individuals with mental disorders. Furthermore, critics highlighted the impact of diagnostic labels as self-fulfilling prophecies (Goffman, 1959, 1963; Scheff, 1966, 1975), such that the psychiatric diagnosis caused the bearer of the disorder to exhibit behaviors implied by the label. Also, critics emphasized the failure of even well-trained clinicians to be reliable when assigning diagnoses. Two particular events occurred in the early 1970s that served to coalesce these criticisms into widespread discomfort with the DSM-II/ICD-8. These events were the outcry by gay activists against the inclusion of homosexuality as a mental disorder and the publication of an article in *Science* titled "On Being Sane in Insane Places" (Rosenhan, 1973). According to this influential article, a group of normal individuals was admitted to psychiatric hospitals with the diagnosis of schizophrenia, and almost all were released after a fairly short hospitalization with the diagnosis of schizophrenia (in remission). Both the debate about homosexuality and the embarrassment engendered by the Rosenhan article not only spurred questions about what constituted a mental disorder but also led to questions about *who* would determine the solutions to these questions. For instance, the final decision about whether homosexuality was a mental disorder was decided by a vote of the membership of the American Psychiatric Association. However, numerous authors challenged the science of Rosenhan's methods and his claim of an invalid psychiatric diagnostic system (Farber, 1975; Millon, 1975; Spitzer, 1975; Weiner, 1975). Despite the demonstration of Rosenhan's methodological limitations, his study brought to light crucial issues concerning classification.

As a result of these criticisms, a revolutionary change occurred in the classification of mental disorders. This change was initiated in the late 1950s when Joseph Zubin, a prominent psychologist, invited a philosopher of science named Carl Hempel to speak on issues of classification at a meeting of psychiatrists and psychologists. Hempel adopted a logical positivist approach to science. Logical positivism holds that science should be founded on data that are verifiable and factual; data can used to test scientific theories. Hempel urged mental health professionals to focus on improving the precision with which they defined diagnostic concepts through the use of operational definitions. Operational definitions require that a construct, such as a diagnosis, be defined by the methods in which the construct is determined or measured (i.e., the operational definition of the construct of intelligence is defined by a score on an intelligence test).

Hempel's ideas exerted substantial influence on the major thinkers of the time who were attempting to wrestle with the issues of classification. In particular, Kendell's (1975) book was a pragmatic translation of Hempel's ideas into the language of psychiatrists. In the early 1970s, Robert Spitzer, who was working with Joseph Zubin, was appointed to head the committee to create the third edition of the DSM (i.e., the DSM-III). Spitzer was aware of a paper (Feighner et al., 1972) by a group of psychiatrists at Washington University in St. Louis, Missouri, who had proposed the use of diagnostic criteria to help clarify the definitions of mental disorders. Diagnostic criteria were specific, behavioral referents that served as decision rules for the characteristics of a disorder that must be present to warrant a diagnosis. The ultimate goal in introducing diagnostic criteria to classification was to enhance diagnostic reliability by increasing the specificity of the category definition. The St. Louis psychiatrists were strongly antipsychoanalytic in their views, and they advocated for a neo-Kraepelinian approach to psychopathology. Klerman (1978) summarized the ideas of the neo-Kraepelinians, specifying such propositions that (a) mental illnesses are discrete entities with a clear boundary from normalcy, (b) psychiatry should focus on biological aspects of mental illnesses, (c) diagnostic criteria should be valued and validated, and (d) research should continuously seek to improve the reliability and validity of classification and diagnosis. Spitzer and these neo-Kraepelinians created the DSM-III, which was published in 1980 (Blashfield, 1984).

The DSM-III was a substantial change from previous editions of the DSM. The DSM-II was a spiral-bound, small, lightweight notebook. The DSM-III was hardbound and was the size of a standard textbook. The DSM-III introduced the use of diagnostic criteria. In addition, the DSM-III was multiaxial so that diagnoses of patients occurred along five separate dimensions. Therefore, a complete diagnosis using the DSM-IV entails:

Axis I   Clinical Disorders or Conditions Needing Clinical Attention
Axis II   Personality Disorders or Mental Retardation
Axis III   Medical Conditions
Axis IV   Psychosocial Difficulties
Axis V   Global Assessment of Functioning (scale of 0–100)

Finally, the number of categories of mental disorders ballooned from 186 in the DSM-II to 265 in the DSM-III. The DSM-III became an instant international success and was used widely in a number of countries around the world (Spitzer, Williams, & Skodol, 1983). The DSM-III also was a stunning financial success (Sadler, 2005; Spiegel, 2005) and generated so much income for the American Psychiatric Association that this professional group created its own publishing company. The DSM-III-R was published in 1987 and was intended to only be a revision of the DSM-III criteria. However, a number of new diagnostic categories were added in the DSM-III-R. The DSM-IV was published in 1994, and its timing was designed to coincide with the publication of the ICD-10.

The ICD-10, published in 1993, represented a sizeable change, both in terms of categories, hierarchical organization, and use of diagnostic criteria. The ICD-10 has never been used in the United States even though, by treaty agreement, American medicine should be using the most recent ICD codes. Most American clinicians and researchers interested in

TABLE 5.1   An Idea Unfolding—

A Timeline of Important Historical Events Regarding Classification

1662	John Grant published the London Bills of Mortality (a classification of causes of death)
1763	Carolus Linneaeus published the Genera Morborum
1768	William Cullen published the Synopsis of Nosologiae Methodicae
1812	Benjamin Rush pushed the first textbook on psychiatry in the United States
1883	William Hammond published the second American textbook on psychiatry
1883	Emil Kraepelin published the first edition of his textbook of psychiatry
1915	Emil Kraepelin published the eighth edition of his textbook
1917	The American Medico-Psychological Association (American Psychiatric Association) published the Statistical Manual for the Use of Hospitals for Mental Disease
1942	The U.S. Army published Medical Bulletin #203 for use in World War II as a classification of mental disorders
1948	The World Health Organization published the International Classification of Diseases (sixth edition) (ICD-6)
1952	The Diagnostic and Statistical Manual of Mental Disorders (first edition) (DSM-I) was published by the American Psychiatric Association
1967	ICD-8
1968	DSM-II
1972	Feighner, et al. published a paper in the Archives of General Psychiatry which advocated using diagnostic criteria to define mental disorder categories
1977	ICD-9
1980	DSM-III
1987	DSM-III-R
1993	ICD-10
1994	DSM-IV
2000	DSM-IV-TR
2011	DSM-V (current estimated publication date)

psychopathology have very little knowledge about the ICD-10 and the diagnostic categories contained in this system.

Table 5.1 contains a timeline of major changes associated with the classification of mental disorders. This timeline focuses primarily on American approaches to classification.

GOALS OF A CLASSIFICATION SYSTEM

From our perspective, there are six goals of a scientific classification system (Blashfield & Draguns, 1976; Blashfield & Livesley, 1999). The derivation of these goals is based on the literature about biological classification (Simpson, 1961; Mayr & Ashlock, 1991). These six goals are briefly outlined here.

First Goal—Nomenclature

A classification system provides a set of nouns that a wide variety of mental health professionals can use to describe objects in their professional world. The objects of study in the mental health field are human beings. Thus, diagnostic categories refer to sets of individuals who descriptively share certain similarities. By using the names associated with these categories, professionals can communicate. For example, diagnostic terms like *dysthymia* or *antisocial personality disorder* contain shorthand meanings that convey information to other professionals. Without diagnostic categories, professionals would have trouble talking to each other about their clientele, about therapy, about changes in their practice, and so on.

Second Goal—Information Retrieval

There is an old dictum in botany: "The name of a plant is the key to its literature." Recently, the bushes in the front yard of this chapter's first author's house began to die; there were black spots on the leaves. We cut off a twig from the bush and took it to the local county agriculture station. The agent immediately told us what the plant was, what the likely source of the fungus was, and what we would need to buy to treat it. He also went to a rack of pamphlets and pulled out one about this plant, its growing patterns in our part of the country, and the intervention needed for the proper care of this bush (see Sadler [2005, pp. 432–436] for another discussion of this metaphor).

The same process occurs in the mental health field. When teaching abnormal psychology to undergraduates, one exercise is to show them movies such as *Ordinary People* or *As Good As It Gets*, and ask the students to diagnose the characters in the movie. In doing this, they look up the meaning of various diagnoses in their textbook. The organization of the abnormal psychology textbook and the representation of categories help them begin to understand the landscape of unusual human behavior. It is no accident that what we now think of as Kraepelin's classification systems were simply the tables of contents to his textbooks of psychiatry.

Third Goal—Description

The first two goals seemed mostly to be pragmatic aims relevant to the usefulness of a classification for clinicians. Description is a goal that researchers value. Ideally, patients with the same diagnosis should share many of the same symptoms. More important, the symptom pattern associated with diagnosis X should be easily differentiated from the symptom pattern associated with diagnosis Y. This descriptive clarity is important to researchers because researchers want to use these diagnoses as ways to define separable populations of patients for study. If the diagnosis of "social phobia" has virtually the same descriptive meaning as the diagnosis of "avoidant personality disorder," then research on the genetics of these two disorders is unlikely to be fruitful because researchers will not be able to consistently keep these disorders separate when diagnosing patients and their family members.

The important organizing concept associated with the goal of description is the concept of a syndrome—a collection of signs (observable indications of a disorder, such as extreme weight loss) and symptoms (reported features of a disorder by the patient, such as a reported fear of gaining weight even though underweight) that tend to co-occur. Sydenham, the important 18th-century British physician, used the concept of the syndrome to generate coherence out of his extensive practical medical experiences. The modern DSMs, with their lists of diagnostic criteria, are attempting to describe syndromes of co-occurring symptom patterns.

Fourth Goal—Prediction

The next goal is one that both researchers and clinicians will value greatly if it is achieved. Knowing the diagnosis of a patient is useful to the extent that it helps us predict various things about the patient (see also Chapter 3, for a discussion of prediction). For instance, a diagnosis should be able to help predict the course of the disorder. Kraepelin used the development and course of the symptoms (i.e., prediction) as the organizing principle for the chapters in his textbook. Clinicians also want to predict what treatment(s) will be best for a patient. Modern drugs are designed to work for certain diagnoses. When drug companies market their products, the drugs are presented in terms of effectiveness in treating patients with particular diagnoses.

Fifth Goal—Concept Formation

The best way to explain this goal is in terms of a historical metaphor. In the 17th century, a major contributor to biological classification was Karl Linnaeus. Linnaeus was a Swedish botanist who had traveled extensively and had collected a large number of specimens of different plants. He needed some way to organize the complex and highly varied specimens that he had collected. He decided to use a hierarchical organizational scheme in which he created basic descriptive categories called *genera*. These genera were then placed in higher order categories based on various physical descriptive characteristics of the specimens (i.e., he organized the categories based on morphology). Thus, he formed families, orders, and even kingdoms. He also recognized that many of the genera could be further subdivided in meaningful ways, so he created species as representing subsets of genera.

The next innovation that profoundly changed biological classification was Darwin's theory of evolution by natural selection. This theory provided a conceptual basis for understanding why a hierarchical organization of biological categories made sense. The hierarchical patterning represented historical patterns of evolutionary descent. Stated more abstractly, Linnaeus's classification and the subsequent attempts to improve on his system generated the concepts that Darwin, with his genius and his experiences on a remote island, were able to blend into a theory about biological change. In effect, the classification created by Linnaeus became the building blocks for Darwin's theory.

The classification of psychopathology is often compared with biological classification. There are two mains reasons for this metaphor. First, the authors of the modern DSMs advocate a biological approach to mental disorders, so it probably makes sense to them that psychiatric classification should be modeled after a biological classification. Second, because research on biological classification has been an important topic since the 1600s, the assumption is that the issues in biological classification are understood and that there are no major controversies in this field (but see immediately below). Thus, questions about psychiatric classification can be solved by seeing how the parallel questions were resolved in biological classification.

Sixth Goal—Sociopolitical

The last important goal of a classification is its social, political, and economic function. Although most of us think of biological classification as an area in which there is no controversy and no political debates, quite the contrary has been true. Hull (1988), in an intriguing book concerning changes in biological classification during the 20th century, documented how three different theoretical approaches to the classification of living things were developed. The political battles that developed among the three approaches to biological classification were intense and acrimonious. These battles extended to struggles over the control of the editorial boards of journals and grant funding committees. Applied to the classification of mental disorders, control over the official diagnostic system affects the models of research that make sense and mental health funding by both the government and the private sector. It also has a strong influence on the types of decisions that mental health professionals can make (if they wish to be reimbursed for their services).

HOW WELL DOES THE CURRENT DSM
(I.E., THE DSM-IV) MEET THESE GOALS?

Science is a process (Hull, 1988). Knowledge gradually accumulates. Although there are breakthroughs and paradigm shifts, the progress of science is often slow and measured. The DSM-III and the subsequent editions of the DSM (i.e., the DSM-III-R and DSM-IV) represent major changes in psychiatric classification. But the fact that those changes were substantial does not mean the DSM-IV has achieved all of the goals we have outlined. We will comment on how well the modern DSMs (i.e., the DSM-III and its progeny) meet these six goals by discussing these goals again in reverse order.

Meeting the Goal of Sociopolitical Functions
The revolution in psychiatry associated with the creation of the DSM-III was stimulated by the ascendancy of the biological model to a position of dominance within American psychiatry. Before the DSM-III, many psychiatrists functioned primarily as psychotherapists, generally with a psychoanalytic approach to treatment (Luhrman, 2000). Since the DSM-III, the practice of psychiatry has been focused on the prescription of psychotropic medications. Currently, most psychiatrists (e.g., Kramer, 1993) view mental disorders as diseases that require biological interventions. Mental disorders that may be more psychological or interpersonal in their etiology are likely to be neglected.

Another sociopolitical function of classification concerns the "turf" issues between psychiatry and psychology (as well as the other mental health professions). Professional psychiatry and professional psychology have increasingly been struggling for dominance and leadership of the mental health field (see Kutchins & Kirk, 1997; Sadler, 2005). The introduction of the DSM-III exacerbated this struggle because organized psychiatry made large sums of money from selling the DSMs and related books (Sadler, 2005) and because the control of diagnoses had a substantial impact on both insurance reimbursement and the pharmaceutical industry. Before the publication of the DSM-III, there was a move within professional psychology to create its own classification of psychopathology to fight the political dominance of psychiatry (Blashfield, 1984). Ownership of the DSM trademark has guaranteed psychiatry's reign over psychopathology because psychiatry controls how mental disorders will be named, determined, described, and diagnosed. This reign has been extremely successful and profitable for the American Psychiatric Association. This ongoing turf battle between psychiatry and psychology is now reappearing in a struggle over whether to use a dimensional measurement system for describing the personality disorders to replace the categorical system in the DSM-IV.

Meeting the Goal of Concept Formation

The authors of the DSM-III and its successors have argued that their classifications were intended to be theory-neutral. Because of the psycho-analytic versus biological schism in psychiatry (Luhrman, 2000), Spitzer and the other neo-Kraepelinians who created the DSM-III did not want to be labeled as siding with either perspective. The goal was to create a classification system whose categories were acceptable to all clinicians, researchers, and professional groups within the mental health field.

Interestingly, this attempt to avoid theoretical allegiance has stimulated a consensual response from the critics of the DSM-III and its successors. Commentators on these classifications believe that (1) the DSMs contain an implicit theoretical model of psychopathology and (2) even more broadly, all classification systems are inherently embedded in theoretical models about the objects being classified (see Faust & Miner, 1986; Hacking, 1999; Margolis, 1994). In other words, classifications and theories about the objects of the classification cannot be separated.

As noted earlier, the implicit theoretical model associated with the recent DSMs has been a biological model of psychopathology. This model was advocated by a group of psychiatrists who believe that all valid mental disorders are diseases of the brain (Klerman, 1978; Woodruff, Goodwin, & Guze, 1974). Two areas of knowledge about psychopathology have been dramatically affected by this perspective: epidemiology and genetics. In contrast, other nonmedical topics, such as the interpersonal context of abnormal behavior, the sociology of deviance in the form of abnormal behaviors, and the longitudinal study of psychopathology, have languished.

One consequence of having an unclear, disputed theoretical foun-dation as a supporting and guiding force underpinning classification is an unclear, disputed definition of mental disorder. The authors of the DSM-IV readily admit that " . . . no definition adequately specifies precise boundaries for the concept of 'mental disorder'" (APA, 1994, p. xxi). Despite the difficulties in defining such a concept, the DSM's purpose of a definition was to serve as the atheoretical bridge to tie all theoretical models to a common depiction of what a mental disorder is. Nonetheless, the theory-neutral DSM definition of a mental disorder (which debuted in the DSM-III) stimulated much research activity con-cerning the importance, necessity, and accuracy of defining a mental disorder. Kendell (1975) documented several themes associated with defining disease and mental disorder, including defining disorders by what doctors treat, as a statistical concept, and as a reaction to stress/ environment. Other attempts have been made to define mental dis-orders (Klein, 1978; Spitzer & Endicott, 1978), but most notable is Wakefield's (1992) introduction of the concept of harmful dysfunction. Wakefield recognized the difficulty of defining mental disorder, given its intrinsically vague and ambiguous nature, but appreciated the need for such a definition to validate and extend the act of classifying mental disorders. In his harmful dysfunction approach, Wakefield (1999) conceptualized mental disorders as " . . . failures of internal mechanisms to perform naturally selected functions" (p. 374) that produce impairment. Wakefield insisted that analyzing what a disorder is requires both a scientific and value judgment to assess the failure of the function and the harm that results from the failure. A 1999 special issue of the *Journal of Abnormal Psychology* (volume 108) features various discussions concerning Wakefield's harmful dysfunction analysis, as well as critiques and alternatives to his conceptualization of mental disorder.

Meeting the Goal of Prediction

The post–DSM-III era has witnessed a marked increase in the number and the range of psychopharmacological tools. The number of new medications that have appeared to treat mental disorders has been growing steadily. The use of drugs to treat mental illness has become standard. In fact, this approach is so valued that clinical psychologists, few of whom currently can prescribe, have been lobbying state legislatures to change the laws so that they can obtain prescription privileges for psychotropic medications (as of this writing, they have been successful in two states: New Mexico and Louisiana, and in one territory, Guam).

A long-standing rule of thumb in medicine has been

History → Diagnosis → Treatment

That is, a competent clinician should observe the patient, take a detailed history of the patient's symptoms, make a diagnosis, and, based on the diagnosis, assign the treatment most likely to alleviate the patient's suffering.

Nevertheless, both research and clinical practice indicate that there is no one-to-one correspondence between categories of psychopathology and available treatments. Roth and Fonagy (1996) reviewed research on the treatment of a variety of mental disorder groupings. They noted that a family of medications normally used to treat psychotic patients, known as neuroleptics, is also used for treating individuals diagnosed with borderline personality disorder and schizotypal personality disorder. Furthermore, Roth and Fonagy observed that neuroleptics also have been known to treat depressive symptoms, anxiety disorders, and impulsive behavior, as well as psychotic-like symptoms in nonpsychotic disorders. Similarly, studies indicate that the popular antidepressant Prozac can treat depression, obsessive-compulsive disorder, panic disorder, some eating disorders, and attention-deficit/hyperactivity disorder.

Psychiatry and psychology have attempted to identify "empirically supported treatments" that clinicians can learn to use to treat various mental disorders. On their Web site, the American Psychiatric Association publishes "Practice Guidelines" that contain a list of disorders that can be cared for based on empirical investigation. The American Psychiatric

Association's objective is to provide mental health professionals with strategies to guide treatment plans and clinical decisions based on "research studies and clinical consensus." Of the sixteen major headings of mental disorders in the DSM-IV, practice guidelines exist only currently for three families of disorders (i.e., *substance use disorders, eating disorders,* and *dementias*) and eight individual diagnostic categories (*acute/posttraumatic stress disorder, bipolar, borderline personality, delirium, major depression, obsessive-compulsive disorder, panic disorder,* and *schizophrenia*). This list of diagnoses with practice guidelines is small relative to the total 300+ categories in the DSM-IV. This shows that psychiatry is still attempting to reach a consensus on the treatment of a majority of mental disorders that the DSM has recognized.

Meeting the Goal of Description

Medical diseases generally are conceptualized as relatively distinct entities with clear boundaries from other disease phenomena. This assumption of isolated diseases that can be clearly separated once their etiologies have been resolved has guided psychiatric classification. Most researchers interested in improving classification systems have attempted to isolate clearly separable, distinct patterns of symptom presentations in patients.

However, this assumption of finding descriptively separable disorders has proven elusive. For instance, Cloninger (1989) noted that there has been an increase over time in "wastebasket" diagnoses with the designation of NOS (i.e., *Not Otherwise Specified*). For example, Eating Disorder NOS is a diagnosis referring to a patient who has some type of eating problem, but in whom the eating problem does not fit any of the known eating disorder diagnoses. The frequent use of these NOS diagnoses in clinical practice (Karterud et al., 2003; Okasha et al., 1996; Seibel & Dowd, 2001) suggests that the DSM categories are not adequately describing the forms of psychopathology that clinicians see in their daily practices.

Related to this issue is what has become known as the "comorbidity problem" (Maser & Cloninger, 1990). The innovation in the DSM-III of using diagnostic criteria was intended to resolve issues with the descriptive clarity of the categories of mental disorders. However, not long after the DSM-III was published, Boyd et al. (1984) published a study showing substantial diagnostic overlap among various mental disorders. For instance, Boyd et al. noted that if a patient had a depressive disorder, the odds of that same patient having an anxiety disorder was roughly 10 times greater than if the patient did not have a depressive disorder. Following writers in epidemiology and medicine, Boyd et al. used the medical term "comorbidity" to refer to this phenomenon. The study by Boyd et al. led to a number of other studies regarding diagnostic overlap (comorbidity). As it turns out, most mental disorders overlap with a number of other mental disorders. In fact, this overlap is sometimes so substantial that new disorders have been named to capture this overlap (e.g., schizoaffective disorder, anxious depression).

The basis for this diagnostic overlap is unclear. One possible reason is the lack of specificity with which mental disorders are defined. Consider, for instance, the personality disorders. The level of diagnostic overlap among these disorders is high. In a study using a structured interview at Iowa, researchers found that the average patient with a mental disorder met the diagnostic criteria for 2.5 of the 11 personality disorders being studied. Even more strikingly, 25% of the patients in this sample met the diagnostic criteria for 5 or more of the 11 personality disorders. One patient in the sample of 151 patients met the criteria for all 11 personality disorders!

To try to understand why this overlap occurred, Blashfield and Breen (1989) sent a scrambled list of personality disorder criteria to a group of psychiatrists and psychologists. We asked the subjects to assign the criteria to their parent categories. The clinicians could accomplish this task with only 67% accuracy. Linde and Clark (1998) replicated this study with the DSM-IV personality disorders. They found that clinicians could accomplish the task with 75% accuracy. Even more interestingly, they mixed criteria from Axis I disorders and found that clinicians could sort those criteria back to their parent categories with less than 70% accuracy. These two studies suggest that at least a substantial portion of the diagnostic overlap of mental disorders is associated with how modern DSMs define these disorders.

Meeting the Goal of Information Retrieval

The information retrieval function of classification can be conceptualized using the metaphor of a spreading activation model of memory. Collins and Loftus (1975) suggested that once a concept has been activated in the mind of an individual, this activation spreads to other related concepts, allowing the individual to retrieve additional information regarding the initial concept. For example, thinking of the word "apple" activates the memory of what this word refers to, which then begins to activate other concepts associated with apple, such as fruit, red, juicy, Adam and Eve, and so on. In the same way, a classification system should serve a similar function in that it should provide a sufficient and efficient system for information retrieval of concepts related to the original concept.

The conceptual network of information retrieval was further advanced by the DSM in stimulating important research in the area of epidemiology. The field of epidemiology (literally meaning "of the people") was developed to study infectious diseases that affected the masses and generally was not applied to clinical settings, in which the focus was on the individual. According to Shepard (1978), Joseph Goldberger's early 20th-century work on the epidemiology of pellagra demonstrated to psychiatrists how epidemiology could be useful in organizing information about mental disorders.

Over the last 90 years, epidemiology began to find its voice in making an impact on classifying mental disorders. Two impressive investigations, which were made possible by the innovations in the DSM-III and its successors, were the Epidemiologic Catchment Area study (ECA; Robins & Regier, 1991) and the National Comorbidity Survey (NCS; Kessler et al., 1994). The ECA and NCS studies provided a massive amount of information about the prevalence of mental disorders in modern American society and the association of these disorders with various demographic characteristics. An important, surprising finding from these two massive surveys was the high frequency of overlap among psychiatric diagnoses (comorbidity), thus suggesting potential problems with how mental disorders are described, diagnosed, and organized. Regier and Narrow (2005) indicated that the knowledge gained from epidemiological research should be used to redefine current diagnostic criteria to increase validity. These potential changes also could have substantial impact on genetic research (Merikangas, 2005).

Meeting the Goal of Nomenclature

When viewed simplistically, the DSM-III seems to meet the goal of a nomenclature. When researchers study mental disorders, the titles of their articles, the descriptions of their participants, and the terms used in discussing subsets of patients almost always are presented in DSM terms. Thus, there are papers about dysthymic disorders, body dysmorphic disorder, binge eating disorders, and so on. Additionally, the DSMs are purchased by virtually every clinician in the United States, and the diagnoses, along with the associated code numbers (which are ICD-9-CM code numbers, incidentally), are routinely reported in the charts that these clinicians keep and in the forms that these clinicians use to request insurance payments.

Thus, the DSMs, as the official diagnostic classificatory systems for mental disorders of the American Psychiatric Association, have become the basis of all language used to discuss and describe patients. In effect, the DSM is like *Webster's Dictionary*—the standard reference source that all clinicians must consult to determine appropriate language usage in the field.

Now we will start with the "howevers."

Although the DSMs are like dictionaries, authors have more frequently pointed to the Bible as a better analogy for the recent DSMs (i.e., editions since the DSM-III). The latter analogy has often been stated in sardonic tones. The implications are that the DSMs, despite their attempt to be based on empirical evidence, actually represent "received wisdom" that the authors pass onto other mental health professionals as if the categories in the DSMs represented the unvarnished truth about mental patients. Moreover, much as many priests carry around pocket Bibles, psychiatrists, psychologists, social workers, and other mental health professionals often carry around pocket editions of the DSMs so that they can look up various mental disorders as they work. Finally, like the Bible, the sections of the DSMs were written by different authors and often seem contradictory. But because all sections of the DSMs, like the Bible, are ostensibly true, the defenders of the DSMs argue that the apparent contradictions exist only in the eyes of the beholder. Thus, the DSMs, like the Bible, stimulate extensive additional literatures that attempt to explain what the DSMs really mean.

Another "however" is that not all mental health professionals adhere to DSM terminology. In particular, psychoanalysts have rejected the neo-Kraepelinian approach to classification. The DSM-III was viewed by psychoanalysts as a major rejection of their approach to viewing individuals with mental disorders. Modern journals that contain the writings of psychoanalysts will use DSM terms at times, but more often use terms and concepts that focus on the interactional process aspects of psychotherapy. When analysts discuss categories of patients, they often do so using colorful, idiosyncratic terms such as the "as if" personality, "patients drawn to the bad breast," or the "stably unstable."

Another example of a small but persistent literature that has grown up around a non-DSM category derives from the cadre of researchers who have focused on "psychopathy." To the casual reader, psychopathy appears to be a variant of the DSM diagnosis of antisocial personality disorder. However, advocates of the psychopathy concept explicitly reject this interpretation (Hare, 1993; Lykken, 1995), citing that psychopathy does not necessarily include criminal or violent activity, as typically seen in antisocial personality disorder. To them, psychopathy is a diagnostic concept whose meaning has only partial overlap with the meaning of antisocial personality disorder. Psychopathy literally means "disease of the mind" and was originally used to describe mental disorders as a whole. Since then, the term has been used more specifically to describe personality disorders in general, and then even further narrowed to include only aggressive, violent, and disruptive behavior (Hare, Cooke, & Hart, 1999)—thus the connection to the DSM description of antisocial personality disorder.

Another problem with DSMs as a nomenclature is that the DSMs and ICDs use common language words to name disorders. Often these common language names serve to obfuscate the meaning of diagnostic concepts rather than clarify them. For instance, the term "hysteria" is one of the oldest recognized diagnostic concepts in the mental health literature. However, the word "hysteria" comes from the Greek word for uterus. Greek physicians at the time of Hippocrates thought that hysteria resulted from a woman's uterus becoming detached and floating around her body, thereby creating pain and discomfort in a variety of bodily areas. This name choice has led to historical controversies over whether men could be hysteric and exhibit the same nonsystematic, mixed collection of attention-gathering medical symptoms that originally had been noted in female patients. Interestingly, the group of researchers who had a great deal of influence on shaping the DSM tried to change the name of "hysteria" to "Briquet's disorder," but without success. However, the end result was that this word disappeared from the DSM-III and subsequent editions.

Common language names often serve to confuse laypersons when they attempt to use diagnostic concepts from the DSM. For instance, when teaching an abnormal psychology course, we asked undergraduate students to explain the meaning of various terms before the course began. With some terms, these undergraduates were surprisingly accurate. For instance, most seemed to have some grasp of the concept of "borderline personality disorder" as referring to an emotionally labile, interpersonally difficult individual who was more likely to be female than male. With other terms, the misinterpretation of these undergraduates was interesting. A consistent minority, for instance, thought that schizophrenia referred to individuals with multiple personalities. More surprising was that another subset of undergraduates thought that an individual with antisocial personality was an individual who was an isolated loner rather than someone who persistently violated the norms of society.

The biggest "however," however, is that the names in the DSMs structure thinking about mental disorders. Consider, for instance, a recent continuing education course for mental health professionals on how to treat personality disorders. The person conducting the presentation had separate, 30-minute lectures on treating each of the personality disorders, as if each of these diagnoses was equally valid and associated with an equal amount of controlled treatment research. In fact, however, the size of the literatures for only three personality disorders are reasonably large (*antisocial personality disorder, borderline personality disorder* and *schizotypal personality disorder*), whereas the size of the literatures on the other disorders range from small (e.g., *histrionic personality disorder*) to almost nonexistent (e.g., *passive-aggressive personality disorder*).

More broadly, categorical thinking is inherent to how we as humans approach all stimuli. As human beings, we impose categorical structures onto what we do. Even when the descriptive literature persistently documents dimensional entities (e.g., intelligence, hypertension, and depression), we still tend to organize our knowledge around categorizations of these dimensions (e.g., we use terms like "the mentally retarded," "hypertensives," and "melancholic depression").

A DIMENSIONAL ALTERNATIVE TO THE CLASSIFICATION OF MENTAL DISORDERS

Primarily because of the comorbidity problem, a number of researchers have suggested that a dimensional system should replace at least a portion of the current classification of mental disorders. For most investigators, the portion to be replaced is the classification of personality disorders. Trull and Durrett (2005) discussed the four dimensions that have been persistently found in descriptive studies of patients with personality disorders and showed how these four dimensions yield a more parsimonious system than does the current 10-category model of the DSM-IV. These four dimensions are (1) neuroticism/negative affectivity/emotional dysregulation, (2) extraversion/positive emotionality, (3) dissocial/antagonistic behavior, and (4) constraint/compulsivity/conscientiousness.

In terms of the six purposes of a classification system listed earlier, the current evidence indicates that a dimensional system of personality disorders better fits the descriptive purpose than does the DSM-IV categorical view (see also Chapter 12). Another advantage of the dimensional approach is that it has an extensive historical basis in personality theory, starting with the seminal work of Eysenck (1953). Thus, the concepts of a dimensional approach are embedded in a theoretical approach that is well known in psychology. Although we are not aware of major empirical tests of whether these four dimensions can predict treatment decisions, the descriptive advantages of the four-dimensional model makes it plausible that this dimensional approach might prove more effective when making predictions than do the DSM-IV categories of personality disorders.

In terms of the other three purposes, however, the strengths of the dimensional model are less clear. First, despite the long history of recognition of these personality dimensions (e.g., Eysenck, 1953), they are not well known to clinicians. Moreover, researchers who study these dimensions still disagree concerning the most appropriate names and conceptualizations for these dimensions. From a nomenclature perspective, the four dimensions are likely to be met with resistance by clinicians because of their unfamiliarity.

Second, how these dimensions will improve information retrieval, at least regarding the personality disorders, is not certain. Large national studies have been performed on these dimensions as normal dimensions of personality, but how abnormality on these dimensions relates to demographic and sociological factors in the general population is unknown.

Third, a dimensional model is likely to generate substantial sociopolitical resistance. As already noted, dimensional models of personality disorders have been advocated primarily by psychologists, and the theoretical basis of these models are trait theories of personality, which were developed by psychologists. Most psychiatrists are not familiar with these approaches or with this way of thinking about human behavior. More important, psychiatrists are unlikely to abdicate control of the personality disorders to a model that has been conceptualized by psychologists and whose measurement is dominated by self-report tests created by psychologists.

Is the classification of mental disorders important to understanding psychopathology? In an odd way, classification is like water. Water is essential for human life. Water exists on two-thirds of the surface of the planet on which we live. Water and its control are central to the economic and sociopolitical development of groups of human beings. Water is so essential to human existence and to human culture that we take it for granted.

Just as water is basic to human existence, classification is fundamental to human cognition. As human beings, we are hardwired to think in categorical terms. Human cognition without categorization is unimaginable. Lakoff (1987), in the opening chapter of his book *Women, Fire, and Dangerous Things*, stated this position eloquently:

> Categorization is a not a matter to be taken lightly. There is nothing more basic than categorization to our thought, perception, action and speech. Every time we see something as a kind of thing, for example, a tree, we are categorizing. When we reason about kinds of things—chairs, nations, illnesses, emotions, any kind of thing at all—we are employing categories. Whenever we intentionally perform any kind of action, say something as mundane as writing with a pencil, hammering with a hammer, or ironing clothes, we are using categories. . . . Without the ability to categorize, we could not function at all, either in the physical world or in our social and intellectual lives. An understanding of how we categorize is central to any understanding of how we think and how we function, and therefore central to an understanding of what makes us human. (pp. 5–6)

Is classification a great idea of clinical science? The answer lies in a comment by John Culkin:

> We don't know who discovered water, but we are certain it wasn't a fish.

Author's Note: The authors wish to thank Jared Keeley, Shannon Reynolds, and Elizabeth Flanagan for their comments on drafts of this chapter.

KEY TERMS

Classification: A systematic organization of objects that share similar properties and features.

Comorbidity: (Diagnostic overlap) the presentation of more than one disorder in the same patient.

Diagnostic and Statistical Manual of Mental Disorders (DSM): The official United States classification system of mental disorders published by the American Psychiatric Association.

International Classification of Diseases (ICD): The official international classification system for all medical diseases, injuries, and causes of death published by the World Health Organization (the classification of mental disorders is subject of this medical classification).

Nomenclature: A form of a classification system in which only the names of the categories are listed (i.e., the names are not defined and examples are not presented).

SUGGESTED READINGS

Four Important Books About the Classification of Mental Disorders

Kendell, R. E. (1975). *The role of diagnosis in psychiatry.* London: Blackwell.
Kutchins, H., & Kirk, S. A. (1997). *Making us crazy: DSM—The psychiatric bible and the creation of mental disorders.* New York: The Free Press.
Millon, T., & Klerman, G. L. (Eds). (1986). *Contemporary directions in psychopathology: Toward the DSM-IV.* New York: Guilford.
Sadler, J. Z. (2005). *Values and psychiatric diagnosis.* New York: Oxford University Press.

Four Important Books About the General Topics of Classification and Categorization

Gelman, S. A. (2003). *The essential child: Origins of essentialism in everyday thought.* New York: Oxford University Press.
Hull, D. L. (1988). *Science as a process: An evolutionary account of the social and conceptual development of science.* Chicago: University of Chicago Press.
Mayr, E., & Ashlock, P. D. (1991). *Principles of systematic zoology* (2nd ed.). New York: McGraw-Hill.
Murphy, G. L. (2002). *The big book of concepts.* Cambridge, MA: MIT Press.

REFERENCES

American Psychiatric Association. (1952). *The diagnostic and statistical manual of mental disorders* (1st ed.). Washington, DC: American Psychiatric Association.
American Psychiatric Association. (1968). *The diagnostic and statistical manual of mental disorders* (2nd ed.). Washington, DC: American Psychiatric Association.
American Psychiatric Association. (1980). *The diagnostic and statistical manual of mental disorders* (3rd ed.). Washington, DC: American Psychiatric Association.
American Psychiatric Association. (1987). *The diagnostic and statistical manual of mental disorders* (3rd ed., revised). Washington, DC: American Psychiatric Association.
American Psychiatric Association. (1994). *The diagnostic and statistical manual of mental disorders* (4th ed.). Washington, DC: American Psychiatric Association.
American Psychiatric Association. (2000). *The diagnostic and statistical manual of mental disorders* (4th ed., text revision). Washington, DC: American Psychiatric Association.
Blashfield, R. K. (1984). *The classification of psychopathology.* New York: Plenum.
Blashfield, R. K., & Breen, M. J. (1989). Face validity of the DSM-III-R personality disorders. *American Journal of Psychiatry, 146,* 1575–1579.

Blashfield, R. K., & Draguns, J. G. (1976). Toward a taxonomy for psychopathology. *British Journal of Psychiatry, 129,* 574–583.

Blashfield, R. K., & Livesley, W. J. (1999). Classification. In T. Millon, P. H. Blaney, and R. D. Davis (Eds.), *Oxford textbook of psychopathology.* Oxford University Press.

Boyd, J. H., Burke, J. D., Gruenberg, E., Holzer, c. e., Rae, D. S., George, L. K., et al. (1984). Exclusion criteria of DSM-III: A study of the co-occurrence of hierarchy-free syndromes. *Archives of General Psychiatry, 41,* 983–989.

Carey, B. (2005, June 12). Who is mentally ill? Deciding is often all in the mind. *New York Times.* (Week in Review).

Cloninger, C. R. (1989). Establishment of diagnostic validity in psychiatric illness: Robins and Guze's method revisited. In L. N. Robins & J. E. Barrett (Eds.), *The validity of psychiatric diagnosis.* New York: Raven Press.

Collins, A. M., & Loftus, E. F. (1975). A spreading-activation theory of semantic processing. *Psychological Review, 82,* 407–428.

Cooper, J. (2003). Remembering Robert Kendell. *British Journal of Psychiatry, 182,* 279–280.

Costa, P. T., & Widiger, T. A. (2002). *Personality disorders and the five-factor model of personality.* Washington, DC: American Psychological Association.

Cottle, M. (1999, August 2). Selling shyness. *New Republic, 221,* 24–29.

Eysenck, H. J. (1953). *The structure of human personality.* London: Methuen.

Farber, I. E. (1975). Sane and insane: Constructions and misconstructions. *Journal of Abnormal Psychology, 84,* 589–620.

Faust, D., & Miner, R. A. (1986). The empiricist and his new clothes: DSM-III in perspective. *American Journal of Psychiatry, 143,* 962–967.

Feighner, J. P., Robins, E., Guze, S. B., Woodruff, R. A., Winokur, G., & Munoz, R. (1972). Diagnostic criteria for use in psychiatric research. *Archives of General Psychiatry, 26,* 57–63.

Goffman, E. (1959). The moral career of the mental patient. *Psychiatry, 22,* 123–142.

Goffman, E. (1963). *Stigma.* Englewood Cliffs, NJ: Prentice-Hall.

Hacking, I. (1999). *The social construction of what?* Cambridge, MA: Harvard University Press.

Hare, R. D. (1993). *Without conscience: The disturbing world of the psychopaths among us.* New York: Simon & Schuster.

Hare, R. D., Cooke, D. J., & Hart, S. D. (1999). Psychopathy and sadistic personality disorder. In T. Millon, P. H. Blaney, and R. D. Davis (Eds.), *Oxford textbook of psychopathology.* Oxford University Press.

Karterud, S., Pedersen, G., Bjordal, E., Brabrand, J., Friis, S., Haaseth, O., et al. (2003). Day treatment of patients with personality disorders. *Journal of Personality Disorders, 17,* 243–262.

Kendell, R. E. (1968). *The classification of depressive illness.* London: Oxford University Press.

Kessler, R. C., McGonagle, K. A., Zhao, S., Nelson, C. B., Hughes, M., Eshleman, S., et al. (1994). Lifetime and 12-month prevalence of DSM-III-R psychiatric disorders in the United States: Results from the National Comborbidity Survey. *Archives of General Psychiatry, 51,* 8–19.

Klein, D. F. (1978). A proposed definition of mental disorder. In D. F. Klein & R. L. Spitzer (Eds.), *Critical issues in psychiatric diagnosis.* New York: Raven Press.

Klerman, G. L. (1978). The evolution of a scientific nosology. In J. C. Shershow (Ed.), *Schizophrenia: Science and practice.* Cambridge, MA: Harvard University Press.

Kramer, P. D. (1993). *Listening to Prozac.* New York: Viking.

Lakoff, G. (1987). *Women, fire, and dangerous things: What categories reveal about the mind.* Chicago: University of Chicago Press.

Linde, J. A., & Clark, L. A. (1998). Diagnostic assignment of criteria: Clinicians & DSM-IV. *Journal of Personality Disorders, 12,* 126–137.

Livesley W. J., Schroeder, M. L., & Jackson, D. N. (1992) Factorial structure of traits delineating personality disorders in clinical and general population samples. *Journal of Abnormal Psychology, 101,* 432–440.

Luhrman, T. M. (2000). *Of two minds: An anthropologist looks at American psychiatry.* New York: Vintage.

Lykken, D. T. (1995). *The antisocial personalities.* Hillsdale, NJ: Lawrence Erlbaum Associates.

Margolis, J. (1994). Taxonomic puzzles. In J. Z. Sadler, O. P. Wiggins, & M. A. Schwartz (Eds.), *Philosophical perspectives on psychiatric diagnostic classification.* Baltimore, MD: Johns Hopkins University Press.

Maser, J. D., & Cloninger, C. R. (Eds). (1990). *Comorbidity of mood and anxiety disorders.* Washington, DC: American Psychiatric Press.

Menninger, K. (1963). *The vital balance.* New York: Viking Press.

Merikangas, K. R. (2005). Implications of genetic epidemiology for classification. In J. E. Helzer & J. J. Hudziak (Eds.), *Defining psychopathology in the 21ˢᵗ century: DSM-V and beyond.* Washington, DC: American Psychiatric Publishing, Inc.

Millon, T. (1975). Reflections on Rosenhan's "On being sane in insane places." *Journal of Abnormal Psychology, 84,* 456–461.

Okasha, A., Omar, A. M., Lotaief, F., Ghanem, M., Seif el Dawla, A., & Okasha, T. (1996). Comorbidity of Axis I and Axis II diagnoses in a sample of Egyptian patients with neurotic disorders. *Comprehensive Psychiatry, 37,* 95–101.

Regier, D. A., & Narrow, W. E. (2005). Defining clinically significant psychopathology with epidemiologic data. In J. E. Helzer & J. J. Hudziak (Eds). *Defining psychopathology in the 21ˢᵗ century: DSM-V and beyond.* Washington, DC: American Psychiatric Publishing, Inc.

Robins, L. N., & Regier, D. A. (1991). *Psychiatric disorders in America.* New York: Free Press.

Rosenhan, D. L. (1973). On being sane in insane places. *Science, 179,* 250–258.

Roth, A., & Fonagy, P. (1996). *What works for whom?* New York: Guilford Press.

Rothman, D. J. (1994, February 14). Shiny happy people. *New Republic, 210,* 34–38.

Scheff, T. J. (1966). *Being mentally ill: A sociological theory.* Chicago: Aldine.

Scheff, T. J. (1975). *Labeling madness.* Englewood Cliffs, NJ: Prentice-Hall.

Seibel, C. A., & Dowd, E. T. (2001). Personality characteristics associated with psychological reactance. *Journal of Clinical Psychology, 57,* 963–969.

Shepard, M. (1978). Epidemiology and clinical psychiatry. *British Journal of Psychiatry, 133,* 289–298.

Simpson, G. G. (1961). *Principles of animal taxonomy.* New York: Columbia University Press.

Spiegel, A. (2005, January 4). The dictionary of disorder. *The New Yorker, 80,* 56–63.

Spitzer, R. L. (1975). On pseudoscience in science, logic in remission and psychiatric diagnosis: A critique of Rosenhan's "On being sane in insane places." *Journal of Abnormal Psychology, 84*, 442–452.

Spitzer, R. L., & Endicott, J. (1978). Medical and mental disorder: Proposed definition and criteria. In D. F. Klein & R. L. Spitzer (Eds.), *Critical issues in psychiatric diagnosis*. New York: Raven Press.

Spitzer, R. L., & Fleiss, J. L. (1974). A re-analysis of the reliability of psychiatric diagnosis. *British Journal of Psychiatry, 125*, 341–347.

Spitzer, R. L., Williams, J. B. W., & Skodol, A. E. (1983). *International perspectives on DSM-III*. Washington, DC: American Psychiatric Press.

Talbot, M. (2001, January 24). The shyness syndrome: Bashfulness is the latest trait to become a pathology. *New York Times*.

Trull, T. J., & Durrett, C. A. (2005). Categorical and dimensional models of personality disorders. *Annual Review of Clinical Psychology, 1*, 355–380.

Wakefield, J. C. (1992). The concept of mental disorder: On the boundary between biological facts and social values. *American Psychologist, 47*, 373–388.

Wakefield, J. C. (1999). Evolutionary versus prototype analyses of the concept of disorder. *Journal of Abnormal Psychology, 108*, 374–399.

Weiner, B. (1975). "On being sane in insane places": A process (attributional) analysis and critique. *Journal of Abnormal Psychology, 84*, 433–441.

Woodruff, R. A., Goodwin, D. W., & Guze, S. B. (1974). *Psychiatric diagnosis*. London: Oxford University Press.

World Health Organization. (1967). *Manual of the international statistical classification of disease, injuries, and causes of death* (eighth edition). Geneva: World Health Organization.

World Health Organization. (1993). *The ICD-10 classification of mental and behavioural disorders: Diagnostic criteria for research*. Geneva: World Health Organization.

6

Psychotherapy Outcome Can Be Studied Scientifically

GORDON L. PAUL

It may be puzzling to readers, midway through the first decade of the 21st century, that "psychotherapy outcome can be studied scientifically" is among the great ideas of clinical science. At the time of this writing, organized initiatives have been undertaken for nearly 15 years to identify and promulgate evidence-based mental health practices (see Paul, 2000). Why the scientific study of psychotherapy outcomes was ever considered less than "usual and customary practice" requires a look at history.

CHAPTER OVERVIEW

In this chapter, I first provide a definition of psychotherapy so that everyone shares the same meaning for the activity. Next, I trace the history of clinical practice and research before there was scientific evidence on outcomes. This history shows how various "schools" of psychotherapy—largely developed in the prescientific era—guided the efforts of both clinical practitioners and applied investigators for a quarter of a century. I then describe the way that continued commitment to such "schools," in the absence of evidence, combined with reports from later superficial and unsophisticated "demonstration studies" to derail outcome research for another 25 years in the early scientific era.

Following the historical context that led to assertions that the study of outcomes was beyond the capabilities of clinical science, I note how this "great idea" was among developments of the radical 1960s. After outlining the central presuppositions and organizing principles, domains and classes of variables, and appropriate questions to be asked for the successful scientific study of outcomes, I end the chapter with some implications of the evidence-based practice movement for both research and everyday clinical work.

WHAT IS PSYCHOTHERAPY?

The best definition follows the fundamentals proposed by Lee Winder in his 1957 *Annual Review* chapter (pp. 309–310). "Psychotherapy" is an activity that involves six essential characteristics:

1. There is an interpersonal relationship of some duration between two or more people.
2. One of the participants (the therapist) has had special experience and/or training in the handling of human problems and relationships.
3. One or more of the participants (clients) have entered the relationship because of their own or others' dissatisfaction with their emotional, behavioral, and/or interpersonal adjustment.
4. The methods used are psychological in nature.
5. The procedures of the therapist are based upon some formal theory regarding mental disorders, in general, and the specific problems of the client, in particular.
6. The aim of the process is the amelioration of the difficulties that cause the client to seek the help of the therapist.

PSYCHOTHERAPY PRACTICES AND RESEARCH BEFORE SCIENTIFIC EVIDENCE ON OUTCOMES

The Prescientific Era

Before 1920, those responsible for the practice of psychotherapy (primarily physicians and clergy) relied on uncontrolled observations and inferences from individual cases for development of theory, procedures, and techniques. As noted elsewhere in this volume (see Chapters 1, 2, and 7), conclusions drawn from such uncontrolled case studies are prone to biases and many other errors. Ideas and procedures attracted followers if they had exciting content and were presented forcefully and repeatedly. The upshot was the development of a variety of "schools" of psychotherapeutic theory and practice.

In the absence of evidence of what worked at all, let alone what worked better, proponents of each school decried the practices of one another. Unsupported assertions were common, such as the following by Brill in 1909: "The results obtained by the treatment are unquestionably very gratifying. They surpass those obtained by simpler methods in two chief respects; namely, in permanence and in the prophylactic value they have for the future" (p. 4). Advocates bemoaned the slowness with which practitioners aligned with other schools accepted the value of their own favored approach (e.g., Jones, 1910).

Critics in the prescientific era were fervent in pointing out the lack of evidence to support claims for superiority of one approach to another. Professor Hoche of Freiburg University was among the most ardent. He maintained that followers of a specific school of psychotherapy constituted "not a scientific school but a cult, concerned with articles of faith rather than facts" (Patrick & Bassoe, 1910, p. 26). The main features of such cults included: fanatic faith, intolerance toward unbelievers, worship of the 'Master,' willingness to swallow the most unreasonable assumptions, and fantastic overestimation of present and possible future attainments. Such movements spread due to the "lack of historic sense and philosophic schooling" among adherents. Because of the absence of facts regarding outcomes, Hoche asserted that history would record followers of a particular school of psychotherapy as only a "psychic epidemic among physicians" (p. 27).

The Demonstration Era

The practical necessity of justifying expenditures (see Chapter 8) in the face of such critics gradually shifted the focus of administrators and practitioners toward outcomes. The period from roughly 1920 through the mid-1940s was filled with attempts to demonstrate the effectiveness of psychotherapy practices. A flurry of detailed case reports by psychotherapists of various persuasions all claimed success. However, the lack of controls for alternative influences and the absence of measurement (see Chapter 4) resulted in little gain in factual information regarding effectiveness for any procedure.

Beyond the information from individual clinicians during this period, clinics, hospitals, institutes, and other organized groups began reporting their percentage-success rates (see Eysenck, 1952). These demonstration studies generally employed retrospective collection of data with the practical goal of justifying operations—rather than a scientific impetus for generating objective knowledge. Although retrospective data and practical goals need not contaminate the findings of any given investigation, other characteristics of studies during this era are now known to seriously limit the conclusions that could be drawn from them (see Kiesler, 1966; Paul, 1967b, 1969, 1986). Such limiting characteristics include:

1. The only criteria for success were overall judgments by psychotherapists and clients. [Involved participant's judgments are especially prone to bias from irrelevant factors.]

2. Beyond noting the "school" affiliation of therapists, there was no specification of either the characteristics of psychotherapists or of the treatment procedures employed. [Lack of knowledge about who were psychotherapists and what they actually did with clients.]
3. Beyond listing diagnostic categories, there was no specification of either the characteristics of clients or of the problems presented for treatment. [Lack of knowledge about who were clients and what was the actual focus of treatment.]
4. Information was gathered only on clients who received psychotherapy. [No knowledge of what might have taken place in the absence of a particular treatment.]

Most of these demonstration studies were little more than accumulated tallies of uncontrolled case reports. A critic of undocumented claims for effectiveness of a particular psychotherapeutic approach recently quipped, "A collection of anecdotes does not data make," and so it was for the "evidence" obtained from the forgoing studies. Nevertheless, how-to-do-it books, lectures, and apprenticeships within each school of psychotherapy flourished—each now touting more confidently that their own way was the best.

With no data on what actually transpired, everyone presumed that practices within each school were relatively homogenous and that practitioners from different schools were engaged in unique activities. Advocates began to express concern about how their own school's approach should be evaluated (e.g., Glover et al., 1937). Such concerns emphasized the theory of psychopathology and change endorsed by each school for the "proper" selection of outcome criteria. Although limited to the "school" approach, concerns about evaluation criteria forecast the early scientific era in psychotherapy research.

The Early Scientific Era

The mid- to late-1940s through the early 1960s was marked by increasingly sophisticated applications of scientific methods to problems posed by and for psychotherapy. During World War II, many psychologists— previously trained in research methodology—first worked with applied problems, including interventions for emotional, behavioral, and interpersonal difficulties. Psychologists' and psychiatrists' experiences during wartime and later in Veterans' Administration (VA) hospitals exposed them to both scientific methods and the need for evidence concerning psychotherapy. However, it was practical necessities, once again, that sparked a flurry of activity in the area. Foremost among these was the need for psychologists to train graduate students how to perform their recently acquired clinical specialty.

The Boulder Conference on Graduate Education in Clinical Psychology (Raimy, 1950). Less than five years following World War II, a national conference was held in Boulder, Colorado. That conference emphasized the lack of firm scientific evidence about psychotherapy upon which to base the training of practitioners. A participant offered the following "somewhat facetious," but often-quoted, assessment to underscore the absence of knowledge about psychotherapy practices and outcomes at the time: "Psychotherapy is an undefined technique applied to unspecified problems with unpredictable outcome. For this technique we recommend rigorous training" (Raimy, 1950, p. 93).

A proposed remedy was for clinical psychology training curricula to prepare students for functioning as both scientists and clinical practitioners—"Boulder-model" scientist-practitioners—as the graduates of such programs would be called. The hope was for increases in the amount and quality of psychotherapy research by incorporating the practitioner and the researcher within the skin of the same individuals.

Hans Eysenck's first review of the effects of psychotherapy was published in a prestigious journal in 1952—only two years after publication of the Boulder proceedings. Eysenck concluded, "The figures fail to support the hypothesis that psychotherapy facilitates recovery from neurotic disorder" (p. 323). This furthered the sense of urgency for science based facts on which to base clinical work.

Although not yet impacting practitioners—or most investigators—the scientific era of psychotherapy research was evident in the publications of methodologists by the early 1950s (e.g., Edwards & Cronbach, 1952; Hunt, 1952; Meehl, 1955; Miller, 1951; Watson, 1952; Zubin, 1953). Rather than the study of some mystical and sacrosanct activity—as psychotherapy had come to be viewed by many clinicians and researchers alike—psychotherapy was viewed simply as one area of the study of interpersonal behavior influence. These methodologists also detailed the classes of variables needing assessment, the minimal methodological requirements for evaluation, and suggested strategies for programmatic investigation.

Psychotherapy research efforts increased dramatically following the Boulder conference. By 1961 psychotherapy was specified in the American Psychological Association (APA) directory as a major interest for more psychologists than any other topic (Strupp & Luborsky, 1962). Between 1958 and 1966, the APA Division of Clinical Psychology (Div. 12) organized three national/international conferences on *Research in Psychotherapy*, with funding for all from the National Institute of Mental Health (NIMH).

The First Conference on Research in Psychotherapy (Rubinstein & Parloff, 1959). Held in 1958 in Washington, DC, this conference first brought together major figures from both psychology and psychiatry. In their summary of the proceedings—notably titled "Research *Problems* in Psychotherapy" [emphasis added]—Morris Parloff and Eli Rubinstein masterfully described the considerable conceptual, sociological, and methodological impediments to scientific progress in the area (Parloff & Rubinstein, 1959).

Guild rights of one profession over another briefly surfaced when a number of members of the medical profession asserted that the M.D. degree should be a prerequisite for the practice of psychotherapy. Some psychologists later retorted that a psychiatrist could be defined as one who practiced psychotherapy without proper *Ph.D.* training, but little effort during the conference was reportedly devoted to such issues.

"Status" concerns, however, were identified as impediments for clinical investigators in both disciplines. Most conferees had academic appointments and were familiar with the methodological publications from the early 1950s. Even so, "outcome research" was acknowledged to be more difficult to undertake than other studies. It was also associated with "applied" rather than "basic" science and further tainted because of previous "superficial and unsophisticated research attempts." It was clear from discussions during the conference (although seldom mentioned in "polite society") that few investigators could afford the disproportionate amount of time and energy required to conduct studies of outcomes when their own personal evaluation was based on the "publish or perish" criteria of major academic settings.

Most large-scale researchers responded to the methodological and status concerns with what Joe Zubin (1964) later called a "flight into process." Rather than study outcomes to determine if clients were helped with problems brought to the therapist, research focused on the therapist-client interaction during the "natural treatment process." Psychotherapy research became personality research *within* psychotherapy. Instead of the clinical goal of external change, within-treatment changes predicted from theory then became the "proper" interest. Such "process research" was more "basic" and therefore more prestigious. Some also claimed that outcome studies could not be meaningful without first identifying important process variables.

Although a few more sophisticated evaluation studies appeared during the early scientific era, the Washington conference revealed additional conceptual problems that were impediments to progress in the study of outcomes. The historical influence of various schools of psychotherapy was so strong for their followers that "naturalistic observation" of practice became an end in itself. The realization that criteria for successful outcomes varied with the theoretical frame of reference of the investigator came explicitly to the fore. Parloff and Rubinstein (1959) joked that researchers affiliated with differing theoretical frameworks had too often "fallen victim to the malady of premature hardening of the categories" (p. 291). The "hardening of the categories" for followers of different schools resulted in statements such as, "[T]he investigator's selection of specific criteria [is] a *premature* and *presumptuous* value judgment" (p. 278) [emphasis added]. People were asserting that psychotherapy outcomes could *NOT* be studied scientifically!

In their epilogue, Parloff and Rubinstein repeated the facetious characterization of psychotherapy from the Boulder conference (quoted earlier), noting that the vigorous research efforts during the ensuing decade had made little progress in establishing a firm body of evidence to support many practices:

> Basic problems in this field of research have remained essentially unchanged and unresolved. This may be due in large part to the fact that both the investigator and the therapist have managed to preserve their favorite concepts, assumptions, values and hypotheses by hermetically sealing them in layers of ambiguity. This conference was successful to the extent that some of this ambiguity was recognized if not actually pierced (Parloff & Rubinstein, 1959, p. 292).

The Second Conference on Research in Psychotherapy (Strupp & Luborsky, 1962). Held in 1961 at the University of North Carolina, Chapel Hill, this conference was conceived in Washington, DC, as a follow-up of the considerable problems identified at the first meeting. Unlike the first, the second conference was to intensively deal with a few selected research issues relevant to individual psychotherapy with adults. The explicit focus on methodology within the broader context of psychological research on interpersonal influence seemed to be liberating. Loosening of traditional school fixations and of the mystique surrounding "psychotherapy" was evident in the titles of invited papers, such as Jerome Frank's "The Role of Cognitions in Illness and Healing," and Len Krasner's "The Therapist as a Social Reinforcement Machine."

Papers and discussions at the Chapel Hill conference resulted in some clarification of the criterion problem and sharpening of the variables necessary for research to provide solid outcome evidence. In addition to client variables, the therapist, the therapist-client interaction, and the client's extratreatment life environment also were emphasized. Multiple examples showed how the importance of process variables came from their interaction with client outcomes, rather than exclusively from personality theory.

In their summary of the proceedings, Lester Luborsky and Hans Strupp noted that everyone "seemed to be going his own way, but not so blithely as was the case three years ago" (1962, p. 308). "Naturalistic" and "experimental" approaches were both valued. Further, the "prejudice against outcome studies" had been "worked through." Instead of deploring the presumptuousness or impossibility of studying outcomes scientifically, conferees acknowledged the difficulty of the task—and proceeded to problem solve. In contrast to earlier conflicts regarding criteria based on school affiliations, "The conciliatory point was made that criteria depend on the purpose of the treatment; as the [client's] aims vary, so might the criteria one would select" (p. 320). A major conceptual breakthrough acknowledged the ultimate test of outcomes to be behavioral criteria that reflect clients' change in functioning in their extratreatment life environment.

In their epilogue, Luborsky and Strupp focused on continuing problems for researchers, but concluded with a list of "growing edges" of progress.

Among the sources of progress, the contribution of audio/visual technology and computers was clear—especially to aid in shedding light on what actually transpires within therapy settings. The last and perhaps most important of these growing edges was the "conceptual analyses of the 'domains' of psychotherapy," with a call for continued efforts to provide an organizing structure to make sense of the "complex territory to be covered" and to guide future work (1962, p. 328).

RESEARCH ON PSYCHOTHERAPY OUTCOMES TO THE MID-1960S

Status of the Outcome Evidence

"Chaos prevails" was Kenneth Colby's verdict on the status of psycho-therapy research in his 1964 *Annual Review* chapter (p. 347)—nearly two decades into the scientific era. Ed Bordin similarly lamented the dilemma of the clinician who wished to base psychotherapy practice on scientific evidence, writing in 1966, "The present state of our knowledge is such that strong doubts can be expressed about virtually all psycho-logical practices . . . none of them rest upon a firmly verified foundation of knowledge" (p. 119).

Hans Eysenck's additional reviews of the outcome literature included an edited book in 1966, reprinting his third review of the evidence for the effects of psychotherapy (or lack thereof) and numerous "discussion" responses to it. With the single exception of methods based on learning theory, little had changed from Eysenck's earlier conclusions. Discussions included polemics of an earlier era, asserting, "The evaluation of the effects of psychotherapy is not a task we can handle with existing tools" (Hyman & Berger, 1966, p. 86). Such assertions were countered by others who pointed out that continued promulgation of specific treatment approaches in the absence of evidence constituted a "kind of cult" (Davidson, 1966, p. 75)—charges not unlike those leveled by Professor Hoche more than 55 years earlier.

Radical Times for Practice and Research

Emphasis on alternative models paralleled the indictments of continued practice in the absence of evidence for effectiveness. The 1960s were radical times of global protests, activism, and countercultural movements in society. Psychotherapy practice and research showed equally bold challenges to established traditions. As in earlier eras, alternatives often took on "school" characteristics, where many clinicians and investigators demonstrated a cult-like zeal, with premature conclusions that they had "found the answer."

Held in 1966 at the University of Chicago, the third conference on *Research in Psychotherapy* (Shlien, 1968b) mirrored the radical times. John Shlien's (1968a) editorial "Introduction and Overview" was the closest approximation to a general summary of the proceedings or epilogue. Discussions were "too sizable" to publish. Related symposia and conferences of the early 1960s were reportedly so numerous that all concerned had "developed a certain weariness, even a wry derision toward such meetings" (p. vii).

The fascination of the counterculture with psychedelic drugs, mescaline and lysergic acid diethylamide (LSD), found applications as both a model for psychotherapy and as an enhancement to treatment. In addition, a flood of case studies and controlled investigations reported a variety of procedures under the general rubric of "behavioral therapies." Because the latter procedures were based on the clinical extension of laboratory-derived principles, even when reports were from adherents of one or another of the behavioral "schools," they brought with them the tradition of operational definitions and assessment of effects that was a departure from previous customs (see Ullmann & Krasner, 1965).

"Candidly questioning" both the products of the field and the worth of another conference, the NIMH provided grant rosters to identify the most active research areas. They were: (a) behavioral therapies, (b) therapist-client interactions, and (c) "psychopharmacology"—"a euphemism for . . . LSD [therapy]." These topics and the "days of grass-roots enthusiasm and libertarian challenges to vested authority" resulted in "a rather robust gathering of confident, sometimes testy researchers . . . [who] not only march to the beat of many separate drummers, but all marched to the call of an uncertain trumpet" (Shlien, 1968a, p. vii).

Shlien (1968a) wrapped up the conference in the following way: "We are poised on the edge of better understanding and better combinations of what constitutes science for our field. Description is essential, but it is not enough. The . . . more rudimentary scientific question, 'What is the evidence?' . . . [requires] existence of a phenomenon of change, thus outcome studies. With more consideration of process, the field moves to a more mature scientific question, 'What are the mechanisms?' . . . The activity of psychotherapy remains not science at all, so far as these works go, but a practical art. . . . Our research still circles around those meanings and struggles to encompass them in a scientific framework" (p. xi).

The Methodological Renaissance

Concurrent "challenges to vested authority" by "testy researchers" also resulted in a resurgent focus on methodology in the 1960s. Methodologists hoped to make the activity of psychotherapy not only an art but also an applied science. Classic methodological papers from the early scientific era were reprinted with commentaries that related research findings to clinical practice (e.g., Goldstein & Dean, 1966; Stollack, Guerney,

& Rothberg, 1966). Books by Len Krasner and Len Ullmann (1965) and by Arnie Goldstein, Ken Heller, and Lee Sechrest (1966) placed therapy studies squarely in the mainstream of research on behavior influence. Designs and controls for evaluation of outcomes were not only elaborated but also demonstrated in application (e.g., Campbell & Stanley, 1966; Frank, 1966; Goldstein et al., 1966; Paul, 1966, 1967a).

The Chapel Hill conference clarified many things, particularly the "criterion problem" for outcome assessment. The clarion call of those proceedings for continued "conceptual analyses of the 'domains' of psychotherapy" to provide a structure for guiding future work was explicitly addressed by Don Kiesler (1966) and by the present writer (Paul, 1967b, 1969). At different times, Kiesler and I were exposed to the same faculty at the University of Illinois at Urbana-Champaign (see Paul, 2001, p. 306), likely contributing to a certain similarity in our approach to problem solving in this area. However, we independently added to the excellent conceptual analyses of the domains and classes of variables resulting from the Chapel Hill conference by Barbara Betz (1962), Jerome Frank (1962), Daniel Levinson (1962), and related discussants.

Under the rubric of *The Uniformity Assumption Myths*, (first labeled by Colby, 1964), Kiesler (1966) elaborated how nearly all of the relevant variables in previous research had been too heterogeneous to allow meaningful conclusions. The "patient uniformity assumption" refers to the belief that "patients at the start of treatment are more alike than they are different" (p. 110). To the contrary, he noted, they "are actually much more different than they are alike" (p. 111)—within diagnostic categories as well as on just about any measure one could devise (demographic, ability, personality, etc.). The "therapist uniformity assumption" refers to the belief that "therapists are more alike than different and that whatever they do with their patients may be called 'psychotherapy'" (p. 112). In contrast, the advent of tape recordings showed "that differences in technique and personality exist, even within schools, and that disagreement prevails" (p. 112). Therapists in previous studies, he pointed out, also differed widely on many dimensions shown to influence treatment outcomes for clientele (e.g., experience, attitudes, personality variables).

Kiesler (1966) further refuted other myths ("spontaneous remission" and "the adequacy of prevailing research paradigms") and clarified confusions ("process-outcome distinction," "lack of utility of diagnostic classifications," "unrealistic expectations" for definitive studies or treatments). Finally, specifying previous research confounds, he delineated the minimal requirements for any psychotherapy research paradigm.

My own formulations, summarized later, attempted to build on the prior work of the Chapel Hill conference and others. For all of us, the "great idea" that psychotherapy outcome could be studied scientifically came together as part of the broader analyses of the entire psychotherapy research enterprise.

HOW PSYCHOTHERAPY OUTCOMES CAN BE STUDIED SCIENTIFICALLY

Central Presuppositions and Organizing Principles

Scientific research consists of a special way of answering questions so that the knowledge obtained and the means by which it is obtained are public, demonstrable, reproducible, and communicable. This requires relevant independent and dependent variables to be specified and quantified with acceptable reliability and validity for the questions asked. The questions also must be answerable ones. Much of the historical problem with therapy research came from confusion of the "context of discovery" and the "context of justification" in asking questions (see Reichenbach, 1938). Psychological science may not be positioned to discover the "real truth" of the experiences that take place between two or more persons (context of discovery), but verifying the degree to which the goals of such an interaction are achieved or not (context of justification) is logically no different for psychotherapy than for any change agency (see also Chapter 7).

As with any activity in which change in people or their behavior is the intended goal, the primary dependent variable should be whether the goal was achieved, assessed in the place where changes should occur. Logically and ethically, the goal of psychotherapy is to help with the problems for which help was asked. People come to a therapist because they have done something that disturbs somebody (themselves or others) to the extent that action results—that is, they enter treatment. The "something" they do occurs under a set of circumstances in the environment outside of the treatment setting. That is the place where assessment of success or failure should occur. The real question of effectiveness is whether the problems that brought the client to therapy change in the desired direction without producing new problems. Assessment should focus on the relevant circumstances in day-to-day living and working environments of clientele.

Apart from the greater number and complexity of variables, the principles and methods of outcome research are the same as for any other research design. The purpose is to discover phenomena (measurable behavioral events or changes), the variables that affect them, and the lawfulness of the effects—that is, cause-effect relations. Through manipulation or selection, experimental methods provide the way in which effects of measurable variables can be observed on other phenomena. "The experimental method is essentially reality testing refined and systematized . . . largely a matter of focusing on answerable questions and of introducing enough controls so that it is possible to trust and understand the answers" (Holt, 1965, p. 41).

Research design, thus, provides the vehicle for obtaining valid knowledge on therapy outcomes. Ben Underwood (1957, p. 86) told us there is really only one principle of design: Devise studies so that the effects of independent variables can be evaluated unambiguously. The questions in outcome research are multivariate ones. "But to draw a conclusion about the influence of any given variable, that variable must have been systematically manipulated alone somewhere in the design" (p. 35). As in other areas of investigation, the greatest difficulties in outcome research stem from "research errors"—discrepancies between what *is* concluded and what *can* be concluded as a consequence of the scientific operations.

Research errors pose threats to both the internal and external validity of psychotherapy studies (see Campbell & Stanley, 1966). Internal validity signifies the degree to which the design has ruled out plausible rival hypotheses. Underwood (1957) calls internal errors in which independent variables are confounded from different classes "lethal errors"(p. 90)—because there is no way that a meaningful conclusion can be reached from the procedures used. Without internal validity, outcome studies are not interpretable. External validity refers to the generalizability of findings from a given study to different populations of variables, which cannot be known without application of findings elsewhere. Although external errors are not likely to be "lethal" ones in outcome studies, overgeneralizations may be more harmful than in other research areas because the results should find their way into ongoing practice.

Relevant Domains and Classes of Variables

Essential ingredients for psychotherapy include at least one client and one therapist interacting over some finite period of time. Thus, clients, therapists, and time constitute the major domains, with specific classes of variables within each. These domains and classes, summarized in Table 6.1, should be taken into account for solid outcome research on psychotherapy, regardless of the theoretical predilections of either therapists or investigators. Adequate description, measurement, or control operations for relevant variables in each class within all three domains allow both internal and external validity to be more readily identified.

Clients (1). People enter treatment to obtain help in changing some aspects of their behavior that they, or someone else, find distressing (1a). Phenomena include the full range of problems that people may present for treatment, from erectile dysfunction to hallucinations. Components of distressing behavior may vary in number and nature and may change over time. *Change in variables within this class must always be included as dependent variables in outcome studies.* Clients also vary on the full range of individual attributes (1b) beyond their distressing behavior. Psychiatric classifications are in (1b) because most traditional "diagnostic" categories lack the specificity needed to detail treatment focus (see Chapter 5).

(1b) variables define role behavior and may interact with other classes to affect outcomes. Relevant variables here must be described and controlled; they may also be treated as independent or dependent

TABLE 6.1.   Major Domains and Classes of Variables in Psychotherapy
Research (adapted from Paul, 1967b)

	1. Clients
a. *Distressing behavior*	[excesses, deficits, or inappropriate timing in aspects of motoric, cognitive, & ideational, or physiological & emotional functioning]
b. *Relatively stable personal-social characteristics*	[social, personality, ability, & motivational variables, demographics, & Dx classifications]
c. *Physical-social life environment*	[family, friends, & work settings & events, external stimuli, economic & social resources]
	2. Therapists
a. *Therapeutic techniques*	[verbal & nonverbal psychosocial procedures defined by their nature, frequency, content, & timing; psychotropic drugs & discrete somatic interventions]
b. *Relatively stable personal-social characteristics*	[social, personality, ability, & motivational variables, demographics, & endorsed theories]
c. *Physical-social treatment environment*	[characteristics of the treatment setting, facility demographics & reputation, fee structure]
	3. Time
a. *Initial contact*	
b. *Pretreatment*	
c. *Initial treatment stage*	
d. *Main treatment stage*	
e. *Termination (pretermination stage)*	
f. *Posttreatment*	
g. *Follow-up*	

variables. The external environment class (1c) includes the intercurrent
life experiences impinging on the client. (1c) variables may set the time
or place for distressing behavior and they may provide assets or liabilities
for change. Phenomena within this class usually require description and
control to prevent confounding, but they can be treated as independent
variables or, occasionally, as dependent variables.

Therapists (2). Therapeutic techniques (2a) include both psychosocial
and biomedical procedures. Psychosocial procedures are what psychotherapists use in attempting to change a client's distressing behavior.
They may be discrete procedures or a series of actions and strategies.
They may vary in number and nature and may change over time

in relation to other variables. They may also differ in breadth, from application of a single principle, to an integrated package (e.g., systematic desensitization), to the conduct of classical psychoanalysis. For outcome research in psychotherapy, psychosocial techniques are nearly always the independent variable of greatest interest. Drugs and other biomedical interventions should be described, controlled, and examined for possible enhancing/worsening interactions with client outcomes.

Therapists also vary on the full range of individual attributes (2b). This class includes characteristics related to treatment, such as experience, prestige, "conditions" established, and "school" affiliation. Variables within this class are important because they may be confounded with specific techniques or interactive with other classes to moderate outcomes. Relevant variables here must be described and controlled; they may also be treated as independent or, occasionally, as dependent variables. The treatment environment class (2c) is important because of interactions that might affect outcomes. Description and control are the minimal operations, but they may be used as independent or dependent variables as well.

Time (3). Time is granted domain status because its importance for specifying the set of circumstances for both assessment and interpretation of relations among variables in other domains is exceeded only by its historical neglect. Temporal variables delineated in relation to client-therapist contact (3a–3f) provide important points for assessment, depending on the questions asked of the research design. The focus and nature of measurement operations are determined by both the moment in time, or "time window," at which information should be gathered and the length of time to which such information applies. As part of therapy conditions, time may vary in terms of the length of treatment contact (e.g., 3b–3f). Within treatment proper (3c, d, e), time and number of sessions may vary within and between different stages. Similarly, durations and activities may vary before initiation of treatment (3a–3b) and during follow-up periods (3e and 3f–3g). All of these temporal aspects must be explicit for precise conclusions to be drawn and accumulated.

The Appropriate Question(s)

Study of the above classes of variables clarifies where research errors have occurred and suggests the operations needed for obtaining answers to the *right* questions. Kiesler's (1966) "uniformity assumption myths" are everywhere evident. "Does psychotherapy work?" is a meaningless question because of the diversified procedures (1a) encompassed and the failure to take into account therapist characteristics (1b) that may contribute to efficacy. Even if psychotherapy were a homogeneous entity—which it clearly is not—this question fails to properly specify the "for what" in "does it work?" "Does it work for neuroses?" or "schizophrenia?" are the wrong questions. Most traditional "diagnoses" not only lack the needed specificity, but allow confounds among all classes in the client domain. The term "work" itself (i.e., the criteria for improvement) is similarly confused without specifying the "for what." Research based on such questions was doomed to lethal errors from the point of conception because of confusions and confounding of variables within Domains 1 and 2.

The "ultimate clinical question(s)" toward which all clinical-intervention research should be directed is the following: "*What* treatment, by *whom*, is most effective for *this* individual with *that* specific problem, under *which* set of circumstances, and *how* does it come about?" (Paul, 1969, p. 44). The "how does it come about?" part refers to the identification of the principles or mechanisms that best account for changes obtained by specified therapeutic techniques, which might not be included in a given outcome study.

The rest of the "ultimate question(s)" is appropriate for any and all studies of psychotherapy outcome (see Paul, 1967b, p. 111). Relating it to the variables listed in Table 6.1: *What* treatment (2a, therapeutic techniques), by *whom* (2b, therapists with relatively stable personal-social characteristics), is most effective (change in 1a, the client's distressing behavior outside the treatment setting, from 3b, pretreatment, to 3f and g, posttreatment and follow-up) for *this* individual (1b, clients with relatively stable personal-social characteristics) with *that* specific problem (1a, distressing behavior) under *which* set of circumstances (1c, physical-social life environment; 2c, physical-social treatment environment, and; 3a–g, time parameters)?

Of course, no single investigation of *any* degree of complexity is capable of answering the entire question. Posing it simply provides the framework for investigators to specify the aspect of the question for which a given study seeks answers and a basis for judging the study's adequacy in providing them. A solid empirical foundation for subsequent research would also be established if every psychotherapy outcome study not only specified the aspect of the question to be answered, but adequately described, measured, and controlled variables within each of the classes listed in Table 6.1 as well. More rapid accumulation of knowledge across reports could occur through identifying components of studies that constitute replications and quasi-replications of one another. Researchers could trust and build on the work of other investigators.

Research Design and Strategies

Having specified the domains and classes of variables requiring description, measurement, or control, the means of obtaining partial answers to the ultimate outcome question(s) becomes a problem of research design and strategies. The "level of product" obtained from a research design varies from those that can produce only correlational conclusions with strengthened hypotheses to those that can establish cause-effect relations for specific variables within and between classes—including analytic conclusions for complex variables. How can we best establish causal relations between specified treatment techniques and changes in classes of identified distressing behavior? How can we best determine the way client and therapist personal-social characteristics and respective physical-social environments moderate the latter relations?

Unconfounded cause-effect relations for therapeutic techniques with classes of distressing behavior can be found within a single study only in factorial or partial-factorial designs that cross multiple therapists and include randomized clients, with both "untreated" and "nonspecific-treatment" controls. "Untreated" controls reflect the state of affairs for clients in the absence of active treatment—conditions such as no-contact, no-treatment, wait-list, minimal-treatment, or custodial-treatment procedures. "Nonspecific treatment" controls serve to partial out the effect of common therapeutic features involved in "receiving treatment" within the particular class of intervention procedures and therapists—that is, features that are "nonspecific" (common) to any treatment technique in the class. Such control conditions might consist of placebo, attention-placebo, pseudo-treatment, component-treatment, or alternative-treatment procedures.

There is no single factorial design, but as many different and complex designs as required by aspects of the ultimate question in a given study. Factors, levels of factors, and different treatment and control conditions are added as needed by the nature of the cause-effect relations to be evaluated. Factorial designs are best to precisely determine the comparative effectiveness of techniques. They are the most efficient for obtaining answers to multiple aspects of the ultimate question as well. Tactical use of less costly designs is important for making clinical and scientific progress. If the relevant variables in all domains are carefully specified, measured, and controlled, lower-level between-group designs, within-subject group designs, intensive single-client experimental analyses, and laboratory simplifications all have an important role. *ALL* can contribute if they are strategically employed with regard to what is already known from accumulated and/or factorial studies—especially for polishing procedures and for testing the limits of generalizability over variations of clients, distressing behavior, therapists, and settings (see Paul, 1967b, 1969, 1986).

CONTRIBUTIONS OF OUTCOME RESEARCH THROUGH THE START OF THE 21ST CENTURY

Lots of activity took place during the nearly four decades since most clinical researchers agreed that psychotherapy outcome could be studied scientifically. My colleagues and I extended the ultimate clinical question(s) and conceptual scheme, from just psychotherapy research and practice, to include investigations of psychotropic drugs, comparative studies of inpatient psychosocial programs, and entire facilities and systems of service (see Hayes, 1991). I offered several studies as models of the kind and scope of programmatic research designs that can establish the comparative efficacy/effectiveness/efficiency of psychosocial treatments for problems ranging from debilitating performance anxiety through chronic psychoses—including evaluation of the principles underlying mechanisms of change (see Paul, 2001).

Few investigators beyond our own group incorporated all of the research recommendations presented earlier. Even so, Peter Nathan (2004) notes, by the early 1980s enough evidence accumulated for effective psychosocial techniques with several classes of distressing behavior that their lack of use in everyday practice became of concern. Dissemination becomes important when procedures can make a difference in clients' lives. Although practitioners were not eager to change activities on the basis of research findings, what was learned about the dissemination of innovations in the mental health field suggested that many techniques were maintained or adopted beyond their scientific evidence. These included a wide variety of psychotherapeutic methods—*some that were harmful*—most just lacking evaluation (see Lilienfeld, 2002).

The Meta-Analytic Revolution

Progress in accumulating evidence continued through the 1980s. "Randomized Clinical Trials" (RCTs) became fashionable terminology for describing outcome studies. Statistical "effect-size" indicants and secondary analysis of data from multiple studies (dubbed "meta-analysis" for "analysis of analyses") were popularized as a way to summarize the literature. Critics were occupied with concerns about "canned analyses" that were blindly applied without consideration of design nuances, hidden faults in meta-analyses, the lack of transportability of effect-size indexes, and the strength, integrity, and effectiveness of procedures both in the transfer of treatments to ongoing practice and across investigations (see Paul, 1986).

Donald Fiske (1983) supported the "meta-analytic revolution" as a way of forcing greater specification of therapeutic goals and procedures. He also thought it demonstrated the need for improved comparability and standardization among investigators—noting that, "Meta-analytic work has brought out . . . the pandemic problem of method specificity" in previous work (p. 65). My perspective in the mid-1980s (see Paul, 1986) was that meta-analytic techniques were "potentially useful tools to aid in ordering, integrating, and examining the results of clinical treatment studies . . . *to the extent* that a precise and accurate data base can be retrieved, and that reliable procedures are made explicit for selecting studies and contrasts, coding variables, calculating comparable effect sizes, and aggregating or disaggregating the information according to meaningful classification schemes" (pp. 72–73). I saw the ultimate question(s) and conceptual scheme described earlier to be especially relevant to the meta-analytic accumulation of knowledge across studies.

Most practitioners hailed early meta-analytic studies that extolled the "benefits of psychotherapy," especially when conclusions claimed to support equal effectiveness for all approaches (see Glass & Kliegl, 1983; Smith, Glass, & Miller, 1980). Such conclusions of psychotherapy equivalence are often called the "Dodo bird verdict," in reference to Lewis Carroll's *Alice in Wonderland*, "At last the Dodo said, '*Everybody* has won, and *all* must have prizes'" (see Hunsley & Di Giulio, 2002, for an evolutionary review of the "Dodo bird" and a critique of both earlier and later studies that clearly refutes the "verdict").

Critics were vehement about research errors that were hidden by the apparent objectivity of the statistical techniques in meta-analytic reviews. Conflicts were so great that a special section of the February 1983 *Journal of Consulting and Clinical Psychology (Vol. 51, No. 1)* was devoted to the approach.

Although among the *many* problems detailed by Jim Mintz (1983) and mentioned by David and Diana Shapiro (1983), Terry Wilson and Stanley Rachman (1983) were especially fervent about meta-analytic research errors perpetuating "the impression that statistical techniques can make acceptable poor-quality data that distort therapeutic process and outcome" (p. 54). Agreeing with Don Fiske in their positive evaluation of the approach, Michael Strube and Don Hartmann (1983) nevertheless warned, "The application of these techniques requires careful attention to a number of potential problems, including biased selection of studies, inadequacies in the studies comprising the database for the review, and violations of the assumptions of meta-analytic statistical procedures" (p. 14). I explored the application of Rosenthal's (1983) recommended indexes for determining the magnitude of effects as well as the design relevance of meta-analytic treatment of several specific studies. My conclusion regarding the approach as of the mid-1980s was, although a "promising one, it is as yet, a promise unfulfilled" (Paul, 1986, p. 73).

The Evidence-Based Practice Movement

The importance of outcome research received a major boost from the evidence-based practice (EBP) movement, which was launched in medicine in the early 1990s. That practices should be based on evidence rather than intuition seemed like a reasonable proposition to people everywhere. By 2005, John Norcross, Larry Beutler, and Ronald Levant wrote, "The EBP movement is truly a juggernaut, racing to achieve accountability in medicine, psychology, education, public policy, and even architecture. The zeitgeist is to require professionals to base their practice, to whatever extent possible, on evidence" (p. 6).

Following on concern for the lack of science-based treatments by practitioners in the 1980s, a major step for mental health EBPs came from the APA Society of Clinical Psychology (Div.12). Under President David Barlow's initiative, a series of task forces identified what came to be called "Empirically Supported Therapies" (ESTs). Phil Kendall (1998, p. 3) introduced a special section of the *Journal of Consulting and Clinical Psychology* by explaining, "The phrase (EST) was chosen because it emphasizes empirical research, requires positive outcomes from the research, and does not prematurely close the process of evaluation." The phrase was also meant to show that the cornerstone for EST endorsement was "the process of empirical evaluation, rather then the polemical talents or charismatic features of an individual promoter."

All the mental health disciplines developed guidelines to encourage EBPs. But, as I've noted before (Paul, 2000), "'evidence-based' and 'empirically supported' often are used as buzzwords with inconsistent meaning—a frequent occurrence when labels or catch phrases replace careful descriptions. . . . [Thus,] so-called 'evidence-based guidelines' [have been proliferated] that are little more than consensus codification of subjective judgments or of research that is severely restricted by political or guild interests" (p. 4).

Most agree that professional activities "should be based on the best available evidence from systematic research, artfully integrated in a careful case formulation, and applied with clinical expertise" (Paul, 2000, p. 4). Articulated criteria, however, as in lists of ESTs and specified guidelines, threaten "money, territory, and livelihoods" (Norcross et al., 2005, p. 8). Special issues or sections of all the major clinical journals have been devoted to controversial aspects of the EBP movement, including: the criteria used to identify and sanction clinical procedures, the generality of "manualized treatments," the utility of "efficacy vs. effectiveness" research, "common vs. specific" effects, "art vs. science," and "equivalency" and "allegiance" effects (see Nathan, 2004; Norcross et al., 2005; Paul, 2000).

Drew Westen, Catherine Novotny, and Heather Thompson-Brenner (2004a) published a review in the *Psychological Bulletin* entitled, "The Empirical Status of Empirically Supported Psychotherapies: Assumptions, Findings, and Reporting in Controlled Clinical Trials." A series of critical responses were elicited by that publication, including those by Stuart Ablon and Carl Marci (2004), Paul Crits-Christoph, Terry Wilson, and Steve Hollon (2005), Marvin Goldfried and Catherine Eubanks-Carter (2004), David Haaga (2004), and John Weisz, Robin Weersing, and Scott Henggeler (2005). These critical responses and replies by Westen et al. (2004b, 2005) serve as a veritable guidebook to the controversial aspects of the EBP movement and to the continuing problems of the meta-analytic approach in literature reviews.

Concerned that ESTs failed to adequately reflect the contribution of relationship factors, the APA Division of Psychotherapy (Div. 29) established a task force under President John Norcross (2002) to examine the effect of the therapeutic relationship on outcomes—resulting in

"Empirically Supported Relationships" (ESRs). Long troubled that, as competing approaches, ESTs *vs.* ESRs failed to capture the inherent interactive nature of the psychotherapeutic enterprise, Louis Castonguay and Larry Beutler (2006) initiated another task force (Div. 12) designed to *integrate* the work of the previous EST and ESR groups. Their work groups creatively focused on the identification of *principles of therapeutic change* (akin to the Empirically Supported Principles—ESPs—recommended by Rosen & Davison, 2003), including client and therapist characteristics, relational conditions, therapist behaviors, and classes of intervention likely to lead to change in psychotherapy. Rather than borrowing from drug studies, this approach appears to better fit the complexity of psychosocial treatments, the ultimate question(s), and related domains and classes of variables.

Status of the Outcome Evidence

In spite of the controversies, Shlien's (1968a) "rudimentary scientific question" regarding evidence of change receives a much different answer at the start of the 21st century than the therapeutic nihilism of the 1960s. Accumulated knowledge regarding the efficacy/effectiveness/ cost-efficiency of a wide range of therapy procedures now has clear empirical support. Diane Chambliss and Tom Ollendick, in their 2001 *Annual Review* chapter, not only summarized the controversies and evidence regarding empirically supported psychological interventions but also provided extensive listings of "condition-treatment" groups that had survived the analysis of several task forces in the United States, United Kingdom, and elsewhere.

David Barlow continued his leadership in the EBP movement, arguing in a powerful article in 2004 that the strength of data supporting psychological treatments warrants their regular inclusion in health care systems around the world. He wrote (p. 873): "[D]iverse but specifically designed psycho-logical treatments emerging from different theoretical persuasions have established proven efficacy compared to alternative treatments, including alternative psychological treatments. . . . [T]hese . . . are characterized by three principle features. First . . . they are specifically tailored to the patho-logical process that is causing the impairment and distress. . . . Second, most of the techniques incorporated into these treatments emerge from the laboratories of psychological science. . . . Third . . . [they] emanate from diverse . . . approaches . . . that are becoming less clearly demarcated as treatments . . . blend theoretically driven strategies based on emerging evidence of effectiveness." Barlow suggests the term "psychological treat-ments" to differentiate these efforts from generic psychotherapy because, in addition to the common strengths of all psychosocial approaches, they include "specific procedures targeted to the psychopathology at hand" (p. 873).

Not a fleeting phenomenon, a quarterly journal of abstracts originating in the United Kingdom, *Evidence-Based Mental Health*, has been online since 1998 (http://ebmh.bmjjournals.com/). Also from the United Kingdom, the Cochrane collaboration (see Gambrill, 1999) and the National Institute for Clinical Excellence (e.g., see NICE, 2003) have included mental health problems and treatments in systematic reviews for years. Books summarizing evidence-based psychotherapy are in their second editions (e.g., Nathan & Gorman, 2002; Roth & Fonagy, 2004) and the literature to 2005 is sufficiently compelling for Hogrefe & Huber Publishers to launch a new book series entitled, *Advances in Psychotherapy—Evidence-Based Practice* (http://www.hhpub.com/books/series/52.html). In summary, Kathleen Carroll closed her part of a briefing of the U.S. Congressional Mental Health Caucus in May 2005 with the following: "If the overriding question for lawmakers is 'Is there evidence that these approaches are effective and cost-effective, and that they work in the real world?' The answer is 'Yes' " (Kersting, 2005, p. 15).

Implications of the EBP Movement for Research and Practice

Norcross et al. (2005) started the epilogue of their volume on the controversies of the EBP movement as follows: "All mental health professions will need to respond to the clarion call for evidence-based practices by demonstrating the safety, efficacy, and efficiency of their work. . . . No amount of kvetching, howling at the moon, or passing resolutions will alter that reality" (p. 403). Reflecting the truth of these words, the Substance Abuse and Mental Health Services Administration (SAMHSA, 2005), with seven cabinet-level federal agencies, released *Transforming Mental Health Care in America: The Federal Action Agenda.* This online document "gives shape to the call for a fundamental transformation of mental health services in America by the President's New Freedom Commission" (see "Preface" in the *Action Plan*). Work with regulatory and funding agencies will "identify evidence-based and promising practices that warrant further research, those ready for field implementation, and those that can and should be funded at the State and local levels." Science, services, and funding will serve as "three legs to the stool" to "establish guidance for practical application of research findings" (see "Principle D" in the *Action Plan*).

Although outcome research per se is important to the entire movement, complementary goals for future research and practice include (a) seeking answers to Shlien's (1968a) "more mature scientific question" regarding the mechanisms underlying effective techniques and (b) bringing evidence-based procedures into the day-to-day work of practicing clinicians. Jerry Davison and Arnie Lazarus (1995) have long advocated interactions between controlled nomothetic inquiries and idiopathic formulations, with applications, as the best way to contribute to both of the latter goals (see also Chapter 7). Don Peterson (2004) articulated similar notions and Dan Fishman's (2005) online journal is intended to assist both goals as well.

The "efficacy versus effectiveness research" distinction is important to the discovery of mechanisms underlying proven techniques and to the goal of dissemination to practice settings. Distinctions between *efficacy*, emphasizing internal validity in controlled "laboratory" settings, and *effectiveness*, emphasizing external validity in "real-world" situations, were popularized by medical research funding agencies (see Raskin & Maklan, 1991). Such distinctions are important for evaluating outcomes in physical medicine, and for some limited psychosocial interventions. Unfortunately, when the "efficacy/effectiveness" terminology was adapted to psychotherapy research, unnecessary attributes of some studies became attached as surplus meanings to the words themselves. "Efficacy" came to imply "unrepresentative but tight," whereas "effectiveness" implied "representative, but untrained and sloppy" (see Nathan, 2004).

In fact, the "efficacy versus effectiveness" distinction need not apply to studies of psychosocial procedures that are explicitly designed and executed in the "real world" to maximize both internal and external validity as well as to elucidate the basic principles underlying change (see Paul, 2000, 2001). Tom Borkovec and Louis Castonguay (1998) are among the strongest advocates of this approach, arguing for "programmatic therapy outcome investigations deliberately designed to acquire basic knowledge" and "therapy research in naturalistic settings whose primary goal is also to answer basic questions" (p. 136). They promote "Practice Research Networks" to organize practitioners and researchers for these purposes.

Michael Lambert (2005) and his colleagues have shown the utility of research in the "real-world" clinic in a different way—by providing feedback to therapists about ongoing cases in real time for "quality management in routine clinical practice." Client-focused research systems to monitor and provide feedback about clients' progress in psychotherapy were developed to enhance outcome for those who are predicted to be treatment failures. In a typical study (e.g., Whipple et al., 2003), feedback to therapists regarding whether their clients were experiencing an average or below-average "therapeutic relationship, motivation to change, or social support network" (determined from brief standardized scales regularly completed by clients) resulted in clients staying in therapy longer and reporting superior outcomes (p. 59).

Such instances in which careful therapy research actually takes place in "real-life" clinical settings, with "real-life" therapists and clients, automatically fulfills the first of Peter Nathan's (2004) two possibilities for increasing the likelihood of evidence-based procedures being applied in practice: that is, when practitioners can "see themselves in the research psychotherapists and their patients in the research patients and the research environment in the real-world settings. . . ." His second possibility is "when more psychotherapists in training receive training" in EBPs (p. 957).

The empirically based set of principles emerging from Castonguay and Beutler (2006) and the "take-home consensus" from Norcross et al. (2005, p. 404) seem to capture the complexity of the enterprise better than anything to date. Accordingly, the treatment method, the therapist, the relationship, the client, and principles of change are vital contributors and all must be studied. Comprehensive evidence-based practices will consider *all* of these determinants and their optimal combinations. "Common and specific effects" and "art and science" appear properly complementary, not as "either/or" dichotomies. The ultimate clinical question(s) is as meaningful now as a basis for study design and the accumulation of knowledge as it was initially. I recommend its explicit use for guidance.

What about the evidence-based practitioner? Day-to-day clinical EBPs differ from research in important ways. Donald Peterson (2004) wrote about the division of research and practice: "The two are related. The two are interdependent. But science and practice are not the same, and no monistic ideology can make them the same. . . . Monism fails because it denies fundamental, irreconcilable differences in the aims and modes of inquiry of science and practice" (pp. 207–208). Researchers seek quandaries in theory and practice—the lifeblood of successful research design. As a researcher, I am ever alert for discrepancies in theory and practice. Our clients, instead, require us to synthesize what is known from the science of the field for their immediate benefit, with or without controls to establish precise cause-effect relations.

As a clinician in the consulting room or supervising others, I agree with Davison and Lazarus (1995) that "technical eclecticism" is the best guiding heuristic. Proven procedures should be incorporated and applied within an overall, internally consistent theoretical formulation, no matter where the techniques or procedures originated. My own working assumptions as a self-defined evidence-based practitioner are:

1. Procedures should be based on the best available evidence from systematic research. [There *ARE* known specific effects.]
2. Evidence should be artfully integrated in a careful case formulation to guide treatment as an ongoing hypothesis-testing activity. [Artful integration *IS* teachable.]
3. Clients should be fully informed partners in the treatment enterprise as quickly as their capabilities allow. [Most *CAN* come to understand probabilistic, personalized explanations.]
4. Procedures should be implemented with clinical expertise to maximize changes in accordance with clients' desires and values. [There *ARE* teachable common factors.]
5. When problems fail to respond to proven techniques or lack specific outcome data, extrapolate from the best science-based principles for related phenomena. [There *ARE* established principles.]

What to do if you are now asked, "Does psychotherapy work?" Have no hesitation in answering on the basis of evidential support for the ultimate clinical question(s)—"It depends."

KEY TERMS

Efficacy-effectiveness research: A distinction popularized by medical research funding agencies, in which *efficacy* research emphasized internal validity in controlled "laboratory" settings (but was often unrepresentative of practice settings), and *effectiveness* research emphasized external validity in "real-world" situations (but often failed to properly train personnel or guard against confounds from irrelevant factors). The distinction need not apply to studies of psychosocial procedures that are explicitly designed and executed in the "real world" to maximize both internal and external validity as well as to elucidate the basic principles underlying change.

Empirically Supported Therapies (ESTs): According to Phillip C. Kendall, a term chosen to describe the treatment techniques for specified conditions that are endorsed by American Psychological Association task forces applying specific requirements for research support; it emphasizes empirical research, requires positive outcomes from the research, does not prematurely close the process of evaluation, and indicates that the process of empirical evaluation, rather then the polemical talents or charismatic features of an individual promoter, underlies endorsement.

Meta-analysis: Literally, "analysis of analyses," referring to the calculation of "effect-size" indicants and secondary statistical analysis of the original data from multiple studies as a way of summarizing the literature in an area. A useful set of techniques that are especially prone to hidden errors.

Psychotherapy: An activity that involves six essential characteristics: (a) An interpersonal relationship of some duration between two or more people; (b) one of the participants (the therapist) has had special experience and/or training in the handling of human problems and relationships; (c) one or more of the participants (clients) have entered the relationship because of their own or others' dissatisfaction with their emotional, behavioral, and/or interpersonal adjustment; (d) the methods used are psychological in nature; (e) the procedures of the therapist are based upon some formal theory regarding mental disorders in general and the specific problems of the client in particular; and (e) the aim of the process is the amelioration of the difficulties that cause the client to seek the help of the therapist.

Ultimate clinical question(s): Gordon L. Paul's question(s) proposed to guide the conduct and accumulation of all research on clinical interventions: "*What* treatment, by *whom*, is most effective for *this* individual with *that* specific problem, under *which* set of circumstances, and *how* does it come about?"

Uniformity assumption myths: Donald J. Kiesler's summary term for incorrect assumptions in psychotherapy research, in the absence of measurement or documentation, that clients (overall and within diagnostic classes), therapists (overall and within endorsed "schools"), and psychotherapy procedures (across therapists and within endorsed "schools") were more alike than different.

SUGGESTED READINGS

Castonguay, L. G., & Beutler, L. E. (Eds.). (2006). *Principles of effective change that work.* New York: Oxford University Press.

Franks, C. M. (Ed.). (1969). *Behavior therapy: Appraisal and status.* New York: McGraw-Hill.

Hayes, S. C., Follette, V. M., Risley, T., Dawes, R. D., & Grady, K. (Eds.). (1995). *Scientific standards of psychological practice: Issues and recommendations.* Reno, NV: Context Press.

O'Donohue, W. T., Henderson, D. A., Hayes, S. C., Fisher, J. E., & Hayes, L. J. (Eds.). (2001). *History of the behavioral therapies: Founder's personal histories.* Reno, NV: Context Press.

Ullmann, L. P., & Krasner, L. (Eds.). (1965). *Case studies in behavior modification.* New York: Holt, Rinehart, & Winston.

REFERENCES

Ablon, J. S., & Marci, C. (2004). Psychotherapy process: The missing link. Comment on Westen, Novotny, and Thompson-Brenner (2004). *Psychological Bulletin, 130,* 664–668.

Barlow, D. H. (2004). Psychological treatments. *American Psychologist, 59,* 869–878.

Betz, B. J. (1962). Experiences in research in psychotherapy with schizophrenic patients. In H. H. Strupp, & L. Luborsky (Eds.), *Research in psychotherapy, Vol. II.* (pp. 41–60). Washington, DC: American Psychological Association.

Bordin, E. S. (1966). Curiosity, compassion, and doubt: The dilemma of the psychologist. *American Psychologist, 21,* 116–121.

Borkovec, T. D., & Castonguay, L. G. (1998). What is the scientific meaning of "empirically supported therapy?" *Journal of Consulting and Clinical Psychology, 66,* 136–142.

Brill, A. A. (1909). Selected papers on hysteria and other psychoneuroses: Sigmund Freud. *Nervous and Mental Disease Monograph Series, No. 4.*

Campbell, D. T., & Stanley, J. C. (1966). *Experimental and quasi-experimental designs for research.* Chicago: Rand McNally.

Castonguay, L. G., & Beutler, L. E. (2006). Common and unique principles of therapeutic change: What do we know and what do we need to know? In L. G. Castonguay, & L. E. Beutler (Eds.), *Principles of therapeutic change that work* (pp. 353–358). New York: Oxford University Press.

Chambless, D. L., & Ollendick, T. H. (2001). Empirically supported psychological interventions: Controversies and evidence. *Annual Review of Psychology, 52,* 685–716.

Colby, K. M. (1964). Psychotherapeutic processes. *Annual Review of Psychology, 15,* 347–370.

Crits-Christoph, P., Wilson, G. T., & Hollon, S. D. (2005). Empirically supported psychotherapies: Comment on Westen, Novotny, and Thompson-Brenner (2004). *Psychological Bulletin, 131,* 412–417.

Davidson, H. A. (1966). Discussion. In H. J. Eysenck (Ed.), *The effects of psychotherapy* (pp. 73–75). New York: International Science Press.

Davison, G. C., & Lazarus, A. A. (1995). The dialectics of science and practice. In S. C. Hayes, V. M. Follette, T. Risley, R. D. Dawes, & K. Grady (Eds.), *Scientific standards of psychological practice: Issues and recommendations* (pp. 95–120). Reno, NV: Context Press.

Edwards, A. L., & Cronbach, L. J. (1952). Experimental design for research in psychotherapy. *Journal of Clinical Psychology, 8,* 51–59.

Eysenck, H. J. (1952). The effects of psychotherapy: An evaluation. *Journal of Consulting Psychology, 16,* 319–324.

Eysenck, H. J. (Ed.). (1966). *The effects of psychotherapy.* New York: International Science Press.

Fishman, D. B. (2005). Editor's introduction to PCSP—From single case to database: A new method for enhancing psychotherapy practice. *Pragmatic Case Studies in Psychotherapy [Online]*, http://hdl.rutgers.edu/1782.1/pcsp1.1.47, *1*(1), Article 2.

Fiske, D. W. (1983). The meta-analytic revolution in outcome research. *Journal of Consulting and Clinical Psychology, 51,* 65–70.

Frank, J. D. (1962). The role of cognitions in illness and healing. In H. H. Strupp & L. Luborsky (Eds.), *Research in psychotherapy, Vol. II.* (pp. 1–12). Washington, DC: American Psychological Association.

Frank, J. D. (1966). Treatment of the focal symptom: An adaptational approach. *American Journal of Psychotherapy, 20,* 564–575.

Gambrill, E. (1999). Evidence-based clinical practice, evidence-based medicine, and the Cochrane collaboration. *Journal of Behavior Therapy and Experimental Psychiatry, 30,* 1–14 (plus Erratum, 30, 153–154).

Glass, G. V., & Kliegl, R. M. (1983). An apology for research integration in the study of psychotherapy. *Journal of Consulting and Clinical Psychology, 51,* 28–41.

Glover, E., Fenichel, O., Strachey, J., Bergler, E., Nunberg, N., & Bibring, E. (1937). Symposium on the theory of the therapeutic results of psychoanalysis. *International Journal of Psychoanalysis, 18,* 125–189.

Goldfried, M. R., & Eubanks-Carter, C. (2004). On the need for a new psychotherapy research paradigm: Comment on Westen, Novotny, and Thompson-Brenner (2004). *Psychological Bulletin, 130,* 669–673.

Goldstein, A. A., & Dean, S. J. (Eds.). (1966). *The investigation of psychotherapy: Commentaries and readings.* New York: Wiley.

Goldstein, A. A., Heller, K., & Sechrest, L. B. (1966). *Psychotherapy and the psychology of behavior change.* New York: Wiley.

Haaga, D. A. F. (2004). A healthy dose of criticism for randomized trials: Comment on Westen, Novotny, and Thompson-Brenner (2004). *Psychological Bulletin, 130,* 674–676.

Hayes, S. C. (1991). Pursuing the ultimate clinical question: An interview with Gordon L. Paul. *The Scientist-Practitioner, 1*(3), 6–16.

Holt, R. R. (1965). Experimental methods in clinical psychology. In B. B. Wolman (Ed.), *Handbook of clinical psychology* (pp. 40–77). New York: McGraw-Hill.

Hunsley, J., & Di Giulio, G. (2002). Dodo bird, phoenix, or urban legend? *The Scientific Review of Mental Health, 1*(1), 11–27.

Hunt, J. McV. (1952). Toward an integrated program of research on psychotherapy. *Journal of Consulting Psychology, 16,* 237–246.

Hyman, R., & Berger, L. (1966). Discussion. In H. J. Eysenck (Ed.), *The effects of psychotherapy* (pp. 81–86). New York: International Science Press.

Jones, E. (1910). The psycho-analytic method of treatment. *Journal of Nervous and Mental Disease, 37,* 285–295.

Kendall, P. C. (1998). Empirically supported psychological therapies. *Journal of Consulting and Clinical Psychology, 66*(1), 3–6.

Kersting, K. (2005). Psychologists publicize behavioral treatments' effectiveness. *Monitor, 36*(7), 15.

Kiesler, D. J. (1966). Some myths of psychotherapy research and the search for a paradigm. *Psychological Bulletin, 65,* 110–136.

Krasner, L. (1962). The therapist as a social reinforcement machine. In H. H. Strupp & L. Luborsky (Eds.), *Research in psychotherapy, Vol. II.* (pp. 61–94). Washington, DC: American Psychological Association.

Krasner, L., & Ullmann, L. P. (1965). *Research in behavior modification: New developments and implications.* New York: Holt, Rinehart, & Winston.

Lambert, M. J. (2005). Emerging methods for providing clinicians with timely feedback on treatment effectiveness: An introduction. *Journal of Clinical Psychology/In Session, 61*(2), 141–144.

Levinson, D. J. (1962). The psychotherapist's contribution to the patient's treatment career. In H. H. Strupp & L. Luborsky (Eds.), *Research in psychotherapy, Vol. II.* (pp. 13–24). Washington, DC: American Psychological Association.

Lilienfeld, S. O. (2002). Our Raison d'Etre. *The Scientific Review of Mental Health, 1*(1), 1–10.

Luborsky, L., & Strupp, H. H. (1962). Research problems in psychotherapy: A three-year follow-up. In H. H. Strupp & L. Luborsky (Eds.), *Research in psychotherapy, Vol. II.* (pp. 308–329). Washington, DC: American Psychological Association.

Meehl, P. E. (1955). Psychotherapy. *Annual Review of Psychology, 6,* 357–378.

Miller, J. G. (1951). Objective methods of evaluating process and outcome in psychotherapy. *American Journal of Psychiatry, 108,* 258–263.

Mintz, J. (1983). Integrating research evidence: A commentary on meta-analysis. *Journal of Consulting and Clinical Psychology, 51,* 71–75.

Nathan, P. E. (2004). Epilogue: The clinical utility of therapy research. Bridging the gap between the present and the future. In A. R. Roberts & K. Yeager (Eds.), *Evidence-based practice manual* (pp. 949–960). New York: Oxford University Press.

Nathan, P. E., & Gorman, J. M. (Eds.). (2002). *A guide to treatments that work* (2nd ed.). New York: Oxford University Press.

National Institute for Clinical Excellence (NICE) (2003). *Schizophrenia: Full national clinical guidelines on core interventions in primary and secondary care.* London: Gaskell.

Norcross, J. C. (Ed.). (2002). *Psychotherapy relationships that work: Therapists contributions and responsiveness to patients.* New York: Oxford University Press.

Norcross, J. C., Beutler, L. E., & Levant, R. F. (2005). Prologue & Epilogue. In J. C. Norcross, L. E. Beutler, & R. F. Levant (Eds.), *Evidence-based practices in mental health: Debate and dialogue on the fundamental questions* (pp. 3–12; 403–06). Washington, DC: American Psychological Association.

Parloff, M. B., & Rubinstein, E. A. (1959). Research problems in psychotherapy. In E. A. Rubinstein & M. B. Parloff (Eds.), *Research in psychotherapy, Vol. I.* (pp. 276–293). Washington, DC: American Psychological Association.

Patrick, H. T., & Bassoe, P. (1910). *Nervous and mental diseases.* Chicago: Year Book Publishers.

Paul, G. L. (1966). *Insight vs. desensitization in psychotherapy: An experiment in anxiety reduction.* Stanford, CA: Stanford University Press.

Paul, G. L. (1967a). Insight vs. desensitization in psychotherapy two years after termination. *Journal of Consulting Psychology, 31,* 333–348.

Paul, G. L. (1967b). Strategy of outcome research in psychotherapy. *Journal of Consulting Psychology, 31,* 109–118.

Paul, G. L. (1969). Behavior modification research: Design and tactics. In C. M. Franks (Ed.), *Behavior therapy: Appraisal and status* (pp. 29–62). New York: McGraw-Hill.

Paul, G. L. (1986). Can pregnancy be a placebo effect? Terminology, designs, and conclusions in the study of psychological and pharmacological treatments of behavior disorders. *Journal of Behavior Therapy and Experimental Psychiatry, 17,* 61–81.

Paul, G. L. (2000). Evidence-based practices in inpatient and residential facilities. *The Clinical Psychologist, 53*(3), 3–11.

Paul, G. L. (2001). The active unconscious, symptom substitution, & other things that went 'bump' in the night. In W. T. O'Donohue, D. A. Henderson, S. C. Hayes, J. E. Fisher, & L. J. Hayes (Eds.), *History of the behavioral therapies: Founder's personal histories* (pp. 295–336). Reno, NV: Context Press.

Peterson, D. R. (2004). Science, scientism, and professional responsibility. *Clinical Psychology: Science and Practice, 11,* 196–210.

Raimy, V. C. (Ed.). (1950). *Training in clinical psychology.* Englewood Cliffs, NJ: Prentice Hall.

Raskin, I. E., & Maklan, C.W. (1991). Medical treatment effectiveness research: A view from inside the Agency for Health Care Policy and Research. *Evaluation & The Health Professions, 14,* 161–186.

Reichenbach, H. (1938). *Experience and prediction.* Chicago: University of Chicago Press.

Rosen, G. M., & Davison, G. C. (2003). Psychology should list empirically supported principles of change (ESPs) and not credential trademarked therapies or other treatment packages. *Behavior Modification, 27,* 300–312.

Rosenthal, R. (1983). Assessing the statistical and social importance of the effects of psychotherapy. *Journal of Consulting and Clinical Psychology, 51,* 4–13.

Roth, A., & Fonagy, P. (Eds.). (2004). *What works for whom? A critical review of psychotherapy research* (2nd ed.). New York: Guilford.

Rubinstein, E. A., & Parloff, M. B. (Eds.). (1959). *Research in psychotherapy, Vol. I.* Washington, DC: American Psychological Association.

Substance Abuse and Mental Health Administration (SAMHSA). (2005). *Transforming mental health care in America: The federal action agenda.* Retrieved July 26, 2005, from http://www.samhsa.gov/Federalactionagenda/NFC_TOC.aspx.

Shapiro, D. A., & Shapiro, D. (1983). Comparative therapy outcome research: Methodological implications of meta-analysis. *Journal of Consulting and Clinical Psychology, 51,* 42–53.

Shlien, J. M. (1968a). Introduction and overview. In J. M. Shlien (Ed.), *Research in psychotherapy, Vol. III* (pp. vii–xii). Washington, DC: American Psychological Association.

Shlien, J. M. (Ed.). (1968b). *Research in psychotherapy, Vol. III.* Washington, DC: American Psychological Association.

Smith, M. L., Glass, G. V., & Miller, T. I. (1980). *The benefits of psychotherapy.* Baltimore, MD: Johns Hopkins University Press.

Stollack, G. E., Guerney, B. C., & Rothberg, M. (Eds.). (1966). *Psychotherapy research.* Chicago: Rand McNally.

Strube, M. J., & Hartmann, D. P. (1983). Meta-analysis: Techniques, applications, and functions. *Journal of Consulting and Clinical Psychology, 51,* 14–27.

Strupp, H. H., & Luborsky, L. (Eds.). (1962). *Research in psychotherapy, Vol. II.* Washington, DC: American Psychological Association.

Ullmann, L. P., & Krasner, L. (Eds.). (1965). *Case studies in behavior modification.* New York: Holt.

Underwood, B. J. (1957). *Psychological research.* New York: Appleton-Century-Crofts.

Watson, R. I. (1952). Research design and methodology in evaluating the results of psychotherapy. *Journal of Clinical Psychology, 8,* 29–33.

Weisz, J. R., Weersing, V. R, & Henggeler, S. W. (2005). Jousting with straw men: Comment on Westen, Novotny, and Thompson-Brenner (2004). *Psychological Bulletin, 131,* 418–426.

Westen, D., Novotny, C. M., & Thompson-Brenner, H. (2004a). The empirical status of Empirically Supported Psychotherapies: Assumptions, findings, and reporting in controlled clinical trials. *Psychological Bulletin, 130,* 631–663.

Westen, D., Novotny, C. M., & Thompson-Brenner, H. (2004b). The next generation of psychotherapy research: Reply to Ablon and Marci (2004), Goldfried and Eubanks-Carter (2004), and Haaga (2004). *Psychological Bulletin, 130,* 677–683.

Westen, D., Novotny, C. M., & Thompson-Brenner, H. (2005). EBP ≠ EST: Reply to Crits-Christoph et al. (2005) and Weisz et al. (2005). *Psychological Bulletin, 131,* 427–433.

Whipple, J. L., Lambert, M. J., Vermeersch, D. A., Smart, D. W., Nielsen, S. L., & Hawkins, E. J. (2003). Improving the effects of psychotherapy: The use of early identification of treatment and problem-solving strategies in routine practice. *Journal of Counseling Psychology, 50,* 59–68.

Wilson, G. T., & Rachman, S. J. (1983). Meta-analysis and the evaluation of psychotherapy outcome: Limitations and liabilities. *Journal of Consulting and Clinical Psychology, 51,* 54–64.

Winder, C. L. (1957). Psychotherapy. *Annual Review of Psychology, 8,* 309–330.

Zubin, J. (1953). Evaluation of therapeutic outcome in mental disorders. *Journal of Nervous and Mental Disease, 117,* 95–111.

Zubin, J. (1964). Technical issues: Discussion. In P. H. Hoch & J. Zubin (Eds.), *The evaluation of psychiatric treatment* (pp. 122–128). New York: Grune & Stratton.

7

Clinical Case Studies Are Important in the Science and Practice of Psychotherapy

GERALD C. DAVISON AND ARNOLD A. LAZARUS

It is our view that innovations by clinicians are the lifeblood of advances in the development of new therapeutic interventions. Major clinical discoveries are usually made by clinicians and then investigated by more experimentally minded workers whose subsequent findings may persuade others that a technique is worth a closer look. Whether or not attention is paid to a discovery—especially if that discovery borders on the unbelievable—can depend in large measure on a prior *pro hominem* judgment about the integrity and standing of the person making the claims.

Many regard the laboratory and the clinic as opposite ends of a continuum. Research is said to be precise, controlled, and uncontaminated. The ideas that flow from applied settings are often regarded as woolly, riddled with bias, purely anecdotal, and even useless. Our abiding belief is that the path between the laboratory and the clinic is a two-way street (Davison & Lazarus, 1994, 1995; Lazarus & Davison, 1971; Woolfolk & Lazarus, 1979). As just stated, we aver that most new methods have come from the work of creative clinicians.

Scientists and practicing clinicians can each offer unique contributions in their own right and can conceivably open hitherto new and unexpected clinical-experimental dimensions for research and practice. Certainly this is inherent to the scientist-professional model that, after all these years, remains a vigorous and widely accepted guide to education and training in clinical psychology (Belar & Perry, 1991). Ideas tested in the laboratory may be applied by the practitioner who, in turn, may discover important individual nuances that remain hidden from the laboratory scientist simply because the tight environment of the experimental testing ground makes it impossible for certain behaviors to occur or for certain observations to be made. Conversely, ideas formulated in the clinic, provided that they are amenable to disproof, can encourage scientists to subject the claims of efficacy to controlled tests. Although it is proper to guard against *ex cathedra* statements based on flimsy and subjective evidence, it is a serious mistake to discount the importance of clinical experience per se.

The constraints of controlled analogue research on what one can discover were suggested years ago by Wachtel (1973) in an analysis of the relative contributions of traits and situational factors in behavior. In arguing against the emphasis placed by Mischel (1968) on the overriding importance of situational variables in predicting behavior, Wachtel suggested that it was Mischel's focus on analogue laboratory research with normal children and adults that led him to conclude that traits were of lesser importance. Wachtel's position, with which we concur, was that enduring dispositions, for example, traits such as dependency and sensitivity to criticism (as well as many DSM categories), are of greater importance in clinical populations than in people whose everyday functioning is adaptive and satisfying.

There is nothing mysterious about the fact that repeated exposure to any given set of conditions makes the recipient aware of subtle cues and contingencies in that setting that elude the scrutiny of those less familiar with the situation. Clinical experience enables a therapist to recognize problems and identify trends that are usually beyond the perceptions of novices, regardless of their general expertise. It is at this level that new ideas can come to the practitioner and often constitute breakthroughs that could not be derived from animal analogues or tightly controlled investigations. It is when they try new things that perceptive clinicians can appreciate relationships that may go unnoticed by less resourceful and less observant workers. Conversely, controlled research is enriched and made more societally relevant when it addresses complex real-world problems that are usually brought to their attention by clinicians. Different kinds of data and differing levels of information are obtained in the laboratory and the clinic. As will be elaborated below, each is necessary, useful, and desirable (Lazarus & Davison, 1971).

Case studies have been used in many disciplines to advance both basic and applied knowledge. They have been widely employed in the study of many areas such as language acquisition, memory, cognitive development, and psychopathology (e.g., Pinker, 1994a, 1994b). Consider the work of Jean Piaget (Piaget & Inhelder, 1969), for example, who sat for hours with little children, listening to them talk out loud (as children do) as they tried to solve problems set before them. The rich idiographic descriptions he published on children's verbalized problem-solving activities laid the foundation for experimental research by other child development investigators. Other disciplines such as education, anthropology, psychiatry, business, and rehabilitation also have relied on case studies to advance knowledge (Yin, 1994).

The entire edifice of Freud's psychoanalytic theory was built on a few cases he saw in therapy. At the same time, much about Freudian theory exemplifies the potential shortcomings of generalizing from single cases. It took decades to expose Freud's penchant to distort what his patients really said, the facts that he omitted, and his failure to consider alternative explanations of their problems (e.g., Crews, 1998; Sulloway, 1991). As Loftus and Guyer (2002a) emphasized, the main hazard of the single case history is that it can mislead, "especially when only half the story is told" (p.24).

Many case studies rest on the perceptions and omissions of the reporter, and it is not uncommon to see how a strong "confirmation bias" can distort the findings (see also Chapters 1 and 2 for discussions of confirmation bias). Of course, as Greenwald and associates pointed out (Greenwald, Pratkanis, Leippe, & Baumgardner, 1986; Greenwald & Pratkanis, 1988), even the most rigorous of scientific inquiries are vulnerable to the desire of investigators to confirm hypotheses rather than test them dispassionately with a welcoming stance toward *dis*confirmation. In any event, some case studies have opened a window into human behavior and physiology that might otherwise have remained shut (see McNally, Cassiday, & Calamari, 1990; Moscovitch, Winocur, & Behrmann, 1997; Sacks, 1990).

In clinical psychology and related disciplines such as counseling and psychiatry, case studies come from practitioners and are based on uncontrolled observations (usually in the context of ongoing therapy) that are qualitative, anecdotal, unsystematic, and not replicable. Some would argue that it would be better from a scientific point of view not to cite cases from routine clinical practice at all. If clinical information from a client is to be presented to one's peers, it is imperative to minimize subjective, individualistic impressions. Strategies to achieve this end could include videotaping or audiotaping sessions and then having them appraised by independent assessors. Also, the services of an impartial researcher to assess the client before, during, and after the therapy and render an objective judgment of outcome would enhance the scientific value of the case presentation.

Although scientifically minded clinical researchers rightly aim for controlled conditions and objective measures, the naturalistic and uncontrolled characteristics of some traditional case studies can nevertheless kindle hypotheses about human behavior and encourage more systematic modes of inquiry. The importance of idiographic analyses of single cases should not be overlooked or dismissed, as they allow maximum flexibility to test new hypotheses. We have emphasized that innovations by clinicians are the lifeblood of advances in the development of new therapeutic interventions (Davison & Lazarus, 1994; Lazarus & Davison, 1971). When launching the journal *Clinical Case Studies* in 2002, Michel Hersen stressed that single case reports have led over the years to the greatest innovations in psychotherapy, and he listed Beck, Frankl, Freud, Lazarus,

Pavlov, Rogers, Skinner, and Wolpe as among the innovators who used the case method (see also Chapter 1 for a discussion of Skinner's methods).

It is imperative to understand what information can and cannot be derived from case studies. The most general and basic caveat is that single cases cannot be the purveyors of "proof." At best, they can be suggestive of a relevant connection, a likely pathway, a potentially important finding, or a positive trend. Two major pitfalls to avoid are confusing correlation with causation, and assuming that a sufficient degree of so-called "anecdotal evidence" is on a par with well-controlled confirmation and proof. (An apt expression is that the plural of "anecdote" is not data.) These two egregious errors bedevil much of our clinical lore.

WHAT CASE STUDIES CAN CONTRIBUTE

We believe there are six characteristics of case studies that earn them a firm place in psychological theory and research (cf. Davison & Lazarus, 1994, 1995; Lazarus & Davison, 1971). These features are listed below and then elaborated on.

1. A case study may cast doubt on a general theory.
2. A case study may provide a valuable heuristic to subsequent and better-controlled research.
3. A case study can provide the opportunity to apply principles and notions in entirely new ways.
4. A case study can, under certain circumstances, provide enough experimenter control over a phenomenon to furnish "scientifically acceptable" information.
5. A case study may permit the investigation, although poorly controlled, of rare but important phenomena.
6. A case study can put "meat" on "the theoretical skeleton."

A Case Study May Cast Doubt on a General Theory

The successful handling of a particular case may underscore an important exception to a theory. For example, a given theory may hold that a certain kind of problem is untreatable. If a therapist were able to make a favorable impact upon the putatively unchangeable problem, this would cast doubt on the tenets of the theoretical viewpoint under consideration. In philosophical terms, this is commonly referred to as existence proof, that is, a demonstration that a given phenomenon can exist and therefore a refutation of a generalization that such a phenomenon cannot exist. An example will make this clearer.

A pervasive theory that dominated the field of psychotherapy for many years was that, unless unconscious conflicts were accessed and fully resolved, treatment gains would be impermanent and, even worse, would lead to symptom substitution (the manifestation of symptoms of the underlying disorder in a different domain) and even deterioration. This psychoanalytic and psychodynamic theory held sway, and the burgeoning field of what is now called cognitive behavior therapy (CBT) struggled for about four decades (during the 1950s until the 1990s) to achieve respectability (see Goldfried & Davison, 1994; Davison & Lazarus, 1994). In this regard, findings from the laboratory and the clinic led to the eventual approbation of CBT procedures for a variety of human problems and cast doubt on the tenets of the aforementioned psychoanalytic framework. Patients who improved did not suffer from symptom substitution (Emmelkamp, 2004; Hollon & Beck, 2004).

In addition, clinicians and researchers alike conducted follow-ups to verify or disconfirm the dire consequences that would allegedly result unless deep-seated conflicts were resolved. For example, Davison and Lazarus (1994) alluded to the case of a client with multiple complaints, including generalized anxiety, depression, obsessive-compulsive problems, somatization, agoraphobia, and social isolation. He responded favorably to a broad-based cognitive-behavioral treatment regimen, but psychodynamic theorists predicted that within 3 to 5 years the client would not only relapse, but he might decompensate and end up in a mental hospital. The psychodynamic argument was brought into serious question when a 7-year follow-up revealed that the client had maintained and extended his gains. Similar findings from other clinicians, as well as follow-up data from many controlled studies, beginning with Paul's (1966) classic desensitization study, strengthened the CBT position—although it should be remembered that only one clearly negative instance is sufficient to discredit any general hypothesis.

A Case Study May Provide a Valuable Heuristic to Subsequent and Better-Controlled Research

Case studies in clinical psychology are probably best known for their heuristic value, for suggesting new directions that can be pursued systematically by laboratory investigators. Case studies bring to mind Reichenbach's (1938) classic distinction between the context of discovery (hypothesis generation) and the context of justification (hypothesis testing). The special utility of case studies is found in the former.

Examples of the heuristic value of case studies are legion. The research in systematic desensitization that virtually exploded in the late 1960s into the 1970s would probably not have been undertaken without the successful clinical cases that were reported by Joseph Wolpe and others in the 1950s (e.g., Lazarus & Rachman, 1957; Wolpe, 1958). The cognitive behavior therapy movement of the later 1970s that extends into the present is derived largely from the clinical reports and theoretical propositions first propounded by Ellis (1962) and Beck (1967). The more recent interest we see in making connections between experimental (nonclinical) cognitive research and clinical research in psychopathology and intervention would probably not have developed without the clinical insights, hunches, and even speculative clinical reports of practitioners such as Ellis and Beck.

After case reports attract the attention of the field, systematic investigations can take us further in understanding favorable outcomes from novel interventions. To discover what aspect of a particular strategy or technique results in therapeutic change, and how this is best achieved, global outcomes must be broken down into a series of specific interrelated factors and precise process experiments must be conducted on the mechanisms of change. Thus, when clinical reports of the effectiveness of systematic desensitization were first published, it was considered essential to draw up precise anxiety hierarchies, to train clients in deep and progressive muscular relaxation, and to proceed to present items from the hierarchy in very small incremental steps (e.g., Wolpe, 1958). Given that several other practitioners had reported positive outcomes with specific phobias and sensitivities by the application of imaginal desensitization (e.g., Lazarus & Rachman, 1957), experimentally minded workers began to take a closer look (e.g., Davison, 1968; Lang & Lazovik, 1963; Lang, Lazovik, & Reynolds, 1965). This led to many laboratory studies by a host of experimenters (see, for example, reviews by Davison & Wilson, 1973, and Wilson & Davison, 1971). In essence, these experiments demonstrated that painstaking hierarchies are usually unnecessary and that relaxation, rather than acting as a substitute or counterconditioning response for anxiety as Wolpe had hypothesized, may be important as an inducement to fearful persons to expose themselves to what they are afraid of.

The area of clinical depression, both unipolar and bipolar, also has attracted a wide experimental and clinical audience, and scores of thorough, careful, and well-controlled studies have been conducted. Indeed, some of the leading and most respected clinical experimenters and laboratory scientists have carried out studies in this area (see Hollon & Beck, 2004). But it, too, was launched mainly by clinical case reports (e.g., Beck, 1967).

A Case Study Can Provide the Opportunity to Apply Principles and Notions in Entirely New Ways

The clinical setting affords the opportunity and challenge to develop new procedures based on techniques and principles already in use. Certain aspects of particular problems may call for a new way of relating old principles and practices to their resolution.

A case in point concerns the use of a procedure usually termed "the empty chair technique" or the "two-chair method," which was devised and introduced by Gestalt therapists for helping the client become more aware of denied feelings (Perls, 1969). The client is asked to imagine having a conversation with someone or something in the empty chair. For example, the therapist may say, "Imagine your mother in this chair (about three feet away), see her vividly, and, now, talk to her about how you felt when she punished you unfairly." There are innumerable other people (e.g., relatives, friends, employers, a deceased friend), objects (e.g., one's car, wedding ring, favorite fruit, a precious ornament), parts of one's own personality (critical parent, frightened child, introversion, obsession with work), emotions and symptoms (anxiety, backaches, fatigue), any aspect of a dream, and so on, that can be imagined in the empty chair. The client is required to shift back and forth between the chairs as he or she also speaks for the person-trait-object in the other chair. This "conversation" supposedly tends to access and clarify the client's feelings and reactions to the other person (or object) and may increase self-understanding as well as empathy for the feelings and motives of the other person. The rationale and methodology underlying this Gestalt procedure were posited to be replete with an intricate mosaic of putative needs, conflicts, feelings, images, memories, emotions, judgments, and expectations about the other person or thing.

Meanwhile, cognitive-behavioral practitioners often use *role-playing* to augment the effects of assertiveness training and social skills training. For instance, the therapist plays the role of an overbearing boss, or enacts the part of an angry spouse, and the client is asked to play-act a series of assertive responses. If the client is at a loss, they switch roles and the therapist then speaks for the client and *models* appropriate rejoinders (Lazarus, 1971). However, in our clinical experience it was common to find clients who were unresponsive to this method, often because they considered the therapist's portrayal of their troublesome others wide of the mark. "My father would never say that!" "You make my wife sound like somebody that simply is not her." We then hypothesized that perhaps "the empty chair technique" would enable these portrayals to be more realistic and emotionally involving for the patient, and we incorporated our version of the procedure into our therapeutic practice.

Note that when borrowing and adapting this technique, cognitive-behavior therapists use it for different purposes than do Gestalt therapists. In a CBT framework its primary purpose is to achieve specific behavior change, usually in terms of better social skills and assertive responses. Thus, clients can focus on problematic interpersonal relationships and speak for themselves as well as the other person's issues. Imagine that the client is a woman who has a problem with her boyfriend. She commences by asking him (supposedly sitting in the other chair) a pertinent question or by sharing an observation. Before moving to the empty chair and speaking for her boyfriend, she may be urged by the therapist to rephrase her statement. "I think you need to be more emphatic. Tell him that you found his behavior at the party unacceptable." The client moves back and forth assuming her boyfriend's position and giving probable rejoinders. As she then restates her own feelings and needs, the therapist might suggest responses that the client had not anticipated, and he would coach her to remain focused and not waver.

The foregoing is an example of how a technique can be applied and understood in entirely different ways from its original structure and purpose. Behavioral clinicians, after incorporating the elements of the procedure, can experiment with the method clinically as an adjunct to behavior rehearsal and may find it advantageous. If case reports of the clinical innovation seem promising to experimentalists, means can be devised to examine it under controlled conditions.

A Case Study Can, Under Certain Circumstances, Provide Enough Experimenter Control Over a Phenomenon to Furnish Scientifically Acceptable Information

It would be incorrect to assert that case reports are ipso facto intrinsically uncontrolled and entirely anecdotal. This point of view is disproved by the work of Skinner and his associates (e.g., Ayllon, Azrin, Baer, Bijou, Krasner, Lindsley, Risley, and Wolf) in laboratories and clinical settings. On establishing a reliable baseline for the occurrence of a given behavior, predictable changes follow the alteration of a particular contingency. Operant researchers have gone on to show how the behavior can be returned to its original level by reinstating the original contingency. This is the familiar A–B–A design; numerous and ingenious variations of the basic reversal design have been described in the vast literature on behavior modification (Hurst & Nelson-Gray, 2006).

A classic case in point was presented by Wolf, Risley, and Mees (1964). The therapists undertook to reinstate walking in a 6-year-old autistic child who had regressed to the point at which he crawled around on his hands and knees more than 80% of the time. Walking was reinstated by instructing his teachers to offer him candy and social reinforcement (attention and praise) intermittently for walking, while completely ignoring him when he was crawling. Within 2 weeks, the child walked normally and seldom crawled. One of the teachers questioned the relevance of the reinforcement contingencies and maintained that it was noncontingent love, attention, and approval that had altered the child's behavior. To test this hypothesis, the teachers were again directed to offer "love and approval," only this time to make it contingent on crawling while ignoring the child when he was walking. In less than a week, the child had reverted to pretreatment levels of crawling. Finally, by reversing the contingencies once more, he stopped crawling and resumed normal walking—an A–B–A–B design. (Under many circumstances, it would be unethical or impractical to reverse contingencies in order to reinstate problem behaviors. There are alternatives in single-subject research, such as multiple baseline designs, that eliminate the need for reversals.)

The scientific status of single-subject research has been recently elaborated by Hurst and Nelson-Gray (2006): "The basic tenet of S-P [single-participant] research is that a treatment effect can be evaluated through the assessment of a reliable and replicated baseline and treatment data from a single participant. S-P designs are especially useful when completing research in an applied setting where RCTs may not be practical, when evaluating treatments for problems that occur infrequently [see our next point], and when assessing exploratory or pilot treatment effects. . . . Not only are S-P designs useful for research but they are also useful as a matter of routine in clinical practice, providing the clinician with data-based evidence about a treatment's effect on a case-by-case basis" (p. 73).

A Case Study May Permit the Investigation, Although Poorly Controlled, of Rare but Important Phenomena

It is the practicing clinician rather than the experimental researcher who is likely to observe rare and unusual human conduct. Many therapists have commented that the actions and interactions they hear about in their consulting rooms expose one to human behavioral variations that are very infrequently encountered in most people's everyday lives. Even a highly imaginative person is unlikely to conjure up many of the non-normative issues that clients share with a trusted therapist. Most practitioners avow that they have heard startling tales that would only be shared one-on-one with a trusted confidant (what Perry London [1964] many years ago called "secrets of the heart").

Kottler and Carlson (2003) have edited a book that tries to capture and convey a sense of what clinicians may encounter behind the closed doors of their sacrosanct consulting rooms. A sampling of the chapter titles gives an idea of what clinicians can encounter: "The Man Who Wanted His Nose Cut Off," "The Woman Who Hanged Herself to Check Her Husband's Response Time," "The Eighty-Two-Year-Old Prostitute," and "The Three-Year-Old Who Was An Alcoholic." To ignore the unique opportunities practitioners have to observe rare phenomena would vitiate the clinical and societal relevance of our science.

A Case Study Can Assist in Placing "Meat" on the "Theoretical Skeleton"

In a related vein, two of the chapters in the Kottler and Carlson (2003) book highlight the fact that there is no manual or empirically supported therapy to guide a therapist when confronted by a client who confesses an urge to eat from garbage cans. One can sometimes tie a highly unusual complaint to obsessive-compulsive tendencies, or to a posttraumatic stress disorder, or to some other DSM Axis I or II diagnosis, but the case itself will call for certain therapeutic artistry. Group designs, such as those used in the usual comparative outcome studies, may verify or disconfirm the value of interventions for large groups of people, but they have limitations in informing the practitioner about how to proceed with a particular individual (Davison & Lazarus, 1994, see especially page 165; Stiles, 2006).

Clinicians approach their work with a given set, a framework for ordering the complex data that are their domain. But frameworks are insufficient. The clinician, like any other applied scientist, must fill out the theoretical skeleton. Individual cases present problems that always call for knowledge beyond basic psychological principles.

LIMITATIONS OF CASE STUDIES

We have emphasized in this chapter what case studies *can* do, what kinds of information they can provide to both the practicing clinician and scientific investigator. We cannot conclude this effort without mentioning what case studies *cannot* do, what their epistemic limitations are.

For many reasons, case studies cannot establish cause-effect relationships. For example, in most instances a case report cannot tell us what would have happened with just the passage of time. Nor can a case study control for the placebo effect. O'Leary and Wilson (1987) underscored, among other factors, that successful clinical outcomes could be a result of changes in the client's life unrelated to therapy. Suggestion or the personal characteristics of the therapist also can have a profound effect. There is no way to control for these factors in a case study.

The generalizability of the findings with a single case design is difficult to determine and usually calls for direct and systematic replications. Yet all clinical research must face the issue of generalizability. Just how much does any method generalize across cases, conditions, and cultures? Perhaps the most flexible yet informative research strategy for evaluating generalizability is "benchmarking," a strategy first described by McFall (1996). In a benchmarking study, treatments of established efficacy in randomized clinical trials are administered in clinical service settings with unselected patients. The outcomes in the service setting are then compared with those from RCTs performed in research clinics (see Westbrook & Kirk, 2005; Wilson, 2006).

The emphasis in case reporting is on demonstrating change that is clinically or socially significant. Because they are usually reported by an individual clinician, however, case studies are prone to biased perceptions and reporting (see also Chapter 2). One cannot be confident that the delineation of therapy outcome is untainted by the clinician's understandable investment in the patient getting better. We phrased this point earlier as the plural of "anecdote" not being "data."

CONCLUDING COMMENT

Researchers and scientifically minded clinicians are both interested in predicting changes following specific procedures. Continuing dialectical interactions between innovations in the applied arena and controlled inquiry in research settings can lead to the discovery of promising strategies for enhancing conceptual and procedural knowledge. Single cases can be useful for drawing some clinical inferences but not others. They are particularly useful for their heuristic functions in a context of discovery, less useful—and often misleading—in a context of justification.

KEY TERMS

Idiographic: Relating to investigative procedures that concentrate on the unique characteristics of a single person, studying them in depth as in case study.

Heuristic: Generative of new directions that scientific study might take; an idea that suggests hypotheses that might be worth pursuing in a systematic manner.

Case study: An in-depth, idiographic study of a single person or other unit, such as a group or a community, with a focus on historical as well as current factors believed to account for the unit's characteristics.

Randomized controlled trial (RCT): An experimental research strategy, adopted by psychology from drug therapy research, that assigns to experimental conditions participants assumed to be homogeneous with respect to the variable of interest—for example, depression. Random assignment itself is a method of assigning people to groups that gives each person an equal chance of being in each group.

Generalizability: Sometimes referred to as external validity, the extent to which research results can be applied to the populations and settings that are of primary interest.

SUGGESTED READINGS

Castonguay, L., & Beutler, L. E. (Eds.) (2005). *Principles of therapeutic change that work*. New York: Oxford University Press.

Kring, A., Davison, G. C., Neale, J. M., & Johnson, S. (2007). *Abnormal psychology* (10th ed.). New York: Wiley.

Lambert, M. J. (Ed.). (2004). *Bergin and Garfield's handbook of psychotherapy and behavior change* (5th ed.). New York: Wiley.

Norcross, J. C., Beutler, L. E., & Levant, R. F. (Eds.). (2006). *Evidence-based practices in mental health: Debate and dialogue on the fundamental questions.* Washington, DC: American Psychological Association.

O'Donohue, W. T., Henderson, D. A., Hayes, S. C., Fisher, J. E., & Hayes, L. J. (Eds.). (2001). *A history of the behavioral therapies: Founders' personal histories.* Reno, NV: Context Press.

REFERENCES

Beck, A. T. (1967). *Depression: Clinical, experimental, and theoretical aspects.* New York: Harper & Row.

Belar, C. D., & Perry, N. W. (Eds.). (1991). National conference on scientist-practitioner education and training for the professional practice of psychology. Sarasota, FL: Professional Resource Press.

Crews, F. (Ed.). (1998). Unauthorized Freud: Doubters confront a legend. New York: Viking.

Davison, G. C. (1968). Systematic desensitization as a counterconditioning process. *Journal of Abnormal Psychology, 73,* 91–99.

Davison, G. C., & Lazarus, A. A. (1994). Clinical innovation and evaluation: Integrating practice with inquiry. *Clinical Psychology: Science and Practice, 1,* 157–168.

Davison, G. C., & Lazarus, A. A. (1995). The dialectics of acience and practice. In S. C. Hayes, V. M. Foulette, R. M. Dawes, & K. E. Grady (Eds.), Scientific standards of psychological practice: Issues and recommendations (pp. 95–120). Reno, NV: Context Press.

Davison, G. C., & Wilson, G. T. (1973). Processes of fear-reduction in systematic desensitization: Cognitive and social reinforcement factors in humans. *Behavior Therapy, 4,* 1–21.

Ellis, A. (1962). *Reason and emotion in psychotherapy.* New York: Lyle Stuart.

Emmelkamp, P. M. G. (2004). Behavior therapy with adults. In M. J. Lambert (Ed.), *Bergin and Garfield's handbook of psychotherapy and behavior change* (5th ed., pp. 393–446). New York: Wiley.

Goldfried, M. R., & Davison, G. C. (1994). *Clinical behavior therapy: Expanded edition.* New York: Wiley-Interscience.

Greenwald, A. G., Pratkanis, A. R., Leippe, M. R. & Baumgardner, M. H. (1986). Under what conditions does theory obstruct research progress? *Psychological Review, 93,* 216–229.

Greenwald, A. G., & Pratkanis, A. R. (1988). On the use of "theory" and the usefulness of theory. *Psychological Review, 95,* 575–579.

Hollon, S. D., & Beck, A.T. (2004). Cognitive and cognitive behavioral therapies. In M. J. Lambert (Ed.), *Bergin and Garfield's handbook of psychotherapy and behavior change* (5th ed., pp. 447–492). New York: Wiley.

Hurst, R. M., & Nelson-Gray, R. (2006). Single-Participant (S-P) design research. In J. C. Norcross, L. E. Beutler., & R. F. Levant (Eds.), *Evidence-based practices in mental health: Debate and dialogue on the fundamental questions* (pp. 64–73). Washington, DC: American Psychological Association.

Kazdin, A. E. (1998). Research design in clinical psychology (3rd ed.). Boston: Allyn and Bacon.

Kottler, J. A., & Carlson, J. (Eds.). (2003). *The mummy at the dining room table: Eminent therapists reveal their most unusual cases.* San Francisco: Jossey-Bass.

Lang, P. J., & Lazovik, A. D. (1963). The experimental desensitization of a phobia. *Journal of Abnormal and Social Psychology, 66,* 519–525.

Lang, P. J., Lazovik, A. D., & Reynolds, D. (1965). Desensitization, suggestibility, and pseudotherapy. *Journal of Abnormal Psychology, 70,* 395–402.

Lazarus, A. A. (1971). *Behavior therapy and beyond.* New York: McGraw-Hill.

Lazarus, A. A., & Davison, G. C. (1971). Clinical innovation in research and practice. In A. E. Bergin & S. L. Garfield (Eds.), *Handbook of psychotherapy and behavior change* (pp. 196–213). New York: Wiley.

Lazarus, A. A., & Rachman, S. (1957). The use of systematic desensitization in psychotherapy. *South African Medical Journal*, 31, 934–937.

Loftus, E. F., & Guyer, M. J. (2002a). Who abused Jane Doe? The hazards of the single case history. Part 1. *Skeptical Inquirer*, 26, 24–32.

Loftus, E. F., & Guyer, M. J. (2002b). Who abused Jane Doe? The hazards of the a single case history. Part 2. *Skeptical Inquirer*, 26, 37–44.

London, P. (1964). *The modes and morals of psychotherapy*. New York: Holt, Rinehart and Winston.

McFall, R. M. (1996, July). Consumer satisfaction as a way of evaluating psychotherapy: Ecological validity and all that versus the good old randomized trial (panel discussion). Paper presented at a panel discussion at the Annual Convention of the American Association of Applied and Preventative Psychology, San Francisco.

McNally, R. J., Cassiday, K. L, & Calamari, J. E. (1990). Tiajin-kyofu-sho in a Black American woman: Behavioral treatment of a culture-bound anxiety disorder. *Journal of Anxiety Disorders*, 4, 83–87.

Mischel, W. (1968). *Personality and assessment*. New York: Wiley.

Moscovitch, M., Winocur, G., & Behrmann, M. (1997). What is special about face recognition? Nineteen experiments on a person with visual object agnosia and dyslexia but normal face recognition. *Journal of Cognitive Neuroscience*, 9, 555–604.

O'Donohue, W. T., Henderson, D. A., Hayes, S. C., Fisher, J. E., & Hayes, L. J. (Eds.). (2001). *A history of the behavioral therapies: Founders' personal histories*. Reno, NV: Context Press.

O'Leary, K.D., & Wilson, G. T. (1987) *Behavior therapy: Application and outcome* (2nd ed.). Englewood Cliffs, NJ: Prentice Hall.

Paul, G. L. (1966). *Insight vs. desensitization*. Stanford: Stanford University Press.

Perls, F. S. (1969). *Gestalt therapy verbatim*. Moab, UT: Real People Press.

Piaget, J., & Inhelder, B. (1969). *The psychology of the child*. New York: Basic Books.

Pinker, S. (1994a). *The language instinct*. New York: Morrow.

Pinker, S. (1994b). How could a child use verb syntax to learn verb semantics? *Lingua*, 92, 377–410.

Reichenbach, H. (1938). *Experience and prediction: An analysis of the foundations and the structure of knowledge*. Chicago: University of Chicago Press.

Sacks, O. (1990). *Awakenings*. New York: Harper Perennial.

Stiles, W. B. (2006). Case studies. In J. C. Norcross, L. E. Beutler, & R. F. Levant (Eds.), *Evidence-based practices in mental health: Debate and dialogue on the fundamental questions* (pp. 64–73). Washington, DC: American Psychological Association.

Sulloway, F. J. (1991). Reassessing Freud's case histories. *ISIS*, *82*, 245–275.

Wachtel, P. L. (1973). Psychodynamics, behavior therapy, and the implacable experimenter: An inquiry into the consistency of personality. *Journal of Abnormal Psychology*, 82, 324–334.

Westbrook, D., & Kirk, J. (2005). The clinical effectiveness of cognitive behaviour therapy: Outcome for a large sample of adults treated in routine practice. *Behaviour Research and Therapy, 43,* 1243–1390.

Wilson, G. T. (2006). Manual-based treatment: Evolution and evaluation. In T. A. Treat, R. R. Bootzin, & T. B. Baker (Eds.), *Psychological clinical science: Papers in honor of Richard M. McFall.* Mahwah, NJ: Lawrence Erlbaum Associates.

Wilson, G. T., & Davison, G. C. (1971). Processes of fear reduction in systematic desensitization: Animal studies. *Psychological Bulletin, 76,* 1–14.

Wolf, M. M., Risley, T. R., & Mees, H. (1964). Application of operant conditioning procedures to the behavior problems of an autistic child. *Behaviour Research and Therapy,* 1, 305–312.

Wolpe, J. (1958). *Psychotherapy by reciprocal inhibition.* Stanford, CA: Stanford University Press.

Woolfolk, R. L., & Lazarus, A. A. (1979). Between laboratory and clinic: Paving the two-way street. *Cognitive Therapy and Research,* 3, 233–244.

Yin, R. K. (1994). *Case study research: Design and methods* (2nd ed.). Thousand Oaks, CA: Sage.

8

Treatment and Assessment Take Place in an Economic Context, Always

NICHOLAS A. CUMMINGS

It's the economy, stupid.

—*James Carville (1992 and 1996), advisor to President Bill Clinton*

This title is hardly a newsflash, and the reader is likely to respond with a flippant, "Of course, I know that." Yet this response belies the extent of psychology practitioners' misunderstanding of the economic forces that impinge on practice, suppress current incomes, and that will shape the future of behavioral healthcare delivery, either positively or negatively. Many practitioners suffer from an antibusiness bias that blinds them to pertinent information that would be helpful to both them and their patients (O'Donohue, 2002). With others, their eyes glaze over when confronted with a spreadsheet, and they are lucky if they can balance and reconcile their own checking accounts. They complain that they are seeing more patients for less money, and the managed care companies pay less an hour for psychotherapy than plumbers are paid for their work. Taking into account the wide educational disparity between doctoral psychologists and plumbers, they despair that society is treating them unfairly. Yet it is not a matter of fairness, for there are economic principles that explain why plumbers are relatively well paid, whereas psychologists are underpaid. These principles remain a mystery to most psychologists. To put it sadly but bluntly, most practitioners are economic illiterates (Cummings,

2002). The purpose of this chapter is to identify these economic forces and to enable practitioners to exercise a greater control over their own destiny.

LABOR IS SUBJECT TO THE LAWS OF SUPPLY AND DEMAND

Most psychologists are well aware that if a product is in short supply, the price goes up, whereas if there is a glut of that product on the market, prices will plummet. Yet they do not realize that the laws of supply and demand apply equally to a unit of labor. A frequent lament on the American Psychological Association (APA) Division 42 (Independent Practice) listserv is, "All I want is an income commensurate with the years of education it took for me to earn my doctorate." The higher income of master's-level nurse practitioners in comparison with that of doctoral psychologists in practice is often invoked as an example of unfairness. These arguments are irrelevant in a free market setting, and all that these sour grapes can produce is whine. The fact remains that there is a shortage of nurses and a glut of psychotherapists, most of the latter at a master's level who are willing to work for less, competing effectively against doctoral psychologists, forcing them to accept reimbursement schedules suppressed by the horde of lower-paid psychotherapists.

The laws of supply and demand are so compelling that in the past corporations have tried to circumvent them through monopolies, cartels, price fixing, and other practices that are now illegal, thanks to antitrust laws. Corporations may still try, but as the plethora of federal and state antitrust suits against Microsoft has shown, it is best to compete in the marketplace with a superior product, not monopolistic practices. Historically, labor was able to form "monopolies" that are not as well remembered by the public as are the so-called robber barons. For example, John L. Lewis of the United Mine Workers could in the 1930s shut down the coal mines in minutes, plunging the nation into an energy crisis. Similarly, Jimmy Hoffa could idle his teamsters and stop every truck in the nation, emptying grocery store shelves, whereas Harry Bridges could suspend shipping on both coasts, curtailing all imports and exports, with a single phone call. Such powerful labor unions were able to impinge on otherwise low-paying jobs and subvert normal marketplace pressures. However, there are now legal restrictions on unions, and both labor and industry are more or less equally subject to the laws of supply and demand.

THE CASE OF THE MORTAR-CARRYING BRICKLAYER AND THE PLIGHT OF PSYCHOLOGY

A former patient who had recently moved into the community from another state was not able to get a job in his skill as a bricklayer, and in desperation accepted a minimum wage laborer's job carrying the mortar up the scaffolding to the bricklayers. He complained that even though he was working as a hod-carrier, he should be paid bricklayer's scale because he was a journeyman bricklayer. One day in a fit of pique he fell off the scaffolding, and, now recovering from two broken bones, insisted that he should be paid bricklayer's workers compensation scale, not that of a laborer. As I listened, he reminded me of so many of our colleagues who are doing the same work as master's-level psychotherapists but want to be paid a higher doctoral pay scale.

A perusal of state rosters of practitioners licensed to do psychotherapy reveals that the ranks of social workers, marriage-family therapists, counselors, psychiatric nurse practitioners, and other master's-level licensees far outweigh the number of psychologists licensed to practice and who are essentially offering their services as psychotherapists. Similarly, the networks of managed behavioral care companies list a plethora of master's-level psychotherapists. This overwhelming number of nondoctoral psychotherapists firmly establishes the reimbursement scale for psychotherapy on a predoctoral level. If doctoral psychologists are to compete, they must offer services that cannot be performed by their master's-level counterparts, and they must reflect doctoral level skills not attained by counselors and social workers.

HISTORICAL PERSPECTIVE

The professional psychologist, defined as a practitioner whose primary income derives from independent practice, was born during World War II. Before 1940, there were scarcely 200 psychologists in private practice scattered throughout the country. Most were women with master's degrees who limited their practices to children. For some reason, women seeing children did not constitute a threat to the predominantly male psychiatric profession. Male psychiatrists even made referrals to them, while shunning their male counterparts. Before World War II, most psychiatrists were older and had European accents, and were not available for military service when the army's chief psychiatrist, General William Menninger, decided that psychotherapists offering immediate interventions on the front lines could prevent the development of more serious and chronic psychiatric conditions. As cofounder with his brother Karl of the Menninger Clinic, he used his skills to create the School of Military Neuropsychiatry at Mason General Hospital on Long Island, New York. It was there that young master's-level psychologists were given the additional training in crash courses to perform as frontline psychotherapists. These young men returned to civilian life determined to become clinical psychologists, and were joined by other graduate students who took advantage of the new stipends and funding for clinical psychology doctoral programs from both the Veterans Administration (VA) and the newly established National Institute of Mental Health (NIMH). Both of these government agencies, believing there would never be enough psychiatrists, sought to train clinical psychologists and psychiatric social workers to meet the swelling public demand for psychotherapy. As a returning World War II veteran, the author was one of these, and all the events of the next half-century occurred in his lifetime and with his direct participation as an activist.

At first, the newly minted clinical psychologists went to work in institutional settings, but chafing under the dominance of psychiatry they soon began to enter independent practice in droves. There was no state licensure of psychologists, so there was an easy transition to private practice. At the same time, there was no public recognition of psychologists, only psychiatrists, and potential patients demanded to see psychiatrists. We bridged this gap by affiliating and working with established psychiatrists who were overwhelmed by the burgeoning number of referrals.

It should be pointed out that in the 1950s the economics pertaining to psychotherapy were much different than they are today. Because of the publicity accorded psychological problems and their solution through psychological interventions during and immediately following World War II, a seemingly insatiable demand for psychotherapy was generated. The public response, coupled with the acute shortage of trained, practicing psychotherapists, resulted in what economists call a "seller's market," and fostered a prosperous endeavor for the newly minted professional psychologists. In addition, it became fashionable for every potential patient to undergo extensive intellectual and personality testing, so much so that seeing a psychotherapy patient who had not completed a battery of psychological tests (in which, along with the Wechsler, the Rorschach and Thematic Apperception Tests were ubiquitous, and the Bender-Gestalt and the Machover Draw-a-Person Tests nearly so) was unthinkable (see also Chapter 4). Psychologists had a total monopoly on the assessment market, adding even another dimension to their flourishing practices.

THE ADVENT OF THIRD-PARTY PAYMENT

Another difference in the economic climate was the absence of third-party payment for psychotherapy. Until the late 1960s and early 1970s, all patients receiving psychotherapy paid out of pocket. This constituted another economic principle, that of free market checks-and-balances. If patients experienced no progress, or were otherwise dissatisfied, they quit therapy, as they did not want to waste their money. With the advent of third-party payment, a new phenomenon surfaced. Called "therapeutic drift," patients were willing to continue treatment in the face of no progress because someone else was paying for it, all the while hoping that sooner or later something positive would happen (Budman & Gurman, 1988). Others, for whom change was not desirable, could bask in the narcissistic experience of having an entire hour once or twice a week to talk about themselves, all the while having the full attention of a prepaid listener who was taking their self-possessions seriously (Bergin & Garfield, 1994; Lambert, 1992). The natural economic checks and balances accorded by the unadulterated doctor-patient relationship and in effect since the era of Hippocrates in 400 B.C.E. were gone from psychotherapy, never to return. In the hope of reinstating something similar, Nobel Laureate Milton Friedman (2004) proposed a system of medical savings accounts (MSAs) that would be tax free and used to pay the doctor. Unused portions of the MSA would eventually revert to the patient, restoring at least partially the economic doctor-patient relationship.

Psychology fought hard for decades to be included by insurers who had been reimbursing only psychiatrists with third-party payment, and rightly so. It would not be long before most Americans had some form of health insurance, and without inclusion in third-party reimbursement, psychology would have lost out in the independent practice marketplace. The successful decades of struggle have been chronicled (Wright & Cummings, 2001), concluding with psychiatry's abandoning psychotherapy in the 1980s for "remedicalization" and becoming essentially a psychotropic-prescribing profession. This change left psychology as the preeminent psychotherapy profession, an economic heaven that went unappreciated until the end of its short life span (c. 1985 to 1995).

THE NULLIFICATION OF THE SUPPLY AND DEMAND RELATIONSHIP

It has long been recognized that the "laws" of supply and demand have not operated in the healthcare sector as they do in the general economy. This is because physicians (along with hospitals, psychotherapists, and other providers) traditionally have controlled both the supply and demand sides of healthcare. It is the doctor who determines what treatment the patient needs, what procedures should be rendered, and how long the treatment should last. Traditionally, psychologists were trained in long-term psychotherapy and showed little inclination to research and develop more efficient, time-sensitive approaches, later to be known as brief therapy.

On the supply side, government subsidized the education and training of healthcare practitioners, including psychologists, psychiatrists, and social workers, not only to relieve the critical shortage of a few decades ago but also to create a surplus of providers. It was widely believed that once there was an ample supply of doctors, costs would go down. This is true in every other industry: A glut of workers results in cheaper wages. In healthcare, however, as the number of providers increased beyond the number needed, costs went up instead of down. Physicians, being in control of both supply and demand, merely rendered more treatment, and particularly more procedures, to a declining number of available patients. In health economics, such practices are termed *demand creation*, which nullify the effects of supply and demand (Feldstein, 1996). Added to this nullification is the tax incentive that accrues to the employer who provides the health insurance, with the employee erroneously believing it is a free benefit. To the contrary, health insurance is provided by companies in lieu of higher wages that would be more costly to the employer, a hidden economic reality that further distorts the system.

HEALTHCARE RATIONING IS UBIQUITOUS

There is not an industrialized nation in which healthcare is not rationed, and it always is what economists call *silent rationing*, whereby various methods of limiting services are undertaken, without the consumer being aware of them, as a deliberate response to scarcity of resources (Feldstein, 1996). Once healthcare is made available at little or no cost to the consumer, patients overuse the health system, especially for minor events that heretofore would not have been taken to the doctor (Sowell, 2003). Termed *artificial demand escalation*, it is inevitable in all third-party payer insurance where there are yet some controls possible, but especially in all government-sponsored healthcare (Feldstein, 1996; Sowell, 2003). The author for 3 years was involved with attempting to modernize the mental health sector of the National Health Service (NHS) in the United Kingdom, where health rationing is reflected not only in long waiting lists, such as 35 months for a hernia repair, but also by the exclusion of newer and more expensive drugs and the costly latest technologies. Several years ago, the Province of Ontario, part of the Canadian universal health system, announced at the beginning of December that the healthcare budget had been exhausted, and no healthcare would be paid for until after the new budget came into effect at the first of the year. Since then, Ontario has learned not to blunder into such crass rationing by using a variety of silent rationings, the latest of which is reinstating a progressive system of premiums, thus ending the tradition of free healthcare for all (Mackie, 2004). The Canadian system would be even more strained were it not for tens of thousands of Canadians who, tiring of waiting for services, cross annually into the United States, where they are willing to pay out-of-pocket. This phenomenon prompted Eli Ginsburg, the Columbia University health economist, to quip a number of years ago that the Mayo Clinic in Rochester, Minnesota, is the annex to the Canadian health system.

Not understanding the ubiquitous nature of healthcare rationing, one psychology journal published an unprecedented series of three articles, all in the same issue, and all by the same author (Miller, 1996a, 1996b, 1996c), decrying that managed care is "invisible rationing." To the credit of the journal's editor, an article was soon published that corrected the lack of economic understanding on the part of the trilogy's author (Cummings, Budman, & Thomas, 1998). It established that although managed care is, indeed, silent rationing, it is a more humane form of rationing than the scarcity of resources inevitably forced on most universal healthcare systems.

DEMAND CREATION IN THE PRACTICE OF PSYCHOLOGY

Once there were too many physicians, doctors merely *created demand* (Feldstein, 1996) by providing more, often marginally necessary, services. Of all the health professionals, behavioral care providers (including psychiatrists, psychologists, social workers, marriage and family therapists, master's-level psychologists, and substance abuse counselors) are in the greatest oversupply. It would be expected, therefore, that such provision of unnecessary services would be prevalent among psychotherapists and others who treat behavioral disorders. Examples abound, but some of the most widely recognized include the following.

The most obvious example of demand creation is to place the declining number of patients available in increasingly longer psychotherapy. One patient seen for 3 years is equivalent to six patients each seen for one-half year. This practice exploded with the glut of psychotherapists, as did the proliferation of assessments, a procedure that was totally within the province of psychologists. The advent of managed care, to be discussed later, curtailed these practices, which only spurred practitioners to greater economic creativity (Weitz, 2000).

Another form of demand creation is to invent a syndrome for which the psychotherapist already has a treatment. Psychotherapy has a number of established treatments for depression, and by a new syndrome, seasonal affective disorder (SAD, the state of feeling "blue" in the gloom of winter), these established techniques could be applied to an entire new population. Stretching our credulity even further, more recently NIMH identified "reverse SAD" that ostensibly afflicts persons during daylight savings time (Spencer, 2003). Psychology already had the treatment, but the new disorders were created, thus expanding the number of persons who could be regarded as patients and for whom insurance coverage could be provided. Similarly, bereavement counseling techniques were transposed to the new "grief and crisis counseling" that is rushed to the scene of every disaster. Interventions developed by military psychologists for treating combat posttraumatic stress syndrome (PTSD) were transposed to civilian stress reactions, whereas long-established therapy techniques were applied to "battered woman syndrome," a newly created disorder that has received wide acceptance in the courts and in forensic psychology. Cummings (2005) delineated the process by which this is done, whereas Lilienfeld, Lynn, and Lohr (2003), and Lilienfeld, Fowler, Lohr, and Lynn (2005) have addressed the proliferation of dubious diagnoses and their treatments that have been spawned in the era of the psychotherapist glut. Any collection of behavioral symptoms can be grouped together, rendered a name, and, once this syndrome becomes a part of the Diagnostic and Statistical Manual, the American Psychiatric Association's billing bible, third-party payment is guaranteed. Even before receiving wide acceptance, trial lawyers latch on to these "syndromes" to bolster their claims, and find willing psychologist accomplices in these legal charades (Wright, 2005b).

In a similar vein, existing disorders can be expanded far beyond their proven utility so that a vast number of potential new patients is created. When the American Psychiatric Association (1994) in its Diagnostic and Statistical Manual, 4th Edition, changed the definitions of attention deficit disorder (ADD) and attention-deficit/hyperactivity disorder (ADHD), it quadrupled the number of patients, especially children and adolescents, who would be eligible for treatment (Cummings & Wiggins, 2001; Rosemond, 2005; Wright, 2005a). The diagnostic criteria for depression are constantly shifting toward including more and more of what previously has been regarded as usual, downward mood swings experienced by virtually all individuals as part of daily living. Stress also has been redefined so that any or all employees suffer from pathological job stress, all parents manifest child rearing anxiety, and all of us who are not millionaires suffer from social status sensitivity syndrome.

A third type of demand creation among psychologists is the invention of new treatments that have wide public appeal just out of compassion, while leaving the treatment unproven or even deleterious. An example is what has been termed critical incidence stress debriefing, which has received broad media attention in everything from the Columbine shooting to the World Trade Center attack. Teams of psychologists converge on every disaster, and the public has been led to believe this treatment is efficacious. Yet recent research suggests it may encourage histrionics, retard resiliency, and even delay the natural process by which trauma effects are healed (McNally, 2003a, 2003b).

Economists would stress that even though the provider may be in a conflict of interest at times with efforts to control demand, few practitioners would cynically set out to inflate costs. Their avowed intent is that the patient should receive all necessary health services. Nonetheless, the term "unconscious fiscal convenience" has been used in describing the conflict between ostensibly sincere providers and the health system (Budman & Gurman, 1988).

ENTER MANAGED BEHAVIORAL HEALTHCARE

During the 1970s and 1980s, the inflationary curve for healthcare began to spiral out of control, often exceeding the inflation rate of the general economy two- or threefold. The federal government grew increasingly concerned, and through a series of unsuccessful initiatives, such as monetary incentives to increase the supply of physicians in the expectation that this would increase competition and lower fees, sought to reduce the rate of inflation in healthcare costs. In 1975, legislation was enacted that allowed the federal government to encourage and fund the formation of health maintenance organizations (HMOs), which, before 1975, had been largely a California and Minnesota phenomenon. The concept, especially as it was administered by Kaiser Permanente, the nation's first and highly successful HMO, captured the interest of health economists as a possible solution to the healthcare economic crisis. It also was seen by Senator Edward Kennedy, who chaired the U.S. Senate Subcommittee on Health, as bringing the nation one step closer to nationalized healthcare. With this empowerment, HMOs proliferated and grew from less than 1% of the insured population to their current status as the dominant health delivery system in the nation. Unfortunately, HMOs did not deliver behavioral care very efficiently, and sought to control costs by either providing crisis care only, or by capping the benefit at 10 or 20 sessions.

Frustrated by the continued high inflationary curve in healthcare, in the mid-1980s Congress put into effect a table of diagnosis-related groups (DRGs) for Medicare and Medicaid reimbursement to hospitals. This mandated a set number of days of hospitalization for each of almost 400 conditions. If the hospital exceeded the allowance, it lost money. If it used less than the allowance, it made a profit. Unable to construct DRGs for mental health and chemical dependency (MH/CD) conditions, the federal government tacitly decided to let the private sector solve the problem. Decades of laws and regulations forbidding the corporate practice of medicine were first ignored, then either repealed or struck down by the courts. Managed behavioral health organizations (MBHOs) were formed and grew rapidly as they "carved out" behavioral care from the parent insurers. Health plans had become alarmed when they saw that without DRGs the mental health costs were now exceeding the inflation rate of the tethered medicine and surgery, and were eager to contract with the emerging MBHOs. A little known or unappreciated fact is that the MBHOs actually saved the MH/CD benefit, obtained after many hard-fought years, from extinction. Faced with an out-of-control inflationary spiral in MH/CD, insurers were beginning to eliminate it as a covered benefit until the carve-out arrangements capped their costs and relieved them of any further financial worry.

OUT OF THE COTTAGE: THE INDUSTRIALIZATION OF HEALTHCARE

Industrialization occurs when an economic endeavor emerges from individual, family, or small group proprietorship with limited production (known as cottage industries) to large-scale production employing large workforces and using innovations in technology, organization, and consolidation, resulting in increases in both productivity and its resulting lower cost to consumers (Feldstein, 1996). Healthcare had been a cottage industry until Congress enacted DRGs and inadvertently ushered in the era of managed care by removing barriers to the corporate practice of medicine. Psychologists, not understanding the economic forces at work, often ask, "Why did healthcare have to industrialize?" Rather, the question should be, "Why did a sector that accounts for one-sixth of our gross national product (GNP), for a total of $1.4 trillion, take so long to industrialize?" Manufacturing industrialized in the early 1900s, energy in the 1930s, transportation in the 1950s, and retail in the 1970s. In the 1980s, the time had finally come for healthcare to industrialize. It was late in the history and development of the economy, but it was inevitable.

Foreseeing this inevitability, Cummings issued a series of warnings, showing how psychology could own what had not yet been named managed care, and published a do-it-yourself kit on how to prevent the industrialization of behavioral care passing into the control of big business (Cummings & Fernandez, 1985; Cummings, 1986). To demonstrate to his colleagues how to accomplish this goal, he founded American Biodyne as a showcase to be emulated. He promised to cap Biodyne's enrollment at a half-million covered lives, leaving 50 or more psychologist-owned mental health plans to be created by colleagues. But Cummings could not even give the golden goose away; no one came to visit other than business executives. Despairing, he took his foot off the brake and in the next 5 years enrollment skyrocketed to 14.5 million covered lives in 39 states. As practitioners lost their authority to make patient care decisions, they ignored the message and blamed the messenger and demonized him (Thomas, J., Cummings, & O'Donohue, 2002). It was not until after the turn of the 21st century that organized psychology recognized the missed opportunity. But it was too late; by the early 1990s, Wall Street and not psychology owned managed behavioral care, and 160 million Americans were receiving their behavioral care through some form of managed care (Cummings, 2000).

One of the lessons to be learned, once industrialization has taken place, is that there cannot be a return to the preceding cottage industry (Feldstein, 19996; Sowell, 2003). For example, once Henry Ford invented the assembly line, automobiles handcrafted in garages could not compete in cost, value, and efficiency. Lacking in economic knowledge, as late as the 1990s officials of the APA were still referring to managed care as a passing fad, and were promising that it would be repealed soon through political, not economic, solutions (Wright, 1992). Psychologists, wanting to maintain their solo practices intact, compounded their economic illiteracy by pouring money into initiatives that promised to roll back the clock. The natural evolution that continues in the industrialization of healthcare brought changes that gave practitioners hope that managed care was being vanquished. Also, a series of court victories that put a stop to egregious practices inflated that hope, but it was not long before disillusion set in.

An important challenge, in which the APA was heavily involved, and which, if successful, would have changed the healthcare landscape significantly, failed in the U.S. Supreme Court (Bradshaw, 2004). In holding that patients cannot use state courts to sue HMOs for malpractice when treatment recommended by their doctors is withheld, the court said that the 1974 federal law, known as ERISA, governs health insurance regulations for millions of Americans who receive health coverage, including mental health benefits, through their workplace. Finally disillusioned, psychologists who are generous in making direct contributions to political campaigns are no longer as generous in giving to their professionally established activist organizations, such as the Association for the Advancement of Psychology (Fox, 2004).

PARITY LEGISLATION

Providers' legislative efforts have been amazingly successful in that laws mandating parity of mental health coverage with that of physical health have been enacted in 39 states and the federal government. Yet they are a complete bust because the nation spends less on mental health and substance abuse after parity than it did before, with estimated total expenditures plummeting from the $60 to $70 billion range to an estimated total of $50 to $60 billion (Carnahan, 2002). The managed care companies, fearing the return of runaway MH/CD costs, put in place more draconian hurdles to access behavioral health than exist for physical health. Just as rent control results in housing shortages because landlords abandon their properties and new building is discouraged, parity is an excellent example of the point that economic "laws" can defy and circumvent legislation. In the end, the successful parity legislation is a feel good façade, enabling lobbyists and advocates to justify their cost to their constituents.

If parity were a serious consideration, either the $1.4 trillion annual health budget would have to be doubled, or the existing expenditure would have to reallocate half a trillion dollars each to physical and mental health. Stated in these terms, it is apparent that enforced parity is not a viable solution to the dwindling behavioral healthcare budget.

Some psychologists also have lobbied successfully in the enactment of what are known as "every willing provider laws." These laws forbid MBHOs to be selective, and mandate that they must accept every licensed practitioner who wants to join their networks. This has done nothing to relieve psychology's dwindling economic base, for larger networks mean more practitioners vying for fewer referrals. Destructively, however, it has contributed to reduced quality and mediocrity as the MBHO cannot discriminate in favor of the superior practitioner. In spite of the fact that licensure proffers that it guarantees expertise, all practitioners are not created equal. As once the employer of nearly 10,000 practitioners in 39 states, the author can attest that the tremendous variability in the effectiveness of psychologists, psychiatrists, and social workers is alarming, and laws dictating use of every willing provider seriously threaten quality delivery of services (Cummings, 2000).

THE PSYCHOPHARMACOLOGY REVOLUTION AND DEMAND REDUCTION

The new generation of psychotropic medications (antidepressant, anti-psychotic, and anxiolytic drugs) has significantly eroded referrals for psychotherapy. For example, in 1990, nearly 95% of patients released from psychiatric hospitals were referred for outpatient psychotherapy and counseling. By 2000, the number had precipitously fallen to only 10%, as discharged patients were given medication instead (Carnahan, 2002). Over 80% of prescriptions for psychotropic medications are written by primary care physicians, bypassing even psychiatrists for whom prescribing constitutes the majority of their practice. This decrease in consumer demand for behavioral care interventions would be known as *demand reduction* (Feldstein, 1996), were it not for the fact that the new psychotropic drugs are expensive and are given for longer and longer periods. Overall costs, therefore, have actually risen (Carnahan, 2002), and evidence is emerging that counseling and brief therapy are not only cheaper but equally (and at times even more) effective (Antonuccio, Danton, & DeNelsky, 1999; Glasser, 2003). Thus, this is not demand reduction but, rather, what is called *demand substitution* (Feldstein, 1996), with questionable benefits.

Feeling the economic pinch of reduced demand for psychotherapy, psychologists have mounted an aggressive campaign to acquire prescription authority that has so far been successful in two states, New Mexico and Louisiana (Ally, 2004). Having essentially given up psychotherapy in favor of medication, psychiatry has mounted a vigorous opposition to further inroads by psychologists into their mainstay practice. It may take 20 years, but psychologists eventually will gain prescription authority nationally for two economic reasons. First, there is a shortage of psychiatrists in rural areas, and patients must wait for weeks for psychiatric medication evaluation. This shortage has been successfully exploited by psychologists who are more widely distributed and could relieve the crisis. Second, society is pushing knowledge downward, with practical nurses doing the work of registered nurses, who in turn are doing much of the work of primary care physicians who have included in their practices the lower tiers of geriatric, obstetrical, surgical, and dermatological procedures. This trend, opposed by medical/surgical specialists, has gained momentum and wide acceptance by the consumer.

It is inevitable that this trend will eventually include psychologists, who will be doing much of the work of psychiatrists, such as prescribing psychotropic medications and achieving full hospital privileges.

Psychologists are looking to prescription authority as a financial boost to their dwindling practices and sagging incomes. Undoubtedly, the acquisition of prescription authority and hospital privileges would significantly expand the economic base of psychological practice. When that day comes, it remains to be seen, however, whether they abandon the hard work of psychotherapy for the expediency of the prescription pad.

TENTATIVE RESPONSES TO A DWINDLING ECONOMIC BASE

A growing number of psychologists have found niche practices, such as the counseling of women undergoing fertility treatment, grief counseling, or treating individuals who seek to change from a homosexual to heterosexual orientation. The ingenuity of some of these niche practices is astounding, successfully providing a good livelihood for practitioners whose standard practices had evaporated. However, a niche reflects a limited clientele, and financial success is inversely proportional to the greater number of practitioners who enter the niche. Much has been written touting the advantages of both niche practice and the abandonment of managed care networks in favor of out-of-pocket paying clientele. However, experience with universal healthcare demonstrates there is a limit to the number of individuals, between 5% to 7% of those eligible, who will forego prepaid care for the convenience, and perhaps better quality, of out-of-pocket services. This refuge from reduced practice is temporary at best, subject largely to relatively few practitioners taking the plunge. The inverse relationship between success and the number of persons filling the niches and opting for fee-for-service practice, foresees economic trouble ahead. Saturation will have simply wiggled sideways.

A surprisingly large number of psychologists are abandoning their psychological practices for the burgeoning and lucrative endeavor known as *coaching* (Fairley & Stout, 2004). This is a 180-degree departure from psychotherapy, a nonjudgmental procedure that eschews advice in favor of the patient's growth and individual choice, to coaching, which is directive, motivational, and advice-giving. There is currently no state licensure for coaching, and because essentially anyone can hang out a shingle, it is attracting both the well trained and the incompetent, and in some instances even the unsavory. It appeals to consumers because it offers the immediate answer and the quick fix, yet it remains to be seen how stable and durable this market will be over the next several years.

Psychological assessment in healthcare has declined to the point where it has all but disappeared. Psychodiagnostic testing still occupies a large portion of the training curriculum for doctoral clinical psychologists, mostly at the insistence of the APA accreditation process, but managed care companies report that referrals for psychological assessment are less than 1% of their referrals to practitioners (Cummings, Pallak, & Cummings, 1996). Moreover, most of these referrals are in geropsychology. The exception is testing in neuropsychology, a time-consuming and lucrative practice that services mostly trial lawyers who see this as a necessary expenditure to bolster their claims in malpractice suits. Lawsuits pay well, attracting a steady migration to neuropsychology and forensic psychology, where practitioners do not have to worry about losing what one neuropsychologist (Thomas, 2003) called their "Cadillac practices." This is another economics-driven opting out of the healthcare system by psychologists.

Perhaps the most misguided attempt to increase the shrinking economic base is that of creating and credentialing specializations through the APA's National College. Paradoxically, a profession that has been unable to define its competencies, or to agree on a core curriculum in nearly 20 national conferences in the more than half a century since the Boulder Conference of 1948, has rushed into credentialing a number of specialties, with others waiting in line to be anointed. The belief is that piling on credentials will increase incomes, but this would be true only if lacking such a credential bars one from practicing that specialty. As long as social workers who are doing the bulk of psychotherapy continue to be able to see any prospective patient, psychology is only tying its economic hands by eliminating the general practice of psychology. Sadly, psychology could become the most credentialed and lowest paid doctoral health profession in America (Cummings, 2003).

MUTUALLY MISPERCEIVED DEMAND: THE IMPORTANCE OF MEDICAL COST OFFSET

In the mid-1950s, the Kaiser Permanente Health System in Northern California discovered that 60% of its patient visits to a physician were by patients who had no physical disease, or whose medical condition was exacerbated by psychological factors (Follette & Cummings, 1967; Cummings & Follette, 1968). The NIMH funded over 20 replications, all of which produced what the government termed *medical cost offset*, the phenomenon in which behavioral interventions reduce medical and surgical expenditures (demand) beyond the costs needed to provide the psychological services (Jones & Vischi, 1979). These early studies showed wide variability in the amount of medical cost offset, a matter addressed by the Bethesda Consensus Conference convened by the NIMH. The conclusion was not surprising; the more innovative and targeted the behavioral interventions, the greater the medical cost offset (Jones & Vischi, 1980). Over the next 35 years, studies numbering in the hundreds have established the phenomenon of medical cost offset, and defined many of its parameters (as summarized in Cummings, Cummings, & Johnson, 1997, and Cummings, O'Donohue, & Ferguson, 2002).

Physicians are trained to find physical disease, and in the face of overwhelming symptoms that are actually undiagnosed manifestations of stress, will order and repeat a multitude of tests and procedures, which persuade the patient even more that the condition is physical. In economics, this is known as *mutually misperceived demand* (Feldstein, 1996), as the demand disappears when the appropriate treatment is administered, in this case, targeted behavioral interventions. It is estimated that this mutually misperceived demand exceeds the costs of all malpractice suits, and in the realm of avoidable costs, is exceeded only by medical errors (Cummings, 2001). Appropriately delivered behavioral interventions can save up to 10% or 15% in medical surgical costs, and only a 5% savings in a national medical cost offset program would exceed the entire annual budget for both mental health and substance abuse (Cummings, O'Donohue, & Ferguson, 2002).

The inelastic barriers found in the healthcare system make it difficult to institute such a far-reaching program. In most health plans, data are not obtained in a way that can connect the necessary cause and effect (i.e., tracing back medical visits for those who received psychotherapy). Furthermore, most behavioral care currently is provided by carve-outs, separate companies that do not connect at all with the computers of the health plan gathering data on medical and surgical visits. For this and other reasons, the policy makers at NIMH and the Substance Abuse and Mental Health Services Administration (SAMHSA) are actively encouraging through research and demonstration projects the integration of behavioral health within primary care, and the inclusion of medical cost offset as an economic tool.

Typically, organized psychology would compound the misperceived demand by perpetuating the traditional fee-for-service office model. The APA, through its friends in Congress, persuaded the government to sponsor a demonstration project intended to show that unlimited access to traditional, nontargeted psychological services would reduce healthcare costs. The Champus program (now called TriCare) in the Fort Bragg, North Carolina area was chosen. Within 3 years, an $8 million mental health program skyrocketed out of control to $80 million, a 1,000% increase, and with no demonstrable improvement in healthcare as acknowledged by the researchers themselves (Bickman, 1996). This is among the greatest healthcare economic debacles of all time, and one that the APA has embalmed in the *American Psychologist*, never to be resurrected in any of its publications, and thus effectively blocking an economic lesson that would be invaluable in revamping education and practice in psychology.

DELIVERING THE NUTS WITHOUT THE BOLTS:
AN ECONOMIC PLIGHT

Healthcare has created two silos, a physical healthcare silo that is enormous, and a tiny mental health silo that is underfunded and underappreciated. As painful as it may be, it is time psychological practice looked at the facts. As much as 85% of behavioral care is provided by nonpsychiatric primary care physicians (PCPs), not psychologists, psychiatrists, or social workers. Allegorically speaking, one silo makes bolts, while our silo makes nuts, the latter believing that you can not have bolts without the nuts. It is as if we are unaware that the bolt silo (i.e., physical healthcare) manufactures almost all the nuts (i.e., behavioral health interventions), leaving us as a somewhat less than necessary service requiring adequate funding. In spite of all the legislative and judicial thrusts by psychology and other advocates, the mental health budget (including substance abuse) has declined to $70 billion (5%) of the total $ 1.4 trillion healthcare annual budget, even though 60% of patients presenting to primary care experience significant psychological problems that are interfering with their physical health. It is time for psychology to vacate an outmoded silo. Unfortunately, few practitioners are prepared by training to become behavioral primary care providers, and only two or three doctoral programs have overhauled their curricula to meet the requirements of the future healthcare system already embraced by the U.S. Air Force, the Veterans Administration, the Community Health Centers, and Kaiser Permanente, to name only the largest of the delivery systems doing so (Cummings, O'Donohue, & Ferguson, 2002).

This model of primary care integration goes beyond current health psychology and collaboration, which retain separate silos but with closer communication. Rather, it places behavioral health in the primary care setting, with behavioral care providers (BCPs) colocated and working side-by-side with primary care physicians (PCPs). Up to 85% of patients receiving behavioral interventions are seen in the primary care setting, with only 15% of the patients, mostly chronically psychotic or brain impaired, being referred to specialty mental health. Thus, the silos are eliminated, and along with them traditional barriers perpetuating mind-body dualism in healthcare delivery vanish. Preliminary data emerging from the aforementioned facilities that have adopted this model indicate that whereas in the traditional model only 10% of referrals for behavioral care ever go into treatment, almost 90% of those so identified undergo behavioral interventions by a BCP in the colocated model (Cummings, O'Donohue, & Ferguson, 2002). This is potentially a ninefold expansion of psychology's current economic base. As APA president, Levant (2004) made colocated behavioral primary care one of his top priorities, and hopefully psychology will not again miss an economic opportunity. It remains to be seen whether our silo-trained practitioners are ready to leave their offices to work in the primary care trenches. It further remains to be seen whether the university training programs rise to the need to train psychologists for the forthcoming era, or whether social workers will once again co-opt the market.

THE ECONOMIC WINNERS AND LOSERS IN THE NEW HEALTHCARE ENVIRONMENT

The psychiatric hospital, which in 1985 was regarded by Wall Street as a growth industry, is undoubtedly the major loser in the new healthcare economy. The advent of DRGs in medicine and surgery prompted the hospitals to convert their empty beds, as many as 50% in some cases, to psychiatric beds that were not subject to DRGs. New and hastily formed psychiatric inpatient programs were extensively advertised, especially those for troublesome adolescents, all at the expense of health insurance. A short-lived boom followed, soon curtailed by the MBHOs that reduced psychiatric hospitalization by 95% using draconian measures, and funneling patients to outpatient psychotherapy. The boom then shifted in favor of the psychotherapist, resulting in a decade (1985–1995) of unprecedented economic prosperity for psychologists and social workers. During this era, psychology became the preeminent psychotherapy profession, a status that had been long in coming, and lulled our colleagues into the false belief it was here to stay.

Hospitals have since reinvented themselves, scaling back psychiatric wards to appropriate sizes, and they are once again doing well. Psychology had ample time to heed the warning as the impact on independent solo practice took somewhat longer to be apparent, but it was no less devastating. By the mid-1990s, the private practitioner was well aware of the tenuous nature of psychotherapy practice that followed the implementation of stringent measures to tether outpatient psychotherapy costs (Oss, 1995). Social workers rapidly adjusted to managed care and are now performing as much as two-thirds of all outpatient psychotherapy. Psychology, by contrast, demonstrated amazing inflexibility as it dug in its heels and set out to roll back the clock by legislative and judicial means, a losing way to attempt the repeal of economic forces (Cummings, 2000; Cummings, Pallak, & Cummings, 1996).

Years have passed and most psychologists still don't get it: Assessment and practice take place in an economic context, and the solutions to their plight are economic. Supply and demand considerations are the farthest from their minds as they wonder what happened to their practices, and our clinical psychology programs pump out more and more graduates looking to go into the private practice of psychotherapy. A prominent practitioner (Sherman, 2004, p. 21), quoted a colleague and proffered the lament as typical of the feelings of psychologist practitioners: "David stated with some angst that, in keeping with inflation, everything attached to his practice—his rent, his billing service, phones, pagers, insurance—all have gone up over the years but not the fee that he is allowed to charge his clients through these plans. He indicated that most of the patients don't have any inkling about pricing structure. Before I could interject a word, he went on to say, 'I used to be proud of my profession but I may have to leave it entirely or supplement my career with some other part-time work.'" What was the author's solution? Contribute more money to psychological organizations to support advocacy that would restore the old, bygone, and still unrecognized economically outmoded days (Sherman, 2004).

A GLIMPSE INTO THE NEAR FUTURE

Medicine is often two decades ahead of psychology in matters of practice, and medical schools are already including business and finance courses in their curricula. Almost a decade ago, medicine created a new degree, master of medical management (MMM), to help physicians cope in the new industrialized environment. Finally, to help current and future psychologists and other behavioral care providers comprehend health-care economics, and in a rare display of solidarity, a number of academics and practitioners have come together to create the electronic master of behavioral health administration degree (MBHA). The curriculum has been written, with courses in health economics, finance, health delivery program evaluation and implementation, and other courses found in the usual business MBA, but with an emphasis on activities and knowledge that pertain specifically to behavioral healthcare delivery. It will be online, available to practicing psychologists and other behavioral care providers who want to upgrade their skills, and become tomorrow's leaders and innovators in behavioral healthcare delivery systems.

In the meantime, it would be prudent for every practicing behavioral care provider, as well as every clinical psychology researcher, to begin by reading Sowell (2003) and Feldstein (1996). This is not merely a practitioner problem, because in the future of psychotherapy development and evaluation we must augment evidence-based treatment (EBT) with economically viable treatment (EVT). Only by understanding the economic forces that predestine practice, and how to successfully employ strategies accordingly, will psychology rise above its current professional and emotional depression.

KEY TERMS

Entrepreneurship: The innovation and founding of a new entrepreneurial endeavor, as contrasted with entrepreneurial, which pertains to the ongoing business and management of an established entity.

Managed care: The first manifestation in the delivery of health services after the health care field industrialized in circa 1985 to 1990, with other alliterations now following.

Professional practitioner: A provider of mental health whose primary livelihood derives from dispensing services in an independent setting, be it in a solo (alone) or in a group arrangement.

Rationing: The ubiquitous and inevitable limitation of healthcare services in response to worldwide shortages of health resources. Rationing may be explicit as practiced in managed care, or silent when it results from long waiting lists, shortages of providers, or unavailability of medications and other healthcare supplies.

Supply and demand: The economic "laws" that influence the cost of goods and services, in which oversupply and low demand tend to suppress prices, while short supply and high demand tend to inflate them.

Third-party payer (also **payor**): An entity, usually private insurer or government, which is independent of both the patient and practitioner, that reimburses either the patient or the provider for approved health services rendered.

RECOMMENDED READINGS

Cummings, N. A., Cummings, J. L., & Johnson, J. N. (Eds.). (1997). *Behavioral health in primary care: A guide for clinical integration.* Madison, CT: Psychosocial Press.

Cummings, N. A., O'Donohue, W. T., & Ferguson, K. E. (Eds.). (2002). *The impact of medical cost offset on practice and research: Making it work for you.* Volume 5: Cummings Foundation for Behavioral Health: Healthcare utilization and cost series. Reno, NV: Context Press.

Cummings, N. A., Pallak, M. S., & Cummings, J. L. (Eds.). (1996). *Surviving the demise of solo practice.* Madison, CT: Psychosocial Press.

Feldstein, P. J. (2001). *Health care economics* (6th edition). Albany, NY: Delmar.

Sowell, T. (2003). *Applied economics.* New York: Basic Books.

Weitz, R. D. (Ed.). (2000). *Psycho-economics: Managed care in mental health in the new millennium.* Binghamton, NY: Haworth.

REFERENCES

Ally, G. (2004, July/August). Louisiana medical psychologists gain prescription authority. *National Psychologist, 13*(4), 1 and 3.

American Psychiatric Association (1994). *Diagnostic and Statistical Manual of Mental Disorders,* 4th Ed., Washington, DC.

Antonuccio, D. O., Danton, W. G., & DeNelsky, G. Y. (1999). Raising questions about antidepressants. *Psychotherapy and Psychosomatic Medicine, 68*(1), 3–14.

Bergin, A. E., & Garfield, S. L. (Eds.). (1994). *Handbook of psychotherapy and behavior change* (4th edition). New York: Wiley.

Bickman, L. (1996). A continuum of care: More is not always better. *American Psychologist, 51,* 689–701.

Bradshaw, J. (2004, July/August). HMOs win Supreme Court challenge. *National Psychologist, 13*(4), 2.

Budman, S. H., & Gurman, A. S. (1988). *Theory and practice of brief therapy.* New York: Guilford.

Carnahan, I. (2002, January 21). Asylum for the insane. *Forbes*, 33–34.

Carville, J. (1992 and 1996). "It's the economy, stupid." Statement frequently repeated on regular television appearances during the Clinton election and reelection campaigns on *Meet the Press*. Washington, DC: NBC News.

Cummings, N. A. (1986). The dismantling of our health system: Strategies for the survival of psychological practice. *American Psychologist, 41*, 426–431.

Cummings, N. A. (2000). The first decade of managed behavioral care: What went right and what went wrong? *Critical Strategies: Psychotherapy in Managed Care, 1*, 19–30.

Cummings, N. A. (2001). A new vision of healthcare for America. In N. A. Cummings, W. O'Donohue, S. C. Hayes, & V. Follette (Eds.), *Integrated behavioral health: Positioning mental health practice with medical/surgical practice*. San Diego, CA: Academic Press.

Cummings, N. A. (2002). Are healthcare practitioners economic illiterates? *Families, Systems, and Health, 20*(4), 383–393.

Cummings, N. A. (2003). Just one more time: Competencies as a refrain. *Register Reports, 29* (Spring), 12–13.

Cummings, N. A. (2005). Expanding a shrinking economic base: The right way, the wrong way, and the mental health way. In R. H. Wright & N. A. Cummings (Eds.), *Destructive trends in mental health: The well-intentioned path to harm*. New York: Brunner-Routledge (Taylor and Francis Group).

Cummings, N. A., Cummings, J. L., & Johnson, J. N. (1997). *Behavioral health in primary care: A guide for clinical integration*. Madison, CT: Psychosocial Press (an imprint of International Universities Press).

Cummings, N. A., Bodman, S. H., & Thomas, J. L. (1998). Efficient psycho-therapy as a viable response to scarce resources and rationing of treatment. *Professional Psychology: Research and Practice, 29*(5), 460–469.

Cummings, N. A., & Fernandez, L. (1985, March). Exciting new opportunities for psychologists in the market place. *Independent Practitioner, 5*, 38–42.

Cummings, N. A., & Follette, W. T. (1968). Psychiatric services and medical utilization in a prepaid health plan setting: Part 2. *Medical Care, 6*, 31–41.

Cummings, N. A., O'Donohue, W. T., & Ferguson, K. E. (2002). *The impact of medical cost offset on practice and research: Making it work for you*. Cummings Foundation for Behavioral Health: Healthcare utilization and cost series, volume 5. Reno, NV: Context Press.

Cummings, N. A., Pallak, M. S., & Cummings, J. L. (1996). *Surviving the demise of solo practice: Mental health professionals prospering in the era of managed care*. Madison, CT: Psychosocial Press (an imprint of International Universities Press).

Cummings, N. A., & Wiggins, J. G. (2001). A collaborative primary care/behavioral health model for the use of psychotropic medication for children and adolescents. *Issues in Interdisciplinary Care, 3*(2), 121–128.

Fairley, S. G., & Stout, C. E. (2004). *Getting started in personal and executive coaching*. San Francisco, CA: Jossey-Bass (a Wiley Company).

Feldstein, P. J. (1996). *Health care economics* (5th edition). Albany, NY: Delmar.

Follette, W. T., & Cummings, N. A. (1967). Psychiatric services and medical utilization in a prepaid health plan setting. *Medical Care, 5*, 25–35.

Fox, R. E. (2004). The cold hard facts. *Independent Practitioner, 24*(3), 110.

Friedman, M. (2004, January 27). Keynote address to the World Health Care Congress, Washington, DC.

Glasser, W. (2003). *Psychiatry can be hazardous to your mental health.* New York: HarperCollins.

Jones, K. R., & Vischi, T. R. (1979). The impact of alcohol, drug abuse, and mental health treatment on medical care utilization.: A review of the research literature. *Medical Care, 17* (suppl.), 43–131.

Jones, K. R., & Vischi, T. R. (1980). *The Bethesda Consensus Conference on Medical Offset: Alcohol, drug abuse and mental health administration report.* Rockville, MD: Alcohol, Drug Abuse, and Mental Health Administration.

Kent, A. J., & Hersen, M. (2000). *A psychologist's proactive guide to managed mental health care.* Mahwah, NJ: Lawrence Erlbaum Associates.

Lambert, M. J. (1992). Psychotherapy outcome research: Implications for integrative and eclectic therapists. In J. C. Norcross & M. R. Goldfried (Eds.), *Handbook of psychotherapy integration* (pp. 94–129). New York: Basic Books.

Levant, R. F. (2004). 21st century psychology: Toward a biopsychosocial model. *Independent Practitioner, 24*(3), 128–1390.

Lilenfeld, S. O., Fowler, K. A., Lohr, J. M., & Lynn, S. J. (2005). Pseudoscience, nonscience, and nonsense in clinical psychology. In R. H. Wright & N. A. Cummings (Eds.), Destructive trends in mental health: The well intentioned path to harm, pp. 187–218. New York: Routledge.

Lilienfeld, S. O., Lynn, S. J., & Lohr, J. M. (Eds.). (2003). *Science and pseudoscience in clinical psychology.* New York: Guilford.

Mackie, R. (2004, June 10). Ontario budget will re-introduce health-care premiums. *Canada,* 1 and 9.

McNally, R. J. (2003a). As extensively quoted in S. Begley, Is trauma debriefing worse than letting victims heal naturally? *Wall Street Journal,* September 12, B1.

McNally, R. J. (2003b). *Remembering trauma.* Cambridge, MA: Belknap/Harvard University.

Miller, I. P. (1996a). Ethical and liability issues concerning invisible rationing. *Professional Psychology: Research and Practice, 27,* 583–587.

Miller, I. P. (1996b). Some "short-term therapy values" are a formula for invisible rationing. *Professional Psychology: Research and Practice, 27,* 577–582.

Miller, I. P. (1996c). Time-limited therapy has gone too far: The result is invisible rationing. *Professional Psychology: Research and Practice, 27,* 567–576.

O'Donohue, W. T. (2002). Introduction to J. L. Thomas, J. L. Cummings, and W. T. O'Donohue (Eds.), *The entrepreneur in psychology: The collected papers of Nicholas A. Cummings* (Vol. 2). Phoenix, AZ: Zeig, Tucker & Theisen.

Oss, M. (1995). More Americans enrolled in managed behavioral care. *Open minds, 12,* 1–3.

Rosemond, J. (2005). The diseasing of America's children: The politics of diagnosis. In R. H. Wright & N. A. Cummings (Eds.), *Destructive trends in mental health: The well-intentioned path to harm.* New York: Brunner-Routledge (Taylor and Francis Group).

Sherman, R. (2004). Professional practice: Reversing a downward trend. *California Psychologist, 37*(4), 21.

Sowell, T. (2003). *Applied economics.* New York: Basic Books.

Spencer, J. (2003, May 22). When blue skies bring on the blues: Research shows why some despair on sunny days and relish gloom of winter. *Wall Street Journal,* D1–2.

Thomas, J. L., Cummings, J. L., & O'Donohue, W. T. (2002). *The entrepreneur in psychology: The collected papers of Nicholas A. Cummings* (Vol. 2). Phoenix, AZ: Zeig, Tucker & Theisen.

Weitz, R. D. (Ed.). (2000). *Psycho-economics: Managed care in mental health in the new millennium.* New York: Haworth.

Wright, R. H. (1992). Toward a political solution to psychology's dilemmas. *Independent Practitioner, 12*(3), 111–113.

Wright, R. H. (2005a). Attention deficit hyperactivity disorder: What it is, and what it is not. In R. H. Wright & N. A. Cummings (Eds.), *Destructive trends in mental health: The well-intentioned road to harm.* New York, NY: Brunner-Routledge (Taylor and Francis Group).

Wright, R. H. (2005b). Introduction to R. H. Wright & N. A. Cummings (Eds.), *Destructive trends in mental health: The well-intentioned road to harm.* New York: Brunner-Routledge (Taylor and Francis Group).

Wright, R. H., & Cummings, N. A. (2002). *The practice of psychology: The battle for professionalism.* Phoeniz, AZ: Zeig, Tucker & Theisen.

The Great Paradigms of Clinical Science

9

Evolution-Based Learning Mechanisms Can Contribute to Both Adaptive and Problematic Behavior

WILLIAM TIMBERLAKE

The experimental study of learning has been a major contributor to the ability of scientists and practitioners to produce, analyze, and control learned behavior in humans and nonhumans, in both the laboratory and in everyday life. During the first half of the 20th century, laboratory research systematically advanced the study of learning beyond descriptive and anthropomorphic accounts by introducing two powerful reinforcement procedures that reliably produced and controlled learned behavior. One of these procedures is Pavlovian conditioning—the presentation of reward contingent on a predictive cue (as in signaling proximate food to your dog by opening the cupboard where food is stored). The other is operant conditioning—the presentation of reward contingent on the performance of a specific behavior (as in presenting a treat to your dog only when it holds up a paw, or giving a weekly allowance to a child only after she does her chores). Elements of Pavlovian and operant procedures often intertwine, as in your signaling a car trip to the dog by picking up your keys (based on Pavlovian pairings of key sounds and trips in the car), followed by requiring the dog to sit before you open the car door (based on an operant contingency in which access to the car follows the required response of sitting).

During the second half of the 20th century, learning procedures increased in complexity and application in areas such as complex reinforcement contingencies, stimulus learning, niche-related learning, and neurophysiological systems. *Complex reinforcement contingencies* (see Ferster & Skinner, 1957; Pear, 2001) include: *schedules of reinforcement*, in which reward is contingent on satisfying combinations of response frequency and timing; *discriminated operants*, in which responding is controlled by cues that signal the reinforcement schedule in effect; *response chaining*, in which the performance of one response requirement produces an opportunity to perform a second response, the performance of which produces access to a third response, and so on, until the terminal response is reached and reward obtained; and *shaping* (see Peterson, 2004), in which the organism is incrementally trained to perform a task by rewarding successively closer approximations to the target behavior.

Complex stimulus contingencies and processing include: computation of predictive relations between cues and rewards (Rescorla, 1967; Baker et al., 2001); perceptual learning (Goldstone, 2003; Kellman, 2002; Hall, 2001) and multiple forms of memory (Atkinson & Shiffrin, 1968; Squire & Knowlton, 2000); and how learning about cues positively or negatively predicting important events may interfere with or facilitate subsequent learning about redundant and contradictory cues (Rescorla & Wagner, 1972; Denniston et al., 2001). For example, learning first that the clothing colors of a street gang predict danger can interfere with subsequent learning that a particular location predicts danger independent of gang colors, but it can facilitate learning that the colors of another gang predict safety.

Niche-related learning refers to learning guided and constrained by evolved mechanisms selected to facilitate specific forms of adaptive learning in particular (niche-related) circumstances. Examples include: generating aversions to the taste and smell of novel foods following an experience of nausea (Garcia & Garcia y Robertson, 1997); acquiring the spatial direction and locations of commodities and dangers relevant to survival (Collett, 2002); and attachment learning between precocial young and their mothers (Bateson & Horn, 1994; Gubernick, 1981). Finally, evidence continues to accumulate about the relation of forms of learning to *specific cellular substrates and neurophysiological systems*, including: specialized neuronal subsystems for sensory analysis (see Krasne, 2002), different circuitry related to types of fear-learning (e.g., Fendt & Fanselow, 1999); cortical locations involved in face recognition in multiple species (e.g., McCarthy, 2000; Peirce & Kendrick, 2002), and the specificity of dominant transmitters involved in different forms of foraging behavior (e.g., see Tinsley et al., 2000, 2001).

However, despite the increased scope and complexity of concepts, procedures, and the role of neurophysiology, the dominant view of learning remains focused on the role of reinforcement in producing adaptive outcomes. Identification of predictive cues, efficient response selection, and engagement of relevant motivational processes are all considered part of the general adaptive qualities of reinforcement (Hollis, 1997; Rescorla; 1988). Skinner (1966) even argued that reinforcement in the form of "selection by consequences" is a common causal process underlying not just responding to learning contingencies but also to the development of culture, and the course of evolution itself.

Given the dominance of the adaptive view of reinforcement learning, most researchers, practitioners, and theorists have viewed maladaptive, problematic behavior as resulting from inappropriate or problematic reinforcement contingencies, like the beatings delivered by Charles Dicken's unsavory character Fagen (in *Oliver Twist*) to compel his band of ragamuffins to steal for him. Other problematic behaviors have been attributed to unrecognized or inadequately enforced reinforcement contingencies, as in the case of children who whine until their parents give them a new computer game, or the case of patients who engage in self-injurious behavior controlled partly by the resultant attention they receive (Iwata et al., 1994).

Given this view, the obvious solution for controlling problematic behavior is to remove the contingencies supporting antisocial, selfish, disruptive, self-defeating, or destructive behaviors and replace them with contingencies promoting more socially effective behaviors. Skinner championed this approach in his groundbreaking books *Walden Two* (Skinner, 1948b) and *Science and Human Behavior* (Skinner, 1953). This conceptual analysis of reinforcement combined with the developed technology of operant conditioning has led to successful interventions related to a variety of problematic behaviors, ranging, for example, from autism (Kamps et al., 2002; Lovaas, 1977) and stuttering (Ingham et al., 2001) to antisocial and self-injurious behavior (Iwata et al., 1994).

However, the point of this chapter is not just to call attention to how inappropriate or inefficient contingencies can be modified to produce more effective behavior (Timberlake, 1980, 1993, 2002). Instead, my major purpose is to clarify how common environmental contingencies can interact with niche-related evolutionary mechanisms to produce problematic and even incapacitating effects, such as misbehavior, phobias, addictions, irrational responses, and conflict behavior. I will focus on why such inappropriate behaviors are often easily learned and yet highly resistant to alteration or redirection using other contingencies. The learning results I review argue for continued effort in developing a complex, nuanced view of learning, one better grounded in how the evolutionary and developmental history of an organism affects the outcome of environmental contingencies.

The reasons that maladaptive behaviors occur in adaptive learning circumstances lie in how the organism's circumstances interact with niche-related (evolution-based) learning mechanisms selected for in the species' evolutionary past. From an evolutionary view, learning mechanisms exist because, on balance, their results have been adaptive; they have differentially promoted survival. In other words, the presence of learning mechanisms increased survival and reproduction by enhancing the flexibility, speed, and/or accuracy with which individuals: (1) identify cues predicting important resources (such as safety, status, food, and mates), (2) select responses to efficiently gain access to these resources, and (3) engage and regulate motivational states that promote efficient behavior related to predictive cues and contexts.

A critical and underappreciated point is that the functions of learning differ sufficiently from one circumstance to another that it is possible to select mechanisms specialized for notably greater effectiveness and efficiency in one context than in another. For example, consider that the memory mechanisms evolved to permanently store song learning in a bird are likely to have been selected for different characteristics than the memory mechanisms evolved to store the momentary spatial location of recent seed caches (see Sherry & Schacter, 1987). Furthermore, analysis of motor system performance (as well as experience with designing machines such as special-purpose robots) provides evidence for the view that selecting for one learning characteristic, such as speed, results in mechanisms that typically place limits on other learning characteristics, such as accuracy or flexibility of outcome.

In short, the more that evolutionary pressures have canalized and restricted learning in specific environmental circumstances, the more likely that a relatively small change in these circumstances will interact with the underlying mechanisms in highly atypical ("unforeseen") ways that can result in problematic outcomes. For example, selection for minimizing the exposure necessary for a newly hatched duckling to identify and follow its mother appears to have placed potential restrictions on the accuracy of such learning. For example, ducklings will persist in following a beach ball or a dog provided it is the first sizable moving stimulus they come in contact with following hatching.

It is true that many such learning mechanisms appear to have evolved with "safety" mechanisms that help avoid completely inappropriate forms of learning. For example, ducklings that imprint on the auditory calls of their mother while in the egg increase the chances they will imprint on a visual stimulus emitting the same call, rather than a silent basketball or whining dog. Humans often use the "safety" mechanisms of planning ahead and modifying their learning in line with an anticipated goal. So if a student is going to visit Spain in 4 months and would like to learn Russian someday, the student usually focuses on learning Spanish first.

However, the usefulness of such safety mechanisms can be compromised by the interaction of evolved mechanisms with changes in circumstances. For example, if a well-meaning duck lover places a portable television in the nest box to keep eggs company, the duckling may remain near the TV after hatching. In general, specific knowledge about the components and circumstances that control learning is important in maintaining or not interfering with the adaptive expression of niche-related learning.

A major goal of the rest of this chapter is to suggest a framework for analyzing circumstances in which evolutionary mechanisms can contribute to both efficient and problematic outcomes of Pavlovian and operant contingencies (see also Chapter 11 for a discussion of evolutionary models of behavior). Such a framework should provide a starting point for helping produce more adaptive and less problematic learned behavior. The first section clarifies the nature of problematic behavior and how we can know that learning mechanisms contributed to it. The second section introduces concepts from a behavior systems approach (Timberlake, 1994, 2001; Timberlake & Lucas, 1989). Clarifying these concepts should identify motivational organization and perceptual-motor reactions and help analyze how they interact with each other and with procedures and circumstances to produce both adaptive and problematic behavior. The third section applies this framework to four types of learning that can produce problematic behavior.

TWO INITIAL QUESTIONS

What is problematic behavior? Although we usually recognize problematic behavior when we see it, providing an adequate universal definition is difficult. For example, behavior judged as problematic by your friends or spouse may include forgetting birthdays and wearing mismatched socks. In the legal system, problematic behavior involves behavior that harms another person directly or indirectly through action against their person, property, future earnings, or reputation. Governments usually define as problematic any behavior that interferes with their functioning and/or fails to follow their edicts. For logicians, problematic behavior is illogical behavior that does not follow from basic premises. In short, to a surprising extent, problematic behavior depends on the audience. Thus, behavior that will get you jailed or worse in one culture is tolerated or even encouraged in another. Despite such obvious definitional difficulties, here is a potentially workable starting point—problematic behavior is recurring behavior that competes or interferes with an organism reaching goals or expectations supported by its evolutionary, biological, and/or environmental context.

How can we determine that problematic behavior is produced by learning? Hopefully, the future will bring assistance from correlations of molar learned behavior with molecular changes in the behavior of the brain as revealed by changes in metabolism or blood flow measured by ever-improving recording and scanning techniques. More information also will accrue as we develop genetic techniques to clarify how a small change in a single gene or the qualities of a transmitter substance can influence an entire network of neurons producing a cascade of changes in early development and later learning (Boldogkoi, 2004). However, even with the next generation of technology, we still will be a notable distance from understanding and predicting the behavioral functions of learning from

neurophysiology alone, and, thus, still distant from identifying the neurological basis of problematic qualities.

At present, the most direct evidence for the involvement of learning
in problematic behavior is that we can produce the behavior by applying learning procedures. Less direct evidence is provided by an ability
to modify already existing problematic behavior by applying learning
procedures. The weakest evidence for a role of learning in problematic
behavior is provided by the resemblance of temporal configurations of
stimuli, responses, and potential reinforcers to the configurations present
in operant or Pavlovian conditioning. It should be clear that neither
familiar temporal configurations of potential learning elements nor the
ability to use learning procedures to generate or modify problematic
behavior compel the conclusion that learning is *necessary* to produce the
behavior. However, the more of these criteria (production, modification,
and stimulus-response-reward configurations) satisfied in a situation,
the more likely that learning contributed to the development and control
of problematic behavior present.

A CONCEPTUAL FRAMEWORK FOR ADAPTIVE AND PROBLEMATIC LEARNED BEHAVIOR

Learning evolved as a function of structures and processes that reliably
linked learned behavior to the survival and reproduction of individuals.
When some circumstances change (due to altered environmental and
social ecology, genetic changes, or their interaction), the niche-related
mechanisms that facilitated survival by improved learning may now
produce problematic behavior (Timberlake, 2002). A popular example of
how the same mechanisms can produce both adaptive and problematic
outcomes relates to the remarkable abilities of humans to recognize
and to strongly prefer foods that taste "fatty," "sweet," or "salty." These
taste abilities appear to have evolved to promote our discovery of these
important and relatively scarce and hard-to-get resources. Ancestors who
used these cues in determining what to eat were more likely to survive
than those who did not. A problematic side of these abilities is revealed
when such resources are constantly available in the environment with
few physical demands for obtaining them. The expected result is already
with us—an increasingly overweight population in less than optimal
health because of food preferences that once promoted survival but
now promote overeating and associated diseases.

A second case, related more directly to the effects of experience, involves
the ability of human immune system cells to "learn" to recognize poisons
or irritants, such as wasp venom or pollen, and to produce histamine with
enhanced speed and volume (Janeway et al., 2004). Problematically, an
enhanced histamine reaction can interfere seriously with breathing. Thus,
an experience-based improvement in a protective reaction can in some

circumstances endanger the same organism it evolved to protect. Similarly, an arousal system designed to mobilize fight or flight in the presence of extreme predation risk or dangerous social ostracization can lead to problematic fear or aggression when linked by learning to minor social status issues such as receiving a "B" on a test, or overhearing an unflattering evaluation of one's wardrobe. In short, when circumstances differ sufficiently from those of the selection environment, evolved learning mechanisms can produce costly, goal-interfering, and even dangerous, outcomes.

A behavior systems approach provides a general conceptual framework intended to capture important aspects of organism-environment interactions in which learning has been selected to occur (Timberlake 1983, 1993, 2001; Timberlake & Lucas, 1989). This framework is based on observational and experimental data and embodies the view that purposive behavior is organized around regulated motivational-emotional systems related to functions such as defense, intake of food and water, reproduction, and social contact and status. Each motivational system is expressed through learned and unlearned, flexible and fixed, perceptual-motor processing "units" (action modules) supported by the environment and memory, primed by the system, and triggered by relevant cues.

The repertoire of specific action modules varies with the environment and with the sequence of search states organized with respect to local goals: a *general search state* controls access to learned and unlearned actions related to persistent, often systematic, search for an absent goal; a *focal search state* controls access to learned and unlearned actions related to local search for an imminent goal, and an *interacting/consuming state* controls access to learned and unlearned actions related to interactive commerce with the goal. Cues prime or inhibit systems, search states, and the expression of specific action modules. For example, a conditioned stimulus predicting food for a deprived animal will prime the feeding system, as well as a search state, and potential perceptual-motor modules appropriate to the perceived temporal and spatial proximity of food. The behavior expressed will depend on the system, the search state, the availability of perceptual triggering filters, and the environmental support (affordances) for particular responses.

Learning takes multiple forms, including response integration and differentiation plus changes in stimulus priming and environmental affordances supporting particular responses. *Positive reinforcement* of specific cues, responses, and contexts is usually based on transitions from a motivational state farther from the goal state to one that is closer. For example, moving from general to focal search for food, or from acute fear to lower fear, are both positively reinforcing because the organism enters a state more proximate to the goal state (consuming food or successfully avoiding harm).

In contrast, circumstances that compel a transition from a positive goal state to a more distant search state are punishing. For example, being forced away from social contact with a friend is punishing, as is being forced out of a safe situation into a fearful one. Furthermore, to the extent that the state transition is unexpected, the effects often are amplified. Although this analysis of reinforcement in terms of transitions between motivational states is largely behavioral, such a systems organization of state transitions and repertoires lends itself to integration with neurophysiology and development (see Fanselow, 1994; Fendt & Fanselow, 1999; and Amorapanth et al., 2000, for neurophysiological analysis of fear/defense components; and see Hogan, 1994, for conceptual ties to development).

In a behavior system learning does not occur *de novo*, based on arbitrarily interchangeable and recombinable stimuli, responses, motivations, and environments. Instead, learning is grounded in the interaction of environmental support with evolved and experientially developed learning mechanisms, motivational states, stimulus sensitivities, and motor organization, which the organism brings with it to the learning situation. How then can we account for the apparent interchangeability of different stimuli, responses, and motivational systems in producing particular learning effects? The answer lies in three interrelated characteristics of learning research.

First, most species have a number of attentional and locomotor behaviors that they use in conjunction with multiple motivational systems. Thus, experimenters can usually identify a repertoire of cues and actions that will work in several circumstances. Second, many species (with humans an obvious example) show great flexibility in the development of sensory control and skilled motor performance. The basis of this flexibility lies in specialized mechanisms organized in frontal and parietal cortexes, which integrate gaze direction and reaching with a wide variety of environmental cues (see Shadmehr & Wise, 2005). Third, successful experimenters routinely "tune" the procedures and apparatus of operant and Pavlovian experimental paradigms to produce more vigorous, reliable, and interpretable responding by selecting cues and response measures that work well for a particular situation and species. The data suggest that such tuning works precisely because it brings elements of specific motivational systems in contact with evolved, niche-related learning mechanisms (see Timberlake, 1994, 2002, 2003). In other words, the common practice of carefully tuning apparatus and procedures can make contact with evolved special-purpose mechanisms, while still allowing experimenters to describe and account for their experiments in terms of abstract, general concepts and models.

Given this view, it seems unlikely that any species evolved primarily to learn about artificial stimuli or produce arbitrary responses; it seems more likely that organisms react to artificial stimuli on the basis of approximate fits to perceptual-motor modules that evolved to fit tasks related to specific ecological niches. This issue has relevance to the recent point of Domjan, Cusato, and Krause (2004) that, compared to artificial stimuli, learning with ecologically relevant CSs is more resistant to blocking, extinction and the debilitating effects of long CS-US intervals. The differences they cite seem consistent with the likelihood that tuned, ecologically relevant CSs engage evolved perceptual-motor mechanisms and search states of a particular behavior system better than do less well-tuned, "artificial" stimuli.

Finally, it is worth pointing out that the behavior systems approach has both general and specific qualities. For example, the transitions between search states that promote learning are similar in many systems, but their timing with respect to reward and, especially, their repertoires of perceptual-motor modules can vary considerably with the system and the species. Similarly, in a behavior system view, both Pavlovian and operant procedures engage the same underlying framework of states and perceptual-motor structures; however, they do not engage and support these states and structures in the same way. The effects of the timing of contingencies, the kinds of cues employed by experimenters, and the focus of the attention on behavior differ in Pavlovian and operant conditioning.

In short, animals respond to "arbitrary" cues based on the best fit of the general and specific perceptual filters and response affordances available, given the circumstances and the activated systems and repertoires. In the "field" the functions of learning and behavior are usually easier to classify into systems and species-specific repertoires. In the laboratory, the selection and tuning of cues, response affordances, and procedures still make contact with evolved special purpose mechanisms but allow experimenters to describe and account for their results using abstract general concepts and models.

HOW EVOLVED LEARNING MECHANISMS CAN PROMOTE PROBLEMATIC BEHAVIOR: FOUR KINDS OF EXAMPLES

We are ready now to ask our basic question—in what circumstances are typical learning procedures likely to produce problematic behavior? In answering this question, I will consider four kinds of examples of how learning can contribute: (1) previous perceptual-motor learning; (2) presenting reinforcers; (3) conditioning predictive cues; and (4) reinforcing responses.

Problematic Effects of Previous Perceptual-Motor Learning

I will begin with a few examples in which common perceptual-motor learning, well practiced in a previous setting, can interfere markedly with learning and behavior in the present circumstance. For many of us, this effect shows up when we buy new consumer electronic gear. A current problem of mine is finding the delete key on the keyboard of my notebook computer after working for many years on a desktop computer. The key is not even close to the same location! Such interference is often just annoying (unless you are working on deadline), but interference arising from switching such "mappings" can be critical in driving a car.

A few of you may recall the awkwardness of changing from a car with a manual transmission to an automatic. In that case when you brake with your right foot, your left foot keeps stomping around searching for the "missing" clutch pedal. Switching from driving in America to driving in England provides an even more riveting experience of interference. In driving in America, you learn to stay on the right side of the road and glance to the left at intersections before turning right. Unfortunately, these well-integrated actions can produce downright dangerous results in England, where the rules are opposite—stay on the left side of the road, and glance to the right before turning immediately left. Tracking such marked reversals requires considerable discriminative control and practice (e.g., when approaching a roundabout in England, repeat the mantra over and over, "look right, turn left").

Examples of interference related to social systems can be even more complex and damaging. Many human adults continue to use behaviors developed in relating to members of their family of origin to deal unsuccessfully with other adults not in their family. In the case of cultural traditions, the failure to adapt to altered environmental circumstances can threaten the group's survival. For example, Diamond (2005) pointed out that long-standing Norwegian cultural practices in building, farming, hunting, and raising livestock appeared to doom the Norse attempt to settle Greenland. The settlers did not adapt their cultural customs to the poorer soil, shorter growing season, and different resources, and starvation finally ended their attempt. The fall of the rich civilization on Easter Island may well have been a result of a similar conflict between cultural practices involving the extravagant use of wood, and the ecological requirements for survival on an isolated island with limited resources of both timber and food.

Problematic Effects of Presenting Reinforcers

Problematic learning effects are not limited to changing circumstances involving complex skills and social customs. Simply presenting a negative event in a particular environment can prime a motivational system, including search states, actions, and sensitivities to environmental affordances, thereby markedly affecting subsequent behavior in that environment. For example, a single shock to a rat in a new environment increases freezing and cautious sniffing in that apparatus. Anecdotal reports indicate that unexpectedly encountering a coiled, poisonous snake along a path produces persistent vigilance and avoidance near the spot. In the case of positive reinforcers, a single presentation of a receptive female Japanese quail in an apparatus is sufficient to semipermanently alter a male's activity and focus of attention in that environment (Domjan, 1994). In humans, the discovery of a quarter on a sidewalk by a 6-year-old boy is sufficient to produce persistent ground watching for days.

Three characteristics of behaviors that follow a single reinforcer presentation in a controlled environment are: (1) behaviors are organized in time; (2) behaviors are problematic in that they are unnecessary, having no current effect on the delivery of the reinforcer; and (3) behaviors are related to perceptual-motor modules in the reinforcer system that could be functional in environments that resemble the circumstances of selection. The first two characteristics are accentuated when reinforcers are regularly presented at short fixed intervals, as well as at long (especially circadian) intervals, the two circumstances I consider next.

Fixed-Time Delivery of Reward
(Superstition and Adjunctive Behavior)

The presentation of small amounts of food to pigeons at fixed intervals in the 6–20 sec range rapidly produces stereotyped, repetitive behavior during the interval between rewards. Skinner (1948a) called this behavior "superstitious." In his view, the behavior was produced by the accidental contingency of a response and reward, which strengthened the response, thereby increasing its probability, and, thus, the likelihood that it would again be accidentally followed by food, and so on. The importance of calling the pigeon's behavior "superstitious" was that it provided a framework for explaining the odd behaviors that humans engage in within the general reinforcement model of a simple perceived connection between their behavior and an important outcome (e.g., wearing a particular pair of socks while your team is winning or hopping over sidewalk cracks to protect your mother's back).

A notable problem is that Skinner's focus on beliefs and arbitrary repetitive behaviors distracted attention from the qualities of reinforcer-related behavior predictable from a behavior system's analysis of niche-related mechanisms. A pigeon's behavior under a 15-sec fixed-time food schedule is organized across the entire interval, beginning with a brief circling away from the hopper after feeding, usually followed by extensive focal search in the form of head bobbing and stepping back and forth at the hopper wall. The behavior is obviously unnecessary and appears related to the feeding system. The stepping, head-bobbing behavior most resembles 14- to 19-day-old nestling squab begging for the regurgitation of food from a recently arrived parent (Timberlake & Lucas, 1985).

However, when food is presented on the same schedule from a hopper under a hole in the floor, distant from any wall, the stimulus conditions are markedly changed, and the pigeon's resultant behavior resembles foraging in a field. Furthermore, when food is presented from a wall hopper at longer intervals, pigeons engage in more extensive locomotor search, including pacing along the wall (Innis et al., 1983). If water rather than food is presented, pigeons show water search (twisting their beak in the hopper, soft pecking of the wall, and waiting motionless by the water source—Reberg et al., 1978). Other species of birds and the laboratory rat show their own characteristic search behaviors when food or water is presented at fixed intervals up to 8 minutes (e.g., Lucas et al., 1988; Timberlake & Lucas, 1991).

An important question is whether superstitious behavior in humans can be framed using similar system concepts. At the least, some superstitious behaviors appear based on task-relevant anticipatory behaviors. For example, many stereotyped motor movements displayed by a batter facing a fast pitcher are potentially task-relevant, including: repeatedly tightening and loosening gloves, gripping the bat, and making rhythmic motions that synchronize bat and body movement with the release of the ball.

Circadian Timing

Both activity and complex metabolic, neural, and endocrine changes show temporal synchronization across repeated circadian intervals (approximately 24 hours). Exposure to a circadian light-dark schedule entrains a rest-activity cycle that incorporates a remarkable number of body processes (including changes in body temperature, blood volume, calcium, pH, and melatonin levels—Moore-Ede et al, 1982). Neither planning nor practice facilitates this cycle, nor can they prevent persistence of the rest-activity cycle in a changed environment. For example, after flying from the United States to Germany, your body rhythms are prepared to go to bed around 4:00 a.m. and get up at noon, regardless of your thoughts and desires. Such persistence of the rest-activity cycle in the absence of a supporting light cycle is adaptive on overcast days, but it is problematic in an era of air travel. Your body must deal with the problem by adjusting to the new light-dark cycle (albeit at its own rate of approximately 2 hours per day).

Circadian and Compensatory Conditioning of Meals. Interestingly, a large, regularly timed daily meal also will entrain an increase in activity, independent of the light-dark cycle (Stephan, 1997; White & Timberlake, 1999), as well as the compensatory insulin release that typically precedes intake (Woods, 1991). These results relate specifically to the feeding system. The entrainment of activity promotes searching for food beginning 2–3 hours before its presentation; the anticipatory release of insulin prepares the digestive system to deal with a large amount of food in a short time. It could be argued that rats that searched for food in the "vicinity" of previous times and previous places probably found food more reliably than organisms that carefully waited until the precise time they last ate or who only searched at a single location. As might be expected, the timing of the anticipatory activity resets (when food is moved) more rapidly than the circadian rest-activity cycle resets to light changes; however, both effects appear focused on circadian intervals. If a meal is regularly presented at a longer interval (e.g., 31 hours), rats do not anticipate that interval; instead their meal "time-keeper," like that in humans, assumes a circadian universe and produces increased activity 22–26 hours after a large meal (White & Timberlake, 1999), the time a reliable circadian food source should reappear (see Crystal, 2003, for possible interval clocks).

Circadian and Compensatory Drug Actions. Other data suggest that a hefty dose of an addictive drug, like amphetamine, resembles food in supporting increased activity preceding the injection time (Kosobud et al., 1998; Pecoraro et al., 2000), and in producing physiological reactions that increase tolerance for the effects of the drug. Similar to the way that conditioned insulin secretion produces "tolerance" for the effects of a large meal, the development of drug tolerance appears based on the body rapidly mobilizing compensatory reactions in advance of drug administration, which counteract the physiological effects of the drug (Siegel, 1999a). Although most research has focused on environmental context mediators of the tolerance effect, it seems possible that tolerance effects also may be related to circadian entrainment processes. For our purposes here, note that experience-based circadian and compensatory reactions can be both adaptive and problematic, depending on the circumstances.

Problematic Effects of Conditioning Responses and Systems to Predictive Cues

In this section, I consider the argument that Pavlovian conditioning procedures, because they typically control specific stimuli predicting proximate reward, should more reliably produce specific adaptive and problematic learning than simply presenting unsignalled reinforcers. I evaluate this possibility by reviewing the use of predictive cues to condition both more variable search and avoidance responses and more proximate stereotyped *defensive* and *appetitive reactions* (e.g., taste aversion and sign-tracking), as well as priming entire motivational and emotional systems related to defense, foraging, and reproduction (see Domjan, 2005, for a review of Pavlovian conditioning in multiple systems, and Timberlake, 1994, for a related account).

Conditioning Defensive Reactions to Predictive Cues

Problematic behavior appears often in learning related to *defensive reactions*, relatively fixed and stereotyped reactions to gut cues (taste-nausea), contamination cues, "skin" (pain) cues, panic cues, and suffocation cues. Learning of proximate *defensive reactions* is often rapid and constrained in terms of controlling cues; it is apparently evolved to facilitate survival given immediate, direct survival threats. However, in circumstances I outline later, the efficient and constrained nature of conditioning *defensive reactions* can overreact to danger (recall the immune system example), as well as make erroneous connections between danger and available cues. Both results can produce highly problematic effects.

Internal Body Defense: Gut Defense Reactions. Taste-aversion learning is a highly organized defensive conditioning reaction experienced by most humans at some time (Garcia & Garcia y Robertson, 1985). The phenomenon involves one-trial emergence of aversion to a novel taste/odor that is followed within 8–12 hours by nausea. My own encounter involved eating snails for the first time followed by stomach flu 5 hours later. The gut defense subsystem combines taste and olfactory inputs with information on gut status and toxicity at the level of the parabracheal nucleus in the brain stem; higher cortical areas have no direct input to this system. Thus, it is understandable that although "I knew" that the snails did not cause my stomach virus, my nose and taste buds unshakably blamed the snails, and, ever since, have defended me vigorously against them. Such problematic learning is not humorous when a patient associates novel taste-smells with nausea due to radiation or chemotherapy treatments and can't continue until this side effect is controlled. The point is that highly integrated defense systems speed learning about predictive cues but can produce debilitating errors of "causal inference" not easily reversed.

Internal Body Defense: Social Contamination Reactions. Paul Rozin and his collaborators have worked extensively on the role of learning in the development of the socially influenced phenomenon of contamination. For example, children at a young age will drink water out of a glass that contains a cockroach (dead and sterilized), but at older ages they will refuse to drink even when the cockroaches are frozen inside sealed plastic cubes. Reactions to assumed contaminants range from the nausea of gut reactions, to the physical "fending off" of skin-defense reactions, and even full-blown panic reactions.

In an evolutionary context, there are clear advantages to avoiding disease-related contaminants (pathogens). But, possibly because humans until recently had no way to observe many pathogens directly, we have created a "magical" perception of contagion based on contact, thereby linking it to social customs and status. Cultural aspects can be seen in the refusal of most Hindus to wear clothing related in any way to an inferior caste (Hejmadi et al., 2004), whereas most Americans refuse to wear clothes previously worn by a murderer, no matter how many times they are washed (Rozin & Nemeroff, 1990). On the good "contamination" side, people will stand in long lines and spend money for the opportunity to gain contact with a cultural hero by means of a look, word, handshake, or signature.

External Body Defense: Pain-Defense (Circa-Strike) Reactions. Similar complex reactions to threatening stimuli can occur with body-defense threats. Bakeless (2004) summarized a journal entry by 18th-century explorer Meriwether Lewis describing a harrowing encounter with an aroused grizzly bear. He narrowly escaped with his life by leaping into a river. Lewis wrote, "It now seemed to me that all the beasts of the neighborhood had made a league to destroy me" (Bakeless, 2004, p. 187). He reported shooting at any movement around him as he hurried back to camp. In neurophysiological terms, we would say that his amygdala was primed by a traumatic encounter and he subsequently reacted to the slightest signs of threat with vigorous defensive attack, a reaction Fanselow (1994) labeled "circa-strike behavior." Although learned, shooting here appears to be extreme "fending off" behavior, depending on fast, low-resolution subcortical visual pathways that use rough recognition algorithms to trigger defensive actions.

Research in the late 1950s unknowingly demonstrated such fast pathway defensive behavior to cues paired with light shock to the fingers. Even when these cues were presented too rapidly to be cognitively distinguished from control cues, the amygdaloid system "knew" them and produced a sizable GSR (galvanic skin response). Social cues also interact with the pain-defense system, both in terms of the involvement of the cingulate cortex with both physical and social pain (Eisenberger & Lieberman, 2004), and in terms of danger cues biasing the perception of an ambiguous object in a picture as a function of the race of the observer and that of the person holding the object (Larsen, 2004).

External Body Defense: Panic and Suffocation Reactions. There is a very large literature on the occurrence of panic and suffocation reactions (some of it summarized in Bouton et al., 2001, and in many therapy texts). Panic reactions appear akin to random escape reactions under extreme threat in many mammals, a behavior of last resort. They involve a near cessation of stimulus processing in favor of escape and "fending off" behavior. Suffocation reactions add persistent exaggerated (and often counterproductive) attempts to breathe and strike out at proximate obstacles under conditions of stress and shortness of breath. Differences among individuals in these reactions make it difficult to observationally separate these reactions from each other and from other acute reactions, like extreme phobias. However, it seems likely that they all engage a common core of stereotyped *defensive reactions*.

Conditioning Defensive Systems to Predictive Cues

Stereotyped *defensive reactions* (circa-strike attack appeasement, panic/suffocation resistance, freezing, and refusal of contact with food or contaminated objects) are characteristic of proximate defense of immediate body functioning and integrity and are triggered initially by relatively specific unconditioned cues, but with learning can be triggered by a broader array of stimuli. More appetitive defensive states are expressed in initially more variable anticipatory behaviors such as vigilance, withdrawal, and avoidance, controlled by more distant cues. Defensive systems appear to have been selected over evolutionary time to prime, learn, and trigger behaviors that reduce the likelihood of reaching a terminal *defensive reaction* but also to increase the effectiveness and speed of the terminal reaction. Unfortunately, learning related to both avoiding a terminal reaction and increasing the effectiveness of the terminal reaction can produce more extensive and generally incapacitating effects than the terminal reaction itself.

In the next several paragraphs, we will consider briefly how Defensive Systems can be involved in common defensive behaviors labeled as: phobias, obsessive-compulsive disorder (OCD), panic disorder, and posttraumatic stress syndrome (e.g., Thorpe & Olson, 1997). First, though, two comments are relevant. In this brief review, I selectively review clusters of primed perceptual-motor reactions that appear related to motivational substates within defensive systems, but without attempting to tie these actions to diagnosis categories (see DSM-IV). Second, it is worth noting that even *gut-defense reactions* can be related to distant vigilance behaviors. For example, a single pairing of odors and smells with nausea immediately controls terminal *defensive reactions;* but with repetition of pairings these stereotyped reactions can be transferred to general environmental cues and locations (e.g., Timberlake & Melcer, 1988). At this point, taste-nausea behavior is controlled more like one of the external defensive system syndromes considered below, with general vigilance effects and avoidance of locations. Similarly, in the case of contamination reactions, predictive taste cues are likely to engage *gut-defense reactions*, whereas visual cues can produce fending off circa-strike reactions.

Phobias refer to specific stimulus objects and environmental circumstances that organisms often fear with little or no experience, and that produce defense system actions, ranging from avoidance and/or freezing, to circa-strike and taste-nausea reactions (as in the case of germs). Like contamination behavior, phobias can be socially transmitted and facilitated. For example, Mineka and Cook (1993; see Mineka & Ohman, 2002) showed that naïve captive-reared rhesus monkeys with no fear of snakes readily learned to fear them if they saw familiar monkeys display fear to a snake or to a bag shown later to contain a snake. However, monkeys did not fear a flower that clever experimental procedures also made appear to be an object of fear in other monkeys. Note that the problematic effect of phobias is a result of the cost of extreme vigilance and avoidance when phobic cues, or cues loosely related to phobic cues, are present. Severely phobic organisms can become incapacitated or show disorganized escape behavior similar to panic in the presence of such cues.

Panic disorder refers to the fear-based avoidance of circumstances and cues associated with increased fear and body sensations similar to those associated with panic breathing. Built-in defensive and compensatory reactions appear to play an important role in the development of panic disorder, such that increased breathing rate and heart-rate acceleration may actually facilitate full-blown panic or suffocation reactions. Many sufferers from panic disorder avoid crowded and noisy public areas because the feelings they produce relate to those preceding a panic attack. It may be that sufferers of multiple chemical sensitivities avoid exposure to particular odors or circumstances because of similar feelings of imminent panic/suffocation. Siegel (1999b) has pointed out that multiple chemical sensitivities often begin with an experience of fear in circumstances with strong novel odors (as would accompany a chemical spill in the workplace). The resultant sensitivity to a broader range of circumstances and/or odors may be caused by flattening of the generalization gradient across stimulus dimensions. In extreme forms, the behavior involved in avoiding stimuli that might trigger a panic attack can be sufficiently time consuming and complex to interfere with daily activities, sometimes reducing people to shut-ins.

Obsessive-Compulsive Disorder. The repetitive "checking" behavior characteristic of OCD appears to reflect repetitive vigilance and avoidance behaviors designed to maintain a distance from fearful, disruptive events, such as losing your wallet or someone breaking into your home. OCD vigilance behaviors are defense system analogues of general search behaviors in appetitive systems in that they are controlled by cues, such as door locks, that are only distantly related to the feared outcome. Thus, as with most appetitive behaviors, they are highly resistant to extinction. People often report being at loss to control OCD behavior, despite that it may add hours to the simple procedure of locking their home for the evening, visiting a public restroom, or preparing to go on vacation.

Posttraumatic stress disorder appears based on a sustained experience of acute danger and trauma with no ability to stop the trauma or control *defensive reactions* to it. A flashback to this experience is generally triggered unexpectedly by a combination of cues (such as sounds, smells, and "feel") that produce sharply accelerated heart rate, increased blood pressure, rapid, shallow breathing, and disruption of thought processes. It is often accompanied by an experience of "reliving" the stimulus conditions and defensive behaviors specific to the traumatic events. Reexperiencing trauma appears related to fast-pathway associations that are only fully activated under extreme arousal, and, thus, unlike typical hippocampally stored memories, they are not subject to ordinary interference or extinction (see LeDoux, 1996).

Dealing With a Defense System. Because so many of the behaviors primed, conditioned, and supported by a defense system are generally maladaptive, there have been many attempts to develop effective treatments. The current dominant approach to maladaptive fear reactions uses combinations of antianxiety drugs, relaxation techniques, controlled exposure (desensitization) to cues, and cognitive restructuring therapy (Bouton, 2002). The slowness of these procedures contrasts with the apparent effectiveness of context flooding in nonhuman animals (i.e., forcing the animal to remain in the fear-producing circumstance as opposed to allowing it to control its own exposure to the fear-producing circumstance; see e.g., Morokoff & Timberlake, 1971).

The argument against using flooding techniques is that the treatment itself may produce dangerous levels of stress as well as potential conditioning of fear and avoidance to still more cues. However, an argument against chemical, calming, and cognitive-based treatments is that they may not evoke enough of the original context to activate the amygdaloid complex and trigger the controlling memories to allow them to extinguish. More recent work by Bouton (2002) and his coworkers has raised this issue by showing that extinction of a specific aversive cue by itself (without the context) does not produce general unlearning. Unless the context has also been extinguished, replacing the organism in the original context reinstates the defense system and the specific behavioral effects of the cue.

A recent approach by McFall and his coworkers (personal communication, 2000) reduced OCD behavior by imposing a disequilibrium schedule (Timberlake, 1980, 1993) that required the person to cut in half their "checking" behavior each week to preserve full access to an important appetitive behavior, such as a leisurely coffee and pastry in the morning. The disequilibrium schedule is recomputed each week so that performing the previous week's average amount of "checking" provides access to only half the participant's coffee and pastry time each day. To regain access to the remainder, the participant must reduce their checking by half in the current week. The success of this procedure in reducing OCD behavior suggests that a schedule linking an appetitive system to the cues that control fear-based vigilance behavior may succeed more rapidly than long-term desensitization to environmental cues. This procedure resembles motivational counterconditioning based on a schedule-based connection between the OCD-related cues and delayed access to an appetitive behavior. In general, what seems clear is that there are common aspects to a fear system underlying the production of maladaptive behaviors, so that reducing the fear and understanding how the problematic behaviors function in the system can facilitate reducing them.

Conditioning Predictive Cues in Appetitive Systems (Including Sign-Tracking)

From a behavior systems view, appropriately engaging an evolved appetitive system, such as feeding or courting, should facilitate rapid, automatic learning in the same way that rapid automatic learning can occur with a defense system. If this assumption is so, problematic effects can occur in appetitive learning provided key requirements and supportive stimuli engage the structure of the system inappropriately. We will consider three examples.

Feeding System. The ability of cues predicting food to elicit foraging behavior has been known for some time. For example, Zener (1937) reported that if a dog trained to salivate in the presence of a light predicting food were released from its harness, it would engage in a variety of food-finding behaviors, including approaching, nosing, and licking the light (see Jenkins et al., 1978, for a well-controlled demonstration of food-begging in dogs to a cue predicting food). This kind of unnecessary search and contact behavior was labeled "sign-tracking" by Hearst and

Jenkins (1974) in their review of research that followed up the discovery of Brown and Jenkins (1968) that naïve pigeons would approach and vigorously peck a lighted key that predicted food without being trained to do so. As might be expected from its strong resemblance to operantly reinforced keypecking, sign-tracking led to a reassessment of the roles of operant and Pavlovian procedures in learning and a growing recognition that animals readily learn system-related terminal responses and actions under multiple training methods.

Given the variety of system-related search behaviors conditioned to predictive stimuli (Hearst & Jenkins, 1974; Suboski, 1990; Timberlake & Lucas, 1989), and their marked variation with the cue's qualities and temporal relation to reward, it seems evident there is a pervasive ability of specific cues predicting reward to engage system-related search reactions (e.g., Matthews & Lehrer, 1987; Silva & Timberlake, 1998). For example, Timberlake et al. (1982) showed that a ball bearing presented to a rat less than 4 sec before the delivery of food produced vigorous nosing in the feeder before food came; whereas a ball bearing presented more than 4 sec before food tended to produce persistent interaction with the bearing. In other words, a weaker focal state can be interrupted by a moving predictive cue related to alternative focal search; a stronger focal state is not disrupted. This variation based on a small timing difference supports the potential for precise temporal control of the differences in focal versus more general search states related to the temporal and physical distance to food.

Sign-tracking actions to predictive cues show problematic aspects of learning in two ways. First, they persist, although they are completely unnecessary to obtain the reward. Second, under a negative (omission) schedule that omits a reinforcer if the organism engages in the sanctioned activity, the organism often loses reinforcers. It is also worth considering that "irrational" impulsive choice behavior may occur because of a strong focal search state conditioned to proximate reward (Logue, 1998).

Reproductive System. The work of Domjan and collaborators has shown extensive evidence that male quail provided a cue predicting access to a willing female will exhibit conditioned courtship behavior (a fetish?) that depends on the support of the predictive cue (see Koksal et al., 2004). If the cue is a light, the quail will approach the location where the female will appear (Domjan, 1994; 1998). If the cue is a terry cloth "body" it will approach and neck grab; if the body has a head, it will attempt to mount it (Cusato & Domjan, 1998). In terms of timing, if a cue light begins over a minute before the female is presented, the quail will extensively search a double chamber, despite never finding a mate during the search (Akins et al., 1994). In all cases, the quail engages in behavior that is not needed to access the reward; further, this behavior is poorly controlled by operant omission contingencies that make access to the female contingent on omitting approach to the CS or area of the US.

Summary. The argument that our ability to identify and control stimuli predicting a reinforcer should produce less problematic learning appears to have a lot of counterevidence. If anything, learned identification of a CS that engages either an aversive or appetitive system can produce complex and extensive forms of unnecessary behavior. In fact, outside the laboratory cues that are not actually predictive of danger are frequently incorporated as supports for defense systems and as triggers for specific problematic actions, such as panic attacks, recurring traumatic episodes, phobic stimuli, or OCD behaviors. Interestingly, unnecessary behaviors also can occur in the presence of predictive stimuli and contexts related to feeding and mating systems.

PROBLEMATIC EFFECTS OF REINFORCING SPECIFIC RESPONSES

This section considers whether operant (instrumental) training, the designated "jewel" of adaptive learning, also shows susceptibility to problematic outcomes. Under operant conditioning procedures in which reward is contingent on the performance of a target response, many organisms rapidly learn and efficiently perform those responses. Furthermore, training response segments separately and then linking them together can produce complex chains of goal-directed responses. For example, in a demonstration, Skinner trained a rat he named "Pliny" to press a lever for a ball bearing, carry the bearing to a "chimney," lift it up, and drop it in to get food (Skinner, 1937).

However, that operant-like sign-tracking responses (keypecking in pigeons and lever manipulation in rats) are produced using only Pavlovian (stimulus-reward) contingencies between a key light and food strongly supports the view that classic operant conditioning is also based on organized systems and sensory-motor units. Further evidence for the contribution of organized systems and environmental support is provided by the analysis of experimenter tuning of apparatus and procedures in producing reliable and interpretable outcomes (Timberlake, 2002). We will add here three areas in which system organization interacts with operant training procedures and environmental support to produce problematic learning and behavior: conflicts between task requirements and system characteristics, the emergence of misbehavior, and interactions between systems.

Coherent Versus Conflicting Tasks and Systems

We all are intuitively aware of potential difficulties in combining just any response with any reinforcer. Rewarding a hyperaggressive dog for sitting in obedience class by allowing it to threaten or attack the next dog in line is inevitably less than optimal. Sevenster (1973), working with stickleback fish, provided a pretty piece of laboratory research in this area. He compared the ability of reproductive males to learn to swim through a wire circle versus biting the tip of a glass rod to produce the opportunity to display to a rival male stickleback versus court a reproductive female. As would be expected from observing reactions typically associated with aggression and with courtship, there was a marked interaction between the type of reward and the ease of performing the different operant requirements. Males found it easier to swim through a ring to court an attractive female, and to bite the tip of the rod to display to a rival male. Thus, based on the fit between the motivational system and the operant task, Sevenster found either highly efficient or problematic learned behavior.

Timberlake and White (1990) provided an example of the importance of the coherence of the environmental task structure with the underlying system structure in the case of rats searching a radial arm maze. Naïve deprived rats searching an unbaited and clean maze showed the same characteristic search efficiency as naïve rats searching a baited maze. Subsequent research showed that baiting only some of the arms did not change the tendency toward exhaustive and efficient search of the entire maze. Further work revealed evidence of a role for tactile orientation to the maze arms (Hoffman et al., 1999; Timberlake et al., 1999). In short, baiting none, some, or all arms of a typical radial maze has similar effects, indicating that the same niche-related search mechanisms underlie all learning in the maze.

Misbehavior and the Interaction of Operant and Pavlovian Contingencies

We owe to Keller and Marion Breland (1961) the careful documentation of misbehavior. The Brelands helped develop the shaping techniques of Skinner's laboratory at Minnesota and applied and expanded them in training animals for commercial purposes. They had considerable success shaping long sequences of behavior using a clicker signal previous closely paired with food. The clicker was an important contributor because it produced a transition to a search state closer to reward without disrupting the animal by the consummatory state of immediate food delivery. However, along with the Brelands' remarkable successes came surprising examples of "misbehavior," cases in which a painstakingly constructed sequence of responses suddenly fell apart when the operant requirements were slightly extended (Breland & Breland, 1961).

The most famous examples of misbehavior involved a miserly raccoon and a rooting pig. Both animals were shaped to pick up and transport coinlike tokens to drop in a container (a "piggy bank" in the case of the pig) to obtain food. All went well until the trainer asked the animals to pick up and transport two tokens in succession to obtain the reward. The animals then began to interact extensively with the first token rather than completing carrying it to and depositing it in the bank and continuing back to pick up the second token. The raccoon repeatedly "rinsed" the token by dipping it inside the can and rubbing it against the side; the pig repeatedly dropped the token and rooted it along the ground. The emergence of washing and rooting behaviors in the middle of an apparently successful learning task turned the animals from well-trained successes to problematic failures.

The Brelands attributed such phenomena to "instinctive drift," but we can now be more precise about the basis. From a behavior system view, the initial training of an operant chain involving picking up and transporting the token to a "bank," dropping it in, and receiving food produces a reliable close temporal pairing between transporting the token and food. The result of such pairings should be a focal search state conditioned to the token. When the trainer adds the requirement of transporting and depositing a second token after the first, the focal search state and its repertoire are no longer reliably interrupted by the delivery of food and the animal is faced with the punishment of a transition from the focal search state to a more general search state to go and fetch the second token. The result is that the animal remains in the focal search state longer, allowing emergence of other behaviors besides carrying. The raccoon's behavior of "washing" the first token is likely supported by the tactile similarity of the hard token to the shells of small crustacea extracted from the muddy bottoms of shallow ponds and stream, whereas the pig's behavior of rooting the tokens is likely related to their tactile similarity to hard ground tubers. In this view, the phenomenon of mis-behavior is a particularly clear example of how the same mechanisms that produce adaptive behavior in one situation can produce problematic behavior when the circumstances are slightly altered.

Conflicting Systems

Historically, a great deal has been made of the role of conflict in creating problematic behavior. For example, early attempts to create experimental neuroses in animals centered on presenting dogs with very difficult dis-criminations in the context of mild fear (Pavlov, 1927), or on creating conflict in cats between approaching food and avoiding a highly noxious blast of air (Masserman, 1943). At least in Masserman's case it is worth noting that the cat was not incapacitated by a within-system processing conflict but by a between-system conflict between approaching the food and avoiding the air blast, or perhaps (having a cat myself) just avoiding movement in the presence of danger regardless of the presence of food. In this section, we will consider three examples of how conflicting systems are involved in several known phenomena, and how they might be manipulated.

Punishment and Conflicting Systems. The use of punishment has been a source of grave ambivalence in American culture. Punishment is both highly recommended and fervently proscribed: "Spare the rod and spoil the child," versus " . . . a term commonly associated with abuse, ridicule, and revenge" (Axelrod, 1983). Two points are worth noting. First, given the behavior systems view of punishment as a transition from a search state more proximate to reward to one further away, punishment provides relevant feedback in most learning. In fact, a learning environment combining clear negative state transitions for wrong responses with clear positive state transitions for correct responses is usually highly effective. Second, most of the problems associated with punishment appear related to engaging a defense system related to avoidance of pain or social shame and rejection.

In other words, some applications of punishment, like some applications of reward, work well in a learning environment. Other applications of both punishment and reward (Perone, 2003) can produce problematic actions that interfere with effective learning. For example, if a mother wants her child not to run into the street, she can grab the child near the street and physically punish him or her. But, depending on the severity of the punishment, the proximity to the street, the attention of the child, and the demeanor of the mother, punishment may produce an avoidance reaction to the parent instead of the street, or to the street under all (undiscriminated) circumstances, or it may even encourage the child to run toward the street. Punishing children until they cry or calling attention in public to their foibles can engage shame and perceived rejection. Just as in the case of reward, the difference between effective and problematic punishment is a matter of circumstances and how underlying system structures and states are engaged.

Loss of Intrinsic Motivation. A long-standing belief in social psychology is that rewarding someone for engaging in a task destroys intrinsic motivation for that task (and perhaps similar tasks; e.g., Lepper & Greene, 1978; although see Eisenberger & Shanock, 2003). For example, if a child spontaneously draws pictures (an important example in this research), s/he is likely engaging in a form of motor exploration that involves refinable perceptual-motor mechanisms related to representing, completing, or extending visual patterns. An interesting aspect of drawing is that it can be related to a number of motivational systems, ranging from foraging to social interaction and constructing shelter. When a social system involving competition for social status is engaged by offering rewards, that system becomes salient and tied to the behavior. It is this tie that gives the appearance of destroying intrinsic motivation. The original perceptual motor substrate for drawing is not destroyed, but the salient reward-related demand characteristics of the circumstances must be changed in order to see it.

System Switching. In addition to the evidence from OCD treatment by contingencies mentioned earlier, I previously presented other evidence of how switching dominant motivational systems can be an efficient means of reducing or eliminating problem behavior (Timberlake, 1995). Peter Borchelt, a pet therapist, told me a lovely example about receiving an emergency call from a couple that had invited a new boss over for dinner. Too late to make other plans, the couple realized that their boss was a stranger to their dog, and their dog barked incessantly at strangers. Peter (who at that point in his career made house calls) went to their apartment and immediately received the severe barking treatment from the dog. Armed with a modest piece of cheese Peter seated himself alone in the front room. When the dog barked, Peter threw it a small piece of the cheese to eat. The result of continuing to throw the cheese to the dog each time it barked was that the dog was soon seated beside Peter's chair, begging for more cheese. Everyone was pleased, until Peter realized that from a strict reinforcement view, this outcome was confusing. Each time the dog barked Peter had reinforced it with cheese, and yet the dog had stopped barking instead of increasing barking. From a motivational system view, the outcome makes sense. By feeding the dog cheese, Peter had switched the dominant system from territorial defense to feeding.

I am indebted to Gary Lucas for an example in which an older man was subjected to noisy neighborhood kids playing in his yard every afternoon. When curmudgeonly behavior didn't help, he offered to pay them $5 a day to run around his yard yelling for an hour every afternoon after school. He paid them at the end of the hour each day, but after a week he told them he couldn't pay them any longer. Their retort was that if he wasn't going to pay them, they weren't going to yell in his yard anymore.

CONCLUSIONS

Research and theorizing about learning have focused on the ability of general reinforcement procedures to rapidly and efficiently change behavior. Maladaptive or problematic behavior usually has been attributed to inappropriate, inconsistent, or inadequate application of contingent reward. In contrast, the focus of this chapter has been on how learning procedures can produce both adaptive and maladaptive behavior, with and without Pavlovian or operant contingencies selecting for specific predictive stimuli or responses. In the present view, both adaptive and problematic behaviors result from the interaction of the environment with the specific organization underlying systems of behavior. It seems evident that learning mechanisms emerged over the course of evolution because they provided more accurate, flexible, and/or rapid adaptive behavior than did more fixed adaptations. But it also seems clear that learning mechanisms evolved within the context of particular regulatory systems involving goal-oriented states, perceptual-motor modules, and supportive environmental characteristics. Thus, learning mechanisms are "designed" to promote effective learning, but in particular types of environmental circumstances. In different circumstances, the same mechanisms may produce problematic learning and behavior. In other words, the same systems that produce adaptive learned behavior under some circumstances can produce problematic learned behavior under others.

Given that the basis of many behavioral and a number of cognitive therapies is provided by Skinner's general reinforcement approach to behavioral control, it may seem puzzling to argue that our best chance to avoid and reduce problematic effects of contingencies is based on a better understanding of the specific motivational organization, perceptual-motor modules, search states, and neural processing that underlie learning. All these concepts appear peripheral to the basic Skinnerian reinforcement approach. However, as I have pointed out elsewhere (e.g., Timberlake, 2003), Skinner's remarkable abilities to fit apparatus and procedures to his subject's capabilities argue that he, at least intuitively, understood the importance of evolved motivational and perceptual-motor structures and environmental support for learning. He simply focused his conceptual account on abstract statements of general procedures, and referred to his skillful use of evolved mechanisms in terms like "carving nature at the joints," "luck," and "selection by consequences," (Skinner, 1938, 1959, 1966).

Combining a niche-related behavior systems approach with common learning circumstances, procedures, and phenomena has the potential to help analyze and understand the circumstances for both adaptive and maladaptive learning, thereby providing a clearer basis for developing and implementing procedures that decrease or prevent problematic learned behavior. I think the continuing development of brain scanning and electophysiological techniques for humans (and nonhumans as well) increases the possibility of applying an integrative motivational and emotional systems approach to the understanding of problematic and adaptive learning in both humans and nonhumans. Among relevant recent discoveries is the evidence of common neural processing for physical pain and social rejection and separation (Eisenberger & Lieberman, 2004), suggesting involvement of a similar motivational-emotional system and similar kinds of related learning. In short, knowledge about the neurophysiological and functional design of niche-related mechanisms relevant to learning should help us understand the motivational, stimulus processing, and response organization underlying learned behavior and its relation to environmental cues and contingencies.

Author Notes. I thank Gary Lucas, Jackson Goodnight, and Rick Viken for helpful comments, Dick McFall for encouragement, and the editors for feedback and patience.

KEY TERMS

Behavior systems: Regulated motivational-emotional systems based on niche-related mechanisms selected during evolution to facilitate the learning and performance of adaptive behavior under a range of environmental circumstances; however, these mechanisms can, in unselected circumstances, produce maladaptive or problematic behavior. System components include a sequence of goal-related substates—ranging from general search to consummatory reactions in *appetitive systems*, and from vigilance to active resistance and protective reactions in *defensive systems*. Each substate primes a repertoire of learned and niche-related, perceptual motor modules. Particular modules are selected for expression by a combination of eliciting stimuli and environmental support for responses (affordances). A behavior system typically organizes combinations of learned and niche-related behavior that facilitate obtaining or avoiding specific regulatory cues or conditions.

Disequilibrium schedule: An operant schedule that links the expression of components of a behavior system in a way that disrupts their freely occurring (baseline) response levels. Under a reward schedule the organism must perform relatively more of the early component to gain access to the baseline amount of the second component. For example, given a baseline meal of consuming four peas and four cookies, a schedule in which a child must eat four peas to get access to each cookie should reinforce eating peas. Under a punishment schedule the organism must perform relatively less of one component to avoid being faced with a requirement to take in more than its baseline of the other component. For example, given the same four-pea, four-cookie baseline, a schedule in which a child must follow each cookie by eating six peas should decrease the number of cookies eaten relative to baseline.

Pavlovian and operant conditioning procedures: A Pavlovian conditioning procedure involves presenting a rewarding or punishing stimulus contingent on the presentation of a cue. An operant conditioning procedure involves presenting access to a reward or avoidance of a punisher contingent on the performance of a response. In both cases, the procedure has its effect because it engages and interacts with a functioning behavior system. The outcome of these procedures depends on the interaction of the stimulus or response contingency with the characteristics and support of the environment and system. Depending on the qualities of the system and the environment, and the timing of cues and responses predicting reward, the conditioning results for *appetitive systems* will involve consummatory, focal search, and/or general search behaviors, and for *defensive systems* will involve vigilance, avoidance, active resistance, and protective reactions. Pavlovian procedures produce multiple phenomena, including: autonomic conditioning, superstitious conditioning, autoshaping, adjunctive behavior, and aspects of misbehavior. Operant procedures include complex and simple schedules of relation between required responses and rewards (e.g., fixed and variable ratios, fixed and variable intervals, chaining, matching, delayed matching to sample, partial reinforcement, maze locomotion and choice, etc.).

Rewards and punishers: An appetitive reward is a stimulus correlated with a transition from a more distant search state to a search state or consummatory reaction more proximal to the goal of a behavior system. An aversive reward is a stimulus correlated with a transition from a reaction state closer to defense and pain reactions toward a reaction state farther away. An appetitive punisher is a stimulus correlated with a forced transition from a more proximal search or consummatory reaction state to a more distant search state. An aversive punisher is a stimulus correlated with a forced transition from vigilance or a distant avoidance state to a reaction state typically related to pain or fear.

Tuning: The often systematic adjustments by the experimenter to eliciting and supporting stimuli, response affordances, and conditioning contingencies to facilitate and support vigorous expression of a behavior system in a way interpretable and usable by the experimenter to control behavior. This frequently means engaging components of a system in the way they were selected to function in an evolutionary niche.

SUGGESTED READINGS

Bouton, M. E. (2002). Context, ambiguity, and unlearning: Sources of relapse after behavioral extinction. *Biological Psychiatry, 52,* 976–986.

Carroll, M. E. (2001). *Animal research and human health: Advancing human welfare through behavioral science.* Washington, DC: American Psychological Association.

O'Donohue, W. T. (1998). *Learning and behavior therapy.* Needham Heights, MA: Allyn & Bacon.

Siegel, S. (1999). Drug anticipation and drug addiction: The 1998 H. David Archibald Lecture. *Addiction, 94,* 1113–1124.

Timberlake, W., & Lucas, G. A. (1989). Behavior systems and learning: From misbehavior to general principles. In S. B. Klein & R. R. Mowrer (Eds.), *Contemporary learning theories: Instrumental conditioning theory and the impact of biological constraints on learning* (pp. 237–275). Hillsdale, NJ: Lawrence Erlbaum Associates.

REFERENCES

Akins, C. A., Domjan, M., & Gutierrez, G. (1994). Topography of sexually conditioned behavior in male Japanese quail (Coturnix japonica) depends on the CS-US interval. *Journal of Experimental Psychology: Animal Behavior Processes, 20,* 199–209.

Amorapanth, P., LeDoux, J. E., & Nader, K. (2000). Different lateral amygdala outputs mediate reactions and actions elicited by a fear-arousing stimulus. *Nature Neuroscience, 3,* 74–79.

Atkinson, R. C., & Shiffrin, R. M. (1968). Human memory: A proposed system and its control processes. In K. W. Spence & J. T. Spence (Eds.), *Psychology of learning and motivation.* New York: Academic Press.

Axelrod, S. (1983). Introduction. In S. Axelrod & J. Apsche (Eds.), *The effects of punishment on human behavior* (pp. 1–11). New York: Academic Press.

Bakeless, J. (2004). *The journals of Lewis and Clark.* New York: Signet.

Baker, A. G., Murphy, R. A., & Mehta, R. (2001). Contingency learning and causal reasoning. In R. R. Mowrer & S. B. Klein (Eds.), *Handbook of contemporary learning theories* (255–306), Mahwah, NJ: Lawrence Erlbaum Associates.

Bateson, P., & Horn, G. (1994). Imprinting and recognition memory: A neural net model. *Animal Behaviour, 48,* 695–715.

Boldogkoi, Z. (2004). Gene network polymorphism if the raw material of natural selection: The selfish gene network hypothesis. *Journal of Molecular Evolution, 59,* 340–357.

Bouton, M. E. (2002). Context, ambiguity, and unlearning: Sources of relapse after behavioral extinction. *Biological Psychiatry, 52*, 976–986.

Bouton, M. E., Mineka, S., & Barlow, D. H. (2001). A modern learning theory perspective on the etiology of panic disorder. *Psychological Review, 108*, 4–32.

Breland, K., & Breland, M. (1961). The misbehavior of organisms. *American Psychologist, 16*, 681–684.

Brown, P. L., & Jenkins, H. M. (1968). Auto-shaping the pigeon's key peck. *Journal of the Experimental Analysis of Behavior, 11*, 1–8.

Collett, T. S. (2002). Spatial learning. In R. Gallistel (Ed.) and H. Pashler (Ed.-in-Chief), *Steven's handbook of experimental psychology* (3rd ed., Vol. 3, pp. 301–364). New York: John Wiley & Sons.

Crystal, J. D. (2003). Nonlinearities in sensitivity to time: Implications for oscillator-based representations of interval and circadian clocks. In W. H. Meck (Ed.), *Functional and neural mechanisms of interval timing* (pp. 61–75). Boca Raton, FL: CRC Press.

Cusato, B., & Domjan, M. (1998). Special efficacy of sexual conditioned stimuli that include species typical cues: Tests with a conditioned stimulus pre-exposure design. *Learning & Motivation, 29*, 152–167.

Denniston, J. C., Savastano, H. I., & Miller, R. R. (2001). The extended comparator hypothesis: Learning by contiguity, responding by relative strength. In R. R. Mowrer & S. B. Klein (Eds.), *Handbook of contemporary learning theories* (pp. 65–117). Hillsdale, NJ: Lawrence Erlbaum Associates.

Diamond, J. (2005). *Collapse: How societies choose to fail or succeed.* New York: Penguin Group, USA.

Domjan, M. (1994). Formulation of a behavior system for sexual conditioning. *Psychonomic Bulletin & Review, 1*, 421–428.

Domjan, M. (1998). Going wild in the laboratory: Learning about species typical cues. In D. L. Medin (Ed.), *The psychology of learning and motivation* (Vol. 38, pp. 155–186). San Diego, CA: Academic Press.

Domjan, M. (2005). Pavlovian conditioning: A functional perspective. *Annual Review of Psychology, 56*, 179–206.

Domjan, M., Cusato, B., & Krause, M. (2004). Arbitrary versus ecological conditioned stimuli: Evidence from sexual conditioning. *Psychonomic Bulletin & Review, 11*, 232–246.

Eisenberger, N. I., & Lieberman, M. D. (2004). Why rejection hurts: A common neural alarm system for physical and social pain. *Trends in Cognitive Sciences, 8*, 294–300.

Eisenberger, R. & Shanock, L. (2003). Rewards, intrinsic motivation, and creativity: A case study of conceptual and methodological isolation. *Creativity Research Journal, 15*, 121–130.

Fanselow, M. S. (1994). Neural organization of the defense behavior system responsible for fear. *Psychonomic Bulletin & Review, 1*, 429–438.

Fendt, M., & Fanselow, M. (1999). The neuroanatomical and neurochemical basis of conditioned fear. *Neuroscience & Biobehavioral Reviews, 23*, 743–760.

Ferster, C. B., & Skinner, B. F. (1957). *Schedules of reinforcement.* New York: Appleton-Century-Crofts.

Garcia, J., & Garcia y Robertson, R. (1985). Evolution of learning mechanisms. In B. L. Hammonds (Ed.), *Psychology and learning* (pp. 191–243). Washington, DC: APA Press.

Goldstone, R. L. (2003). Perceptual learning/Invatarea perceptual. *Cognitie Creier Comportament, 7*, 31–59.

Gubernick, D. J. (1981). Mechanisms of maternal "labeling" in goats. *Animal Behaviour, 29*, 305–306.

Hall, G. (2001). Perceptual learning: Association and differentiation. In R. R. Mowrer & S. B. Klein (Eds.), *Handbook of contemporary learning theories* (pp. 367–408), Mahwah, NJ: Lawrence Erlbaum Associates.

Hearst, E., & Jenkins, H. M. (1974). Sign-Tracking: The stimulus-reinforcer relation and directed action. *Monograph of the Psychonomic Society.* Austin, TX: The Psychonomic Society.

Hejmadi, A., Rozin, P., & Siegel, M. (2004). Once in contact, always in contact: Contagious essence and conceptions of purification in American and Hindu Indian children. *Developmental Psychology, 40*, 1612–49.

Hoffman, C. M., Timberlake, W., Leffel, J., & Gont, R. (1999). How is radial-arm maze behavior related to locomotor search tactics? *Animal Learning & Behavior, 27*, 426–444.

Hogan, J. A. (1994). Structure and development of behavior systems. *Psychonomic Bulletin & Review, 1*, 439–450.

Hollis, K. L. (1997). Contemporary research on Pavlovian conditioning: A "new" functional analysis. *American Psychologist, 52*, 956–965.

Ingham, R. J., Kilgo, M., Ingham, J. C., Moglia, R., Belknap, H., & Sanchez, T. (2001). Evaluation of a stuttering treatment based on reduction of short phonation intervals. *Journal of Speech, Language, & Hearing Research, 44*, 1229–1244.

Innis, N. K., Simmelhag-Grant, V. L., & Staddon, J. E. R. (1983). Behavior introduced by periodic food delivery: The effects of interfood interval. *Journal of the Experimental Analysis of Behavior, 39*, 309–322.

Iwata, B. A., Pace, G. M., Dorsey, M. F., Zarcone, J. R., Vollmer, T. R., Smith, R. G., et al. (1994). The functions of self-injurious behavior: An experimental-epidemiological analysis. *Journal of Applied Behavior Analysis, 27*, 215–240.

Janeway, C. A., Travers, P., Walport, M., & Shlomchik, M. (2004). *Immunobiology* (6th ed.). New York: Garland Science Publishing.

Jenkins, H. M. Barrera, C. Ireland, C., & Woodside, B. (1978). Signal-centered action patterns of dogs in appetitive classical conditioning. *Learning & Motivation, 9*, 272–296.

Kamps, D., Royer, J., Dugan, R., Kravits, R., G. Gonzalez-Lopez, A. Garcia, J., et al. (2002). *Exceptional Children, 68*, 173–187.

Kellman, P. J. (2002). Perceptual learning. In R. Gallistel (Ed.) & H. Pashler (Ed.-in-Chief), *Steven's handbook of experimental psychology* (3rd ed., Vol. 3, pp. 259–299). New York: John Wiley & Sons.

Koksal, F., Domjan, M., Kurt, A., Sertel, O., Orung, S., Bowers, R., et al. (2004). An animal model of fetishism. *Behaviour Research & Therapy, 42*, 1421–1434.

Kosobud, A. E. K., Pecoraro, N. C., Rebec, G. V., & Timberlake, W. (1998). Circadian activity precedes daily methamphetamine injections in the rat. *Neuroscience Letters, 250*, 99–102.

Krasne, F. (2002). Neural analysis of learning in simple systems. In R. Gallistel (Ed.) & H. Pashler (Ed.-in-Chief), *Steven's handbook of experimental psychology* (3rd ed., Vol. 3, pp. 131–200). New York: John Wiley & Sons.

Larsen, R. J. (2004). Emotion and cognition: The case of automatic vigilance. *Psychological Science Agenda* (APA online), *18*, No. 11, 1–4.

LeDoux, J. E. (1996). *The emotional brain: The mysterious underpinnings of emotional life.* New York: Simon & Schuster, Inc.

Lepper, M. R., & Greene, D. (Eds.). (1978). *The hidden costs of reward: New perspectives on the psychology of human motivation.* Oxford, UK: Lawrence Erlbaum.

Logue, A. W. (1998). Self-control. In W. T. O'Donohue (Ed.), *Learning and behavior therapy* (pp. 215–226). Needham Heights, MA: Allyn & Bacon.

Lovaas, O. I. (1977). *The autistic child: Language development through behavior modification.* New York: Irvington.

Lucas, G. A., Timberlake, W., & Gawley, D. J. (1988). Adjunctive behavior in the rat under periodic food delivery in a 24-hr environment. *Animal Learning & Behavior, 16,* 19–30.

Masserman, J H. (1943). *Behavior and neurosis.* Chicago: University of Chicago Press.

Matthews, T. J., & Lerer, B. E. (1987). Behavior patterns in pigeons during autoshaping with an incremental conditioned stimulus. *Animal Learning & Behavior, 15,* 69–75.

McCarthy, G. (2000). Physiological studies of face processing in humans. In Gazzaniga (Ed.), *The new cognitive neurosciences* (2nd ed; pp. 393–410). Cambridge MA: MIT Press.

Mineka, S., & Cook, M. (1993). Mechanisms underlying observational conditioning of fear in monkeys. *Journal of Experimental Psychology: General, 122,* 23–38.

Mineka, S., & Ohman, A. (2002). Phobias and preparedness: The selective, automatic, and encapsulated nature of fear. *Biological Psychiatry, 52,* 927–937.

Moore-Ede, M. C., Sulzman, F. M., & Fuller, C. A. (1982). *The clocks that time us.* Cambridge, MA: Harvard University Press.

Morokoff, P., & Timberlake, W. (1971). Cue exposure and overt fear responses as determinants of extinction of avoidance in rats. *Journal of Comparative and Physiological Psychology, 77,* 432–438.

Pavlov, I. P. (1927). *Conditioned reflexes: An investigation of the physiological activity of the cerebral cortex.* Oxford, UK: Oxford University Press.

Pear, J. J. (2001). *The science of learning.* New York: Psychology Press.

Pecoraro, N., Timberlake, W., & Tinsley, M. (1999). Incentive downshifts evoke search behavior in rats (*Rattus norvegicus*). *Journal of Experimental Psychology: Animal Behavior Processes, 25,* 153–167.

Pecoraro N., Kosobud, A. E., Rebec, G. V., & Timberlake, W. (2000). Long Tau methamphetamine schedules produce circadian ensuing drug activity in rats. *Physiology and Behavior, 70,* 1–12.

Peirce, J. W., & Kendrick, K. M. (2002). Functional asymmetry in sheep temporal cortex. *Neuroreport: For Rapid Communication of Neuroscience Research, 13,* 2395–2399.

Perone, M. (2003). Negative effects of positive reinforcement. *The Behavior Analyst, 26,* 1–14.

Peterson, G. (2004). A day of great illumination: B. F. Skinner's discovery of shaping. *Journal of the Experimental Analysis of Behavior, 82,* 317–328.

Reberg, D., Innis, N. K., Mann, B., & Eizenga, C. (1978). "Superstitious" behavior resulting from periodic response-independent presentations of food or water. *Animal Behaviour, 26,* 506–519.

Rescorla, R. A. (1967). Pavlovian conditioning and its proper control procedures. *Psychological Review, 74,* 71–80.

Rescorla, R. A. (1988). Behavioral studies of Pavlovian conditioning. *Annual Review of Neuroscience, 11,* 329–352.

Rescorla, R. A., & Wagner, A. R. (1972). A theory of Pavlovian conditioning: Variations in the effectiveness of reinforcement and nonreinforcement. In A. H. Black & W. F. Prokasy (Eds.), *Classical conditioning: I. Current research and theory.* New York: Appleton-Century-Crofts.

Rozin, P., & Nemeroff, C. (1990). The laws of sympathetic magic: Psychological analysis of similarity and contagion. In J. Stigler, R. A. Shweder, & G. Herdt (Eds.), *Cultural psychology: Essays on comparative human development.* Cambridge: Cambridge University Press.

Sevenster, P. (1973). Incompatibility of response and reward. In R. A. Hinde & J. Stevenson-Hinde (Eds.), *Constraints on learning: Limitations and predispositions* (pp. 263–283). New York: Academic Press.

Shadmehr, R., & Wise, S. P. (2005). The computational neurobiology of reaching and pointing: A foundation for motor learning. Cambridge, MA: MIT Press.

Sherry, D. F., & Schacter, D. L. (1987). The evolution of multiple memory systems. *Psychological Review, 94,* 439–454.

Siegel, S. (1999a). Drug anticipation and drug addiction: The 1998 H. David Archibald Lecture. *Addiction, 94,* 1113–1124.

Siegel, S. (1999b). Multiple chemical sensitivity as a conditional response. *Toxicology and Industrial Health, 15,* 323–330.

Silva, K. M., & Timberlake, W. (1998). A behavior systems view of responding to probe stimuli during an interfood clock. *Animal Learning & Behavior, 26,* 313–325.

Skinner, B. F. (1937). Rat works slot machine for a living. *Life, 2,* 80–81.

Skinner, B. F. (1948a). Superstition in the pigeon. *Journal of Experimental Psychology, 38,* 168–172.

Skinner, B. F. (1948b). *Walden two.* Oxford: Macmillan.

Skinner, B. F. (1953). *Science and human behavior.* Oxford: Macmillan.

Skinner, B. F. (1959). A case history of the scientific method. In S. Koch (Ed.), *Psychology: A study of a science. Study I.: Conceptual and systematic. Volume 2. General systematic formulations, learning, and special processes* (pp. 359–379). New York: McGraw-Hill.

Skinner, B. F. (1966). The phylogeny and ontogeny of behavior. *Science, 153,* 1205–1213.

Squire, L. R., & Knowlton, B. J. (2000). The medial temporal lobe, the hippocampus, and the memory systems of the brain. In M. Gazzaniga (Ed.), *The new cognitive neurosciences* (2nd ed., pp. 765–780). Cambridge, MA: MIT Press.

Stephan, F. K. (1997). Calories affect zeitgeber properties of the feeding-entrained circadian oscillator. *Physiology & Behavior, 62,* 995–1002.

Suboski, M. D. (1990). Releaser-induced recognition learning. *Psychological Review, 97,* 271–284.

Thorndike, E. L. (1932). *The fundamentals of learning.* New York: Teachers College, Columbia University.

Thorpe, G. L., & Olson, S. L. (1997). *Behavior therapy: Concepts, procedures, and applications.* Needham Heights, MA: Allyn & Bacon.

Timberlake, W. (1980). A molar equilibrium theory of learned performance. In G. H. Bower (Ed.), *Psychology of learning and motivation* (Vol. 14). New York: Academic Press.

Timberlake, W. (1983). The functional organization of appetitive behavior: Behavior systems and learning. In M. D. Zeiler & P. Harzem (Eds.), *Advances in the analysis of behavior: Vol. 3. Biological factors in learning,* (pp. 177–221). Chichester: Wiley.

Timberlake, W. (1993). Behavior systems and reinforcement: An integrative approach. *Journal of the Experimental Analysis of Behavior, 60,* 105–128.

Timberlake, W. (1994). Behavior systems, associationism, and Pavlovian conditioning. *Psychonomic Bulletin & Review, 1,* 405–420.

Timberlake, W. (1995). Reconceptualizing reinforcement: A causal system approach to reinforcement and behavior change. In W. O'Donohue & L. Krasner (Eds.), *Theories in behavior therapy* (pp. 59–96). Washington, DC: APA Books.

Timberlake, W. (2001). Motivational modes in behavior systems. In R. R. Mowrer and S. B. Klein (Eds.), *Handbook of contemporary learning theories* (pp. 155–209). Hillsdale, NJ: Lawrence Erlbaum Associates.

Timberlake, W. (2002). Niche-related learning in laboratory paradigms: The case of maze behavior in laboratory rats. *Behavioural Brain Research, 134,* 355–374.

Timberlake, W. (2004). Is the operant contingency enough for a science of behavior? *Behavior and Philosophy, 32,* 197–229.

Timberlake, W., Leffel, J., & Hoffman, C. M. (1999). Stimulus control and function of arm-following by rats on a radial-arm floor maze. *Animal Learning & Behavior, 27,* 445–460.

Timberlake, W., & Lucas, G. A. (1985). The basis of superstitious behavior: Chance contingency, stimulus substitution, or appetitive behavior? *Journal of the Experimental Analysis of Behavior, 44,* 279–299.

Timberlake, W. & Lucas, G. A. (1989). Behavior systems and learning: From misbehavior to general principles. In S. B. Klein & R. R. Mowrer (Eds.), *Contemporary learning theories: Instrumental conditioning theory and the impact of biological constraints on learning* (pp. 237–275). Hillsdale, NJ: Erlbaum.

Timberlake, W., & Lucas, G. A. (1991). Periodic water, interwater interval, and adjunctive behavior in a 24-hour multi-response environment. *Animal Learning and Behavior, 19,* 369–380.

Timberlake, W., & Melcer, T. (1988). Effects of poisoning on predatory and ingestive behavior toward artificial prey in rats (*Rattus norvegicus*). *Journal of Comparative Psychology, 102,* 182–187.

Timberlake, W., Wahl, G., & King, D. (1982). Stimulus and response contingencies in the misbehavior of rats. *Journal of Experimental Psychology: Animal Behavior Processes, 8,* 62–85.

Timberlake, W., & White, W. (1990). Winning isn't everything: Rats need only food deprivation not food reward to traverse a radial arm maze efficiently. *Learning and Motivation, 21,* 153–163.

Tinsley, M. R., Rebec, G. V., & Timberlake, W. (2000). Facilitation of preparatory behavior in an artificial prey paradigm by D1 dopamine receptor activation. *Behavioral Brain Research, 114,* 23–30.

Tinsley, M. R., Rebec, G. V., & Timberlake, W. (2001). Facilitation of efficient search of an unbaited radial-arm maze in rats by D1, but not D2, dopamine receptors. *Pharmacology, Biochemistry, and Behavior, 70,* 181–186.

White, W., & Timberlake, W. (1999). Meal-engendered circadian ensuing activity in rats. *Physiology and Behavior, 65,* 625–642.

Woods, S. C. (1991). The eating paradox: How we tolerate food. *Psychological Review, 98,* 488–505.

Zener, K. (1937). The significance of behavior accompanying conditioned salivary secretion for theories of the conditioned response. *American Journal of Psychology, 50,* 384–403.

10

Behavior Genetic Approaches Are Integral for Understanding the Etiology of Psychopathology

IRWIN D. WALDMAN

Understanding the etiology of traits and disorders is one of the corner-stones of clinical psychology. Along with classification and diagnosis, treatment response, and course and outcome, investigations regarding the causes underlying disorder are fundamental to research on psycho-pathology. Historically, a multitude of approaches to understanding the etiology of psychopathological conditions have been proposed, each with its own advocates and followers. Unfortunately, this proliferation of etiological approaches can lead to a fractionated portrait of the causes underlying a given disorder, and result in substantial confusion in researchers, practitioners, and consumers of mental health services. For example, it is often unclear which etiological approach is the "correct" one for a given disorder, or even which among the many causal perspectives are overlapping versus truly distinct from one another.

In this chapter, I present a behavior genetic approach to understanding the etiology of a disorder or trait, and portray how it represents a com-prehensive, overarching conceptual and analytic framework for under-standing cause that is free of some of the conceptual and methodological concerns of other etiological approaches. To provide a tangible example of the application of behavior genetic designs and analyses to a disorder or trait, I draw on behavior genetic studies of antisocial behavior, which represents one of the most extensive research domains in the behavior genetic literature. After a brief overview of the nature and importance of behavior genetic approaches to etiology and a short primer on behavior genetic methods as implemented in the typical twin or adoption study, I briefly review some of the pertinent findings on genetic and environmental influences on antisocial behavior that have emerged from a recent meta-analytic review of the literature on twin and adoption studies. I conclude the chapter by reviewing some extensions of traditional twin designs and with a précis of some promising future directions.

BEHAVIOR GENETIC APPROACHES TO THE ETIOLOGY OF DISORDERS AND TRAITS

The nature and importance of behavior genetic approaches to psychopathology

Behavior genetics is an approach to research that is concerned primarily with understanding the etiology (causes) of either traits indicative of "normal" functioning or of disorders indicative of disruptions to adaptive functioning. What distinguishes behavior genetics from the many other approaches to etiology that are common in clinical psychology is a focus on disentangling genetic from environmental causes and characterizing the magnitude of their influence. Indeed, it is this ability to distinguish unambiguously among different causes that sets behavior genetic approaches apart from most other etiological approaches, and underscores the importance of clinical psychologists becoming familiar with behavior genetic methods and findings throughout the course of their training. Perhaps the most prevalent misconception about behavior genetic designs is that they are somehow "biased" or predisposed toward detecting genetic influences. Nothing could be further from the truth. In fact, as we'll soon discover, such designs are actually the ideal vehicle for uncovering *environmental* contributions to a trait or disorder.

An example of the complexities of inferring the causes underlying a disorder, the shortcomings of conventional approaches to studying etiology, and the advantages of behavior genetic approaches may be useful before elaborating on the details of behavior genetic methods and findings. Depression, like the majority of psychiatric disorders, has been shown to run in families (Goodwin & Guze, 1989). This means that many (but not all) children who develop depression will have had depressed parents, and that some (but not all) depressed parents will have children who develop depression (see also Chapter 14). In a family study, researchers investigate whether a disorder of interest (e.g., depression) is more common in the relatives of focal affected individuals (who are often called the "probands") than in the relatives of focal unaffected individuals (who are often called the "matched controls") who are similar on many characteristics other than the presence of disorder. Although it may be relatively easy to document that depression is familial in this way, it is unfortunately quite difficult to understand the reasons for it. It is quite possible that the children of depressed parents who become depressed themselves are treated in certain ways by their depressed parents that cause them to develop depression. It may be the case, for example, that as a consequence of their disorder depressed parents provide less warmth to their children than nondepressed parents, which over time leads them to be more likely to develop depression. Alternatively, it may be the case that depression has a genetic basis, so that the same genes that predispose to the disorder in parents are transmitted to their children and lead them to be more likely to develop the disorder as well. The decreased warmth observed in depressed parents may simply be a result of their depression or another manifestation of the same genes that predispose to their depression. This would imply that the relation of lower parental warmth to the increased risk of developing later depression in the children of depressed parents may be an epiphenomenon of the parents' depression, rather than playing a causal role in the development of the disorder (see also Chapter 14, for a discussion of developmental approaches to psychopathology).

The foregoing example highlights the fundamental shortcoming of family studies, namely, that genetic and environmental influences on the etiology of a disorder cannot be disentangled, because they both contribute to the similarity of individuals in intact families. This methodological limitation is unfortunate because such distinctions are important to clinical researchers and practicing clinicians alike. Knowing whether the etiology of a disorder comprises predominantly genetic or environmental influences can—and should—have a profound effect on the search for specific genetic or environmental causal mechanisms that underlie the disorder. If the etiology is primarily genetic, the subsequent search may focus on the involvement of specific candidate genes, whereas if the etiology is primarily environmental, the search may instead focus on the role of specific environmental mechanisms and risk factors.

Fortunately, although family studies fall short in this regard, twin and adoption designs permit valid inferences regarding the genetic and environmental components of the etiology of a disorder. Adoption studies disentangle genetic and environmental influences by contrasting the similarity of family members who share rearing environment, but not genes, with family members who share genes, but not rearing environment. This separation may be accomplished by contrasting the correlations between adoptive and biologically related siblings, or the correlations between adoptees and their adoptive parents with the correlations between adoptees and their biological parents and adoptive parents and their biological children. All of these comparisons contrast the similarity of family members who differ in their genetic and environmental relatedness, thus permitting such influences to be teased apart. For example, if the familiality of depression is due to environmental mechanisms that family members share, the similarity of depression should be greater between adoptees and their adoptive parents than between adoptees and their biological parents. Alternatively, if the familiality of depression is due to genetic mechanisms that family members share, the similarity of depression should be greater between adoptive parents and their biological children and adoptees and their biological parents than between adoptees and their adoptive parents. Similarly, if the familiality of depression is a result of genetic mechanisms that family members share, the similarity of depression should be greater between biologically related siblings than between adoptive siblings.

Although adoption studies are useful behavior genetic designs, twin studies have at least two advantages over adoption studies. First, they can be considerably larger, given the greater accessibility of and ease of sampling twins than adoptive families. Hence, they typically afford greater statistical power for resolving genetic and environmental influences. Second, twin studies typically afford greater generalizability to the general population. Like adoption studies, twin studies also disentangle genetic and environmental influences by contrasting the similarity of family members (i.e., twins) who share features of the environment to the same extent but differ in the extent to which they share genes.

A common misunderstanding of twin studies is that it is only twins reared apart that permit genetic and environmental influences to be disentangled. In fact, these influences can be validly distinguished as long as a study includes twins who differ in zygosity, that is, monozygotic (identical) twins that result from the splitting of a single fertilized egg and dizygotic (fraternal) twins that result from the fertilization of two separate eggs. Genetic and environmental influences can be distinguished in a twin study by contrasting the similarity of monozygotic twins who share 100% of the genes transmitted by their parents, and dizygotic twins who share on average 50% of the genes transmitted by their parents.

A crucial assumption of twin studies is that both identical and fraternal twins share features of the environment *that influence the disorder or trait* to the same extent, even as they differ in the extent to which they share genes. This is termed the equal environments assumption, and also is frequently misinterpreted to mean that identical twins cannot be any more similar than fraternal twins for aspects of their environments. As highlighted in the aforementioned description, however, this assumption is not violated merely by identical twins showing greater similarity than fraternal twins for aspects of their environments but is violated only if those environmental features *influence* the trait or disorder under study. For example, it is frequently the case that as children identical twins are dressed more similarly than fraternal twins (e.g., in matching cute sailor or cowboy outfits), and critics of behavior genetic studies (e.g., Lewontin, Rose, & Kamin, 1984) often have raised this observation as a violation of the equal environments assumption in twin studies of disorders or traits (e.g., schizophrenia or intelligence). Nonetheless, this observation would only violate the equal environments assumption if it could be shown that being dressed in a cute sailor or cowboy outfit was a risk (or protective) factor for schizophrenia, or contributed to higher versus lower intelligence (or vice versa), a position that is implausible at best. This assumption has been tested in a number of ways and has led to the conclusion that it appears to be met for the majority of twin studies of disorders and traits (e.g., Kendler, Neale, Kessler, Heath, & Eaves, 1993).

Twin and adoption studies have made several singular contributions to our understanding of a variety of psychopathological conditions. First, beginning in the mid-1960s, disorders such as schizophrenia, major depression and bipolar disorder, autism, anxiety disorders, antisocial personality disorder, and attention-deficit/hyperactivity disorder all were shown to have a substantial genetic basis (Plomin, DeFries, McClearn, & McGuffin, 2002).

Genetic influences on these disorders have come to be assumed by most current psychopathology researchers (Bouchard, 2004), obscuring the controversy that once surrounded this etiological position, as well as the fact that until recently most researchers strongly believed that the etiology of these disorders was predominantly if not entirely environmental.

Second, behavior genetic studies of such disorders also have shown that the environmental influences that underlie their etiology are primarily nonshared, rather than shared (Harris, 1998; Rowe, 1994). These findings also may have significant implications for the search for subsequent environmental risk factors, suggesting some as plausible while ruling out others. Third, twin studies of a variety of disorders have found that much of their genetic influences are shared in common across overlapping disorders, suggesting that if specific candidate genes are found to be risk factors for one of these disorders they will similarly predispose to the overlapping disorders as well. Common (shared) genetic influences have been found for depression and anxiety disorders in adults (Kendler et al., 1992), changing our conception of the relation between such disorders as Major Depression and Generalized Anxiety Disorder, as well as among disruptive disorders in childhood (e.g., Waldman et al., 2001) and externalizing disorders in adults (Krueger et al., 2002).

DRAWING INFERENCES REGARDING GENETIC AND ENVIRONMENTAL INFLUENCES USING TWIN DATA

As the reader is no doubt aware, there have been many theoretical approaches posited to explain the etiology of antisocial behavior and other psychopathological conditions (e.g., schizophrenia, attention-deficit/hyperactivity disorder [ADHD]) and adaptive traits (e.g., intelligence, extraversion). With regard to antisocial behavior, a variety of etiologies have been proposed. For example, in their attempts to explain the etiology of antisocial behavior researchers have focused on the role of antisociality in one's peers (Vitaro, Boivin, & Tremblay, in press), developmental models (Moffitt, in press; Nagin, in press), sex differences

(Crick, Ostrov, & Kawabata, in press), social-cognitive processes (Pettit & Mize, in press), neurobiological factors (Lee & Coccaro, in press), and cross-national differences (van Wilsem, in press), to mention just a few approaches. Unfortunately, in their typical form most of these theories are often more casual than causal (Rogosa, 1987), in that it often is hard to envision what data or pattern of results could result in their falsification. This highlights a vital property of rigorous theories, namely their testability and the possibility that they can be subject to serious challenge and be rejected given particular results that contradict their predictions. This property, unfortunately rare in the social sciences, can be summarized by the position that a theory that cannot be mortally endangered cannot be alive (Meehl, 1978; Popper, 1959). Thus, perhaps the most important feature of behavior genetic designs and their attendant analyses is their testability, particularly their inherent comparison of alternative, a priori etiological hypotheses. A brief description of the use of data from twins to test alternative hypotheses regarding the genetic and environmental influences underlying a trait or disorder and to estimate these influences may be helpful before presenting a summary of the results of behavior genetic studies of antisocial behavior. Behavior geneticists typically are interested in disentangling three broad sets of influences that may cause individual differences or variation in a given trait. First, heritability, or h^2, refers to the proportion of variance in the trait that is due to genetic differences among individuals in the population. Second, shared environmental influences, or c^2, refer to the proportion of variance in the trait that is due to environmental influences that family members experience in common, which increase their similarity for the trait. For example, if two siblings go to a school that has particularly strong effects on enhancing intelligence and academic achievement, this would represent a shared environmental influence on these traits. Third, nonshared environmental influences, or e^2, refer to the proportion of variance in the trait that is due to environmental influences that are experienced uniquely by family members, which decrease their similarity for the trait. For example, if two siblings are enrolled in two different schools, one of which has programs that enhance intelligence and academic achievement and the other not as much, this would represent a non-shared environmental influence on these traits.

It is worth noting that many misconceptions exist regarding heritability. For example, many people believe that it refers to the proportion of an *individual's* trait that is influenced by genes, that it implies that a trait or disorder cannot be changed, or that it is a meaningless concept because genes and environments are inextricably intertwined throughout an individual's development. Although it makes sense to refer to the proportion of variability (e.g., 60%) in a trait (e.g., intelligence) that is due to genetic differences among individuals in a population, it makes no sense to refer to 60% of a particular child's intelligence being due to his or her genes.

Heritability also refers only to the proportion of variability in a trait or disorder that is due to genetic differences among individuals in a given population at a given time, and it bears few or no implications for the potential malleability of that trait or disorder due to any particular (environmental or genetic) intervention. Indeed, it is easy to think of traits or disorders that have a substantial genetic basis but are quite malleable, such as heritable vision problems that are correctable through the use of eyeglasses.

Finally, many critics of behavior genetic methods and findings have asserted that indices such as heritability are meaningless because genes and environments act together throughout development and their effects therefore cannot be distinguished. The example that some critics offer to support this is that one could not say which is more important to the size of a particular cardboard box, its length or its width (Ehrlich, 2000). Similar to the earlier example regarding intelligence, although one may not be able to ascribe differential importance to length or width as they contribute to the size of an individual box, one most certainly could determine whether *differences* in size among a collection of boxes were due more to *differences* in their lengths or widths. Thus, what may be inextricably intertwined in the development of an individual is indeed distinguishable when one examines individual differences.

In order to estimate genetic and environmental influences, twin studies rely on the fact that monozygotic (MZ) twins are identical genetically whereas fraternal or dizygotic (DZ) twins, just like nontwin siblings, are on average only 50% similar genetically. As explained earlier, it also is assumed that MZ twins are no more similar than DZ twins for the *trait-relevant* aspects of the shared environment; that is, that environmental influences on the trait of interest are shared in common between members of fraternal twin pairs to the same extent as between members of identical twin pairs (as earlier, the *equal environments assumption*). It also is assumed that the parents of the twins mate at random with respect to the trait being studied (i.e., that there is no *assortative mating*). Similar to the assumptions underlying other statistical analyses (e.g., normality of the residuals in a regression analysis), these assumptions are unlikely to be completely met, but quantitative genetic analyses are quite robust to minor violations of them. Given these assumptions, the correlation between identical twins comprises heritability and shared environmental influences (i.e., $r_{MZ} = h^2 + c^2$), as these are the two sets of influences that can contribute to identical twins' similarity for the trait. In contrast, the correlation between fraternal twins comprises one-half of heritability and shared environmental influences (i.e., $r_{DZ} = 1/2h^2 + c^2$), reflecting the smaller degree of genetic similarity between fraternal twins. Algebraic manipulation of the two equations for twin similarity allows one to estimate h^2, c^2, and e^2 (viz., $h^2 = 2 [r_{MZ} - r_{DZ}]$, $c^2 = 2r_{DZ} - r_{MZ}$, $e^2 = 1 - r_{MZ}$).

Although estimation of these influences using the twin correlations can be done simply by hand, contemporary behavior geneticists use biometric model-fitting analytic methods that can incorporate additional information on familial relationships (e.g., correlations between nontwin siblings or parents and their children), provide statistical tests of the adequacy of

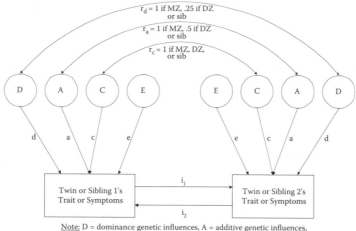

Note: D = dominance genetic influences, A = additive genetic influences,
C = shared environmental influences, E = non-shared environmental influences, and
i = influence of one twin/sibling's trait or symptoms on their cotwin/cosibling's trait or symptoms.

Figure 10.1. Path Model for Univariate Behavior Genetic Analyses of a Trait or Symptom Dimension.

these three influences (viz., h^2, c^2, and e^2) in accounting for the observed familial correlations, and test alternative models for the causal influences underlying the trait (e.g., a model including genetic and nonshared environmental influences versus a model that also includes shared environmental influences). These analyses also can be extended to examine genetic and environmental influences on the covariation among different traits or symptom dimensions. A recent trend in behavior genetic analyses has been to extend the investigation of genetic and environmental influences on traits considered singly (i.e., univariate behavior genetic analyses) to the case of multiple traits considered conjointly (Neale & Cardon, 1992). Multivariate behavior genetic analyses seek to explain the covariation among different traits by examining the genetic and environmental influences that they share in common. Such analyses can shed considerable light on the classification and etiology of psychopathology by permitting tests of common versus unique genetic and environmental influences.

A comprehensive biometric model for the genetic and environmental influences on a single trait for two twins or siblings is presented in the path diagram in Figure 10.1. This path diagram shows the basic biometric model (Neale & Cardon, 1992) for estimating additive and dominance genetic influences, shared and nonshared environmental influences, and the direct influence of one twin or sibling's behavior problems on their cotwin or cosibling's behavior problems. Additive genetic effects are those in which risk for disorder or effects on a trait increase monotonically for individuals who have zero, one, or two copies of a particular allele or form of a gene. Dominant genetic effects are those in which risk for disorder or effects on a trait increase given the presence of either one or two copies of a particular allele or form of a gene. In certain circumstances, the latter path may also indicate rater contrast effects, in which raters (e.g., parents) show a tendency to rate twins or siblings as different from one another. Note that there are now two types of genetic influences, dominance and additive genetic influences, which are summed to arrive at an estimate of broad-sense heritability, or h^2. Although this path model represents the full set of potential causes on twins' traits or symptom scores, there is not enough information in the conventional twin study design to estimate all five of these parameters simultaneously. As a consequence, contemporary twin studies present and contrast the results of a series of restricted models (i.e., models containing a subset of all potential causes) in order to find the most parsimonious model that fits the data well.

In the path diagram in Figure 10.1, D represents dominance genetic influences, A represents additive genetic influences, C represents shared environmental influences, E represents nonshared environmental influences, and i represents the direct influence of one twin or sibling's dispositions or conduct problems on their cotwin or cosibling's dispositions or conduct problems (or alternatively, rater contrast effects). The circles containing these capital letters represent these latent causal genetic and environmental variables, whereas the corresponding lowercase letters (viz., d, a, c, e, and i) represent the magnitude of these influences (i.e., the parameter estimates, which are regression coefficients) on each twin or sibling's dispositions or conduct problems. The square of these parameter estimates (viz., d^2, a^2, c^2, and e^2) represent the variance components corresponding to dominance and additive genetic influences, and shared and nonshared environmental influences. The three correlations in the model—r_d, r_a, and r_c—represent the similarity of particular causal influences between twins or siblings. For example, MZ and DZ twins and nontwin siblings all are correlated 1.0 for shared environmental influences (viz., r_c) consistent with the equal environments assumption. In contrast, MZ twins are correlated 1.0 for both dominance and additive genetic influences (viz., r_d and r_a), whereas DZ twins and nontwin siblings are both correlated .25 and .5 for dominance and additive genetic influences, respectively, consistent with their average level of genetic similarity.

Structural equation modeling programs such as LISREL and MX (Jöreskog & Sörbom, 1993; Neale et al., 1995) can iteratively fit such models to twin and sibling correlations (or variances and covariances) to provide the best estimates of the parameters; that is, parameter estimates that minimize the difference between the twin and sibling correlations implied by the model and those observed in the data. The fit of the model to the data is summarized by an χ^2 statistic, which allows both the fit of a given model and the comparative fit of alternative models to be tested statistically. This property often results in restricted models—models containing only a subset of the parameters in the full model (e.g., only a and e)—that provide an adequate fit to the data. In addition, although we presented the biometric model as applied to data from twins, the model is equally applicable to adoption study data on biologically related and adoptive siblings, and can be extended to analyze data from biologically related and adoptive parent-offspring pairs.

Perhaps because of the name *behavior genetics,* many believe that whereas such designs are ideal for identifying and estimating the magnitude of genetic influences, they are not well suited to characterizing environmental influences and the magnitude of these effects. Fortunately, this is not the case. Indeed, behavior genetic designs represent one of the strongest set of methods for elucidating environmental influences underlying a trait or disorder because genetic influences are simultaneously estimated and controlled (Rutter et al., 2001). In the typical study that seeks to demonstrate environmental influences on a trait or disorder (e.g., childhood antisocial behavior), a putative environmental variable (e.g., parental warmth) is correlated with a trait or disorder and in the presence of such a correlation, environmental influences are inferred. The problem with this conventional approach is that almost all putative environmental variables, such as parental warmth or other aspects of parental behavior and personality, are likely to reflect not only aspects of the environment that the child experiences but also genetically influenced characteristics of the parent that the child inherits. Unfortunately, this problem is not just relegated to parenting variables for which such genetic confounds are more obvious but instead may be pervasive and nonobvious, in that most putative environmental variables may be genetically influenced to some degree, even those that are thought to be a pure reflection of the environment. Two examples along these lines for which genetic as well as environmental influences have been shown to contribute to their underlying etiology are stressful life events (e.g., Saudino et al., 1995) and geographical place of residence (Whitfield et al., 2005). Studies that correlate a trait or disorder with such variables to infer environmental influences may very well be capturing genetic influences instead, at least to some extent. Toward the end of the chapter, I briefly describe two extensions of the traditional biometric model that are particularly well suited for elucidating specific shared and nonshared environmental influences.

A META-ANALYSIS OF BEHAVIOR GENETIC STUDIES OF ANTISOCIAL BEHAVIOR

To illustrate the application of behavior genetic methods to the elucidation of the etiology of a trait or disorder, I present the results of a recent meta-analysis of behavior genetic studies of antisocial behavior (Rhee & Waldman, 2002). In contrast to conventional studies, in which the data to be analyzed come from individual participants, in meta-analyses the relevant data are effect sizes from individual studies (e.g., correlations between measures or family members, mean differences between disordered and nondisordered comparison groups). Meta-analyses serve an important function in reviewing the research literatures pertinent to many topics, as they allow for the systematic, quantitative review of studies that in turn facilitates more conclusive answers to research questions. Such reviews are particularly important in research domains in which studies have especially small samples, resulting in their being quite low in statistical power, or in which the findings across studies appear quite variable, such that conclusions are hard to reach. Such is the case for behavior genetic studies of antisocial behavior, as although over a hundred twin and adoption studies of antisocial behavior have been published, it is difficult to draw clear conclusions regarding the magnitude of genetic and environmental influences given the extant literature. For example, the heritability of antisocial behavior in the published literature ranges from .00 (Plomin, Foch, & Rowe, 1981) to moderately high (e.g., .71; Slutske et al., 1995). Several reasons have been posited to explain such variability in the heritability estimates across studies, including differences in the age of the sample (e.g., Cloninger & Gottesman, 1987), the age of onset of antisocial behavior (e.g., Moffitt, 1993), and differences in the operationalization of, and the methods used to assess, antisocial behavior (e.g., Plomin, Nitz, & Rowe, 1990).

Given the uncertainty in the results of behavior genetic studies of antisocial behavior, and hence its etiology, we conducted a meta-analysis of 51 twin and adoption studies (N = 52 samples; 149 relative groups; 55,525 pairs of participants) in order to provide a clearer and more comprehensive picture of the magnitude of genetic and environmental influences on antisocial behavior (Rhee & Waldman, 2002). We also tested several alternative hypotheses regarding moderating variables that may explain the heterogeneity in the magnitude of these influences on antisocial behavior. Specifically, we examined the possible moderating effects of three study characteristics (i.e., the operationalization of antisocial behavior, assessment method, and zygosity determination method) and two participant characteristics (i.e., the age and sex of the participants) on the magnitude of genetic and environmental influences on antisocial behavior. These study and participant characteristics were chosen because clarifying their moderating effects should improve our understanding of the etiology of antisocial behavior. To test for differences among alternative, a priori hypothesized models we used differences in the aforementioned χ^2 statistic and a supplementary fit index (the Akaike Information Criterion, or AIC), which reflects both the fit of the model and its parsimony (Loehlin, 1997). Among competing models, that with the lowest AIC and the lowest χ^2 relative to its degrees of freedom is considered to be the best fitting model. I summarize the results of these meta-analyses. More technical details about the specific studies included in the meta-analyses, the search procedures used to locate the studies and the criteria used for the inclusion of the studies analyzed, as well as regarding the specific statistical analytic procedures employed, are provided in previous publications (Rhee & Waldman, 2002; Waldman & Rhee, 2005).

Considering all of the data from the twin and adoption studies simultaneously, the full ACDE model fit best relative to the more restrictive, competing alternative models. This suggests that additive and nonadditive genetic influences (accounting for 32% and 9% of the variance, respectively), as well as shared and nonshared environmental influences (accounting for 16% and 43% of the variance, respectively), all contribute importantly to the etiology of antisocial behavior. Given the heterogeneity across studies in estimates of the magnitudes of genetic and environmental influences, we next tested the significance of each of the aforementioned moderators.

With the exception of the sex of study participants, all of the other moderators were significant in explaining heterogeneity in the estimates of the magnitudes of genetic and environmental influences across studies. We first tested the moderating effects of operationalization, namely, whether results of studies varied as a function of characterizing antisocial behavior in terms of diagnoses (i.e., of Conduct Disorder or Antisocial Personality Disorder), criminality, aggression, or antisocial behavior in general (Rhee & Waldman, 2002). We found that results varied significantly by operationalization, such that the ACE model was the best fitting model for diagnosis ($a^2 = .44$, $c^2 = .11$, $e^2 = .45$), aggression ($a^2 = .44$, $c^2 = .06$, $e^2 = .50$), and general antisocial behavior ($a^2 = .47$, $c^2 = .22$, $e^2 = .31$), whereas the ADE model was the best fitting model for criminality ($a^2 = .33$, $d^2 = .42$, $e^2 = .25$). Within the operationalization of diagnosis, significant differences were found between studies examining ASPD (8 samples; 17 groups; 5,019 pairs of participants) and CD (5 samples; 22 groups; 6,560 pairs of participants). Although the magnitude of shared environmental influences (i.e., c^2) was similar, the heritability estimate (i.e., a^2) was higher in studies examining CD ($a^2 = .50$, $c^2 = .11$, $e^2 = .39$), whereas the magnitude of nonshared environmental influences (i.e., e^2) was higher in studies examining ASPD ($a^2 = .36$, $c^2 = .10$, $e^2 = .54$). We next tested the moderating effects of assessment method, contrasting the results for studies that assessed antisocial behavior using self-report, report by others, objective tests, reactions to aggressive material, and official records. We found that results again varied significantly by assessment method, such that the ACE model was the best fitting model for self-report ($a^2 = .39$, $c^2 = .06$, $e^2 = .55$) and report by others ($a^2 = .53$, $c^2 = .22$, $e^2 = .25$), whereas the AE model was the best fitting model for reactions to aggressive stimuli ($a^2 = .52$, $e^2 = .48$). All of the studies using the assessment method of records were also studies examining criminality, hence the ADE model was the best fitting model ($a^2 = .33$, $d^2 = .42$, $e^2 = .25$). Model-fitting could not be conducted for the assessment method of objective test due to lack of information (i.e., only one study used an objective test).

We also tested whether the results of behavior genetic studies of antisocial behavior varied by zygosity determination method and participants' age (Rhee & Waldman, 2002). Our tests of heterogeneity indicated that zygosity determination method was a significant moderator, as the magnitude of genetic and environmental influences differed significantly across studies using blood grouping (8 samples; 18 groups; 1020 pairs of participants), a combination of blood grouping and the questionnaire method (15 samples; 55 groups; 27,631 pairs of participants), and the questionnaire method (11 samples; 39 groups; 8,249 pairs of participants). The ADE model was the best fitting model for studies using blood grouping ($a^2 = .14$, $d^2 = .33$, $e^2 = .53$), whereas the ACE model was the best fitting model for studies using the questionnaire method ($a^2 = .43$, $c^2 = .27$, $e^2 = .30$) and a combination of the two methods ($a^2 = .39$, $c^2 = .11$, $e^2 = .50$). Age also was a significant moderator of the magnitude of genetic and environmental influences on antisocial behavior in children (15 samples; 54 groups; 7,807 pairs of participants), adolescents (11 samples; 31 groups; 2,868 pairs of participants), and adults (17 samples; 50 groups; 27,671 pairs of participants). The ACE model was the best fitting model for children ($a^2 = .46$, $c^2 = .20$, $e^2 = .34$), adolescents ($a^2 = .43$, $c^2 = .16$, $e^2 = .41$), and adults ($a^2 = .41$, $c^2 = .09$, $e^2 = .50$). These results suggest that the magnitude of familial influences (a^2 and c^2) on antisocial behavior decrease with age, whereas the magnitude of nonfamilial influences (e^2) increase with age.

THE IMPORTANCE OF CONSIDERING THE CONFOUNDING AMONG MODERATORS

The results of our meta-analysis (Rhee & Waldman, 2002) suggest that operationalization, assessment method, and age all are significant moderators of the magnitude of genetic and environmental influences on antisocial behavior, but the possible effects of confounding between operationalization, assessment method, and age should be considered when interpreting these results. Parent report was more frequently used in studies examining the general characterization of antisocial behavior than in studies examining diagnosis or aggression in which self-reports were more frequently used, and there were more studies examining the general characterization of antisocial behavior in children and adolescents than in adults. Also, all of the behavior genetic studies of criminality entailed the examination of adults using the assessment method of official records. The specific comparison between studies examining the diagnoses of ASPD and CD showed that the magnitude of genetic influences was higher for CD, whereas the magnitude of nonshared environmental influences was higher for ASPD. These results may be explained by age differences (ASPD being assessed in adulthood and CD being assessed in childhood) or differences in assessment method (self-report being used more often to assess ASPD and parent report being used more often to assess CD).

When there is confounding among the moderators being tested in a meta-analysis, as occurred in our meta-analysis of behavior genetic studies of antisocial behavior (Rhee & Waldman, 2002), there is the possibility that a particular variable may appear to be a significant moderator only because it is confounded with another moderating variable. The role of confounding among moderators in our meta-analysis was assessed between the following pairs of moderators: operationalization and assessment method, age and operationalization, and age and assessment method. All of these analyses revealed significant effects for each moderator even after the effects of the confounding moderator were controlled statistically. For example, the model estimating separate parameter estimates for each level of operationalization and each level of assessment method fit significantly better than the model estimating separate estimates for each level of operationalization only, and the model estimating separate estimates for each level of assessment method only. Similarly, assessment method was a significant moderator after controlling for age, operationalization was a significant moderator after controlling for age, and age was a significant moderator after controlling for operationalization and after controlling for assessment method. Thus, each moderator remained significant even after the effects of other potentially confounding moderators were controlled for statistically.

In summary, our meta-analysis suggested that additive and nonadditive genetic influences, and shared and nonshared environmental influences, all contribute to the etiology of antisocial behavior. These findings are important, as they suggest that the search for both candidate genes and candidate environments will be important in subsequent studies of specific risk factors and etiological mechanisms. The findings also suggest that some of the genes will act in an additive manner, but that others will act in a nonadditive fashion. Likewise, some of the environmental risk factors can be expected to be experienced in common by family members, whereas others will discriminate between those family members who develop antisocial behavior and those who do not. The substantial heterogeneity in results across studies, as well as the fact that almost all of the moderators examined were significant in explaining some of that heterogeneity, also has important implications for future research in this domain. Such heterogeneity suggests that antisocial behavior may be a particularly sensitive phenotype, the etiology of which may differ substantially depending on the age and environmental circumstances of the study participants, as well as on the methods used to operationalize and assess antisociality. Future researchers should thus explore the circumstances under which antisocial behavior shows substantial genetic influences, in general and in terms of the effects of specific genes, as well as those situations that lead environmental influences to be more pronounced. These directions should lead to a more nuanced and accurate depiction of the etiology of antisocial behavior.

FUTURE DIRECTIONS

Candidate Genes and Environments for Antisocial Behavior

Broadly speaking, there are two general strategies for identifying genes that contribute to the etiology of a disorder or trait. The first is a genome scan, in which linkage is examined between a disorder or trait and evenly spaced DNA markers (e.g., approximately 10,000 base pairs apart) distributed across the entire genome (Lander & Schork, 1994). Linkage refers to the statistical relation among family members between their diagnostic status for a particular disorder and their similarity in their genotype for a given DNA marker, or polymorphism. Evidence for linkage between any of these DNA markers and the trait or disorder of interest implicates a broad segment of the genome that may contain hundreds of genes, and lack of evidence for linkage can, in some cases, be used to exclude genomic segments. Subsequent fine-grained can then use a new set of more tightly grouped markers within the implicated genomic region to locate the functional mutation. Thus, genome scans may be thought of as exploratory searches for putative genes that contribute to the etiology of a disorder. The fact that major genes have been found for many Mendelian medical diseases (i.e., diseases in which the relation between genotype and disease is largely or entirely deterministic, rather than probabilistic) by means of genome scans testifies to the usefulness of this method. Unfortunately, the power of linkage analyses in genome scans is typically quite low, making it very difficult, if not impossible, to detect genes that account for less than ~15% of the variance in a disorder. Given this, the promise for genome scans of complex traits remains largely unknown.

The second strategy for finding genes that contribute to the etiology of a disorder is the candidate gene approach. In many ways, candidate gene studies are polar opposites of genome scans. In contrast to the exploratory nature of genome scans, well-conducted candidate gene studies represent a targeted test of the role of specific genes in the etiology of a disorder as the location, function, and etiological relevance of candidate genes is most often known or strongly hypothesized a priori. Thus, an advantage of well-conducted candidate gene studies in comparison with genome scans is that positive findings are easily interpretable because one already knows the gene's location, function, and etiological relevance, even if the specific polymorphism(s) chosen for study in the candidate gene is not functional and the functional polymorphism(s) in the candidate gene is as yet unidentified. There are also disadvantages to the candidate gene approach given that only previously identified genes can be studied. Thus, one cannot find genes that one has not looked for or have yet to be discovered, and because there are relatively few strong candidate genes for psychiatric disorders, the same genes are examined as candidates for almost all psychiatric disorders, regardless of how disparate the disorders may be in terms of their symptomatology or conjectured pathophysiology.

In well-designed studies, however, knowledge regarding the biology of the disorder is used to select candidate genes based on the known or hypothesized involvement of their gene product in the etiology of the trait or disorder (i.e., its pathophysiological function and etiological relevance). With respect to antisocial behavior, genes underlying various aspects of the dopaminergic and serotonergic neurotransmitter pathways may be conjectured based on several lines of converging evidence suggesting a role for these neurotransmitter systems in the etiology and pathophysiology of these traits and their relevant disorders. For example, there is considerable overlap between antisocial behavior and childhood ADHD (e.g., Lilienfeld & Waldman, 1990), thus candidate genes for ADHD also may be relevant candidates for antisocial behavior. Several genes within the dopamine system appear to be risk factors for ADHD (see Waldman & Gizer, 2006, for a recent review). Dopamine genes are plausible candidates for ADHD, given that the stimulant medications that are the most frequent and effective treatments for ADHD appear to act primarily by regulating dopamine levels in the brain (Seeman & Madras, 1998; Solanto, 1984), and also affect noradrenergic and serotonergic function (Solanto, 1998). In addition, "knock-out" gene studies in mice, in which the behavioral effects of the deactivation of specific genes are examined, have further demonstrated the potential relevance of genes within these neurotransmitter systems. Results of such studies have markedly strengthened the consideration of genes within the dopaminergic system as candidate genes for ADHD, such as the dopamine transporter gene (*DAT1*; Giros, Jaber, Jones, Wightman, & Caron, 1996) and the dopamine receptor D3 and D4 genes (*DRD3* and *DRD4*; Accili et al., 1996; Dulawa, Grandy, Low, Paulus, & Geyer, 1999; Rubinstein et al., 1997), as well as genes within the serotonergic system, such as the serotonin 1β receptor gene (*HTR1β*; Saudou et al., 1994). Serotonergic genes also are plausible candidates for antisocial behavior, given the demonstrated relations between serotonergic function and aggression and violence (Berman, Kavoussi, & Coccaro, 1997).

Candidate genes for neurotransmitter systems may include: (1) *precursor genes* that affect the rate at which neurotransmitters are produced from precursor amino acids (e.g., tyrosine hydroxylase for dopamine, tryptophan hydroxylase for serotonin); (2) *receptor genes* that are involved in receiving neurotransmitter signals (e.g., genes corresponding to the 5 dopamine receptors, *DRD1*, *D2*, *D3*, *D4*, and *D5*, and to the serotonin receptors, such as *HTR1β* and *HTR2A*); (3) *transporter genes* that are involved in the reuptake of neurotransmitters back into the presynaptic terminal (e.g., the dopamine and serotonin transporter genes, *DAT1* and *5HTT*); (4) *metabolite genes* that are involved in the metabolism or degradation of these neurotransmitters (e.g., the genes for catechol-o-methyltransferase, *COMT*, and for monoamine oxidase A and B [i.e., *MAOA* and *MAOB*]); and (5) genes that are responsible for the *conversion* of one neurotransmitter into another (e.g., dopamine beta hydroxylase, or $D\beta H$, which converts dopamine into norepinephrine).

There are many environmental variables that have been posited as risk factors for antisocial behavior. Relevant environmental domains include: pre- and perinatal influences, such as maternal smoking and drinking and obstetrical complications; parenting variables, such as warmth, control, harsh discipline, supervision, and monitoring; family background variables, such as family poverty, size, disruption, divorce, and single versus dual parent status; sibling and peer influences, such as aggression and antisocial behavior, substance-use or -abuse, academic achievement, and aspirations; and neighborhood characteristics, such as economic inequality, cohesion, crime rates, and collective efficacy. Unfortunately, as mentioned earlier, it is difficult to interpret much of the literature on the relation between such putative environmental variables and antisocial behavior because the environmental and genetic influences that potentially underlie such relations are confounded. We present two designs that are especially useful for inferring the causal mechanisms that underlie such putative environmental risk factors. The first of these designs is tailored particularly to examining nonshared environmental influences, whereas the second of these designs is directed toward inferring environmental influences that are transmitted from parents to their children. These designs and their application are described in turn later.

The Discordant MZ-Twins Design

The discordant-MZ twin design is perhaps both the simplest behavior genetic design and one of the most effective for revealing nonshared environmental influences on traits or disorders. In this design, one correlates differences between MZ twins on a phenotype of interest (e.g., a measure of antisocial behavior) with differences on some putative environmental measure (e.g., parental supervision or monitoring). The presence of such a correlation in discordant MZ twins suggests that the putative environmental variable is a nonshared environmental influence on the target trait or disorder. Although the search for nonshared environmental influences in behavior genetic studies has recently been criticized for its low yield and very small effect sizes (Turkheimer & Waldron, 2000), more recent studies of differences between MZ twins (e.g., Asbury et al., 2003) have suggested that harsh parenting and negative feelings of the parent toward the child are nonshared environmental influences on conduct problems among 4-year-old children, with harsher parenting and more negative parental feelings associated with greater conduct problems. A potential criticism of such findings is that the differences in conduct problems may have given rise to the differences in parenting, rather than resulting from them (e.g., greater conduct problems leads parents to discipline more harshly and feel more negatively, rather than vice versa). Thus, inferences regarding specific nonshared environmental influences are stronger to the extent that the putative environmental influence precedes the development of the target phenotype, occurs early in infancy or childhood, and is such that few plausible alternative 'third variables' can be postulated to account for the observed relation.

The Children-of-Twins Design

As suggested earlier, the relations between putative environmental variables such as parental warmth and control and psychopathological outcomes such as antisocial behavior may reflect direct causal environmental effects or may be due to genetic or environmental confounds. For example, the relation between parental harsh discipline and children's antisocial behavior could be due to a direct environmental influence, to background environmental influences such as socioeconomic status, or to shared genetic influences, in which the same genes that underlie parents' tendencies to discipline harshly also underlie their children's antisocial behavior. Given these confounds, such specific candidate environmental influences on antisocial behavior can best be considered putative, and require examination in genetically informative designs to validate their mechanism of effect as truly environmental.

One approach to this problem has been to incorporate specific putative environmental measures into traditional behavior genetic designs. A recent example is a study by Jaffee et al. (2004) in which the putative environmental effects of physical maltreatment on children's antisocial behavior were assessed within the context of a twin study design. Although the twins' physical maltreatment was significantly and substantially related to their parents' antisocial behavior, and the heritability of their own antisocial behavior was appreciable ($h^2 = .67$), the effects of parental physical maltreatment on their twin children's antisocial behavior appeared to remain after controlling for the genetic influences on antisocial behavior (which accounted for 56% of the physical maltreatment effect). Unfortunately, problems with this design, in particular with inferring that the residual relation of the putative environmental variable and the target variable (e.g., antisocial behavior) is indeed causal and environmental in nature, have recently come to light (Purcell & Koenen, 2005; Turkheimer et al., 2005), calling into question the authors' claims that such measured variables indeed reflect direct, causal environmental influences.

Fortunately, several authors have recently proposed novel, alternative behavior genetic designs and analyses that are well suited to discriminating among these causal possibilities. In particular, the Children-of-Twins design (e.g., D'Onofrio et al., 2003) appears to be particularly effective for disentangling the direct effects of putative parental environmental variables from confounding background genetic or environmental influences. In this design, the twins sampled are parents (e.g., female MZ and DZ twins who are mothers) and are studied along with their children. Specifically, the putative causal parental environmental variable (e.g., harsh discipline or smoking during pregnancy) is measured in the twin parents, whereas the target phenotype of interest (e.g., childhood conduct problems) is measured in their children. Given the fact that the parents are twins, coupled with the inclusion of pertinent data on the target phenotype in their children, permits one to draw valid inferences on the nature and etiology of the relation between the parental (putative environmental) variable and the child's phenotype in ways that other research designs (including other behavior genetic designs) cannot. Studies are beginning to investigate the relations of such putative environmental variables with antisocial behavior using the Children-of-Twins design and thus to move their status from the putative to the actual.

Gene-Environment Interactions

Researchers also have begun to investigate the possibility that candidate genes and candidate environments may not simply act in an additive manner in their influence on antisocial behavior. Developmental psychopathology researchers have long been intrigued by the prospect of gene-environment interaction, and many have contended that one cannot understand the development of psychopathology without considering such processes (see Chapter 14). One recent, high-profile example of gene-environment interaction for psychopathology that has garnered considerable attention and interest showed that the risk for adolescent antisocial behavior and violence based on abuse during early childhood depended on alleles at the *MAOA* gene (Caspi et al., 2002). Notable features of this study were the careful measurement of both the psychopathology outcome and the environmental risk factor, as well as the use of functional mutations in the *MAOA* gene. It is important to recognize the symmetrical nature of such gene-environment interactions, that is, that gene-environment interaction refers both to the moderation of the effects of environmental risk factors as a function of individuals' genotypes at a particular gene, as well as to the moderation of individuals' genetic predispositions for a certain disorder as a function of aspects of the environments to which they are exposed and experience. It would be fairly straightforward to test whether the effects of the candidate genes mentioned above vary as a function of many of the aforementioned environmental risk factors for antisocial behavior. I expect that more studies of gene-environment interaction for antisocial behavior will emerge in the near future.

SUMMARY

In this chapter, I described the advantages of behavior genetic designs for studying the etiology of traits and disorders over other more commonly used approaches in the personality and psychopathology literature. After a brief primer on behavior genetic designs and analyses using twins, I presented results from a recent meta-analysis of twin and adoption studies on antisocial behavior which suggested the importance of additive and dominant genetic influences and shared and nonshared environmental influences, as well as highlighting the heterogeneity in these influences across studies and the explanation of such using moderators such as the operationalization and assessment of antisocial behavior, the age of study participants, and the method of determining zygosity in twin studies. I concluded the chapter with a brief discussion of future directions, including the search for specific candidate genes and candidate environments that may account for some of the genetic and environmental influences revealed in the meta-analysis, as well as novel behavior genetic designs that may be particularly useful for revealing specific environmental causal mechanisms, as well as interactions between candidate genes and environments.

KEY TERMS

Zygosity: In a twin study, the number of eggs that are fertilized that give rise to the multiple offspring. Monozygotic twins result from the splitting of a single fertilized egg and share 100% of the genes transmitted by their parents, whereas dizygotic twins that result from the fertilization of two separate eggs and share on average 50% of the genes transmitted by their parents.

Equal environments assumption: A crucial assumption of twin studies, in which both identical and fraternal twins share features of the environment *that influence the disorder or trait* to the same extent, even as they differ in the extent to which they share genes.

Heritability (h^2): The proportion of variance in a trait or disorder that is due to genetic differences among individuals in a population.

Shared environmental influences (c^2): The proportion of variance in a trait or disorder that is due to environmental influences that family members experience in common, which increase their similarity for the trait or disorder.

Nonshared environmental influences (e^2): The proportion of variance in a trait or disorder that is due to environmental influences that are experienced uniquely by family members, which decrease their similarity for the trait or disorder.

SUGGESTED READINGS

Lander, E. S., & Schork, N. J. (1994). Genetic dissection of complex traits. *Science, 265,* 2037–2048.

Neale, M. C., & Cardon, L. C. (1992). *Methodology for genetic studies of twins and families.* Kluwer.

Plomin, R. (1996). *Nature and nurture: An introduction to human behavioral genetics.* San Francisco: Wadsworth.

Plomin, R., DeFries, J. C., Craig, I. W., & McGuffin, P. (2002). *Behavioral genetics in the postgenomics era.* Washington, DC: American Psychological Association.

Plomin, R., DeFries, J. C., McClearn, G. E., & McGuffin, P. (2000). *A primer of behavioral genetics* (4th ed.). San Francisco: Worth.

Rhee, S. H., & Waldman, I. D. (2002). Genetic and environmental influences on antisocial behavior: A meta-analysis of twin and adoption studies. *Psychological Bulletin, 128,* 490–529.

REFERENCES

Accili, D., Fishburn, C. S., Drago, J., Steiner, H., Lachowicz, J. E., Park, B. H., et al. (1996). A targeted mutation of the D3 dopamine receptor gene is associated with hyperactivity in mice. *Proceedings of the National Academy of Sciences of the United States of America, 93,* 1945–1949.

Asbury, K., Dunn, J. F., Pike, A., & Plomin, R. (2003). Nonshared environmental influences on individual differences in early behavioral development: A monozygotic twin differences study. *Child Development, 74,* 933–943.

Berman, M. E., Kavoussi, R. J., & Coccaro, E. F. (1997). Neurotransmitter correlates of human aggression. Ch. 28, In D. M. Stoff, J. Breiling, & J. D. Masur (Eds.), *Handbook of Antisocial Behavior.* New York, NY: John Wiley.

Bouchard, T. J. (2004). Genetic influence on human psychological traits. *Current Directions in Psychological Science, 13,* 148–151.

Caspi, A., McClay, J., Moffitt, T. E., Mill, J., Martin, J., Craig, I. W., Taylor, A., & Poulton, R. (2002). Role of genotype in the cycle of violence in maltreated children. *Science, 297,* 851–854.

Cloninger, C. R. & Gottesman, I. I. (1987). Genetic and environmental factors in antisocial behavior disorders. In S. A. Mednick, T. E. Moffitt, & S. A. Stack (Eds.), *The causes of crime: New biological approaches* (pp. 92–109). New York: Cambridge University Press.

Crick, N. R., Ostrov, J. M., & Kawabata, Y. (in press). Relational aggression and gender: An overview. In D. Flannery, A. Vazonsyi, & I. Waldman (Eds.), *The Cambridge handbook of violent behavior.* New York: Cambridge University Press.

D'Onofrio, B. M., Turkheimer, E., Eaves, L. J., Corey, L. A., Berg, K., Solaas, M. H., & Emery, R. E. (2003). The role of the children of twins design in elucidating causal relations between parent characteristics and child outcomes. *Journal of Child Psychology and Psychiatry, 44,* 1130–1144.

Dulawa, S. C., Grandy, D. K., Low, M. J., Paulus, M. P., & Geyer, M. A. (1999). Dopamine D4 receptor-knock-out mice exhibit reduced exploration of novel stimuli. *Journal of Neuroscience, 19,* 9550–9556.

Ehrlich, P. R. (2000). *Human natures: Genes, cultures, and the human prospect.* Washington, DC: Island Press.

Giros, B., Jaber, M., Jones, S. R., Wightman, R. M., & Caron, M. G. (1996). Hyperlocomotion and indifference to cocaine and amphetamine in mice lacking the dopamine transporter. *Nature, 379,* 606–612.

Goodwin, D. W., & Guze, S. B. (1989). *Psychiatric diagnosis* (4th ed.). New York: Oxford University Press.

Harris, J. R. (1998). *The nurture assumption: Why children turn out the way they do.* New York: The Free Press.

Jaffee, S. R., Caspi, A., Moffitt, T. E., & Taylor, A. (2004). Physical maltreatment victim to antisocial child: Evidence of an environmentally mediated process. *Journal of Abnormal Psychology, 113*, 44–55.

Joreskog, K. G. & Sorbom, D. (1993). *LISREL VIII: User's guide.* Mooresville, IN: Scientific Software, Inc.

Kendler, K. S., Neale, M. C., Kessler, R. C., Heath, A. C., & Eaves, L. J. (1992). Major depression and generalized anxiety disorder: Same genes, (partly) different environments? *Archives of General Psychiatry, 49*, 716–722.

Kendler, K. S., Neale, M. C., Kessler, R. C., Heath, A. C., & Eaves, L. J. (1993). A test of the equal environment assumption in twin studies of psychiatric illness. *Behavior Genetics, 23*, 21–27.

Krueger, R. F., Hicks, B. M., Patrick, C. J., Carlson, S. R., Iacono, W. G., & McGue, M. (2002). Etiologic connections among substance dependence, antisocial behavior and personality: Modeling the externalizing spectrum. *Journal of Abnormal Psychology, 111*, 411–424.

Lander, E. S. & Schork, N. J. (1994). Genetic dissection of complex traits. *Science, 265*, 2037–2048.

Lee, R., & Coccaro, E. F. (in press). Neurobiology of impulsive aggression: Focus on serotonin and the orbitofrontal cortex. In D. Flannery, A. Vazonsyi, & I. Waldman (Eds.), *The Cambridge handbook of violent behavior.* New York: Cambridge University Press.

Lewontin, R. C., Rose, S., & Kamin, L. J. (1984). *Not in our genes: Biology, ideology and human nature.* New York: Pantheon.

Lilienfeld, S. O. & Waldman, I. D. (1990). The relation between childhood Attention-Deficit Hyperactivity Disorder and adult antisocial behavior reexamined: The problem of heterogeneity. *Clinical Psychology Review, 10*, 699–725.

Loehlin, J. C. (1997). *Latent variable models (3rd Edition).* Hillsdale, NJ: Lawrence Erlbaum Associates.

Moffitt, T. E. (1993). Adolescence-limited and life course persistent antisocial behavior: A developmental typology. *Psychological Review, 100*, 674–701.

Moffitt, T. E. (in press). A review of research on the taxonomy of life-course persistent versus adolescence-limited antisocial behavior. In D. Flannery, A. Vazonsyi, & I. Waldman (Eds.), *The Cambridge handbook of violent behavior.* New York: Cambridge University Press.

Nagin, D. S. (in press). Overview of a semi-parametric, group-based approach for analyzing trajectories of development. In D. Flannery, A. Vazonsyi, & I. Waldman (Eds.), *The Cambridge handbook of violent behavior.* New York: Cambridge University Press.

Neale, M. C., Boker, S. M., Xie, G., & Maes, H. (1999). *Mx: Statistical Modeling* (5th ed.). Richmond, VA: Department of Psychiatry.

Neale, M. C. & Cardon, L. C. (1992). *Methodology for genetic studies of twins and families.* Amsterdam: Kluwer.

Pettit, G. S., & Mize, J. (in press). Social-cognitive processes in the development of antisocial and violent Behavior. In D. Flannery, A. Vazonsyi, & I. Waldman (Eds.), *The Cambridge handbook of violent behavior.* New York: Cambridge University Press.

Plomin, R., DeFries, J. C., Craig, I. W., & McGuffin, P. (2002). *Behavioral genetics in the postgenomics era.* Washington, DC: American Psychological Association.

Plomin, R., Foch, T. T., & Rowe, D. C. (1981). Bobo clown aggression in childhood: Environment, not genes. *Journal of Research in Personality, 15*, 331–342.

Plomin, R., Nitz, K., & Rowe, D. C. (1990). Behavioral genetics and aggressive behavior in childhood. In M. Lewis & S.M. Miller (Eds.), *Handbook of Developmental Psychopathology*. New York: Plenum.

Plomin, R., DeFries, J. C., McClearn, G. E., & McGuffin, P. (2000). *A primer of behavioral genetics* (4th ed.). San Francisco: Worth.

Purcell, S. and Koenen, K. (2005). Environmental mediation and the twin design. *Behavior Genetics, 35*, 491–498.

Rhee, S. H. & Waldman, I. D. (2002). Genetic and environmental influences on antisocial behavior: A meta-analysis of twin and adoption studies. *Psychological Bulletin, 128*, 490–529.

Rowe, D. C. (1994). *The limits of family influence*. New York: Guilford.

Rubinstein, M., Phillips, T. J., Bunzow, J. R., Falzone, T. L., Dziewczapolski, G., Zhang, G., Fang, Y., Larson, J. L., McDougall, J. A., Chester, J. A., Saez, C., Pugsley, T. A., Gershanik, O., Low, M. J., & Grandy, D. K. (1997). Mice lacking dopamine D4 receptors are supersensitive to ethanol, cocaine, and methylphenidate. *Cell, 90*, 991–1001.

Rutter, M., Pickles, A., Murray, R., & Eaves, L. (2001). Testing hypotheses on specific environmental causal effects on behavior. *Psychological Bulletin, 127*, 291–324.

Saudino, K. J., McGuire, S., Hetherington, E. M., Reiss, D., & Plomin, R. (1995). Parent ratings of EAS temperaments in twins, full siblings, half siblings, and step siblings. *Journal of Personality and Social Psychology, 68*, 723–733.

Saudou, F., Amara, D. A., Dierich, A., LeMeur, M., Ramboz, S., Segu, L., et al. (1994). Enhanced aggressive behavior in mice lacking 5-HT1B receptor. *Science, 265*, 1875–1878.

Seeman P., Madras B. K. (1998). Anti-hyperactivity medication: methylphenidate and amphetamine. *Molecular Psychiatry*. 3, 386–396.

Slutske, W. S., Heath, A. C., Dinwiddie, S. H., Madden, P. A. F., Bucholz, K. K., Dunne, M. P., Statham, D. J., & Martin, N. G. (1995). Modeling genetic and environmental influences in the etiology of conduct disorder: A study of 2,682 adult twin pairs. *Journal of Abnormal Psychology, 106*, 266–279.

Solanto, M. V. (1984). Neuropharmacological basis of stimulant drug action in attention deficit disorder with hyperactivity: a review and synthesis. *Psychological Bulletin, 95*, 387–409.

Solanto, M. V. (1998). Neuropsychopharmacological mechanisms of stimulant drug action in attention-deficit hyperactivity disorder: a review and integration. *Behavioural Brain Research, 94*, 127–152.

Turkheimer, E., D'Onofrio, B. M., Maes, H. H., & Eaves, L. J. (2005). Analysis and interpretation of twin studies with measured environments, *Child Development, 76*, 1217–1233.

Turkheimer, E. & Waldron M. (2000). Nonshared environment: A theoretical, methodological, and quantitative review. *Psychological Bulletin, 126*, 78–108.

Van Wilsem, J. (in press). Cross-national data on violent victimization. In D. Flannery, A. Vazonsyi, & I. Waldman (Eds.), *The Cambridge handbook of violent behavior*. New York: Cambridge University Press.

Vitaro, F., Boivin, M., & Tremblay, R. E. (in press). Peers and violence: A two-sided developmental perspective. In D. Flannery, A. Vazonsyi, & I. Waldman (Eds.), *The Cambridge handbook of violent behavior*. New York: Cambridge University Press.

Waldman, I. D. & Gizer, I. (2006). The Genetics of ADHD. *Clinical Psychology Review 26*, 396–432.

Waldman, I. D., Rhee, S. H., Levy, F., & Hay, D. A. (2001). Genetic and environ-
    mental influences on the covariation among symptoms of attention deficit
    hyperactivity disorder, oppositional defiant disorder, and conduct disorder.
    In D. A. Hay & F. Levy (Eds.), *Attention, Genes and ADHD*. East Sussex, UK:
    Brunner-Routledge.
Waldman, I. D. & Rhee, S. H. (2005). Genetic and Environmental Influences
    on Psychopathy and Antisocial Behavior. in Patrick, C. (Ed.), *Handbook of
    Psychopathy*. New York: Guilford Press.
Whitfield, J. B., Zhu, G., Heat, A. C., & Martin, N. G. (2005). Choice of residential
    location: Chance, family influences, or genes. *Twin Research, 8*, 22–26.

11

Evolutionary Theory Provides a Framework for Understanding Abnormal Behavior

RICHARD J. SIEGERT AND TONY WARD

There has been a profound increase in the influence of evolutionary theory (ET) within psychology since the early 1980s (Barkow, Cosmides, & Tooby, 1992; Barrett, Dunbar, & Lycett, 2002; Buss, 1999; Siegert & Ward, 2002b). One important aspect of the increasing acceptance of the relevance of evolutionary thinking for psychology has been the proliferation of evolutionary explanations for various forms of psychopathology (Baron-Cohen, 1995; Gilbert et al., 2001; Price, Sloman, Gardner, Gilbert, & Rohde, 1994; Siegert & Ward, 2002a; Thornhill & Palmer, 2000). It is our contention that evolutionary theory has much to offer clinical science in attempting to understand many different types of abnormal behavior. Indeed, we consider this notion to be one of the *great ideas of clinical science*.

In arguing that evolutionary theory has much to contribute to our understanding of psychopathology we will attempt the following. First, we offer a brief historical account of the impact of ET on psychology, noting that for much of the 20th century, evolutionary ideas were distinctly unfashionable in psychology. Second, we attempt to explain the fundamental principles comprising Darwin's theory and then summarize the five leading contemporary approaches to its application in *evolutionary psychology* (EP). Third, we briefly describe two attempts at developing an evolutionary perspective on depression, as an example of how ET can be helpful in understanding abnormal behavior (Allen & Badcock, 2003; Price et al., 1994; Price, 1967). Finally, we will consider some possible implications of an evolutionary perspective on psychopathology for everyday clinical practice.

A HISTORICAL PERSPECTIVE ON EVOLUTIONARY THEORY AND PSYCHOLOGY

Darwinian Influences on Psychology

The influence of Darwinian thought upon psychology was notable in the 19th century, but declined quickly in the early 20th century, until it experienced something of a revival in the mid-1960s (Durrant, 1998; Siegert & Ward, 2002a). In the 19th century, Darwin's evolutionary theory was a major influence on his cousin Frances Galton, who pioneered the mental testing movement. The concept of individual variation then became a central theme in that movement (Hergenhahn, 1992; Nietzel, Bernstein, & Milich, 1998). Darwin also influenced Freud, who wrote his earliest works in the wake of Darwin. Butler and Strupp (1991) have noted that Freud's training in medicine and neurology occurred at a time when Western scientific thinking was rapidly absorbing Darwinian ideas and concepts. They also observed that central to Freud's thinking were the concepts of *drives* and *instincts*, which stemmed from humans' evolutionary past. Hergenhahn (1992) commented that in demonstrating the continuity between humans and other animals, Darwin strengthened Freud's contention that human behavior was motivated by instincts rather than reason. In North America, Darwinian theory was evident in the work of William James and most notably in the writings of the eminent social psychologist James Baldwin (Richards, 1987). However, the influence of evolutionary theory on psychology declined markedly in the early 20th century.

Durrant (1998) noted a decline in evolutionary thinking in psychology from the early part of the 20th century and a renewal of interest beginning in the 1960s. He noted that several factors were influential in its decline. The first was social, as evolutionary thinking became associated with social Darwinism and the eugenics movement. The second was theoretical, as a growing number of psychologists came to view evolutionary explanations of behavior as narrow, limited, and lacking in explanatory breadth. A third was the rise of behaviorism, which decreed that minds (be they animal or human), and instincts, were not a fit subject for scientific study. A similar picture also has been observed in the history of psychiatry (McGuire & Troissi, 1998).

Since the early 1960s, however, there has been a resurgence of interest in evolutionary theory and its relevance for psychology and psychopathology.

A number of factors have contributed to this change. There was increasing evidence from animal research that species-specific differences in conditioning of behavior not only existed but actually seemed to set the limits of learning. Breland and Breland, two ex-pupils of B. F. Skinner, had applied Skinner's operant psychology in a successful business, training animals for zoos, department stores, television, and advertising (Breland & Breland, 1961). After several years experience of successfully shaping the behavior of pigs, chickens, porpoises, raccoons, reindeer, whales, and numerous other species, they came to the conclusion that J. B. Watson had got it wrong. Watson had argued in the 1930s that instinct was no longer a useful concept for psychology. However, Breland and Breland found that species differences had repeatedly frustrated their operant conditioning techniques. They reported this in an influential and immensely readable *American Psychologist* article entitled "The Misbehavior of Organisms." Shortly afterward, Seligman (1971) argued that not all fears were equally conditionable and that most phobias, such as fears of heights, animals, and germs, had obvious biological consequences. Around that time, Skinner himself wrote a paper clarifying his view of the relationship between operant psychology and evolutionary principles, and answering some of the criticisms of operant psychology from ethologists (Skinner, 1966). However, in the evolution of evolutionary psychology, it was the publication of E. O. Wilson's book *Sociobiology: The New Synthesis* in 1975 that really marked the return of Darwinian concepts to center stage (Wilson, 1975).

From Sociobiology to Evolutionary Psychology

The publication of *Sociobiology* sparked a controversy that is still simmering today. In a scientific tour de force, Edward O. Wilson, a Harvard entomologist, argued for a unified science of behavior firmly based within the framework of evolutionary biology, and in particular, population biology. Wilson (1975) defined sociobiology as "the systematic study of the biological basis of all social behavior" (p. 4) and asserted that "the organism is only DNA's way of making more DNA" (p. 3). In a scholarly book that integrated evolutionary theory with a sweeping range of data on the social behavior of insects, fish, reptiles, birds, carnivores, elephants, and primates, Wilson tackled such diverse topics as altruism, communication, aggression, dominance, roles and casts, ethics, and aesthetics. However, what really upset people was that Wilson asserted that genetics were as relevant for understanding the social behavior of humans as for understanding honeybees or hummingbirds. Wilson entitled the final chapter of *Sociobiology* "Man: From Sociobiology to Sociology" and speculated on topics including ethics, sex, the division of labor, religion, ritual, and culture. Even homosexuality, it seemed, could be explained by sociobiology—as witnessed by the following passage: "The homosexual members of primitive societies may have functioned as helpers. . . . Freed from the special obligations of parental duties, they could have operated with special efficiency in assisting close relatives. Genes favoring homosexuality could then be sustained at a high equilibrium level by kin selection alone" (Wilson, 1975, p. 555). It seemed that evolutionary biologists were no longer satisfied to exclude humans from the scope of their study—politely leaving this species for anthropologists, sociologists, and psychologists to call their own.

The reaction at the time was fierce, to say the least. Ruse (1985) noted that although the initial reaction from scientific peers was generally positive, within a year a savage attack was launched upon Wilson and his book. In particular, a group of scientists from the Boston area, under the banner "The Science for the People Sociobiology Study Group," launched a concerted campaign against sociobiology in both the popular and academic presses (Rose, 1998; Ruse, 1985). This group included scientific luminaries such as Richard Lewontin and Stephen Jay Gould. Wilson was criticized not only on scientific grounds but also for being reactionary, reductionist, and sexist. At a major conference he was doused with water by angry students. The Sociobiology Study Group even responded to a favorable review of Wilson's book in the *New York Review of Books* with a letter that likened sociobiology to the eugenics movement and the Nazi ideology that resulted in the Holocaust (Brown, 1999; Rose, 1998; Ruse, 1985). However, after the initial furor eventually died down, evolutionary biologists and sociobiologists returned to their fieldwork and laboratories. In fact, sociobiology flourished, although this was mostly within academic journals and at conferences and well away from the sensationalism and glare of the popular press. Most sociobiologists continued to concentrate on the study of nonhuman species.

Thus, sociobiology came of age in the 1970s. The controversy surrounding it seemed to have died down by the 1980s, and the field continued to develop and flourish. Evolutionary psychology, at least the use of that term rather than the term sociobiology, is a phenomenon of the 1990s. In 1992, Barkow, Cosmides, and Tooby published an edited book entitled *The Adapted Mind: Evolutionary Psychology and the Generation of Culture*, in which the contributors applied evolutionary psychology to issues such as cooperation, mate preference, sexual attraction, pregnancy sickness, language, environmental aesthetics, psychological defense mechanisms, and culture (Barkow et al., 1992). The book opens with a 118-page chapter by Tooby and Cosmides entitled "The Psychological Foundations of Culture," which reads like a veritable manifesto for evolutionary psychology. Tooby and Cosmides launched a blistering attack on the "Standard Social Science Model" of culture and in a dazzling mixture of scholarship and zealotry announced the arrival of evolutionary psychology. Other signs that evolutionary psychology is here to stay have been the first undergraduate textbooks on the topic (Barret, Dunbar, & Lycett, 2002; Buss, 1999) and a handbook of evolutionary psychology (Crawford & Krebs, 1998). In addition, the journal *Ethology and Sociobiology* changed its name to *Evolution and Human Behavior.*

THE FUNDAMENTALS OF DARWIN'S THEORY OF EVOLUTION BY NATURAL SELECTION AND FIVE CONTEMPORARY APPROACHES TO EVOLUTIONARY PSYCHOLOGY

Charles Darwin and the Origin of Species

In 1859, Charles Darwin published *On the Origin of Species*. In this text, he marshaled a vast array of observations and facts about plant and animal life forms into a coherent and integrated theory that provided a plausible scientific explanation for the great diversity of species on the Earth and also explained the fossil evidence of extinct life forms. The concept of biological evolution itself was by no means original. Darwin's grandfather Erasmus Darwin, himself a noted scientist, had entertained similar ideas in a somewhat vaguer form (Richards, 1987). The French biologist Lamarck had proposed a theory of evolution based on the (faulty) notion that the physical structure of individual organisms adapted to meet environmental challenges, and that these adaptations were passed on to descendants (Richards, 1987, Rose, 1998). Thus, evolutionary ideas, if fragmentary and at times simply incorrect, were already a part of the intellectual atmosphere when the *Origin of Species* was published. Charles Darwin's great achievement was in synthesizing and integrating the plethora of existing ideas concerning evolution with the known biological facts to develop a single theory that was both internally and externally consistent. This was only possible because Darwin discovered the process by which the evolution of species occurred—the process known as natural selection.

There are three essential elements in Darwin's ideas about natural selection. First, individual members of a species (be they plant or animal) all *vary*. Thus, no two elephants, aphids, starlings, or oak trees, when examined closely, are ever completely identical. Second, some individual members of a species will demonstrate variations that make them better able to survive or adapt to changing environmental conditions. For example, the faster antelope is more likely to escape predatory lions. Third, those individuals better equipped to survive will be more likely to breed and in doing so will pass on these characteristics to their progeny. Consequently, these inherited characteristics will become more common within that species. In addition to natural selection, Darwin also discerned one other important process in evolution—sexual selection. This is the idea that male and female members of a particular species will demonstrate distinct preferences in their choice of mates based on physical or behavioral characteristics. Consequently, those individuals with characteristics or traits that are highly preferred in mates will leave behind more offspring and those characteristics will become more frequent in the population. For example, in certain species of birds, the females demonstrate a preference for mates with extravagant, brightly colored plumage. Perhaps the best-known example of this, the peacock, is a flightless, wild bird of India, also home to the leopard and other "peacock eaters" (Jolly, 1999, p. 84). Sexual selection explains how a characteristic that seems to fly in the face of natural selection (i.e., a profuse, colorful plumage on a flightless bird may make hiding from leopards difficult) can be selected for.

Five Contemporary Evolutionary Approaches to Human Behavior

There are at least five different ways of applying evolutionary theory to human behavior (see Laland & Brown [2002] for a comprehensive introduction to the five theories). These are sociobiology, human behavioral ecology, memetics, evolutionary psychology, and gene-culture coevolution theory. These alternative evolutionary perspectives adopt distinct views on a number of related issues including the relationship between genes and human development, the role of learning in explaining human behavior, and the degree to which human nature is "hardwired" versus subject to modification through intentional (cultural) interventions (Laland & Brown, 2002). Each of the five evolutionary theories has its strengths and weaknesses and is the focus of continued research and theoretical development (Laland & Brown, 2002). For reasons that are not entirely clear, evolutionary psychology has had the most influence in psychology and is the approach underpinning the majority of the current evolutionary work on psychopathology (see Siegert & Ward, 2002).

One important aspect of all five approaches is that they draw a distinction between *ultimate* and *proximate* causes of behavior. This distinction between ultimate and proximate explanations for animal behavior has long been accepted by evolutionary biologists. Ultimate explanations attempt to identify the function of a given trait or mechanism by determining its role in solving a particular adaptive problem while a proximate explanation focuses on the nature of the causal mechanisms that underpin its functional role (Buss, 1999). In the language of EP, ultimate means all the evolutionary factors that contribute to the development of a psychological mechanism or pattern of behavior. By contrast, proximate refers to the more recent factors involved. Thus, ultimate causes will include such things as the ancestral environment, sexual selection, and natural selection. Proximate causes will include such variables as the person's genes, developmental history, learning, and environmental stimuli. Symons (1979) comments that ultimate causes explain *why* an animal exhibits a specific behavior pattern—in ancestral environments that behavior pattern promoted the reproductive success of the individuals displaying it. Proximate causes, says Symons, explain *how* animals eventually develop and display specific behavior patterns. Thus, given a certain genetic endowment, the right developmental circumstances, and appropriate contingencies of reinforcement, the pattern of behavior will emerge. Moreover, any comprehensive explanation of a pattern of behavior should invoke both ultimate and proximate causes and suggest how proximate causes might activate the relevant mental mechanisms involved. Thus, ultimate causes might help explain why humans frequently become depressed. Proximate causes might help explain how a specific individual becomes depressed.

The *sociobiological approach* to explaining human behavior was first introduced to the general public by Edward Wilson in 1975, as recounted earlier. Wilson and his colleagues adapted methods and ideas from ethnology to the study of human beings and systematically investigated the functional significance of human social behavior. The essence of the sociobiological perspective is nicely captured in a quote by Wilson, in which he stated that it is "the systematic study of the biological basis of all social behavior" (Wilson, 1975, p. 4). The basic assumptions underlying this theory are actually straightforward. First, human beings are animals and therefore should be studied using methods derived from researchers studying other animals because all are part of the natural world. Second, humans inherit the capacity for culture and social behavior. It is only the fact that genes code for language and higher cognitive capacities that makes it possible for people to construct art, philosophy, and engage in cultural activities. Third, the ways in which human development proceeds are deeply influenced by genetic constraints. Fourth, these inherited traits constitute human nature and are evident in all cultures: they are universal. Fifth, genes are the basic units of selection, not organisms or groups, and are selected upon the basis of increasing organisms (which are essentially vehicles for genes), reproductive success, and survival. Therefore, a successful gene is more likely to be represented in greater numbers in a future population than its less successful competitors. Finally, genetic processes directly influence human *behavior* as is evident in such phenomena as incest avoidance, sexual division of labor, and male dominance. According to the sociobiological approach, genes directly influence forms of psychopathology, such as depression and anxiety disorders (see Chapter 10 for a discussion of behavior genetic approaches).

Human behavioral ecology is directly concerned with investigating the degree to which human behavior is *currently adaptive* in the environments in which it is expressed (Laland & Brown, 2002). It is important to note the distinction drawn by evolutionary theorists between two quite different, although related, questions: (1) Is a behavior an adaptation? and (2) Is a behavior adaptive? The former refers to a trait selected for in the past because it increased reproductive success. Such a trait may currently be adaptive or maladaptive. In contrast, an adaptive behavior is defined as one that *currently* results in increased reproductive success. It may not have been directly selected for in the past and could be the by-product of another trait that was selected by natural selection. Human behavioral ecologists focus on the second question, namely, is the behavior in question currently adaptive? Typically, researchers construct mathematical models depicting the most adaptive or optimal behavior (based on efficiency considerations) in a specific context and then evaluate its accuracy in predicting behavioral outcomes. Examples of problem domains are the relationship between food choice and caloric value or the best size for a hunting party. If the model is supported it is assumed that the behavior in question could have evolved by means of natural selection. The populations used to test the models are chosen because of their presumed similarity to prehistoric humans and are typically engaged in hunting and gathering practices to survive (Laland & Brown, 2002). According to human behavioral ecology, psychopathology is generally the result of inefficient or maladaptive attempts to secure important human goods.

The *memetic perspective* adapts a gene-focused evolutionary approach to the issue of cultural evolution and was first articulated by Richard Dawkins in his book *The Selfish Gene* (Dawkins, 1989). In this theory, memes are viewed as units of cultural knowledge and function to instruct behavior in some respects, that is, inform individuals how to behave and what to do in certain situations. Examples of memes are songs, ideas, rituals, and skills. In formulating the theory of memes, Dawkins used the gene-organism relationship as a model for the meme-human mind relationship. Memes are viewed as cultural replicators, whereas the vehicles or carriers of memes are human brains. According to Dawkins, memes spread throughout the population through social learning processes such as imitation and are transmitted across the generations throughout a society (and the world potentially) at a given period of time. Their primary purpose, to use anthropomorphic language, is to replicate. In a real sense then, human beings are exploited by memes to propagate themselves. Memes may confer little or no functional advantages on their hosts and in some situations may prove quite deadly (e.g., memes associated with terrorism or suicide). A powerful, although disturbing, way to think of memes is that they infest or infect the minds of persons, and in this sense, are cultural viruses. Some memes are grouped together in larger complexes to form clusters of ideas, such as religions or political ideologies. A concerning feature of some memes is that they "defend" themselves against rejection. For example, some types of religious or ideological doctrines may contain component ideas that make it virtually impossible to falsify them. From the point of view of memetics, psychopathology is directly related to the dominance of certain types of memes (e.g., extreme individualism, perfectionism) that result in stressful or negative experiences (e.g., failure, social isolation).

According to *evolutionary psychologists*, evolution resulted in human beings acquiring a range of specific cognitive mechanisms designed to solve certain adaptive problems. As a consequence, the mind is believed to be a set of hundreds or thousands of domain-specific mental modules that operate independently but in a coordinated fashion (Tooby & Cosmides, 1992). Such modules are considered to be independent, self-contained information-processors that function quickly and automatically, mostly outside of conscious awareness. The fact that they are self-contained or informationally encapsulated means that they are unable to be altered by external factors, such as learning or cultural processes. Rather, external influences function to trigger or calibrate the mechanisms to one of several predetermined settings. For example, sexual competition for access to females might result in one of three mating strategies being adopted by a particular male: honest courtship, deception, or rape (Ward & Siegert, 2002).

In contrast to behavioral ecologists, evolutionary psychologists argue that these modules or information processing mechanisms rather than specific behaviors are selected for. It is important to note that these inherited mechanisms are not necessarily operating at birth. In fact, they may come "on line" at different developmental stages. So, for example, mate selection modules only really start to exert a profound influence during adolescence. Additionally, modules are only activated once the relevant environmental conditions obtain and specific information is available as input to the mechanism. The nature of these inputs also may channel individuals down one of several possible developmental pathways by virtue of their effect on the relevant mechanism. From the perspective of evolutionary psychology, psychopathology results from malfunctioning mental modules (e.g., failure of the "theory of mind" module in autism) or their activation in inappropriate environments or contexts (e.g., fear responses in benign situations—Siegert & Ward, 2002a).

The version of gene-culture coevolution theory we prefer is that developed by Odling-Smee et al., (2003), and is best defined by its focus on the construct of *niche construction*. According to Odling-Smee et al., niche construction occurs when organisms alter the environment and thereby modify the relationship between their characteristics and the features of the environment. A good example is leaf-cutter ants: they store plant material in their nests to cultivate a specific type of fungus (i.e., they construct fungal gardens), which they use as a food source. The process of constructing this niche results in systematic changes to the soil and ecosystem within and around the nest and also alters the selection environment of their offspring. This alteration may effectively reduce selection pressures (i.e., reduce the pressure on organisms to adapt or be eliminated) in ways that benefit the long-term survival chances of the ant and its offspring. Examples of niche construction in human beings are the building of houses, implementation of farming practices (e.g., dairy farming), and the development of technology. All these changes modify the niche in which human beings live and thereby change the relationship or match between humans and features of the environment.

According to Odling-Smee et al., three types of processes are involved in niche construction in a population of diverse phenotypes (living organisms): *genetic processes, ontogenetic processes* (individual learning within a lifetime), and *cultural processes*. Each of these processes is associated with unique ways of acquiring, storing, and transmitting information, and also with distinct means of interacting with the environment. An example of genetic processes is that of the orb-web spider, in which the spinning of webs on a nightly basis is thought to be rigidly determined by genes (Avital & Jablonka, 2000). An example of ontogenetic or learning processes is the use of pine needles by wood-pecker finches in the Galapagos Islands to dislodge insects from the bark of trees. This behavior is thought to be relearned by each generation of finches on a trial and error basis (Avital & Jablonka, 2000), and enables the finches to exploit resources (i.e., create a new niche) that were not previously available to them, thereby "creating a stable selection favoring a bill able to manipulate tools rather than the sharp, pointed bill and long tongue characteristic of woodpeckers" (Odling-Smee et al., 2003, p. 22). The advantage of an ontogenetic process such as learning is that organisms are able to rapidly adapt to changing circumstances and not rely on inbuilt genetic solutions. Odling-Smee et al. maintained that this type of learning may well be regulated by a general principle such as the law of effect, so that actions that are followed by a positive outcome are more likely to be repeated in the future. An example of cultural processes in animals is the discovery by macaque monkeys that washing potatoes nested in the sand improves their edibility (Avital & Jablonka, 2000). A human example is the cultural discovery of dairy farming.

We can utilize niche construction theory to understand psychological and social problems such as the predisposition of some individuals to commit sexual assaults. An example of a genetic predisposition might be males' hypothesized tendency to seek impersonal sex and to attempt to exert power and control over females (Ellis, 1989). An example of an ontogenetic process leading to impersonal sex could be learning to use sex as a way of coping with negative mood states and feelings of inadequacy (Marshall & Barbaree, 1990). An example of a relevant cultural process might be the portrayal of females as sexual objects and males as sexually entitled to have sex when and where they want (Polaschek & Ward, 2002)

UNDERSTANDING DEPRESSION FROM AN EVOLUTIONARY PERSPECTIVE

It may seem odd at first that ET could help to shed light on the phenomenon of depression in humans. After all, evolution is about adaptations: those changes in anatomy, physiology, cognition, and behavior that are passed from one generation to the next because they promote survival (and hence reproduction). Consider then the nature of clinical depression. Major depression is a mental disorder characterized by the presence of five of the following symptoms for at least 2 weeks: a sad mood for most of the day/most days; a loss of pleasure or interest in one's usual activities; sleeping problems; fatigue; psychomotor retardation or agitation; reduced appetite with weight loss (or the converse); a negative self-image; feelings of guilt and self-blame; reduced concentration; and suicidal thinking (American Psychiatric Association, 2000). The five symptoms must include sad, depressed mood or loss of interest and pleasure in usual activities. A recent Australian study reported a 12-month prevalence rate for major depression in the community of 6.3% (Andrews, Henderson, & Hall, 2001).

Depression, almost by its very nature, seems maladaptive. It is a condition that seems likely to be most disadvantageous in survival terms. How could such troubling symptoms as fatigue, sadness, guilt, sleeplessness—not to mention loss of libido—help anyone to survive and reproduce? In answering this question, we will consider two evolutionary based theories: the Social Competition Hypothesis and the Social Risk Hypothesis.

The Social Competition Hypothesis of Depression. As noted earlier, the 1960s witnessed a revival of interest in the relevance of ET for understanding human behavior including abnormal behavior. One further example of this shift in attitude was Price's (1967) paper in which he advanced an explanation of depression in terms of dominance hierarchies. This theory was subsequently developed into the social competition hypothesis of depression (Price et al., 1994).

Price et al. hypothesized that depression evolved as a "mechanism for yielding in competitive situations" (p. 242). Yielding is considered an involuntary mechanism that inhibits aggression toward more dominant individuals and signals to those competitors that the individual is not a threat. It is also posited to produce a state of mind conducive to giving up and accepting the situation, which Price et al. call "voluntary yielding." Price et al. suggested that this mechanism of depression evolved out of "ritual agonistic behavior" (i.e., aggression), which, as they noted, is the primary form of social competition underlying sexual selection in most vertebrates. They argued that agonistic behavior is closely related to a self-concept known as *resource-holding potential*, which equates with the fighting capacity of an individual as perceived by that individual and others. Price et al. go as far as to hypothesize that self-esteem evolved out of resource-holding potential.

In some ways, this all seems rather removed from our contemporary social context, in which physical combat is rarely used in settling disputes. However, the theory becomes less esoteric when we note Price et al.'s comment that "ritual agonistic behavior is not the main form of human social competition" any longer but rather that "competition by attraction has largely replaced competition by intimidation" (pp. 245–246). Thus, we can no longer gain social status simply by physically dominating our fellows (except perhaps in the sporting arena and certain criminal subcultures) but, rather, we must rely upon our interpersonal skills, personality, physical attractiveness, and so on. Therefore, it follows that depression may represent a failure to achieve or maintain status and control in the interpersonal realm and a subsequent withdrawal both physically and psychologically. It is also worth noting that Price et al. stated that the simplest hierarchy is the two-person relationship. They suggest that in many dyads, the depressed person occupies a permanently "one-down" position in the relationship, which serves to avoid a psycho-logical "arms race." The depressed person's status is chronically diminished while their partner's is magnified, and this is associated with cognitive distortions in the depressed partner.

Gilbert (2000) recently reported a questionnaire study that examined the relationships among depression, shame, social anxiety, and self-evaluations of social rank in university students and in depressed patients. He reported that depression and social anxiety were strongly related to self-reported submissive behaviors and feelings of inferiority—although not to guilt. Such a pattern of emotions and behaviors is quite consistent with the social competition hypothesis (now known as the social rank hypothesis). Gilbert speculates as to whether social anxiety in depressed people may be somewhat different in nature from social anxiety in general. Gilbert also draws several implications for therapy from the results of this study. For example, he suggests that therapy might need to involve encouraging more assertiveness and better skills for managing conflict within relationships. At the same time, this new assertiveness should be balanced with developing new relationship schemas—ones that emphasize cooperative, equal relationships that function in "less competitive rank-centred ways" (p.185).

The Social Risk Hypothesis of Depression. Allen and Badcock (2003) have recently proposed an evolutionary account of depression that is heavily based on Price et al.'s social competition hypothesis but also draws from attachment theory, social cognition, and neurobiology. Their theory is based on the assumption that most of recent human evolution occurred in relatively small social groups that lived as hunter-gatherers. Consequently, an individual who could not "fit in" and who fell out with the group risked physical punishment and social ostracism. In its extreme form, this probably meant death at the hands of group members or simply being left to survive the ancestral environment alone. Either way, it must have reduced the probability of that individual forming pair-bonds, copulating, reproducing, and thus passing on his or her genes to the next generation.

In essence, the theory posits that the social environment was one of the most important sources of selection pressures, and as a consequence, humans have evolved to be acutely sensitive to a wide range of social factors. Humans who were poor at negotiating their way through the social maze were presumably less likely to be chosen as mates and more likely to be ostracized or even killed. According to Allen and Badcock, depressed mood is a natural response in human beings to various forms of interpersonal tension and conflict. The theory suggests that when people perceive the resources they provide to others (their *social value*) to be outweighed by the costs to others (known as *social burden*), a reduction in self-esteem occurs. This loss in self-esteem (or *social investment potential*) is the mechanism that sets in play a range of behaviors designed to avoid social risk. These include a reduction in risky behaviors (i.e., confident, assertive, acquisitive behaviors), a hypersensitivity to social threats, and an increase in withdrawal behaviors designed to elicit care and support from others.

According to such a theory, we might view mood as a biological alarm system that is uniquely sensitive to the state of our social environment. In some individuals, because of genetic or developmental vulnerability factors, when there is a prolonged state of social stress a full-blown clinical depression can occur. In other words, depression results from a faulty calibration of a naturally occurring mechanism that evolved in response to environmental selection pressures. This is not dissimilar to how panic attacks are currently viewed as a "false alarm" occurring in the "fight-or-flight" response (Bouton, Mineka, & Barlow, 2001). The fight-or-flight response is an adaptation designed to provide a rapid and energetic response to physical threats. But if it is triggered while driving down the freeway on a sunny day or in a university lecture theater, it becomes pathological.

A critical evaluation of either or both of these theories is well beyond the scope of the present chapter. Instead, we will briefly consider some of the common criticisms of EP in general, and where appropriate, use the social risk hypothesis to illustrate how that particular line of criticism might or might not apply. However, for a more in-depth consideration of the most frequent criticisms of EP, we refer the reader elsewhere (Siegert & Ward, 2002a, 2002b). For a sophisticated consideration of the scientific status of EP, and in particular, the falsifiability of evolutionary explanations, see Ketelar and Ellis, 2000; for a more detailed consideration of depression as an adaptation, see Nesse, 2000; and for a blistering attack on evolutionary concepts of psychopathology, see Murphy, in press.

SOME CRITICISMS OF EP

Is EP Reductionist? Like their sociobiological predecessors, evolutionary psychologists have been accused of reductionism (Rose, 1998; Rose & Rose, 2000). Reductionism is an essential strategy for understanding complex phenomena in most branches of science. It refers to a process whereby complex phenomena are broken down into components, which are then divided into subcomponents for analytic purposes. The epistemological assumption at work here is that we can best understand how a whole system works if we can first understand how each of its parts works separately (Nagel, 1998).

Critics of reductionism, as applied to human behavior, typically invoke the notion that different levels of explanation are appropriate for explaining behavior at different levels of organization. Rose (1998, p. 178) put it thus: "Each level of complexity of nature involves new interactions and relationships between the component parts which cannot be inferred simply by taking the system to pieces." Implicit in such criticisms is the idea that certain explanatory variables or causal mechanisms may only *emerge* (i.e., come into existence) at a specific level. For example, our understanding of group dynamics is unlikely to be enhanced by our knowledge of how neurotransmitters function at the synapses of the individual group members.

The first point to make in answering this criticism of EP is that there is not, as detailed earlier, *one* EP. Rather, there are at least five major approaches as identified by Laland and Brown (2002), and considerable diversity exists in theory and methodology among those approaches. The second point is that scientists inevitably use reductionism to understand the parts so that they might eventually comprehend the whole. And why not? It has been a fairly successful strategy so far. The third point is that if one takes Allen and Badcock's (2003) social risk theory of depression as an example, this approach is not reductionist. To the contrary, they draw on a rich foundation of research from several different levels of explanation: developmental psychology, social cognition, and neurobiology. Most important, they seem to be saying that depression is not "all in the genes" but rather that depression is an interpersonal phenomenon.

Is EP Sloppy Science? or How the Leopard Got Its Spots. A common concern about evolutionary explanations for human behavior centers on the fact that they involve speculation about events and environments about which we have very limited knowledge (Rose, 1998). Moreover, these ancestral people and places have not existed for thousands, if not millions, of years. Evolutionary psychologists argue that our minds evolved to suit an environment radically different from the one in which we live today (Barkow et al., 1992). Although no one disputes that claim, what is hotly disputed is how accurately we can reconstruct the physical and social environments of our hominid ancestors. It is only too easy to invent plausible hypotheses about how living in hunter-gatherer society on the Savannah plains of Africa might have influenced behavioral or cognitive evolution. Whether such hypotheses accurately reflect the situation a million years ago is debatable. In fact, evolutionary biologists have a name for this kind of speculation—they call it inventing "just so" stories. The name comes from Rudyard Kipling's charming and imaginative children's tales such as *How the Leopard Got His Spots* and *How the Camel Got His Hump.*

The arguments about the credibility of evolutionary explanations of behavior are complex and difficult to evaluate in any depth without a consideration of relevant issues in the philosophy of science (e.g., Ketelar & Ellis, 2000). However, we have attempted this evaluation elsewhere (Siegert & Ward, 2002a, 2002b). The only point we make here is that the ultimate test of any such hypothesis is the degree to which it furnishes empirically testable hypotheses that can be corroborated. In this regard, the social competition hypothesis has already proven highly fruitful in yielding hypotheses that have stood up to substantive empirical scrutiny (e.g., Gilbert, 2000; Gilbert et al., 2001; Price, Gardner Jr., & Erickson, 2004).

IMPLICATIONS OF EVOLUTIONARY PSYCHOLOGY FOR CLINICAL PRACTICE

We have argued previously that an evolutionary perspective on psycho-pathology will have important implications for clinical practice with regard to etiology, assessment, treatment, and ethics (Siegert & Ward, 2002a). In this chapter, we will confine ourselves to speculating on some of the implications for the treatment of depression of adopting an evolutionary perspective such as the social risk hypothesis (Allen & Badcock, 2003). One positive implication of such an account of depression is that it could help to normalize depression and thus reduce the stigma for the client. From this perspective, depression is thus viewed as an extreme form of a natural and universal tendency for humans to respond in a certain ways to adverse social circumstances. Although acknowledging the distressing and potentially harmful aspects of depression, it can be seen as the extreme end of a continuum of human experience, and one to which we are all prone. Nesse (2000) has similarly argued that many aspects of mental disorders are actually defensive systems gone amok. Thus, anxiety or depression might be likened to a cough that originates as defense against accumulated phlegm in the lungs but then becomes disabling if it persists. Indeed, an evolutionary perspective implies a radical shift in our thinking about the nature of mental disorder. Many of the "maladaptive behaviors" that fill the pages of undergraduate texts on abnormal psychology may actually be behavioral systems that had survival value and have been selected by evolution over millions of years.

Gilbert (1998) made a similar argument in relation to cognitive distortions, noting that human cognition evolved to react rapidly to threats, both social and nonsocial. He argued that much of human cognition is not fundamentally rational. A further implication for treatment that Gilbert mentioned is that some therapists may want to share evolutionary explanations with their clients. He suggested that cognitive therapy can be explained partly as a process of learning to switch off or attenuate normal defensive mechanisms. This means there is less need to hold up some ideal standard of rational thinking as the norm, and in doing so emphasize the patient's own thoughts as irrational, distorted, and inadequate. Rather, distorted cognitions can be normalized so as to reduce the client's feelings of failure, inadequacy, and unworthiness. At the same time, it can be clearly stated to the client that although a tendency toward such thinking is normal in its origins, in the current environment it is self-defeating because it is too intense, too prolonged, and too pervasive.

Perhaps the most interesting implication for treatment is that far from being "all in the genes," an evolutionary perspective on depression seems to indicate that both cognitive behavioral therapy and interpersonal psychotherapy would be treatments of choice. Is it just a coincidence that these two therapies also happen to be the two most effective, evidence-based, nondrug treatments for depression?

CONCLUSION

In this chapter, we have tried to provide a general introduction to the field of evolutionary psychology and to outline its relevance for understanding and treating mental disorder. In doing so, we have been acutely aware of the fine balance inherent in explaining complex concepts in a simple and coherent way without oversimplifying them to the extent that all their subtlety and technical sophistication is sacrificed. Consequently, we would like to conclude by spelling out what we believe are the four most important "take home messages" here: (1) Evolutionary psychology is a species that has several distinct subspecies and they vary considerably in their theoretical assumptions, models, methods, and implications. Much of the controversy surrounding this field has been associated with one particular approach and some of its more extreme claims. However, this ignores the breadth and diversity of the field; (2) there is an important distinction between ultimate and proximate explanations of behavior. Evolutionary psychology is primarily concerned with the former and psychology with the latter. The interface between these two types of explanation remains largely unexplored; (3) an evolutionary perspective on psychopathology does not mean that abnormal behavior is "all in the genes" or that it cannot be treated by psychotherapy. Rather, it suggests that interpersonal relations in the "here and now" should be an important focus in therapy for most psychological problems; and (4) models of human nature, according to evolutionary theory, were not necessarily fixed eons ago on the plains of Africa. Much of the current thinking in the field, such as the niche-construction approach, suggests a more dynamic, evolving concept of human nature. We are an unfinished work of nature.

KEY TERMS

Evolution: A natural process of incremental change in the physiology or behavior of a species through which organisms become better able to survive and reproduce.

Evolutionary psychology: The application of evolutionary theory to understanding and explaining contemporary human behavior.

Natural selection: The process by which variations in individual members of a species that increase the probability of the organism surviving and breeding become more frequent among that species.

Sexual selection: The second important process in Darwin's evolutionary theory described in his book *The Descent of Man*. Features of an individual that make that individual more attractive to members of the opposite sex, and hence more likely to be chosen as a mate, will increase in frequency among that species. Laland and Brown noted that "Darwin introduced the concept of sexual selection in order to provide an additional explanation for physical and mental differences between the sexes" (p. 34).

Sociobiology: The precursor to contemporary evolutionary psychology, which used evolutionary theory to explain much of the social behavior of animals, including humans. Sociobiology and its founder, entomologist E. O. Wilson, were the targets of much controversy in the late 1970s.

SUGGESTED READINGS

Allen, N. B., & Badcock, P. B. T. (2003). The social risk hypothesis of depressed mood: Evolutionary, psychosocial and neurobiological perspectives. *Psychological Bulletin, 129*(6), 887–913.

Buss, D. M. (2004). *Evolutionary psychology: The new science of mind* (2nd ed.). Boston, MA: Allyn and Bacon.

Laland, K. N., & Brown, G. R. (2002). *Sense and nonsense: evolutionary perspectives on human behaviour.* Oxford: Oxford University Press.

Siegert, R. J., & Ward, T. (2002). Evolutionary psychology: Origins and criticisms. *Australian Psychologist, 37*(1), 20–29.

Siegert, R. J., & Ward, T. (2002). Clinical psychology and evolutionary psychology: Toward a dialogue. *Review of General Psychology, 6*(3), 235–259.

REFERENCES

Allen, N. B., & Badcock, P. B. T. (2003). The social risk hypothesis of depressed mood: Evolutionary, psychosocial and neurobiological perspectives. *Psychological Bulletin, 129*(6), 887–913.

American Psychiatric Association. (2000). *Diagnostic and statistical manual of mental disorders—DSM-IV-TR.* Arlington, VA: American Psychiatric Publishing, Inc.

Andrews, G., Henderson, S., & Hall, W. (2001). Prevalence, comorbidity, disability and service utilisation: Overview of the Australian National Mental Health Survey. *British Journal of Psychiatry, 178,* 145–153.

Avital, E., & Jablonka, E. (2000). *Animal traditions: Behavioural inheritance in evolution.* Cambridge: Cambridge University Press.

Barkow, J. H., Cosmides, L., & Tooby, J. (1992). *The adapted mind: Evolutionary psychology and the generation of culture.* New York: Oxford University Press.

Baron-Cohen, S. (1995). *Mindblindness: an essay on autism and theory of mind.* Cambridge, MA: MIT Press.

Barrett, L., Dunbar, R., & Lycett, J. (2002). *Human evolutionary psychology.* Princeton, NJ: Princeton University Press.

Barrett, L., Dunbar, R., & Lycett, J. (2002). *Human evolutionary psychology.* New York: Palgrave.

Bouton, M. E., Mineka, S., & Barlow, D. (2001). A modern learning theory perspective on the etiology of panic disorder. *Psychological Review, 108*(1), 4–32.

Breland, K., & Breland, M. (1961). The misbehavior of organisms. *American Psychologist, 16,* 681–684.

Brown, A. (1999). *The Darwin wars: The scientific battle for the soul of man.* London, U.K.: Simon & Schuster UK Ltd.

Buss, D. M. (1999). *Evolutionary psychology: The new science of mind.* Boston, MA: Allyn & Bacon.

Butler, S. F., & Strupp, H. H. (1991). Psychodynamic psychotherapy. In M. Hersen & A. E. Kazdin (Eds.), *The clinical psychology handbook.* New York: Pergamon Press.

Crawford, C. & Krebs, D. L. (Eds.) (1998). *Handbook of evolutionary psychology: Ideas, issues and applications.* Hillsdale, N.J.: Erlbaum.

Dawkins, R. (1989). *The selfish gene* (2nd ed.). Oxford: Oxford University Press.

Durrant, R. (1998). *A natural history of the mind: The role of evolutionary explanations in psychology.* Unpublished Ph.D. dissertation, University of Canterbury, New Zealand, Christchurch.

Ellis, L. (1989). *Theories of rape: Inquiries into the causes of sexual aggression.* New York: Hemisphere Publishing Corp.

Gilbert, P. (2000). The relationship of shame, social anxiety and depression: The role of the evaluation of social rank. *Clinical Psychology and Psychotherapy, 7,* 174–189.

Gilbert, P., Birchwood, M., Gilbert, J., Trower, P., Hay, J., Murray, B., et al. (2001). An exploration of evolved mental mechanisms for dominant and subordinate behaviour in relation to auditory hallucinations in schizophrenia and critical thoughts in depression. *Psychological Medicine, 31,* 1117–1127.

Hergenhahn, B. R. (1992). *An introduction to the history of psychology.* Belmont, CA: Wadsworth.

Jolly, A. (1999). *Lucy's legacy: Sex and intelligence in human evolution.* Cambridge, MA: Harvard University Press.

Ketelar, T., & Ellis, B. (2000). Are evolutionary explanations unfalsifiable? Evolutionary psychology and the Lakatosian philosophy of science. *Psychological Inquiry, 11*(1), 1–21.

Laland, K. N., & Brown, G. R. (2002). *Sense and nonsense: Evolutionary perspectives on human behaviour.* Oxford: Oxford University Press.

Marshall, W. L., & Barbaree, H. E. (1990). An integrated theory of the etiology of sexual offending. In W. L. Marshall, D. R. Laws, & H. E. Barbaree (Eds.), *Handbook of sexual assault: Issues, theories, and treatment of the offender* (pp. 257–275). New York: Plenum.

McGuire, M., & Troisi, A. (1998). *Darwinian psychiatry.* New York: Oxford University Press.

Murphy, D. (in press). Can evolution explain insanity? *Biology and Philosophy.*

Nagel, T. (1998). Reductionism amd antireductionism. In N. F. Symposium (Ed.), *The limits of reductionism in biology.* Chichester, UK: Wiley.

Nesse, R. M. (2000). Is depression an adaptation? *Archives of General Psychiatry, 57,* 14–20.

Nietzel, M. T., Bernstein, D. A., & Milich, R. (1998). *Introduction to clinical psychology.* Englewood Cliffs, NJ: Prentice Hall.

Odling-Smee, F. J., Laland, K. N., & Feldman, M. W. (2003). *Niche construction: The neglected process in evolution.* Princeton, NJ: Princeton University Press.

Polaschek, D. L. L. & Ward, T. (2002). The implicit theories of potential rapists. What our questionnaires tell us. *Aggression and Violent Behavior, 7,* 385–406.

Price, J., Sloman, L., Gardner, R. J., Gilbert, P., & Rohde, P. (1994). The social competition hypothesis of depression. *British Journal of Psychiatry, 164,* 309–315.

Price, J. S. (1967). The dominance hierarchy and the evolution of mental illness. *Lancet 2,* 243–246.

Price, J. S., Gardner, R., Jr., & Erickson, M. (2004). Can depression, anxiety and somatization be understood as appeasement displays? *Journal of Affective Disorders, 79*, 1–11.

Richards, R. J. (1987). *Darwin and the emergence of evolutionary theories of mind and behavior.* Chicago: University of Chicago Press.

Rose, H., & Rose, S. (2000). *Alas poor Darwin: Arguments against evolutionary psychology.* London: Jonathon Cape.

Rose, M. R. (1998). *Darwin's spectre: Evolutionary biology in the modern world.* Princeton, NJ: Princeton University Press.

Ruse, M. (1985). *Sociobiology: Sense or nonsense?* (2nd ed.). Dordrecht, Holland: D. Reidel Publishing Co.

Seligman, M. E. P. (1971). Phobias and preparedness. *Behavior Therapy, 2*, 307–320.

Siegert, R. J., & Ward, T. (2002a). Clinical psychology and evolutionary psychology: Toward a dialogue. *Review of General Psychology, 6*(3), 235–259.

Siegert, R. J., & Ward, T. (2002b). Evolutionary psychology: Origins and criticisms. *Australian Psychologist, 37*(1), 20–29.

Skinner, B. F. (1966). The phylogeny and ontogeny of behavior. *Science, 153*, 1205–1213.

Symons, D. (1979). *The evolution of human sexuality.* New York: Oxford University Press.

Thornhill, R., & Palmer, C. T. (2000). *A natural history of rape: Biological bases of sexual coercion.* Cambridge, MA: MIT Press.

Tooby, J. & Cosmides, L. (1992). "The psychological foundations of culture." pp. 19–136. Chapter 1 in J. H. Barkow, L. Cosmides & J. Tooby (Eds.). *The adapted mind: Evolutionary psychology and the generation of culture.* New York: Oxford University Press.

Ward, T., & Siegert, R. J. (2002). Rape and evolutionary psychology: A critique of Thornhill and Palmer's theory. *Aggression and Violent Behavior, 7*(2), 145–168.

Wilson, E. O. (1975). *Sociobiology.* Cambridge, MA: Harvard University Press.

12

Personality Traits Are Essential for a Complete Clinical Science

ALLAN R. HARKNESS

Suppose you read that powerful forces influence human biographies. You read that these forces are linked to anxiety, sexuality, drug use, and success and failure in relationships and work. You read that we tend not to perceive these forces. What if you learned that these claims are on solid scientific ground? That these influences are measurable, their effects predictable? And what if you discovered that these influences had rarely appeared in the grand theories of psychology; that they tend not to be included in the treatment plans of clinical psychologists; that they are rarely parameters in empirically supported treatments? In short, they are overlooked. Anyone wanting to help patients could regard these forces as unexploited opportunities. These powerful, rarely perceived, yet scientifically respectable influences really do exist. They are called personality traits.

Traits? The word conjures the dull, the static, the boring. But traits are dynamic, interesting, and pregnant with clinical opportunity. Traits have measurability, assessment technology, structural analysis, behavior genetics, and longitudinal studies standing behind them. This chapter presents the viewpoint that traits are enduring properties of real psychobiological systems inside the people we work with. Not all trait theorists and not all personality psychologists share this viewpoint.

This chapter provides clinicians-in-training with an introduction to this view. The chapter is not a comprehensive review. Literature citations are held to a minimum, selecting a few key papers that illustrate theory and critical research. In this chapter, I explore the nature of traits, show how researchers decide which traits to study, suggest which traits might be useful for clinical applications, describe how traits are linked with human biography, and examine some biological perspectives essential for understanding traits.

PERSONALITY TRAITS SHOULD BE CENTRAL IN CLINICAL SCIENCE

The typical approaches used in clinical sciences are: (a) the *general laws* approach, (b) the *developmental* approach, and (c) the *failure analysis* approach. The general laws approach finds principles that apply across groups such as all humans, all mammals, or all vertebrates. For example, a general law of learning is habituation—subjects showing less and less orienting response following repeated exposure to an innocuous stimulus. Another example is the pleasure principle of classic psycho-analysis. Many psychological interventions apply general laws, such as operant and classical conditioning, as well as the general principles guiding cognitive therapies.

Another major scientific approach is developmental (see also Chapter 14). The developmental perspective asks: How did the units of observation come to be? Across the sciences, such theories are quite broad ranging, including cosmology (what are the steps from the big bang to the large-scale structures seen now?) and biological evolution. Psychologically oriented clinicians think of individual development. They try to under-stand the life-course processes and transformations of the patient. With evolutionary psychology, we also broaden the developmental question: How did modern humans come to be (see also Chapter 11)? From the 1940s to the 1980s, the general laws approaches, reflected in behaviorism and psychoanalysis, and psychoanalytic versions of developmental theory, dominated clinical formulations.

The failure analysis approach examines complex systems that have reached some catastrophic failure point. We are all familiar with the National Transportation Safety Board teams that quickly arrive at the scene of an air disaster. They focus on understanding systems that failed with catastrophic results. The words "catastrophic" and "failure" signal that this perspective is intimately tied with the human evaluative response determining what is experienced as a bad or undesirable result. In clinical science, the psychopathology perspective is a prime example. Diagnostic categories focus attention on typically adaptive systems seen in breakdown and failure. Did typically adaptive systems encounter environmental excursions that pushed them beyond their functional limits? Did variations in the genetic blueprints produce nonfunctioning variants of typically adaptive systems? Does the diagnosis focus attention on the combination of the two—diathesis and stress? The psychopathology approach uses categorical diagnosis to collect a volume of case information allowing studies of etiology, epidemiology, course, prognosis, and therapeutics.

However, by the 1950s, studies showing the unreliability of diagnostic decisions across clinicians had deeply eroded confidence and interest in diagnostic formulations. In the 1980s, a movement within psychiatry sought to improve the reliability of diagnoses and restore respectability to the pathology perspective. With the publication of the DSM-III, the mental health field underwent a dramatic reversal. Diagnosis, consideration of prevalence, course, and prognosis, again became central to case conceptualization in the clinical sciences of mental health. This historic arc is detailed in an excellent volume by Blashfield (1984; see also Chapter 5). The pendulum has swung so far back toward the psychopathological position that it now seems difficult to get students to consider general laws, development, or, as we shall see, personality traits.

General laws, the developmental perspective, and failure analysis provide the central perspectives of clinical science. However, these three approaches are like a jigsaw puzzle with an important piece missing, a piece that would make the full clinical picture more comprehensible. The missing piece is (d) the *individual differences approach to personality*. Personality traits provide an essential complement to the other perspectives.

Personality traits complement general laws. Traits are personalized parameters by which general laws are played out in individual existence. For example, almost all people can learn avoidance or escape responses to unpleasant stimuli. But how sensitive is our patient to aversive stimuli? How rapidly does he or she learn to avoid or escape? Individual differences provide the stable and clinically essential personal parameters that link general laws to individual existence.

Evolution asked the broad developmental question, how does life change? The answers radically changed biology, leading to a dramatic synthesis of ideas ranging from the mathematics of population size to the facts of molecular genetics. Evolution has moved us from platonic ideals of fixed species to recognize living populations as fuzzy sets of individuals characterized by genetic diversity. Within this new view of nature, individual differences, and thus, of course, personality traits, are central.

Personality traits also provide perspective on the failure analysis or psychopathology perspective. The psychopathology perspective, with its ability for a high degree of focus on symptomatic classes, may not be able to detect the themes in disparate phenomena generated by naturally occurring individual differences. What are seen as relatively qualitative types may result from case-picking regions of a more continuous descriptor space (Clark & Watson, 1999a; Krueger, Caspi, Moffitt, Silva, & McGee, 1996). Understanding personality traits brings the perspective that life is characterized by variation. The idea of natural variation is a corrective to the default perspective that there is some ideal, perfect state of health from which we have been cast by disease. Personality traits alone do not a clinical science make. But without them, general laws, developmental laws, and the psychopathological perspective are incomplete and misleading.

WHAT ARE PERSONALITY TRAITS?

. . . Trait is here defined as a psychological (therefore, organismic) structure underlying a relatively enduring behavioral disposition, i.e., a tendency to respond in certain ways under certain circumstances. In the case of a personality trait some of the behaviors expressing the disposition have substantial adaptational implications. (Tellegen, 1988, p. 622)

This chapter is deeply influenced by the clear definitions and concepts offered by Tellegen (1988, 1991). To introduce personality traits, we start with a realistic description of a hypothetical character.

Beth

As Beth stands in line to board a plane, she strikes up a conversation with the woman ahead of her. Beth forgets an object in her pocket and sets off an alarm. She shares a smile and some self-deprecating humor with the security agent wielding the metal detecting wand. Her smile is a Duchenne smile (Ekman, 2003, p. 207); the smile is genuine, and there seems to be a sparkle in her eyes.

On board, Beth scans the cabin and sees blond curls on the head of a chubby baby. She crosses the aisle to make baby-pleasing faces and sounds. The baby responds with one of his first social smiles. The added wave of enjoyment strengthens her mood. Even in the dry desert of commercial air travel, flowers of pleasure bloom for Beth.

Why did Beth behave like that? Did Beth just learn of great news? Had she taken amphetamines or cocaine? Was she drunk? Did she just experience a bright mood with little apparent cause? Or did enduring characteristics of important, prominent biological systems exert an influence on her behavior? This last possibility—the steady steering of enduring parameters of important biological systems—that is the stuff of personality traits.

Traits as enduring settings of biological systems. Long before human evolution, vertebrates evolved such systems as an exploratory/approach/ seeking system, an anger/rage system for detecting and dealing with frustration of one's goals, a fear system for dealing with dangers, and several other systems (Panksepp, 1998). Each system recognizes major classes or themes of adaptively significant events. The systems then mobilize and organize relevant response systems. Personality traits are enduring operating characteristics of central psychobiological systems such as the danger detection system and the appetitive approach system. Panksepp (2000) referred to such systems as "homologous in all mammals" (p. 137). Traits characterize enduring settings of those systems such as input threshold, breadth of definition of releasing stimuli, and the onset speed, vigor, and topography of responses.

The systems are dynamic, sensitively responding in real time to the moment-to-moment flow of information. A mouse moving from cover to the edge of an open field has a danger detection system calculating the net dangers inherent in moving out into the open field. The mouse also has an explore-approach system that responds to the possibility of food—cut grains in the open field. The dynamic balance of these systems provides inputs to the ongoing behavior stream. The dynamic, moment-to-moment responses of each system are called states or emotions. But the enduring properties—these make for a nervous mouse or a Magellan explorer mouse. The enduring properties are traits.

To read outlines of real biological systems thought to underlie some personality traits, see, for example Depue (1996), Clark and Watson (1999b), Siever and Davis (1991), and Zuckerman (1991). Elegant experimental work sketching out a danger detection system is described in an engaging manner by LeDoux (1996). And see Gosling (2001) for a fascinating and comprehensive review of personality traits in other species.

Traits and Theory

The place of traits in psychological science has advanced over the last 50 years because of better data and methods, such as major longitudinal and behavior genetic studies. Personality also has advanced because of improved theory. We now have better ways of thinking about traits. Up through the 1950s, much of psychology had adopted a strict operationist approach to the philosophy of science. In this approach, you could decide to measure the love between a couple by timing how many seconds they gazed at each other during a 5-minute observation period. In the strict operationist approach, love would then mean nothing more than *seconds of gaze per 5-minute period*.

In the 1950s, psychologists such as Cronbach and Meehl (1955) and Jane Loevinger (1957) helped psychology move beyond strict operationism to use theoretical constructs or open concepts. A construct is part of a theory. It gains part of its meaning from the other parts of theory. To be a scientific theory, the network of constructs has to be connected, in a restricting way, to the things we observe. But a construct, say, "love," might be connected to many other constructs and a nearly infinite possible list of ways of measuring love. The list of potential measures is open, that being one of several ways in which the concepts are open (Meehl, 1978).

The acceptance of the construct in psychological theories necessitated whole new methodologies. We went beyond predictive, criterion-oriented validity to *construct validity* (Cronbach & Meehl, 1955; see also Chapter 4), in which we started to realize that when we collect data on

TABLE 12.1 Elements of Trait Theory

Element	What is it?	Where is it?
Trait	Real psychobiological structure yielding functioning dispositions	In patients, human (and other species) subjects of study
Trait construct	Theory of trait and trait dimension, refined through research	In minds of psychologists, on pages of textbooks and journals
Trait indicators	Observable, measurable signs that are statistically related to the trait	Live behavior, life history, on rating forms, test responses, test profiles
Trait dimension	A distribution of values of the trait, inferred from trait indicators measured in each individual of the population	In a population of individuals who vary on the trait
Characteristic adaptation	Psychological structures such as habits, attitudes, roles that are causally close to behavior and develop in a person within a cultural and life-history context	In patients, human (and other species) subjects of study

personality tests, we need to learn simultaneously about the performance of the measure and the performance of the theory (Tellegen & Waller, in press). Statistical methods that can deal with constructs with many potential markers can be broadly referred to as latent variable models or structural equation models (e.g., Loehlin, 2004). Such approaches are incredibly flexible, allowing the comparison of theories, examination of multitrait–multimethod problems, the simultaneous analysis of multi-sample data, behavior genetic models, hierarchical models, and developmental models.

Tellegen (1988, 1991) clarified the distinctions among traits, constructs, and trait indicators. Essential distinctions are summarized in Table 12.1. *Traits* arise from stable operating characteristics of real structures inside the people we observe. Beth has a real system that readily creates context-appropriate outgoing and sociable behaviors, drives interest in people, yields energy, engagement, and approach, and strong and ready pleasure responses to species-typical satisfactions. As noted in Table 12.1, psychologists must distinguish between the real *traits* in the people we observe and our *trait constructs*, which are parts of theory. The constructs, to paraphrase Loevinger (1957), are found in the minds of theorists and are represented by symbols in their writings.

The next distinction is a difficult one for psychologists trained after Watson and Skinner. *Traits are not behavior.* Traits are dispositions arising from stable characteristics of underlying systems, and thus are detectable and falsifiable scientific entities. Traits influence behavior, but they are not behavior (Meehl, 1986). This is shown in Table 12.1 in the distinction between *trait indicators* and traits. Because of trait influence, many behaviors, including test responses and life events, can function as trait indicators. However, a single trait is just one of many causal influences on how a person behaves.

Table 12.1 also conveys the population concept of *trait dimension* (Tellegen, 1988). Consider this physical example: each individual has a weight, and that weight can be used to locate the person along the population distribution of weights. The population distribution defines the dimension. In personality, a population of people are distributed from Low Positive Emotionality to High Positive Emotionality (Tellegen, 1985; Watson & Clark 1997). That is a dimension of personality. An individual, like Beth, is located somewhere along that trait dimension.

Major theoretical advance: Some traits are emotion dispositions. Traits are dispositions arising from enduring settings of biological systems subserving broad categories of adaptive behavior. Which systems? Tellegen (1982, 1985) and Watson and Clark (1984, 1997) advanced theory by clearly connecting emotion and personality. A classic personality trait, referred to as Neuroticism (vs. Emotional Stability), was reinterpreted in terms of its relationship to mood, affect, and emotion. People high in Neuroticism were seen as having a disposition to experience a range of negative emotions (e.g., anxiety, self-doubt, anger). Tellegen (1982) suggested the label Negative Affectivity (subsequently changed to Negative Emotionality). Similarly, Extraversion (versus Introversion) was reinterpreted in terms of a disposition to experience positive emotions. There is an emerging synthesis between the emotion and personality literatures (see, e.g., Izard, Libero, Putnam, & Haynes, 1993; Watson & Clark, 1992). Emotion systems are dynamic moment-to-moment mammalian adaptive systems, but within the individual, those systems have enduring and individuating parameters. Some of those enduring and individuating settings are personality traits. It is also important to note that some personality traits may not be part of emotion systems.

A broad psychological framework for traits. McCrae (1993) offered the distinction between Basic Tendencies (a term he used for personality traits) and Characteristic Adaptations. For clinical applications, this is a critically important distinction. If Beth has a trait that entails the parameters of her positive emotion systems yielding easy enjoyment, readiness for social engagement, and so on, this will have an impact on many nontrait psychological structures such as attitudes ("people are fun"), self-concept ("I'm friendly"), and the types of life history, relationships, memories, habits, and skills she will develop. These are the Characteristic Adaptations, the final entry on Table 12.1. McCrae and Costa (1995) theorized that Self-Concept is a specialized and important Characteristic Adaptation.

McCrae and Costa (1995) developed a broad theoretical framework that postulated that information flows, via dynamic processes, only in the following direction:

Biological Bases → Basic Tendencies → Characteristic Adaptations.

Although this part of their theory shocked me at first, I came to realize that like Frances Crick's Central Dogma of Molecular Biology,[1] this is a paradigm giver. That important exceptions crop up here and there (like retroviruses for Crick's Dogma) just show the overall power of the paradigm for helping scientists and clinicians think through problems.

There is more to McCrae and Costa's (1995) framework, and it is essential reading for the clinician. External influences work by changing characteristic adaptations. And characteristic adaptations effect life events, or *objective biography*. Characteristic adaptations drive both the thematic coherence of traits and the cultural variation characteristic of human behavior. I have found that asking students to frame a case in terms of the McCrae and Costa (1995) theory helps them to move their case conceptualization beyond a disconnected list of diagnoses to become an integrated, coherent picture of the patient.

WHICH PERSONALITY TRAITS?

Anyone can think of hundreds, perhaps thousands of ways people differ psychologically. The clinician looking at the glut of trait labels experiences a sinking feeling and suspects there is a disorganized and chaotic mess in personality. That suspicion would be wrong. In fact, there is quite a bit of order among traits. The predominant method used to discover order has been *exploratory factor analysis*. A brief, nontechnical description of exploratory factor analysis will be presented. Some psychologists have been skeptical about the ability of factor analysis to reveal underlying structure, such as hierarchical biological systems. However, exploratory factor analysis has already scored a well-documented success with tests of mental ability. Burt (1949), based on a review of factor analyses, deduced that general mental ability has two underlying components to which he ascribed functions much like those that we would recognize as functions of left and right cerebral hemispheres. Burt provided a framework that neatly integrated and informed later well-controlled experimental evidence on asymmetry of function of the cerebral hemispheres. In personality, the same pattern is emerging: Factor analysis is a starting point. It helps us to arrive at a first approximation answer to the "Which Traits?" question. More refined pictures of trait systems

---

[1] A reader of my original draft brought to my attention that Allik and McCrae (2002) had made the same connection to the central dogma.

can then emerge from the integration of measurement, developmental, longitudinal, behavior genetic, and neuroscience work.

Brief Introduction to Exploratory Factor Analysis[2]

To answer the question "Which traits?" researchers look at relationships between measures such as scales, item responses, and ratings. Suppose that you asked 400 people to rate how willingly they would make a parachute jump. You also ask them to rate how willingly they would walk across a field inhabited by poisonous snakes. Those more willing to parachute jump will generally be more willing to take the snake walk. And those refusing one will tend to refuse the other. Across the sample of people, there is a positive correlation between the self-ratings. Some will feel sure about one task and less sure of the other. Some will have specific reactions to heights or snakes. This means the correlation will not be a perfect 1.0, but it will probably be positive. If there is a stable personality trait that affects responses to both of these items, then using the language of Table 12.1, we could call those items *trait indicators*.

Suppose further that we had asked the same 400 people to rate how easily and strongly they feel joy when something good happens. And we also ask them how much they enjoy talking with other people. People who are depressed would tend to rate themselves low on both. Some fortunate people would rate themselves high on both. It turns out that items about joy and the enjoyment of conversation also tend to be positively correlated. Another fact emerges: The parachute item, although related to the snake walk item, bears a clearly smaller relationship to the joy and talking questions.

There is structure in the relationship of the items, structure seen across a sample of people. Some items seem to work together as closely coordinated teams. The parachute item and the snake item are a closely coordinated team. The joy and the conversation items also form a team. But the two teams are not strongly coordinated with each other.

Exploratory factor analysis is a technique for taking the correlations among many scales, or items, or ratings, and looking for structure in the patterns of those relationships. Exploratory factor analysis can look for teams of items that are working together. Such a team, when identified, is called a factor. Although this example is not a real factor analysis, the "teams of items" concept provides an intuitive understanding of two

---

[2] Readers familiar with exploratory factor analysis will quickly realize that this chapter provides only a simplified conceptual introduction to the topic. Some of the teaching shortcuts involved using only two indicators per factor (obviously inadequate), not discussing methods that could guide the level of extraction, and not even addressing rotation (although results are discussed as though rotated to idealized simple structure). I hope the sophisticated reader is willing to grant didactic latitude to bring along readers who are new to the topic.

factors underlying the structural relationships among the four items. Finding teams offers a substantial simplification: We may be able to describe people on the basis of two factors rather than on the basis of all four items. How do the factors from factor analysis relate to trait theory? From Table 12.1, we know that a trait indicator is an observable behavior that should be affected by a trait. A trait dimension is a population concept, created by people varying on the trait. This variation causes the indicators to show correlations, or to evidence teamwork. Thus, a factor found in the analysis could be an indication of a trait dimension.

In a famous 1950s study, Tupes and Christal (1992) conducted exploratory factor analyses of ratings of U.S. Air Force personnel. Comparing analyses from different samples, they found they could extract five factors that would replicate. The five factors were called surgency, agreeableness, dependability, emotional stability, and culture. A variant of this model is called simply the Five Factor Model (FFM) and it underlies Costa and McCrae's (1992) NEO PI-R. The NEO PI-R measures five broad domains: Neuroticism (in Tupes and Christal's terms, low emotional stability), Extraversion (surgency), Agreeableness, Conscientiousness (dependability), and Openness to Experience (a variant of some themes in culture).

The NEO PI-R measures each of the domains by measuring six different facets, or narrower traits thought to contribute to the domain. For example, the Extraversion domain is composed of six facets: Warmth, Gregariousness, Assertiveness, Activity, Excitement-Seeking, and Positive Emotions. The Conscientiousness domain is composed of Competence, Order, Dutifulness, Achievement Striving, Self-Discipline, and Deliberation. This type of organization is called hierarchical organization. Understanding it is a key to properly interpreting the diversity of tests, measures, and theoretical conceptions of personality traits. Hierarchical organization of personality traits will be described immediately after two more hypothetical characters, Tommy and Ed, are introduced. Our set of three characters, Beth, Tommy, and Ed, will be critical in illustrating hierarchical organization.

Tommy

Tommy is a teen. His favorite game involves virtual carjackings. He loves the unpredictability, never knowing when rival gangs or cops may pop up. He loves the surprise on the faces of the victims. Right now he is unhappy because he is sitting down to his first class of the day. He is bored already. He knows what will happen.

He spots a pile of books on the next desk and nudges them, sending the books tumbling. The irritated victim looks right at him and loudly says, "Thanks," alerting the teacher.

"Tommy," she says, "pick up the books."

Tommy's lips tighten. He flushes with anger at being ordered around, at being made the focus of attention. He glares at the victim and utters a threat. The teacher is angry now, professionalism gone.

"Tommy, get the hell out of this classroom and go to the principal's office."

Tommy has been to the principal's office many times. He is not worried. He is relieved. Out of class, he is back into the unpredictable. Something could happen now. He knows it will not be horrible. He is curious, engaged. This will be more interesting than class.

Ed

Ed is riding a train. His fear of flying led him to buy train tickets. As he rides, he thinks of terrorist attacks on Spanish trains and tubes in London. He had thought he could travel without worry, but here he is, imagining his own blood on the seat cover ahead. With the first finger of his right hand, he twirls his hair. He has twirled his hair since he was a baby. He feels the first sensations of a tickle in his throat.

"Oh great," he thinks, "I'm getting sick on a trip." Ed thinks of the time he got the flu on the road. He remembers weakness, exhaustion. He remembers having to carry bags, sit up in an airplane seat. He remembers laryngitis that began with just such a tickle in the throat. The train seems to be going so slowly. His legs are cold.

"Did I bring the hotel information?" He begins to rummage through his briefcase. Unnoticed, some papers fall out. A heavy-set man grunts as he picks them up and hands them to Ed.

"Oh, my credit card bill!" Ed, thinking of identity theft, snatches the papers from the helper. The man's brow furrows at Ed's rudeness. Ed's mood is really down now. The down mood allows him to associate fluidly to the next worry.

"The credit cards," he thinks, "Why can't I control my spending? I'm undisciplined. Spend, spend, spend. I'm back to the limit again."

Ed coughs and feels the tickle. To check it out, he loudly clears his throat—yes, irritation—he clears again. Other travelers shift their bodies away from Ed. He runs his tongue over the roof of his mouth, as far back as he can. "Yes, tender. I feel the bumps."

Tommy, Ed, and Beth can be used to illustrate hierarchical structure.

Hierarchical Structure of Personality Traits

When we first think about hierarchy, we might think: The peasant is under the earl, who in turn is under the king. This is a hierarchy in which any individual must be classified as either peasant, earl, or king. Hierarchical structure, as found in the realm of personality, is really quite different. This type of hierarchy again involves teams of items, scales, ratings, or other trait indicators that can subsequently be used to describe people. In this hierarchy, big, loosely knit teams of indicators are made up of highly coordinated subteams. The subteams are subordinate to, and play for, big, more loosely coordinated teams. This is a challenging but critical idea. The personality hierarchy is not a hierarchy of individuals classified into categories. Instead, this hierarchy involves narrow but more tightly coordinated teams of trait indicators playing on the teams of higher-order operators or factors that underlie the structure of observed correlations. This is a hierarchical structure of correlation or covariation.

An exemplary study of personality structure was a meta-analysis (an analysis combining the data from many previous studies) by Markon, Krueger, and Watson (2005). They identified 44 scales (scores on relatively homogeneous collections of items) from five widely used families of personality instruments.[3] The relationships between 44 scales are described by 946 correlations. These were assembled into an organized arrangement called a correlation matrix. The authors set out to find as many studies as possible from which to form 946 best estimates of each correlation. Markon, Krueger, and Watson (2005) noted that they produced estimates based on 77 different samples ranging in size from $n = 158$ to $n = 52,879$.

After 946 values were estimated from all available data, the correlation matrix was mathematically conditioned for factor analysis. The researchers then extracted 2, 3, 4, and 5 factor solutions. The authors argued that taken together, the factor solutions comprise a single coherent hierarchical structure. There are very broad traits at the two-factor level, and more differentiated, narrow traits at each subsequent level of extraction.

Markon et al. found, at the two-factor level, two massive traits—many scales with substantial loadings on each factor, thus comprising two loosely coupled teams of scales. The first factor has loadings from scales tapping worry, anxiety, the experience of negative emotions, emotional instability, aggressiveness, negative distortion of thinking, lack of conscientiousness, oppositionality, identity disturbance, and poor self-control. Tommy, the boy who enjoys the carjacking game, would probably score high on a scale constructed from this factor. He seems more aggressive, oppositional, and displays less self-control than the average child. The description would be a bit coarse for him, though; he does not seem to be much of a worrier or an anxiety prone person.

Ed, the train traveler, would probably also score above average on a scale made from this factor. He seems very anxious, readily detecting problems in the incoming stream of information. He experiences many negative emotions; and he has negative distortions in his thinking. When

---

[3] "Families" refers to the fact that scales from several different versions of the instruments were used. The families of personality instruments were the DAPP, EPQ, MPQ, NEO PI-R, and the TCI. Refer to Markon, Krueger, and Watson (2005) for full citations of the tests and various versions.

worried, he can be a bit impulsive. However, noting that he is high on this scale would also mislead a bit. He does not seem particularly aggressive. We do not know if he is oppositional. Beth, our airline traveler, might score low on such a scale.

The second factor had high loadings on scales measuring extraversion, a sense of well-being, and social ease. Beth would score high on a scale made to measure this factor. Where would Tommy and Ed score? We might guess low, but we have little information on which to base our guess. Can they have fun and enjoy things? Are they interested in people, in seeking social contact? At this point we do not know. It would be very useful to measure them with a scale made to measure this factor. The two-factor solution lacks detail—it is too coarse to accurately describe many people.

Markon et al. next extracted three factors. The three factors are very coherently related to the earlier two factors. The big negative factor split into two more narrow factors. They found that the massive factor with worry, anxiety, and being easily stressed split off from being aggressive and poorly self-controlled. This combination of aggressiveness and impulsive poor self-control was found in the work of Siever and Davis (1991). The third factor remained extraversion, social interest, and well-being.

At this three-factor level, we can better capture Tommy and Ed. Tommy would be elevated on the aggressiveness and poor self-control scale. He would not be elevated on a scale built from the tension, worry, and negative emotions factor. Ed is just the reverse. He would be high on the worry, stress, and tension factor, but we would not expect him to be particularly elevated on the aggressiveness and poor self-control factor. Beth remains the only person we would have strong expectations for on the extraversion well-being factor. We can see that the factors of the three-factor level are quite coherently related to the factors of the two-factor level, but greater resolution of individual cases can be obtained.

Markon et al. (2005) found that at the four-factor level, aggressiveness split off from poor self-control. Aggressiveness separated from what Watson and Clark (1993) referred to as Behavioral Disinhibition. Tellegen referred to the trait dimension as Constraint. In work with my collaborators, I used Tellegen's trait construct and labeled the same trait dimension from the reverse end as Disconstraint (Harkness, McNulty, Ben-Porath, & Graham, 2002). Markon et al.'s four-factor solution clearly maps onto the four constructs arrived at by Trull and Durrett's (2005) literature review. Trull and Durrett suggested that there is converging support for dimensional systems that tap four broad domains of personality: "neuroticism/negative affectivity/emotional dysregulation; extraversion/positive emotionality; dissocial/antagonistic behavior; and constraint/compulsivity/conscientiousness" (p. 13.1). Widiger (1998) and Watson, Clark, and Harkness (1994) also singled out these four trait dimensions as particularly relevant to clinical issues related to personality. A well-constructed measure at this four-factor level would allow us to try to index Tommy's level of aggressiveness separately from his lack of constraint and conscientiousness.

At the five-factor level, Markon et al. identified the model that underlies the NEO-PI-R, with Openness splitting off from positive emotionality. This yields Neuroticism, Agreeabless, Conscientiousness, Extraversion, and Openness.

Markon et al. produced a top-down derivation of the hierarchy. My colleagues and I (Harkness, 1992; Harkness and McNulty, 1994) produced a bottom-up study of hierarchical structure, and arrived at a similar solution: Aggressiveness, Disconstraint, Negative Emotionality/ Neuroticism, Introversion/Low Positive Emotionality. However, for our fifth dimension, we identified degree of reality contact, a trait dimension we called Psychoticism. This model is the Personality Psychopathology Five, or PSY-5 (Harkness & McNulty, 1994; Harkness, McNulty, Ben-Porath, & Graham, 2002). The PSY-5 can be scored if the patient has completed the Minnesota Multiphasic Personality Inventory—Revised (MMPI-2).

The concepts of factor analysis and hierarchical structure provide practitioners with tools to understand how specific trait measures fit into broader or narrower levels of the hierarchy. These concepts allow clinicians to understand how different measures can be located relative to the levels spelled out by the hierarchical consensus structure found by Markon, Krueger, and Watson (2005).

Traits Influence Environments and Our Biographies

Traits help create the environments we live in. The narrative of Beth, with high Positive Emotionality, described her as flying on a commercial airline, an activity that is rarely a source of pleasure. Yet she saw an opportunity to converse in the waiting line. Extraverts, high Positive Emotionality people, value the chance to talk, to interact. Talking led her to forget something in her pocket, triggering a search. Her response? The search became an opportunity to interact, to joke with the security agent, to see humor in her predicament. In the plane, she sought out a baby and interacted with him, evoking the baby's smile. Beth's high Positive Emotionality/Extraversion helps create the social environment she lives in.

Tommy created an environment too. Disconstrained and Aggressive, he reacted to the predictability and authoritarian structure of the class-room by knocking down a classmate's books. The teacher responded by asserting more authority. Both teacher and victim responded with anger and hostility to Tommy's threat.

Ed's trait of high Negative Emotionality/Neuroticism helped create an environment. He chose the train, a slow mode of transport, and then felt irritated by its speed. He alienated other passengers by snatching a letter, being in a dark mood, and continuous throat clearing.

Buss (1987) described how personality is linked to the social environment by three processes: selection, evocation, and manipulation. *Selection* refers to personality guiding active choice of environment. The Extravert selects environments with opportunity for social interaction. The person with high Negative Emotionality may select environments so as to avoid anxiety. *Evocation* means that people with different levels of traits cause the environment to react differently. Beth's personality caused a baby to smile at her. Tommy evoked hostility and punishment. Ed's high Negative Emotionality caused people to pull back from him. *Manipulation* refers to active change of the environment. Like an extravert sparking up a dull party, Beth may actually change the mood of passengers on the plane. Selection, evocation, and manipulation are dynamic processes intimately tying the environments we inhabit and the events we experience to our personalities. Traits entrain clinical dynamics.

Here is a small selection of studies examining links between personality and the events in one's life. Magnus, Diener, Fujita, and Pavot (1993) conducted a 4-year longitudinal study on 62 women and 35 men. The participants had filled out the NEO Personality Inventory (Costa & McCrae, 1985) when taking a psychology class. The 97 respondents located 4 years later reported on the experience of objectively verifiable life events classified as either good events (e.g., got a pet) or bad events (victim of nonviolent crime). Negative Emotionality predicted objective bad events: the higher the Negative emotionality, the more bad events. Positive Emotionality/Extraversion predicted objective good events: the more Extraverted the participant, the higher the number of positive events. Why more positive events? Is it possible that greater activity, energy, interest, engagement, warmth, and social interest create good possibilities?

Ormel and Wohlfarth (1991) conducted a 7-year longitudinal study with 296 Dutch adults. The participants completed a Negative Emotionality measure and then 6 years later had interviews to determine the number and severity of long-term difficult conditions in their lives. Examples included having a child with a handicap or having marital problems. Difficult conditions were classified into two types: *endogenous*, over which the participant had some control, and *exogenous*, those difficulties judged to be causally independent of the participant. At the 6-year follow-up interview, the researchers also measured the level of psychological distress experienced by the participant. At the 7th year, researchers again interviewed the participants and determined degree of change in their life situation, from improvement to deterioration. They again measured the level of psychological distress. They found that Negative Emotionality correlated $r = .39$ ($p < .05$) with the incidence of endogenous (participant has some control) long-term difficulties, measured 6 years later. Exogenous (participant had no control) long-term difficulties only correlated $r = .06$ (ns) with Negative Emotionality measured 6 years earlier. Structural equation modeling revealed that the personality trait of Negative Emotionality, measured 6 or 7 years before the environmental measures, had "strikingly stronger" (p. 751) causal pathways influencing psychological distress than did the measured long-term difficulties themselves or change in life situation. This should be a clear signal to the clinician that personality traits must be central to understanding any case.

As you conduct an intake interview, or gain extensive biographical information over the course of therapy, how do you understand the emotional coloration of events provided by the patient? What defined the promotion at work as an opportunity or a danger? All the events of the patient's life have been filtered through emotion systems. The long-term parameters, the enduring biases on those systems are personality traits. But the effect of personality traits is not limited to perception. Through selection, evocation, and manipulation, traits influence the creation of objective biographies. The clinician needs a sound measure of personality traits to understand, in a psychologically sophisticated way, the narrative of the patient's life.

As Caspi (2000) eloquently summarized it: "Across the life course—from one's family of origin to one's family of destination—behavioral development takes place in environments that are correlated with individual differences in personality. And even though it is not possible to predict chance encounters, personality differences influence how even these fortuitous events are subjectively experienced" (p. 170).

BIOLOGY AND PERSONALITY

Behavior genetics was introduced in Chapter 10 of this volume. Fundamental genetic analysis begins with the distinction between the genotype and the phenotype. The genotype is composed of the genes possessed by an individual. The phenotype is the realized expression of characteristics of the individual. Behavior genetics methods provide a better understanding of traits by using the natural experiments of different types of twinning, adoption, and other naturally occurring variations in the degree of genetic relatedness between people. Behavior genetics research also capitalizes on variations in the degree of environmental sharing between research participants; for example, some research participants share a home environment, others do not (see Chapter 10). Research has also incorporated molecular methods. The result has been increased understanding of the genetic contribution to personality trait variation, and equally important, a better understanding of the environmental contribution (see Plomin, DeFries, McClearn, & McGuffin, 2001).

Loehlin and Rowe (1992) simultaneously examined large twin studies, adoption studies, and data on the relatives of twins. Their subjects had completed questionnaire measures of the five-factor model personality traits. Loehlin and Rowe were able to study the degree of personality similarity between subjects in light of varying degrees of genetic related-ness and whether the subjects shared a family environment or not. Recall from Chapter 10 that the *heritability* of a trait is the proportion of the variance of that trait that is due to genetic variation in the population. Heritability is symbolized by h^2. Loehlin and Rowe estimated h^2 of these personality traits to range from .40 to .50. Thus, about 40 to 50% of the variation in five-factor personality traits was estimated to be genetic in origin. It also follows that 50% to 60% of the variation in five-factor personality traits was estimated to be nongenetic in origin.

A major contribution of behavior genetic research methods has been the ability to parse environmental contributions to traits into two types (see also Chapter 10). One type of environmental effect causes similarity in pairs of people who have grown up in the same home. The proportion of phenotypic variation due to environmental factors making family members similar to each other is called *shared environmental influence*, symbolized in the models as c^2. In this type of effect, environment creates personality covariance in people who share a family. The other type of environmental influence does not make family members similar to each other. It is called *nonshared environmental influence*, and it is symbolized as e^2. Nonshared environmental influence adds variance into pairs of observations.

Loehlin and Rowe (1992) showed that environmental influence on personality tends to be predominantly e^2, not c^2. That is, environment tends to inject variance rather than inducing covariance between people who share a home environment. Based on these findings, an adoptive parent should not expect the home environment to mold the child to have traits like the parent's traits.

Rowe (1994) noted that this runs counter to socialization models. However, it should not be surprising to theorists who hold the psychobiological view of constructive realism. In this view, personality traits are the stable, enduring features of biological systems—cell networks. What then is the environment of a personality trait? Is it what humans see through their eyes or hear through their ears? Is environment the stream of events that could be enacted on a Shakespearian stage? Yes, those are parts of environment. But not all. Environment for a cell system is also the microns-deep wetlands around each cell of the system. Environment for the genes of each cell includes the nanometer scale molecules in and around the nucleus of each cell in the system. Much of what goes on in these critical parts of the environment is not noise—it is systematic dynamic process. However, it is environment that cannot possibly be shared with anyone, including an MZ twin. It is *nonshared* environment.

Loehlin and Rowe's (1992) findings have stood up well to many replications. The behavior genetics of self-reported personality individual differences is well summarized as moderate heritabilities in the 40 to 50% range, with the rest of the variation due to environment. Furthermore, sharing a home environment does not tend to strongly make people similar in personality traits, at least as measured by self-report. And yet we have learned some new, interesting things since the early 1990s.

A finding that surprised many is that life events, biographical histories of people, are to some degree heritable (Plomin, 1994). They are influenced by our genes. MZ twins, starting life with identical genetics, lead more similar lives than DZ twins resulting from two separate conception events. In a sample of older Swedish twins, Saudino, Pedersen, Lichtenstein, McClearn, and Plomin (1997) found a genetic effect for life events for controllable, desirable, and undesirable events in the lives of women. For those events and women, all of the genetic influence on life events appeared to act through personality. The measure of personality is central for the clinician who desires a psychological understanding of the life events of patients.

The Behavior Genetics of the Hierarchy of Traits

As described earlier, the structure of personality traits is hierarchical (e.g., Guilford, 1975; Harkness, 1992; Watson Clark, & Harkness, 1994; Markon, Krueger, & Watson, 2005). At the top of the hierarchy are a small number of dimensions with wide, broad psychological implications. At lower levels, there are more numerous dimensions that are psychologically narrow. The lower-level, narrow dimensions contain themes from the higher-order dimension to which they belong, but they also contain specific features not shared with the higher level.

Jang, McCrae, Angleitner, Riemann, and Livesley (1998) studied the behavior genetics of lower level traits using the NEO PI-R (Costa & McCrae, 1992). As previously noted, the NEO PI-R was constructed to have a hierarchical structure. The higher-level, broad domains are Neuroticism, Extraversion, Openness, Agreeableness, and Conscientiousness. The scales measuring these five domains are each composed of six subscales measuring more narrow dimensions. Thus, 30 facet-level scales are nested within the 5 domain scales of the NEO PI- R. Jang et al. studied the behavior genetics of these 30 lower-level scales.

They studied the *specific variance* of the subscales. Specific variance is the residual variance left after the variance of the five broad domain scales was removed. They found that the specific variance of 26 of the 30 facets had a significant heritable component. And at each level of the personality hierarchy, from broad domains down to narrow subscales, a consistent pattern is found: Personality is substantially influenced by both genetic and environmental factors. But the environmental influence does not tend to create similarities between persons who share the family environment.

Factor Analytic Structure, Behavior Genetics, and Biological Systems

Krueger (2000) examined the behavior genetics of structural relations among MPQ (Tellegen, 1982) scores. The MPQ is also based on a hierarchical model. MPQ primary scales, composed of tightly coordinated teams of items, relate in a pattern suggestive of higher-order, broader teams that Tellegen (1982) called super-factors. Krueger was able to decompose the phenotypic correlations into matrices of (additive) genetically mediated correlations among MPQ subscales, and nonshared environmentally mediated correlations among those scales. There is strong structural resemblance in all three matrices—structure that is summarized by the super-factors of Negative Emotionality, Positive Emotionality, and Constraint. Krueger raised the question of what would create the same structure in all three matrices. He offered an answer:

> These mechanisms may be three distinct neural systems undergirding affective and motivational temperament. A first hypothesized system mediates responses to appetitive stimuli and is manifested phenotypically as frequency of positive emotional experience; a second system mediates responses to aversive stimuli and is manifested phenotypically as frequency of negative emotional experience; a third system coordinates responses to motivationally significant stimuli and is manifested phenotypically as the tendency to express versus constrain the expression of affect and impulse [cf. Tellegen, 1985] (Krueger, 2000, p. 1065).

Thus, variation—genetic, environmental, and resulting phenotypic—exerts coherent patterns of influence by flowing through the aqueducts of a hierarchical personality system. Personality shows the hallmarks of biological structure: hierarchical organization.

Beyond Self-Report

The German Observational Study of Adult Twins (GOSAT; Borkenau, Riemann, Angleitner & Spinath, 2001) makes an extremely informative contribution to the behavior genetics of personality. Most behavior genetics studies of personality have been conducted using self-report and some have used observer ratings for measurement. In GOSAT, these methods were complemented with extensive observational measurement. Three hundred twin pairs were classified into MZ (168 pairs) and DZ (132 pairs) using predominantly molecular genetic methods (only 17 pairs were classified by questionnaire assessment of phenotypic similarity). Each participant was videotaped performing 15 different tasks, yielding approximately 60 minutes of tape per participant. One hundred twenty independent judges provided comprehensive and replicated ratings on the 300 participants' performances on the 15 tasks. No judge rated both cotwins of a twin pair. Videotaped performances on the 15 tasks were separately rated on scales designed to tap the five-factor model of personality (additional ratings were also made for the Big 5 factor of intellect). The authors noted that they collected some 1.26 million ratings on the videotapes!

Borkenau et al. replicated previous findings on self-report and peer ratings with estimates of 40% genetic and 60% environmental on personality, with, once again, little or no evidence that sharing a family environment makes people similar. Self-reported Extraversion was the single exception, with some evidence of sharing family environment producing increased similarity. What about the observational measures? Aggregated ratings of personality by the independent judges, on the five-factor model at the domain level, did not, in a single case, result in a statistically significant effect of shared environment. However, using the alternative theory of the fifth factor, intelligence rather than openness, did result in a statistically significant effect of sharing a family environment. Several subscales or intelligence ratings showed the same phenomenon.

Borkenau et al. reported the results of the full model that allowed estimation of additive genetic effects, the effect of environment that does not cause family members to be similar, and also the size of environmental factors that do cause family members to resemble each other. When the ongoing stream of behavior is rated by independent judges, the authors estimated the relative size of influence on judges ratings as 40% genetic, 35% environment acting in a way that does not cause similarity within families, and 25% of the influence is due to environment acting to cause similarity among family members. How can the estimate of the effect of shared environmental influence be 25% when it is statistically nonsignificant? Even if an effect is not statistically significant, the best estimate of the size of the effect, in a maximum likelihood sense, may not be zero.

Another important factor to consider in interpreting the GOSAT findings is that personality is not the same thing as behavior. In the view presented in this chapter, personality is composed of the stable properties of important systems that steer behavior. No one would confuse "saying something smart" with "being smart." Intelligence is a stable property of the systems that generate intelligent behavior. To adequately infer intelligence or personality from behavior would involve many observations, across many times, involving varied situations demanding adaptive behaviors. To read the descriptions of the 15 tasks presented in the GOSAT research, it seems that many would allow for inferences about extraversion and intelligence, but only one seems to engage imagined frustration. However, the authors were not proposing to replace questionnaire self-report or peer ratings with observation measurement. Instead, the GOSAT authors used observation of streams of behavior to escape measurement problems that could result in spurious findings from self-report and memory-based peer report. They achieved this in a landmark study that replicates the baseline estimate of heritability of personality at 40%. This study also raises the possibility that when the measurement problems of self-report and peer ratings are removed, sharing a family environment may have some homogenizing effect. However, it is also possible that sharing family environment has nonpersonality effects on behavior, perhaps stylistic effects, that influence judges. Perhaps the judges were rating characteristic adaptations as much as personality traits.

Not Breeding True

Finally, evidence is accumulating that some of the genetic influence on personality may be of a type that does not create resemblance between parent and offspring. There are two major classes of genetic effects detectable by some behavior genetic designs. One type of genetic effect produces easily observable resemblances between family members. This is called an additive genetic effect. Many genes affect personality. And if genes impact phenotypes additively, then family members will be similar to each other in proportion to the number of genes they share. Resemblance becomes proportional to relatedness. MZ twins will be twice as similar as those who share 50% of variant form genes, such as parent-offspring pairs, DZ twins, and other full siblings (see also Chapter 10). Grandparents and cousins will have degrees of similarity on traits in proportion to their degree of relatedness given substantial additive genetic effects. In physically observable traits with a good degree of heritability, additive genetic effects are hard to miss. Much of variation in height is of this form.

But not all genes work like this. You may recall Mendel's pea plants and know that some forms of genes dominate other forms, requiring knowledge of the configuration of pairs of genes to predict their effects. If many of the genes affecting personality have such dominance or nonadditive effects, then the expected pattern of resemblance between relatives changes. The predicted pattern of similarity is no longer simply proportional to percentage of genes shared. Instead, certain relationships have privileged status: MZ twins should have more than twice the similarity of DZ twins. Siblings should be more similar than parent-offspring pairs. When these nonadditive effects are pronounced, genetic effects are much harder to intuit from looking at or interacting with families. Resemblance seems unpredictable. Although there is a genetic effect, the trait does not "breed true."

Recent articles (Finkel & McGue, 1997; Plomin, Corley, Caspi, Fulker, & DeFries, 1998) have suggested that dominance effects may play an important role in personality. This would explain a number of important phenomena. First, it would help us understand why genetic effects on personality tend not to be noticed. If dominance effects are important, smooth gradations of phenotypic similarity are not easily observed, and thus it is primarily through the natural experiment of the MZ twin pair that we see the true potency of genetic influence on personality.

Second, dominance effects would suggest that passive matching of genetics and environment would not be a very powerful effect. Parents contribute both genes and environment to their children, but if the genetic effect does not produce resemblance, the passive match of genes with environment would lack the predictable directionality that would make it a potent force. Thus, a recent addition to our knowledge is that personality may not strongly "breed true."

People sometimes "assort," or choose like mates, on certain traits, such as height. They do not assort much based on personality, except for modest correlations in the Disconstraint versus Constraint domain (Lykken & Tellegen, 1993). Bouchard and Loehlin (2001) remarked that the failure to observe assortative mating in personality is an interesting and important issue. One possible answer is that attraction mechanisms would only tend to evolve for predominantly additive traits, where the phenotype is a fairly good guide to the genotype. Personality traits, with a healthy dose of nonadditive genetic variance, may not provide good guidance for assortative mating. Traditionalism, one of the primary traits within Disconstraint–Constraint, was one of only two MPQ scales to lack dominance effects in Finkel and McGue's (1997) study. So a personality trait that shows a rare degree of assortative mating also happens to lack dominance effects—to be predominantly additive. This conjecture on the relation between additivity and assortment is, of course, testable.

The Evolution of General Mechanisms, Such as Personality Traits

Personality traits, as dispositional systems such as Negative Emotionality/ Neuroticism, generate equivalences between very different classes of input (Tellegen, 1991). Ed worried about the tickle in his throat, his credit card bill, and identity theft. Emotion and personality systems are general, not specific, systems. However, evolutionary psychology, as a field, has emphasized very specific mechanisms: "An evolutionary perspective leads one to view the mind as a crowded zoo of evolved, domain specific programs" (Cosmides & Tooby, 2000, p. 91). I would agree that evolution starts its work on specific problems facing whole organisms. However, evolution ends up with much more than a zoo of isolated specific mechanisms. A fundamental observation of biological structure, taught in introductory biology courses, is hierarchical organization. Molecules are organized, packaged, and coordinated in organelle systems, which are organized, packaged, and coordinated within cell systems, and then cells are organized, packaged, and coordinated within organ systems, and on up through multicellular organisms. What evolutionary mechanisms lead beyond single purpose mechanisms (see Chapter 11, for a discussion of the evolution of behavior)?

At least two processes can generate general problem-solving systems. First, if an organism evolves a specific problem-solving system, that system becomes a preadaptation for solving other problems. For example, an opening in the body used to circulate oxygenated water becomes a perfect place to collect nutrients. Teeth could be situated in the opening as well, solving a further specific problem of breaking into defended foods. The teeth in a mouth are a preadaptation for defensive and offensive applications of those teeth. The teeth in a jawless mouth are a preadaptation for a jaw that can give mechanical advantage to the teeth. I have taken poetic license with evolution of the general purpose mouth from *Aplysia* ancestors forward, but the point holds. We do not have separate speaking, eating, drinking, sneezing, breathing, and laughing mouths.

A second mechanism for the evolution of general problem-solving systems also starts with the evolution of specific adaptations. Say an organism plagued by a light-guided predator evolves photosensitive cells that allow the avoidance of lighted areas. Such cells could be preadaptations for even more narrowly targeted specific adaptations, such as very low light rodlike cells that allow navigation in very low light, and parallel evolution of narrow bandwidth, that is, "color"-sensitive conelike cells that might allow identification of color bands on predators. We now have two rather specific systems: rodlike low light cells, and conelike color-detecting cells. The two specific adaptations are in fact preadaptations for the evolution of a system that hooks them together. Students of the retina will recognize amacrine cells, horizontal, and bipolar cells as real biological entities that hook rods and cones together to yield a very general light analysis system.

This last process, of specific problem-solving systems being preadaptations for the evolution of integrators, is clearly a basis for that fundamental hallmark of biological structure: hierarchical organization. Cosmides and Tooby (2000) acknowledged that such integrating systems exist:

> Emotions are such programs. To behave functionally according to evolutionary standards, the mind's many subprograms need to be orchestrated so that their joint product at any given time is functionally coordinated, rather than cacophonous and self-defeating. This coordination is accomplished by a set of superordinate programs—the emotions. They are adaptations that have arisen in response to the adaptive problem of mechanism orchestration. . . . " (Cosmides & Tooby, 2000, p. 92).

Recognition of the critical role played by emotion systems, which are indeed general problem-solving systems, could bring together natural allies: the individual differences perspective and evolutionary psychology. Personality traits are the enduring long-term differentiating properties of just such systems.

ESSENTIAL KNOWLEDGE AND SKILLS FOR CLINICAL APPLICATION

Harkness and Lilienfeld (1997) provided a broad framework for applying personality individual differences in clinical work. We may, for example, help the patient understand themes in his or her biography (Harkness & McNulty, 2002). We can help the person understand the personal parameters by which general laws are played out in his or her life, bringing reasonable and achievable expectations to therapy. Harkness and McNulty (2006) described how personality traits can be used by clinicians to anticipate and head off difficulties in the therapeutic alliance.

As clinicians, we can develop a deeper understanding of patient vulnerabilities, not as disconnected diagnoses, but as the expression of powerful enduring forces at work in the lives of our patients—personality traits.

To successfully apply personality individual differences science on behalf of patients, both conceptual knowledge and procedural skills must be developed. The clinician should be able to administer and interpret a psychometrically sound test that provides an overview of major personality individual differences. A few examples include the MPQ (Tellegen, 1982), ZKPQ (Zuckerman, Kuhlman, Joireman, Teta, & Kraft (1993), PSY-5 (MMPI-2; Harkness, McNulty, Ben-Porath, & Graham, 2002), and the NEO PI-R (Costa & McCrae, 1992). The edited volume by DeRaad and Peruguini (2002) provides background and research on a wide range of personality measures, both Five Factor and alternative models.

AUTHOR NOTES

I deeply appreciate the comments on an earlier draft that I received from the editors, and from Claire Harkness, Robert Krueger, John Loehlin, Jeff McCrae, John McNulty, Kristian Markon, and Auke Tellegen. Special thanks go to the students in a graduate seminar entitled "Personality Traits as a Central Concept in Clinical Science." Jennifer Bristow, Christina Cantrell, Aimi Nelson, Nina Schneider, Michelle Streich, Sara Tiegreen, Jill Wanner, Taeh Ward, and Kate Witheridge provided comments on my attempts to write about and teach this material in an understandable manner.

SUGGESTED READINGS

Caspi, A. (2000). The child is the father of the man: Personality continuities from childhood to adulthood. *Journal of Personality and Social Psychology, 78,* 158–172.

Harkness, A. R., & McNulty, J. L. (2006). An overview of personality: The MMPI-2 Personality Psychopathology—Five Scales (PSY-5). In J. N. Butcher (Ed.), *MMPI-2: A practitioner's guide* (pp. 73–97). Washington, DC: American Psychological Association.

Markon, K. E., Krueger, R. F., & Watson, D. (2005). Delineating the structure of normal and abnormal personality: An integrative hierarchical approach. *Journal of Personality and Social Psychology, 88,* 139–157.

Tellegen, A. (1985). Structures of mood and personality and their relevance to assessing anxiety, with an emphasis on self-report. In A. H. Tuma & J. D. Maser (Eds.), *Anxiety and the anxiety disorders* (pp. 681–706). Hillsdale, NJ: Lawrence Erlbaum Associates.

Wiggins, J. S. (Ed.). (1996). *The five-factor model of personality: Theoretical perspectives.* New York: Guilford.

REFERENCES

Allik, J., & McCrae, R. R. (2002). A Five-Factor Theory perspective. In R. R. McCrae & J. Allik (Eds.), *The Five-Factor Model of personality across cultures* (pp. 303–322). New York: Kluwer Academic/Plenum.

Blashfield, R. K. (1984). *The classification of psychopathology: Neo-Kraepelinian and Quantitative approaches*. New York: Plenum.

Borkenau, P., Riemann, R., Angleitner, A., & Spinath, F. M. (2001). Genetic and environmental influences on observed personality: Evidence from the German Observational Study of Adult Twins. *Journal of Personality and Social Psychology, 80*, 655–668.

Bouchard, T. J., Jr., & Loehlin, J. C. (2001). Genes, evolution, and personality. *Behavior Genetics, 31*, 243–273.

Burt, C. (1949). The structure of the mind: A review of the results of factor analysis. *British Journal of Educational Psychology, 19*, 100–111, 176–199.

Buss, D. M. (1987). Selection, evocation, and manipulation. *Journal of Personality and Social Psychology, 53*, 1214–1221.

Caspi, A. (2000). The child is the father of the man: Personality continuities from childhood to adulthood. *Journal of Personality and Social Psychology, 78*, 158–172.

Clark, L. A., & Watson, D. (1999a). Personality, disorder, and personality disorder: Towards more rational conceptualization. *Journal of Personality Disorders, 13*, 142–151.

Clark, L. A., & Watson, D. (1999b). Temperament: A new paradigm for trait psychology. In L. A. Pervin & O. P. John (Eds.), *Handbook of personality: theory and research* (2nd ed., pp. 399–423). New York: Guilford.

Cosmides, L., & Tooby, J. (2000). Evolutionary psychology and the emotions. In M. Lewis & J. M. Haviland-Jones (Eds.), *Handbook of emotions* (2nd ed., pp. 91–115). New York: Guilford.

Costa, P. T., Jr., & McCrae, R. R. (1985). *NEO Personality Inventory manual*. Odessa, FL: Psychological Assessment Resources.

Costa, P. T., Jr., & McCrae, R. R. (1992). *NEO PI-R: Professional Manual*. Odessa, FL: Psychological Assessment Resources.

Cronbach, L. J., & Meehl, P. E. (1955). Construct validity in psychological tests. *Psychological Bulletin, 52*, 281–302.

de Road, B., & Peruguini, M. (Eds.) (2002). *Big Five Assessment*. Seattle, WA: Hogrefe & Huber.

Depue, R. A. (1996). A neurobiological framework for the structure of personality and emotion: Implications for personality disorders. In J. F. Clarkin & M. L. Lenzenweger (Eds.), *Major theories of personality disorder* (pp. 347–390). New York: Guilford.

Ekman, P. (2003). *Emotions revealed: Recognizing faces and feelings to improve communication and emotional life*. New York: Times Books.

Finkel, D., & McGue, M. (1997). Sex differences and nonadditivity in heritability of the multidimensional personality questionnaire scales. *Journal of Personality and Social Psychology, 72*, 929–938.

Gosling, S. D. (2001). From mice to men: What can we learn about personality from animal research? *Psychological Bulletin, 127*, 45–86.

Guilford, J. P. (1975). Factors and factors of personality. *Psychological Bulletin, 82*, 802–814.

Harkness, A. R. (1992). Fundamental topics in the personality disorders: Candidate trait dimensions from lower regions of the hierarchy. *Psychological Assessment, 4,* 251–259.

Harkness, A. R., & Lilienfeld, S. O. (1997). Individual differences science for treatment planning: Personality traits. *Psychological Assessment, 9,* 349–360.

Harkness, A. R., & McNulty, J. L. (1994). The personality psychopathology five (PSY-5): Issue from the pages of a diagnostic manual instead of a dictionary. In S. Strack & M. Lorr (Eds.), *Differentiating normal and abnormal personality* (pp. 291–315). New York: Springer.

Harkness, A. R., & McNulty, J. L. (2002). Implications of personality individual differences science for clinical work on personality disorders. In P. T. Costa, Jr. & T. A. Widiger (Eds.), *Personality disorders and the five-factor model of personality* (2nd ed., pp. 392–403). Washington, DC: American Psychological Association.

Harkness, A. R., & McNulty, J. L. (2006). An overview of personality: The MMPI-2 Personality Psychopathology—Five Scales (PSY-5). In J. N. Butcher (Ed.), *MMPI-2: A practitioner's guide* (pp. 73–97). Washington, DC: American Psychological Association.

Harkness, A. R., McNulty, J. L., Ben-Porath, Y. S., & Graham, J. R. (2002). *The Personality Psychopathology Five (PSY-5) scales: Gaining an overview for case conceptualization and treatment planning.* Minneapolis: University of Minnesota Press.

Izard, C. E., Libero, D. Z., Putnam, P., & Haynes, O. M. (1993). Stability of emotion experiences and their relations to traits of personality. *Journal of Personality and Social Psychology, 64,* 847–860.

Jang, K. L., McCrae, R. R., Angleitner, A., Riemann, R., & Livesley, W. J. (1998). Heritability of facet-level traits in a cross-cultural twin sample: Support for a hierarchical model of personality. *Journal of Personality and Social Psychology, 74,* 1556–1565.

Krueger, R. F. (2000). Phenotypic, genetic, and nonshared environmental parallels in the structure of personality: A view from the multidimensional personality questionnaire. *Journal of Personality and Social Psychology, 79,* 1057–1067.

Krueger, R. F., Caspi, A., Moffitt, T. E., Silva, P. A., & McGee, R. (1996). Personality traits are differentially linked to mental disorders: A multitrait-multidiagnosis study of an adolescent birth cohort. *Journal of Abnormal Psychology, 105,* 299–312.

LeDoux, J. (1996). *The emotional brain: The mysterious underpinnings of emotional life.* New York: Simon and Schuster.

Loehlin, J. C. (2004). Latent variable models: An introduction to factor, path, and structural equation analysis (4th ed.). New York: Lawrence Erlbaum Associates.

Loehlin, J. C., & Rowe, D. C. (1992). Genes, environment, and personality. In G. Capara & G. L. Van Heck (Eds.), *Modern personality psychology: Critical reviews and new directions* (pp. 352–370). New York: Harvester Wheatsheaf.

Loevinger, J. (1957). Objective tests as instruments of psychological theory. *Psychological Reports, 3,* 635–694 (Monograph 9).

Lykken, D. T., & Tellegen, A. T. (1993). Is human mating adventitious or the result of lawful choice? A twin study of mate selection. *Journal of Personality and Social Psychology, 65,* 56–86.

Magnus, K., Diener, E., Fujita, F., & Pavot, W. (1993). Extraversion and neuroticism as predictors of objective life events: A longitudinal analysis. *Journal of Personality and Social Psychology, 65,* 1046–1053.

Markon, K. E., Krueger, R. F., & Watson, D. (2005). Delineating the structure of normal and abnormal personality: An integrative hierarchical approach. *Journal of Personality and Social Psychology, 88,* 139–157.

McCrae, R. R. (1993). Moderated analyses of longitudinal personality stability. *Journal of Personality and Social Psychology, 65,* 577–585.

McCrae, R. R., & Costa, P. T., Jr. (1995). Trait explanations in personality psychology. *European Journal of Personality, 9,* 231–252.

Meehl, P. E. (1978). Theoretical risks and tabular asterisks: Sir Karl, Sir Ronald, and the slow progress of soft psychology. *Journal of Consulting and Clinical Psychology, 46,* 806–834.

Meehl, P. E. (1986). Trait language and behaviorese. In T. Thompson & M. D. Zeiler (Eds.), *Analysis and integration of behavioral units* (pp. 315–334). Hillsdale, NJ: Erlbaum.

Ormel, J., & Wohlfarth, T. (1991). How neuroticism, long-term difficulties, and life situation change influence psychological distress: A longitudinal model. *Journal of Personality and Social Psychology, 60,* 744–755.

Panksepp, J. (1998). *Affective neuroscience: The foundations of human and animal emotions.* New York: Oxford University Press.

Panksepp, J. (2000). Emotions as natural kinds within the mammalian brain. In M. Lewis & J. M. Haviland-Jones (Eds.), *Handbook of emotions* (2nd ed., pp. 137–156). New York: Guilford.

Plomin, R. (1994). *Genetics and experience: The developmental interplay between nature and nurture.* Newbury Park, CA: Sage.

Plomin, R. Corley, R., Caspi, A., Fulker, D. W., & DeFries, J. (1998). Adoption results for self-reported personality: Evidence for nonadditive genetic effects? *Journal of Personality and Social Psychology, 75,* 211–218.

Plomin, R., DeFries, J. C., McClearn, G. E., & McGuffin, P. (2001). *Behavior genetics.* New York: Worth.

Rowe, D. C. (1994). *The limits of family influence: Genes, experience, and behavior.* New York: Guilford.

Saudino, K. J., Pedersen, N. L., Lichtenstein, P., McClearn, G. E., & Plomin, R. (1997). Can personality explain genetic influences on life events? *Journal of Personality and Social Psychology, 72,* 196–206.

Siever, L. J., & Davis, K. L. (1991). A psychobiological perspective on the personality disorders. *American Journal of Psychiatry, 148,* 1647–1658.

Tellegen, A. (1982). *Brief manual for the Differential Personality Questionnaire.* Unpublished manuscript, University of Minnesota, Minneapolis. [Renamed Multidimensional Personality Questionnaire].

Tellegen, A. (1985). Structures of mood and personality and their relevance to assessing anxiety, with an emphasis on self-report. In A. H. Tuma and J. D. Maser (Eds.), *Anxiety and the anxiety disorders* (pp. 681–706). Hillsdale, NJ: Lawrence Erlbaum Associates.

Tellegen, A. (1988). The analysis of consistency in personality assessment. *Journal of Personality, 56,* 621–663.

Tellegen, A. (1991). Personality traits: Issues of definition, evidence, and assessment. In D. Cichetti & W. Grove (Eds.), *Thinking clearly about psychology: Essays in honor of Paul Everett Meehl* (pp. 10–35). Minneapolis: University of Minnesota Press.

Tellegen, A. & Waller, N.G. (in press). Exploring personality through test construction: Development of the Multidimensional Personality Questionnaire. In S. R. Briggs & J. M. Cheek (Eds.), *Personality measures: development and evaluation* (Vol. 1). Greenwich, CT: JAI Press.

Trull, T. J., & Durrett, C. A. (2005). Categorical and dimensional models of personality disorder. *Annual Reviews of Clinical Psychology.*

Tupes, E. C., & Christal, R. E. (1992). Recurrent personality factors based on trait ratings. *Journal of Personality, 60,* 225–251.

Watson, D., & Clark, L.A. (1984). Negative affectivity: The disposition to experience aversive emotional states. *Psychological Bulletin, 96,* 465–490.

Watson, D., & Clark, L. A. (1992). On traits and temperament: General and specific factors of emotional experience and their relation to the five-factor model. *Journal of Personality, 60,* 441–476.

Watson, D., & Clark, L. A. (1993). Behavioral disinhibition versus constraint: A dispositional perspective. In D. M. Wegner, & J. W. Pennebaker (Eds.), *Handbook of mental control* (pp. 506–527). New York: Prentice Hall.

Watson, D., & Clark, L. A. (1997). Extraversion and its positive emotional core. In R. Hogan, J. Johnson, & S. Briggs (Eds.), *Handbook of personality psychology* (pp. 767–793). San Diego, CA: Academic Press.

Watson, D., Clark, L. A., & Harkness, A. R. (1994). Structures of personality and their relevance to psychopathology. *Journal of Abnormal Psychology, 103,* 18–31.

Widiger, T. A. (1998). Four out of five ain't bad. *Archives of General Psychiatry, 55,* 865–866.

Wiggins, J. S. (Ed.). (1996). *The five-factor model of personality: Theoretical perspectives.* New York: Guilford.

Zuckerman, M. (1991). *Psychobiology of personality.* New York: Cambridge University Press.

Zuckerman, M., Kuhlman, D. M., Joireman, J., Teta, P., & Kraft, M. (1993). A comparison of three structural models for personality: The big three, the big five, and the alternative five. *Journal of Personality and Social Psychology, 65,* 757–768.

13

The Cognitive Neuroscience Perspective Allows Us to Understand Abnormal Behavior at Multiple Levels of Complexity

STEPHEN S. ILARDI, KEVIN RAND, AND
LESLIE KARWOSKI

Sarah had always thought of herself as a confident, happy person. At least that was true until a few months ago, when it felt like her world began to unravel. It all started when her longtime boyfriend, Kurt, broke up with her unexpectedly just before their final exams. Distraught, Sarah tried at first to lose herself in schoolwork, but instead wound up agonizing about Kurt for the better part of each day. Although her friends and family rallied to her side and did their best to cheer her up, they eventually grew weary of her self-deprecating tirades. "I always knew he'd find somebody better," she insisted. "It's no wonder he dumped a fat loser like me." Nothing anyone did seemed to help. Sarah grew increasingly tearful and withdrawn, and started spending most of her days curled up on the sofa with the shades drawn tight. She failed to show up for any of her finals, and lost the energy to complete even the most basic of tasks. In fact, she went without showering for days at a time. Her mother eventually grew so concerned that she tried to talk Sarah into getting treatment, a suggestion that met with considerable resistance. "A shrink? No way. I'm not crazy." Sarah did agree, however, to start taking the St. John's wort her mother bought for her at a local health food store. Pessimistic at first, Sarah nevertheless felt her depression begin to lift gradually over the next several weeks, and within 3 months she felt like she was mostly back to her old self.

Sarah's struggle with major depression is one echoed in the experience of literally millions of Americans each year. But what actually *causes* depression? Looking at Sarah's case, we find a bewildering array of factors to consider:

1. Her nasty breakup stands out as an obvious candidate. After all, depression is often preceded—as it was in Sarah's case—by the loss of one or more important social relationships (Brown & Harris, 1989; Monroe, Rohde, Seeley, & Lewinsohn, 1999). However, most people who experience such painful setbacks do not descend into full-blown depressive illness (Brown, Bifulco, & Harris, 1987); they merely become sad. What was it about *Sarah* that led to such a debilitating, pathological response?

2. A behavioral geneticist would likely highlight the significant heritability of depression (Hamet & Tremblay, 2005; Merikangas & Kupfer, 1995)—i.e., the existence of a genetic vulnerability to the disorder. It is possible, in other words, that Sarah was genetically predisposed to the experience of depression, and a thorough assessment of her extended family might well reveal a greater-than-chance number of genetic relatives with a history of major mood disorder (see Chapter 10 for a discussion of behavior genetic approaches to psychopathology).

3. At a lower-order level of analysis, a molecular geneticist might want to assess Sarah for the presence of a specific variation of the *serotonin transporter gene* implicated as a risk factor for depression onset (Caspi et al., 2003; Eley et al., 2004; Kendler, Kuhn, Vittum, Prescott, & Riley, 2005). Specifically, individuals with two "short" copies of a key serotonin transporter gene sequence appear to be much more likely than those with two "long" copies to become depressed in the face of adverse life events.

4. As its name suggests, this transporter gene plays an important role in regulating the brain's *serotonergic* (serotonin-using) neural pathways. Thus, at the level of neurotransmitter function, one might hypothesize the existence of abnormally low activity in many of Sarah's serotonergic circuits, especially those involved in the regulation of mood, sleep, appetite, and the body's stress response (Nemeroff, 2002; Wirz-Justice, 1995). This hypothesis is rendered more plausible by the fact that St. John's wort, which appeared helpful in Sarah's case, is known to enhance serotonergic neurotransmission (Calapai et al., 2001)

5. At a psychological level of analysis, a cognitively oriented investigator might attend to Sarah's relentless cascade of self-deprecating thoughts, and the robust body of research that links such negative thoughts to the experience of negative mood states (reviewed in Ingram, Scott & Siegle, 1999).

6. At an even higher-order, social level of analysis, it could be noted that depression is frequently characterized by the relative absence of effective social support (Paykel, 1994). Even friends who are initially supportive, as in Sarah's case, will tend to withdraw in the face of

persistent depressive symptoms (Stice, Ragan, & Randall, 2004; see also Chapter 14 for a discussion of developmental approaches to depression).

Remarkably, the above explanations barely scratch the surface of the vast set of phenomena implicated as potential etiological factors in major depressive disorder, an array of factors ranging from inadequate light exposure (Espiritu et al., 1994) to decreased left frontal cortical activity (Davidson, 1998) to excessive activation of the body's hypothalamic-pituitary-adrenal axis (Nemeroff, 2002) to feelings of hopelessness (Abramson, Metalsky, & Alloy, 1989) to reduced levels of brain-derived neurotrophin factor (BDNF) (Vaidya & Duman, 2001) to attenuated access to reinforcing activities (Lewinsohn, 1975) to inadequate dietary intake of omega-3 fatty acids (Peet, Murphy, Shay & Horrobin, 1998). How are we to make sense of it all? Is there any way to arrive at a coherent understanding of this large set of causal interrelationships that span the molecular, genetic, neurophysiological, behavioral, cognitive, affective, and social levels of organizational complexity?

Although a newcomer to the study of abnormal behavior might hope to discover a satisfactory answer to the question—and might even hope to find that the field's researchers have long since developed a comprehensive theory that integrates the causal influence of all relevant phenomena seamlessly across all appropriate levels of complexity—such a hope would be in vain. Much of the field's research is conducted by investigators working within the confines of fairly narrow conceptual frameworks, that is, theories that focus on a small subset of relevant phenomena, typically those operating only at a single causal level. For example, the influential *hopelessness theory* of depression (Abramson et al., 1989) attends almost exclusively to the causal role of one specific form of cognition (hopelessness), with relatively little attention to the task of integrating known genetic, physiological, or social causal factors. Likewise, the venerable *catecholamine hypothesis* (Schildkraut, 1965) is essentially limited in scope to the role of disordered neurotransmitter function. Comparable examples abound, not just in the depression research literature, but in the investigation of virtually all psychological disorders (Ilardi & Feldman, 2001a). When it comes to the study of abnormal behavior, meaningful integration across all relevant areas of inquiry is not yet the norm.

In fact, the broader discipline of psychology has long existed in a state of theoretical disunity (Ilardi & Feldman, 2001a; Miller, 1992; Rand & Ilardi, 2005; Staats, 1983, 1999), and *clinical* psychology—the subdiscipline concerned with assessment and treatment of psychological disorders—has been marked by conceptual fragmentation from its inception (Miller, 1992; Staats, 1983). This unfortunate absence of a unifying theoretical framework, or *paradigm*, has been identified by science historians (e.g., Kuhn, 1970) as one of the telltale signs that a discipline has not yet progressed beyond the practice of *immature science*. In his seminal analysis of the historical development of scientific disciplines, Kuhn suggested that the early, immature stage of a discipline's development is typically marked by battling among various theoretical factions over disciplinary "turf"—a process that serves as a rate-limiting factor on the pace of genuine scientific progress. Clinical psychology, of course, has at present a dizzying array of such theoretical factions (behaviorists, cognitivists, Rogerians, psychoanalysts, gestaltists, feminists, and so on). Therefore, it is perhaps not surprising that the field has witnessed relative stagnation in recent years regarding the introduction of effective new interventions for psychological disorders (Foa & Kozak, 1997).

In striking contrast, the mature natural sciences (e.g., physics, chemistry, biology, astronomy, geology) are each characterized by the existence of widely embraced conceptual frameworks within which investigators carry out their respective programs of paradigmatic research. These mature sciences are also marked by extraordinary linkage of theory and method across disciplines, a phenomenon known as *consilience* (Wilson, 1998). Such linkage means that each distinct area of natural science inquiry is now fundamentally interwoven with many other areas at multiple levels of complexity, from the subatomic to the organismic to the cosmological. As observed by Tooby and Cosmides (1992), "These disciplines are becoming integrated into an increasingly seamless system of interconnected knowledge and remain nominally separated more out of educational convenience and institutional inertia than because of any genuine ruptures in the underlying unity of the achieved knowledge" (p. 19). This remarkable integration in the natural sciences has led to numerous discoveries than transcend traditional disciplinary boundaries (for example, the use of chemical spectroscopy to determine the elemental composition of distant stars), and has catalyzed an accelerating pace of scientific discovery on myriad fronts. It also has sparked the creation of many novel, hybrid domains of scientific investigation (e.g., molecular genetics) at the intersection of previously distinct fields.

Perhaps not surprisingly, the study of abnormal human behavior has been revolutionized in recent years by the emergence of one such hybrid scientific domain—cognitive neuroscience (Gazzaniga, 2000; Gazzaniga, Ivry, & Mangun, 2002). The focus of cognitive neuroscience (CN) can be expressed in a single question: How do the physical operations of the brain give rise to people's thoughts, feelings, and behavior? (At this juncture, a brief word of clarification is in order. Because the word "cognitive" is most commonly used to refer to people's *thoughts*, some investigators have suggested the need for a parallel discipline of "affective neuroscience" [Panskepp, 1998] to investigate the important neural underpinnings of emotional states. However, "cognitive neuroscience" is generally understood as subsuming the neural bases of *all* mental phenomena—emotions, moods, motivations, and behavioral impulses, not just thoughts, per se [Posner & DiGirolamo, 2000]—and it is in this broader sense that we employ the term.)

CN encompasses the work of a broad range of researchers—psychologists, neuroscientists, computer scientists, linguists, geneticists, neuropsychologists, mathematicians, and many others—collaborating across formal disciplinary boundaries to shed light on the age-old "mind-body problem" (Gazzaniga, Ivry, & Mangun, 1998; Ilardi & Feldman, 2001a). Linked in a web of consilience with the natural sciences (Ilardi & Feldman, 2001b), CN is now witnessing what has been deemed a "heroic period" of scientific discovery (Wilson, 1998).

COGNITIVE NEUROSCIENCE: A BRIEF PRIMER

The dream of a psychology erected on the neural underpinnings of mental events was expressed by such founding luminaries as Wundt and Freud. However, the dream went unfulfilled for the better part of the 20th century, as the field awaited the development of methodologies adequate to the task of measuring brain structure and function at fine-grained levels of detail. In fact, it was not until the 1980s that the confluence of two important developments led to the emergence of cognitive neuroscience as a distinct area of inquiry: (a) the increasing availability of neuroimaging techniques such as positron emission tomography (PET) scans and functional MRI used to measure activity levels in localized brain regions; and (b) the formulation of computational models (especially simulated neural network models; cf. Rumelhart & McClelland, 1986) that provide a valuable conceptual bridge connecting the physical architecture of the brain with its associated cognitive processes (we will describe such models in greater detail in the next section). With these developments in place, the stage was set for an extraordinary convergence of researchers drawn together from disparate fields to investigate how the brain gives rise to the mind.

The Basic Tenets of Cognitive Neuroscience

Although CN investigators come from diverse disciplinary backgrounds, they are able to collaborate effectively by virtue of a set of shared assumptions about the relationship of mind and brain (Gazzaniga et al., 2002). These assumptions are the fundamental concepts on which the CN conceptual framework is built (Ilardi, 2002), and we believe attempts to explain abnormal behavior in the 21st century will increasingly need to incorporate them.

Tenet #1: *The brain is an organ designed by natural selection to process information.*

The human brain is a large, metabolically costly organ, and yet it performs no important mechanical or chemical function for the body (Tooby & Cosmides, 1995). In fact, the brain's only adaptive significance lies in its ability to process information for the real-time regulation of behavioral and physiological processes (Dennett, 1995; Tooby & Cosmides, 1995; Wilson, 1998). But how, exactly, does a 3-pound lump of neural tissue go about the task of processing information? This was a mystery that baffled scientists for hundreds of years, remaining opaque even late into the 20th century. However, over the past few decades, computational theorists have begun the process of modeling the brain's functional architecture—with its latticelike network of 100 billion nodes (i.e., neurons) and 100 trillion modifiable interconnections (neural *synapses*) (Kosslyn & Koenig, 1992; McClelland & Rumelhart, 1988). The resulting brain-inspired simulation models have convincingly demonstrated that the brain's neural architecture is capable of: (a) encoding information in the changeable *connection strengths* between neurons; and (b) processing encoded information with each wave of neural firing (i.e., *depolarization*). Indeed, investigators have discovered that simulated neural network arrays are especially adept at difficult computational tasks such as object recognition, visual pattern detection, and speech recognition—feats that our own brains accomplish with relative ease, but that are fiendishly difficult to implement on traditional (serial-processing) computers.

Tenet #2: *Mental events arise directly from physical events in the brain.*

The mystery of how mind and body are interrelated is one of the oldest and most widely debated questions in all of philosophy. Mind-body *dualism*, which conceptualizes the mind and the body (brain) as radically distinct, independent entities, is a view that has dominated Western culture for several centuries, a view that has shaped our very language and—at least implicitly—much of the field's thinking about psychology (Goodman, 1991). In fact, dualism is a widespread assumption across virtually all cultures, as it appears to match most people's deepest intuitions about the human condition (after all, it is not at all apparent at any intuitive level how "brain stuff" could possibly yield "mind stuff"; cf. Pinker, 2002). There is even some evidence from the field of developmental cognitive psychology that children spontaneously generate dualistic assumptions, prompting the suggestion that we're all "natural born dualists" (Astuti, 2001; Bloom, 2004). Nevertheless, cognitive neuroscience claims that every thought, impulse, feeling, perception, and motivation arises from distinct patterns of neural activity in the brain, that mental events are physical events. It claims, in brief, that "the mind is what the brain does" (Minsky, 1986).

A number of recent research findings lend strong support to this CN assumption. First, an extensive neurology literature documents that damage to specific brain regions (e.g., Wernicke's area, amygdala) results in the predictable alteration or loss of corresponding mental functions (Gazzaniga et al., 1998, 2002; Kosslyn & Koenig, 1992). Serious damage to the occipital cortex, for example, inevitably leads to disordered visual perception that varies according to the focal visual processing regions that sustain damage. Furthermore, neuroimaging procedures have identified dozens of localized brain regions that are differentially active in tandem with the experience of highly specific mental events (Liotti et al., 2000;

Turk, Rosenblum, Gazzaniga, & Macrae, 2005). So, for example, clinically depressed individuals (such as Sarah, described previously), have been observed to experience increased activity in the regions of the brain's frontal cortex associated with the process of rumination, that is, dwelling on negative thoughts (Phan et al., 2002)—a hallmark of depressive thinking. And, in a compelling corollary finding, depressed patients successfully treated with either cognitive therapy or with antidepressant medication show pronounced reductions in activity in a rumination-linked area known as the ventral prefrontal cortex (Goldapple, et al., 2004).

In its rejection of mind-body dualism and its corresponding assumption that all human mental activity arises from brain activity, CN places our thoughts and feelings within the domain of lawful, material events that can be studied with a high degree of scientific rigor. As such, CN provides a robust conceptual and methodological bridge between the field of psychology and the natural sciences.

Tenet #3: *All human mental events are the result of neural information processing.*

This claim is often referred to as the "computational theory of mind" (Pinker, 1997), and it represents the conjunction of the two preceding tenets. In other words, not only is there a direct, one-to-one correspondence between neural and mental events, but every facet of our rich mental lives is actually the result of the brain's computational activity.

Although the specific algorithms (or "programs") governing neural computation in the human brain are still not well understood (Kandel, 1998), a number of research findings support the computational theory of mind. First, based on their very structure and physical character-istics, neurons are extremely well suited to the task of receiving and transmitting information; indeed, neurons exhibit many design features consistent with having been naturally selected by virtue of their infor-mational function (Bownds, 1999). Second, as alluded to previously, rich mathematical models now verify that networks of neurons are capable of representing and processing information (McClelland & Rumelhart, 1986; Phillips, 1997). Third, functional neural-network simulation models are capable of capturing important facets of human information processing, such as visual object recognition and hippocampal memory consolidation (Atallah, Frank, & O'Reilly, 2004; Dayan & Abbott, 2001). Fourth, damage to specific portions of the brain leads to predictable alterations in consciously experienced mental events (Gazzaniga, et al., 2002). Finally, it is worth noting that the computational theory of mind is at present the only viable, substantive scientific explanation for how the physical events of the brain could give rise to mental events (Pinker, 1997).

Tenet #4: *The brain's structure and function are largely determined by genes and the protein products they produce.*

Genes do not directly program behavior. Rather, they control the production of proteins that determine the way in which neural connections are formed and many details of their functioning. The genes themselves (i.e., molecular patterns in our DNA) cannot be altered by our experience, but the *expression* of particular genes—their being turned on or off in specific cells to regulate cellular functioning—is a process susceptible to environmental influences. Such environment-gene transactions have much to do with the way information is represented and processed in the brain; thus, genes influence how behavioral and mental events are expressed (Kandel, 1998). Increasingly, researchers are now turning their attention to the identification of specific genetic alleles (variations) that confer heightened vulnerability to mental illnesses by virtue of their direct regulatory effects on relevant neural circuits. For example, researchers have identified a variation on a specific neuroregulatory gene (called monoamine oxidase A, or *MAOA*) that renders its male carriers likely to engage in violent, antisocial behavior, especially when they have themselves experienced violent abuse as children (Caspi et al., 2002; Stokstad, 2002).

How Can CN Make Sense of Abnormal Behavior?

Having summarized the core assumptions of the CN perspective, we now turn our attention to the value of the CN perspective in making sense of abnormal behavior. We begin with a story.

When this chapter's first author was a fledgling graduate student many years ago, his advisor (Ed Craighead, a noted depression researcher) issued a memorable challenge. Pointing to a recently published outcome study of cognitive therapy versus antidepressant medication for depression, he observed that patients in the two treatment conditions experienced an equivalent decrease in negative thinking over the course of treatment. "We expect to see less negative thinking with cognitive therapy," he said, "since that's the whole focus of the intervention. But how can someone's thoughts change just as much when they simply swallow a pill every day? How, exactly, does a pill change the way a person thinks about himself, the way he views the world around him? Can you explain that? And I mean really *explain it*, not just put labels on a diagram with some boxes and arrows." The student shrugged, so Craighead continued with a smile, "No, and neither can I. But someone needs to find a way to explain it. And until they do, we ought to be pretty humble about what we claim to understand about depression."

Craighead's challenge echoes a key point made at the chapter's outset; namely, that the range of phenomena implicated in the experience of depression spans so many different levels of complexity—from the molecular to the mental to the social—that the task of making sense of the causal interrelationships among these various phenomena has historically proven quite daunting. The same can be said, of course, regarding every other major form of mental illness (e.g., schizophrenia, autism, anorexia nervosa, panic disorder, alcohol dependence, obsessive-compulsive disorder, antisocial personality disorder). However, the cognitive neuroscience

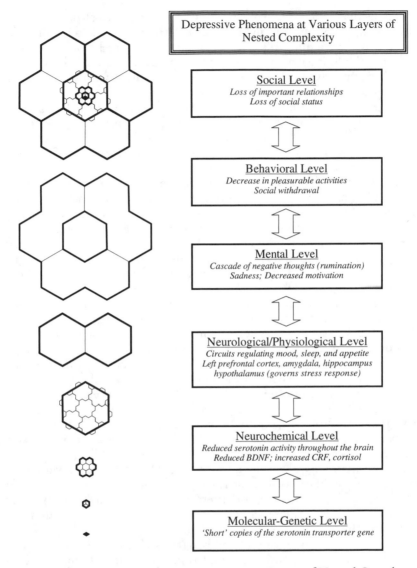

Figure 13.1. Depressive Phenomena at Various Layers of Nested Complexity.

perspective now provides an enormously useful framework within which investigators have recently begun to elucidate such causal interrelationships across many different levels of complexity, and to fit the various pieces of the puzzle of abnormal behavior into a coherent whole. Craighead's questions and others like them are now yielding tentative answers.

As shown in Figure 13.1, the phenomena of greatest interest to depression researchers involve six hierarchically nested levels of complexity:

(1) molecular-genetic; (2) biochemical; (3) neurological/physiological; (4) mental; (5) behavioral; and (6) social. Although the field is still many years away from a full explication of all possible interrelationships across all levels, the following cursory overview serves to illustrate the value of the CN perspective in providing a conceptual context within which such a process of discovery is gradually unfolding.

When someone becomes clinically depressed—like Sarah in the chapter's opening vignette—she is likely to have had the recent experience of interpersonal loss or setback (Brown & Harris, 1989), an event at the (high-order) social level of complexity depicted in Figure 13.1. Of course, virtually everyone experiences such aversive social events at some point, yet most people never become depressed. Some people are much more vulnerable than others, and we noted previously that the risk of depressive illness in the face of negative life events appears to be increased by a specific genetic diathesis—two "short" copies of a key serotonin transporter gene sequence (Caspi et al., 2003). In other words, phenomena at a very low level of complexity (the molecular-genetic) somehow interact with events at a very high level of complexity (the social) to bring about depressive illness. How?

At the level of neurochemistry, just above the molecular-genetic, we see that the serotonin transporter gene helps regulate the activity of brain circuits that use serotonin as a key neurotransmitter. Among other things, serotonergic circuits play a role in regulating the body's stress response (Andrews & Matthews, 2004; Lowry, 2002). These serotonin-using neural pathways influence activity in the brain's *amygdala* and *hypothalamus*, which in turn regulate the release of key stress hormones like cortisol and CRF. People with two short copies of the transporter gene tend to have reduced serotonergic activity, and a tendency toward an excessive, runaway stress response (Hariri et al, 2005), resulting in an abnormally high production of stress hormones.

At the neurological level, the influence of prolonged elevations in stress hormones like CRF and cortisol is pronounced, with effects of great relevance to the experience of depression, among them: (a) suppressed activity in the left *prefrontal cortex* (PFC), a brain region that mediates both the experience of positive mood states and the motivation to initiate and pursue goal-directed behaviors (Buss et al., 2003; Kalin, Larson, Shelton, & Davidson, 1998); (b) increased activity in circuits of the *amygdala* that mediate the experience of sad mood (Sajdyk, Shekhar, & Gehlert, 2004); and (c) disrupted consolidation of new memories in the brain's *hippocampus* through the suppressed production of a key protein—brain-derived neurotrophin factor (BDNF)—which stimulates the sprouting of new neural (*dendritic spine*) connections in the brain (Nestler et al., 2002; Vaidya & Duman, 2001). These neurological effects in turn appear linked to other important changes in brain function, such as increased activity in the *ventral prefrontal cortex*, which mediates the experience of rumination (Mayberg, 2003), and the *subgenual cingulate*, which is centrally involved in the conscious perception of emotional pain (Phillips, 2003).

Thus, we see a multifaceted set of causal pathways that connect a specific gene with an identified vulnerability to a runaway depressive stress response. This leads in turn to important alterations in neurological functioning. Because brain states and mental states are merely flip sides of the same coin, such stress-linked neurological changes are reflected in corresponding changes in mood (decreased positive affect, increased sadness), motivation (reduced goal pursuit), cognition (rumination, decreased memory function, cognitive impairment), and behavior (reduced levels of activity and decreased behavioral initiative). These mental and behavioral effects may in turn lead to impaired social functioning and withdrawal—hallmark manifestations of depression—which then have the potential to exacerbate the runaway stress response, the harmful effects of which we have just delineated. So it is that we find six nested levels of complexity linked in a reciprocal cycle of causation.

The CN perspective also provides a useful framework for making sense of otherwise perplexing facets of the treatment outcome literature. For example, because the aforementioned levels of complexity (depicted in Figure 13.1) are entwined in reciprocal chains of causation, one should actually *expect* to find that interventions that succeed in producing therapeutic changes at any level in the diagram have the potential to generate corresponding effects that ripple across adjacent levels. Thus, when it was reported by researchers that cognitive therapy for depression brings about observable changes in the brain (Goldapple et al., 2004)—a finding breathlessly heralded by some in the news media as profoundly mysterious—those informed by the CN perspective were not at all surprised. *Of course* effective therapy changes the brain! In fact, only a dualist could expect otherwise, as any experience that changes our thoughts and feelings must, by definition, be capable of producing changes in the corresponding neural substrates of those very thoughts and feelings. Likewise, it is unsurprising to observe that medications, which exert a direct influence at the level of neurochemical function, can bring about corresponding changes at the higher-order level of thoughts and feelings encoded in neural tissue. Nor is it unexpected to find that simple behavioral changes, like engaging in aerobic exercise, can induce alterations in neural functioning similar to those brought about by medications (e.g., Adlard & Cotman, 2004). In fact, the CN perspective yields an important insight with extensive applicability in any clinical context: *Experience changes the brain.*

The preceding discussion only hints at the enormous complexity of the many reciprocal causal pathways involved in the onset, maintenance, and treatment of depression—it represents at most a cursory, speculative sketch of a very limited subset of relevant factors. However, we believe it helps illustrate the value of the CN perspective in providing a coherent conceptual framework for understanding effects that ripple across multiple levels of complexity, from the molecular to the social. If space permitted, CN's utility in this respect could be demonstrated vis-à-vis numerous other psychological disorders (e.g., schizophrenia, obsessive-compulsive disorder, autism, bipolar disorder, antisocial personality disorder) that have, in recent decades, given rise to a similarly vast array of research findings at the genetic, neurochemical, neurological/physiological, mental, behavioral, and social levels of analysis. (We leave this task as an exercise for the reader!)

How the CN Perspective Can Be Useful in Applied Settings

At this juncture, some readers may be wondering, "Do I really need to know any of this? Can't I just keep on doing good, evidence-based treatment and not worry about the cognitive neuroscience stuff?" It's certainly a reasonable question. Fortunately, there are two important ways in which the CN perspective can be of practical utility to clinicians, and these are briefly outlined below:

Enhanced Credibility. Psychotherapy patients are increasingly exposed to explanations of abnormal behavior at the neurobiological level of analysis—for example, the notion that "mental illness is caused by 'chemical imbalance'"—and many will ask their therapists how it is, exactly, that a behavioral intervention can be useful in treating a "brain disorder." Likewise, numerous prospective therapy patients enter treatment having already been prescribed psychotropic medications, and they often want to know in some detail how both the drugs and the therapy will differentially affect their presenting symptoms. To the extent that the therapist cannot provide coherent answers to such questions, his or her credibility (and thus the therapeutic alliance itself) may be badly compromised. Fortunately, the CN perspective provides a cogent framework within which such questions can be meaningfully addressed, and abnormal behavior explained at multiple interrelated levels of complexity.

Enhanced Treatment Efficacy. Despite their "empirically supported" designation, most research-tested psychotherapies are helpful for only a subset of patients who enter treatment (see also Chapter 6). For example, cognitive-behavior therapy for depression (Beck, Rush, Shaw, & Emery, 1979)—the most heavily researched of all therapies—brings about remission for only about 50–60% of severely depressed patients (DeRubeis, Gelfand, Tang, & Simons, 1999). Clearly, there is still ample room for improvement, and this point applies to the bulk of the field's most widely disseminated psychotherapies. The CN perspective, however, provides a promising avenue for enhancing the efficacy of existing interventions.

For example, one of us (SSI) recently treated a depressed, middle-aged man named Bill, who had been referred after failing to respond to an adequate dose of antidepressant medication and supportive psychotherapy. Treatment initially followed Beck's CBT (cognitive-behavioral therapy) protocol, but it became clear over the first few sessions that Bill's symptoms were not improving at all. As I reflected on the situation following Session 4, two pernicious problems stood out in particular: (a) Bill was chronically distressed about his impaired memory and concentration, which caused numerous work-related difficulties and led to his legitimate concern about an eventual loss of employment; and (b) his symptoms had their onset during the short, gloomy days of winter, and his sleep had been characterized ever since by a circadian phase-shift pattern (with resultant terminal insomnia) that left him chronically sleep-deprived and lethargic. Informed by the CN perspective, which facilitates conceptualization of the patient's problems at multiple levels of complexity, I was able to formulate adjuvant treatment strategies that proved to be of enormous clinical benefit.

First, chronic suppression of the neural growth hormone BDNF (brain-derived neurotrophin factor) is strongly implicated in depression's characteristic profile of cognitive impairment, and it is known that aerobic exercise is a potent means of reversing this BDNF suppression (Adlard & Cotman, 2004). Accordingly, I discussed with Bill the potential desirability of his resuming the schedule of regular aerobic activity that he had dropped during the onset of his symptoms. Although he expressed some enthusiasm about this idea when I brought it up, I knew (again, in light of the CN perspective) that depression's typical suppression of left frontal cortical activation would likely make it difficult for him to initiate a goal-directed activity like exercise (Henriques & Davidson, 1991). When I asked him about it, Bill acknowledged that his ongoing difficulty with initiating activities had derailed each of his previous self-directed attempts at "getting back in shape." But he also observed he was usually able to complete tasks that others prompted him to do, and he suggested that if I would be willing to help him schedule specific workout times, dates, places, and so on, he would be capable of following the schedule. After two weeks of regular aerobic activity, Bill reported, "Dr. Ilardi, I think I'm starting to get my memory back. It just seems like I'm thinking a little more clearly. My boss even told me he could see some improvement in my work." Not surprisingly, his mood began to improve as well.

On the sleep front, I discussed with Bill the fact that his seasonal-onset pattern of depression and chronic early awakening might indicate dysregulation of the neural circuits governing his "body clock" (circadian cycle)—a condition often brought about by insufficient exposure to bright light, especially during the winter months. (Natural sunlight, at a luminance of about 10,000 lux, is 25 times brighter than standard indoor lighting.) He found this explanation compelling, and agreed to purchase a 10,000-lux light box (we found one online for a cost of about $200) and to use it for at least a half hour each day. Within a week of beginning this light exposure routine, he noticed that the terminal insomnia was improving, and his cumulative nightly sleep total had increased from an average of "about 5 hours a night" to "between 7 and 8 hours most nights." His lethargy also gradually disappeared, roughly in lockstep with his diminishing sleep deprivation.

Buoyed by Bill's newfound improvement in cognitive function
and his heightened energy, we quickly resumed treatment with more
traditional CBT. It was only a matter of weeks before his depression
was in complete remission for the first time in over 4 years. So it was
that a chronically treatment-refractory depressed patient experienced a
favorable outcome when a standard CBT intervention was supplement-
ed with adjuvant strategies derived from a CN-informed perspective on
major depressive disorder.

If space permitted, we could provide dozens of other examples of
enhanced intervention by virtue of the ability to conceptualize and address
abnormal behavior at multiple levels of complexity. In fact, we note that
the cognitive neuroscience perspective now serves as an increasingly
potent catalyst for innovative treatment research. Recent CN-informed
advances range from: (a) the integrative use of *d-cycloserine*—a drug that
promotes the formation of new memories—to accelerate the pace of
habituation to fear-inducing stimuli during exposure-based treatment for
phobias (Ressler et al., 2004) to (b) the employment of neurocognitive
rehabilitation exercises (e.g., exposure to a modified serial attention task)
as an effective means of increasing activity in frontal cortical circuits that
help suppress rumination in depression (Siegle, in press) to (c) the short-
term use of beta-blocker medications to promote ultra-rapid habituation to trauma-based cues during exposure therapy for posttraumatic
stress disorder (Debiec & Ledoux, 2004; Przybyslawski, Roullet, & Sara,
1999). Given the extraordinary pace of discovery that now characterizes
CN-inspired clinical research, these exciting examples surely represent
merely the tip of the proverbial iceberg, as the years ahead will witness
myriad new ways in which the CN framework proves to be of profound
clinical utility.

CONCLUDING REMARKS

The ability of researchers to integrate across multiple levels of complexity—and thereby to collaborate effectively across formerly rigid disciplinary boundaries—has become a hallmark of every mature natural
science discipline, and has helped to catalyze innumerable scientific
advances in recent decades. Likewise, the integrative cognitive neuroscience enterprise—which delineates how brain gives rise to mind—is
now experiencing what has aptly been termed a "heroic period" of
scientific discovery (Wilson, 1998). To the degree that psychopathology
research in coming years is informed by CN theory and methodology,
we may thus expect to see an unprecedented degree of conceptual
integration and collaboration among clinical researchers, and an unpar-
alleled pace of scientific discovery regarding the causes, consequences,
and treatments of abnormal behavior. Accordingly, students of abnormal
behavior who choose to embrace this approach—to pursue appropriate

training in the neural bases of cognition, affect, and behavior—will have the opportunity to participate in one of the most exciting scientific developments of our time.

KEY TERMS

Cognitive neuroscience: A cross-disciplinary field of inquiry focused on elucidating the manner in which neural events give rise to cognition, affect, and behavior.

Consilience: The integration of knowledge across disciplinary boundaries to create a unified conceptual framework.

Paradigm: The set of common beliefs and agreements—shared among scientists within a given domain of inquiry—about how problems should be understood and addressed (Kuhn, 1962).

Psychopathology: The study of mental illness.

Major depressive disorder: A debilitating syndrome characterized by dysphoria, sleep and appetite disturbance, reduced concentration, psychomotor retardation, social withdrawal, and suicidal thoughts and behavior.

RECOMMENDED READINGS

Ilardi, S. S., & Feldman, D. (2001). The cognitive neuroscience paradigm: A unifying meta-theoretical framework for the science and practice of clinical psychology. *Journal of Clinical Psychology, 57,* 1067–1088.

Panksepp, J. (2004). *Affective neuroscience:* The foundations of human and animal emotions. New York: Oxford University Press.

Pinker, S. (1999). *How the mind works.* New York: Norton.

Rand, K., & Ilardi, S. S. (2005). Toward a consilient science of psychology. *Journal of Clinical Psychology, 61,* 7–20.

Wilson, E. O. (1998). *Consilience: The unity of science.* New York: Knopf.

REFERENCES

Abramson, L. Y., Metalsky, G. I., & Alloy, L. B. (1989). Hopelessness depression: A theory-based subtype of depression. *Psychological Review, 96,* 358–372.

Adlard, P. A., & Cotman, C. W. (2004). Voluntary exercise protects against stress-induced decreases in brain-derived neurotrophic factor protein expression. *Neuroscience, 124,* 985–92.

Andrews M. H., & Matthews S. G. (2004). Programming of the hypothalamo-pituitary-adrenal axis: Serotonergic involvement. *Stress, 7,* 15–27.

Astuti, R. (2001). Are we all natural dualists? A cognitive developmental approach. *Journal of Royal Anthropological Institute, 7*(3), 429.

Atallah, H. E., Frank, M. J., & O'Reilly, R. C. (2004). Hippocampus, cortex, and basal ganglia: Insights from computational models of complementary learning systems. *Neurobiology of Learning and Memory, 82,* 253–267.

Beck, A. T., Rush, A. J., Shaw, B. F., & Emery, G. (1979). *Cognitive therapy of depression.* New York: The Guilford Press.

Bloom, P. (2004). *Descartes' baby: How the science of child development explains what makes us human.* New York: Basic Books.

Bownds, M. D. (1999). *The biology of mind: Origins and structures of mind, brain, and consciousness.* Bethesda, MD: Fitzgerald Science Press.

Brown, G. W., Bifulco, A., & Harris, T. O. (1987). Life events, vulnerability and onset of depression: Some refinements. *The British Journal of Psychiatry, 150,* 30–42.

Brown, G. W., & Harris, T. O. (1989). *Life events and illness.* New York: Guilford Press.

Buss, K. A., Schumacher, J. R., Dolski, I., Kalin, N. H., Goldsmith, H. H., & Davidson, R. J. (2003). Right frontal brain activity, cortisol, and withdrawal behavior in 6-month-old infants. *Behavioral Neuroscience, 117,* 11–20.

Calapai, G., Crupi, A., Firenzuoli, F., Inferrera, G., Squadrito, F., Parisi, A., et al. (2001). Serotonin, norepinephrine and dopamine involvement in the antidepressant action of hypericum perforatum. *Pharmacopsychiatry, 34,* 45–49.

Caspi, A., McClay, J., Moffit, T., Mill, J., Martin, J., Craig, I., et al. (2002). Role of genotype in the cycle of violence in maltreated children. *Science, 297*(5582), 851–854.

Caspi, A., Sugden, K., Moffitt, T. E., Taylor, A., Craig, I. W., Harrington, H., et al. (2003). Influence of life stress on depression: moderation by a polymorphism in the 5-HTT gene. *Science, 301,* 386–389.

Davidson, R. J. (1998). Anterior electrophysiological asymmetries, emotion, and depression: Conceptual and methodological conundrums. *Psychophysiology, 35,* 607–614.

Dayan, P., & Abbott, L. F. (2001). *Theoretical neuroscience: Computational and mathematical modeling of neural systems.* Cambridge, MA: MIT Press.

Debiec, J., & Ledoux, J. E. (2004): Disruption of reconsolidation but not consolidation of auditory fear conditioning by noradrenergic blockade in the amygdala. *Neuroscience, 129,* 267–72.

Dennett, D. C. (1995). *Darwin's dangerous idea.* New York: Simon & Schuster.

DeRubeis, R. J., Gelfand, L. A., Tang, T. Z., & Simons, A. D. (1999). Medications versus cognitive behavior therapy for severely depressed outpatients: Mega-analysis of four randomized comparisons. *American Journal of Psychiatry, 156,* 1007–1013.

Eley, T. C., Sugden, K., Corsico, A., Gregory, A. M., Sham, P., McGuffin, P., et al. (2004). Gene-environment interaction analysis of serotonin system markers with adolescent depression. *Molecular Psychiatry, 9,* 908–915.

Espiritu, R. C., Kripke, D. F., Ancoli-Israel, S., Mowen, M. A., Mason, W. J., Fell, R. L., et al. (1994). Low illumination experienced by San Diego adults: Association with atypical depressive symptoms. *Biological Psychiatry, 35,* 403–407.

Foa, E. B., & Kozak, M. J. (1997). Beyond the efficacy ceiling? Cognitive behavior therapy in search of theory. *Behavior Therapy, 28,* 601–612.

Gazzaniga, M. S. (Ed.). (2000). *Cognitive neuroscience: A reader.* Malden, MA: Blackwell.

Gazzaniga, M. S., Ivry, R., & Mangun, G. R. (1998). *Fundamentals of cognitive neuroscience.* New York: W.W. Norton.

Gazzaniga, M. S., Ivry, R., & Mangun, G. R. (2002). *Cognitive neuroscience: The biology of the mind* (2nd ed.). New York: W.W. Norton.

Goldapple, K., Segal, Z., Garson, C., Lau, M., Bieling, P., Kennedy, S., et al. (2004). Modulation of cortical-limbic pathways in major depression. *Archives of General Psychiatry, 61*, 34–41.

Goodman, A. (1991). Organic unity theory: The mind/body problem revisited. *American Journal of Psychiatry, 148*, 553–563.

Hamet, P., & Tremblay, J. (2005). Genetics and genomics of depression. *Metabolism, 54* (Supplement 2), 10–15.

Hariri, A. R., Drabant, E. M., Munoz, K. E., Kolachana, B. S., Mattay, V. S., Egan, M. F., et al. (2005). A susceptibility gene for affective disorders and the response of the human amygdala. *Archives of General Psychiatry, 62*, 146–152.

Henriques, J. B., & Davidson, R. J. (1991). Left frontal hypoactivation in depression. *Journal of Abnormal Psychology, 100*, 535–545.

Ilardi, S. S. (2002). The cognitive neuroscience perspective: A brief primer for clinical psychologists. *Behavior Therapist, 25*, 49–52.

Ilardi, S. S., & Feldman, D. (2001a). The cognitive neuroscience paradigm: A unifying metatheoretical framework for the science and practice of clinical psychology. *Journal of Clinical Psychology, 57*, 1067–1088.

Ilardi, S. S., & Feldman, D. (2001b). Toward rapprochement: Comments on the role of biological science within cognitive neuroscience and radical behaviorism. *Journal of Clinical Psychology, 57*, 1121–1124.

Ingram, R. E., Scott, W., & Siegle, G. (1999). Depression: Social and cognitive aspects. In T. Millon, P. H. Blaney, & R. D. Davis (Eds.), *Oxford textbook of psychopathology* (pp. 203–226). New York: Oxford Press.

Kalin, N. H., Larson, C., Shelton, S. E., & Davidson, R. J. (1998). Asymmetric frontal brain activity, cortisol, and behavior associated with fearful temperament in Rhesus monkeys. *Behavioral Neuroscience, 112*, 286–292.

Kandel, E. R. (1998). A new intellectual framework for psychiatry. *American Journal of Psychiatry, 155*, 457–469.

Kosslyn, S. M., & Koenig, O. (1992). *Wet mind: The new cognitive neuroscience.* New York: Free Press.

Kendler, K. S., Kuhn, J. W., Vittum, J., Prescott, C. A., & Riley, B. (2005). The interaction of stressful life events and a serotonin transporter polymorphism in the prediction of episodes of major depression: a replication. *Archives of General Psychiatry, 62*, 529–535.

Kuhn, T. S. (1970). *The structure of scientific revolutions* (2nd ed.). Chicago: University of Chicago Press.

Lewinsohn, P. M. (1975). Engagement in pleasant activities and depression level. *Journal of Abnormal Psychology, 84*, 729–31.

Liotti, M., Mayberg, H. S., Brannan, S. K., McGinnis, S., Jerabek, P., & Fox, P. T. (2000). Differential limbic—cortical correlates of sadness and anxiety in healthy subjects: Implications for affective disorders. *Biological Psychiatry, 48*, 30–42.

Lowry, C. A. (2002). Functional subsets of serotonergic neurones: Implications for control of the hypothalamic-pituitary-adrenal axis. *Journal of Neuroendocrinology, 14*, 911–923.

Mayberg, H. S. (2003). Modulating dysfunctional limbic-cortical circuits in depression: Toward development of brain-based algorithms for diagnosis and optimised treatment. *British Medical Bulletin, 65*, 193–207.

McClelland, J. L., & Rumelhart, D. E. (1988). *Explorations in parallel distributed processing,* Cambridge, MA: MIT Press.

Merikangas, K. R., & Kupfer, D. J. (1995). Mood disorders: Genetic aspects. In H. I. Kaplan & B. J. Sadock (Eds.), *Comprehensive textbook of psychiatry* (6th ed., pp. 1102–1116). Baltimore, MD: Walkins.

Miller, R. B. (1992). Introduction to the philosophy of clinical psychology. In R. B. Miller (Ed.), *The restoration of dialogue: Readings in the philosophy of clinical psychology* (pp. 1–28). Washington, DC: American Psychological Association.

Minsky, M. (1986). *Society of mind*. New York; Simon and Schuster.

Monroe, S. M., Rohde, P., Seeley, J. R., & Lewinsohn, P. M. (1999). Life events and depression in adolescence: Relationship loss as a prospective risk factor for first onset of major depressive disorder. *Journal of Abnormal Psychology, 108*, 606–614.

Nemeroff, C. B. (2002). Recent advances in the neurobiology of depression. *Psychopharmacology Bulletin, 36* (Supplement 2), 6–23.

Nestler, E., Barrot, M., DiLeone, R., Eisch, A., Gold, S., & Monteggia, L. (2002). Neurobiology of depression. *Neuron, 34*, 13–25.

Panskepp, J. (1998). *Affective neuroscience: The foundations of human and animal emotions*. New York: Oxford University Press.

Paykel, E. S. (1994). Life events, social support and depression. *Acta Psychiatrica Scandinavica, 89*, 50–58.

Peet, M., Murphy, B., Shay, J., & Horrobin, D. (1998). Depletion of omega-3 fatty acid levels in red blood cell membranes of depressive patients. *Biological Psychiatry, 43*, 315–319.

Phan, K. L., Wager, T., Taylor, S. F., & Liberzon, I. (2002) Functional neuroanatomy of emotion: A meta-analysis of emotion activation studies in PET and fMRI. *NeuroImage, 16*, 331–348.

Phillips, M. (2003). Understanding the neurobiology of emotion perception: Implications for psychiatry. *The British Journal of Psychiatry, 182*, 190–192.

Phillips, W. A. (1997). Theories of cortical computation. In M. D. Rugg (Ed.), *Cognitive neuroscience* (pp. 169–196). Cambridge, MA: MIT Press.

Pinker, S. (1997). *How the mind works*. New York: W. W. Norton and Co.

Pinker, S. (2002). *The blank slate: The modern denial of human nature*. New York: Viking.

Posner, M. I., & DiGirolamo, G. J. (2000). Cognitive neuroscience: Origins and promise. *Psychological Bulletin, 126*, 873–889.

Przybyslawski, J., Roullet, P., & Sara, S. J. (1999): Attenuation of emotional and nonemotional memories after their reactivation: role of beta adrenergic receptors. *Journal of Neuroscience, 19*, 6623–6628.

Rand, K. L., & Ilardi, S. S. (2005). Toward a consilient science of psychology. *Journal of Clinical Psychology, 61*, 7–20.

Ressler, K. J., Rothbaum, B. O., Tannenbaum, L., Anderson, P., Graap, K., Zimand, E., et al. (2004). Cognitive enhancers as adjuncts to psychotherapy: Use of D-cycloserine in phobic individuals to facilitate extinction of fear. *Archives of General Psychiatry, 61*, 1136–1144.

Rumelhart, D. E., & McClelland, J. L. (Eds.). (1986). *Parallel distributed processing: Explorations in the microstructure of cognition* (Vol. 1). Cambridge, MA: MIT Press.

Sajdyk, T. J., Shekhar, A., & Gehlert, D. R. (2004). Interactions between NPY and CRF in the amygdala to regulate emotionality. *Neuropeptides, 38*, 225–234.

Schildkraut, J. (1965). The catecholamine hypothesis of affective disorders: A review of supporting evidence. *American Journal of Psychiatry, 122*, 509–522.

Siegle, G. J. (in press). From brain imaging to intervention: Disruptions of emotional reativity in unipolar depression. *Japanese Journal of Research on Emotions.*

Staats, A. W. (1983). *Psychology's crisis of disunity: Philosophy and methods for a unified science.* New York: Praeger.

Staats, A. W. (1999). Unifying psychology requires new infrastructure, theory, method, and a research agenda. *Review of General Psychology, 3,* 3–13.

Stice, E., Ragan, J., & Randall, P. (2004). Prospective relations between social support and depression: Differential direction of effects for parent and peer support? *Journal of Abnormal Psychology, 113,* 115–119.

Stokstad, E. (2002) Violent effects of abuse tied to gene. *Science, 297,* 5582, 752.

Tooby, J., & Cosmides, L. (1992). The psychological foundations of culture. In J. Barkow, L. Cosmides, & J. Tooby (Eds.), *The adapted mind: Evolutionary psychology and the generation of culture.*

Tooby, J., & Cosmides, L. (1995). Mapping the evolved functional organization of mind and brain. In M. S. Gazzaniga (Ed.), *The cognitive neurosciences* (pp. 1185–1198). Cambridge, MA: MIT Press.

Turk, D. J., Rosenblum, A. C., Gazzaniga, M. S., & Macrae, C. N. (2005). Seeing John Malkovich: The neural substrates of person categorization. *Neuroimage, 24,* 1147–1153.

Vaidya V. A., & Duman, R. S. (2001). Depression: Emerging insights from neurobiology. *British Medical Bulletin, 57,* 61–79.

Wilson, E. O. (1998). *Consilience: The unity of knowledge.* New York: Vintage Books.

Wirz-Justice, A. (1995). Biological rhythms in mood disorders. In F. E. Bloom & D. J. Kupfer (Eds.), *Psychopharmacology: The fourth generation of progress* (pp. 999–1017) New York: Raven Press.

The Great Crosscutting Perspectives of Clinical Science

14

Early Developmental Processes Inform the Study of Mental Disorders

ERIN C. TULLY AND SHERRYL H. GOODMAN

Annie is a 35-year-old wife and mother of two small children. For the past year, she has not enjoyed her family, friends, or her work, and each day feels like a burden. She lies awake at night, ruminating that she was the most negligent mother at the playground and that her husband has lost interest in her. When she wakes up in the morning, she feels tired and drags herself through the day. She cannot find the energy to clean the house or prepare dinner and on occasion has even forgotten to pick up her children at school. As a result, Annie feels worthless and believes that the feeling of being overwhelmed by normal daily tasks will never end.

One might wonder how Annie became so depressed, impaired, and hopeless. The answer is probably very complex, involving the interplay of biological, psychological, and social factors through continually changing processes that began very early in her life and continue into her adulthood. One also might wonder about the likelihood that her children will also bear the burden of depression. The answer, similarly, is very complex.

GREAT IDEA: STUDYING EARLY DEVELOPMENTAL PROCESSES TO BETTER UNDERSTAND AND TREAT MENTAL DISORDERS

Psychopathology does not typically appear suddenly but, rather, emerges gradually through the course of development. Knowledge of early developmental processes is crucial for understanding mental disorders, even those that emerge in adolescence or adulthood. Imagine an army officer determining how to command his army after hearing only the last few dits and dahs of a Morris Code message, or imagine a baker trying to recreate the recipe for a cake after tasting the cake but without knowledge of the ingredients. In the same way, it is both inefficient and inadequate to study mental disorders by investigating either clinically significant levels of symptoms or diagnosable disorders (i.e., the outcome of a long developmental course) without knowledge of developmental psychopathology and, especially, of the role of early experience. Freud and others have said that "The child is father to the man." Studying early developmental processes is the *key* to understanding the emergence of psychopathology.

In this chapter, we will first outline core concepts that elucidate the importance of early development for later functioning. Then, we will describe how these concepts are relevant at various stages of early development for understanding later mental illness. Finally, we will discuss the implications of understanding early developmental processes for clinical practice.

DEVELOPMENTAL PROCESSES

From a developmental psychopathology perspective, psychopathology is most usefully conceptualized in terms of pathways that extend through time, rather than in terms of endpoints or outcomes (Cummings, Davies, & Campbell, 2000). Thus, understanding the emergence of Annie's depression requires us to study the maladaptive pathways that led to her depression (Sroufe & Rutter, 1984).

Maladaptive pathways are identified by studying connections between normal developmental processes and the emergence of behavioral and emotional problems across time. Children adapt to the new challenges posed at each stage of development by means of changes in biological, cognitive, behavioral, and socioemotional processes (Cicchetti & Schneider-Rosen, 1986; Cicchetti & Toth, 1995). By studying individual patterns of adaptation to salient developmental issues and the consequences of those patterns of adaptation for emotional and behavioral functioning, maladaptive developmental pathways can be distinguished from more adaptive (or normative) developmental pathways. Perhaps Annie's adaptation to certain developmental tasks, such as her development of the ability to regulate emotional responses as a young child, was incomplete or unsuccessful and was a component of developmental processes leading to her depression as an adult.

RISK AND PROMOTIVE FACTORS

Risk factors are characteristics of persons or their situations that are associated with an increased likelihood of developing patterns of maladaptation and that can predict the onset of disorder (Garmezy, Masten, & Tellegen, 1984). Although these associations alone are not necessarily indicative of causal mechanisms, risk factors are markers for underlying mechanisms that can intensify maladaptive processes and thwart the achievement of successful adaptation (Cicchetti & Toth, 1995; Masten et al., 1999). High levels of conflict and negativity in Annie's family may have been a risk factor that made it less likely that Annie developed more normative, healthy views of herself and her relationships, which subsequently contributed to depressogenic cognitions and depression itself.

In contrast, *promotive factors* are associated with patterns of successful adaptation and healthy outcomes (Gutman, Sameroff, & Eccles, 2002). They are markers for mechanisms that promote successful adaptation and reduce the chances of developing psychopathology. Promotive factors probably also affected Annie's developmental pathways. Strong cognitive abilities may have helped Annie to develop coping strategies to deal with high levels of conflict and stress in her family, which consequently reduced her risk of developing even more serious depression than she experienced. These risk and promotive factors, as well as the patterns of adaptation to normative tasks, are constantly evolving, with implications for current and future functioning.

TRANSACTIONAL MODELS

Psychopathology emerges from developmental pathways involving complex interplays among multiple influences that change over the course of development. Children and the context within which they develop are multifaceted and continually changing over time, which creates innumerable variables that mediate and moderate associations between influences on development and outcomes in multiple domains of functioning. A *mediator* is a variable that accounts for all or part of the relation between a predictor and an outcome (Baron & Kenny, 1986). It should be distinguished from a *moderator*, which is a variable that affects the direction and/or strength of the relation between a predictor variable and an outcome (Baron & Kenny, 1986). A mediator explains *how* or *why* a predictor variable is related to an outcome variable, whereas a moderator explains *when* or *under what conditions* a predictor variable is related to an outcome variable. Diverse pathways may lead to the same outcome, a concept termed *equifinality* (Cicchetti & Rogosch, 1996; Harrington, Rutter, & Fombonne, 1996). In other words, different childhood precursors may lead to the same adult outcome. Thus, the processes underlying Annie's depression may be very different from the processes underlying the depression of other women in her support group.

Transactional models have been particularly useful for studying risk and promotive factors as they relate to the development of psychopathology (Rolf, Masten, Cicchetti, Nuechterlein, & Weintraub, 1990). Transactional models recognize the importance of mutually influencing genetic, neurobiological, biochemical, psychological, and sociological factors in the development of psychopathology and describe the progressive evolution of developmental domains through mutual exchange with the environment (Cicchetti & Toth, 1995). It follows, then, that from a developmental psychopathology and transactional perspective, understanding mechanisms associated with the development of psychopathology requires us to study: (1) normal developmental processes, (2) individual differences in pathways of adaptation to normative tasks, (3) associations between these individual pathways and the development of psychopathology, and (4) the interplay among genetic, neurobiological, psychological, and environmental factors as they influence these developmental processes over time.

EARLY DEVELOPMENTAL PERIODS

Prenatal Influences

Although infancy has typically been considered the earliest opportunity for experiences that might influence the development of psychopathology, researchers are increasingly recognizing the potential role of prenatal influences. Such influences include not only genes (Goodman, 2003) but also experiences that can disrupt the healthy development of brain structures and neuroendocrine functions, which bear important implications for the later development of psychopathology (see Chapter 10 for a discussion of the interplay between genetic and environmental influences).

Studies of animals, typically rhesus monkeys and rats, have been particularly revealing of an important role of stress during pregnancy (for a recent review, see DiPietro, 2004). Offspring of prenatally stressed animals are born smaller, with less mature neuromotor functioning, and delayed cognitive development. They explore their environments less, vocalize less, and exhibit abnormal neuroendocrine responses to stress that persist beyond infancy. Although these studies provide interesting insights about the potential role of prenatal stress in pathways of maladaptation, the findings cannot be directly generalized to humans. There are basic differences in the physiology of humans and animals that preclude direct comparisons. Moreover, the nature of the stressors experimentally imposed on animals is very different from the distressed mood and other naturally occurring stressors that may affect pregnant women. Another important distinction between studies of animals and humans is that, with animal studies, random assignment of the animals to high-stress or low-stress groups is possible. This design, which involves direct manipulation of a variable, allows for direct inferences about causal mechanisms. Studies in humans are necessarily quasi-experimental, as random assignment to high- and low-stress groups are not practically or ethically possible. Thus, definitive inferences about causal mechanisms cannot be drawn from the studies of humans.

Surprisingly, few studies have tested associations between pregnant women's stress, anxiety, or depression and the development of psycho-pathology in their children. This is especially true when considering only studies that both collected data prospectively during pregnancy (rather than relying on mothers' retrospective recall of their mood during pregnancy) and used independent sources of information on the children's problem behaviors (rather than relying exclusively on the mothers' reports, which may be influenced by their mood). Of the few studies that meet these criteria, the findings for the most part suggest that women's psychological distress during pregnancy is associated with more maladaptive outcomes in their children, including problems with attention and behavioral or emotional control (DiPietro, 2004). Although statistically significant, more studies are needed before we can draw conclusions about how large these effects are and whether they might be moderated by such variables as the severity or timing of the women's distress.

At a more basic level, researchers have found that fetuses of anxious mothers experience reduced blood flow and that levels of stress hormones in mothers and their fetuses are highly intercorrelated. Fetuses' first transactions with their mothers occur at gestational days 13–14, when uterine blood flow is established. Thus, fetuses may be affected by the neuroendocrine correlates of mothers' mood during most of fetal development. High levels of cortisol exposure prenatally may initiate a cascade of neuroendocrine events, resulting in persistent changes in corticotropin-releasing-factor (CRF)-containing neurons, the hypotha-lamic-pituitary-adrenal (HPA) axis, and the sympathetic nervous system, all of which may mediate the development of depression either in child-hood or later, in adulthood (Nemeroff, 1998).

In the case of Annie's depression, stress and anxiety experienced by Annie's mother during her pregnancy may have resulted in Annie's prenatal exposure to high levels of cortisol and other hormones. Then, through alterations in HPA axis functioning, biological predispositions to self-regulation difficulties may have triggered a developmental process of emotion regulation difficulties that later in the developmental pathway bore implications for Annie's depression as an adult.

Other researchers suggest that brain development may be altered during fetal development in ways that hold implications for the emergence of psychopathology. The prefrontal cortex has been of particular inter-est because it plays a central role in emotion regulation and expression. For example, Dawson and her colleagues found that infants of prena-tally depressed mothers demonstrate increased relative right to left frontal cortical activation, a pattern associated with the experience of "withdrawal" emotions (e.g., distress and fear) and withdrawal strategies in response to stress (Ashman & Dawson, 2002). This association appears to be related directly to the prenatal exposure to mothers' depression and is not mediated by the infants' experience with parenting associated with postnatal depression in mothers (e.g., insensitivity). Thus, genetic or intrauterine factors are the probable mechanisms.

Together these findings are consistent with the idea that the prenatal period is a time when development can go awry and may be the initial stage in developmental pathways leading to psychopathology. Whether because of genes, exposure to high levels of cortisol, reduced uterine blood flow, or other mechanisms that are not yet understood, some infants are born with biological systems that predispose to psychopathology. As a result, these infants may be born with physical and psychological disadvantages, such as low birth weight, being difficult for parents to console, and problems with self-regulation, all of which may be initial steps in pathways of risk for psychopathology.

In summary, although research is still somewhat limited, knowledge of prenatal influences is almost certainly crucial for a comprehensive understanding of the emergence of Annie's depression. Fetal exposure to cortisol may have resulted in alterations in Annie's HPA axis system functioning and, thus, persistent changes in how she responds to stress. Her mother's depression during pregnancy may have led to changes in frontal cortical activation and, consequently, to patterns of withdrawal from stress. In these and other ways, Annie's biological system may be primed to react in maladaptive ways to future challenges and adverse conditions.

EXPERIENCES IN INFANCY

Researchers have long been interested in development during infancy for its potential to affect mental health. Infancy is a critical period for several reasons: (1) the extensive biological and socio-emotional development that occurs during this stage, (2) the potential for environmental influences on these aspects of development, and (3) known associations between these aspects of development and the later emergence of psychopathology.

In terms of biological development during infancy, the brain undergoes a period of particularly rapid development in the first 6 months of postnatal life. Notably, frontal lobe development continues postnatally. As described in the previous section of this chapter, relative increased right to left frontal activation is related to problems with emotion self-regulation, which bears direct implications for the development of depression and other forms of psychopathology (Ashman & Dawson, 2002; Graham, Heim, Goodman, Miller, & Nemeroff, 1999). Correspondingly, reduced left frontal brain activity is associated with vulnerability to experience and express negative affect in stressful situations, a tendency to withdraw and avoid interaction, and lower behavioral initiation (Davidson & Fox, 1989; Dawson, Frey, Panagiotides, Osterling, & Hessl, 1997; Fox, 1994). Research is also beginning to show that these brain patterns are associated with a diminished capacity to experience joy and a heightened tendency to experience negative affect and thus may contribute to risk for developing depression and other emotional problems later in life (Davidson & Fox, 1989; Dawson et al., 1997; Fox, 1994).

With respect to socioemotional development, developing secure attachment relationships is an important task during infancy that has implications for functioning later in life. Throughout the first year, infants are acquiring a sense of themselves in relation to others and the world that, ideally, results in a secure attachment strategy. If infants fail to develop secure attachment relationships, they are at increased risk for the later development of emotional and behavioral problems (Sroufe, Egeland, Carlson, & Collins, 2005). Infants' temperament may moderate the association between attachment and the development of psycho-pathology, although the role of temperament in relation to attachment has been the subject of an as yet unresolved debate among researchers (Zeanah & Fox, 2004).

A key environmental influence on both the biological and socio-emotional aspects of development is parenting. Warm and contingently responsive care is necessary for healthy infant development, and failure to provide such care may impede healthy maturation of biobehavioral mechanisms. Even children who did not experience adverse fetal environments and are born with well-functioning neuroregulatory systems may acquire dysfunctions by means of interaction with a caregiver who is not sufficiently warm or responsive. Given the current understanding that important aspects of brain functions and neurobehavioral mechanisms are still developing after birth, researchers are beginning to learn the extent to which the infant brain is sensitive to early life stress, with the major focus being on the frontal lobes given the major role they play in the regulation of emotion. Researchers are finding that good quality parenting is required to support healthy brain development that continues into the first few years of postnatal life (Ashman & Dawson, 2002; Field, 1994). Specifically, neurobiological development during early postnatal life may be adversely influenced by mothers being nonresponsive, intrusive, or with-drawn, and by both expressing and eliciting an excess of negative emotion in interactions with the infants. Both Dawson and Field are accumulat-ing evidence that such adverse early parenting is related to the reduced left frontal electrical brain activity that has previously been described as associated with withdrawal in children and with depression in adults.

Similarly, a pattern of less sensitive, responsive, and reciprocal parenting is the strongest predictor of insecure attachment (Cassidy & Shaver, 1999) and, more broadly, of infants' premature, ineffective efforts to self-regulate (Gianino & Tronick, 1988). In turn, each of these aspects of infant functioning is associated with vulnerability to depression. Specifically, insecure attachment leads children to develop negative expectancies for other relationships and negative self-perceptions, leaving the child vulnerable to depression (Cummings & Cicchetti, 1990). Similarly, infants' frustrated attempts to obtain needed external regulation from their parents have been observed to lead to their engaging in self-directed regulatory behaviors, foretelling a retreat from engagement with the social world (Gianino & Tronick, 1988). Negative affect itself is related to later learning difficulties (Bugental, Blue, Cortez, & Fleck, 1992). Less ability to self-regulate might emerge as a generalized dysregulation of emotion and behavior, or, more specifically, as heightened sensitivity to stressors (e.g., interparental conflict, parents' distress), a threatened sense of emotional security, undercontrolled behavior with parents and peers, including aggression, or, alternatively, overcontrolled behavior or suppressing emotions as a way of coping with stressful situations.

Infants' more predominant negative affect, whether a function of the suggested problems in brain development or the failure of parents to meet infants' basic needs, may be associated with a tendency to elicit sad affect in other interacting partners (Field, Healy, Goldstein, & Perry, 1988) and with a predisposition to negatively biased perceptions, and it may predict subsequent learning difficulties (Bugental et al., 1992; Singer & Fagen, 1992). Thus, parents' failure to adequately support their infants' needs, the critical component of experience in infancy, bears implications for aspects of adaptation to situations encountered later in development, suggesting multiple pathways for the development of depression.

Again, then, it is evident that several promising keys to understanding the emergence of Annie's depression lie in early developmental processes. Continued postnatal development of relatively increased right frontal activation and, consequently, expressions of negative affect, may have been related in complicated ways to negative interactions between Annie and her mother. Annie's fussiness as a baby and withdrawal from interactions with her mother may have been reciprocally related to her mothers' difficulty in calming Annie and with a harsh and uncaring style of interacting with her. These negative interactions may have led to negative expectations about future interpersonal relationships and a sense of social incompetence, cognitions that contribute to the developmental processes resulting in Annie's depression.

EXPERIENCES IN THE PRESCHOOL YEARS

As Annie entered the preschool years, pathways of adaptation and maladaptation continued to develop as different salient challenges became relevant over time. The preschool years are particularly critical for emotional, cognitive, and social development. Failure to achieve stage-salient milestones, such as developing the capacity for self-regulation, has been associated with emotional and behavioral problems in preschool-aged children (Zahn-Waxler, Cole, Welsh, & Fox, 1995).

Beginning with emotional development, during this period children learn to identify and regulate their emotions, to cope autonomously with emotional demands, to differentiate their own emotions from those of others, and to incorporate feedback about their emotional expressivity (Cole, Michel, & Teti, 1994; de Roten, Favez, Drapeau, & Stern, 2003;

Kopp, 1989). The capacity to exercise self-control over the expression of negative emotion and behavior is an important developmental task to be accomplished during the preschool years. Failure to achieve self-regulation of emotions may lead to the development of psychopathology (Calkins, 1994; Calkins & Keane, 2004; Eisenberg et al., 1995; Keenan, 2000; Thompson, 1994).

Many processes affect the development of emotion regulation abilities, including the maturation of various biological systems. Regulation of behavior and emotions is largely determined by maturation of the frontal lobes (Fox, 1994), particularly the prefrontal cortices (Posner & Rothbart, 2000) and the parasympathetic nervous system (Calkins, 1997). For example, Fox and colleagues (Fox et al., 1995) found that children who displayed social competence during play sessions exhibited greater relative left frontal activation, whereas children who displayed social withdrawal exhibited greater relative right frontal activation. Perhaps slow maturation of these biological systems influenced early withdrawal behavior in Annie that evolved through developmental pathways into social isolation later in life.

Moving on to cognitive development, normative changes in cognitive abilities provide preschool-aged children with the abilities to evaluate the self, explain the causes of events and outcomes in their lives, and develop expectancies about which situations will be distressing and which will be enjoyable (Harter, 1999; Kaslow, Adamson, & Collins, 2000). In a complex interplay of various developing systems, young children's rapidly developing cognitive abilities also play a role in their capacity for emotion regulation as their level of cognitive development influences perception and understanding of emotions and emotional events (Cole et al., 1994; Kopp, 1989).

Again, various risk processes may thwart the development of positive cognitions of the self early in life. For example, exposure to chronic or traumatic stress may lead children to believe that they are not effective causal agents (Segal, 1988). If Annie experienced chronic negative emotion-producing events during this critical period of cognitive development, such as exposure to her parents' unresolved marital conflict or their excessive criticism of her behavior, she may have developed negatively biased representations of herself that could have set the foundation for the emergence of her depressogenic cognitions later in life.

A final major developmental task of the preschool years is learning to interact socially as social networks expand to include the classroom, teachers, and peers. These changing social environments provide new information about emotions, regulatory influences, and social acceptability that affects the development of emotion regulation systems (Saarni & Crowley, 1990). Illustrating the complex, reciprocal nature of developmental pathways, children's successful communication of emotions through emotionally expressive behavior likewise affects social relationships. For adaptive social functioning, young children must develop social skills and appropriate interpersonal behaviors. Normative social tasks for preschool-aged children include developing the capacity for empathy and learning to respond to other people's problems with attempts to change the situation by helping, sharing, and soothing (Radke-Yarrow & Zahn-Waxler, 1984; Zahn-Waxler & Radke-Yarrow, 1982).

Interacting risk processes may also interfere with successful development of social skills and appropriate interpersonal behavior. For instance, an empathetic response to another's distress coupled with an attribution of having caused the distress may result in interpersonal guilt (Hoffman, 1982). Because early development is characterized by egocentrism and difficulty with self-other differentiation, young children may be particularly likely to make overgeneralized assumptions of personal responsibility for distress in others, and thereby experience guilt (Radke-Yarrow, Zahn-Waxler, Richardson, Susman, & Martinez, 1994). Again, children's cognitive abilities affect their social functioning in a complex reciprocal fashion.

Maturation of hypothalamic pituitary adrenal (HPA) axis systems during early development adds another layer of complexity to emotional, cognitive, and social development during the preschool years. Normatively, the HPA system continues to mature through infancy and toddlerhood as baseline cortisol production becomes more stable and a pattern of diurnal decline begins to emerge (Watamura, Donzella, Kertes, & Gunnar, 2004). As preschool-aged children develop self-regulatory abilities, they begin to produce lower concentrations of cortisol (Gunnar & Cheatham, 2003; Watamura et al., 2004). Children who experience the normal developmental challenges of the preschool period as particularly stressful may develop chronic activation of the HPA axis and also may be less able to inhibit behaviors and regulate emotions. Given that HPA functioning has been implicated in the pathophysiology of various forms of psychopathology (Ressler & Nemeroff, 2000), it is plausible that through developmental pathways that involve a reciprocal relationships between chronic stress, HPA overactivation, and regulation difficulties, early imbalances in Annie's HPA system may be implicated in the later emergence of her depression. Annie's strong cognitive abilities may have acted as a promotive factor if they facilitated the development of effective coping strategies for dealing with stress and positively altered the maladaptive developmental pathways from stress to her depression.

In summary, inadequate development in various domains of functioning during the preschool years may contribute to maladaptive developmental pathways. Suboptimal development of the ability to regulate emotions and behaviors, evaluate the self, explain and cope with life events, and interact socially with peers, as well as immature development of biological processes (e.g., frontal lobes, cardiac vagal regulation, HPA-axis) may play a role in pathways that over time lead to mental disorders.

CLINICAL IMPLICATIONS

Knowledge of early experiences and hypotheses about early developmental processes involved in the emergence of psychopathology hold particular implications for case conceptualization and treatment planning. Recognizing that developmental pathways leading to psychopathology are initiated early in development underscores the importance of early intervention and prevention. Imagine the potential differences in Annie's developmental pathways that may have resulted from interventions early in her life. For example, if Annie's mother had received treatment for her anxiety during pregnancy, Annie's prenatal exposure to cortisol and other hormones and, thus, her risk for alterations to her HPA axis system may have been greatly reduced. Interventions during infancy or the preschool years targeted at increasing maternal warmth and reciprocally positive mother-child interactions may have helped Annie to develop more positive views of herself and others. Later, when Annie began interacting with peers, interventions to help her learn to self-regulate emotions may have resulted in better peer relationships and coping skills. Any changes in the developmental processes may have initiated very different developmental pathways that could have drastically reduced her risk for later depression.

Even in the absence of early interventions, knowledge of basic developmental processes informs clinical interventions with adults. The developmental psychopathology literature provides insight, beyond the treatment outcome literature, about potential processes underlying psychopathology and thus provides clues about potential targets for interventions. Given the research on prenatal exposure to depression and the implications for HPA system functioning, knowledge that Annie's mother was anxious during pregnancy might lead to hypotheses about maladaptive developmental processes involving the HPA system and predispositions to experiencing negative emotions. Treatment goals based on knowledge of this developmental process may involve increasing Annie's awareness of her tendency to experience negative affect and developing a plan for regular pleasurable activities to counter her tendencies toward negative affect. In a similar way, knowledge of early relationships with parents or peers, such as relationships characterized by criticism or social rejection, may help uncover core beliefs of being unlovable or unworthy. These core beliefs may form the foundation for cognitive-behavioral interventions aimed at restructuring Annie's depressogenic thinking patterns. Thus, developmental psychopathology bears substantial implications for treatment of disorders throughout the life span.

CONCLUSIONS

In summary, understanding Annie's depression at any particular point in time requires the study of many diverse systems that mutually influence one another in complex transactional ways, unfolding over time. From a developmental psychopathology perspective, adaptation to developmental challenges is ongoing throughout the lifespan. Thus, patterns of adaptation and maladaptation are constantly changing across the entire life course from prenatal development until death. Merely considering the potential influences from the first few years of life raises innumerable questions, the answers to which reveal the importance of early development. Did prenatal exposure to her mothers' stress and anxiety, and thus high levels of cortisol, lead to an imbalance in Annie's HPA axis functioning? How were the alterations in HPA axis functioning related to Annie's difficulty with self-regulation as an infant? Were Annie's self-regulation difficulties reciprocally related to negative mother-infant interactions? Did negative mother-infant interactions contribute to expectations of negative interpersonal interactions in the future and thus to social withdrawal from peers? Did these relationships lead to the development of negative beliefs of the self and the world and later to depressogenic thinking patterns? Hypotheses about potential early influences on later psychopathology are virtually endless.

KEY TERMS

Developmental psychopathology: An interdisciplinary scientific field that seeks to elucidate the interplay among biological, psychological, and social aspects of normal and abnormal development as they relate to multiple outcomes, including patterns of emotional and behavioral adaptation and maladaptation, that change constantly across the life course (Cummings, Davies, & Campbell, 2000).

Equifinality: A term that refers to the idea that there may be different childhood precursors of the same adult outcome (Cicchetti & Rogosch, 1996).

Mediator: A variable that accounts for all or part of the relation between a predictor and an outcome (Baron & Kenny, 1986).

Moderator: A variable that affects the direction and/or strength of the relation between a predictor variable and an outcome (Baron & Kenny, 1986).

Promotive factors: Characteristics of persons or their situations that are associated with a positive outcome (Gutman et al., 2002).

Risk factors: Characteristics of persons or their situations that are associated with a negative outcome (Garmezy et al., 1984).

Transactional models: Integrative models that explain the development of psychopathology as the complex interplay among neurobiological, biochemical, psychological, and sociological factors that evolve through mutual exchange with the environment (Cicchetti & Toth, 1995).

SUGGESTED READINGS

Cummings, M. E., Davies, P. T., & Campbell, S. B. (2000). *Developmental psychopathology and family process: Theory, research, and clinical practice.* New York: Guilford Press.

Davidson, R. J., Ekman, P., Saron, C., Senulis, R., & Friesen, W. V. (1990). Approach-withdrawal and cerebral asymmetry: Emotional expression and brain physiology I. *Journal of Personality and Social Psychology, 58,* 330–341.

Del Carmen-Wiggins, R., & Carter, A. (2004). *Handbook of infant, toddler, and preschool mental health assessment*. New York: Oxford University Press.

Gunnar, M., & Cheatham, C. L. (2003). Brain and behavior interface: Stress and the developing brain. *Infant Mental Health Journal, 24*, 195–211.

Sroufe, L. A., Egeland, B., Carlson, E. A., & Collins, A. W. (2005). *The development of the person: The Minnesota study of risk and adaptation from birth to adulthood*. New York: Guilford Press.

REFERENCES

Ashman, S. B., & Dawson, G. (2002). Maternal depression, infant psychobiological development, and risk for depression. In S. H. Goodman & I. H. Gotlib (Eds.), *Children of depressed parents: Mechanisms of risk and implications for treatment* (pp. 37–58). Washington, DC: American Psychological Association Books.

Baron, R. M., & Kenny, D. A. (1986). The moderator-mediator distinction in social psychological research: Conceptual, strategic, and statistical considerations. *Journal of Personality and Social Psychology, 51*, 1173–1182.

Bugental, D. B., Blue, J., Cortez, V., & Fleck, K. (1992). Influences of witnessed affect on information processing in children. *Child Development, 63*, 774–786.

Calkins, S. D. (1994). Origins and outcomes of individual differences in emotion regulation. *Monographs of the Society for Research in Child Development, 59*(2–3), 53–72.

Calkins, S. D. (1997). Cardiac vagal tone indices of temperament reactivity and behavioral regulation in young children. *Developmental Psychobiology, 31*, 125–135.

Calkins, S. D., & Keane, S. P. (2004). Cardiac vagal regulation across the preschool period: Stability, continuity, and implications for childhood adjustment. *Developmental Psychobiology, 45*(3), 101–112.

Cassidy, J., & Shaver, P. R. (1999). *Handbook of attachment: Theory, research, and clinical applications*. New York: Guilford Press.

Cicchetti, D., & Rogosch, F. A. (1996). Equifinality and multifinality in developmental psychopathology. *Development and Psychopathology, 8*, 597–600.

Cicchetti, D., & Schneider-Rosen, K. (1986). *An organizational approach to childhood depression*. New York: Guilford.

Cicchetti, D., & Toth, S. L. (1995). Developmental psychopathology and disorders of affect. In D. Cicchetti & D. J. Cohen (Eds.), *Developmental psychopathology* (Vol. 2: Risk, disorder, and adaptation, pp. 369–420). Oxford: John Wiley & Sons.

Cole, P. M., Michel, M. K., & Teti, L. O. (1994). The development of emotion regulation and dysregulation: A clinical perspective. *Monographs of the Society for Research in Child Development, 59*, 73–100.

Cummings, E. M., & Cicchetti, D. (1990). Toward a transactional model of relations between attachment and depression. In M. T. Greenberg & D. Cicchetti (Eds.), *Attachment in the preschool years: Theory, research, and intervention. The John D. and Catherine T. Macarthur Foundation series on mental health and development* (pp. 339–372). Chicago: University of Chicago Press.

Cummings, E. M., Davies, P. T., & Campbell, S. B. (2000). *Developmental psychopathology and family process: Theory, research, and clinical practice*. New York: Guilford Press.

Davidson, R. J., & Fox, N. A. (1989). Frontal brain asymmetry predicts infants' response to maternal separation. *Journal of Abnormal Psychology, 98,* 127–131.

Dawson, G., Frey, K., Panagiotides, H., Osterling, J., & Hessl, D. (1997). Infants of depressed mothers exhibit atypical frontal brain activity: A replication and extension of previous findings. *Journal of Child Psychology and Psychiatry, 38,* 179–186.

de Roten, Y., Favez, N., Drapeau, M., & Stern, D. N. (2003). Two studies on autobiographical narratives about an emotional event by preschoolers: Influence of the emotions experienced and the affective closeness with interlocutor. *Early Child Development and Care, 173,* 237–248.

DiPietro, J. A. (2004). The role of prenatal maternal stress in child development. *Current Directions in Psychological Science, 13,* 71–74.

Eisenberg, N., Fabes, R. A., Murphy, B., Maszk, P., Smith, M., & Karbon, M. (1995). The role of emotionality and regulation in children's social functioning: A longitudinal study. *Child Development, 66*(5), 1360–1384.

Field, T. (1994). The effects of mother's physical and emotional unavailability on emotion regulation. *Monographs of the Society for Research in Child Development, 59*(2–3), 208–227.

Field, T., Healy, B., Goldstein, S., & Perry, S. (1988). Infants of depressed mothers show depressed even with nondepressed adults. *Child Development, 59,* 1569–1579.

Fox, N. (1994). Dynamic cerebral processes underlying emotion regulation. *Monographs of the Society for Research in Child Development, 59*(2–3).

Fox, N., Rubin, K. H., Calkins, S. D., Marshall, T. R., Coplan, R. J., Porges, S. W., et al. (1995). Frontal activation asymmetry and social competence at four years of age. *Child Development, 66*(6), 1770–1784.

Garmezy, N., Masten, A., & Tellegen, A. (1984). The study of stress and competence in children: A building block for developmental psychopathology. *Child Development, 55,* 97–111.

Gianino, A., & Tronick, E. Z. (1988). The mutual regulation model: The infant's self and interactive regulation and coping and defensive capacities. In T. M. Field & P. M. McCabe (Eds.), *Stress and coping across development.* (pp. 47–68). Hillsdale, NJ: Lawrence Erlbaum Associates.

Goodman, S. H. (2003). Genesis and epigenesis of psychopathology in children with depressed mothers: Toward an integrative biopsychosocial perspective. In D. Cicchetti & E. Walker (Eds.), *Neurodevelopmental mechanisms in psychopathology* (pp. 428–460). New York: Cambridge University Press.

Graham, Y. P., Heim, C., Goodman, S. H., Miller, A. H., & Nemeroff, C. B. (1999). The effects of neonatal stress on brain development: Implications for psychopathology. *Development and Psychopathology, 11,* 545–565.

Gunnar, M. R., & Cheatham, C. L. (2003). Brain and behavior interface: Stress and the developing brain. *Infant Mental Health Journal, 24*(3), 195–211.

Gutman, L. M., Sameroff, A. J., & Eccles, J. S. (2002). The academic achievement of African-American students during early adolescence: An examination of multiple risk, promotive, and protective factors. *American Journal of Community Psychology, 39,* 367–399.

Harrington, R., Rutter, M., & Fombonne, E. (1996). Developmental pathways in depression: Multiple meanings, antecedents, and endpoints. *Development and Psychopathology, 8,* 601–616.

Harter, S. (1999). *The construction of the self: A developmental perspective.* New York: Guilford Press.

Hoffman, M. L. (1982). Development of prosocial motivation: Empathy and guilt. In N. Eisenberg (Ed.), *The development of prosocial behavior* (pp. 281–313). San Diego, CA: Academic Press.

Kaslow, N. J., Adamson, L. B., & Collins, M. H. (2000). A developmental psycho-pathology perspective on the cognitive components of child and adolescent depression. In A. J. Sameroff, M. Lewis, & S. M. Miller (Eds.), *Handbook of developmental psychopathology* (2nd ed.). New York: Kluwer Academic/ Plenum Publishers.

Keenan, K. (2000). Emotion dysregulation as a risk factor for child psycho-pathology. *Clinical Psychology: Science & Practice, 7*(4), 418–434.

Kopp, C. B. (1989). Regulation of distress and negative emotions: A developmental view. *Developmental Psychology, 25*, 343–354.

Masten, A. S., Hubbard, J. J., Gest, S. D., Tellegen, A., Garmezy, N., & Ramirez, M. (1999). Competence in the context of adversity: Pathways to resilience and maladaptation from childhood to late adolescence. *Development and Psychopathology, 11*, 143–169.

Nemeroff, C. B. (1998). The neurobiology of depression. *Scientific American, 278*, 42–49.

Posner, M. I., & Rothbart, M. K. (2000). Developing mechanisms of self-regulation. *Development and Psychopathology, 12*(3), 427–441.

Radke-Yarrow, M., & Zahn-Waxler, C. (1984). Roots, motives and patterning in children's prosocial behavior. In E. Staub, D. Bar-Tal, J. Karylowski, & J. Reykowski (Eds.), *The development and maintenance of prosocial behavior: International perspectives on positive morality* (pp. 155–176). New York: Plenum Press.

Radke-Yarrow, M., Zahn-Waxler, C., Richardson, D. T., Susman, A., & Martinez, P. (1994). Caring behavior in children of clinically depressed and well mothers. *Child Development*, (65), 1405–1414.

Ressler, K. J., & Nemeroff, C. B. (2000). Role of serotonergic and noradrenergic systems in the pathophysiology of depression and anxiety disorders. *Depression and Anxiety, 12*, 2–19.

Rolf, J., Masten, A., Cicchetti, D., Nuechterlein, K., & Weintraub, S. (1990). *Risk and protective factors in the development of psychopathology*. New York: Cambridge University Press.

Saarni, C., & Crowley, M. (1990). The development of emotion regulation: Effects on emotional state and expression. In E. A. Blechman (Ed.), *Emotions and the family: For better or for worse*. Hillsdale, NJ: Lawrence Erlbaum Associates.

Segal, Z. V. (1988). Appraisal of the self-schema construct in cognitive models of depression. *Psychological Bulletin, 103*, 147–162.

Singer, J. M., & Fagen, J. W. (1992). Negative affect, emotional expression, and forgetting in young infants. *Developmental Psychology, 28*, 48–57.

Sroufe, L. A., Egeland, B., Carlson, E. A., & Collins, A. W. (2005). *The development of the person: The Minnesota study of risk and adaptation from birth to adult-hood*. New York: Guilford Press.

Sroufe, L. A., & Rutter, M. (1984). The domain of developmental psychopathology. *Child Development, 55*, 17–29.

Thompson, R. A. (1994). Emotion regulation: A theme in search of defini-tion. *Monographs of the Society for Research in Child Development, 59*(2–3), 25–52.

Watamura, S. E., Donzella, B., Kertes, D. A., & Gunnar, M. R. (2004). Developmental changes in baseline cortisol activity in early childhood: Relations with napping and effortful control. *Developmental Psychobiology*, 45(3), 125–133.

Zahn-Waxler, C., Cole, P. M., Welsh, J. D., & Fox, N. A. (1995). Psychophysiological correlates of empathy and prosocial behaviors in preschool children with behavior problems. *Development and Psychopathology*, 7, 27–48.

Zahn-Waxler, C., & Radke-Yarrow, M. (1982). The development of altruism: Alternative research strategies. In N. Eisenberg (Ed.), *The development of prosocial behavior* (pp. 109–137). New York: Academic Press.

Zeanah, C. H., & Fox, N. A. (2004). Temperament and attachment disorders. *Journal of Clinical Child & Adolescent Psychology*, 33, 32–41.

15

Mental and Physical Health Influence Each Other

NEIL SCHNEIDERMAN AND SCOTT D. SIEGEL

INTRODUCTION

The idea that mental and physical health can influence each other has a long but controversial history. Hippocrates, a Greek physician born in 460 BC, and often considered the father of medicine, believed that illness had a physical and rational explanation (Asimov, 1982; Porter, 1994). He asserted that each of four circulating fluids (blood, black bile, yellow bile, phlegm) is associated with bodily temperaments. According to Hippocrates, diseases arise when the four circulatory fluids get out of balance. In essence, then, Hippocrates believed that disturbances in temperament lead to disease and conversely that disturbances in bodily functions influence temperament.

The advent of physical medicine during the Renaissance brought new approaches to the investigation of physical phenomena. Andreas Vesalius (1543), a Dutch physician, published his anatomical text *De Humani Corporis Fabrica* (*On the Make-Up of the Human Body*) based on dissections of the human body. Subsequently, William Harvey (1628) described how blood circulates in the body and is propelled by the heart. Men such as Versalius and Harvey used scientific experimentation instead of conjecture to explain physical functioning.

The proposition that body functioning can be explained entirely by physical mechanisms reflects a *biological reductionism*, which holds that concepts such as the mind or soul are not needed to explain disease processes. René Descartes, a 17th-century French philosopher, argued that the mind was a separate entity parallel to, but incapable of influencing, somatic processes (Descartes, 1637/1956). The Cartesian dualism of mind and body provided a philosophical justification for Western medicine to adopt biological reductionism and reject possible interactions between *psyche* and *soma*. Thus, many Western physicians tended to adopt the view that the onset and course of a physical illness can be reduced to a purely biological explanation without consideration of mental processes (i.e., thoughts and emotions).

The emphasis on biological reductionism received strong impetus from the work of Robert Koch (1881/1987), who demonstrated that the infectious disease anthrax developed in mice only when the material injected into a mouse's bloodstream contained spores of *Bacillus anthraces*. Koch (1882/1987) also discovered the tubercle bacillus for which he was awarded the Nobel Prize in Physiology or Medicine in 1905. Thus, it became clear that infectious diseases were caused by specific micro-organisms. In spite of the strong evidence that microorganisms cause infectious diseases, scientists in the late 19th and early 20th century began to make observations suggesting that external forces other than microorganisms might influence disease processes.

Claude Bernard (1865/1961) pointed out that the maintenance of life is dependent upon keeping an organism's internal environment constant in the face of a changing external environment. He noted that physical challenges to the integrity of an organism provoke responses to counteract those threats. Subsequently, Walter Cannon (1929) coined the term *homeostasis* to describe the process of maintaining stability in the face of environmental change. Cannon (1928, 1935) provided evidence that homeostasis can be threatened by psychologically meaningful as well as physical challenges. Hans Selye (1956) used the term *stress* to describe the effects of any agent that seriously threatens homeostasis. Although Selye recognized that stress responses are designed to be adaptive, he also found that severe, prolonged stress responses can result in tissue damage and disease.

Based on the work of Cannon, Selye, and others, George Engel (1977) argued that a biopsychosocial model is needed to replace the narrow biological reductionism that was prevalent in Western medicine. Engel wrote that "Medicine's crisis stems from the logical inference that since 'disease' is defined in terms of somatic parameters, physicians need not be concerned with psychosocial issues that lie outside medicine's responsibilities and authority" (Engel, 1977, p. 129). He contended that a growing body of evidence justifies the belief that mental and physical health can influence each other. However, as recently as 1985, much of the medical community in the United States appeared to agree with Marcia Angell's editorial in the *New England Journal of Medicine* that the "belief in disease as a direct reflection of mental state is largely folklore" (Angell, 1985).

The rapprochement of biological reductionism and a biopsychosocial medical model was dependent on establishing (a) statistically significant associations in well-controlled epidemiological studies between "mental states" (i.e., thoughts and emotions) and disease outcomes, and (b) discovery of plausible biological pathways that can mediate these associations. During the past two decades both significant associations and plausible pathways have been documented.

ASSOCIATIONS BETWEEN MENTAL STATES AND DISEASE

The initial step required to demonstrate that mental health can influence physical health is to show in well-controlled prospective studies that statistically significant associations exist between specific mental states and disease outcomes. Such studies need to rule out demographic, behavioral, and biological variables that might be correlated with the mental state and lead to spurious conclusions about the nature of the association between the mental state and the disease outcome. Well-controlled, prospective studies have demonstrated relationships between mental states (e.g., depression, perceived stress) and a number of diseases including coronary heart disease (CHD), cancer, HIV/AIDS, and the common cold.

Cardiovascular Disease

In a prospective study of 2,832 healthy men and women aged 45–88 years, Anda et al. (1993) found that depressed mood or severe feelings of hopelessness were associated with 50% and 100% increases, respectively, in the relative risk of dying from CHD during an average follow-up period of more than 12 years. Several other large-scale, well-controlled studies have confirmed the prospective relationship between depressed affect and an increased death rate from CHD (Barefoot & Schroll, 1996; Ferketich, Schwartzbaum, Frid, and Moeschberger, 2000; Penninx et al., 2001).

Numerous prospective studies also have found depression to be an independent risk for new events in the progression of existing CHD (Wulsin & Singal, 2003). Lespérance et al. (2002), for example, examined in 896 patients the effect of depression diagnosed in the hospital after a heart attack (i.e., myocardial infarction) on death from CHD during the next 5 years. Those with at least a moderately elevated Beck depression score (i.e., greater than 10) had more than three times the relative risk of dying as people with a low Beck depression score (i.e., less than 5).

Several prospective studies have shown that proneness to anger or hostility places middle-aged men and women at risk for having nonfatal and fatal heart attacks independent of established biological risk factors (Barefoot, Dahlstrom, & Williams, 1983; Shekelle, Gale, Ostfeld, & Paul, 1983; Williams et al., 2000). An association between anxiety and fatal CHD also has been observed in a large scale study that controlled for traditional risk factors, including advancing age, obesity, smoking, elevated blood pressure, high serum cholesterol, family history of CHD, and a high level of alcohol consumption (Kawachi, Sparrow, Vokonas, & Weiss, 1994).

Cancer

Psychosocial factors have also been associated with the onset and progression of cancer. Everson et al., (1996) followed 2,428 men in Finland aged 42 to 60 years for up to 6 years. Moderate and high hopelessness scores predicted an 80% increase in relative risk of developing cancer. In another study, Watson, Haviland, Greer, Davidson, & Bliss (1999) followed 578 women with early-stage breast cancer for 5 years. High depression scores were associated with more than three times the risk of dying. Thus, there is some evidence that depression and feelings of hopelessness may influence the development and course of some cancers.

HIV/AIDS

Two major studies have shown that depressed affect is positively associated with increased death rates in men and women infected with HIV. In one study, Mayne, Vittinghoff, Chesney, Barrett, & Coates (1996) studied 402 HIV infected men who had sex with men. The men were assessed every 6 months for up to 6 years. Depressed affect was associated with a 67% greater relative risk of dying after controlling for such confounds as initial severity of disease, lymphocyte count, HIV medication usage, and so on. In a similar study, Ickovics et al. (2001) assessed each of 765 HIV-infected women every 6 months for up to 7 years. The investigators found that women with chronic depressive symptoms were twice as likely to die as women with few or no symptoms.

The impact of life stressors also has been studied in HIV-infected men who had sex with men. In men with HIV who did not have AIDS symptoms during their initial assessment, Leserman et al. (2000) found that faster progression to AIDS over a 7.5-year period was associated with more cumulative stressful life events (rated as being independent of personality), low satisfaction with social support, and the use of denial as a primary coping mechanism. Thus, it appears that psychosocial factors are associated with HIV/AIDS outcomes.

Upper Respiratory Diseases

Observational studies suggested that stress might predict susceptibility to the common cold (e.g., Graham, Douglas, & Ryan, 1986). However, such studies did not control for viral exposure, and it is conceivable that stressed people seek more outside contact and thus are exposed to more viruses. Therefore, Cohen, Tyrrell, & Smith (1991) quarantined volunteers for several days at the beginning of which they received nose drops containing one of several strains of cold virus or a saline solution. Those individuals who reported experiencing the most stressful life events and highest levels of perceived stress and negative mood had the greatest likelihood of developing cold symptoms. In a subsequent study of volunteers who received cold virus, Cohen et al. (1998) observed that people who had recently endured chronic stressful life events (i.e., events lasting a month or longer, including unemployment, chronic underemployment, or continued interpersonal difficulties) had a higher likelihood of catching cold than people who had experienced stressful events lasting less than a month.

Comment

Numerous well-controlled prospective studies have demonstrated significant associations between specific mental states and subsequent disease outcomes. An important aspect of these studies is that they examined and ruled out important demographic, behavioral, and biological variables that might be correlated with the mental state and lead to spurious conclusions about the relationship between the mental state and disease outcome. Thus, in the studies examining associations between psychosocial factors and CHD in nonpatient populations, statistical adjustments were typically made for demographic (e.g., age, race, sex, educational attainment), behavioral (e.g., smoking, physical inactivity, alcohol use), and biological (e.g., blood pressure, cholesterol level, obesity) variables (e.g., Anda et al., 1993). Similar adjustments were made in the study relating feelings of hopelessness to an increased risk for developing cancer (Everson et al., 1996). In patients with established CHD, adjustments have additionally been made for cardiac function, medication regimen, and severity of previous heart attack, if relevant (e.g., Lespérance, Frasure-Smith, Talajic, & Bourassa, 2002). Studies examining the relationship between psychosocial variables and disease progression or death in HIV/AIDS patients have typically used statistical controls for clinical features of the disease, medications prescribed, substance use, and demographic characteristics (e.g., Ickovics et al., 2001). In studying the stress-illness relationship for common colds, the investigators ruled out potential behavioral (e.g., smoking, alcohol use, exercise, diet, quality of sleep), biological (e.g., white-cell counts, total immunoglobulin level), demographic, and personality variables as mediators (Cohen et al., 1991).

Although the judicious use of statistical controls can provide reasonable confidence that a particular mental state is specifically related to the development, progression, or consequences of a disease, it provides neither direct evidence of a causal relationship nor specification of the mediating variable(s) per se. Determination of a causal relationship between a mental state and a disease outcome requires description of plausible biological mechanisms and evidence that removal of the mental state can prevent the development, progression, or consequences of the disease.

MEDIATORS OF THE MENTAL STATE-DISEASE
RELATIONSHIP

Hippocrates believed that disturbances in temperament lead to disease (Asimov, 1982; Porter, 1994) but was unable to describe plausible biological mediators based on scientific evidence. Acceptance of the Cartesian model of separate, independent realms for mind, *res cogitans*, and body, *res extensa* (Descartes, 1637/1956), made the concept of mind irrelevant to the functioning of the body (see also Chapter 13). Ryle (1949, p. 11) referred disparagingly to mind as the "ghost in the machine." Given the wide acceptance of Cartesian doctrine in biomedicine throughout most of the 20th century, studies examining relationships between mental states and disease processes were often discouraged in the biomedical community.

There is, however, a countervailing trend that also developed during the 20th century. This trend was in part based on Cannon's (1928, 1935) finding that homeostasis could be threatened by psychologically meaningful challenges and Selye's (1956) observations that prolonged stress could result in tissue damage and disease. The trend also gained impetus from documentation that the mammalian brain not only transduces sensory information but is capable of organizing perceptions, thoughts, and emotional responses in ways that can influence health (Institute of Medicine, 2001). In response to perceived threat, the brain causes the sympathetic nervous system, including the adrenal medulla, to release epinephrine and norepinephrine, and the adrenal cortex, which is also part of the adrenal gland, to release cortisol. In threatening environments requiring active coping (e.g., fight or flight), activation of the sympathetic nervous system produces transitory adaptive and protective effects, including maximizing the possibilities for muscular exertion (Cannon, 1929). If the threat is too persistent, however, the long-term release of stress hormones from the sympathetic nervous system and adrenal cortex may damage health (Schneiderman, 1983; Selye, 1956). These stress hormones act on metabolism, the immune system, and bodily tissues.

The exact causal pathways linking mental states to disease outcomes, as well as illnesses or disease processes to mental states, have not been thoroughly explored. However, their broad outlines are emerging and have stimulated exciting research (see Chapter 14 for discussions of mediators in the context of developmental psychopathology).

Cardiovascular disease, including CHD and stroke, is currently the leading cause of death in the United States. Epidemiological data indicate that depression, hostility, and social isolation are risk factors for CHD (Anda et al., 1993; Casc, Moss, Case, McDermott, & Eberly, 1992; Williams et al., 2000). As shown in Figure 15.1a, the increased risk may be caused by behavior (i.e., lifestyle), pathobiological responses, or an interaction between behavioral and biological responses. In terms of behavior, depression is associated with an unhealthy lifestyle, including excess alcohol intake, increased calories, and decreased physical activity (Cruess,

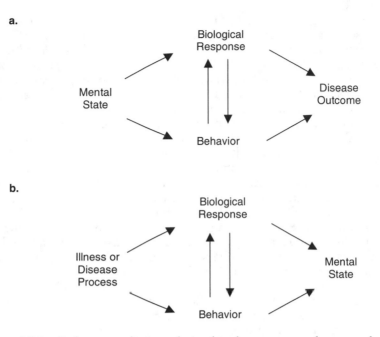

Figure 15.1. Pathways mediating relationships between mental states and disease outcomes (a), and illnesses or disease processes and mental states (b)

Schneiderman, Antoni, & Penedo, 2004), smoking (Glassman et al., 1990), and poor medical adherence (Zigelstein et al., 1998). In terms of direct pathophysiological mechanisms, depression is also associated with increased levels of cortisol (Caroll, Curtis, Davies, Mendels, & Sugarman, 1976) and sympathetic nervous system activation (Yeith et al., 1994), which can increase platelet reactivity to promote clotting of blood (Musselman et al., 1996).

A number of mental states and behaviors, including depression, hostility, and increased consumption of calories, cigarettes, and alcohol, often co-occur. These characteristics are not only associated with increased CHD risk but also with low levels of brain serotonin. Reduced levels of brain serotonin are associated with depression (Risch & Nemeroff, 1992), hostility (Coccaro et al., 1989) and alcoholism (Ballenger, Goodwin, Major, & Brown, 1979). Thus, it appears that the pathways shown in Figure 15.1a provide plausible biological and behavioral pathways mediating the relationship between mental states such as depression and CHD outcomes.

Just as plausible biological and behavioral mechanisms indicate how mental states can influence disease outcomes, there is now considerable evidence that illness or disease processes can influence mental states (see Figure 15.1b). Because disease represents a major threat to homeostasis, animals, including humans, have evolved important strategies to counter this threat. The immune system, in particular, promotes homeostasis by detecting and eliminating pathogens, but at a sizeable metabolic cost. To offset some of these metabolic costs during times of illness, the immune system communicates with the central nervous system to influence behavior, mood, and motivation in ways that conserve energy. This set of changes is often referred to as *sickness behavior* (Hart, 1988). By conserving energy, sickness behavior facilitates the return to homeostasis and is therefore adaptive. However, during times of chronic illness, sickness behavior can become maladaptive to the extent that it impairs mental health. In this section, we review the adaptive nature of the acute sickness behavior response and its implications for mental health during chronic illness.

In response to an acute infection, the immune system generates both local and systemic changes (see Roitt, Brostoff, & Male, 2001 for a more extensive review). Both sets of responses are orchestrated by a class of communicatory molecules known as *cytokines*. At the local level, the actual site of infection, cytokines coordinate the work of containing and eliminating invading pathogens. Cytokines also disperse beyond the local level to other tissues, including those in the central nervous system, to induce systemic changes. The systemic reaction to infection, the *acute-phase response*, includes fever, changes in metabolism and liver protein production, and an increase in blood level of white blood cells. This systemic response is adaptive in the sense that it promotes the intensity of local immune responses and impairs microbial growth. For example, fever speeds white blood cell replication *and* retards bacterial replication. But for every 1°C increase in body temperature, there is a corresponding 10% increase in metabolic cost (Kluger, 1979). Coupled with the fact that illness tends to suppress eating (see later), an ongoing immune response can create a caloric deficit that itself, over time, can pose a threat to homeostasis. How is this new metabolic threat to homeostasis resolved?

It has been long recognized that disease is associated with subjective feelings of malaise and listlessness. Sick individuals are generally less active than their healthy counterparts. Research with rodents and other animals injected with bacteria has shown decreases in exploratory behavior, social and sexual behavior, food and water intake, self-care, and motivation for pleasurable stimuli (e.g., sweetened liquids) and increases in sleep compared to healthy controls (Larson & Dunn, 2001). It has not been until relatively recently, however, that these behavioral and motivational changes have been considered within an evolutionary context. Benjamin Hart, who coined the term *sickness behavior*, noted that " . . . the behavior of a sick individual is not a maladaptive and undesirable effect of illness but rather a highly organized strategy that is at times critical to the survival of the individual if it were living in the wild state" (Hart, 1988, p. 124). In other words, feeling bad when sick is good for you. But how? Decreases in overall activity and increases in sleep largely function to reduce exertion so that metabolic resources can be allocated to immune-mediated functions, such as fever (Dantzer, 2001; Maier & Watkins, 1998). But what of decreased feeding behavior? Although not initially apparent, feeding during illness is maladaptive for several reasons. First, searching for food, eating, and digestion are metabolically costly in the short-term, diverting energy away from the task of fighting infection. Second, in the "wild state," animals are vulnerable when ill. Less able to evade predators, foraging for food can be risky for the sick. Third, feeding raises blood levels of zinc and iron, minerals utilized by microorganisms during replication (Maier & Watkins, 1998). Thus, loss of appetite during illness would appear to be adaptive.

The behavioral changes associated with sickness are believed to reflect a shift in underlying motivational systems (Dantzer, 2001). Sick individuals are less active not because of depleted metabolic resources, but because they are motivated to prevent a depletion of metabolic resources. There is more to this difference than semantics, including important implications for the relationship between physical illness and mental health. Recall that cytokines coordinate local and systemic immune response to infection. Cytokines alone, even in the absence of an actual infection, are sufficient to induce sickness behavior. It has been extensively documented that injecting rodents and other animals with cytokines induces all aspects of sickness behavior (see Larson & Dunn, 2001). Similar observations have been made in people who have been treated with cytokines for certain types of cancer (Capuron & Dantzer, 2003; see later). It is the body's signals that cause sickness, *not* the pathogen. Furthermore, sick animals are not uniformly less active than healthy animals. Indeed, sick animals are *less motivated* by rewarding stimuli, but they are also *more motivated* to avoid aversive stimuli than healthy animals. Research has shown, for example, that sick animals make more bar presses to avoid electrical shock than healthy animals, even if they also make fewer bar presses for rewarding brain stimulation (see Dantzer, 2001; Miller, 1964). Dantzer wrote, "It is easy to imagine that if a sick person lying in bed hears a fire alarm ringing in the house and sees smoke coming out of the basement, the person should be able to momentarily overcome sickness behavior to escape danger" (Dantzer, 2001, p. 15). Differences between rodents injected with cytokines and control animals become more apparent when nesting safely in their home cage than when exposed to some novel, dangerous environment. That is, when faced with the prospect of an imminent threat, the symptoms of sickness recede so the sick animal can fight or flee. When home and safe, the sickness behavior symptoms reemerge. Parallels have been drawn to the "vacation effect" observed in people who frequently report becoming ill soon after going on vacation, just after meeting some deadline at work, or following exams in school (e.g., Vingerhoets, Van Huijgevoort, & Van Heck, 2002). Thus, sickness behavior is more than the mere consequence of depleted metabolic resources; it is a highly organized strategy that conserves energy when possible and allows for flexibility in responding to risk.

Although in the short term sickness behavior is adaptive, chronic illness can lead to a protracted state of sickness behavior and poor mental health outcomes. Cardiovascular disease is a good example. Research in the last decade has demonstrated a consistent relationship between depressive symptomatology and CHD (Rugulies, 2002); specifically, depression predicts both the development of CHD in initially healthy people and poorer survival after a heart attack. These relationships are retained even after controlling for traditional risk factors (e.g., hypertension, elevated cholesterol, smoking, increasing age, male sex) and markers of disease severity. Furthermore, nearly 20% of CHD patients meet criteria for major depression (Carney et al., 1987) and an additional 27% meet criteria for minor depression (Schleifer et al., 1989). In contrast, the point prevalence of major depression in individuals without CHD of comparable age and gender is only 3% (Myers et al., 1984).

Historically, the relationship between depression and CHD has been described in behavioral terms. For instance, depression is associated with poor health behaviors, which predict the onset of CHD. Alternatively, experiencing depression following a heart attack may be understood as a psychological reaction to a stressful event. There is yet another way to understand this relationship: inflammation. Although generally accepted today, it was not until recently that CHD was thought to contain an inflammatory component. Previously, cardiologists thought infarctions were caused by gradually expanding, yet generally static, accumulations of lipids. Atherosclerotic lesions today are typically understood as dynamic, immunological responses to vascular injury (see Ross, 1999). The exact causes of vascular injury are unknown, but the usual suspects include cholesterol (Kaul, 2001); blood flow shear from frequent, sudden shifts in blood pressure (Leopold & Loscalzo, 2000); oxygen-derived free radicals (Touyz, 2000); viral pathogens (e.g., Vercellotti, 1998); and cigarette smoke. The immunological responses to vascular injury are mediated by cytokines.

There is considerable overlap between the symptoms of depression and sickness behavior. The Diagnostic and Statistical Manual of Mental Disorders, fourth edition (DSM-IV-TR; American Psychiatric Association, 2000) criteria for a major depressive episode require either depressed mood or anhedonia and four other symptoms, including change in appetite or weight, altered sleeping patterns, psychomotor retardation (or agitation), fatigue/loss of energy, feelings of worthlessness/excessive guilt, difficulties concentrating, and recurrent thoughts of death (see also Chapters 13 and 14 for a discussion of models of depression). As reviewed earlier, in both animals and humans, the administration of exogenous cytokines can induce anhedonia, a change in eating habits, altered sleeping patterns, reduced overall activity levels, fatigue, and cognitive difficulties. Thus, exogenous cytokines are sufficient (but not always necessary; see Capuron & Dantzer, 2003; de Beaurepaire, 2002) to produce the symptoms of a major depressive episode. Appels, Kop, & Schouten (2000) proposed the construct of *vital exhaustion* to distinguish between traditional depression and the state of unusual fatigue associated with CHD. Vital exhaustion also includes feelings of demoralization and increased irritability, though these symptoms are conceptualized as secondary to the fatigue. That is, CHD patients who experience a sudden, unusual bout of exhaustion may become demoralized and irritable because of their unexplainable fatigue. Supporting the inflammation link, a number of studies have found associations between depressive symptomatology and increased levels of inflammatory molecules in both healthy and cardiac populations (Appels et al., 2000; Maes et al., 1995; Suarez, 2004).

Elevated levels of depressive symptomatology have been observed in other chronic illnesses in which chronic inflammation is central to its pathophysiology (see Figure 15.1b). This is especially true for the autoimmune diseases, such as multiple sclerosis (MS), a condition in which an overactive immune system targets and destroys the myelin surrounding nerves, contributing to a host of symptoms that include paralysis and blindness. Granted, because individuals with MS face a number of stressors, reports of depression are not surprising. However, when compared with individuals facing similar disability who do not have MS (e.g., car accident victims), MS patients still report higher levels of depression (Ron & Logsdail, 1989). As in CHD, research has documented associations between markers of inflammation and depressive symptomatology in MS patients. Cancer patients undergoing cytokine therapy are also more likely to report sickness behavior. Administering cytokines (i.e., cytokine therapy) to cancer patients is thought to activate immune cells capable of curtailing cancerous growth. The efficacy of such therapies aside, physicians have observed that cytokine therapy causes a host of side effects that resemble sickness behavior, including fatigue, flulike symptoms, and cognitive impairment. Randomized studies have substantiated these observations (Bonaccorso, BMSM, 2000; Meltzer, & Maes, 2000; Capuron et al., 2002).

In summary, physical disease represents a threat to homeostasis and thus a threat to life itself. The body's responses to disease are usually effective and generally short-lived. During these periods, the body signals to itself that rest is in order and exertion should only be reserved for those situations in which it is absolutely necessary. By heeding these messages, people and animals alike speed the recovery process. But in cases of chronic illness, such as heart disease, or autoimmune conditions in which the immune system becomes overactive, sickness behavior fails to resolve itself without outside intervention.

CONCLUDING REMARKS

Hippocrates was a keen observer of the human condition. Approximately 2,400 years ago, he noted that people's emotional states and coping skills could influence physical health, and vice versa (Asimov, 1982; Porter, 1994). For more than two millennia many people shared this view. However, it was not until the 20th century that science provided the conceptual basis and tools required to explore the relationships between mind and body. For Descartes (1637/1936), the mind was synonymous with soul and could live on after the body perished. In contrast, for scientists in the late 20th century, mind came to refer to thoughts and emotions organized by the brain. Once this conception was formulated, and became subject to observation and experimentation, it became possible for scientists to determine how the neuronal outflow from the brain could organize hormones and behavior to determine health outcomes (see also Chapter 13).

Scientific observations that mental and physical health can influence each other bear important implications for the management of chronic diseases. Findings that psychosocial interventions, such as cognitive behavioral stress management, can decrease negative mood (e.g., depression) and thereby facilitate problem-focused coping (Schneiderman, Antoni, Saab, & Ironson, 2001), suggest that such interventions can help to decrease high-risk behaviors (e.g., unprotected sex) leading to reinfection from new viral strains in HIV/AIDS patients. These interventions also can improve health behaviors in patients at high risk for diabetes and CHD. Recently, a large randomized clinical trial examining behavioral and pharmacological strategies for preventing Type 2 diabetes in people at high risk found that both strategies worked but that the behavioral approach was significantly more effective than the use of medication (Diabetes Prevention Program Research Group, 2002). Psychosocial interventions also have been shown to help chronic-pain patients reduce their distress and perceived pain as well as increase their physical activity and ability to return to work, and decrease their use of medication and overuse of the health care system (Morley, Eccleston, & Williams, 1999).

Clinical trials have reported both positive and null results for psychosocial treatment of patients following heart attack (Schneiderman et al., 2001). The largest randomized controlled trial reporting positive results for reducing recurrent heart attack or death from CHD was the Recurrent Coronary Prevention Project (Friedman et al., 1986), which found that the group-based psychosocial intervention decreased hostility and depressed affect (Mendes de Leon, Powell, & Kaplan, 1991). In contrast, the major psychosocial intervention study reporting null results for medical endpoints was the Enhancing Recovery in Coronary Heart Disease (ENRICHD) clinical trial (ENRICHD, 2003), which found that the intervention modestly decreased depression and increased perceived social support, but did not affect the composite medical endpoint of death or nonfatal heart attack recurrence. However, a secondary analysis, which examined the effects of the psychosocial intervention within gender by ethnicity subgroups, found significant decreases approaching 40% for both cardiac death and nonfatal heart attacks in white men but not in other subgroups such as minority women (Schneiderman, Saab, Catellier, Powell, & DeBusk, 2004). It should be noted that findings based on secondary analyses are post hoc in nature, thereby increasing the risk for Type 1 error. Such findings need to be replicated although the difference in findings among subgroups in the Schneiderman et al. (2004) study indicates that future studies need to attend to important variables that prevented morbidity and mortality benefits among gender and subgroups other than white men.

In summary, the relationship between mental and physical health is reciprocal. Mental states such as depression can lead to the development, progression, or death from some diseases due to behavioral factors (e.g., smoking) or biological stress responses. Conversely, the stress of physical illness, or such disease processes as inflammation, can lead to sickness or depression as a function of cytokine activity or behavior (e.g., excessive alcohol intake). Thus, the case has been made that one of the great ideas of clinical science is that mental and physical health influence each other. Large-scale epidemiological investigations have demonstrated significant associations between mental states and disease. Innovative experiments have identified important mediators of the mental state-disease relationship. And along the frontier of knowledge, behavioral intervention studies have begun to show that physical health can be improved by influencing mental processes. Consequently, clinical scientists need to be aware of the reciprocal nature of mind-body relationships. More research is needed, and tools developed, that can uncover these relationships in patient populations and individuals.

Acknowledgements: Supported by Research Grant HL36588 and Research Training Grant HL07426 from the National Heart, Lung, and Blood Institute of the National Institutes of Health.

KEY TERMS

Biological reductionism
Biopsychosocial model
Homeostasis
Mind-body interaction
Sickness behavior

RECOMMENDED READINGS

Cruess, D. G., Schneiderman, N., Antoni, M. H., & Penedo, F. (2004). Biobehavioral bases of disease processes. In T. J. Boll, R. G. Frank, A. Baum, & J. L. Wallander (Eds.), *Handbook of clinical health psychology: Vol. 3, Models and perspectives in health psychology.* Washington, DC: American Psychological Association.

Rozanski, A., Blumenthal, J. A., & Kaplan, J. (1999). Impact of psychological factors on the pathogenesis of cardiovascular disease and implications for therapy. *Circulation, 99,* 2192–2217.

Schneiderman, N. (2004). Psychosocial, behavioral and biological aspects of chronic diseases. *Current Directions in Psychological Science, 18,* 247–251.

Schneiderman, N., Antoni, M. H., Saab, P. G., & Ironson, G. (2001). Health psychology: Psychosocial and biobehavioral aspects of chronic disease management. *Annual Review of Psychology, 52,* 555–580.

Schneiderman, N., Ironson, G., & Siegel, S. D. (2005). Stress and health: Psychological, behavioral and biological determinants. *Annual Review of Clinical Psychology, 1,* 607–628.

REFERENCES

American Psychiatric Association. (2000). *Diagnostic and statistical manual of mental disorders* (4th ed., text revision). Washington, DC: American Psychiatric Association.

Anda, R., Williamson, D., Jones, D., Macera, C., Eaker, E., Glassman, A., et al. (1993). Depressed affect, hopelessness, and the risk of ischemic heart disease in a cohort of U.S. adults. *Epidemiology, 4,* 285–294.

Angell, M. (1985). Disease as a reflection of the psyche. *New England Journal of Medicine, 312,* 1570–1572.

Appels, A., Kop, W. J., & Schouten, E. (2000). The nature of depressive symptomatology preceding myocardial infarction. *Behavioral Medicine, 26,* 86.

Asimov, I. (1982). *Asimov's biographical encyclopedia of science and technology* (2nd rev. ed.). Garden City, NY: Doubleday.

Ballenger, J. C., Goodwin, F. K., Major, L. F., & Brown, G. L. (1979). Alcohol and central serotonergic metabolism in man. *Archives of General Psychiatry, 36,* 224–227.

Barefoot, J. C., Dahlstrom, G., & Williams, R. B. (1983). *Psychosomatic Medicine, 45,* 59–63.

Barefoot, J. C., & Schroll, M. (1996). Symptoms of depression, acute myocardial infarction, and total mortality in a community sample. *Circulation, 93,* 1976–1980.

Bernard, C. (1865/1961). *An introduction to the study of experimental medicine* (H. C. Greene, trans.). New York: Collier.

Bonaccorso, S., Meltzer, H., & Maes, M. (2000). Psychological and behavioural effects of interferons. *Current Opinion in Psychiatry, 13,* 673–677.

Cannon, W. B. (1928). The mechanism of emotional disturbance of bodily functions. *New England Journal of Medicine, 198,* 165–172.

Cannon, W. B. (1929). *Bodily changes in pain, hunger, fear and rage* (2nd ed.). New York: Appleton.

Cannon, W. B. (1935). Stresses and strains of homeostasis (Mary Scott Newbold Lecture). *American Journal of Medicine Sciences, 189,* 1–14.

Capuron, L., & Dantzer, R. (2003). Cytokines and depression: the need for a new paradigm. *Brain, Behavior, and Immunity, 17,* S119–S124.

Capuron, L., Gumnick, J. F., Musselman, D. L., Lawson, D. H., Reemsnyder, A., & Nemeroff, C. B. (2002). Neurobehavioral effects of interferon-alpha in cancer patients: phenomenology and paroxetine responsiveness of symptom dimensions. *Neuropsychopharmacology, 26,* 643–652.

Carney, R. M., Rich, M. W., Tevelde, A., Saini, J., Clark, K., & Jaffe, A. S. (1987). Major depressive disorder in coronary artery disease. *American Journal of Cardiology, 60,* 1273–1275.

Caroll, B. J., Curtis, G. C., Davies, B. M., Mendels, J., & Sugarman, A. A. (1976). Urinary free cortisol excretion in depression. *Psychology in Medicine, 6,* 43–50.

Case, R. B., Moss, A. S., Case, N., McDermott, M., & Eberly, S. (1992). Living alone after myocardial infarction. *Journal of American Medical Association, 267,* 515–519.

Coccaro, E. F., Siever, L. J., Klar, H. M., Maurer, G., Cochrane, K., & Cooper, T. B. (1989). Serotonergic studies in patients with affective and personality disorders. *Archives of General Psychiatry, 46,* 587–599.

Cohen, S., Frank, E., Doyle, W. J., Skoner, D. P., Rabin, B. S., & Gwaltney, J. M., Jr. (1998). Types of stressors that increase susceptibility to the common cold in healthy adults. *Health Psychology, 17,* 214–223.

Cohen, S., Tyrrell, D. A., & Smith, A. P. (1991). Psychological stress in humans and susceptibility to the common cold. *New England Journal of Medicine, 325,* 606–612.

Cruess, D. G., Schneiderman, N., Antoni, M. H., & Penedo, F. (2004). Biobehavioral bases of disease processes. In Boll, T.J., Frank, R.G., Baum, A., & Wallander, J. L. (Eds.), *Handbook of clinical health psychology (Vol. 3), models and perspectives in health psychology* (pp. 31–79). Washington, DC: American Psychological Association.

Dantzer, R. (2001). Cytokine-induced sickness behavior: Where do we stand? *Brain, Behavior, and Immunity, 15,* 7–24.

de Beaurepaire, R. (2002). Questions raised by the cytokine hypothesis of depression. *Brain, Behavior, and Immunity, 16,* 610–617.

Descartes, R. (1637/1956). *Discourse on Method* (L. J. LaFleur, Trans.). Indianapolis, IN: Sammes

Diabetes Prevention Program Research Group. (2002). Reduction in the incidence of Type 2 diabetes with lifestyle intervention and metformin. *New England Journal of Medicine, 346,* 393–403.

Engel, G. L. (1977). The need for a new medical model: A challenge for biomedicine. *Science, 196,* 129–136.

ENRICHD. (2003). Effects of treating depression and low perceived social support on clinical events after myocardial infarction: The Enhancing Recovery in Coronary Heart Disease patients (ENRICHD) randomized trial. *Journal of the American Medical Association, 289,* 3106–3116.

Everson, S. A., Goldberg, D. E., Kaplan, G. A., Cohen, R.D., Pukkala, E., Tuomilehto, J., et al. (1996). Hopelessness and risk of mortality and incidence of myocardial infarction and cancer. *Psychosomatic Medicine, 58,* 113–121.

Ferketich, A. K., Schwartzbaum, J. A., Frid, D. J., & Moeschberger, M. L. (2000). Depression as an antecedent to heart disease among women and men in the NHANES I study. National Health and Nutrition Examination Survey. *Archives of Internal Medicine, 160,* 1261–1268.

Friedman, M., Thoresen, C. E., Gill, J. J., Ulmer, D., Powell, L. H., Price, V. A., et al. (1986). Alteration of Type A behavior and its effect on cardiac recurrences in post myocardial infarction patients: Summary results of the recurrent coronary prevention project. *American Heart Journal, 112,* 653–665.

Glassman, A. H., Helzer, J. E., Covey, L. S., Cottler, L. B., Stetner, F., Tipp, J. E., et al. (1990). Smoking, smoking cessation and major depression. *Journal of American Medical Association, 264,* 1546–1549.

Graham, N. M. H., Douglas, R. B., & Ryan, P. (1986). Stress and acute respiratory infection. *American Journal of Epidemiology. 124,* 389–401.

Hart, B. L. (1988). Biological basis of the behavior of sick animals. *Neuroscience Biobehavioral Reviews, 12,* 123–37.

Harvey, W. (1628). *Exercitatio anatomica de motu cordis et sanguinis in animalibus* (Anatomical exercise on the motion of the heart and blood in animals). Frankfurt, Germany: np.

Ickovics, J. R., Hamburger, M. E., Vlahov, D., Schoenbaum, E. E., Schumm, P., & Boland, R. J. (2001). Mortality: CD4 cell count decline, and depressive symptoms among HIV-seropositive women. *Journal of American Medical Association, 285,* 1466–1474.

Institute of Medicine (2001). *Health and behavior: The interplay of biological, behavioral, and societal influences.* Washington, DC: National Academy Press.

Kaul, D. (2001). Molecular link between cholesterol, cytokines and atherosclerosis. *Molecular & Cellular Biochemistry, 219,* 65–71.

Kawachi, I., Sparrow, D., Vokonas, P. S., & Weiss, S. T. (1994). Symptoms of anxiety and risk of coronary heart disease: The normative aging study. *Circulation, 90,* 2225–2229.

Kluger, M. J. (1979). *Fever: It's biology, evolution and function.* Princeton, NJ: Princeton University Press.

Koch, R. (1881/1987). On the etiology of anthrax. In *Essays of Robert Koch.* (K. C. Carter, Trans.). Westport, CT: Greenwood Press.

Koch, R. (1882/1987). The etiology of tuberculosis. In *Essays of Robert Koch.* (K. C. Carter, Trans.). Westport, CT: Greenwood Press.

Larson, S. J., & Dunn, A. J. (2001). Behavioral effects of cytokines. *Brain, Behavior, and Immunity, 15,* 371–387.

Leopold, J. A., & Loscalzo, J. (2000). Clinical importance of understanding vascular biology. *Cardiology in Review, 8,* 115–123.

Leserman, J., Petitto, J. M., Golden, R. N., Gaynes, B. N., Gu, H., Perkins, D. O., et al. (2000). Impact of stressful life events, depression, social support, coping, and cortisol on progression to AIDS. *American Journal of Psychiatry, 157,* 1221–1228.

Lespérance, F., Frasure-Smith, N., Talajic, M., & Bourassa, M. G. (2002). Five-year risk of cardiac mortality in relation to initial severity and one-year changes in depression symptoms after myocardial infarction. *Circulation, 105,* 1049–1053.

Maes, M., Meltzer, H. Y., Bosmans, E., Bergmans, R., Vandoolaeghe, E., & Ranjan, R. (1995). Increased plasma concentrations of interleukin-6, soluble interleukin-6, soluble interleukin-2, and transferrin receptor in major depression. *Journal of Affective Disorders, 34,* 301–309.

Maier, S. F., & Watkins, L. R. (1998). Cytokines for psychologists: implications of bidirectional immune-to-brain communication for understanding behavior, mood, and cognition. *Psychological Review, 105,* 83–107.

Mayne, T. J., Vittinghoff, E., Chesney, M. A., Barrett, D. C., & Coates, T. J. (1996). Depressive affect and survival among gay and bisexual men infected with HIV. *Archives of Internal Medicine, 156,* 2233–2238.

Mendes de Leon, C. F., Powell L. H., & Kaplan, B. H. (1991). Change in coronary-prone behaviors in the recurrent coronary prevention project. *Psychosomatic Medicine, 53,* 407–419.

Miller, N. E. (1964). Some psychophysiological studies of motivation and the behavioral effects of illness. *Bulletin of the British Psychological Society, 17,* 1–20.

Morley, S., Eccleston, C., & Williams, A. (1999). Systematic review and meta-analysis of randomized controlled trials of cognitive behavior therapy and behavior therapy for chronic pain in adults, excluding headache. *Pain, 80,* 1–13.

Musselman, D. L., Tomer, A., Manatunga, A. K., Knight, B. T., Porter, M. R., Kasey, S., et al. (1996). Exaggerated platelet reactivity in major depression. *American Journal of Psychiatry, 153,* 1313–1317.

Myers, J. K., Weissman, M. M., Tischler, G. L., Holzer, C. E., III, Leaf, P. J., & Orvaschel, H. (1984). Six month prevalence of psychiatric disorders in three communities, 1980 to 1982. *Archives of General Psychiatry, 41*, 959–967.

Penninx, B. W., Beckman, A. T., Honig, A., Deeg, D. J., Schoevers, R. A., van Eijk, J. T., et al. (2001). Depression and cardiac mortality: results from a community-based longitudinal study. *Archives of General Psychiatry, 58,* 221–227.

Porter, R. (1994). *The biographical dictionary of scientists.* (2nd ed.). New York: Oxford University Press.

Risch, S. C., & Nemeroff, C. B. (1992). Neurochemical alterations of serotonergic neuronal systems in depression. *Journal of Clinical Psychiatry, 53*, 3–7.

Roitt, I., Brostoff, J., & Male, D. (2001). *Immunology* (6th ed.). London: Mosby.

Ron, M., & Logsdail, S. (1989). Psychiatric morbidity in multiple sclerosis: A clinical and MRI study. *Psychological Medicine, 19*, 887–95.

Ross, R. (1999). Atherosclerosis—An inflammatory disease. *New England Journal of Medicine, 340*, 115–126.

Rugulies, R. (2002). Depression as a predictor for coronary heart disease. *American Journal of Preventive Medicine, 23*, 51–61.

Ryle, G. (1949). *The concept of mind.* London: Hutchinson.

Schleifer, S. J., Macari-Hinson, M. M., Coyle, D. A., William, W. R., Kahn, M., & Gorlin, R. (1989). The nature and course of depression following myocardial infarction. *Archives of Internal Medicine, 149*, 1785–1789.

Schneiderman, N. (1983). Behavior, autonomic function and animal models of cardiovascular pathology. In: T. M. Dembroski, T. H. Schmidt, & Gerhard Blümchen (Eds.), *Biobehavioral bases of coronary heart disease* (pp. 304–363). Basel, Switzerland: Karger.

Schneiderman, N., Antoni, M. H., Saab, P. G., & Ironson, G. (2001). Health psychology: Psychosocial and biobehavioral aspects of chronic disease management. *Annual Review of Psychology, 52*, 555–580.

Schneiderman, N., Saab, P. G., Catellier, D. J., Powell, L. H., & DeBusk, R. F. (2004). Psychosocial treatment within gender by ethnicity subgroups in the enhancing recovery in coronary heart disease (ENRICHD) clinical trial. *Psychosomatic Medicine, 66*, 475–483.

Selye, H. (1956). *The stress of life.* New York: McGraw-Hill.

Shekelle, R. B., Gale, M., Ostfeld, A. M., & Paul, O. (1983). Hostility, risk of coronary disease, and mortality. *Psychosomatic Medicine, 45*, 219–228.

Suarez, E.D. (2004). C-reactive protein is association with psychological risk factors of cardiovascular disease in apparently healthy adults. *Psychosomatic Medicine, 66*, 684–691.

Touyz, R. M. (2000). Oxidative stress and vascular damage in hypertension. *Current Hypertension Reports, 2*, 98–105.

Vercellotti, G. M. (1998). Effects of viral activation of the vessel wall on inflammation and thrombosis. *Blood Coagulation & Fibrinolysis, 9*, S3–6.

Versalius, A. (1543). *De humani corporis fabrica (On the make up of the human body).* Amsterdam, Netherlands.

Vingerhoets, A. J., Van Huijgevoort, M., & Van Heck, G. L. (2002). Leisure sickness: A pilot study on its prevalence, phenomenology, and background. *Psychotherapy & Psychosomatics, 71*, 311–317.

Watson, M., Haviland, J. S., Greer, S., Davidson, J., & Bliss, J. M. (1999). Influence of psychological response on survival in breast cancer: A population based cohort study. *Lancet, 354*, 1331–1336.

Williams, J. E., Paton, C. C., Siegler, I. C., Eigenbrodt, M. L., Nieto, F. J., & Tyroler, H. A. (2000). Anger proneness predicts coronary heart disease risk: Prospective analysis from the Atherosclerosis Risk in Communities (ARIC) Study. *Circulation, 101,* 2034–2039.

Wulsin, L. R., & Singal, B. (2003). Do depressive symptoms increase the risk for the onset of coronary disease? A systematic quantitative review. *Psychosomatic Medicine, 65,* 201–210.

Yeith, R. C., Lewis, L., Linares, O. A., Raskin, M. A., Villacres, E. C., Murburg, M. M., et al. (1994). Sympathetic nervous system in major depression: Basal and desipramine-induced alterations in plasma norepinephrine kinetics. *Archives of General Psychiatry, 51,* 411–422.

Zigelstein, R. C., Bush, D. E., & Fauerbach, J. A. (1998). Depression, adherence behavior, and coronary disease outcomes. *Archives of Internal Medicine, 158,* 808–809.

CHAPTER
16
Some Forms of
Psychopathology Are Partly
Socially Constructed

STEVEN JAY LYNN, ABIGAIL MATTHEWS,
JOHN C. WILLIAMS, MICHAEL N. HALLQUIST, AND
SCOTT O. LILIENFELD

Culture embodies institutions, traditions, beliefs, and values. Culture
establishes the parameters for what is considered a psychological disorder
and for what is not, and shapes the expression of personal distress and
the way in which abnormal or unusual behavior is conceptualized and
treated (Millon & Davis, 1999; see also Chapter 17). These parameters
are further shaped by historical time periods, which may partly dictate
preferred idioms of psychological distress. The thesis of our chapter
is that a rich and complete understanding of psychological disorders
cannot be disentangled from the cultures and historical time periods
in which they occur (Dean, 1997; Young, 1995). Or, put another way,
some psychological disorders are partly socially constructed.

GENERAL CONCEPTUAL ISSUES

When we say "partly" socially constructed, we mean that social construction rarely, if ever, operates in a vacuum to mold the manifestation of
psychopathology. Instead, cultural and historical variables almost always
operate on a backdrop of a preexisting psychopathological *diathesis*, that

is, predisposition. From the perspective of a *diathesis-stressor* model of psychopathology, cultural and historical influences can be conceptualized as variables that interact statistically with a preexisting liability to mental disorder—often one that is partly genetic in origin—to produce psychopathology. For example, as we will learn later in the chapter, some eating disorders (e.g., bulimia nervosa) may be a product of a preexisting liability that is partly genetic in origin (the diathesis) interacting with culturally derived norms for thinness and physical beauty (the stressor; see Keel & Klump. 2003). Although systematic research evidence for the diathesis-stressor model is not easily obtained (largely because it requires investigation of the manifestation of the same diathesis across different cultures, different time periods, or both), it remains a plausible heuristic framework for the social construction of psychopathology.

The Mental Disorder Category as Socially Constructed

When psychopathologists speak of the social construction of mental disorder, they are typically referring to one of two separable issues. First, they may be referring to the social construction of the higher-order concept of "mental disorder" itself. That is, some authors maintain that the very concept of mental disorder is entirely a social construction. The best known and most vocal proponent of this view is psychiatrist Thomas Szasz (1961/1972), who argued famously that "mental disorder is a myth." For Szasz, the mental illness label is ascribed by society to behavior that is socially devalued or noxious. From this radical perspective, mental illness is no more than a pejorative appellation that society attaches to behavior that it dislikes.

Clearly, Szasz is on to something here. There can be little question that most, if not all, mental disorders, including schizophrenia, obsessive-compulsive disorder, psychopathy, alcoholism, and autism, are regarded as harmful by society. Moreover, as we'll learn later in the chapter, homosexuality was removed from the American Psychiatric Association's diagnostic manual not primarily on the basis of scientific evidence but, rather, on the basis of society's more accepting view of same-sex attraction.

Yet Szasz's position, which is still influential in some circles, is refuted by several clear-cut counterexamples. As Wakefield (1992) observed, laziness, rudeness, and racism are socially devalued but are not considered mental disorders (or in most cases, even indicators of mental disorders). Therefore, Szasz's claim that mental illness is isomorphic with socially devalued behavior appears to be falsified.

Wakefield (1992) instead posited that the higher-order category of disorder, including mental disorder, is a hybrid concept that encompasses both social values and biological abnormalities. Specifically, Wakefield argued that mental disorders are "harmful dysfunctions," meaning that they are (a) viewed by society as producing impairment for the individual, others, or both *and* (b) failures or breakdowns of an evolutionarily selected psychological system. For example, according to Wakefield, panic disorder is a mental disorder because it is (a) (correctly) perceived as harmful to the individual and (b) an activation of an evolutionarily selected alarm system in an inappropriate setting (i.e., a "false alarm"; Barlow, 2002).

A number of authors (e.g., Houts, 2001; Lilienfeld & Marino, 1995; McNally, 2001) have criticized Wakefield's harmful dysfunction analysis as problematic. For example, Lilienfeld and Marino (1995) took issue with Wakefield's assertion that all disorders can be thought of as break-downs of evolutionarily derived systems, because some widely agreed-on disorders, such as amusia and agraphia (i.e., an inability to appreciate music and an inability to write, respectively), are failures of systems that have not been evolutionarily selected per se. These and other criticisms notwithstanding, Wakefield's conceptualization of mental disorder as a hybrid concept is a significant advance, as it helps to distinguish those features of the mental illness concept that are socially constructed from those that are not. Clearly, Wakefield is correct that mental illness is partly, but not entirely, a socially constructed concept. In this respect, Szasz (1961/1972) was partly right and partly wrong.

Specific Mental Disorders as Socially Constructed

Second, many authors contend that specific mental disorders, such as schizophrenia, psychopathy, and alcoholism, are socially constructed. Influenced largely by such cultural anthropologists as Frans Boaz, Margaret Mead, and Ruth Benedict, these authors typically contend that behavior that is regarded as psychopathological in some cultures is commonly viewed as entirely normal in others (e.g., see Benedict, 1934). A frequently invoked example is that of the shaman, who ostensibly would be viewed as pathological, even psychotic, in Western cultures but is revered in some non-Western cultures.

Nevertheless, evidence does not support this stance of extreme cultural relativism. As Jane Murphy (1976) discovered in her landmark study of the Yorubas of Nigeria and the Yupik-speaking Eskimos on an island in the Bering Sea, some mental disorders, such as schizophrenia, psychopathy, and alcoholism, are readily recognized in cultures that are markedly different from our own (see also Chapter 18). Moreover, Murphy reported that the Yorubas readily distinguished between shamans and mentally ill individuals. For the Yorubas, the shaman is "out of mind but not crazy," whereas the mentally ill individual is "out of mind and crazy." More broadly, evidence from behavior genetic and evolutionary investi-gations strongly suggests that an extreme "blank slate" model of human nature, in which psychopathology is imposed by culture on a *tabula rasa* within the individual, is no longer scientifically tenable (Pinker, 2002; see also Chapters 10 and 11).

As a consequence, in this chapter we stake out a middle ground position. We acknowledge that "human nature" exists and that most, if not all, cultures share certain propensities toward personality traits and psychopathology. At the same time, we argue that culture and history can mold the overt expression of these diatheses in clinically important ways (see Kleinman, 1988, for a discussion of the pathogenic-pathoplastic model of psychopathology).

The Role of Social Construction in the Diagnostic Manual

The impact of sociocultural factors has been explicitly recognized in the most recent edition of the Diagnostic and Statistical Manual of the American Psychiatric Association (DSM-IV; APA, 1994). The introduction to the manual asserts that it is incumbent on clinicians to "take into account the individual's ethnic and cultural context in the evaluation of each of the DSM-IV axes . . . and ways in which the cultural context is relevant to clinical care" (p. xxiv). To underscore the ubiquity and diversity of sociocultural influences, and the need to calibrate treatment to each individual's unique background, the appendix of DSM-IV provides formulae to supplement multiaxial diagnoses with cultural factors, and catalogues 25 distinct "culture-bound syndromes" (CBSs). CBSs are defined as recurrent patterns of locality-specific aberrant behavior or distress that can be considered "folk diagnostic categories," and reflect community beliefs regarding the presentation, course, treatments, and causes of the conditions they indicate (DSM-IV, 1994).

At the outset of our discussion, we present a sampling of culture-bound syndromes to illustrate the protean ways in which sociocultural influences may shape how psychological distress is manifested and explained. We then consider two culture-bound syndromes that are largely specific to industrialized cultures: bulimia nervosa (better known simply as "bulimia") and dissociative identity disorder (DID; known formerly as multiple personality disorder). Before concluding, we discuss sociocultural influences on the conceptualization of homosexuality and PTSD, consider the role of sociocultural factors, and present a number of clinical considerations regarding the impact of sociocultural variables on psychotherapy (see also Chapter 17 for a discussion of the impact of culture on the expression of psychopathology).

Culture-Bound Syndromes

CBSs are widely distributed across the globe. They can be described in terms of ethnicity (e.g., Latino), particular nations or locales (e.g., Korea, Portugal), or racial categories (e.g., Eskimo, Native American). CBSs often include symptoms that at least superficially resemble symptoms included in Western diagnostic categories, and often span multiple diagnostic categories. For example, the symptoms of *Nervios* ("nerves"), found across North and South America, variously resemble anxiety, adjustment, depressive, dissociative, somatoform, and psychotic disorders. Given the local nature of CBSs, they often are not recognized by Western classification systems and may well be misconstrued and misdiagnosed apart from their context of origin. For instance, in the southern United States, a *spell* or trance state during which communication with spirits or the deceased takes place might be described as a psychotic episode in terms of traditional psychiatric nomenclature, although in the folk tradition in which it arises it may not be considered a medical or psychiatric event.

Anxiety and somatic symptoms are very common in CBSs. Nearly two-thirds of the syndromes include somatic symptoms, which seem to be a preferred idiom of distress in some non-Western cultures (Keyes & Ryff, 2003; Kleinman, 1988). Some examples of somatic syndromes include *brain fag*, a West African syndrome of aches, visual and sensory symptoms, and poor concentration, experienced by students whose brain is said to be fatigued from too much thinking. *Shenjing shuairuo* is an officially classified Chinese syndrome of physical disturbances, which often meets the Western criteria for mood or anxiety disorder. In China, depression is much less commonly diagnosed compared with Western cultures. Rather, mood-related complaints more typically center on such somatic symptoms as dizziness, physical pains, and sleeping problems (Flaherty, Gavira, & Val, 1982), as is also the case with Hispanic populations (Stoker, Zurcher, & Fox, 1965). For example, in Portugal, *sangue dormido* is a diverse aggregation of somatic complaints known as "sleeping blood."

Approximately half of the 25 identified syndromes include anxiety, as exemplified by the following: (a) *dhat:* anxiety and hypochondriasis related to the discharge of semen; (b) *koro,* an intense, at times even epidemic, anxiety that one's sex organs will retract into the body and cause death; (c) *latah*, a trancelike hypersensitivity to fright with imitation of others and command obedience; and (d) *taijin kyofusho,* a Japanese phobia (probably related to DSM-IV social phobia) that one's body or its functions will offend others.

A number of CBSs include mild to severe dissociation. In cases of *falling out*, which occur in the southern United States and Caribbean, the sufferer collapses suddenly and experiences temporary blindness and an inability to move. Other syndromes include dissociation along with a violent or destructive outburst, often with features that resemble Western psychotic symptoms. *Amok* is a dissociative syndrome prevalent in Southeast Asia, which can result from interpersonal slights and insults that elicit brooding and a subsequent homicidal or otherwise violent outburst (giving rise to the colloquial phrase, "running amok"). At times, amok occurs in tandem with a psychotic episode. Relatedly, *pibloktoq,* a dissociative rampage among the Eskimo that includes reckless or destructive behavior and retrograde amnesia, often ends with convulsions or a coma lasting as long as 12 hours. *Ataque de nervios,* frequent in Latino cultures, describes fits of shouting, crying, physical or verbal aggression, dissociation, and amnesia. A central feature is the sense of being out of control, which often follows on the heels of a stressful life event. *Boufee delirante* is an African syndrome that involves acute aggressive or destructive behavior, sometimes accompanied by paranoia or hallucinations, which, in Western terms, would be considered a Brief Psychotic Disorder.

Two other syndromes, the first of Latino and the second of Korean origin, are thought to arise from intense anger or rage. *Bilis and colera* indicate supposed core bodily imbalances caused by the experience of anger or rage, and subsequent aches, tension, screaming, trembling, or loss of consciousness. The symptoms of *Hwa-byung*, attributed to the suppression of anger, include aches, pains, palpitations, insomnia, and panic.

Western and folk diagnostic categories often diverge with respect to the causes attributed to particular conditions. For example, the presentation of *susto*, known throughout Latin America by a variety of names (*espanto, pasmo, tripa ida*), resembles certain depressive, stress, and somatoform disorders. However, in cases of susto, unhappiness and sickness are attributed to the soul having left the body from a sudden fright. Folk treatments include cleansing to restore spiritual equilibrium, and ritually calling the soul back to the body. Alternatively, blacks and whites in the southern United States and the Caribbean may blame *rootwork* (also known as voodoo or hexes) for an acute fear of death thought to result from sorcery perpetrated by a malevolent individual who seeks to engender physical and psychological distress. Before recovery is possible, the subject must be treated by a *root doctor.* A similar phenomenon, *mal puesto*, exists among Latinos, and exposure to *mal de ojo*—the "evil eye"—known widely across cultures, is presumed to cause a myriad of unsettling affective and somatic symptoms. Similarly, *ghost sickness*, a preoccupation with death among Native American tribes, is sometimes attributed to witchcraft.

Across Asia, folk traditions attribute certain untoward experiences and behaviors to decidedly non-Western causes. For instance, *Chi-gong psychotic reaction* is an official Chinese diagnosis that describes dissociative, paranoid, or psychotic symptoms ascribed to the practice of Chi-gong, an energy exercise similar to yoga or tai chi. Those who are "overly involved" in the practice of Chi-gong are judged most at risk. Physical and metaphysical causes are commonly attributed to CBSs in Asia. *Shenkui*, for example, is a Chinese folk somatic syndrome accompanied by anxiety or panic that is attributed to excessive semen loss from sexual activity or "white turbid urine," which is believed to contain semen. *Shin byung* is a Korean folk syndrome of anxiety, somatic symptoms, and dissociation attributed to possession by ancestral spirits. Similarly, North Africans and Middle Easterners may experience *zar*, a purported possession state during which a host of otherwise aberrant behaviors are considered normal.

Eating Disorders

Western Idealization of Thinness

Closer to home, bulimia and dissociative identity disorder have been described as culture-bound disorders (DSM-IV, 1994) because they are diagnosed with much greater frequency in industrial and often Western cultures, and appear to vary in prevalence as a function of sociocultural variables. Weight and body shape are central determinants of female attractiveness in contemporary Western societies, in which the ideal female body is extremely thin, often to an unhealthy and unattainable degree (Garner, Garfinkel, Schwartz, & Thompson, 1980; Stice, 2002). Media presentations of beauty, which we detail in the course of our discussion, promote the idea that achieving an attractive appearance is tantamount to attaining happiness (Thompson, Heinberg, Altabe, & Tantleff-Dunn, 1999).

Sociocultural influences are among the best predictors of body image dissatisfaction (Anderson & DiDomenico, 1992), and are associated with food restriction and the onset of binge eating and purging (Katzman & Wolchik, 1984; Leon, Fulkerson, Perry, & Cudeck, 1993; Stice, Spangler, & Argas, 2001). Relatedly, decreases in body dissatisfaction predict decreases in bulimic eating patterns (Polivy & Herman, 2004; Stice & Agras, 1999). Women dissatisfied with their bodies tend to self-impose stringent weight goals, and they diet to achieve a culturally prized body type (Heinberg & Thompson, 1995; Thomspon & Stice, 2001). In time, futile attempts to reach an unrealistic weight can perpetuate pathological dieting behaviors that meet diagnostic criteria for eating disorders. According to a sociocultural perspective, males account for only 5%–10% of eating disorder cases (Hoek & vanHoecken, 2003) because society's stringent weight ideals do not target males.

Influence of the Media

A variety of media outlets propagate and reinforce the importance of thinness, and equate a slender figure with beauty. Movies, sitcoms, and magazines feature extremely underweight females, typically 15% below the average weight of women (Johnson, Tobin, & Steinberg, 1989). In fact, images of women displayed in the media are often thin enough to meet diagnostic criteria for anorexia nervosa (Wiseman, Gray, Moismann, & Ahrens, 1990). The media's ideal woman is "biogenetically difficult, if not impossible, for the majority of women" to achieve (Hawkins, Richards, Granley, & Stein, 2004, p. 36; see also Banks, 1992).

Ironically, although the cultural ideal has become progressively thinner, women have, on average, become progressively larger (Garner & Garfinkel, 1980; Wiseman, Gray, Mosimann, & Ahrens, 1992), magnifying pressure to appear thin at all costs. During this period, media icons have evolved from curvaceous to tubular (Garner, Garfinkel, Schwartz, & Thompson, 1980). Women often identify media figures as a relevant comparison group (Heinberg & Thompson, 1995), and consequently cannot escape noting blatant discrepancies between their own bodies and those of celebrities and models. Heinberg and Thompson (1995) found that women who rated celebrities as important exhibited greater body image disturbance and eating disorder symptoms than other women.

The print media also has placed greater emphasis on female attractiveness in recent years: Fashion models are routinely featured in full-body shots, rather than headshots, a dramatic change from the past. Magazine content analyses indicate that the number of diet-related advertisements and articles have also significantly increased since the 1980s (Sypeck, Gray, & Ahrens, 2004). Exposure to print media's thin models predicts low self-esteem, depression, stress, guilt, shame, insecurity, and body dissatisfaction (Irving, 1990; Stice & Shaw, 2002). Interestingly, these dramatic changes coincide with a significant increase in the incidence of eating disorders (Gordon, 2000).

Tiggermann and Pickering (1996) found that females who viewed programs that portrayed idealized, stereotyped women (e.g., soap operas, music videos) experienced body dissatisfaction relative to individuals who watched sports and news broadcasts. However, it is possible that women who are already concerned about their bodies tend to watch many television programs that focus on idealized, stereotyped images of women.

At any rate, it is difficult to escape television commercials that tout the message that "thin is good" and "thinner is best." The average U. S. citizen views approximately 35,000 television commercials each year (Thompson et al., 1999), many of which feature "beautiful people" to sell products that improve appearance or help individuals to lose weight. Among 4,000 commercials aired on network television, 1 out of every 3.8 commercials portrayed the importance of beauty and 1 out of every 11 commercials indicated explicitly that physical attractiveness is desirable (Downs & Harrison, 1985).

Adolescents, who are at the greatest risk for developing anorexia or bulimia, watch an average of 4 hours of television daily (Fouts & Burgraff, 1999). They are the primary targets of appearance enhancement advertisements, 86% of which are geared at young female viewers (Ogletree, Williams, Raffeld, Mason, & Fricke, 1990). Girls ages 11–14 who rate magazines as important sources of information about physical appearance and girls who report a strong desire to attain the thin ideal are more likely to exhibit drive for thinness, disordered eating behavior, and weight-management behavior (Levine, Smolak, & Hayden, 1994). Indeed, body dissatisfaction prospectively predicts restrictive eating behaviors in adolescent girls (Cattarin & Thompson, 1994).

The media's reach extends to children. Schur, Sanders, and Steiner (2000) found that up to 52% of first- to third-grade girls want to lose weight and desire a thinner body shape. Twenty-three percent of adult women reported that their body image was influenced by television or movie stars when they were children, whereas 22% said that fashion models in magazines influenced their body image when they were young (Garner, 1997). Indeed, children's books, videos, and commercials portray thin-as-ideal messages wherein beauty is associated with goodness, and obesity is associated with negative attributes (Herbozo, Tantleff-Dunn, Gokee-Larose, & Thompson, 2004). Accordingly, children, like adults, associate positive traits with thin individuals and negative traits with overweight individuals (Tiggermann & Wilson-Barrett, 1998).

At all ages, the media probably fosters social comparisons of physical appearance, which is known to play a role in body dissatisfaction (Striegel-Moore, McAvay, & Rodin, 1986). Childhood teasing about weight, which arguably derives from a sociocultural thin ideal, is positively related to eating disturbance and body dissatisfaction (Edlund, Halvarsson, Gebre-Medhin, & Sjöden, 1999; Thompson & Heinberg, 1993). Whether the media create the sociocultural physical ideal or whether the media simply reflect the views and beliefs of the culture is difficult to determine. Most likely, there is a reciprocal causality between culture and media (Raphael & Lacey, 1992).

Eating Disorders in Non-Western Nations

Eating disorders are prevalent in cultures that emphasize a thin ideal but are relatively rare in cultures that do not (McCarthy, 1990; but see Keel & Klump, 2003). However, in the past few decades, epidemiological data indicate that the increasing prevalence of eating disorders has become an international health concern (see Gordon, 2000). Eating disorders were previously considered to be ethnospecific insofar as the vast majority of anorexia and bulimia cases have been reported in Western industrialized societies. However, non-Western nations have recently reported an upsurge in eating pathology. Whereas the mechanisms that link culture to maladaptive eating behaviors have not been elaborated, the diffusion of the thin body ideal to non-Western nations via media technology appears to be at least a correlate, if not an etiological factor, in the development of eating disorders (Gordon, 2000).

The industrialization and modernization of many non-Western nations has promoted the infiltration of Western-oriented media into areas previously impervious to Western influence. Today, the popular media regularly exposes parts of Africa, India, Latin America, the Middle East, and Asia to Western standards of thinness (Gordon, 2000). British *Vogue*, published in 40 countries along with international and local fashion magazines, features weight loss articles and promotes clothing and cosmetics that implicitly, if not explicitly, invite women to adopt the Western ideals and reject more traditional standards in which larger body sizes were preferred (Gordon, 2000).

Alternatively, Western diagnostic criteria for eating disorders are not universally applicable and may account for differential prevalence rates across the world (Mumford, 1993). The DSM-IV necessitates body image concerns and body size distortion in the diagnosis of anorexia. Furthermore, according to the DSM-IV, an intense fear of fatness must motivate an individual's weight loss attempts. Lee (1995) suggests that these criteria are biased to reflect Western society's construction of eating disorders. In a study of anorexic Asian females, Lee found that many women failed to report body size concerns. Instead, bloating and the absence of hunger were attributed to food refusal and emaciation. These findings suggest that the DSM-IV may not be culturally sensitive to the symptom presentation of eating disorders, and could partially account for global prevalence rate disparities.

Based on a meta-analysis of incidence rates of eating disorders over time, an examination of the geographic prevalence of anorexia and bulimia, and an analysis of historical accounts of eating disorders, Keel and Klump (2003) claimed that the etiology of bulimia is culturally bound in terms of Western influences, but that the etiology of anorexia is not. They argued that a primary role for genetic influence is suggested by the fact that anorexia cases have been reported in some non-Western countries (e.g., areas of the Middle East, India, and Asia) that have not been exposed to thinness messages. However, an alternative hypothesis is that sociocultural factors other than media thinness messages are at work in these non-Western countries. Keel and Klump (2003) propose that bulimia is probably a culture-bound disorder given the dearth of cases in nations that lack Western influences.

Dissociative Identity Disorder

Dissociative identity disorder (DID) is a perplexing and controversial condition in which a person displays two or more personalities or "personality states" (i.e., alters) that recurrently take control over the individual's behavior. According to the sociocognitive model of DID, patients actively seek to undertand their psychological distress and do so in terms of available cultural narratives as well as suggestive therapeutic procedures. More specifically, proponents of the sociocognitive contend that DID results from inadvertent therapist cueing (e.g., suggestive questioning regarding the existence of possible alters, hypnosis, guided imagery), media influences (e.g., television and film portrayals of DIDs, such as *Sybil*), and broader sociocultural expectations regarding the presumed clinical features of DID.

The sociocognitive model (SCM; Spanos, 1994, 1996; see also Aldridge-Morris, 1989; Lilicnfcld, et al., 1999; Lynn & Pintar, 1997; McHugh, 1993; Merskey, 1992; Sarbin, 1995) contrasts with the traditional posttraumatic model (PTM; Gleaves, 1996, Gleaves, May, & Cardena, 2001; Ross, 1997) of DID, which holds that dissociation or compartmentalization of the personality arises in childhood as a means of coping with severe trauma (e.g., sexual, physical abuse). Advocates of the PTM cite data suggesting that perhaps 90% or more of individuals with DID report a history of severe child abuse (Gleaves, 1996).

Proponents of the SCM (Lilienfeld et al., 1999; Lilienfeld & Lynn, 2003; Merckelbach & Muris, 2001) noted that significant questions can be raised concerning the child abuse-DID link for the following reasons: (a) Many ostensible confirmations of this association derive from studies that lack objective corroboration of child abuse (e.g. Coons, Bowman, & Milstein, 1988) or are plagued with methodological shortcomings (e.g., inadequate comparison groups); (b) the reported high levels of child abuse among DID patients may be attributable to selection and referral biases common in psychiatric samples (e.g., patients who are abused are more likely to enter treatment); (c) correlations between abuse and psychopathology tend to decrease substantially or disappear when the person's perception of family pathology is statistically controlled; and (d) it has not been established that early abuse plays a causal role in DID (see also Chapter 2). These considerations do not exclude an etiological role for early trauma in DID, but they suggest the need for further controlled research before strong conclusions (e.g., Gleaves, 1996; Gleaves et al., 2001) can be drawn.

Advocates of the SCM cite the following findings (see Lilienfeld & Lynn, 2003; Lilienfeld et al., 1999) as consistent with the SCM or as a challenge to the PTM: First, the number of patients with DID has increased dramatically over the past few decades (Elzinga et al., 1998), along with the number of alters per DID individual (North, Ryall, Ricci, & Wetzel, 1993). However, over this period, the number of alters at the time of initial diagnosis appears to have remained constant (Ross, Norton, & Wozney, 1989). Moreover, both of these increases coincide with dramatically increased therapist and public awareness of the major features of DID (Fahy, 1988).

Second, evidence suggests that the overt expression of multiple identity enactments is shaped by cultural and historical factors. Consistent with this claim is the fact that until fairly recently DID was largely unknown outside of North America (see also Hochman & Pope, 1997, for data suggesting considerably greater acceptance of DID in North American countries compared with non–North American English-speaking countries). For example, a 1990 survey in Japan (Takahashi, 1990) revealed no known cases of DID in this country. In addition, until recently DID was rare in England, Russia, and India (Spanos, 1996). Interestingly, the cross-cultural expression of DID appears to be different in India than in North America. In the relatively rare cases of DID reported in India, the transition between alters is almost always preceded by sleep, a phenomenon not observed in North American cases of DID. Media portrayals of DID in India similarly include periods of sleep before the transitions between alters (North et al., 1993).

Gleaves (1996) noted that DID has recently been diagnosed in Holland (see also Sno & Schalken, 1999) and several other European countries, and used this finding to argue against the SCM. Nevertheless, this finding is difficult to interpret. In Holland, for example, the writings of several well-known researchers (e.g., van der Hart, 1993; van der Kolk, van der Hart, & Marmar, 1996) have resulted in substantially increased media and professional attention to DID.

Moreover, "culturally influenced" is not equivalent to "culture bound." In other words, the fact that a condition initially limited to only a few countries subsequently spreads to other countries does not necessarily indicate that this condition is independent of cultural influence. To the contrary, the fact that the features of DID are becoming better known in certain countries would lead one to expect DID to be diagnosed with increasing frequency in these countries. Indeed, the spread of DID to countries in which the characteristics of this condition are becoming more familiar constitutes one important and potentially falsifiable prediction of the SCM.

Third, mainstream treatment techniques for DID appear to reinforce patients' displays of multiplicity, reify alters as distinct personalities, and encourage patients to establish contact with presumed latent alters (Spanos, 1994, 1996). Indeed, many or most DID patients show few or no clear-cut signs of this condition (e.g., alters) before psychotherapy (Kluft, 1988). In fact, the number of alters per DID individual tends to increase substantially over the course of DID-oriented psychotherapy (Piper, 1997).

Fourth, the majority of diagnoses of DID derive from a relatively small number of psychotherapists, many of whom are specialists in DID (Mai, 1995). Relatedly, psychotherapists who use hypnosis, which is clearly a suggestive technique, tend to have more DID patients in their caseloads than do psychotherapists who do not use hypnosis (Powell & Gee, 1999).

Finally, laboratory studies suggest that nonclinical participants who are provided with appropriate cues and prompts can reproduce many of the overt features of DID (Stafford & Lynn, 2002; Spanos, Weekes, & Bertrand, 1985). Laboratory research also does not support the assertion that consciousness can be separated into multiple streams by amnesic barriers to form an independently functioning alter personality (Lynn, Knox, Fassler, Lilienfeld, & Loftus, 2004).

The five sources of evidence cited strongly suggest that DID is a socially constructed and culturally influenced condition, rather than a naturally occurring response to early trauma. Although none of these lines of evidence is by itself dispositive, the convergence of evidence across all of these sources of data provides a potent argument for the validity of the SCM (see Lilienfeld et al., 1999).

Moreover, it is important to note that the diagnosis of DID has a short history but a long ancestry. Historically, dissociative and somatoform disorders were grouped together under the broader rubric of hysteria. Beginning with DSM-III (APA, 1980), these conditions were dissociated from each other and the overarching construct of hysteria was eliminated (Hyler & Spitzer, 1978). This decision was understandable given that the concept of hysteria was vague and poorly defined. Nevertheless, the SCM suggests that the dissociation of dissociative and somatoform disorders may have been an error (Kihlstrom, 1994). These superficially different groups of disorders may reflect variegated expressions of a shared diathesis (Goodwin & Guze, 1996; Lilienfeld, 1992), although the nature of this diathesis (e.g., fantasy proneness) remains to be determined. Slater (1965) similarly noted that many conditions that would today be subsumed under the rubric of somatoform and dissociative disorders can assume a variety of superficially different manifestations across individuals.

Moreover, the behavioral expression of these conditions may be shaped by cultural and historical factors. For example, *latah*, a condition characterized by sudden and transient episodes of profanity, command obedience, trancelike states, and amnesia, is limited primarily to women in Malaysia and Indonesia (Bartholomew, 1994). Conversion disorders were prevalent at the end of the 19th century but are apparently much rarer now (Jones, 1980). In moving from one fin-de-siècle to the next, conversion disorders and DID may have merely changed places as the disorder in fashion (Hacking, 1995).

Vieth (1995) argued that the manifestations of somatoform and dissociative conditions have changed dramatically over time in accord with prevailing cultural conceptions. For example, Vieth observed that Victorian England in the 19th century experienced a dramatic increase in the prevalence of dramatic and unexplained somatic symptoms (e.g, paralyses, aphasias), which were subsequently displaced by less florid episodes of fainting ("the vapors"). He noted that:

> The manifestations of [these conditions] tended to change from era to era much as did the beliefs as to etiology and the methods of treatment. The symptoms, it seems, were conditioned by social expectancy, tastes, mores, and religion, and were further shaped by the state of medicine in general and the knowledge of the public about medical matters. . . . Thus we have seen departures from and returns to the generalized convulsion, the globus hystericus, the loss of consciousness, the cessation of breathing. We have watched the acting-out of demonic possession and the vast variety of delusions related to it. (p. 209)

These shifting manifestations of what may be a similar underlying diathesis offer further support for the SCM (see also Lilienfeld et al., 1999).

Generalizability of Sociocultural Influences

Our discussion of culture-bound syndromes in industrialized and non-Western, nonindustrialized societies suggests that cultural influences play a role in relation to diverse symptoms and psychological conditions (see also Chapter 17). Consideration of two very different disorders, substance abuse and schizophrenia, although clearly not culture-bound, will, nevertheless, illuminate the generalizability of sociocultural influences.

Substance use and abuse. One of the most consistent findings regarding the abuse of drugs and alcohol is that patterns of use vary widely across cultures in line with sociocultural variables. For example, in cultures or groups in which drinking is strictly prohibited, as with Muslims or Mormons, very low rates of alcoholism are evident (Kinney & Leaton, 1995). In contrast, in some societies there are virtually no controls or sanctions against drinking. In France, which has the highest rate of alcoholism in the world, drinking alcohol is seen as a healthy, useful part of daily life. Valiant and Milofsky (1982) found that men of Irish extraction were seven times more likely to manifest alcohol dependence than men of Jewish, Italian, Syrian, or Portuguese extraction. The researchers attributed these differences to differences in attitudes toward alcohol and its abuse, although the differences could be a result of genetic influences as well.

Pihl (1999) has summarized five ways in which culture contributes substantially to the use and possible abuse of drugs: (1) The general cultural environment affects cultural norms concerning drug use, as in the examples above, and availability of drugs; (2) the individual's specific community affects values and norms that determine drug regulations that, in turn, affect access to drugs; (3) subcultures within community including workplace, groups at school, and gangs can influence drug use; (4) family and peers model permissive or restrictive drug use, and can provide direct access to drugs; and (5) the drug-using context that includes the physical and social environment influences drug-using practices. For example, the combination of poverty, neighborhood deterioration, and high crime rates places people at especially high risk (Fagen, 1989).

Schizophrenia. The fact that the prevalence of schizophrenia across diverse cultures is approximately 1% (Cornblatt, Green, & Walker, 1999) might be interpreted to mean that cultural factors do not play a role in schizophrenia. Nevertheless, a number of noteworthy differences are apparent in terms of the symptoms and course of schizophrenia across cultures: (a) Catatonic symptoms are less common in the United States than in non-Western countries (Maslowski, Jansen van Rensburg, & Mthoko, 1998), although these differences could be a function of differences in patterns of medication across countries, as well as sociocultural influences; (b) what is considered a "delusion" varies among cultures. Claims regarding the ability to communicate with God in primitive societies and certain subcultures in industrialized societies may be regarded as legitimate, whereas in other cultures these claims would be regarded as delusional. Moreover, the content of delusions often reflects dominant cultural themes, concerns, and preoccupations. Accordingly, the delusions of patients in technological nations not infrequently involve surveillance with "high-tech" equipment (e.g., satellites, brain implants), whereas the delusions of patients in religion-oriented Ireland, for example, are more likely to revolve around grandiose themes of sainthood; (c) The prevalance of schizophrenia is greater in urban than rural populations (Jenkins & Barrett, 2004); and (d) Based on a 2-year follow-up, schizophrenics in developing countries recover in a shorter time and experience fewer residual symptoms than their counterparts in industrialized countries (Sass, 1997; Tanaka-Matsumi & Draguns, 1997; WHO, 1979). The fast-paced, high-stress, work-oriented, competitive lifestyle of industrialized nations, combined with relatively less social and familial support for schizophrenic patients, may well account for the latter differences across developing and industrialized countries (Tanaka-Matsumi & Draguns, 1997). Another possibility is that differences in clinician diagnostic behavior vary across cultures and across different cultural groups.

Sociocultural Factors and Psychological Diagnosis

Homosexuality

Over time, psychiatric diagnoses have been added and deleted from the psychiatric nomenclature in response to prevailing scientific and cultural views. In relatively recent times, homosexuality has been deleted from the diagnostic manual, whereas posttraumatic stress disorder (PTSD) has been added.

What is considered normal or pathological has differed across historical time periods. For instance, in the 18th and 19th centuries, masturbation and homosexuality were viewed as sexual perversions. However, they are no longer considered pathological as a result of survey research findings (Kinsey, Pomeroy, & Martin, 1948), which revealed that masturbation and homosexuality are among the most common and therefore least deviant unconventional behaviors, and more tolerant societal attitudes.

Today, homosexuality is no longer considered a pathological condition by mainstream mental health professionals. The history-making 1974 decision by the American Psychiatric Association to support a motion to remove homosexuality from its list of mental disorders was highly controversial and flew in the face of opposition from traditional psychoanalysts who viewed homosexuality as an "illness." The change in nomenclature was spurred by confrontation spearheaded by gay activist groups and psychiatrists who demonstrated at meetings of the American Psychological Association, and marshaled both political support and credible scientific evidence for changes in the diagnosis of homosexuality. The depathologizing of homosexuality has resonated widely in the broader culture and facilitated the acceptance of treatment approaches that help patients surmount difficulties in accepting their homosexuality. Today, an active scientific and ethical debate surrounds the issue of the use of treatments designed to change homosexual patients' sexual orientation (Yarhouse & Throckmorton, 2002).

Posttraumatic Stress Disorder

The diagnosis of posttraumatic stress disorder is an example of how a diagnostic category can be created, at least in some measure, in response to sociocultural forces. Psychiatrists have long understood that symptoms of acute stress often follow traumatic experiences (Kolb, 1984; Shephard, 2001). Medical personnel working with veterans from World War I described a class of "war neuroses" that included shell shock, hysteria, and "disordered action" of the heart (Young, 1995). Shell shock was thought to occur following exposure to an event presumed to cause neurological damage—most typically the nearby explosion of an artillery shell—followed by the apparent loss of such central nervous system functions as speech, attention, or motor coordination (Young, 1995). Similarly, World War II psychiatrists diagnosed veterans with "gross stress reaction" (Kardiner, 1947)—a collection of anxiety symptoms including sweating, heart palpitations, and intrusive images included in the DSM-I—following combat.

Veterans from wars before Vietnam were thought to experience transient combat-related disturbances. Indeed, military psychiatrists believed that when a soldier was removed from the battlefield, psychological distress would soon dissipate (Wilson, 1994). Dean (1997) noted that "These problems were 'washed away' by the ritual of acceptance and celebration by appreciative civilians that came in the wake of a successful military effort" (p. 6). However, on returning home, many veterans were met with hostility and were blamed for civilian massacres and drug addiction (Dean, 1997, p. 10).

During Vietnam, a growing number of veterans and mental health professionals believed that exposure to combat necessarily involved massive trauma that left a lasting impact, and that trauma was a result of the horrific nature of war, not the psychological profile or constitutional weaknesses of the veteran (Lifton, 1973; Young, 1995). Some psychiatrists believed that veterans returning home from the war were at a particularly high risk for psychiatric disturbances, with symptoms including guilt, alienation, psychic numbing, and rage. Shatan (1973) described the "post-Vietnam syndrome" as a massive trauma resulting from the inability to grieve losses suffered during combat, the sequelae of which emerged long after service (i.e., 9 to 30 months after combat).

A handful of psychiatrists and Vietnam veterans formed the Vietnam Veterans Working Group (VVWG), and decided that the inclusion of "postcombat disorder" in the upcoming edition of DSM was crucial to the recognition of the psychological suffering endured by many veterans. Robert Spitzer, chief organizer of DSM-III, challenged the VVWG to provide evidence for the inclusion of combat-specific disorders, the idea of which was contrary to extant research (e.g., Helzer, Robbins, & Davis, 1976). Psychiatrists affiliated with the VVWG marshaled hundreds of case histories and chart reviews of Vietnam veterans, many of which detailed symptoms of combat-related anxiety and symptoms similar to what psychiatrists of an earlier generation had termed "war neuroses" (e.g., psychic numbing and intrusive images). Nevertheless, many psychiatrists continued to insist that veterans' psychiatric symptoms could best be described by the existing diagnostic categories of depression, substance abuse, and schizophrenia (Scott, 1990; Young, 1995).

Ultimately, the DSM Committee on Reactive Disorders included "posttraumatic stress disorder" in the third edition of the DSM (DSM-III; APA, 1980). Scott (1990) noted that "PTSD is in the DSM-III because a core of psychiatrists and veterans worked consciously and deliberately for years to put it there. They ultimately succeeded because they were better organized, more politically active, and enjoyed more lucky breaks than the opposition" (pp. 307–308). However, the committee was particularly compelled by the case made by VVWG members that PTSD could result from natural disasters, rape, or other traumatic events (McNally, 2003). Evidence for the similarity of posttraumatic symptoms resulting from a diversity of traumatic stressors provided strong empirical grounds for the inclusion of a trauma-related diagnosis.

The debate surrounding trauma and the PTSD diagnosis has continued virtually unabated (McNally, 2003). For example, Lembcke (1998) argued that conceptualizing psychological distress as a mental disorder inappropriately pathologizes the painful combat experiences endured by Vietnam veterans. Summerfield (2001) staunchly criticized the PTSD diagnosis as heavily socially constructed, arguing that "Posttraumatic stress disorder legitimized their 'victimhood,' gave them moral exculpation, and guaranteed them a disability pension because the diagnosis could be attested to by a doctor" (p. 95). Veterans who receive a military disability pension for combat-related PTSD can earn as much as $36,000 per year for life (Burkett & Whitley, 1998). In their provocative publication, *Stolen Valor,* Burkett and Whitley (1998) found that nearly 30% of Vietnam ex-POWs had never been held captive, and that as many as 75% of PTSD claims are not legitimate.

The PTSD diagnosis has been applied to an increasingly expansive range of problems, such as being exposed to news of a traumatic event, leading to the tenuous equation of psychological distress with trauma (Andreasen, 1995; McNally, 2003; Rosen, 2004; Summerfield, 2001). Some individuals who experienced negative, though relatively common, events such as car accidents and verbal sexual harassment have filed litigation for compensation relating to PTSD symptoms (Summerfield, 2001). In short, there is probably an interaction between the social climate and the definition of psychological trauma that has led to an increasingly broad application of the PTSD diagnosis (sometimes referred to as "criterion creep"). Nevertheless, individuals with PTSD may have distinct neurological and psychological profiles that support the validity of the diagnosis (see McNally, 2003; Stein et al., 1997). Even if the PTSD diagnosis is partially socially constructed, it does not discount the impact of trauma on survivors.

The Role of Sociocultural Influences

Sociocultural influences per se cannot account completely for psycho-pathology. Members of a given society or subculture often "swim in the same cultural sea." Nevertheless, there are often impressive individual variations within a particular culture. For instance, alcoholics are not at all uncommon even in groups with strong sanctions against drinking, and many nonalcoholics live in societies with a high prevalence of alcohol dependence. Whereas the majority of women in our society are repeatedly bombarded with media portrayals of thin women (Hoek & van Hoecken, 2003), only approximately 1 in 100 individuals develops anorexia, and 2–3 in 100 develop bulimia. Individual differences (e.g., genetic, personality, and biochemical factors), which are not well delineated, clearly render some women vulnerable to internalizing ubiquitous thinness standards, and to using dieting and other compensatory behaviors (e.g., purging) to cope with psychological distress. Indeed, it is unlikely that psychological disorders can typically be created *in vacuo* by iatrogenic or sociocultural influences. Rather, sociocultural and iatrogenic influences often operate on a backdrop of preexisting psychopathology or psychological distress.

In the case of DID, sociocognitive influences exert their impact primarily on individuals who are seeking a causal explanation for their instability, identity problems, and impulsive and seemingly inexplicable behaviors. Some important aspects of the competing models we reviewed may prove commensurable (Lilienfeld et al., 1999). For example, early trauma might predispose individuals to develop high levels of fantasy proneness (Lynn, Rhue, & Green, 1988) or related personality traits. In turn, such traits may render individuals susceptible to the iatrogenic and cultural influences posited by the SCM, thereby increasing the likelihood that they will develop DID following exposure to suggestive influences.

Clinical Considerations

A careful assessment of sociocultural influences on the genesis and presentation of psychopathology can be invaluable (see also Chapter 17), a point appreciated by the DSM-IV, which contends that a consideration of sociocultural factors is fundamental to a complete diagnostic assessment. Accordingly, the manual provides an outline for a narrative summary that includes the following categories: (a) cultural identity of the individual (e.g., ethnic or cultural reference group of culture of origin and host culture for immigrants); (b) cultural explanations of the individual's illness (e.g., predominant idioms of distress through which symptoms are communicated, such as possessing spirits, "nerves," somatic complaints); (c) cultural factors related to psychosocial environment and levels of functioning (e.g., relevant interpretations of social stressors, social and informational supports, role of religion, kin networks);

(d) cultural elements of the relationship between the individual and the clinician (e.g., cultural differences between patient and clinician, status differences); and (e) overall cultural assessment for diagnosis and care (e.g., how cultural considerations specifically influence comprehensive diagnosis and care).

An appreciation for the unique cultural background of each patient can enrich psychotherapy as well as assessment (Tseng, 2001). For example, research suggests that therapy tactics that decrease bulimic women's tendency to internalize cultural appearance standards can be beneficial (Piran, Levine, & Steiner-Adair, 2000). Therapists can educate bulimic women about the repercussions of idealized messages with respect to dieting and compensatory behaviors, and devise strategies to help women eat in moderation and develop personal standards independent of messages promoted by the media. With respect to dissociative identity disorder, it is imperative for therapists to do the following: (a) Discuss the potential influence of the media with respect to patients' perceptions of having distinct indwelling personalities; (b) avoid prompting and reifying alters that emerge; (c) refrain from using such suggestive procedures as hypnosis to excavate purportedly repressed or dissociated experiences with memory recovery procedures; and (d) empathize with patients' distress and their need to understand their puzzling life experiences. Beyond these recommendations, the therapist's sensitivity to the patient's family heritage and cultural values and standards will, in all likelihood, strengthen the therapeutic alliance and enable the therapist to have a greater appreciation for nuances in the patient's communications and experience of the world.

CONCLUSIONS

We leave the reader with the following take-home messages:

1. The higher-order concept of mental illness, although partly socially constructed, is not merely a label attached to all socially undesirable behavior (cf., Szasz, 1961). Instead, mental illness may be a hybrid concept that involves not only social values of harm, but also the perception of a biological dysfunction within the organism (e.g., Wakefield, 1992).
2. Although some forms of psychopathology are partly socially constructed, cultural and historical factors almost always combine or interact with a preexisting diathesis (predisposition) toward psychological distress. This diathesis is often at least partly genetic in origin and may be cross-culturally generalizable, even universal in some instances.
3. Many mental disorders, including eating disorders, DID, and PTSD, are in part shaped by prevailing social, cultural, and historical norms, although the underlying personality dispositions to these conditions

may be shared across most or even all cultures. Many culture-bound disorders recognized in the Appendix of DSM-IV may similarly reflect manifestations of diatheses that exist across many cultures.

4. An understanding of sociocultural variables that shape the expression of psychopathology can be beneficial for diagnosis, assessment, and treatment planning.

KEY TERMS

Bulimia: A disorder characterized by recurrent episodes of binge eating, inappropriate compensatory behavior to prevent weight gain (e.g., self-induced vomiting), and self-image unduly influenced by weight and body shape. Binge eating and compensatory eating occur, on average, for 3 months, at least twice a week (DSM-IV-TR, 2000).

Culture-bound syndrome: Recurrent patterns of locality-specific aberrant behavior or distress that can be considered "folk diagnostic categories," and reflect community beliefs regarding the presentation, course, treatments, and causes of the conditions they indicate (DSM-IV, 1994).

Dissociative identity disorder: A controversial diagnosis characterized by the presence of two or more distinct identities or personality states that recurrently take control of the person's behavior. The patient displays a significant inability to recall personal information (DSM-IV-TR, 2000).

Harmful dysfunction: Definition of mental disorder. According to Wakefield (1992), mental disorders are "harmful dysfunctions." More specifically, "They are (a) viewed by society as producing impairment for the individual, others, or both *and* (b) failures or breakdowns of an evolutionarily selected psychological system." For example, according to Wakefield, panic disorder is a mental disorder because it is (a) (correctly) perceived as harmful to the individual and (b) an activation of an evolutionarily selected alarm system in an inappropriate setting (i.e., a "false alarm"; Barlow, 2002).

Shell shock: A condition that anticipated the diagnosis of posttraumatic stress disorder, first observed in World War I. It was thought to occur following exposure to an event presumed to cause neurological damage—most typically the nearby explosion of an artillery shell—followed by the apparent loss of such central nervous system functions as speech, attention, or motor coordination (Young, 1995).

SUGGESTED READINGS

Keel, P. K., & Klump, K. L. (2003) Are eating disorders culture-bound syndromes? Implications for conceptualizing their etiology. *Psychological Bulletin, 129,* 747–769.

Rosen, G. R. (2004). *Posttraumatic stress disorder: Issues and controversies.* Chichester, UK: Wiley.

Spanos, N. P., Weekes, J. R., & Bertrand, L. D. (1985). Multiple personality: A social psychological perspective. *Journal of Abnormal Psychology, 94,* 362–376.

Szasz, T. S. (1961), *The myth of mental illness: Foundations of a theory of personal conduct.* New York: Hoeber-Harper.

Wakefield, J. C. (1992). The concept of mental disorder: On the boundary between biological facts and social values, *American Psychologist, 47,* 373–388.

REFERENCES

Aldridge-Morris, R. (1989). *Multiple personality: An exercise in deception.* Hillsdale, NJ: Erlbaum.

American Psychiatric Association. (1980). *Diagnostic and statistical manual of mental disorders* (3rd ed.). Washington, DC: American Psychiatric Association.

American Psychiatric Association. (1994). *Diagnostic and statistical manual of mental disorders* (4th ed.). Washington, DC: American Psychiatric Association.

Andreasen, N. C. Posttraumatic stress disorder: Psychology, biology, and Manichaean warfare between false dichotomies. *American Journal of Psychiatry, 152,* 963–965.

Banks, C. G. (1992). "Culture" in culture-bound syndromes: The case of anorexia nervosa. *Social Science Medicine, 34(8),* 867–884.

Barlow, D. H. (2002). *Anxiety and its disorders: The nature and treatment of anxiety and panic* (2nd ed.). New York: Guilford Press.

Bartholomew, R. E. (1994). Disease, disorder, or deception? Latah as habit in a Malay extended family. *Journal of Nervous and Mental Disease, 182,* 331–338.

Benedict, R. (1934). Anthropology and the abnormal. *Journal of General Psychology, 10,* 59–82.

Bourne, P. G. (1972). *Men, stress, and Vietnam.* Boston: Little, Brown.

Burkett B. G., & Whitley, G. (1998). *Stolen valor: How the Vietnam generation was robbed of its heroes and its history.* Dallas, TX: Verity.

Cattarin, J., & Thompson, J. K . (1994), A three-year longitudinal study of body image and eating disturbance in adolescent females. *Eating Disorders: Journal of Treatment and Prevention, 2,* 114–125.

Coons, P. M., Bowman, E.S., & Milstein, V. (1988). Multiple personality disorder: A clinical investigation of 50 cases. *Journal of Nervous and Mental Disease, 176,* 519–527.

Cornblatt, B. A., Green, M. F., & Walker, E. F. (1999). Schizophrenia: Etiology and neurocognition. In T. Millon, P. H. Blaney, & Roger D. Davis (Eds.), *Oxford textbook of psychopathology* (pp. 277–310). New York: Oxford University Press.

Dean, E. T. (1997). *Shook over hell: Post-traumatic stress, Vietnam, and the Civil War.* Cambridge, MA: Harvard University Press.

Downs, C. A., & Harrisson, S. K. (1985). Embarrassing age spots or just plain ugly? Physical attractiveness stereotyping as an Instrument of sexism on American television commercials." *Sex Roles, 13,* 9–19.

Elzinga, B.M., van Dyck, R., & Spinhoven, P. (1998). Three controversies about dissociative identity disorder. *Clinical Psychology and Psychotherapy, 5,* 13–23.

Fahy, T. A. (1988). The diagnosis of multiple personality disorder: A critical review. *British Journal of Psychiatry, 153,* 597–606.

Flaherty, J. A., Gavira, F. M., & Val, E. R. (1982). Diagnostic considerations. In E. R. Va., F. M. Gavira, & J. A. Flaherty (Eds.), *Affective disorders: Psychopathology and treatment.* Chicago: Year Book Medical Publishers.

Fouts, G., & Burgraff, K. (1999). Television situation comedies: Female body images and verbal reinforcements. *Sex Roles, 40*(5/6), 473–481.

Garner, D. M., Garfinkel, P. E., Schwartz, D., & Thompson, M. (1980). Cultural expectations of thinness in women. *Psychological Reports, 47*, 483–491.

Garner ̇D. M. (1997). Psychoeducational principles in the treatment of eating disorders. In: D. M. Garner, & P. E. Garfinkel (Eds.), *Handbook for treatment of eating disorders* (pp. 145–177). New York: Guilford Press.

Gleaves, D. H. (1996). The sociocognitive model of dissociative identity disorder: A reexamination of the evidence. *Psychological Bulletin, 120*, 42–59.

Gleaves, D. H., May, M. C., & Cardena, E. (2001). An examination of the diagnostic validity of dissociative identity disorder. *Clinical Psychology Review, 21*, 577–608.

Goodwin, D. W., & Guze, S. B. (1996). *Psychiatric diagnosis* (5th ed.). New York: Oxford University Press.

Gordon, R. A. (2000). Eating disorders: Anatomy of a social epidemic. Blackwell Publishers: Oxford.

Hacking, I. (1995). *Rewriting the soul: Multiple personality and the science of memory.* Princeton, NJ: Princeton University Press.

Hawkins, N., Richards, P. S., Granley, H. M., & Stein, D. M. (2004). The impact of exposure to the thin-ideal media image on women. *Eating Disorders, 12*, 35–50.

Heinberg, L. J., & Thompson, J. K. (1995). Body image and televised images of thinness and attractiveness: A controlled laboratory investigation. *Journal of Social and Clinical Psychology, 14*, 325–338.

Helzer, J. E., Robins, L. N., & Davis, D. H. (1976). Antecedents of narcotic use and addiction: A study of 898 Vietnam veterans. *Drug and Alcohol Dependence, 1*, 183–190.

Herbozo, S., Tantleff-Dunn, S., Gokee-Larose, J., & Thompson, K. (2004). Beauty and thinness messages in children's media: A content analysis. *Eating Disorders, 12*, 21–34.

Hochman, J., & Pope, H. G. (1997). Debating dissociative diagnoses. *American Journal of Psychiatry, 153*, 887–888.

Hoek, H. W., & van Hoecken, D. (2003). Review of the prevalence and incidence of eating disorders. *International Journal of Eating Disorders, 34*, 383–396.

Houts, A. C. (2001). The diagnostic and statistical manual's new white coat and circularity of plausible dysfunctions: Response to Wakefield, Part 1. *Behaviour Research and Therapy, 39*, 315–346.

Hyler, S. E., & Spitzer, R. L. (1978). Hysteria split asunder. *American Journal of Psychiatry, 135*, 1500–1504.

Jenkins, J. H., & Barrett, R. J. (Eds.). (2004). *Schizophrenia, culture, and subjectivity.* Cambridge: Cambridge University Press.

Johnson, C. L., Tobin, D. L., & Steinberg, S. L. (1989). Etiological, developmental and treatment considerations for bulimia. Special issue: The bulimic college student: Evaluation, treatment and prevention. *Journal of College Student Psychotherapy, 3*(2–4), 57–73.

Jones, M. M. (1980). Conversion reaction: Anachronism or evolutionary form? A review of the neurologic, behavioral, and psychoanalytic literature. *Psychological Bulletin.* 87, 421–441.

Kardiner, A. (1947). *War, stress and neurotic illness.* New York: Paul B. Hoeber.

Katzman, M. A., & Wolchik, S. A. (1984). Bulimia and binge eating in college women: A comparison of personality and behavioral characteristics. *Journal of Consulting & Clinical Psychology, 52*(3), 423–428.

Keel, P. K., & Klump, K. L. (2003) Are eating disorders culture-bound syndromes? Implications for conceptualizing their etiology. *Psychological Bulletin, 129*(5), 747–769.

Keyes, C. L. M., & Ryff, C. D. (2003). Somatization and mental health: A comparative study of the idiom of distress hypothesis. *Social Science and Medicine, 57*, 1833–1845.

Kihlstrom, J. F. (1994). One hundred years of hysteria. In S. J. Lynn & J. W. Rhue (Eds.), *Dissociation: Clinical and theoretical perspectives* (pp. 365–394). New York: Guilford Press.

Kinney, J., & Leaton, G. (5ᵗʰ ed. 1995). St. Louis: C. V. Mosby.

Kinsey, A. C., Pomeroy, W. B. & Martin, C. E. (1948). *Sexual behavior in the human male*. Philadelphia: WB Saunders.

Kleinman, A. (1988). *Rethinking psychiatry: From cultural category to personal experience*. New York: Free Press.

Kluft, R. P. (1988). The phenomenology and treatment of extremely complex multiple personality disorder. *Dissociation, 1*, 47–58.

Kolb, L. (1984). The posttraumatic stress disorders of combat: A subgroup with a conditioned emotional response. *Military Medicine, 149*, 237–243.

Lee, S. (1995). Self-starvation in contexts: Towards the culturally sensitive understanding of anorexia nervosa. *Social Science and Medicine, 41*, 25–36.

Lembcke, J. (1998). *The spitting image: Myth, memory, and the legacy of Vietnam*. New York: New York University Press.

Leon, G. R., Fulkerson, J. A., Perry, C. L., & Cudeck, R. (1993). Personality and behavioral vulnerabilities associated with risk status for eating disorders in adolescent girls. *Journal of Abnormal Psychology, 103*, 438–444.

Levine, M. P., Smolak, L., & Hayden, H. (1994). The relation of sociocultural factors to eating attitudes and behaviors among middle school girls. *Journal of Early Adolescence, 14*, 471–490.

Lifton, R. J. (1973). *Home from the War: Vietnam veterans, neither victims nor executioners*. New York: Simon and Schuster.

Lilienfeld, S. O. (1992). The association between antisocial personality and somatization disorders: A review and integration of theoretical models. *Clinical Psychology Review, 12*, 641–662.

Lilienfeld, S. O., & Marino, L. (1995). Mental disorder as a Roschian concept: A critique of Wakefield's "Harmful Dysfunction" analysis. *Journal of Abnormal Psychology, 104*, 411–420.

Lilienfeld, S. O., Lynn, S. J., Kirsch, I., Chaves, J. F., Sarbin, T. R., Ganaway, G. K., et al. (1999). Dissociative identity disorder and the sociocognitive model: Recalling the lessons of the past. *Psychological Bulletin, 125*, 507–523.

Lilienfeld, S. O., & Lynn, S. J. (2003). Dissociative identity disorder: Multiple personality, multiple controversies. In S.O. Lilienfeld, J. M. Lohr, & S. J. Lynn (Eds.), *Science and pseudoscience in clinical psychology* (pp. 109–142). New York: Guilford Press.

Lynn, S. J., & Pintar, J. (1997). A social narrative model of dissociative identity disorder. *Australian Journal of Clinical and Experimental Hypnosis, 25*, 1–7.

Lynn, S. J., Knox, J., Fassler, O., Lilienfeld, S. O., & Loftus, E. (2004). Trauma, dissociation, and memory (pp. 163–186). In J. Rosen (Ed.), *Posttraumatic stress disorder: Issues and controversies*. New York: Wiley.

Lynn, S., Rhue, J., & Green, J. (1988). Multiple personality and fantasy proneness: Is there an association or dissociation? *British Journal of Experimental and Clinical Hypnosis, 5, 138–142.*

Mai, F. M. (1995). Psychiatrists' attitudes to multiple personality disorder: A questionnaire study. *Canadian Journal of Psychiatry, 40,* 154–157.

Maslowski, J., Jansen van Rensburg, D., & Mthoko, N. (1998). A polydiagnostic approach to the differences in the symptoms of schizophrenia in different cultural and ethnic populations. *Acta Psychiatrica Scandinavica, 98,* 41–46.

McCarthy, M. (1990). The thin ideal, depression, and eating disorders in women. *Behavioral Research and Therapy, 28,* 205–215.

McHugh, P. R. (1993). Multiple personality disorder. *Harvard Mental Health Newsletter, 10,* 4–6.

McNally, R. J. (2001). On Wakefield's harmful dysfunction analysis of mental disorder. *Behaviour Research and Therapy, 39,* 309–314.

McNally, R. J. (2003). Progress and controversy in the study of posttraumatic stress disorder. *Annual Review of Psychology, 54,* 229–252.

Merckelbach, H., & Muris, P. (2001). The causal link between self-reported trauma and dissociation: A critical review. *Behaviour Research and Therapy, 39,* 245–254.

Merskey, H. (1992). The manufacture of personalities: The production of multiple personality disorder. *British Journal of Psychiatry, 160,* 327–340.

Miller, M. N., & Pumariega, A. J. (2000). Culture and eating disorders: A historical and cross-cultural review. *Psychiatry, 64*(2), 93–107.

Mumford, D. B. (1993). Eating disorders in different cultures. *International Review of Psychiatry, 158,* 222–228.

Murphy, J. B. (1976). Psychiatric labeling in cross-cultural perspective: Similar kinds of disturbed behavior appear to be labeled abnormal in diverse cultures. *Science, 191,* 1019–1028.

Nagel, K. L., & Jones, K. H. (1992). Sociological factors in the development of eating disorders. *Adolescence, 27,* 107–113.

North, C. S., Ryall, J.-E. M., Ricci, D. A., & Wetzel, R. D. (1993). *Multiple personalities, multiple disorders.* New York: Oxford University Press.

Ogletree, S. M., Williams, S. W., Raffeld, P., Mason, B., & Fricke, K. (1990). Female attractiveness and eating disorders: Do children's television commercials play a role? *Sex Roles, 22,* 791–797.

Pihl, R. O. (1999). Substance abuse: Etiological considerations. In T. Millon, P. H. Blaney, & Roger D. Davis (Eds.), *Oxford textbook of psychopathology* (pp. 249–276). New York: Oxford University Press.

Pinker, S. (2002). *The blank slate: The modern denial of human nature.* New York: Viking.

Piper, A. (1997). *Hoax and reality: The bizarre world of multiple personality disorder.* Northvale, NJ: Jason Aronson.

Piran, N., Levine, M. P., & Steiner-Adair, C. (2000). *Preventing eating disorders: A handbook of interventions and special challenges.* Philadelphia: Brunner/Mazel.

Polivy, J., & Herman, C. P. (2004). Sociocultural idealization of thin female body shapes: An introduction to the special issue on body image and eating disorders. *Journal of Social and Clinical Psychology, 23*(1), 1–6.

Raphael, F. J., & Lacey, J. H. (1992). Sociocultural aspects of eating disorders. *Annals of Medicine, 24,* 293–296.

Reston, J. (1974). The forgotten veterans. *New York Times,* June 2, 1974, section IV, p. 21:1.

Rosen, G. M. (2004). Traumatic events, criterion creep, and the creation of pretraumatic stress disorder. *The Scientific Review of Mental Health Practice, 3*, 39–42.

Ross, C. A. (1997). *Dissociative identity disorder: Diagnosis, clinical features, and treatment of multiple personality.* New York: John Wiley & Sons.

Ross, C. A., Norton, G. R., & Wozney, K. (1989). Multiple personality disorder: An analysis of 236 cases. *Canadian Journal of Psychiatry, 34*, 413–418.

Sarbin, T. R. (1995). On the belief that one body may be host to two or more personalities. *International Journal of Clinical and Experimental Hypnosis, 43*, 163–183.

Sass, L. A. (1997). The consciousness machine: Self and subjectivity and schizophrenia and modern culture. In U. Neisser & D. A. Jopling (Eds.), *The conceptual self in context: Culture, experience, self-understanding* (pp. 203–230). Cambridge: Cambridge University Press.

Schur, E. A., Sanders, M., & Steiner, H. (2000). Body dissatisfaction and dieting in young children. *International Journal of Eating Disorders, 27*, 74–82.

Scott, W. J. (1990). PTSD in DSM-III: A case in the politics of diagnosis and disease. *Social Problems, 37*, 294–310.

Shatan, C. F. (1973). The grief of soldiers in mourning: Vietnam combat veterans' self help movement. *American Journal of Orthopsychiatry, 43*, 640–653.

Shatan, C. F., Smith, J. R., & Haley, S. (1976, June). *Proposal for the inclusion of combat stress reactions in DSM-III.* Paper presented for DSM-III Task Force of American Psychiatric Association.

Shephard, B. (2001). *A War of nerves: Soldiers and psychiatrists in the twentieth century.* Cambridge, MA: Harvard University Press.

Slater, E. (1965). Diagnosis of "hysteria." *British Medical Journal, 1*, 1395–1399.

Sno, H. N., & Schalken, H. F. (1999). Dissociative identity disorder: Diagnosis and treatment in the Netherlands. *European Psychiatry, 5*, 270–277.

Spanos, N. P. (1994). Multiple identity enactments and multiple personality disorder: A sociocognitive perspective. *Psychological Bulletin, 116*, 143–165.

Spanos, N. P. (1996). *Multiple identities and false memories: A sociocognitive perspective.* Washington, DC: American Psychological Association.

Spanos, N. P., Weekes, J. R., & Bertrand, L. D. (1985). Multiple personality: A social psychological perspective. *Journal of Abnormal Psychology, 94*, 362–376.

Stafford, J., & Lynn, S. J. (2002). Cultural scripts, childhood abuse, and multiple identities: A study of role-played enactments. *International Journal of Clinical and Experimental Hypnosis, 50*, 67–85.

Stice, E., & Agras, W. S. (1999). Subtyping bulimics along dietary restraint and negative affect dimensions. *Journal of Consulting and Clinical Psychology, 67*, 460–469.

Stice, E. (2002). Sociocultural influences on body image and eating disturbance. In C. G. Fairburn and K. D. Brownell (Eds.), *Eating disorders and obesity: A comprehensive handbook.* New York: Guilford.

Stice, E., & Shaw, H. E. (2002). Role of body dissatisfaction in the onset and maintenance of eating pathology: A synthesis of research findings. *Journal of Psychosomatic Research, 53*, 985–993.

Stice, E., Spangler, D., & Agras, W. S. (2001). Exposure to media-portrayed thin-ideal images adversely affects vulnerable girls: A longitudinal experiment. *Journal of Social and Clinical Psychology, 20*(3), 270–288.

Stoker, D. H., Zurcher, L. A., & Fox, W. (1968). Women in psychotherapy: A cross-cultural comparison. *International Journal of Social Psychiatry, 15*, 5–22.

Striegel-Moore, R. H., Silberstein, L. R., & Rodin, J. (1986). Toward an understanding of risk factors for bulimia. *American Psychologist, 41(3)*, 246–263.

Striegel-Moore, McAvay, G., & RJ. (1986). Psychological and behavioral correlates of feeling fat in women. *International Journal of Eating Disorders, 5*, 935–947.

Summerfield, D. (2001). The invention of post-traumatic stress disorder and the social usefulness of a psychiatric category. *British Medical Journal, 322*, 95–98.

Sypeck, M. F., Gray, J. J., & Ahrens, A. H. (2004). No longer just a pretty face: Fashion magazines' depictions of ideal female beauty from 1959 to 1999. *International Journal of Eating Disorders, 36*, 342–347.

Szasz, T. S. (1961). *The myth of mental illness: Foundations of a theory of personal conduct.* New York: Hoeber-Harper.

Takahashi, Y. (1990). Is multiple personality really rare in Japan? *Dissociation, 3*, 27, 57–59.

Tanaka-Matsumi, J., & Draguns, J. G. (1997). Culture and psychopathology. In J. W. Berry, M. H. Segall, & C. Kagitcibasi (Eds.), *Handbook of cross-cultural psychology* (pp. 449–491). Boston: Allyn & Bacon.

Thompson, J. & Heinberg, L. (1993). Preliminary test of two hypothesis of body image disturbance. *International Journal of Eating Disorders, 14*, 59–63.

Thompson, J. K., Heinberg, L., K., Altabe, M., & Tanleff-Dunn, S. (1999). *Exacting beauty: Theory, assessment, and treatment of body image disturbance.* Washington, DC: American Psychological Association.

Thompson, J. K., & Stice, E. (2001). Internalization of the thin-ideal: A potent risk factor for body image and eating disturbances. *Current Directions in Psychological Science, 10*, 181–183.

Tiggermann, M., & Pickering, A. S. (1996). Role of television in adolescent women's body dissatisfaction and drive for thinness. *International Journal of Eating Disorders, 20(2)*, 199–203.

Tiggermann, M., & Wilson-Barrett, E. (1998). Children's figure ratings: Relationship to self-esteem and negative stereotyping. *International Journal of Eating Disorders, 23*, 83–88

Tseng, W. (2001). *Handbook of cultural psychiatry.* New York: Academic Press.

Vaillant, G. E., & Milofsky, F. S. (1982). The etiology of alcoholism: A prospective viewpoint. *American Psychologist, 37*, 494–503.

van der Hart, O. (1993). Multiple personality disorder in Europe: Impressions. *Dissociation, 6*, 102–118.

van der Kolk, B. A., van der Hart, O., & Marmar, C. R. (1996). Dissociation and information processing in posttraumatic stress disorder. In B. A. van der Kolk, A. C. McFarlane, & L. Weisaeth (Eds.), *Traumatic stress: The effects of overwhelming stress on mind, body, and society* (pp. 303–327). New York: Guilford Press.

Vieth, I. (1965). *Hysteria: The history of a disease.* Chicago: University of Chicago Press.

Wakefield, J. C. (1992). The concept of mental disorder: On the boundary between biological facts and social values. *American Psychologist, 47*, 373–388.

Wilson, J. P. (1994). The historical evolution of PTSD diagnostic criteria: From Freud to DSM-IV. *Journal of Traumatic Stress, 7*, 681–698.

Wiseman, C. V., Gray, J. J., Moismann, J. E., & Ahrens, A. H. (2002). Cultural expectations in thinness in women: An update. *International Journal of Eating Disorders, 11(1)*, 85–89.

World Health Organization. (1979). *Schizophrenia: An international follow-up study.* Geneva, Switzerland: Author.

Yarhouse, M. A., & Throckmorton, W. (2002). Ethical issues in attempts to ban reorientation therapies. *Psychotherapy, 39,* 66–75.

Young, A. (1995). *The harmony of illusions: Inventing post-traumatic stress disorder.* Princeton, NJ: Princeton University Press.

CHAPTER

17

Cultural Factors Influence the Expression of Psychopathology

YULIA E. CHENTSOVA-DUTTON AND JEANNE L. TSAI

Because we live in an increasingly multicultural world, many mental health professionals are faced with the challenge of assessing and treating individuals whose cultural contexts vary significantly from their own. Consider the following scenario: A young woman complains that she is suffering from attacks by angry spirits. She tells you that these spirits visit her at night (she can see vague outlines of the spirits and hear them whispering) and sit on top of her, rendering her immobile and helpless. Do you think that this woman's behavior is normal or abnormal? The answer to this question depends in part on the woman's cultural context. In mainstream American contexts, these symptoms are rare and often associated with schizophrenia. However, in Hmong contexts, these symptoms (referred to as the *tsog tsuam*, or evil spirit who smothers) are common and not associated with mental illness (Adler, 1991). Thus, the same behavior may be interpreted very differently depending on the cultural context in which it occurs. Therefore, in addition to functional impairment and subjective distress, mental health professionals must consider cultural norms and values when assessing and treating mental illness (see also Chapter 16).

DEFINING CULTURE

Before discussing how culture shapes the expression of mental illness, we must define "culture." We refer to Kroeber and Kluckhohn's (1952) widely cited definition of culture as:

> Patterns, explicit and implicit, of and for behaviour acquired and transmitted by symbols . . . including their embodiment in artifacts; the essential core of culture consists of traditional . . . ideas and especially their attached values; culture systems may, on the one hand, be considered as products of action, on the other, as conditional elements of future action.

This definition not only highlights the complex and dynamic nature of culture but also emphasizes the mutual constitution of culture and psychological processes. That is, culture shapes patterns of behavior and, in turn, is shaped by them (Adams & Markus, 2004). For example, cultural products such as child-rearing advice manuals can influence the choice of child-rearing practices adopted by parents. In turn, when writing the manuals, parenting experts respond to common child-rearing practices of their time (Hulbert, 2003).

Concepts related to "culture" include "ethnicity," "nationality," and "race." Although these terms are often used interchangeably, they also differ in significant ways. Although the term "culture" is typically used to describe systems of shared meanings, values, customs, and beliefs as well as social institutions and physical products (e.g., American versus Chinese culture) (Betancourt & Lopez, 1993; Kroeber & Kluckhohn, 1952), the term "ethnicity" is used to characterize a discrete group of individuals "in terms of common nationality, culture and language" (e.g., Asian Americans or Hispanic Americans) (Betancourt & Lopez, 1993, p. 631). Furthermore, although "ethnicity" is most often used when describing minority groups within a larger culture, the term "nationality" is often used to differentiate among individuals within an ethnic group by their country of origin (e.g., Chinese Americans versus Japanese Americans). Finally, "race" is often used to differentiate groups in terms of their physical characteristics such as skin color (e.g., White Americans and Black Americans) and has been typically used in the context of studying group differences in power, status, and opportunity (Betancourt & Lopez, 1993; Matsumoto, 2000). We use the term "culture" because we are interested in the effects of practices, values, and perspectives (rather than common language, country of origin, or skin color) on psychopathology.

CULTURAL UNIVERSALISM VERSUS CULTURAL RELATIVISM

What is the role of culture in shaping mental illness? Does culture matter, and if so, which aspects of mental illness are shaped by cultural factors? Is the influence of culture on mental illness pathogenic (meaning that cultural factors cause the illness) or pathoplastic (meaning that cultural factors shape the symptoms of the illness)? To what extent do cultural and biological factors in mental illness interact with each other? Can diagnoses be compared across cultural contexts?

Before answering these questions, it is important to acknowledge the historical tension between cultural universalism and cultural relativism (see also Chapter 16 for a discussion). Although few, if any, scholars hold either perspective in its purest form, these perspectives reveal the critical issues and challenges that have confronted cross-cultural investigations of psychopathology. The cultural universalism perspective argues that the fundamental processes that underlie different forms of psychopathology are similar across cultures and that cultural variation in the expressions of these fundamental processes is minimal (Maslowski, Jansen van Rensburg, & Mthoko, 1998; Murphy, 1982). For example, in a classic article, Murphy (1976) provided evidence for cultural universalism in the expression of mental illness. She investigated patterns of psychological and behavioral disturbances across two non-Western cultural contexts (Eskimo and Yoruba villages) and compared them to Western categories of mental illness. The content of particular symptoms was observed to be "colored by culture" (Murphy, 1976, p. 191). For example, Eskimo delusions were based on Eskimo cultural beliefs, whereas Yoruban delusions were based on Yoruban cultural beliefs. However, these differences in content were overshadowed by important similarities. Despite differences in cultural norms and in the availability of labels for aberrant behavior patterns, Murphy observed that markedly similar forms of mental illness (such as psychotic symptoms, anxiety, and antisocial behavior) existed in Western and non-Western contexts. These findings were interpreted as evidence of similarities in fundamental processes underlying mental illness (see Chapter 16).

These universalist claims received much criticism from anthropologists, cultural psychologists, and psychiatrists who asserted that psychological functioning is culturally constructed, or embedded in and shaped by cultural meaning systems (the "cultural relativism" approach) (Boas, 1948; Geertz, 1984; Markus & Kitayama, 1991; Shweder, & Haidt, 2000). These researchers cautioned that uncritically imposing Western mental illness categories on individuals in non-Western cultural contexts might lead to a *category fallacy*, or an overidentification of universals and omission of cultural differences (Lewis-Hernandez & Kleinman, 1994; Kleinman, 1977; Kleinman, 1988). For example, Kleinman (1988) criticized a "pathogenic/pathoplastic" model embedded in many cross-cultural studies of psychopathology. In this model, "Biology is presumed to 'determine' the cause and structure of . . . mental disease, while cultural and social factors at most 'shape' or 'influence' the 'content' of disorder" (p. 24). He noted that this model is faulty because it does not account for the interaction and mutual influence of cultural and biological factors in mental illness (see Chapter 16). Not surprisingly, this perspective has motivated research on the expression of psychopathology across diverse cultural contexts (Kleinman, 1986; Marsella, 1980). For instance, Kleinman (1986) interviewed Chinese patients with a diagnosis of neurasthenia (a syndrome that is common in China, and that is characterized by chronic fatigue, weakness, and associated bodily and emotional complaints) in an effort to understand the relationship between neurasthenia and depression. A large percentage of Chinese neurasthenics met the criteria for a Western diagnosis of major depression. However, the chief complaints of the Chinese neurasthenics were somatic (or affecting the body, from the Greek "soma," or body) rather than emotional (e.g., headaches and dizziness). Kleinman noted that in the Chinese cultural context, somatic complaints are sanctioned ways to elicit support and treatment without evoking the stigma of mental illness. However, neurasthenia was not just another form of Western depression. For instance, antidepressant medications did not alleviate the somatic complaints of the Chinese patients. Instead, their physical symptoms improved only when the patients were able to resolve interpersonal or occupational problems in their lives. Based on this evidence, Kleinman (1986) concluded that emotional distress is the product of an interaction between cultural, psychosocial, and biological factors.

As mentioned earlier, few scholars endorse either the universalist or the cultural relativist positions in their extreme forms, especially as increasing evidence suggests that mental illness is both universal and culturally shaped. In this chapter, we highlight the aspects of mental disorders that are known to be culturally shaped.

We begin with several examples of cultural variability in the prevalence rates of several common mental disorders and their expression. Each of these examples is based on evidence from studies using emic (based on indigenous concepts and instruments) or etic (based on Western concepts and instruments, adapted for use in a non-Western context) approaches. We then outline possible mechanisms by which cultural ideas and practices may shape mental illness. Finally, we discuss the implications of cultural differences in mental illness for clinical practice.

CULTURE AND THE EXPRESSION OF COMMON MENTAL DISORDERS

Major Depression

Major depression is a disorder that is common across cultures and is associated with significant global economic burden and disability (Murray & Lopez, 1997; Ormel et al., 1994). Using Western-based criteria for depressive symptoms, etic studies reveal significant cross-cultural differences in the prevalence rates of major depression, with Western and Latin American countries having higher rates of depression than Asian countries (Kawakami, Shimizu, Haratani, Iwata, & Kitamura,

2004; Simon, VonKorff, Picvinelli, Fullerton, & Ormel, 1999). Depression also has higher recurrence rates in Western and Latin American cultural contexts than in Asian cultural contexts (Simon, Goldberg, Von Korff, & Ustun, 2002). For example, 33–44% of patients in Western and Latin American cultural contexts experienced recurrence of their depressive symptoms after 1 year, compared to 9% of patients in Asian cultural contexts. Moreover, studies of immigrant groups living in Western cultures suggest that lifetime exposure to Western culture is associated with increased rates of depression. For example, American-born Mexican Americans have higher rates of depression than Mexican-born Mexican Americans and Mexicans living in Mexico (Vega et al, 1998; Vega, Sribney, Aguilar-Gaxiola, & Kolody, 2004). Moreover, individuals who moved to the United States as children show higher prevalence rates of psychiatric disorders than individuals who moved to the United States as teenagers and young adults. These differences cannot be explained by economic and educational disparities between individuals in these cultural contexts (Vega, Sribney, Aguilar-Gaxiola, & Kolody, 2004).[1] Instead, the higher rates of depression among American-born Mexican Americans may in part be caused by the erosion of cultural factors (such as family stability and cohesiveness) that protect individuals from becoming depressed. Similarly, internalization of the North American "pursuit of happiness" and having minority status in North American culture may place American-born Mexican Americans at higher risk for depressive symptoms compared to their counterparts living in Mexico.

In addition to influencing the prevalence and recurrence rates of depression, cultural factors appear to shape the expression of depression. In many Western contexts, depression is characterized by "affective" or emotional complaints, such as sad mood or a sense of hopelessness (Manson, 1995). As stated earlier, in many Asian contexts, depression is characterized by somatic symptoms (e.g., Korean [Pang, 1995], Japanese [Waza et al., 1999], and Punjabi cultures [Krause, 1989]). For example, ethnographic evidence suggests that a Punjabi indigenous disorder called the "sinking heart" is similar to depression in that it is often precipitated by social stress and characterized by emotional distress and worry (Krause, 1989). Unlike Western individuals with major depression, however, sinking heart sufferers complain primarily of somatic (e.g., a painful sensation in one's heart) rather than emotional (e.g., sadness and sense of worthlessness) symptoms. In contrast, in some cultural contexts, depressed individuals complain primarily of interpersonal distress rather than somatic and emotional symptoms. For example, in rural Ecuador an illness named "pena" is a depressive illness that is characterized by

---

[1] It is possible that the differences between immigrants and Mexicans living in Mexico are due to a self-selection bias, such that individuals genetically predisposed to depression may be more likely to migrate away from their families. Future studies should assess whether this is the case.

a breakdown in social functioning and by appeals for social reciprocity (Tousignant & Maldonado, 1989).

Ethnographic evidence of cultural differences in the somatization of depression, however, has been recently challenged by findings from etic studies (see Kirmayer & Young, 1998, for review). For example, a study conducted by a World Health Organization research team (Simon et al., 1999) examined the links between somatic and psychological symptoms in 14 countries. The authors found that, contrary to the notion that patients in non-Western cultures somatize their psychological symptoms, the proportion of somatic symptoms to psychological symptoms did not differ across countries. Instead, across cultures, patients were more likely to initially report somatic symptoms when they used walk-in clinics and did not have an ongoing relationship with their physicians. These findings seem to indicate that both somatic and emotional symptoms are at the core of depression across cultural contexts and that patients tend to make initial somatic complaints to their physicians when they do not feel comfortable disclosing information about their emotional distress. It is important to note that findings of this study may be biased by its use of Western-based instruments to assess somatic complaints (see also Chapter 15 for a discussion of links between physical health and psychological adjustment).

In summary, ethnographic studies suggest that patients in non-Western cultural contexts are more likely to express their distress through somatic complaints than patients in Western cultural contexts, whereas epidemiological data uncover cultural similarities in somatization. To integrate these disparate findings, cross-cultural studies of somatization that combine emic and etic research approaches are sorely needed (see Guarnaccia & Rogler, 1999, for an example of such comprehensive research programs). Only by combining these research approaches we can uncover the extent of cultural similarities and differences in the somatization of distress.

Social Anxiety Disorder

In the DSM-IV, social anxiety disorder (social phobia) is characterized by "marked and persistent fear of social situations in which embarrassment may occur" (APA, 1994, p. 411). Etic studies find that the lifetime prevalence of this disorder varies significantly across cultural contexts, ranging from an average low of 0.4–0.6% in Asian countries (such as Korea and Taiwan) to an average high of 7–16% in Western countries (such as the United States, Canada, the Netherlands, and Norway). In rural Russia, the lifetime prevalence of social anxiety disorder is 53% (see Furmark, 2002 for a complete review). Studies using both emic and etic approaches also suggest that social anxiety is expressed differently across cultural contexts. For example, in Japan, Taijin Kyofusho (TKS) resembles social anxiety disorder in its incapacitating fear related to social situations. However, whereas individuals with social anxiety disorder in Western cultures fear that they may humiliate or embarrass *themselves* (e.g., "I am making a fool of myself"; APA, 1994), individuals with TKS in Japan are more concerned with the impact of their behavior on *others* (e.g., "I am bringing shame on my parents"). Specifically, they are afraid of offending or bringing shame on close others (Kleinknecht, Dinnel, Kleinknecht, Hiruma, & Harada, 1997).

Alcohol Abuse

Abuse of alcohol is another mental disorder that is associated with significant global burden (World Health Organization, n.d.). The World Health Organization reported that in 2000, consumption of alcohol varied considerably across cultures (World Health Organization, n.d.). Not surprisingly, alcohol consumption is higher in "wet" or "vinocultural" (wine-producing and wine-drinking) countries, in which social drinking is an essential part of gatherings and celebrations (e.g., France, Germany, Eastern European countries, and Thailand) and lower in "dry" countries in which social drinking is strongly discouraged (e.g., Egypt, Indonesia, and Iraq). For example, the lowest recorded annual consumption rate (0.02 liters of alcohol per capita) was recorded for the predominantly Muslim country of Mauritania, whereas the highest recorded rate (21 liters per capita) was recorded in the Republic of Moldova, a "wet" country.

Because the definition of "normal" drinking varies considerably across cultures, it is difficult to establish universal criteria for "pathological" levels of alcohol consumption (Bennett, Janca, Grant, & Sartorius, 1993; Gureje, Vazquez-Barquero, & Janca, 1996). For example, in Korea, disturbing others is commonly considered an indicator of excessive drinking, whereas in the United States, having physical symptoms, such as passing out or developing a yellow eye tint, is commonly considered an indicator of excessive drinking (Bennett, Janca, Grant, & Sartorius, 1993). Thus, reliance on standardized Western criteria for alcohol abuse or dependence may miss cases of problematic drinking in some cultural contexts.

Keeping this limitation in mind, let us consider evidence based on etic studies that have assessed the prevalence of alcohol-related disorders (alcohol abuse, dependence and harmful use) across cultural contexts (World Health Organization, 2004). These studies report considerable cultural variability in rates of alcohol-related disorders. This variability appears to be due at least in part to cultural strategies for regulating drinking, such as socialization of moderate drinking or religious proscriptions against drinking. For example, rates of alcohol-related mental health problems are lower in "wet" cultural contexts such as among Jewish Americans and Mediterranean Americans (Italian, Greek), as compared with other cultural groups in the United States (e.g., Irish Americans) (Calahan & Room, 1974; Glassner & Berg, 1980; Vaillant, 1983). These results suggest that in "wet" cultural contexts, high levels of alcohol use are integrated into social and religious practices and regulated by tradition, resulting in paradoxically low prevalence rates of alcoholism. Interestingly, the opposite approach of cultural proscription against the use of alcohol also lowers the prevalence of alcoholism. For example, Islam calls for complete abstinence from alcohol. Cultural contexts that are influenced by Islam show not only low alcohol consumption rates but also very low rates of alcohol abuse and dependence. Whereas the annual prevalence of alcohol dependence is 9.9% for Canada and 3% for Germany, it is only 0.2% for Egypt (World Health Organization, 2004). Thus, different cultures can provide drastically different norms regarding the use of alcohol (e.g., incorporation of alcohol into social rituals or proscription against the use of alcohol) that lead to low levels of alcohol-related problems.

POSSIBLE CULTURAL MECHANISMS

Extant research has identified a number of potential cultural variables that can help us account for cultural differences in mental illness. In this section, we will focus on the impact of cultural models of mental health and beauty on the occurrence and expression of mental illness.

Across cultures, people differ in what emotions they would like to feel, what kinds of relationships they would like to have, and how they would like to look. People in different cultural contexts also vary in the extent that they perceive the emotional, social, and physical aspects of themselves to be interrelated. Because notions of mental health are inversely related to notions of mental illness, these cultural models have implications for the occurrence and expression of mental illness. By cultural models we mean shared assumptions that are widely held by individuals in a particular cultural context. These assumptions are typically reinforced by cultural products (e.g., advertisements, child-rearing manuals), institutions (e.g., educational settings), and practices (e.g. parenting practices; see Chapter 14) (see Holland & Quinn, 1987; Markus & Kitayama, 2003; Shore, 1996). These cultural models provide implicit and explicit guidance on desirable and undesirable feelings and behaviors.

Cultural Models of Mental Health

Emotional Functioning. One core aspect of healthy psychological functioning is emotional balance. Views of healthy emotional responses differ across cultural contexts. For example, in European American cultures, healthy emotional functioning is associated with open emotional responding (Bellah, Madsen, Sullivan, Swindler, & Tipton, 1985; Wierzbicka, 1992; 1999), whereas in Asian cultures, healthy emotional functioning is associated with emotional moderation and control (Bond, 1991). Recent studies also indicate that although most individuals want to feel positive, the nature of valued positive emotions differs across cultures (Tsai, Knutson, & Fung, 2006). For instance, high arousal positive emotions such as excitement and enthusiasm are more highly valued in European American than in Asian cultural contexts, whereas low arousal positive emotions such as calmness and serenity show the opposite pattern. These differences in valued positive emotions are consistent with cultural differences in the expression of emotions. A laboratory study in which European Americans and Asian Americans were asked to relive different emotional episodes or engage in emotional conversations with their romantic partners revealed that European Americans express positive emotions (e.g., smile) more often and more intensely than Asian Americans, despite there being no group differences in subjective reports of positive emotional experience or in levels of physiological responding (Tsai, Chentsova-Dutton, Freire-Bebeau, & Przymus, 2002; Tsai, Levenson, McCoy, in press). Intense smiles may be indicative of European American cultural norms of open emotional expression, particularly for high arousal positive emotions such as excitement. Thus, healthy emotional functioning varies for Asian Americans and European Americans in ways that are consistent with their ideal emotions.

Notions of abnormal emotional functioning also can be expected to vary in ways that are consistent with cultural models of emotional functioning. That is, emotional symptoms of psychopathology may represent deviations from culturally specific norms of emotional expression. As mentioned earlier, healthy functioning is associated with open expression of emotions in European American cultural contexts, and with emotional moderation in Asian cultural contexts. One study examined whether the impact of depression on emotional responding differs as a function of cultural norms regarding emotional expression (Chentsova-Dutton, Chu, Tsai, Rottenberg, Gross, & Gotlib, 2006). We predicted that depression may reduce attention to, or concern with, cultural norms of emotional responding, resulting in emotional responses that contradict these norms. That is, in European American cultural contexts, a depressed individual may fail to openly express his or her feelings. In contrast, in Asian cultural contexts, a depressed individual may fail to moderate his or her emotions. To test this hypothesis, we presented depressed and nondepressed European Americans and Asian Americans with a sad film. While watching the sad film, depressed European Americans reported *less* sadness and cried *less* than did nondepressed European Americans. This finding is consistent with evidence that depressed European Americans show dampened emotional responses to emotional imagery, slides, and films compared with nondepressed controls (Allen, Trinder, & Brennan, 1999; Berenbaum, 1992; Rottenberg, Kasch, Gross & Gotlib, 2002). Importantly, despite similar severity levels of depression, this pattern was reversed for Asian Americans: Depressed Asian Americans reported *more* sadness and cried *more* than did nondepressed Asian Americans. Therefore, depression was associated with *diminished* emotional responding to a sad film for

European Americans and with *enhanced* emotional responding for Asian Americans. Thus, within each cultural group, the depressed participants demonstrated the culturally inappropriate emotional response. These findings suggest that the impact of depression on emotional responding may be in part shaped by cultural models of healthy emotional functioning. Future studies need to examine whether these findings hold for patterns of emotional functioning in other forms of mental illness across cultural contexts.

Interpersonal Functioning. Another key aspect of normal functioning is the ability to engage in meaningful social relationships. Models of meaningful social relationships, however, vary significantly across cultures. Western industrialized cultures such as the United States, Australia, and Great Britain have been characterized as *individualistic*. In individualistic cultures, being able to maintain one's autonomy and independence even in the context of close social relationships is valued (Triandis, 1994). Even young infants are expected to develop independent skills, such as being able to sleep through the night or play on their own. In contrast, non-Western cultural contexts, such as Latin American and Asian cultures, have been characterized as *collectivist*.[2] In collectivist cultures, a state of mutual interdependence with close others is considered optimal, and priority is given to the goals of in-groups over one's individual goals (Markus & Kitayama, 1991; Triandis, 1972; Triandis, 1994). According to these values, parental socialization aims to foster children's interdependence with their family (Vereijken, Riksen-Walraven, & Van Lieshout, 1997). For example, infants and toddlers in Japanese families are more likely to regularly share a bed with their parents than infants and toddlers in U.S. families (Latz, Wolf, Lozoff, 1999). As a result, healthy psychological functioning may be more strongly associated with being able to achieve the goals of independence in individualist cultures, and interdependence in collectivist cultures. Thus, the expression of mental illness may emphasize individual concerns in individualist cultures and relational concerns in collectivist cultures (as illustrated earlier in our discussion of social anxiety disorder).

---

[2] It is important to note that there is considerable within-culture heterogeneity in individuals' engagement with individualistic or collectivistic models of self, goals, and pursuits. While all individuals are likely to be exposed to the dominant values and practices of their cultural context, they may respond in different ways. For example, Triandis, Chen, and Chan (1998) found that only 61–67% of individuals in Western cultures (the United States, Australia, The Netherlands, and Germany) reported individualistic tendencies, whereas only 40–56% of individuals in Asian cultures (Japan, Hong Kong, and Korea) reported collectivistic tendencies. When we characterize cultural contexts, we describe dominant cultural norms and values without making an assumption that behavior of all individuals within the cultural context is uniformly shaped by the dominant norms and values.

Strong social ties also can provide protection against occurrence or exacerbation of mental illness. For example, low rates of major depression and social anxiety disorder in Asian cultures can be explained in part by cohesive social structures in these collectivist cultural contexts. Such built-in social networks offer a stable source of social support for its members and may allow them to manage stress more effectively (Chen, Copeland, & Wei, 1999). However, when an individual becomes mentally ill, tightly knit social networks also may increase stigma associated with mental illness. Thus, interpersonal factors can influence the course as well as the occurrence of mental health disorders.

For example, despite the strong evidence for a genetic predisposition to schizophrenia (Jablensky, 2000; Prescott & Gottesman, 1993; see also Chapter 10), aspects of family environment are associated with relapse in patients treated for this disorder (Kanter, Lamb, & Loeper, 1987).[3] Interestingly, different aspects of the family environment predict relapse rates of patients in individualistic and collectivistic cultural contexts. Schizophrenic patients in individualistic European American cultural contexts who return to overly critical family environments are more likely to relapse than patients returning to less critical families (Butzlaff & Hooley, 1998; Lopez et al., 2004). In European American culture, achieving independence is viewed as an important goal. Critical comments from family members may undermine patients' independence and create high levels of stress, ultimately contributing to a relapse. The goal of achieving independence is less important in collectivistic Mexican American culture, and critical comments from family members assert patients' culturally appropriate dependence on family. As a result, family criticism does not predict relapse for Mexican American patients (Lopez et al., 2004).

What interpersonal factors are associated with relapse in collectivistic cultural contexts? Lopez and colleagues (2004) argued that family warmth (or expression of positive emotions and concern for the patient) serves as a critical indicator of healthy interdependence within a Mexican American family. Because achieving interdependence and harmony with one's family is more salient in Mexican American than in European American cultural contexts, lack of family warmth predicts relapse for Mexican American, but not European American, patients with schizophrenia (Lopez et al., 2004). These studies illustrate that cultural models of healthy interpersonal functioning can shape the expression and course of psychopathology.

Mind-Body-Social Context Relationships. The views of what types of symptoms constitute mental illness are deeply embedded in our cultural

---

[3] It is important to note that prediction of relapse does not imply causation of relapse; in fact, family communication patterns may be caused by ill relatives' severe symptoms of psychopathology, as shown by King and colleagues (King, 2000; King, Ricard, Rochon, Steiger, & Nelis, 2003).

models of psychological functioning. Current definitions of mental disorders reflect Western biases of viewing mental illness as primarily characterizing individuals rather than families or communities, and as fundamentally different from physical illnesses (mind-body dualism; see Chapter 15) (Marsella & White, 1982; Manson, 1995). These ideas are not universally shared by other cultures. In many cultures, social, physical, and emotional aspects of functioning are not differentiated. As evident in our examples of major depression, social anxiety, and alcohol-related disorders, emotional distress can be expressed as physical or interpersonal distress in non-Western cultural contexts. For example, recall that depression is expressed primarily in somatic terms in Punjabi culture, and social anxiety disorder and alcohol abuse are defined by their social effects in Asian cultures. Moreover, the tendency to describe distress in emotional (rather than somatic or interpersonal) terms increases as individuals from non-Western cultural contexts acculturate to Western culture and pay increasingly more attention to their own emotions (Chen, Guarnaccia, & Chung, 2003).

The fusion of interpersonal, somatic, and emotional distress is common in non-Western cultural contexts. This fusion can become encoded in the local language, creating a culture-specific "language of affect" (Manson, 1995, p. 491) or the local idioms of distress. Emotional distress may be verbalized as physical or relational symptoms depending on the terms and metaphors available in a particular language and on the appropriate codes for expression and communication of emotions. For instance, in Polynesian Tongan, idiomatic expressions for distress emphasize kinship connections and collective coping (Parsons, 1984), and in Chinese, such somatic terms as "heart discomfort" serve as shared metaphors for affective states or emotions (Tung, 1994). These cultural differences are preserved even when English is used instead of native languages. Tsai, Simeonova, and Watanabe (2004) compared English word use among Chinese Americans and European Americans during discussion of emotional events. They found that Chinese Americans, particularly those who were less oriented to American culture, used more somatic and social words than did European Americans, even though they experienced similar levels of emotion.

Cultural Models of Beauty

Cultural models can foster the occurrence of some types of psychopathology (see Chapter 16). One notable example of this is the growing epidemic of eating disorders such as anorexia nervosa (characterized by refusal to maintain normal body weight) and bulimia nervosa (characterized by binge eating and using inappropriate methods such as purging or laxatives to prevent weight gain). These eating disorders appear to be associated with a cultural idealization of the thin body type for women (Miller & Pumariega, 2001). Data show that cultural models of the ideal body weight as presented in the media and reinforced in specific social groups, such as sororities, contribute to the development of eating disorders (Crandall, 1988; Markey, 2004). Rapid culture change and exposure to Western cultural ideals appear to be associated with increases in the incidence of disordered eating in non-Western cultural contexts (Miller & Pumariega, 2001). For example, the introduction of Western television programming to the island of Fiji in 1995 was followed by a sharp rise in disordered eating behavior and unhealthy attitudes about eating among Fijian girls (Becker, Burwell, Herzog, Hamburg, & Gilman, 2002).

Interestingly, cultural ideals appear to shape some aspects and forms of eating disorders, but not others. For example, weight concerns and bulimic behavior appear to be limited to Western or Westernized cultural settings. These differences occur against a background of cultural similarities in the occurrence of self-starving behaviors (Keel & Klump, 2003). This pattern of disordered eating does not occur exclusively in Western or Westernized contexts. For example, some cases of anorexia nervosa have been reported for women from Pakistan, India, and the United Arab Emirates with no exposure to Western cultural influences. Prevalence rates of anorexia nervosa are also similar across cultures (see Keel & Klump, 2003, for a review; see also Chapter 16). Thus, Western cultural models of beauty combined with abundant food resources in most modern industrialized countries may foster culturally dependent forms of disordered eating (i.e., excessive concerns about one's weight and the occurrence of binging and purging behaviors), whereas other factors, such as genetic predispositions or similar sociocultural pressures, may foster culturally universal forms of disordered eating (i.e., self-starvation).

We have argued that the individuals' models of optimal psychological functioning and beauty are influenced by culture. These core cultural ideas regarding emotions, social relationships, the relationship between emotions and physical sensations, and desirable body size may shape the expression of mental illness in a particular cultural context. How do we translate these data to clinical settings and apply them to developing assessment and treatment techniques that can be used with diverse patient populations? Research on cultural models of mental health and mental illness can help clinical practitioners integrate their own conceptions of the patients' symptoms with those of the patients and their cultural contexts.

Implications for Clinical Practitioners

In an increasingly diverse world, mental health workers are striving to effectively deliver services to individuals from different cultural contexts. Delivering mental health services to diverse populations can be challenging. For example, members of minority cultural groups (particularly Asian Americans and Hispanic Americans) in the United

States underutilize psychological services, are more likely to withdraw from treatment prematurely, and are more likely to exhibit poor treatment outcomes than European American patients (Cheung & Snowden, 1990; Sue, Zane, Young, 1994). In part, these results may be a result of Western biases inherent in assessment and psychotherapy (Hahn & Kleinman, 1983; Wohl, 1989). That is, assessment and psychotherapy typically target individual patients rather than their families, and focus on emotional or cognitive rather than somatic and interpersonal symptoms of distress. Steps can be taken by mental health workers to bridge the client's and practitioner's cultural worldviews.

Clinicians' cultural biases. During clinical assessment and treatment, clinicians working with diverse populations may notice that their conceptions of mental illness are shaped by their own cultural values and assumptions. We need to recognize that thoughts, feelings, and behaviors of clinicians and their clients alike are culturally shaped. In some cases, clinicians' values and assumptions may even come into conflict with the values and assumptions of their patients. In addition to cultural differences that are easily accepted and tolerated by outsiders, cultural models of optimal functioning also give rise to some controversial practices (such as female genital modifications in African cultures, arranged marriage in India, or plastic surgery in Western cultures). These practices can engender misunderstanding, discomfort, or even moral criticism from members of other cultures. There are no easy answers to distinguishing ethically impermissible behavior from culturally rooted and meaningful practices (Rice & O'Donohue, 2002; Shweder, 2003). The highest standards of rigorous scientific evidence (including etic and emic approaches) should be used when evaluating normative cultural practices that engender moral criticism from members of other cultures (see also Chapter 2 for a discussion of other biases in clinical judgment).

Risk of misdiagnosis. Western diagnostic tools may pathologize behaviors that are considered functional in particular cultural contexts, or fail to detect maladaptive behaviors that are normative in Western cultures. For example, one study found that the General Health Questionnaire, a standardized instrument designed to screen for psychological disorders, requires different thresholds to detect mental illness in different cultural contexts (Goldberg, Oldehinkel, & Ormel, 1998).

In addition to standardized assessment tools, clinician's judgments can also result in misdiagnosis. Clinicians' expectations of open expression of positive emotions and positive self-evaluations may be culturally biased and should not be equated with mental health among individuals from other cultural contexts. As we discussed, healthy individuals from non-Western cultural contexts (particularly individuals from Asian cultures) may exhibit lower, but culturally normative, levels of positive emotions (Tsai et al., 2002), self-esteem (Heine & Lehman, 2003), optimism (Heine & Lehman, 1995), and satisfaction with life (Diener, Diener, & Diener, 1995). Thus, healthy individuals from Asian cultures are at risk of being overdiagnosed with mental illness, particularly depression.

Clinicians need to be aware that baselines of healthy and adaptive functioning may differ across cultural contexts. As Draguns (1995) advocated, deviance from the norms of the majority culture should not be mistaken for psychological disturbance (see Chapter 4 for a discussion of norms).

Clinicians also need to be aware of underdiagnosing individuals from non-Western cultural contexts who express their distress in somatic terms, interpersonal terms, or both. Research suggests that around the world, presentation of mental illness in somatic terms is likely to occur when patients do not feel comfortable confiding to their physicians because they do not have an ongoing relationship with them (Simon et al., 1999). This pattern is probably caused by an enduring stigma regarding mental illness that is particularly salient in non-Western cultural contexts. Thus, it is crucially important to establish rapport with clients from diverse cultural backgrounds before taking their responses about emotional functioning at face value. During initial visits, clinicians need to pay close attention to complaints about physical ailments and interpersonal difficulties, because these complaints may serve as signals of mental illness.

Despite these issues, diagnoses of mental illness can be made across cultural contexts by carefully integrating local conceptions of mental illness (symptoms that constitute illness, boundaries between normalcy and illness, precipitating factors, treatment options, course and outcome expectations) with Western-based diagnostic criteria and knowledge. For example, a Western diagnosis of depression given to Asian patients should be complemented with thorough assessment of the patients' interpersonal and somatic complaints and an exploration of the patients' own conceptions of their illness. The DSM-IV proposed a useful and comprehensive strategy for cultural case formulation that focuses on identification of cultural factors related to explanatory models of the individual illness, psychosocial environment, relationship between the individual and the clinician, and the desired treatment (APA, 1994; see also Chapter 5). Unfortunately, empirical reports of the effectiveness of this approach are still limited to isolated case reports. More empirical studies examining the effects of this approach on patient treatment continuation, compliance, and effectiveness are clearly needed.

Assessment of cultural orientation. No clinician can be expected to become an expert in the cultural values and norms of all of his or her patients. Directly consulting patients about their culture is not always helpful, because they may not be explicitly aware of their own cultural norms and values. That is, culture can be "invisible, in large part, to its bearer" (Lutz, 1985, p. 65). In such cases, consulting cultural experts or literature on cultural norms and values can be useful and should be considered an essential part of psychological assessment when working with diverse populations.

One important caveat is that in gathering such information, a clinician needs to be aware of within-culture heterogeneity in values and beliefs and be able to resist ethnic stereotyping based on group membership. Information about cultural values and beliefs should not be blindly applied to every patient from a particular cultural context. Instead, a strategy for cultural case formulation needs to start with assessment of cultural identity of the individual (APA, 1994). Assessing the cultural orientation of the client can range from asking "How Chinese/Mexican/Polish are you?" to administering validated measures of cultural orientation, such as the General Ethnicity Questionnaire (Tsai, Ying, & Lee, 2000). Knowing the level of cultural identity would help the clinician determine whether cultural norms and values may apply to an individual patient from a particular cultural context. Taking such steps can ensure that principles of patient-centered care are implemented in each case.

Future Directions

An important question to consider in our discussion of cultural differences in the prevalence rates and expressions of mental illness is the role of genetic factors. It is possible that some populations may be more genetically predisposed to developing a particular type of mental illness than other populations. It is also possible that the underlying genetic vulnerability may be expressed differently in different cultural contexts. Indeed, behavioral genetics studies have shown that the contribution of genes to many mental disorders is substantial (see Cooper, 2001, for review; see also Chapter 10). It is important to note that the high heritability estimates obtained in behavioral genetics research may be determined by low levels of cultural variability in the primarily monocultural Western study samples. Future studies need to include samples of twins from a variety of cultural contexts or examine the occurrence and expression of mental illness among overseas adoptees living in Western cultural contexts to begin to distinguish genetic from cultural influences of the expression of psychopathology. In turn, studies of culture and psychopathology need to examine within-culture and across-time differences in the expression of mental disorders to establish that variability or changes in cultural values or norms are associated with corresponding changes in the prevalence and expression of mental illness within populations. More studies that take into account genetic and cultural factors and their interaction are sorely needed.

In summary, culture plays an important role in shaping mental illness (see also Chapter 16). Examples from emic and etic research illustrate that prevalence rates and symptom expression of common mental disorders vary across cultures. Cultural factors such as conceptions of healthy emotional and interpersonal functioning can account for these differences. Between-culture and within-culture differences in emotions, social relationships, cognition, and behavior deserve more attention in clinical diagnosis and treatment. In an increasingly multicultural world, it is critically important to consider how culture shapes the expression of psychopathology and to develop effective treatment strategies for individuals from diverse cultural contexts.

KEY TERMS

Culture: By culture, we refer to "patterns, explicit and implicit, of and for behaviour acquired and transmitted by symbols, constituting the distinctive achievements of human groups, including their embodiment in artifacts; the essential core of culture consists of traditional (i.e., historically derived and selected) ideas and especially their attached values; culture systems may, on the one hand, be considered as products of action, on the other, as conditional elements of future action" (Kroeber & Kluckhohn, 1952). The behavior (including abnormal behavior) is shaped by the cultural contexts and simultaneously shapes the culture in the process of mutual constitution.

Emic/etic research approaches: Emic research approaches focus on culture-bound and culture-specific aspects of psychological distress. In contrast, etic research approaches focus on features of psychological functioning that appear to be similar across cultures.

Individualism/collectivism: Individualism/collectivism is a dimension of cultural variability that describes the degree to which a cultural context gives priority to needs, goals, preferences, and values of individuals versus those of groups.

Universalism/relativism: The Universalist approach assumes that the fundamental processes that underlie different forms of psychopathology are culturally universal and that the overt expressions of these fundamental processes may be subject to cultural influences. The Relativist approach assumes that psychopathology is embedded in and shaped by cultural beliefs and practices.

RECOMMENDED READINGS

Draguns, J. (1995). Cultural influences upon psychopathology. Clinical and practical implications. *Journal of Social Distress and the Homeless, 4*, 79–103.

Lewis-Hernandez, R., & Kleinman, A. (1994). Culture, personality and psychopathology. *Journal of Abnormal Psychology, 103*, 67–71.

Markus, H., & Kitayama, S. (1991). Culture and the self: Implications for cognition, emotion, and motivation. *Psychological Review, 98*, 224–253.

Marsella. A. J., & White, G. M. (Eds.). (1982). *Cultural conceptions of mental health and therapy*. Dordrecht, Netherlands: Reidel and Company.

Simon, G. E., Goldberg, D. P., Von Korff, M., & Ustun, T. B. (2002). Understanding cross-national differences in depression prevalence. *Psychological Medicine, 32*, 585–594.

Tsai, J. L., & Chentsova-Dutton, Y. (2002). Understanding depression across cultures. In I. H. Gotlib & C. L. Hammen (Eds.), *Handbook of depression* (pp. 467–491). New York: Guilford Press.

REFERENCES

Adams, G., & Markus, H.R. (2004). Toward a conception of culture suitable for a social psychology of culture. In M. Schaller & C. S. Crandall (Eds.), *The psychological foundations of culture* (pp. 335–360). Mahwah, NJ: Lawrence Erlbaum Associates.

Adler, S. R. (1991). Sudden unexpected nocturnal death syndrome among Hmong immigrants: Examining the role of the nightmare. *Journal of American Folklore, 104,* 54–71.

Allen, N. B., Trinder, J., & Brennan, C. (1999). Affective startle modulation in clinical depression: Preliminary findings. *Biological Psychiatry, 46,* 542–550.

American Psychiatric Association. (1994). *Diagnostic and statistical manual of mental disorder* (4th ed.). Washington, DC: American Psychiatric Association.

Becker, A. E., Burwell, R. A., Herzog, D. B., & Hamburg, P., Gilman, S. E. (2002). Eating behaviours and attitudes following prolonged exposure to television among ethnic Fijian adolescent girls. *British Journal of Psychiatry, 180,* 509–514.

Bellah, R. H., Madsen, R., Sullivan, W. M., Swindler, A., & Tipton, S. M. (1985). *Habits of the heart: Individualism and commitment in American life.* New York: Harper & Row Publishers.

Bennett, L. A., Janca, A., Grant, B. F., & Sartorius, N. (1993). Boundaries between normal and pathological drinking: A cross-cultural comparison. *Alcohol Health and Research World, 17,* 190–195.

Berenbaum, H. (1992). Posed facial expressions of emotion in schizophrenia and depression. *Psychological Medicine, 22,* 929–937.

Betancourt, H., & Lopez, S. (1993). The study of culture, ethnicity, and race in American psychology. *American Psychologist, 48,* 629–637.

Boas, F. (1948). *Race, language and culture.* New York: Macmillan.

Bond, M. H. (1991). *Beyond the Chinese face.* New York: Oxford University Press.

Butzlaff, R. L., & Hooley, J. M. (1998). Expressed emotion and psychiatric relapse. *Archives of General Psychiatry, 55,* 547–552.

Calahan, D., & Room, R. (1974). *Problem drinking among American men.* New Brunswick, NJ: Rutgers Center of Alcohol Studies Publication Division.

Chen, H., Guarnaccia, P. J., & Chung, H. (2003). Self-attention as a mediator of cultural influences on depression. *International Journal of Social Psychiatry, 49,* 192–203.

Chen, R., Copeland, J. M. R., & Wei, L. (1999). A meta-analysis of epidemiological studies in depression of older people in the People's Republic of China. *International Journal of Geriatric Psychiatry, 14,* 821–830.

Chentsova-Dutton, Y., Chu, J. P., Tsai, J. L., Rottenberg, J., Gross, J., & Gotlib, I. H. (2006). *Too depressed to care? Depression influences sadness differently in Asian Americans and European Americans.* Manuscript submitted for publication.

Cheung, F. K., & Snowden, L. R. (1990). Community mental health and ethnic minority populations. *Community Mental Health Journal, 26,* 277–291.

Cooper, B. (2001). Nature, nurture and mental disorder: Old concepts in the new millennium. *British Journal of Psychiatry, 178,* 91–101.

Crandall, C. S. (1988). Social contagion of binge eating. *Journal of Personality & Social Psychology, 55,* 588–598.

Diener, E., Diener, M., & Diener, C. (1995). Factors predicting the subjective well-being of nations. *Journal of Personality and Social Psychology, 69,* 851–864.

Draguns, J. (1995). Cultural influences upon psychopathology: Clinical and practical implications. *Journal of Social Distress and the Homeless, 4,* 79–103.

Furmark, T. (2002). Social phobia: Overview of community surveys. *Acta Psychiatrica Scandinavica, 105,* 84–93.

Geertz, C. (1984). Anti-anti-relativism. *American Anthropologist, 86,* 263–278.

Glassner, B., & Berg, B. (1980). How Jews avoid alcohol problems. *American Sociological Review, 45,* 647–664.

Goldberg, D. P., Oldehinkel, T., & Ormel, J. (1998).Why GHQ threshold varies from one place to another. *Psychological Medicine, 28,* 915–921.

Guarnaccia, P. J., & Rogler, L. H. (1999). Research on culture-bound syndromes: New directions. *American Journal of Psychiatry, 156*(9), 1322–1327.

Gureje, O., Vazquez-Barquero, J. L., & Janca, A. (1996). Comparisons of alcohol and other drugs: Experience from the WHO Collaborative Cross-Cultural Applicability Research (CAR) study. *Addiction, 91,* 1529–1538.

Hahn, R. A., & Kleinman, A. (1983). Biomedical practice and anthropological theory: Frameworks and directions. *Annual Reviews of Anthropology, 12,* 305–333.

Heine, S. J., & Lehman, D. R. (1995). Cultural variation in unrealistic optimism: Does the West feel more invulnerable than the East? *Journal of Personality and Social Psychology, 68,* 595–607.

Heine, S. J., & Lehman, D. R. (2003). Move the body, change the self: Acculturative effects on the self-concept. In M. Schaller & C. Crandall (Eds.), *Psychological foundations of culture* (pp. 305–331). Mahwah, NJ: Lawrence Erlbaum Associates.

Holland, D., & Quinn, N. (1987). *Cultural models in language and thought.* Cambridge, England: Cambridge University Press.

Hulbert, A. (2003). *Raising America: Experts, parents, and a century of advice about children.* New York: Knopf Publishing Group.

Jablensky, A. (2000). Epidemiology of schizophrenia: The global burden of disease and disability. *European Archives of Psychiatry and Clinical Neuroscience, 250,* 274–85.

Kanter, J., Lamb, H. R., & Loeper, C. (1987). Expressed emotion in families: A critical review. *Hospital and Community Psychiatry, 38,* 374–380.

Kawakami, N., Shimizu, H., Haratani, T., Iwata, N., & Kitamura, T. (2004). Lifetime and six-month prevalence of DSM-III-R psychiatric disorders in an urban community in Japan. *Psychiatry Research, 121,* 293–301.

Keel, P. K., & Klump, K. L. (2003). Are eating disorders culture-bound syndromes? Implications for conceptualizing their etiology. *Psychological Bulletin, 129,* 747–769.

King, S. (2000). Is expressed emotion cause or effect in the mothers of schizophrenic young adults? *Schizophrenia Research, 45,* 65–78.

King, S., Ricard, N., Rochon, V., Steiger, H., & Nelis, S. (2003). Determinants of expressed emotion in mothers of schizophrenia patients. *Psychiatry Research, 117,* 211–222.

Kirmayer, L. J., & Young, A. (1998). Culture and somatization: Clinical, epidemiological, and ethnographic perspectives. *Psychosomatic Medicine, 60,* 420–430.

Kleinknecht, R. A., Dinnel, D. L., Kleinknecht, E. E., Himura, N., & Harada, N. (1997). Cultural factors in social anxiety: A comparison of social phobia symptoms and *Taijin Kyofusho. Journal of Anxiety Disorders, 11,* 157–177.

Kleinman, A. (1977). Depression, somatization and the new cross-cultural psychiatry. *Social Science and Medicine, 11,* 3–10.

Kleinman, A. (1986). *Social origins of distress and disease: Depression, neuraesthenia, and pain in modern China.* New Haven, CT: Yale University Press.

Kleinman, A. (1988). *Rethinking psychiatry.* New York: The Free Press.

Krause, I. B. (1989). Sinking heart: A Punjabi communication of distress. *Social Science and Medicine, 29,* 563–575.

Kroeber, A. L., & Kluckhohn, C. (1952). Culture: A critical review of concepts and definitions. *Papers Peabody Museum of Archaeology & Ethnology, Harvard University, 47*(1), 223.

Latz, S., Wolf, A. W., & Lozoff, B. (1999). Co-sleeping in context: Sleep practices and problems in young children in Japan and the United States. *Archives of Pediatric and Adolescent Medicine, 153*, 339–46.

Lewis-Hernandez, R., & Kleinman, A. (1994). Culture, personality and psychopathology. *Journal of Abnormal Psychology, 103*, 67–71.

Lopez, S. R., Nelson Hipke, K., Polo, A. J., Jenkins, J. H., Karno, M., Vaughn, C., et al. (2004). Ethnicity, expressed emotion, attributions, and course of schizophrenia: Family warmth matters. *Journal of Abnormal Psychology, 113*, 428–439.

Lutz, C. (1985). Depression and the translation of emotional worlds. In A. Kleinman & B. Good (Eds.), *Culture and depression: Studies in the anthropology and cross-cultural psychiatry of affect and disorder* (pp. 63–100). Berkeley: University of California Press.

Manson, S. (1995). Culture and major depression: Current challenges in the diagnosis of mood disorders. *Psychiatric Clinics of North America, 18*, 487–501.

Markey, C. (2004). Culture and the development of eating disorders: A tripartite model. *Eating Disorders: The Journal of Treatment & Prevention, 12*, 139–156.

Markus, H., & Kitayama, S. (1991). Culture and the self: Implications for cognition, emotion, and motivation. *Psychological Review, 98*, 224–253.

Markus, H. R., & Kitayama, S. (2003). *Models of agency: Sociocultural diversity in the construction of action*. In V. Murphy-Berman & J. Berman (Eds.), *Nebraska symposium on motivation: Vol. 49. Cross-cultural differences in perspectives on self* (pp. 1–57). Lincoln: University of Nebraska Press.

Marsella, A. J. (1980). Depressive experience and disorder across cultures. In H. C. Triandis & J. G. Draguns (Eds.), *Handbook of cross-cultural psychology, Vol. 6: Psychopathology* (pp. 237–291). Boston: Allyn and Bacon.

Marsella, A. J., & White, G. M. (Eds.). (1982). *Cultural conceptions of mental health and therapy*. Dordrecht, Netherlands: Reidel and Company.

Maslowski, J., Jansen van Rensburg, D., & Mthoko, N. (1998). A polydiagnostic approach to the differences in the symptoms of schizophrenia in different cultural populations. *Acta Psychiatrica Scandinavica, 98*, 41–46.

Matsumoto, D. (2000). *Culture and psychology: People around the world*. Stanford, CT: Wadsworth.

Miller, M. N., & Pumariega, A. J. (2001). Culture and eating disorders: A historical and cross-cultural review. *Psychiatry, 64*, 93–110.

Murphy, H. B. M. (1982). *Comparative psychiatry: The international and intercultural distribution of mental illness*. Berlin: Springer-Verlag.

Murphy, J. M. (1976). Psychiatric labeling in cross-cultural perspective. *Science*, 1019–1028.

Murray, C. J. L., & Lopez, A. D. (1997) Alternative projections of mortality and disability by cause 1990–2020: Global burden of disease study. *Lancet, 349*, 1498–1504.

Nichter, M. (1981). Negotiation of the illness experience: Ayurvedic therapy and the psychosocial dimension of illness. *Culture, Medicine & Psychiatry, 5*, 5–24.

Ormel, J., VonKorff, M., Ustun, T.B., Pini, S., Koren, A., & Oldenhinkel, T. (1994). Common mental disorders and disability across cultures. *Journal of the American Medical Association, 272*, 1741–1748.

Pang, K. A. (1995). Cross-cultural understanding of depression among Korean elderly immigrants: Prevalence, symptoms, and diagnosis. *Clinical Gerontologist, 15*, 3–20.

Parsons, C. (1984). Idioms of distress: Kinship and sickness among the people of Tonga. *Culture, Medicine and Psychiatry, 8*, 71–93.

Prescott, C. A., & Gottesman, I. I. (1993). Genetically mediated vulnerability to schizophrenia. *Psychiatric Clinics of North America, 16*, 245–268.

Rice, N., & O'Donohue, W. (2002). Cultural sensitivity: A critical examination. *New Ideas in Psychology, 20*, 35–48.

Rottenberg, J., Kasch, K. L., Gross, J. J., & Gotlib, I. H. (2002). Sadness and amusement reactivity differentially predict concurrent and prospective functioning in major depressive disorder. *Emotion, 2*, 135–146.

Shore, B. (1996). *Culture in mind cognition, culture, and the problem of meaning.* New York: Oxford University Press.

Shweder, R. A. (2003). *Why do men barbecue? Recipes for cultural psychology.* Cambridge, MA: Harvard University Press.

Shweder, R., & Haidt, J. (2000). The cultural psychology of the emotions, ancient and new. In M. L. J. Haviland (Ed.), *Handbook of emotions* (2nd ed.). New York: Guilford Press.

Simon, G. E., Goldberg, D. P., Von Korff, M., & Ustun, T. B. (2002). Understanding cross-national differences in depression prevalence. *Psychological Medicine, 32*, 585–594.

Simon, G. E., VonKorf, M., Piccinelli, M., Fullerton, C., & Ormel, J. (1999). An international study of the relation between somatic symptoms and depression. *New England Journal of Medicine, 341*, 1329–1335.

Sue, S., Zane, N., & Young, K. (1994). Research on psychotherapy in culturally diverse populations. In A. Bergin & S. Garfield (Eds.), *Handbook of psychotherapy and behavior change* (pp. 783–817). New York: Wiley.

Tousignant, M., & Maldonado, M. G. (1989). Sadness, depression and social reciprocity in highland Ecuador. *Social Sciences and Medicine, 28*, 899–904.

Triandis, H. C. (1972). *The analysis of subjective culture.* New York: Wiley-Interscience.

Triandis, H. C. (1994). *Culture and social behavior.* New York: McGraw-Hill.

Triandis, H. C., Chen, Z. P., & Chan, D. K.-S. (1998). Scenarios for the measurement of collectivism and individualism. *Journal of Cross-Cultural Psychology, 29*, 275–289.

Tsai, J. L., Chentsova-Dutton, Y., Freire-Bebeau, L., & Przymus, D. E. (2002). Emotional expression and physiology in European Americans and Hmong Americans. *Emotion, 2*(4), 380–397.

Tsai, J. L., Knutson, B., & Fung, H. (2006). Cultural variation in affect valuation, *Journal of Personality and Social Psychology, 90*, 288–307.

Tsai, J. L., Levenson, R. W., & McCoy, K. (in press). Cultural and temperamental variation in emotional response. *Emotion.*

Tsai, J. L., Simeonova, D., & Watanabe, J. (2004). Somatic and social: Chinese Americans talk about emotion. *Personality and Social Psychology Bulletin, 30*, 1226–1238.

Tsai, J. L., Ying, Y., & Lee, P. A. (2000). The meaning of "being Chinese" and "being American": Variation among Chinese American young adults. *Journal of Cross-Cultural Psychology, 31*, 302–322.

Tung, M. P. M. (1994). Symbolic meanings of the body in Chinese culture and "somatization." *Culture, Medicine and Psychiatry, 18*, 483–492.

Vaillant, G. E. (1983). *The natural history of alcoholism.* Cambridge, MA: Harvard University Press.

Vega, W. A., Kolody, B., Aguilar-Gaxiola, S., Alderete, E., Catalano, R., & Caraveo-Anduaga, J. (1998). Lifetime prevalence of DSD-III-R psychiatric disorders among urban and rural Mexican Americans in California. *Archives of General Psychiatry, 55,* 771–778.

Vega, W. A., Sribney, W. M., Aguilar-Gaxiola, S., & Kolody, B. (2004). 12-month prevalence of DSM-III-R psychiatric disorders among Mexican Americans: Nativity, social assimilation, and age determinants. *Journal of Nervous and Mental Disease, 192,* 532–541.

Vereijken, C. M., Riksen-Walraven, M. & Van Lieshout, C. (1997). Mother-infant relationships in Japan—Attachment, dependency, and amae. *Journal of Cross-Cultural Psychology, 28,* 442–462.

Waza, K., Graham, A. V., Zyzanski, S. J., & Inoue, K. (1999). Comparison of symptoms in Japanese and American depressed primary care patients. *Family Practice, 16,* 528–533.

Wierzbicka, A. (1992). Talking about emotions: Semantics, culture and cognition. *Cognition and Emotion, 6,* 285–319.

Wierzbicka, A. (1999). *Emotions across languages and cultures: Diversity and universals.* Cambridge: Cambridge University Press.

Wohl, J. (1989). Cross-cultural psychotherapy. In P. B. Pedersen, J. G. Draguns, W. J. Lonner, & J. E. Trimble (Eds.), *Counseling across cultures* (3rd ed., pp. 79–113). Honolulu: University of Hawaii Press.

World Health Organization (n.d.). Global Alcohol Database. Retrieved September 18, 2004, from http://www3.who.int/whosis/menu.cfm?path=whosis,alcohol&language=english.

Zhang, D. (1995). Depression and culture—A Chinese perspective. *Canadian Journal of Counseling, 29,* 227–233.

18

The Great Ideas of Clinical Science Redux: Revisiting Our Intellectual Roots

SCOTT O. LILIENFELD AND WILLIAM T. O'DONOHUE

Why are the Great Ideas of Clinical Science useful? Why are they essential to the intellectual life of all clinical scientists?

We can glean some insight into these questions by revisiting our intellectual roots in the Boulder, or scientist-practitioner, model of clinical training, formulated in the late 1940s at a major conference in Boulder, Colorado. Over half a century later, it is all too easy to forget that David Shakow, the prime mover behind this model, urged programs to train aspiring clinical psychologists to be *psychologists first and clinical psychologists second* (see Shakow, 1969). That is, according to Shakow, clinical psychologists should first and foremost be intimately acquainted with the basic science of psychology, and they should apply this broad knowledge to every aspect of their clinical practice and research. Moreover, Shakow maintained that clinical psychology graduate programs should focus on teaching courses in general theoretical and research principles rather than in specialized methods, such as the MMPI or Rorschach Inkblot Test. Clinical psychologists, Shakow argued, should be critical thinkers, not technicians.

Shakow's sage advice is often lost in the fast-paced modern era of hyper-specialization in academia. Mounting pressures on graduate students to publish papers in premier journals and accumulate large numbers of clinical hours, and on young academics to publish still more papers in premier journals and obtain large federal grants, mitigate against intellectual generalization. In research-oriented clinical psychology programs, there is less and less time for students and faculty to think broadly—even to think at all—and more and more demand on them to generate highly focused, programmatic research. Moreover, the past several decades have witnessed an information explosion that renders it increasingly difficult to stay informed about all domains that abut clinical psychology. Indeed, in many areas of research in clinical science (e.g., mood disorders, schizophrenia, psychotherapy outcome research), it is difficult enough to keep abreast of recent developments in one's own circumscribed "neighborhood" of knowledge, let alone developments in clinical science, psychology, and social and natural science more broadly.

As a consequence, we worry that forthcoming generations of clinical psychologists may be unduly narrow thinkers, constrained by rigid and often artificial disciplinary boundaries. In our view, such thinkers can neither be complete therapists nor complete researchers.

The Great Ideas of Clinical Science, we believe, are a healthy and necessary antidote against recent trends toward intellectual hyperspecialization. By becoming conversant with the overarching intellectual traditions that have animated clinical psychology, clinical students in training and even current clinical practitioners and researchers can become integrative thinkers capable of bringing basic psychological science to bear on important clinical questions, whether they arise in the therapy room or the laboratory. Indeed, many or most of the Great Ideas in this book find their principal origins outside of clinical psychology per se, although they have gradually become assimilated into the study of psychotherapy and psychopathology. For example, much of the research on clinical judgment and prediction (see Chapters 1, 2, and 3) derives from the field of social cognition; much of the research on trait approaches to psychopathology (see Chapter 12) derives from basic personality psychology; much of the research on developmental psychopathology (see Chapter 14) derives from work on normal social and emotional development; and much of the research on cultural influences on psychopathology (see Chapters 16 and 17) derives from cultural anthropology and sociology. Indeed, much of what makes the ideas in this book great is that they are cross-cutting psychological principles that inform not merely clinical science but psychological science more broadly.

In this context, psychologist Lee Sechrest (see Sechrest & Smith, 1994) argued persuasively that "psychotherapy is the practice of psychology." For Sechrest, the effective psychotherapist continually imports insights from the broader field of psychological science into the consulting room (see Chapters 6 and 7). Many of these insights, we maintain, emanate from the Great Ideas presented in this book. Among other things, successful therapists:

- remain alert to their propensities toward confirmation bias and illusory correlation and strive to find ways of compensating for them (Chapters 1, 2, and 3);
- are alert to the problem of distinguishing "noise" from "signal" in their measurements (Chapter 4);
- recognize the value of accurate diagnosis as a means of acquiring new and clinically useful information about their clients (Chapter 5);
- attempt whenever possible to measure the outcomes of their interventions to ascertain how well they are working (Chapters 6 and 7);
- trace the origins of their clients' unhealthy behaviors to basic learning processes, typically in concert with genetic predispositions (Chapters 9 and 10);
- understand how their clients' dysfunctional behaviors often reflect failed adaptations to their environments (Chapter 11);
- remain cognizant of the importance of individual differences in personality and their implications for selecting and crafting psychological interventions (Chapter 12);
- appreciate the complex interplay among clients' cognition, affect, and overt behavior (Chapter 13);
- obtain clinically useful information concerning the early developmental underpinnings of their clients' problems (Chapter 14);
- consider bidirectional influences between their clients' psychological status and their physical health (Chapter 15);
- bear in mind that the expression of their clients' psychopathology may be molded in important ways by cultural variables (Chapters 16 and 17),

and so on (see also Davison, 1992, for apt examples of how basic psychological research can be applied to important clinical problems).

In this way, effective clinicians are fulfilling the laudable ideals of the Boulder model: They are always operating as psychological scientists, even if they do not conduct formal research (see also McFall, 1991). They are also fulfilling the ideals of the Vail Model of PsyD training, which expects practicing clinicians to function as "scholars" and as avid consumers of the psychological research literature (see Norcross, Gallagher, & Prochaska, 1989). Regrettably, over the past several decades, most clinical training PhD and PsyD programs appear to have drifted progressively from Sechrest's vision of psychotherapy and psychotherapy training. An increasing number of these programs have adopted an instrumental, "preprofessional" mindset whose goal is to train specialized clinicians, psychometricians, or narrowly focused clinical investigators rather than integrative scholars.

The prominent Harvard philosopher Wilford Van Orman Quine has invoked the metaphor of a "web of belief" to capture the interconnections among all the beliefs in an individuals's belief system. The relationships are complex, but to give one example, beliefs about the sensitivity of outcome measures can affect one's beliefs about the efficacy of psychotherapy.

To take one more example, one's knowledge of developments in the Human Genome Project, for example, can affect one's beliefs about research priorities in physiological pathways, which in turn can affect one's beliefs regarding treatment priorities for such problems as depression. One critical task shared by practitioners and researchers is to develop alternative hypotheses or explanations for clinical phenomena. The broad base of psychological knowledge covered in this book provides all clinical scientists with the knowledge toolkit to perform this task better.

The past several years have witnessed the passing of some of the genuine giants in clinical science and adjoining fields (e.g., educational psychology, psychometics, individual differences) that have profoundly shaped clinical science (Waller & Lilienfeld, 2005). These figures include Paul Meehl, Lee J. Cronbach, Donald Campbell, Donald Fiske, Lloyd Humphreys, John B. Carroll, Michael Mahoney and David Lykken. All of these individuals were scholars of extraordinary intellectual breadth as well as depth, and they transcended interdisciplinary boundaries by embracing great ideas from intellectual traditions outside of their own. In response to the deaths of these scholars, one of our close friends and colleagues recently asked us rhetorically and despairingly, "Who is left to replace them?"

Like our good friend and colleague, we are concerned that few, if any, giants of psychology are looming on the horizon. Perhaps that is because some of these figures, including Meehl, published numerous nonempirical articles and might well have had difficulty obtaining tenure in today's intensely research- and grant-driven environment (Waller & Lilienfeld, 2005). Nevertheless, we remain cautiously optimistic concerning the future of clinical psychology, especially if the crucial need for intellectual breadth in the training of clinical psychologists is not neglected. The Great Ideas of Clinical Science should help to remind the next generation of clinical psychology scholars that the field of psychology is not only intellectually rich, vibrant, and dynamic, but that it offers invaluable insights into the assessment, causes, and alleviation of human suffering.

REFERENCES

Davison, G. C. (1992). Issues in psychotherapy as the practice of psychology. *Journal of Psychotherapy Integration, 4,* 39–45.

McFall, R. M. (1991). Manifesto for a science of clinical psychology. *The Clinical Psychologist, 44,* 75–88.

Norcross, J. C., Gallagher, K. M., & Prochaska, J. O. (1989). The Boulder and/or the Vail model: Training preferences of clinical psychologists. *Journal of Clinical Psychology, 15,* 822–828.

Sechrest, L., & Smith, B. (1994). Psychotherapy is the practice of psychology. *Journal of Psychotherapy Integration, 4,* 1–29.

Shakow, D. (1969). *Clinical psychology as a science and as a profession: A forty-year odyssey.* Chicago: Aldine.

Waller, N. G., & Lilienfeld, S. O. (2005). Paul Everett Meehl: The cumulative record. *Journal of Clinical Psychology, 61,* 1209–1230.

Index